D1756457

HEARING THE OLD TESTAMENT

2 0 MAY 2025

HEARING THE OLD TESTAMENT

Listening for God's Address

Edited by

Craig G. Bartholomew *&* David J. H. Beldman

WILLIAM B. EERDMANS PUBLISHING COMPANY

GRAND RAPIDS, MICHIGAN / CAMBRIDGE, U.K.

Published 2012 by
Wm. B. Eerdmans Publishing Co.
2140 Oak Industrial Drive N.E., Grand Rapids, Michigan 49505 /
P.O. Box 163, Cambridge CB3 9PU U.K.
www.eerdmans.com

Printed in the United States of America

17 16 15 14 13 12   7 6 5 4 3 2 1

Library of Congress Cataloging-in-Publication Data

Hearing the Old Testament: listening for God's address / edited by
    Craig G. Bartholomew & David J. H. Beldman.
        p.   cm.
    Includes bibliographical references (p.   ) and index.
    ISBN 978-0-8028-6561-8 (pbk.: alk. paper)
    1. Bible. O.T. — Criticism, interpretation, etc.
    I. Bartholomew, Craig G., 1961-   II. Beldman, David J. H., 1977-

    BS1175.3.H43   2012
    221.6 — dc23

                                        2012004719

Publication of this book was supported by a generous grant from The Paideia
Centre for Public Theology.

To Al Wolters,
on the occasion of his retirement

Contents

III: **Hearing the Old Testament**

Abbreviations

NIBCOT	New International Biblical Commentary on the Old Testament
NICNT	New International Commentary on the New Testament
NICOT	New International Commentary on the Old Testament
NIVAC	New International Version Application Commentary
NSBT	New Studies in Biblical Theology
OBT	Overtures to Biblical Theology
OTG	Old Testament Guides
OTL	Old Testament Library
OTM	Oxford Theological Monographs
OTS	Old Testament Studies
PBM	Paternoster Biblical Monographs
PL	Patrologia Latina
SAHS	Scripture and Hermeneutics Series
SBLDS	Society of Biblical Literature Dissertation Series
SBLSymS	Society of Biblical Literature Symposium Series
SBT	Studies in Biblical Theology
SJT	*Scottish Journal of Theology*
SOTSMS	Society for Old Testament Study Monographs
STI	Studies in Theological Interpretation
TBS	Tools for Biblical Studies
TLZ	*Theologische Literaturzeitung*
TRE	*Theologische Realenzyklopädie*
VT	*Vetus Testamentum*
VTSup	Supplements to Vetus Testamentum
WBC	Word Biblical Commentary
WMANT	Wissenschaftliche Monographien zum Alten und Neuen Testament
WTJ	*Westminster Theological Journal*
WUNT	Wissenschaftliche Untersuchungen zum Neuen Testament
ZAW	*Zeitschrift für die alttestamentliche Wissenschaft*
ZNW	*Zeitschrift für die neutestamentliche Wissenschaft*

Contributors

Craig G. Bartholomew is the H. Evan Runner Professor of Philosophy and Professor of Religion and Theology at Redeemer University College. He is also the principal of The Paideia Centre for Public Theology. He has written and edited numerous books, including a commentary on Ecclesiastes (Baker Academic, 2009), a volume on a Christian view of place (Baker Academic, 2011), and an introduction to Old Testament wisdom (co-authored with Ryan O'Dowd; IVP Academic, 2011).

David J. H. Beldman is a part-time faculty member at Redeemer University College and is conducting doctoral research at the University of Bristol on the topic of endings in Old Testament narratives. He currently serves on the committee for the Scripture and Hermeneutics Seminar.

Mark J. Boda is Professor of Old Testament at McMaster Divinity College and Professor in the Faculty of Theology at McMaster University. His published works range from commentaries on the books of Judges, Chronicles, Haggai, and Zechariah to works on the practices and theology of prayer and penitence in the Old Testament. He has served in various leadership roles within the academic guild (including the Society of Biblical Literature and the Institute for Biblical Research) while also seeking to enrich the life of the church through teaching, preaching, and mentoring.

M. Daniel Carroll R. (Rodas) is Distinguished Professor of Old Testament at Denver Seminary. Prior to this post he was Professor of Old Testament and

Ethics at El Seminario Teológico Centroamericano in Guatemala, where he continues to serve as adjunct faculty. He has written and edited several books on Old Testament ethics and on the book of Amos. His latest publication is *Christians at the Border: Immigration, the Church, and the Bible* (Baker Academic, 2008).

Stephen G. Dempster is Professor of Religious Studies at Crandall University. He has written *Dominion and Dynasty: A Theology of the Hebrew Bible* (IVP Academic, 2003) and many articles in the fields of biblical theology and Old Testament canon. He is currently writing commentaries on Genesis and Micah.

Tremper Longman III is the Robert H. Gundry Professor of Biblical Studies at Westmont College. He has written a number of books, including commentaries on Proverbs, Ecclesiastes, Song of Songs, Jeremiah, Lamentations, and Daniel.

J. Clinton McCann Jr. is the Evangelical Professor of Biblical Interpretation at Eden Theological Seminary. He is the author of numerous essays, especially on the Psalms, as well as the author of several books, including the Psalms commentary in the New Interpreter's Bible series and Judges in the Interpretation series.

Iain Provan is the Marshall Sheppard Professor of Biblical Studies at Regent College, Vancouver. He has written numerous books, including commentaries on Lamentations, 1 and 2 Kings, Ecclesiastes, and Song of Songs.

Richard Schultz is the Carl Armerding and Hudson T. Armerding Professor of Biblical Studies at Wheaton College. He is the author of *The Search for Quotation: Verbal Parallels in the Prophets* (JSOTSup 180) and several essays on the book of Isaiah.

Aubrey Spears is pastor of the Church of the Incarnation, Harrisonburg, Virginia. He is also a fellow in practical theology at The Paideia Centre for Public Theology. His book on hermeneutics, application, and preaching is forthcoming from Wipf and Stock, and he is currently writing a commentary on Esther for the Two Horizons Old Testament Commentary Series (Eerdmans).

Heath Thomas is Assistant Professor of Old Testament and Hebrew at Southeastern Seminary and fellow in Old Testament Studies at The Paideia Centre for Public Theology. He also serves on the Scripture and Hermeneutics Seminar committee. He is the author of the forthcoming *Poetry and Theology in Lamentations* (Sheffield Phoenix), coeditor with Robin Parry of the forthcoming *Great Is Thy Faithfulness? Toward Reading Lamentations as Sacred Scripture* (Paternoster/Pickwick), and is currently writing a commentary on Habakkuk for the Two Horizons Old Testament Commentary Series (Eerdmans).

Gordon J. Wenham is Professor Emeritus of Old Testament at the University of Gloucestershire and Tutor in Old Testament at Trinity College, Bristol. He has written many books, including major commentaries on Genesis, Leviticus, and Numbers; books on the Old Testament and ethics, including *Story as Torah: Reading Old Testament Narrative Ethically* (Baker Academic, 2004) and *Psalms as Torah: Reading Biblical Song Ethically* (Baker Academic, 2012); as well as numerous articles. He is currently writing a commentary on the book of Psalms.

Al Wolters is Professor Emeritus of Religion and Theology and Classical Languages at Redeemer University College and is associated with The Paideia Centre for Public Theology. His publications include studies of Plotinus, biblical worldview, Proverbs 31, and the Copper Scroll, and he is currently completing a commentary on the book of Zechariah. He has an interest in the history of biblical interpretation and is a lay preacher.

Christopher J. H. Wright is international director of the Langham Partnership International, a network of ministries founded by John Stott in support of churches in the majority world. Formerly he was principal of All Nations Christian College, England, and taught Old Testament at the Union Biblical Seminary, India. Among his books are *Ethics for the People of God* (IVP Academic, 2004), *The Mission of God* (IVP Academic, 2006), *The Mission of God's People* (Zondervan, 2010), *The God I Don't Understand* (Zondervan, 2008), and commentaries on Deuteronomy and Ezekiel.

The Love of the Old Testament and the Desire for God

Margaret Silf begins her introduction to Ignatian spirituality, *Landmarks*,[1] with a story about a salad bowl. She tells of a friend's induction as vicar in a new parish and of the feast that followed. The members of the congregation tucked into the feast, and soon hardly anything was left . . . except for a large bowl of rice salad. Eventually she realized why: someone had forgotten to put a serving spoon in the dish. Silf compares this to the church, which she says is too often like that salad bowl. People are hungry and longing to receive — but where is the spoon?

As the major part of Christian Scripture, the Old Testament, too, is a feast. And yet far too often Christians do not experience it this way. In the West we live amid growing biblical illiteracy, so that the content of the Old Testament is increasingly unknown, and in the academy far too few of the endless publications seem to provide a "spoon" to allow us to tuck into the feast that awaits.

Essentially this volume is an attempt to map out a "spoon approach" to the Old Testament. At the heart of the hermeneutic advocated in this book is the belief that our love for the Old Testament and our desire for God will come together only when we make the goal of our interpretation to *listen for God's address*. If Scripture is God's Word, then any other goal is inadequate. Craig Bartholomew, one of the editors of this volume, likes to compare Scripture to the field in which is hidden the incomparable treasure of the Christ. This means that a healthy hermeneutic for the Old Testament would find us emerging again and again into the presence of God.

1. London: DLT, 1998.

Not surprisingly, we welcome the current renaissance of interest in theological interpretation. However, this remains a diverse movement, and much work remains to be done in it. Our hope is that this volume will contribute toward a renewal of best practice when it comes to theological interpretation of the Old Testament. As we have discovered in writing and editing this volume, contemporary Old Testament scholars are not trained for work along these lines. Amid the plurality of hermeneutical approaches in Old Testament studies today, it is rare to find listening for God's address as the telos of interpretation. Our attempt to push the envelope in this respect is particularly clear in Part III, in which authors attend to the major parts of the Old Testament in the light of a trinitarian hermeneutic.

We are grateful to our authors for cooperating with us in the careful planning and close editorial process involved in the production of this volume. While collections of essays have a reputation for being more or less random assortments of chapters, readers should note that this is definitely *not* the case here. Craig Bartholomew's chapter "Listening to God's Address," proposing a trinitarian hermeneutic for the Old Testament, was written first, and all authors were asked to engage with this, whether positively or critically. The authors of the chapters in Part II, dealing with methodology, wrote in the light of this chapter; and those who wrote the chapters in Part III were asked to interact with both this chapter and the Part II chapters as they wrote. Finally, the chapter in the last section, on preaching, was written in light of the whole. All of us have continually had all chapters available to us so that we could interact with one another as the volume achieved its final form. While allowing for individual freedom and insights, we have sought to produce a coherent volume.

Doubtless some will question the validity of such an approach in the academy. In response, we offer two points. First, we do not see a trinitarian hermeneutic as in any way relinquishing the utmost rigor in Old Testament studies. As Augustine noted, all truth is God's truth, and this volume is not pre-critical in the sense that it bypasses the advances made by modern Old Testament studies. If anything, it is better described as post-critical, in that it seeks to learn from all the progress in Old Testament studies, but never uncritically. We think that this commitment to rigor and an openness to learn from all approaches is evident throughout the book.

Second, we affirm the right of different groups to develop their own readings of the Old Testament. One effect of postmodern thought in the academic discipline of Old Testament studies has been to alert us unequivocally to the diversity of hermeneutics at work. Amid this "wild pluralism," the way forward in the academy, in our view, is to allow different approaches to come to fruition in their readings of the Old Testament so that the real discussions can begin between alternative approaches. Doubtless Jewish or Muslim scholars, or those committed to secular paradigms, would produce volumes very different from this one. We welcome such difference as the basis on which real dialogue can take place.

This volume has been produced as a project of the Scripture and Hermeneutics Seminar (SAHS), now part of The Paideia Centre for Public Theology (www.paideiacentre.ca). In November 2008 we had the opportunity to outline our vision for this volume at the annual meeting of the SAHS, and we are grateful to the members of the SAHS community (including many of our authors) who interacted with us. We have intentionally encouraged authors to refer to the eight-volume Scripture and Hermeneutics Series where appropriate. The Paideia Centre is a delightful new initiative, and we are grateful for its support in the production of this volume.

Readers should note that we do not in any sense regard this volume as the final word in theological interpretation of the Old Testament. A great deal of work remains to be done to facilitate a renewal in the field. Our hope is that our efforts will inspire new generations to take up the task of serving up the feast of the Old Testament ever anew.

Finally, we are delighted to dedicate this volume to Al Wolters on the occasion of his retirement. Al has made a substantial contribution to Christian scholarship over many years, and not least to Old Testament studies. His *Creation Regained,* probably the most famous work on a long and impressive curriculum vitae, has been translated into multiple languages and continues to inspire new generations, and he has been involved in the Scripture and Hermeneutics Seminar from its inception.

DAVID J. H. BELDMAN *and*
CRAIG G. BARTHOLOMEW

Part I   THE GOD WHO SPEAKS

1 Listening for God's Address: A *Mere* Trinitarian Hermeneutic for the Old Testament

Craig G. Bartholomew

The unique feature of this book is that it makes the telos of reading the Old Testament *listening for God's address*. The bifurcation of theology and biblical studies is well documented, and recent decades have witnessed welcome attempts to overcome this chasm. Nevertheless, the renaissance of theological interpretation of the Bible is still in its early years, and it remains rare to find scholarship on the Old Testament that embodies the kind of integrated theological hermeneutic that retains critical rigor while aiming throughout to hear God's address. This volume aims to fill that gap.

Any theological hermeneutic worth its salt must be Christocentric. As Karl Barth says of Jesus, "This man is the secret of heaven and earth, of the cosmos created by God."[1] Similarly, Lesslie Newbigin asserts that Christ is the clue to the whole of creation.[2] And as Aquinas puts it, "This human be-

1. Karl Barth, *Church Dogmatics* III/1, *The Doctrine of Creation, Part 1*, ed. G. W. Bromiley and T. F. Torrance (Edinburgh: T&T Clark, 1958), p. 21.
2. Lesslie Newbigin, *The Light Has Come: An Exposition of the Fourth Gospel* (Grand Rapids: Eerdmans, 1982).

My use of the adjective "mere" in the title of this essay follows that of C. S. Lewis in his *Mere Christianity*, in that it emphasizes the common ground, rather than the differences, between various trinitarian hermeneutics. The renaissance of interest in trinitarian theology initiated by Karl Barth has yielded a large and complex corpus including works by authors such as Wolfhart Pannenberg, Jürgen Moltmann, Eberhard Jüngel, Colin Gunton, John Zizioulas, T. F. Torrance, and many others. It is not the intention of this introduction to explore the intricacies of trinitarian debate but to demonstrate the radicality and fecundity of "mere" trinitarianism for OT interpretation.

ing is divine truth itself."[3] And precisely because a theological hermeneutic is Christocentric it will be trinitarian. In the context of first-century Jewish monotheism, the New Testament awareness of Jesus as "truly God" made the post-canonical development of the doctrine of the Trinity inevitable. The credit for full elaboration of the doctrine of the Trinity goes to Athanasius,[4] the three Cappadocians, and Augustine.[5]

In our late modern age of wild pluralism it may seem strange, but it needs to be said, that a trinitarian hermeneutic aims at *truthful* interpretation of the Old Testament. Let me elaborate. There are many biblical entrances into the concept of truth, but here I will follow several theologians in entering through John's Gospel.[6] The question of truth comes famously to the fore in Pilate's interrogation of Jesus in John 18:28–19:16a. At stake is whether or not Jesus is "king of the Jews." Jesus replies (18:37) that he came into the world to testify to *the truth,* and that everyone who belongs to *the truth* listens to his voice. As Herman Ridderbos notes,

> Jesus' kingship consists in the utterly unique authority with which he represents the truth in the world. His birth and coming has no other purpose than to "bear witness to the truth," in the absolute sense in which the Fourth Gospel continually speaks of the truth: Jesus testifies to what "he has seen and heard of the Father" (cf. 3:31-36), indeed to the truth that he himself is (14:6) and for which he answers with his life, person, and work. By speaking of himself as "witness," Jesus — standing before the judgment seat of Pilate — is using the language of the courtroom (cf. 1 Tim. 6:13), but not as the accused testifying on his own behalf but as the one who, in the suit that God brings against the world, has come to testify against the rule of the lie and for the "truth," that is,

3. Thomas Aquinas, *Super Evangelium S. Ioannis Lectura,* ed. and trans. P. Raphaelis Cai (Casale Monferratto: Edizione Piemme, 1972), pp. 1, 8.

4. Athanasius, "Ad Serapion," in *Historical Tracts of St. Athanasius,* trans. Miles Atkinson (Oxford: John Henry Parker, 1843).

5. Herman Bavinck notes, "Even more profoundly and philosophically Augustine expounded the doctrine of the trinity in his fifteen books *De Trinitate,* which comprise the most learned discourse on the dogma that was ever written." See his *The Doctrine of God,* trans. William Hendriksen (Edinburgh: Banner of Truth, 1978), p. 283.

6. So, for example, Bruce D. Marshall, *Trinity and Truth* (Cambridge: Cambridge University Press, 2000), pp. 1-3; Hans Urs von Balthasar, *Theologik II: Wahrheit Gottes* (Einsiedeln: Johannes Verlag, 1985), pp. 13-23, and *Theologik III: Der Geist der Wahrheit* (Einsiedeln: Johannes Verlag, 1987), pp. 61-75; Newbigin, *The Light Has Come.*

for God and for God's claim on the world. In that testimony Jesus' kingship consists.[7]

In a postmodern idiom, Pilate replies, "What is truth?" Doubtless many today would see Pilate as the winner of this debate, as Nietzsche famously did. However, Jesus, by reversing his role in the interrogation and thus reframing Pilate's court case in the context of a larger narrative,[8] alerts us unequivocally to the resistance a trinitarian view of truth affords to the relativism of so much postmodernism.[9] The reader of John's Gospel knows the answer to Pilate's question; it is Jesus himself. "Truth is not simply personal; for John truth is a person. Even this is too weak: truth is not just any person, but this human being in particular: Jesus of Nazareth, and among human beings only he. Knowing what truth is and deciding about truth, so this Gospel suggests, finally depend on becoming adequately acquainted with this person."[10] However, Jesus is not the truth all by himself but by virtue of his unique relationship with the Father (5:30; 16:15), who sent him into the world, and by virtue of his unique relationship with the Spirit, whom he sends into the world (16:13-14). "So as John's Gospel and Letters depict it, 'truth' is an attribute of the triune God. Indeed, truth is in some deep sense identical with the persons of the Trinity. Apparently both saying what truth is and deciding what is true depend on identifying the triune God, and on being the subject of his community-forming action."[11]

It is this trinitarian view of God that distinguishes the Christian church from other communities. Bruce Marshall notes the comprehensive scope of the doctrine of the Trinity: "The one God is identified as Trinity through the unfolding of a complex narrative which links Israel, Jesus, and the church; this narrative identification of the triune God organizes a

---

7. Herman Ridderbos, *The Gospel of John: A Theological Commentary,* trans. John Vriend (Grand Rapids: Eerdmans, 1997), p. 596.

8. In *Truth on Trial: The Lawsuit Motif in the Fourth Gospel* (Peabody, MA: Hendrickson, 2000), Andrew Lincoln examines the centrality of the lawsuit to John's Gospel; see especially pp. 123-38. He notes that "Jesus' assertion to Pilate, then, puts his judge on trial regarding the truth" (p. 129). As regards Pilate's famous question, Paul Duke in *Irony in the Fourth Gospel* (Louisville: John Knox, 1985), p. 130, notes: "The dramatic irony of the question lies in our knowledge that the one to whom the question about truth is asked is himself the Truth."

9. See Marshall, *Trinity and Truth,* pp. 168-69, for a cogent defense of the view that Scripture does indeed provide us with a God's-eye view of our world.

10. Marshall, *Trinity and Truth,* p. 2.

11. Marshall, *Trinity and Truth,* pp. 2-3.

comprehensive view of all things, and especially of human nature, history, and destiny."[12]

The post-Enlightenment legacy in theology was to marginalize the doctrine of the Trinity.[13] Much modern theology has been an attempt to *correlate* Christian doctrine with the modern worldview (or worldviews), in a quest for an epistemic middle.[14] However, as Bruce Marshall rightly notes, such an approach has turned out to be not so much mistaken as empty.[15] "Correlation holds out the promise that theologians can do justice both to the contents of Christian beliefs and to the epistemic priorities of modernity while keeping each in its place. Like the dependence thesis generally, correlation makes a promise which in the end it lacks the logical resources to keep."[16] Not surprisingly, the doctrine of the Trinity was a major fatality of this sort of approach.[17]

In contrast, the latter half of the twentieth century, partially in the con-

---

12. Marshall, *Trinity and Truth*, p. 3.

13. This is especially true of twentieth-century English theology. See, for example, Maurice Wiles, *The Making of Christian Doctrine: A Study in the Principles of Early Doctrinal Development* (Cambridge: Cambridge University Press, 1967). Brian Hebbelthwaite, with his "Recent British Theology," in *One God in Trinity: An Analysis of the Primary Dogma of Christianity*, ed. Peter Toon and James D. Spiceland (London: Samuel Bagster, 1980), p. 158, notes: "The most striking feature of recent British trinitarian theology — at least where England is concerned — is the frankness with which orthodox trinitarianism is being questioned or even rejected. . . . Indeed the collapse of trinitarian theology is an inevitable consequence of the abandonment of incarnational Christology."

14. See Marshall, *Trinity and Truth*, pp. 4, 56-71. My working definition of "epistemology" is how to go about knowing something so that you can trust the results of the knowing process. For a critique of correlation see Craig Bartholomew, "In Front of the Text: The Quest of Hermeneutics," in *The Bible in Pastoral Practice: Readings in the Place and Function of Scripture in the Church*, ed. P. Ballard and S. R. Holmes (Grand Rapids: Eerdmans, 2005), pp. 144-47. *Correlation* is the attempt to connect theology with modern thought while respecting the epistemic foundations of both. *Integration* of faith and modern thought is highly desirable, but conceding the epistemic foundations of modern thought insofar as they are non-Christian is not, since it ends up sacrificing the comprehensive trinitarian metanarrative to a different metanarrative.

15. Marshall, *Trinity and Truth*, p. 139.

16. Marshall, *Trinity and Truth*, pp. 139-40. The dependence thesis is the view that Christians have the right to hold Christian beliefs only if these are consistent with beliefs that are not distinctively Christian, namely the results of modern science.

17. Thus, Wiles in *The Making of Christian Doctrine* says that "patristic reasoning about the Trinity can only be saved from the charge of inconsistency by allowing that it is grounded on an appeal to Scripture of a kind which is totally at variance with one that would find general acceptance in the modern world" (p. 129).

text of the reaction to modernity signified by postmodernism, has witnessed a remarkable flowering of trinitarian theology. Undoubtedly the father of this renaissance was Karl Barth,[18] but major contributions have also been made by Jürgen Moltmann, John Zizioulas, Colin Gunton, and many others. This renaissance is of great importance to theological hermeneutics because "prime reality" for the Christian is the God who has come to us in Jesus, and epistemologically it is essential that a theological hermeneutic take this prime reality as its starting point. An exciting development of our time is that a multitude of scholars have come to this view via a variety of theological traditions. Some, such as Hans Frei, George Lindbeck, and Bruce Marshall, have journeyed to this point via the Barthian tradition; others, such as Alvin Plantinga and Nicholas Wolterstorff, via the neo-Calvinist one; still others have come to it via Catholic and Orthodox routes. All have in common Marshall's point that "Christians can and should have their own ways of thinking about truth and about deciding what to believe."[19]

For Christians "God" is the starting point from which everything else is to be understood.[20] And in Christian thought the doctrine of the Trinity specifies the meaning and reference of "God"; as such it is the primary Christian doctrine, with major epistemic significance, and not least in relation to the Old Testament.[21] The link between the Trinity and the Bible is unavoidable:

> The action whereby the Spirit induces us to love God by sharing in the mutual love of the Father and the Son is epistemically decisive: from it ultimately stems our willingness *to hold true the narratives which identify Jesus and the triune God, and to order the rest of our beliefs accordingly.* We cannot love the triune God, let alone love him with his own love, unless we hold a complex collection of beliefs which together pick out and describe the actions in time by which this God identifies himself in the world, and thereby makes his life available to our desires.[22]

18. See Karl Barth, *Church Dogmatics* I/1, *The Doctrine of the Word of God, Part 1*, ed. G. W. Bromiley and T. F. Torrance (Edinburgh: T&T Clark, 2000).

19. Marshall, *Trinity and Truth*, p. xi.

20. In this sense, from a Christian perspective, ontology takes priority over epistemology. In *Naming the Elephant: Worldview as a Concept* (Downers Grove: IVP, 2004), esp. pp. 51-75, James Sire notes the radicality of the post-Enlightenment shift in reversing the order by making how we know, i.e., epistemology, primary. See also Michael Buckley, *At the Origins of Modern Atheism* (New Haven: Yale University Press, 1990).

21. I take it that the "immanent" and the "economic" Trinity are one and the same.

22. Marshall, *Trinity and Truth*, p. 209, emphasis mine.

James Barr articulates this clearly: "All Christian use of the Old Testament seems to depend on the belief that the one God who is the God of Israel is also the God and Father of Jesus Christ."[23] Again: "All our use of the Old Testament goes back to this belief. What is said there that relates to 'God' relates to our God. Consequently that which can be known of our God is known only when we consider the Old Testament as a place in which he is known."[24]

How, then, does the doctrine of the Trinity shape a theological hermeneutic for the Old Testament? In the remainder of this chapter I will propose five ways in which it does so.

1. The Doctrine of the Trinity Implies an Acceptance of the Old Testament as Authoritative Scripture

The doctrine of the Trinity commits us to the view that Scripture as a whole is authoritative in that it renders Jesus Christ to us adequately.[25] This implies, contra Marcion and his many successors, an acceptance of the authority of the Old Testament as just that, the Old Testament. Where did this highly creative grafting of the new onto the old come from? Henri de Lubac rightly asserts that

> it was the consequence of the fact of the Incarnation on the conscience of some few Jews. In the end what was originally known by intuition was developed into a skillfully constructed theory capable of withstanding Jewish attacks on the one hand and those of Gnostics on the other, at the same time providing the means for preserving the scriptures and using them as a basis . . . right from the beginning the essential was there, the synthesis was made, in the dazzling and confused light of revelation. *Novum testamentum in Vetere labet: Vetus nunc in Novo patet.* . . . Very early, of course, separate traditions in the interpretation of scripture were established, different schools arose. . . . But the same fundamental principle compelled the recognition of all. From the beginning "the harmoni-

23. James Barr, *Old and New in Interpretation: A Study of the Two Testaments* (London: SCM, 1966), p. 149.

24. Barr, *Old and New in Interpretation*, pp. 153-55. See also Christopher Seitz, *Figured Out: Typology and Providence in Christian Scripture* (Louisville: Westminster John Knox, 2001), pp. 4-6.

25. See Kevin J. Vanhoozer, *The Drama of Doctrine: A Canonical Linguistic Approach to Christian Theology* (Louisville: Westminster John Knox, 2005), pp. 286-88.

ous agreement of the Law and the Prophets with the Testament delivered by the Lord" was the "rule of the Church."[26]

De Lubac here perceptively notes that central to Christian faith from its inception is an intuitive sense of the unity of the Testaments in Christ. In this respect a view of the canon as a whole originates, as it were, in the Christ event and in the Bible itself. According to Henning Graf Reventlow, the relationship of the Testaments is *the* issue in (modern) biblical theology,[27] and de Lubac helpfully points us to the source of the Christian commitment to — and concern to articulate the logic of — the inner unity of the Bible. Not surprisingly, therefore, this pattern and concern are evident in different ways in catechesis and homiletics from the outset and in all the major Christian thinkers who follow the church fathers, not least Augustine, Aquinas, Luther, Calvin, and so on.

In his struggle with Marcion and the Gnostics over the unity of the Bible, Irenaeus articulates the unity of the Bible as a single story, as Robert Louis Wilken explains:

> Two histories converge in the biblical account, the history of Israel and the life of Christ, but because they are also the history of God's actions in and for the world, they are part of a larger narrative that begins at creation and ends in a vision of a new, more splendid city in which the "Lord God will be their light." The Bible begins, as it were, with the beginning and ends with an end that is no end, life with God, in Irenaeus's charming expression, a life in which one is "always conversing with God in new ways." Nothing falls outside its scope.[28]

With Irenaeus's narrative approach to the Bible we have an incipient biblical theology seeking to articulate the inner unity of the Bible in response to Marcion. The unity of the Testaments is affirmed — there is one God who called Abraham, spoke with Moses, sent the prophets, and is also the Father of our Lord Jesus Christ — and is articulated in terms of the story shape of the Bible as a whole. Furthermore, the story is explained in terms of the theme of renewal or re-creation.

26. Henri de Lubac, *Catholicism: Christ and the Common Destiny of Mankind* (San Francisco: Ignatius, 1947), p. 88.

27. Henning Graf Reventlow, *Problems of Biblical Theology in the Twentieth Century* (London: SCM, 1986).

28. Robert Louis Wilken, *The Spirit of Early Christian Thought: Seeking the Face of God* (New Haven: Yale University Press, 2003), p. 63.

Yet trinitarian theology has sometimes led to neglect of Scripture. An example of this is David S. Cunningham's dealing with the question of same-sex desire in the context of a trinitarian framework. He asserts,

> I have already suggested that the doctrine of the Trinity can help us to understand and evaluate the nature of the relationships among bodies, including relationships that involve sexual desire. And as far as I can see, there is nothing in trinitarian doctrine that has a word to say, in any *prima facie* sense, against monogamous gay or lesbian relationships. In such relationships, mutual participation is clearly possible, just as it is in opposite-sex relationships. The same-sex partner is still an "other," and fully capable of embodying the trinitarian virtue of particularity. The doctrine of the Trinity does not seem to address anatomical features of the desired body; God manifests yearning, desire, and love for the *otherness* of the other, but this is not limited to — nor does it necessarily even involve — questions of sexual difference.[29]

What is striking here is the absence of close attention to the very biblical narratives out of which trinitarian theology emerges. If the doctrine of the Trinity has a prima facie connection with creation, which in terms of the Christian tradition is impossible to deny, and if redemption involves, as Oliver O'Donovan argues, the reaffirmation of creation,[30] then the Trinity has much to say about sexual and gender differences and about marriage and relationships.

This is not to suggest that the hermeneutics of same-sex desire are necessarily simple, but it is to insist that a trinitarian theology cannot become an excuse for bypassing Scripture. Rather, a healthy trinitarian hermeneutic will lead us more deeply into the Old Testament rather than away from it. Calvin is alert to this when he says of his *Institutes*: "It has been my purpose in this labor to prepare and instruct candidates in sacred theology for the reading of the divine Word, in order that they may be able both to have easy access to it and to advance in it without stumbling."[31] As we have noted

29. David S. Cunningham, *These Three Are One: The Practice of Trinitarian Theology* (Oxford: Blackwell, 1998), p. 300.

30. Oliver O'Donovan, *Resurrection and Moral Order: An Outline for an Evangelical Ethics* (Grand Rapids: Eerdmans, 1994).

31. John Calvin, *Institutes of the Christian Religion* I.4, trans. Henry Beveridge (Peabody, MA: Hendrickson, 2008). On the Trinity see Calvin, *Institutes* I.13, especially section 3: "The expressions 'Trinity' and 'Person' aid the interpretation of Scripture and are therefore admissible."

above, the doctrine of the Trinity implies an acceptance of the Scriptures as an authoritative rendering of Jesus Christ, so that a trinitarian hermeneutic should always lead us deeply into Scripture.

2. The Doctrine of the Trinity Alerts Us to the Fact That the Old Testament Is Part of a Larger Whole

The Old Testament by itself is not Christian Scripture; it functions as such only within *tota Scriptura*. We do not read the Old Testament truthfully unless we read it as the Old Testament that is "fulfilled" in the New. Thus, a trinitarian hermeneutic commits us to biblical theology with its quest for the inner unity of the Bible. If we imagine the Bible as a grand cathedral, it becomes apparent that there are many entrances into such a cathedral, so that biblical theology can adopt a variety of methodologies to uncover the unity of Scripture.[32] A particularly fecund approach is that of Irenaeus, whereby the Bible is approached as an overarching narrative. Recently N. T. Wright has developed such a hermeneutic by suggesting that we view the Bible as a drama in multiple acts.[33] Such a dramatic hermeneutic is inherently trinitarian with its sense of perichoretic narrative development.[34]

A trinitarian hermeneutic for the Old Testament also provides the basis for typological or figural analysis of the Bible, which rests on the trinitarian assumption that the footsteps we observe in the New Testament are from the same God we find active in the Old. According to Christopher Seitz,

> Figural reading is not an exegetical technique. It is an effort to hear the two-testament witness to God in Christ, taking seriously its plain sense, in

---

32. See Gerhard F. Hasel, *Old Testament Theology: Basic Issues in the Current Debate*, 4th ed. (Grand Rapids: Eerdmans, 2001).

33. N. T. Wright, "How Can the Bible Be Authoritative?" *Vox Evangelica* 21 (1991): 7-32, suggests five. Craig Bartholomew and Michael Goheen suggest six; see *The Drama of Scripture* (Grand Rapids: Baker Academic, 2004) and "Story and Biblical Theology," in *Out of Egypt: Biblical Theology and Biblical Interpretation*, ed. Craig Bartholomew, Mary Healy, Karl Möller, and Robin Parry, SAHS 5 (Grand Rapids: Zondervan, 2004), pp. 144-71.

34. Kathryn Greene-McCreight notes: "The Rule is thus a basic 'take' on the subject matter and plot of the Christian story, which couples the confession of Jesus the Redeemer with the confession of God the Creator, and thus 'rules out' heretical statements that do not honor the content of the Rule." See her "Rule of Faith," in *Dictionary for Theological Interpretation of the Bible*, ed. Kevin J. Vanhoozer et al. (Grand Rapids: Baker Academic, 2005), p. 704.

conjunction with apostolic teaching. This teaching is guided by the conviction that the persons of the Trinity are to be seen in their fundamental unity, as the Father, the Son, and the Holy Ghost, one God. And this teaching is derived from the two-testament witness itself.[35]

3. The Doctrine of the Trinity Alerts Us to the Importance of Attending to the Discrete Witness of the Old Testament

Too often a Christological hermeneutic has been imposed on the Old Testament, thus restricting its voice from being heard on its own terms.[36] A trinitarian hermeneutic alerts us to the historical unfolding of God's revelation and does full justice to his revelation of himself in and through the life of his elect people, Israel. The emphasis on perichoresis in trinitarian doctrine similarly points in this direction, with its stress that, while all three persons of the Trinity are involved in all their acts, the Father is particularly associated with creation and Israel, the Son with the fulfillment of redemption, and the Spirit with mission. In this respect James Barr rightly notes that

> it is an illusory position to think of ourselves as in a position where the New Testament is clear, is known and accepted, and where therefore from this secure position we start out to explore the much more doubtful and dangerous territory of the Old Testament. . . . Insofar as a position is Christian it is related to the Old Testament from the beginning.[37]

As Brevard Childs notes, therefore, a trinitarian hermeneutic will attend to what he calls the discrete witness of the Old Testament.[38] God's revelation of himself in the life of Israel, an ancient Near Eastern nation, will be taken with full seriousness, and all critical tools will be brought to bear in articu-

---

35. Seitz, *Figured Out*, p. 10.

36. See in this respect Christopher Seitz, "Christological Interpretation of Texts and Trinitarian Claims to Truth," *Scottish Journal of Theology* 52 (1999): 209-26; and Francis Watson, "The Old Testament as Christian Scripture: A Response to Professor Seitz," *Scottish Journal of Theology* 52 (1999): 227-32.

37. Barr, *Old and New in Interpretation*, pp. 153-55.

38. Brevard S. Childs, *Biblical Theology of the Old and New Testaments: Theological Reflection on the Christian Bible* (Minneapolis: Fortress, 1992), pp. 95-118; see also Childs, "The Nature of the Christian Bible: One Book, Two Testaments," in *The Rule of Faith: Scripture, Creed, and Canon in a Critical Age*, ed. Ephraim Radner and George Sumner (Harrisburg: Morehouse, 1998), pp. 115-26.

lating this witness. Critical tools are never neutral, and their underpinnings may require reconfiguration in relation to the epistemic priority of the Trinity, but the historical dimension of Israel's life will be open to rigorous scrutiny.

Does this mean that Christians should read the Old Testament with no sense of the subsequent acts in the story? This is simply impossible, but we should nevertheless be sensitive to the "otherness" of the Old Testament where it does not fit easily with our New Testament sensibilities. Kevin Vanhoozer gets at this point in his assertion that "Of all the canonical dialogues, perhaps the most important is that between the Old and New Testaments. Bakhtin rightly cautions us against thinking of dialogue as the merging of two or more voices into one. . . . In a genuine dialogue, each voice retains its integrity, yet each is also mutually enriched."[39] "Dialogue" is a limited metaphor for the relationship between the Testaments, because the doctrine of the Trinity implies that in the canon of Scripture God speaks with one voice and not two. But Vanhoozer's point is well taken — a trinitarian hermeneutic will listen to the Old Testament on its own terms, trusting that the voice of the Father will be found to be in concord with that of the Son and the Spirit. J. Clinton McCann's work on the Psalter seems to me an excellent example of this sort of hermeneutic in practice.[40]

But let me elaborate on the notion of reconfiguring critical approaches referred to above. Methods are never philosophically and theologically neutral, and it is important to avoid importing methods of interpretation that are at root in conflict epistemologically with the epistemic primacy of the Trinity.[41] Thus Wright, for example, in his *The New Testament and the People of God*, notes that we need a more Jewish and less Greek style of form criticism for the Gospels.[42] The bifurcation between biblical studies and theol-

---

39. Vanhoozer, *The Drama of Doctrine*, pp. 290-91. Childs also makes use of the metaphor of dialogue: "The dialogical move of theological reflection that is being suggested traverses the partial and fragmentary grasp of reality found in both Testaments to the full reality that the church confesses to have found in Jesus Christ"; see "On Reclaiming the Bible for Christian Theology," in *Reclaiming the Bible for the Church*, ed. Carl E. Braaten and Robert W. Jenson (Edinburgh: T&T Clark, 1995), pp. 1-19 (here p. 15).

40. J. Clinton McCann Jr., *A Theological Introduction to the Book of Psalms: The Psalms as Torah* (Nashville: Abingdon, 1993).

41. See Craig Bartholomew, "Uncharted Waters: Philosophy, Theology, and the Crisis in Biblical Interpretation," in *Renewing Biblical Interpretation*, ed. Craig Bartholomew et al., SAHS 1 (Grand Rapids: Zondervan, 2000), pp. 1-39.

42. N. T. Wright, *The New Testament and the People of God* (Minneapolis: Fortress, 1992), p. 427.

ogy has often meant that methods are regularly applied to the Old Testament with the assumption built in that God can neither act nor speak; clearly this sort of emphasis is ruled out by the Trinity.

This is not to suggest that a trinitarian hermeneutic provides an easy way out of the many issues that historical, literary, and postmodern criticism have raised in relation to the Old Testament. At their best, all these approaches involve very close readings of the Old Testament, and the data they point to cannot and should not be ignored. But data is never neutral; it always comes within a particular framework or paradigm so that, as philosophers of science have noted, all theory is underdetermined. A trinitarian hermeneutic should not avoid any of these issues, but, as Stephen Neill noted of a theology of history in relation to New Testament interpretation, it provides the appropriate ring within which solutions may be found.

The relationship between a trinitarian hermeneutic and philosophy is explored in Chapter 3 below. For now it suffices to note that philosophical hermeneutics has much to offer theological hermeneutics.[43] At the same time it must not be assumed that the openness to "the other" in contemporary hermeneutics is equivalent to an openness to the trinitarian God.[44] Careful critical discernment is always required in appropriating contemporary tools that are clearly not rooted in a trinitarian view of the world. And it is important to note that the Trinity implies a worldview:

> The thoughtful person places the doctrine of the trinity in the very center of the full-orbed life of nature and mankind. The confession of the Christian is not an island in mid-ocean but a mountain-top overlooking the entire creation. And it is the task of the Christian theologian to set forth clearly the great significance of God's revelation for (and the relation of that revelation to) the whole realm of existence. The mind of the Christian is not satisfied until every form of existence has been referred to the triune God and until the confession of the trinity has received the place of prominence in our thought and life.[45]

43. See Thiselton's several works on this topic as well as the eight-volume Scripture and Hermeneutics Series.

44. See Jens Zimmermann, *Recovering Theological Hermeneutics: An Incarnational-Trinitarian Theory of Interpretation* (Grand Rapids: Baker, 2004), chapter 8; and Romano Guardini, *The World and the Person* (Chicago: Regnery, 1965).

45. Bavinck, *The Doctrine of God*, p. 329. On a trinitarian worldview see Marshall, *Trinity and Truth*, chapter 5. On p. 118, Marshall notes: "Believing the gospel (that is, the narratives which identify Jesus and the triune God), therefore, necessarily commits believers to a comprehensive view of the world centered epistemically on the gospel narrative itself. On

4. The Doctrine of the Trinity Alerts Us to the Proper Goal of, and Primary Context for, Reading the Old Testament

So much academic exegesis falls short of what must be the goal of a theological hermeneutic, namely, attention to God's address through his Word. From a trinitarian perspective, any hermeneutic that fails to make this its goal is woefully inadequate. Athanasius makes the point that God is not incommunicative; he is always speaking![46] The Trinity reveals God to us as the living and true God: "God is fullness of being: 'ocean of essence.'"[47] And as Charles M. Wood rightly notes, "To read the Bible, at least if one is properly prepared and disposed toward the task, is, on this view, to be addressed by God."[48]

The Trinity is important for a doctrine of creation since it maintains against deism the relation between God and creation and against pantheism the distinction between God and creation. The Trinity teaches "that God is able to impart himself: in an absolute sense to the Son and to the Spirit; in a relative sense, also to the creature."[49] And of course it is particularly through his Word that God imparts himself to his image bearers. Above all others Christ is his Word, but we find Christ by the Spirit in the field of the written Word, both Old and New Testaments. The Word, then, is the means by which God gives himself to us so that a receptivity to receive God is fundamental to any theological interpretation of the Old Testament. As Jean Vanier poignantly notes,

> At one moment in time
> the "Logos"
> became flesh
> and entered history.
> He came to lead us all
> into this communion,
> which is the very life of God.[50]

---

such a view there will be no region of belief and practice which can isolate itself from the epistemic reach of the gospel."

46. Bavinck, *The Doctrine of God*, p. 282.

47. Bavinck, *The Doctrine of God*, p. 330.

48. Charles M. Wood, *The Formation of Christian Understanding: Theological Hermeneutics* (Eugene, OR: Wipf & Stock, 2000), p. 39.

49. Bavinck, *The Doctrine of God*, p. 333.

50. Jean Vanier, *Drawn into the Mystery of Jesus through the Gospel of John* (Ottawa: Novalis, 2004), p. 17.

A theological hermeneutic will therefore always have as its goal to hear God's address, to facilitate communion. This is not for a moment to deny the cognitive, propositional element in God's communication, but it is to insist that "an important aspect of truth gets lost when testimony is 'objectified.' Simply to preserve the content is to catch only half the sacred fish."[51] If the Old Testament is part of God's address to his people, then the primary context for its reception will be ecclesial. It is in the liturgy that "the Word is living and active *maximally* though not *exclusively*."[52] And a close second to this primary context will be *lectio divina* as the appropriate preparation for liturgical hearing of the Old Testament. As Mariano Magrassi notes,

> The passage that leads to the understanding of Scripture leads to life in Christ. When the Scriptures are opened, he admits us to his private domain. Every deeper reading of the text is a movement toward him. The essential task of exegesis . . . is to apply everything to the mystery of Christ. . . . He is the one center where all the lines of the biblical universe meet.[53]

Lectio divina is thus

> not so much a matter of reading a book as of seeking Someone: "With all its ardor, the Church seeks in Scripture the One whom she loves." Exegesis is not technique; it is mysticism. The meaning of Scripture is not an impersonal truth but the fascinating figure of Christ. . . . The whole science of exegesis is the ability to recognize Christ.[54]

From this perspective, academic interpretation of the Bible is secondary in relation to the primary ecclesial reception of the Old Testament.[55] The

51. Vanhoozer, *The Drama of Doctrine,* p. 288.

52. Mariano Magrassi, *Praying the Bible: An Introduction to Lectio Divina* (Collegeville: Liturgical Press, 1998), p. 4. See also in this respect Scott W. Hahn, "Canon, Cult, and Covenant: The Promise of Liturgical Hermeneutics," in *Canon and Biblical Interpretation,* ed. Craig Bartholomew et al. (Grand Rapids: Zondervan, 2006), pp. 207-35; Scott W. Hahn, *Letter and Spirit: From Written Text to Living Word in the Liturgy* (New York: Doubleday, 2005); Robert W. Jenson, "Hermeneutics and the Life of the Church," in *Reclaiming the Bible for the Church,* pp. 89-106; Aidan Kavanagh, "Scriptural Word and Liturgical Worship," in *Reclaiming the Bible for the Church,* pp. 131-50.

53. Magrassi, *Praying the Bible,* p. 44.

54. Magrassi, *Praying the Bible,* pp. 52-53. Readers unfamiliar with *lectio divina* will find Eugene H. Peterson's *Eat This Book: A Conversation in the Art of Spiritual Reading* (Grand Rapids: Eerdmans, 2005), especially Part II, helpful.

55. On study and *lectio divina* see Magrassi, *Praying the Bible,* pp. 72-76.

crucial question is their *interrelationship*. Academic Old Testament exegesis is often construed as a necessary corrective to ecclesial use of the Old Testament. Undoubtedly this can be the case, just as the reverse can be true, but lurking behind this construal is something closely akin to the hermeneutic of correlation.

The common view in this respect goes something like this: a trinitarian approach to Scripture is committed and therefore ideological. It is thus crucial that a non-committed academic study of the Old Testament be developed as a healthy corrective to the excesses and dangers of trinitarian interpretation. The problem with this is that there is no such thing as a non-committed interpretation of the Old Testament; one ends up conceding the epistemic grounds of academic interpretation and hoping that edifices erected on incongruous epistemic grounds can somehow be brought together.[56] But the very nature of the doctrine of the Trinity implies that the metanarrative it embodies is the true story of the world and in conflict with alternative metanarratives.

Thus the difference between academic and ecclesial reception of the Old Testament must not be construed as consisting of different epistemic foundations. Both Old Testament scholar and faithful layperson are called to make the Trinity their prime reality, and rigorous, critical Old Testament exegesis is to be as trinitarian as liturgical reception of the Old Testament. Academic interpretation should rather be seen as a deepening of the church's reading of the Old Testament through rigorous analysis of the text. However, as Barth notes, such analysis must always be directed ultimately toward attending to God's address.

It is also important to note that such an academic trinitarian hermeneutic begins and proceeds with communion: "To fall in love with this God, to be drawn into the love of this Father and this Son for one another, seems an outcome which only their Spirit can bring about."[57] Thus prayer and being present to God should accompany the hermeneutical process, both academic and ecclesial, from beginning to end and back again. It is the Spirit who leads ordinary Christian readers as well as the academic into the truth of Scripture.[58]

---

56. It is precisely this move that Michael Buckley warns against in *At the Origins of Modern Atheism*.

57. Marshall, *Trinity and Truth*, p. 208.

58. Marshall, *Trinity and Truth*, pp. 180-216, and John Webster, *Word and Church: Essays in Church Dogmatics* (Edinburgh: T&T Clark, 2001), p. 80, note the sinful resistance to approaching Scripture as God's address. Webster notes, "Crucially, this means that to read

The ecclesial primacy of Old Testament interpretation also means that Old Testament scholars should have a vested interest in the renaissance of reception history in Old Testament studies, since this provides an important avenue through which to read it in the context of the Christian tradition. Trinitarian interpretation will also be communal, as can be seen in both this volume and the Scripture and Hermeneutics Seminar, which has worked tirelessly to promote community amid an individualistic and often narcissistic academy.

5. The Doctrine of the Trinity Does Not Close Down but Opens Up Interpretation of the Old Testament

A trinitarian hermeneutic is one among many approaches to the Old Testament in our increasingly pluralistic academy. However, this should not be taken to imply that from a Christian perspective one approach is as valid as another, so that a trinitarian hermeneutic is simply a matter of personal preference. From a Christian perspective a trinitarian hermeneutic is the right, truthful way to read Scripture and is *the* way that will yield a truthful understanding of the Old Testament.

But this way is spacious and fecund and creates room for a variety of genuinely theological readings. As Seitz notes,

> Concern with the figural linguistic world of Scripture did not mean single-meaning exegesis! No one reading Justin, Irenaeus, Clement, Origen, the Antiochenes, or Athanasius should expect anything like uniformity, yet all of these, including Origen, bear a decided family resemblance. The dynamic character of scripture in its two-testament form does not allow for propositional or technical flattening, given that this

---

Scripture well is to undergo a chastening of the will, even, perhaps, 'the death of the subject and of the will.' Anything less would fail to take seriously the eschatological character of Christian life and therefore of Christian reading." For analyses of the role of the Spirit in interpretation see Marshall, *Trinity and Truth*, pp. 180-216, and Kevin Vanhoozer, "The Spirit of Understanding: Special Revelation and General Hermeneutics," in *Disciplining Hermeneutics: Interpretation in Christian Perspective*, ed. Roger Lundin (Grand Rapids: Eerdmans, 1997), pp. 131-65. Henri De Lubac, in *Scripture in the Tradition* (New York: Crossroad, 2000), pp. 106-7, asserts that "Just as he is the exegesis of Scripture, Jesus Christ is also its exegete. . . . It is he and he alone who explains it to us, and in explaining it to us he is himself explained."

witness is received in faith, under the guidance of the Holy Spirit, disciplined by prayer, Eucharistic fellowship, and the teaching of the church in its baptismal interrogatories and creedal affirmations.[59]

Similarly, Anthony Thiselton notes that "the inexhaustible, multilayered, multifunctional polyphony of biblical texts transcends repeatedly any single way of saying it; but this does not, need not, and should not invite the disastrous hospitality to radical pluralism that brings anarchy."[60] A trinitarian hermeneutic is radical in that it does exclude certain readings of the Old Testament: Seitz notes how it opposes the historicism rampant in contemporary Old Testament studies;[61] Elizabeth Achtemeier notes how a theological hermeneutic is incompatible with the developmentalism of so much Old Testament study;[62] and we have noted above how a trinitarian hermeneutic resists any theological move that disengages with Scripture.[63] Having said this, a trinitarian hermeneutic opens up the feast of Scripture with its endless possibility of fecund, theological interpretation. As Richard John Neuhaus comments in his foreword to Thomas Oden's *Requiem,*

> Origen, Irenaeus, Cyril of Alexandria, Thomas Aquinas, Teresa of Ávila, Martin Luther, John Calvin, John Wesley — the names fall trippingly from Oden's tongue like a gourmet surveying a most spectacular table. Here are arguments [and we would say interpretations of the Old Testament] you can sink your teeth into, conceptual flights of intoxicating complexity, and truths to die for. Far from the table, over there, *way* over there, is American theological education, where prodigal academics feed starving students on the dry husks of their clever unbelief.[64]

59. Seitz, *Figured Out,* pp. 8-9.

60. Anthony Thiselton, "Communicative Action and Promise in Hermeneutics," in *Disciplining Hermeneutics,* p. 138.

61. Seitz, *Figured Out.*

62. Elizabeth Achtemeier, "The Canon as the Voice of the Living God," in *Reclaiming the Bible,* pp. 119-30.

63. On same-sex blessing and Scripture, see Seitz, "Dispirited: Scripture as Rule of Faith and Recent Misuse of the Council of Jerusalem: Text, Spirit, and Word to Culture," in *Figured Out,* pp. 117-30.

64. Richard Neuhaus, "Foreword," in Thomas C. Oden's *Requiem: A Lament in Three Movements* (Nashville: Abingdon, 1995), p. 10.

Part II LEARNING TO LISTEN

2 The History of Old Testament Interpretation: An Anecdotal Survey

Al Wolters

In keeping with the general purpose of the present volume, the following historical sketch will focus on the *Christian* interpretation of the Old Testament, thus dealing only secondarily with Jewish and other kinds of interpretation. Furthermore, the focus can only be on selected *highlights* in the history of Christian interpretation, with a special interest in the religious appropriation of the Old Testament as *Scripture,* that is, as authoritative canon for believers.

The New Testament

The history of the Christian interpretation of the Old Testament begins with the writings of the New Testament. In these writings it is assumed as a matter of course that the Jewish Scriptures are the divinely inspired and authoritative sacred writings that the Jewish rabbis took them to be. There is no hint anywhere in the New Testament that these Scriptures are to be treated with anything but reverence and awe; they are to be unquestioningly accepted as the very oracles of God. In Paul's classic formulation in 2 Timothy 3:16-17: "All Scripture [that is, the Hebrew Bible] is God-breathed and is useful for teaching, rebuking, correcting and training in righteousness, so that the man of God *(ho tou theou anthrōpos)* may be thoroughly equipped for every good work" (NIV).

This is not to say that the New Testament interpretation of the Jewish Scriptures did not differ decisively from the interpretation that was current among Jewish rabbis in the first century. The most important difference is of course that the New Testament writers understood Jesus Christ to be the fulfillment of the messianic prophecies of the Old Testament. In fact, Luke's Gospel tells us that Jesus explained to his fellow-travelers on the road to Emmaus that the Jewish Scriptures were all about himself: "And beginning with Moses and all the Prophets, he explained to them what was said in all the Scriptures concerning himself" (24:27). Throughout the New Testament, the Old is read as pointing forward in some way to the person of Jesus Christ, to his earthly life from conception to ascension, to the new post-ethnic community of believers that he established, and to the worldwide eschatological kingdom that he inaugurated.

Although the New Testament interpretation of the Old shows many traces of exegetical practices that were also current in contemporary Jewish exegesis, the differences are usually more significant than the similarities.[1] It is particularly striking that Jesus himself repeatedly challenged the rabbinic interpretation of the Hebrew Scriptures, for example in the so-called antitheses of the Sermon on the Mount.[2]

Another striking difference, especially with the interpretation of Scripture that we find in Hellenized Jews like Philo, is the avoidance of allegory in the New Testament. To understand this point, we need to make a careful terminological distinction, following Jean Daniélou, between "allegory" and "typology."[3] The New Testament is full of the latter, in which a person or event in the Old Testament is seen as foreshadowing or prefiguring something in the New. The key point here is that a historical reality earlier in the redemptive metanarrative of Scripture anticipates another historical reality later in that same narrative.[4] Allegory, on the other hand, takes some feature of Scripture and makes it a symbol of some supra-historical spiritual truth in general. Unfortunately, there is some terminological confusion here. "Al-

---

1. See Richard Longenecker, *Biblical Exegesis in the Apostolic Age*, 2nd ed. (Grand Rapids: Eerdmans, 1999).

2. Matt. 5:21-48.

3. Jean Daniélou, *Qu'est-ce que la typologie?* in *L'Ancien Testament et les chrétiens*, ed. P. Auvray et al. (Paris: Éditions du Cerf, 1951), pp. 199-205. Daniélou elaborated on this distinction in many subsequent publications. For a more recent defense of the distinction, see Frances M. Young, *Biblical Exegesis and the Formation of Christian Culture* (Peabody, MA: Hendrickson, 2002), pp. 161-62, 189-201.

4. See Leonhard Goppelt, *Typos: The Typological Interpretation of the Old Testament in the New*, trans. D. H. Madvig (Grand Rapids: Eerdmans, 1982), originally published in German as *Typos: Die typologische Deutung des Alten Testaments im Neuen* (Gütersloh: Gerd Mohn, 1939).

legory" has often been used as including typology as well. When Paul makes a connection between Hagar and "the present city of Jerusalem," he is engaging in typological exegesis, but the Greek word that he uses to describe it is *allēgoroumena* (Gal. 4:24).[5]

The Patristic Era

The field of patristic biblical interpretation is vast, and certain areas are still largely unexplored. In recent decades, with the renewed appreciation for "pre-critical" biblical interpretation and the publication of patristic exegetical works in translation, greater attention has been paid to this crucial period of Christian interpretation of the Bible. It is foundational for everything that follows.

Gnosticism and Marcion

A particularly dangerous challenge to the early church was the movement known as Gnosticism. This movement, which the church fathers traced back to Simon Magus, and which Daniélou[6] plausibly understood as a Jewish movement against Yahweh occasioned by the destruction of Jerusalem in A.D. 70, identified the God of the Old Testament as the evil creator of an evil world, who is to be contrasted with a higher good God named Anthropos, with whom the Gnostic initiates considered themselves ultimately identical.[7] A part of the Gnostic movement was the second-century Marcion, who declared himself a Christian but rejected the authority of the Old Testament and much of the New. The vigorous anti-Gnostic polemic of such church fathers as Irenaeus and Clement of Rome saved the church from this rejection of the Old Testament. Instead, virtually all subsequent patristic writers took over from the New Testament the belief that the Old Testament is inspired,

5. For a useful discussion of the debate surrounding the legitimacy of distinguishing between "typology" and "allegory," see Peter W. Martens, "Revisiting the Allegory/Typology Distinctions: The Case of Origen," *Journal of Early Christian Studies* 16 (2008): 283-317.

6. See Jean Daniélou, "Judéo-Christianisme et Gnose," in *Aspects du Judéo-Christianisme, Colloque de Strasbourg, 23-25 avril, 1964* (Paris: Presses Universitaires de France, 1965), pp. 139-64.

7. Hans Jonas, *The Gnostic Religion: The Message of the Alien God and the Beginnings of Christianity* (Boston: Beacon Press, 1958).

reliable, and authoritative. Henceforth both Testaments were considered to be integral parts of the Christian Scriptures, whose relationship can be characterized by the Augustinian formulation *Novum Testamentum in Vetere latet, Vetus in Novo patet,* "The New is in the Old concealed, the Old is in the New revealed."

The Septuagint

A feature of patristic biblical interpretation that must not be overlooked is the fact that, for the first half-millennium of the Christian era, the Old Testament was known to the church almost exclusively in the form of the Septuagint, which consisted of a Greek translation of the Hebrew Bible (made by many hands over several centuries, beginning in the third century B.C.), supplemented by a number of other Jewish religious writings, most originally written in Greek. It was the Septuagint, both in its original Greek form and in the various daughter translations into other languages that were made from it, which provided the Old Testament text on which the church fathers wrote their commentaries and from which they preached their sermons. As far as they were concerned, the Septuagint *was* the Old Testament. In fact the Septuagint itself was considered inspired.[8] This fundamental fact about patristic exegesis has two significant implications. The first has to do with the extent of the canon. Although the New Testament writers cite as authoritative only the twenty-two books included in the Hebrew Bible,[9] the church fathers accepted as canonical also the so-called apocryphal or deuterocanonical books found in the Septuagint. The second implication is that patristic exegesis is based on a translation that in many places is not an accurate rendering of the underlying Hebrew text. Not only are individual Hebrew words and expressions often not understood, but the original is not infrequently misrepresented or shortened. The translation of the book of Proverbs, for example, is quite tendentious, significantly hellenizing its thought world, while the books of Job and Jeremiah fail to translate a substantial portion of the parent text.

---

8. Mogens Müller, *The First Bible of the Church: A Plea for the Septuagint,* JSOTSup 206 (Sheffield: Sheffield Academic Press, 1996).

9. R. T. Beckwith, *The Old Testament Canon of the New Testament and Its Background in Early Judaism* (Grand Rapids: Eerdmans, 1985). The one exception may be the citation from the book of Enoch in Jude 14.

Philo and Allegory

The reticence that the New Testament writers show with respect to allegory is not generally shared by the writers of the patristic era, traditionally reckoned to end with Gregory the Great and the sixth century A.D. Here the fathers were significantly influenced by the Jewish philosopher Philo of Alexandria. Philo was a Greek-speaking contemporary of the apostles, who sought to combine Platonic philosophy with his Jewish faith. He undertook this project with the aid of allegory, a hermeneutical method that had been developed in Greek philosophy (especially the Stoics) as a means of harmonizing philosophy and the Greek myths. Thus the Stoics interpreted the Zeus of mythology with the All of their own cosmology. Philo used the methodology of allegory to have the Jewish Scriptures, especially the Pentateuch, teach essentially Platonic philosophy.[10] Although he had little influence in Jewish circles, Philo was eagerly read by the Christian church fathers, who not only preserved his writings for posterity, but also adopted his allegorical method for their own purposes. In fact, for many centuries Philo himself was regarded as a kind of "honorary church father."[11]

Alexandrian and Antiochene Schools

In speaking of patristic exegesis, it is customary to distinguish two dominant schools, the Alexandrian and the Antiochene, the former characterized by the uninhibited use of allegory, and the latter by a more sober emphasis on the literal or historical sense. Like all such generalizations, this distinction is a useful oversimplification. The oversimplification lies first of all in the fact that in both "schools" attention was paid to both the literal or historical sense and the more-than-literal spiritual senses, including allegory. In addition, it should be remembered that the Alexandrian "school" in fact set its stamp on the great majority of patristic biblical interpreters, especially those writing in Greek and Latin. It is perhaps more accurate to speak of the Antiochene school as a relatively short-lived protest movement against the excessive allegorizing of the Alexandrians, but without much lasting impact

---

10. Jean Pépin, *Mythe et allégorie. Les origines grecques et les contestations judéo-chétiennes* (Paris: Éditions Montaigne, 1958).

11. David T. Runia, *Philo in Early Christian Literature: A Survey* (Assen: Van Gorcum/Minneapolis: Fortress, 1993), pp. 3-7.

in the long run. Nevertheless, the distinction of schools is useful, since it reminds us that patristic exegesis was not monolithically allegorical.

The Alexandrian school of interpretation was associated with the Catechetical School of Alexandria, founded in the late second century and counting among its early leaders Clement of Alexandria and Origen. It is significant that Alexandria was also the home of Philo, as well as a long tradition of pagan philological scholarship.

Origen

Like his fellow Alexandrian Philo two centuries earlier, Origen defended and used the allegorical method to read the Scriptures in a Platonizing way. It is significant that Origen, like his contemporary Plotinus, the founder of Neoplatonism, was probably a student of Ammonius Sakkas, an Alexandrian Christian who had reverted to paganism and who in his philosophy sought to work out a synthesis of Plato and Aristotle. Origen was no doubt the greatest biblical scholar of antiquity, notable for his vast erudition, which included a thorough knowledge of Hebrew. He was an unabashed promoter of allegorical interpretation. Although he was later condemned as a heretic, he died a martyr for his faith, and his influence on subsequent patristic writers was enormous. He more than anyone else was responsible for the vast influence of the Alexandrian school.

Theodore of Mopsuestia

Theodore was the key figure in the Antiochene school. Together with his close friend John Chrysostom he studied in Antioch of Syria under Diodore of Tarsus, who is generally considered the founder of the school. Although like Origen he was anathematized by later church councils in the West, he was held in high honor as an exegete in the Syriac churches. His hermeneutics is characterized by a strong rejection of allegory (even for the Song of Songs) and a great reluctance to see Old Testament texts as referring to New Testament realities. In fact, the history to which the Hebrew Bible refers is in his view restricted almost entirely to the period ending with the Maccabean revolt in 168-165 B.C. Although he is sometimes depicted as a forerunner of modern historical criticism, his acceptance of typology (however restricted in actual practice), as well as the general authority and reliability of Scripture, shows that this judgment needs to be significantly qualified. Together with Theodore we should mention his friend John Chrysostom, whose sermons popularized the school's basic hermeneutical approach, and his students Nestorius and Theodoret of Cyrrhus.[12]

Jerome

With the exception of Origen, Jerome was the only church father with a good command of Hebrew. He is largely responsible for the new Latin translation of the Bible now known as the Vulgate, although significantly the book of Psalms in the Vulgate is still based on the Greek of the Septuagint. Jerome does not fit neatly into either the Alexandrian or the Antiochene school. In the course of his life he moved gradually away from the kind of allegorizing found in Origen; in his commentary on Jeremiah, which Jerome left unfinished at his death, there is relatively little non-literal interpretation. In other commentaries, such as that on the Minor Prophets, he gives both a literal interpretation, for which he draws very largely on the Jewish interpretive tradition, and a "spiritual" one, where he draws on his Christian predecessors. Oddly enough, for every pericope he gives a translation both of the Hebrew and the Septuagint and treats both as authoritative sources for his exposition.

Syriac Fathers

The preceding account has been largely limited to the works of church fathers who wrote in Greek and Latin. There are others who wrote in other languages, notably Syriac. A significant figure in this tradition is Ephrem the Syrian, whose exegetical work is distinctive in that it is much less influenced by Greek philosophy than were his counterparts in the Greco-Roman world. Furthermore, a noteworthy feature of the Syriac exegetes is that they had a particularly high regard for Theodore of Mopsuestia, whose exegetical works were widely translated into Syriac and in many cases survive today only in Syriac translation. Theodore was often referred to as simply "the Interpreter" *(mephasqana)* in Syriac commentaries on Scripture.

---

12. On Theodore see Dimitri Z. Zaharopoulos, *Theodore of Mopsuestia on the Bible: A Study of His Old Testament Exegesis* (Mahwah, NJ: Paulist Press, 1989).

Preaching and Lectio Divina

Finally, it needs to be stressed that much of the patristic engagement with the Old Testament, as with the Bible as a whole, was concerned with the edification of Christian believers. It was all about the religious appropriation of the Scripture as the Word of God, that is, about hearing the text as divine address, which served to instruct as well as comfort, exhort as well as warn. As a result, much of the surviving literature with respect to the fathers' interpretation of the Old Testament comes in the form of sermons or homilies addressed to an audience of Christian believers at Sunday worship services. In addition, beginning with the fourth century, we also see the development of the practice of *lectio divina*, a meditative way of reading, listening to, and reflecting on portions of Scripture as part of an individual believer's private prayers and devotions. This was a form of Scripture engagement that flourished especially in monastic communities.

The Medieval Period

It is convenient to call the post-patristic period "medieval," but this designation is burdened with the Renaissance prejudice that the centuries which separated classical Greco-Roman culture from the "revival of learning" in fifteenth-century Europe were a dark interlude best forgotten. In fact, it was a period of flourishing as well as decline, both spiritually and intellectually, and in both the Greek-speaking East of the Byzantine Empire and the Latin-speaking West of the Holy Roman Empire. We will focus on a few highlights in the Latin West, where the Bible was the Vulgate.

Respect for Tradition

A pervasive characteristic of medieval biblical interpretation is its respect for the foregoing patristic exegetical tradition. With few exceptions, this means that the commentaries and sermons of this period are generally derivative and lacking in originality. As one example among many, we can refer to the commentary on Zechariah by the ninth-century Frenchman Haimo of Auxerre (*PL* 117.221-78). At a rough estimate, some 90 percent of this commentary can be traced directly to Jerome's commentary on Zechariah. Haimo's own contribution consists of usually condensing and summarizing, sometimes quoting verbatim, and occasionally rephrasing the words of the revered church father. Nevertheless, he refers to Jerome as his source on only three occasions (262C, 266C, 277C). In fact, much of the work of Latin medieval commentators on Zechariah consists of a rehash of Jerome's commentary. Another telling illustration is a remark made by the thirteenth-century Hugh of St. Cher in his *Postilla super totam Bibliam*. On the Valiant Woman of Proverbs 31:10, traditionally interpreted as an allegory of the church, he writes that, although she could also be interpreted literally, "yet, because the Glossators make no mention of a literal interpretation, we shall proceed with the mystical exposition, not wishing to play the prophet (*vaticinari*) at this point." To depart from the traditional allegorical interpretation of the Valiant Woman would be like claiming for oneself the authority of a prophet.[13]

The Predominance of the Vulgate

Just as the Greek Septuagint continued to be the universal Bible of the Byzantine biblical scholars, so the Latin Vulgate, having now replaced the earlier Vetus Latina, ruled supreme as *the* Bible of the Latin West. It too included the Apocrypha.

The Four Senses

The standard hermeneutical paradigm of medieval biblical interpretation is the so-called *quadriga*, the doctrine of the fourfold meaning of Scripture, which actually goes back to the church father John Cassian. It was later summarized in the following mnemonic lines:

> *Littera gesta docet: quid credas allegoria.*
> *Moralis quid agis: quo tendas anagogia.*

> (The letter teaches what happened, allegory what you believe;
> The moral sense what you must do, anagogy where you are headed.)

According to this scheme, "Jerusalem," for instance, means literally the Jewish city, allegorically the church, morally the believer's soul, and anagogically heaven (i.e., the hereafter).

Beginning in the thirteenth century, there was an emphasis on the literal

---

13. See A. Wolters, *The Song of the Valiant Woman: Studies in the Interpretation of Proverbs 31:10-31* (Carlisle: Paternoster, 2001), p. 93.

sense as foundational to the others.[14] This is especially true of Albertus Magnus and Nicholas of Lyra. Albert's student Thomas Aquinas put it this way: "All interpretations are based on one, that is, the literal form, from which alone we can argue."[15]

Glossa Ordinaria

A kind of compendium of standard late medieval biblical interpretation is represented by the so-called *Glossa Ordinaria*. Apparently initiated by Anselm of Laon (c. 1050-1117), first compiled by Anselm himself and a number of associates, this was a series of short exegetical notes *(glossae)* on the complete Bible, drawn almost entirely from patristic and early medieval authorities. By the end of the twelfth century it had achieved its definitive form, as well as its definitive place in the scribal layout of the biblical text. That is, it was positioned in the margin and between the lines of the portion of Scripture to which it applied. As Beryl Smalley writes, "The Gloss became the standard aid to the study of Scripture, the 'tongue' of the biblical text, and an essential part of the *pagina sacra* itself. The text and the Gloss were studied together" [*TRE* 13.452]. It continued to be included as a part of printed Bibles well into the sixteenth century.[16] It is significant that the *Glossa* identifies the apocryphal books as non-canonical.

The Reformation

The significance of the Reformation for the history of biblical interpretation is difficult to overstate. In many ways the Bible was read afresh, through new eyes. This was not only because it was now read in the original languages, because it became widely available in the vernaculars of Europe, was read in a plain and literal sense, and was given supreme authority, even over the fathers and councils of a millennium and a half of church history, but especially because it was rediscovered as the bearer of the gospel of Jesus Christ, with immediate relevance to everyone's existential situation. As Jaroslav Pelikan once put it, "The church did not need a Luther to tell it that the Bible

---

14. Beryl Smalley, *The Study of the Bible in the Middle Ages,* 3rd ed. (Oxford: Blackwell, 1983), pp. 281-308.

15. Thomas Aquinas, *Summa Theologica* I-I, q. 10, ad 3.

16. Smalley, *Study of the Bible,* pp. 46-66.

was true. But it did need a Luther to tell it what the truth of the Bible was."[17] This applied as much to the Old Testament as the New.

Ad fontes

The Reformation shared with the Renaissance an emphasis on returning "to the sources" *(ad fontes)* of Western civilization in antiquity, and thus on recovering a knowledge of the original languages, especially Greek, Hebrew, and Aramaic. For the first time in history, Christians began to take the lead in the study of biblical Hebrew, beginning with Reuchlin. The new knowledge of Hebrew also led to familiarity with the great medieval Jewish commentators, especially the philological masters who concentrated on the literal sense, like Rashi, the Kimchis, and Ibn Ezra. Both Luther and Calvin achieved an amazing mastery of Hebrew. Among other things, this new interest in studying the Old Testament in the original languages led to an explosion of new commentaries and to an undermining of the authoritative position of the Vulgate. We can take almost any book of the Old Testament (with the possible exception of the Song of Songs) and observe that the number of published commentaries on the book in question increases exponentially in the sixteenth century, most of them based on a study of the text in the original languages.

The Attack on Allegory

One prominent feature that distinguished the new Protestant exegesis of Scripture from most of the foregoing tradition, both patristic and medieval, was the widespread rejection of allegory. In this the Reformation represented a kind of return to the hermeneutical principles of the Antiochene school of Christian antiquity. Although Theodore of Mopsuestia was still under a cloud of doctrinal suspicion and many of his works were lost or unknown, the exegetical writings of John Chrysostom were warmly embraced. Next to Augustine, Chrysostom was Calvin's most-quoted church father. The attitude of the Reformers and their followers can be summed up in a telling formulation by the English Reformer and Bible translator William Tyndale: "God is a Spirit, and all his words are spiritual. His literal sense is spiritual, and all his words are spiritual."[18] However, the allegorical interpre-

---

17. Jaroslav Pelikan, *Obedient Rebels* (New York: Harper and Row, 1964), p. 21.
18. William Tyndale, "The Obedience of a Christian Man," in *The Works of the English*

tation of the Song of Songs was still *de rigueur*. Calvin, for example, was highly incensed by Castellio's literal reading of this work.

Luther

Fundamental to Luther's view of the Old Testament is his understanding of the relationship between law and gospel. The Word of God comes to us in two forms: as law and as gospel. Both are in Scripture, and both are to be preached, but they must never be confused. The law says: "Do this." It is God's demand upon us. The gospel says: "This I have done for you." It is God's gift to us. The law itself is holy and good; in itself it is the expression of God's will. But when it is used as the way to salvation, it becomes devilish and a "tyrant." As a way of salvation it has been abolished by Christ. Nevertheless, it still has two functions in the Christian's life. It has a civil function, regulating our neighborly relationships. It also has a divine, spiritual function: it increases our transgressions and so prepares the way unto grace. Thus it can serve as "our schoolmaster to bring us to Christ." In Luther's preface to the New Testament, he states that the Old Testament is a volume containing God's laws and commandments and the New Testament is a volume containing God's promised gospel, although he elsewhere qualifies this bald contrast.

Calvin

Calvin stands in fundamental continuity with Luther, but lacks his law-gospel dialectic. For him the Old Testament law also has a *tertius usus*, namely to regulate, as a "rule of thanksgiving," the life of believers today. He was generally more sympathetic to Jewish interpreters than Luther.

Vernacular Translations

One reason why the Reformation made such an impact was the fact that it prioritized the translation of the Bible (including the Apocrypha, though these books were clearly distinguished from the canonical ones) into the ver-

---

Reformers: William Tyndale and John Frith, 3 vols., ed. Thomas Russell (London: Ebenezer Palmer, 1831), vol. 1, p. 346.

nacular languages of the various countries of Europe and beyond. Here again Luther took the lead, producing a fresh translation of the entire Bible into a colloquial and idiomatic German that could be easily understood. William Tyndale did similar work for English, although he did not live to complete his translation. Suddenly (also because of the invention of the printing press) the entire Bible, four-fifths or more of which is the Old Testament, was made available to almost everyone.

Counter-Reformation

It would be a mistake to think of the new flourishing of biblical studies as an exclusively Protestant affair. Although the Council of Trent in 1546 had declared the Vulgate to be the only "authentic" (i.e., authoritative) Bible translation for public use, Catholic biblical scholars of great erudition also arose. However, they generally still followed the pattern of the medieval *quadriga,* or some variation of it. A good example is the massive work by the Belgian Jesuit Cornelius à Lapide (1567-1637) entitled *Commentaria in Sacram Scripturam,* which was completed shortly before his death.[19] On the one hand, à Lapide demonstrates great philological and historical erudition in elucidating the literal sense and proves himself the equal of any Protestant exegete in his mastery of the ancient languages, including (besides Latin) Greek, Hebrew, Aramaic, Syriac, and Arabic. On the other hand he also treats the supra-literal "spiritual" senses in great detail, drawing on the entire tradition of patristic and medieval exegesis. His work is thus a kind of encyclopedia of the entire history of interpretation, omitting only to cite (except for the occasional polemical aside against "heretics") his Protestant predecessors and contemporaries. He also goes to great lengths to defend the Vulgate, even when Jerome's Latin clearly did not match the Hebrew or Greek of the received original text.

The Seventeenth and Eighteenth Centuries

The seventeenth and eighteenth centuries are marked initially by the period of Protestant scholasticism and later by the Enlightenment. Scholasticism

---

19. One of its many editions is C. à Lapide, *Commentaria ad Sacram Scripturam. Editio Xysto Riario Sfortiae dicata,* 10 vols. (Naples: Nagar, 1854-1859).

tended to read the Old Testament as a quarry or repository of texts that could establish this or that point of dogmatic theology or Christian ethics, for example, the omnipresence of God, or the relation of circumcision to baptism, or how ceremonial laws could be distinguished from civil and moral laws. The commentaries of this period are monuments of philological and historical erudition, but with little value for building up the life of faith. Examples include the works of the Dutch Calvinist Campegius Vitringa Sr. (1659-1722), especially his celebrated commentary on Isaiah.[20] In reaction to this heavily dogmatic and devotionally somewhat sterile tradition there arose various forms of pietism and mysticism. A characteristic representative of the pietist reaction was Johann Heinrich Michaelis (1668-1738), an Old Testament scholar in the pietist center Halle in Germany, who published a text-critical edition of the Old Testament.

Although the hermeneutical approach to the Bible in these centuries (and indeed in all centuries preceding the Enlightenment) is nowadays often called "pre-critical," to distinguish it from the modernist historical criticism that became dominant in the nineteenth and twentieth centuries, this is something of a misnomer. For one thing, the words "critical" and "criticism" were often used, from the seventeenth century onward, to refer in general to the scholarly analysis of classical texts, as in "textual criticism." *Critica sacra* is a common title for publications dealing with the historical and philological aspects of scriptural study. In fact, as late as the nineteenth century in Britain, a popular multivolume commentary on the Bible was called *A Commentary, Critical, Experimental, and Practical of the Old and New Testaments,* in which the word "critical" of the title did not preclude the taking of conservative positions on such issues as the date of Deuteronomy and Daniel, or the unity of Isaiah.[21] For another, the biblical scholars of the seventeenth and eighteenth centuries, many of whom were respected and orthodox churchmen, were remarkably free in matters of textual criticism and other kinds of diachronic analysis. An example of the latter is the assignment of the last six chapters of Zechariah to a pre-exilic author or authors, either to Jeremiah (on the basis of Matt. 27:9) or to one or more unknown prophets. The former view was defended by Joseph Mede in the sev-

---

20. Campegius Vitringa, *Commentarius in librum prophetarum Jesajae,* 2 vols. (Leeuwarden: Halma, 1714-1720).

21. The editors of six volumes were Robert Jamieson, A. R. Fausset, and David Brown (Glasgow: William Collins & Sons/London: James Nisbet, 1864-1870).

enteenth century,[22] and the latter by William Newcome, Archbishop of Armagh, in the eighteenth.[23]

This freedom with respect to the Old Testament text was not without its shadow sides. It was not uncommon to accuse the Jews of having deliberately corrupted the text of the Hebrew Bible. Thus, the Cambridge scholar William Whiston (1667-1752) wrote a book in which he argued that the Masoretic Text is a corrupt text, deliberately altered by the Jews, whereas the true Hebrew text was that underlying the Septuagint and the citations in the New Testament.[24] Similarly, the English theologian John Hutchinson (1674-1737) was a strong defender of the unpointed Hebrew text of the Old Testament, which he believed taught the Christian doctrine of the Trinity. In his view the Masoretic points represented a Jewish corruption of the biblical text. Far from being an isolated eccentric, Hutchinson (and the "Hutchinsonianism" that he inspired) gained a considerable following, among them the respected Hebrew lexicographer John Parkhurst (1728-1797).[25]

A word needs to be said about the Jewish philosopher Benedict de Spinoza (1632-1677), even though he could be excluded from a survey that focuses on the Christian interpretation of the Old Testament. His importance lies in the fact that he is perhaps the first to take a truly rationalistic approach to the task of biblical exegesis. Even though, as a philosopher and a Jew, he had little influence among the Christian (or, for that matter, the Jewish) biblical scholars of his day, he is nonetheless significant as a harbinger of later modernist historical criticism. His purpose, he writes in the eighth chapter of his *Tractatus theologico-politicus* (1670), was "to improve the foundations of the understanding of Scripture, and to get rid, not just of some few, but of the prejudices of theology in general."[26] He was one of the

---

22. Joseph Mede, *Dissertationum Ecclesiasticarum Triga: De Sanctitate Relativa, Veneratione Sacra, Sortitione & Alea, quibus accedunt Fragmenta Sacra* (London: Roycroft, 1653), pp. 89 and 113.

23. William Newcome, *An Attempt Towards an Improved Version, a Metrical Arrangement, and an Explanation of the Twelve Minor Prophets* (Dublin: Marchbank, 1785), pp. 194-95.

24. William Whiston, *An Essay Towards Restoring the True Text of the Old Testament and for Vindicating the Citations Made Thence in the New Testament* (London: Senex, 1722).

25. See Derya Gurses, "The Hutchinsonian Defence of an Old Testament Trinitarian Christianity: The Controversy over Elahim, 1735-1773," *History of European Ideas* 29 (2003): 393-409.

26. As quoted in Hans-Joachim Kraus, *Geschichte der historisch-kritischen Erforschung des Alten Testaments von der Reformation bis zur Gegenwart* (Neukirchen: Verlag der Buchhandlung des Erziehungsvereins Neukirchen Kreis Moers, 1956), p. 55.

first to argue that the Pentateuch could not have been written by Moses. Instead, perhaps Ezra was its true author. As Kraus puts it, "The principles of a historical-critical hermeneutic are formulated for the first time in Spinoza."[27] Because of his radical views, he was expelled from the synagogue in Amsterdam in 1656.

It needs to be remembered that the academic world was much less specialized in early modern times than it is now. One could combine being a biblical scholar with being a philosopher (so Spinoza), a mathematician (so Whiston) or a physicist (so Isaac Newton).

Another example of such an interdisciplinary polymath was Hugo Grotius (1583-1645), the Dutch thinker who is today chiefly remembered for his work in international law. However, he was also a theologian of considerable attainments and wrote annotations on all the books of the Bible, based on the original Hebrew and Greek.[28] He also worked for a theological rapprochement between Protestants and Catholics and accordingly took the Vulgate as the base text of his Latin commentaries. Because he was an Arminian in theology and focused on the literal and historical aspects of the text, with little regard for their religious relevance in the present, he is sometimes depicted as a forerunner of modern historical criticism.[29] However, as in the case of Theodore of Mopsuestia, this is a rather misleading claim. Grotius did not dispute or bracket the classical Christian confession concerning the inspiration, reliability and unity of the Scriptures. Nor did he deny the fulfillment of the messianic prophecies in Jesus Christ, although he was fairly reticent in seeing direct references to Christ in the Old Testament.

A younger Dutch contemporary of Grotius was the Calvinist Johannes Coccejus (1603-1669), a gifted systematic theologian as well as an accomplished biblical scholar, and the author of a highly regarded dictionary of biblical Hebrew.[30] Unlike Grotius, he had a Christological interpretation of almost every passage in the Old Testament, often resorting to allegory to make the connection. It used to be said that Grotius found Christ nowhere

---

27. Kraus, *Geschichte der historisch-kritischen Erforschung*, p. 57.

28. On the Old Testament, see Hugo Grotius, *Annotata ad Vetus Testamentum* (1644), included in his *Opera omnia theologica in tres tomos divisa* (London, 1679).

29. See W. S. M. Knight, *The Life and Works of Hugo Grotius* (London: Sweet & Maxwell, 1925), pp. 245-66, and Kraus, *Geschichte der historisch-kritischen Erforschung*, pp. 46-49.

30. Johannes Coccejus, *Lexicon et Commentarius Sermonis Hebraici et Chaldaici Veteris Testamenti*, in vol. 10 of his *Opera Omnia Theologica, Exegetica, Didactica, Polemica, Philologica*, 3rd ed. (Amsterdam: P. & J. Blaeu, 1701-1706).

in the Old Testament, but Coccejus found him everywhere.[31] A distinctive and controversial aspect of Coccejus's teaching was his view that in the biblical history of redemption we need to distinguish three covenantal dispensations, with each succeeding one abolishing its predecessor. There is first the covenant of works, established with Adam. Subsequently, there is the covenant of grace, established with Moses. Finally there is the new covenant in Christ. Consequently, God's covenant with his people repeatedly changed in content. Furthermore, Coccejus argued that true forgiveness of sins was not available to the Old Testament saints; what God granted them was a *paresis* (overlooking) of sin, not the *aphesis* (forgiveness) of the New Testament.[32]

The eighteenth century was of course the century of the Enlightenment, the broad intellectual and cultural movement that emphasized the supreme authority of reason and decried the prejudices of the past. It believed that reason gave humans access to universally valid truths. All claims to knowledge, including religious knowledge, were called before the bar of the supposedly impartial judge of reason to justify themselves. Not all religion was excluded, but it had to be a *rational* religion, available to all right-thinking human beings. This attitude is summed up in the title of one of the influential works of the philosopher Immanuel Kant: *Religion within the Bounds of Reason Alone* (1793). In the Enlightenment project, reason was thought to transcend all historical particularity of race, nationality, language, gender, and religion, and to lead unerringly, through objective *Wissenschaft*, to a trans-historical truth. Among other things this led to the crucial distinction, in the philosophy of Kant and others, between knowledge and belief. The former is objective and deals with facts; the latter is subjective and deals with values.

This is the epistemological background to the rise of historical criticism in biblical studies, as it came to dominate the field in the nineteenth and twentieth centuries, first in Germany and then throughout the world. Within this tradition, *Kritik* came to mean investigation and analysis of the biblical writings that resolutely sought to bracket all "dogmatic" assumptions about inspiration, historical reliability, prophetic prediction, or God's action in history. To be "scientific" meant to be "critical" (now in the new sense of "fearlessly un-religious"), and this in turn meant to be *voraussetzungslos*, "without presuppositions." In the study of the Old Testament it

---

31. Knight, *Hugo Grotius*, p. 252: "Grotium nusquam in sacris litteris invenire Christum, Cocceium ubique."

32. G. P. van Itterzon, "Coccejus, Johannes," in *Christelijke Encyclopaedie*, ed. F. W. Grosheide and G. P. van Itterzon (Kampen: Kok, 1957), pp. 230-31.

led to various kinds of "scientifically" assured results, notably the detachment of the Pentateuch from the person of Moses, the dating of Deuteronomy to the time of Josiah and that of Daniel to the time of the Maccabees, and the attribution of the book of Isaiah to two or three different authors living in widely differing times and places.

It would be a mistake, however, to characterize the late eighteenth century as being completely dominated by the kind of modernist historical criticism that emerged out of the Enlightenment. Apart from the majority of pastors and theologians who still held to a traditionally orthodox view of Scripture, we can mention a number of creative and influential thinkers who were not in thrall to the Enlightenment, or who actively opposed it. Among these are Robert Lowth (1710-1787), an English churchman and scholar who wrote the famous *Praelectiones de sacra Poesi Hebraeorum* (1754), in which he explored the poetic character of much of the Old Testament and for the first time analyzed parallelism as one of the fundamental features of Hebrew poetry — an analysis that has dominated subsequent Old Testament scholarship to the present day. We find a somewhat similar emphasis in the German philosopher and literary critic Johann Gottfried Herder (1744-1803), who wrote the book *Der Geist der ebräischen Poesie* (1782-83), in which he treated the poetry of the Old Testament as the unsophisticated folk art of a naïve and primitive people. Herder was a student of Johann Georg Hamann (1730-1788), an eccentric philosopher who passionately opposed the spirit of the Enlightenment out of a powerful Christian conversion experience. Hamann notably pointed out that the Enlightenment's commitment to reason was itself a kind of faith.

The Nineteenth Century

The cultural and intellectual milieu associated with German idealism around the turn of the nineteenth century, when the Enlightenment provoked and engaged Romanticism, a milieu that is associated with such names as Kant and Fichte, Hegel and Schelling, Herder and Goethe, in many ways set the tone for the major intellectual developments in the Western world for the next two centuries. There is a sense in which German idealism and its associated movements and individuals gave birth to the modern age.

One of the fundamental features of this milieu and its age was "the rise of historical consciousness," an increasing awareness that cultures and epochs were incommensurable, each with its own unique and irreplaceable identity shaped by time and place. Among other things, this had the effect of enlarging the gap between the culture and mentality of the biblical authors, especially of the Old Testament, and the outlook of post-Enlightenment Europeans. The question of bridging this gap (which Lessing famously referred to as the "ugly ditch") became an acute hermeneutical problem. The problem became even more acute later in the nineteenth century, when the dramatic discoveries in Mesopotamia and Egypt showed how firmly ancient Israel was embedded in its ancient Near Eastern context. More and more the Old Testament seemed to belong to a strange and unfamiliar world. The problem was only exacerbated by the way the new historical criticism challenged the historical trustworthiness of the Old Testament.

The rise of Enlightenment-inspired historical criticism thus introduced a massive discontinuity into the history of the interpretation of the Bible, not least of the Old Testament. It is difficult to overstate the radicality of this discontinuity. It is far greater than that between typological and allegorical interpretation in the patristic era, or that between medieval and Reformation hermeneutical approaches. What had bound together all the previous centuries was a common acceptance of the fundamental Christian confession regarding the unity, inspiration, authority, and veracity of the Bible, as well as its Christocentricity. All of this was now put aside as a matter of dogmatic prejudice that had no business in truly critical scholarship. Such theological tenets might continue to be held in the private sphere of one's subjective "belief," but were out of bounds in the public sphere of objective "knowledge" *(Wissenschaft)*. The history of interpretation can thus henceforth be divided neatly into "pre-critical" and "critical" eras. The discontinuity between the two is so great that it is in a sense illegitimate to include modernist historical criticism of this description in a survey of the *Christian* interpretation of the Old Testament, since it by definition excludes any religious designation. Nevertheless, it is true that the Christian interpretation of the Old Testament has been massively impacted by this kind of historical criticism.

The result has been that a great chasm has opened up between academic scholarship (at least prestigious and publicly acceptable scholarship) and the way Scripture is read and interpreted by the majority of Christian believers as they hear (or preach) sermons and engage in their private devotions.

This has not infrequently led to a loss of faith on the part of Christian students when they were exposed to modernist biblical criticism. This was the case for Friedrich Delitzsch (1850-1922), who was to become one of the pioneers of Assyriology. He dates his loss of faith to a conversation with an unnamed professor of his who had argued for a Josianic date of Deuteronomy. In reply to Delitzsch's question, whether this didn't mean that Deuteronomy was a hoax, the professor replied: "For God's sake! That may be true, but you can't say something like that!"[33] This story is the more poignant because Friedrich was the son of the famous orthodox Lutheran Old Testament scholar Franz Delitzsch (1813-1890), who had devoted most of his life to opposing this kind of historical criticism.

As another illustration of the chasm that had arisen between historical criticism and the life of faith we can mention an episode in the life of Julius Wellhausen (1844-1918), the great scholar who more than anyone embodies the strengths and weaknesses of Enlightenment-inspired historical criticism. After the first edition of his *History of Israel* (1878) was published, in which he had outlined his controversial thesis that the prophets of the Old Testament, rather than coming after the Torah in history, actually came before it, he was severely criticized on all sides. As a result, he asked to be transferred from the faculty of theology to the faculty of Semitic languages. In the letter accompanying this request he wrote: "I became a theologian because I was interested in the scientific treatment of the Bible. It has only gradually dawned on me that a professor of theology also has the practical task of preparing the students for ministry in the evangelical churches, and that I am deficient in that task. In fact, despite all the restraint I have exercised, I do more to make my students unfit for their ministry than otherwise."[34] Wellhausen clearly realized the incompatibility of his views with the requirements of the Christian ministry.

There were of course strong critiques of the kind of radical historical reconstruction that Wellhausen proposed. Virtually all confessionally conservative Christian scholars and communions rejected its major claims. Franz Delitzsch and his erudite co-worker Carl Friedrich Keil (1807-1888), authors of the famous Keil-Delitzsch commentary series on the Old Testament, are impressive examples. The Roman Catholic Church stoutly resisted the new criticism as well. Here we should also mention J. N. Darby (1800-1882) and the rise of dispensationalism, which broke with the long tradition of Christian interpretation that had understood the Old Testament promises to Israel to apply to the church of the New Testament. Instead, these promises were taken to apply to ethnic Israel after a future massive conversion to Christianity. In other ways, too, Darby and his followers insisted on literal interpretations of Old Testament prophecies. Despite these innovations, however, the

33. Kraus, *Geschichte der historisch-kritischen Erforschung*, p. 279.
34. Kraus, *Geschichte der historisch-kritischen Erforschung*, p. 236.

dispensationalists sided with the classical Christian tradition with respect to the inspiration and reliability of the Scriptures. However, none of these negative reactions to modernist historical criticism could prevent the latter from becoming the dominant ideological force in the Western academy.

The Twentieth Century

For most of the twentieth century the academic study of Scripture has been dominated by this ideological force. Christian believers have come to terms with it in various ways. In the early twentieth century, during the heyday of the fundamentalist-modernist controversies, the fundamentalist side in effect rejected historical criticism altogether as a kind of godless rationalism. However, they rarely identified the fundamental epistemological issue: the commitment to a religiously neutral reason. In fact, they often argued as though their opponents were using faulty reasoning and that truly rational thought would come to orthodox Christian conclusions. They thus took over from their opponents the fundamental premise of the Enlightenment. As the twentieth century wore on, the evangelical heirs of the fundamentalists became more and more accommodating to the consensus conclusions of mainline historical criticism. A good example is the recent book by Kenton L. Sparks.[35] Other Christians took a more dualistic tack, arguing that faith and scholarship occupied essentially separate spheres, which should be understood as complementary to each other, or perhaps standing in dialectical tension with each other. It is perhaps in the second way that Barth and his followers, though profoundly critical of theological liberalism, in large measure accepted the results of modernist historical criticism. In my opinion, the same is true of Brevard Childs and his canonical approach to Scripture.[36] As for the Roman Catholic Church, it has undergone a dramatic transformation in its approach to historical criticism in the twentieth century. From a position closely resembling fundamentalism at the beginning of the century it has moved to a practice of biblical scholarship that is virtually indistinguishable from mainline historical criticism.[37]

---

35. Kenton L. Sparks, *God's Word in Human Words: An Evangelical Appropriation of Critical Biblical Scholarship* (Grand Rapids: Baker Academic, 2008).

36. See my "Reading the Gospels Canonically: A Methodological Dialogue with Brevard Childs," in *Reading the Gospels Today,* ed. Stanley E. Porter (Grand Rapids: Eerdmans, 2004), pp. 179-92, especially pp. 187-92.

37. See Luke Timothy Johnson, "What's Catholic about It? The State of Catholic Biblical Scholarship," *Commonweal* (1998): 12-16.

One of the few thinkers who has challenged the epistemological foundations of classical historical criticism is the Christian philosopher Alvin Plantinga. In a seminal essay entitled "Two (or More) Kinds of Scripture Scholarship" he gives a penetrating analysis of the ideological foundations of this kind of criticism.[38]

Curiously enough the late twentieth century has seen a fundamental critique of historical criticism from within the secular establishment. Postmodernism (perhaps better called "late modernism") has come to realize that the Enlightenment project, with its faith in reason and progress, has failed and that rationality is always a function of historically situated human beings whose identities are shaped in multiple ways. As a consequence, classical historical criticism, as a product of the Enlightenment project, needs to be critically re-evaluated.[39]

Fortunately, the climate in biblical scholarship has changed considerably in recent years. Not only is the formerly regnant secular critical paradigm now being challenged from a number of directions (not only from orthodox Christian ones), but there is a thriving movement that seeks to recover the (somewhat unhappily named[40]) "theological interpretation" of Scripture.[41] There is considerable interest in retrieving the exegetical riches of the patristic and medieval periods.[42] The time is ripe for a renewed, unabashedly Christian, scholarly appropriation of the Old Testament, which is in touch with the "pre-critical" Christian past, and simultaneously equipped to handle discerningly the critical tools and resources of modern scholarship.

---

38. A. Plantinga, "Two (or More) Kinds of Scripture Scholarship," *Modern Theology* 14 (1998): 243-77. An expanded version of this essay appears as chapter 12 in A. Plantinga, *Warranted Christian Belief* (New York: Oxford University Press, 2000).

39. See A. K. M. Adam, *What Is Postmodern Biblical Criticism?* (Minneapolis: Fortress, 1995).

40. "Theological" implies that this is the preserve of theologians. But the religious appropriation of Scripture is not restricted to an academic discipline; it is the calling of all believers.

41. See for example the *Dictionary for Theological Interpretation of the Bible*, ed. Kevin J. Vanhoozer et al. (Grand Rapids: Baker Academic, 2005), and the recently launched *Journal for the Theological Interpretation of Scripture*. Of course, many other journals also include exegetical articles from an overtly Christian confessional perspective.

42. See for example the series *Ancient Christian Commentary on Scripture*, ed. Thomas C. Oden (Downers Grove: IVP, 2000), which is remarkable for being published under Protestant auspices. Catholic series like the French *Sources Chrétiennes* have of course existed for a long time.

3 Philosophy and Old Testament Interpretation: A Neglected Influence

Craig G. Bartholomew

[O]ne can say with some justification that the beginnings of biblical criticism are initially far more a philosophical than a theological problem . . . in dealing with these questions. . . . The church historian finds himself or herself transported into the largely uncharted area which lies between philosophy and theology.[1]

Those who devote themselves to the study of Sacred Scripture should always remember that the various hermeneutical approaches have their own philosophical underpinnings, which need to be carefully evaluated before they are applied to the sacred texts.[2]

Nowadays it is rare to find the relationship between philosophy and Old Testament interpretation attended to. Prior to Wellhausen it was, however, common practice for Old Testament scholars to be up front about their philosophical presuppositions and to spend considerable parts of their writings setting these out before applying them. Johann Vatke, who influenced Wellhausen, was quite open about his indebtedness to Hegel and devotes the

1. Klaus Scholder, *The Birth of Modern Critical Theology: Origins and Problems of Biblical Criticism in the Seventeenth Century* (London: SCM, 1990), pp. 5-6.
2. John Paul II, *Faith and Reason* (London: The Incorporated Catholic Truth Society, 1998), p. 85.

45

opening 170 and closing 120 pages or so of his *Biblical Theology* (1835) to a Hegelian understanding of the nature of religion in general and Old Testament religion in particular.[3]

De Wette: Founder of Modern Biblical Criticism

W. M. L. de Wette was the first to use a critical methodology to articulate a view of Israel's history quite different from that implied in the Old Testament.[4] De Wette is most well known as an Old Testament critic because of his work on Deuteronomy, which he dated to the seventh century and connected to the reign of King Josiah. However, he wrote substantially on the New Testament and on Christian theology as well. He stands therefore at the origin of biblical criticism as a whole.

De Wette grew up in a Protestant family and studied at the University of Jena, where his teachers included Fichte, Schelling, Hegel, and Griesbach. For de Wette, though, the major challenge to his faith came from Kant. In 1798, the year before de Wette came to Jena, Kant published his *Der Streit der Fakultäten* in which he outlines an understanding of religion within the bounds of reason alone.[5] As John Rogerson puts it,

> However illustrious his Jena teachers were, the greatest initial impact that was made upon de Wette came from the philosophy of Kant. Indeed, for the remainder of his life, de Wette remained, intellectually, a sort of

3. See John W. Rogerson, *Old Testament Criticism in the Nineteenth Century: England and Germany* (London: SPCK, 1984), pp. 69ff.; H. J. Kraus, *Geschichte der historisch-kritischen Erforschung des Alten Testaments* (Neukirchen-Vluyn: Neukirchener Verlag, 1988), pp. 194-99.

4. Rogerson, *Old Testament Criticism*, pp. 28-29. Where to locate the origins of modern biblical criticism is controversial. I think that de Wette is *a* key figure in terms of the radical application of Enlightenment philosophy to the Bible, but the impetus in this direction lies earlier with Spinoza. On de Wette and biblical criticism see John W. Rogerson, *W. M. L. de Wette, Founder of Modern Biblical Criticism: An Intellectual Biography* (Sheffield: Sheffield Academic Press, 1992), and also Thomas Albert Howard, *Religion and the Rise of Historicism: W. M. L. de Wette, Jacob Burckhardt, and the Theological Origins of Nineteenth-Century Historical Consciousness* (Cambridge: Cambridge University Press, 2000).

5. *Religion within the Limits of Reason Alone* is the title of an earlier book (1793) by Kant, in which he develops the view of religion also expressed in *Der Streit* (1798). Recently the debate about Kant's view of religion and the interpretation of his *Religion within the Limits of Reason Alone* has been reignited. See Chris L. Firestone and Steven Palmquist, eds., *Kant and the New Philosophy of Religion* (Bloomington: Indiana University Press, 2006); Chris L. Firestone and Nathan Jacobs, *In Defense of Kant's Religion* (Bloomington: Indiana University Press, 2008).

Kantian; and he spent many years of his life trying to reconcile his intellectual acceptance of Kant with his aesthetic and almost mystical instinct for religion.[6]

Kant's view had radical implications for religion and biblical interpretation. There is no universally agreed upon interpretation of the Bible, but a religion of reason, because it gets at universal truths, can yield this. Religion is thus reduced to morality and Christian theology is adjusted accordingly. The contingent truths of history cannot be revelatory, since revelation is disclosed through reason. Schelling helped de Wette to develop a critique of Kant's overprivileging of philosophy as final arbiter in all disciplines. For Schelling God as the Absolute was primary and reason a part of the Absolute by which the individual could perceive the Absolute in the particular. Religion is the contemplation of the Absolute as it is manifested in nature, history, and art. Mythology, in this context, is to be regarded positively, because it is an attempt to grasp the Absolute. Schelling's understanding of mythology profoundly influenced de Wette's approach to the Bible, especially to the Old Testament.

In his dissertation (submitted in 1804) and in his *Aufforderung zum Stadium der hebräischen Sprache und Literatur* (1805), de Wette developed a portrait of the history of Israelite religion that differed radically from that of the Old Testament itself and that formed the basis for the development of the nineteenth and twentieth centuries' critical scholarship. But where did de Wette get this portrait? From reading the text, from reading it in a way not constricted by theories of unity of authorship, but also, says Rogerson, by reading the Old Testament through the grid of a certain view of religion, a view of religion as developing from a simple to a complex phenomenon that de Wette probably got from Schelling's *Philosophie der Kunst*. The *Aufforderung* contains a devastating attack on the historicity of the Old Testament, motivated by de Wette's view of religion and mythology. From Kant de Wette had learned, and learned well, that the contingent truths of history cannot be revelatory. Probably from Karl Philipp Moritz's *Die Götterlehre* (1791) de Wette learned that myths were never history but poetry, and although myths were fantasy they could contain sublime ideas.

Thus the Pentateuchal stories are generally of no value for the historian but of great value for the theologian because of their witness to religion. The Pentateuch "is a product of the religious poetry of the Israelite people, which reflects their spirit [*Geist*], way of thought, love of the nation, philosophy of

---

6. Rogerson, *W. M. L. de Wette*, p. 27.

religion."[7] Similarly, in his 1811 commentary on the Psalms, de Wette argues that in many cases it is impossible to determine the historical contexts of many Psalms but this does not matter because what is important is religion expressed in poetic form.[8]

One is struck by the profound influence of philosophical and theological issues on de Wette's thought. According to Rogerson,

> De Wette was convinced that biblical interpretation and theology were concerned with reality, and that reality could only be understood with the help of philosophy. In this he was surely right. Implicit in Christian belief are claims about the nature of reality, about the sort of world in which we live and about the sort of things human beings are. Although philosophy in a broad sense does not seek to provide answers to these questions, it does offer critiques of attempted answers, it exposes contradictions and tautologies and offers conceptual frameworks for deeper reflection. Those who claim to have no philosophy are simply unaware of their philosophical presuppositions.
>
> In using philosophy so unashamedly in his biblical interpretation, theology and ethics, de Wette was standing in an honorable tradition reaching back through Protestant scholasticism to Aquinas and the church of those centuries that produced the classical creeds of Christian orthodoxy. This was one reason why de Wette rejected such orthodoxy, believing that it was based upon inadequate philosophy. . . . we cannot fault de Wette's sincerity in making his views about the nature of reality affect his biblical interpretation and his theology.[9]

Three ways in which de Wette is of major significance for our discussions are as follows: First, he recognized that human perspectives or worldviews are unified and he saw the unavoidable connections between individuals' views of reason and history and religion, i.e., their philosophy, and how they read the Bible. De Wette has much to teach us in this respect. Modernity has been characterized by an explosion in knowledge and a strong differentiation into disciplinary and sub-disciplinary areas. An effect of this is that scholars take longer and longer to specialize in less and less. There is little time and often no encouragement for scholars to descend into the subtexts of their disci-

7. Quoted by Rogerson, *W. M. L. de Wette*, p. 55.

8. See Parker's comment that de Wette is a rationalist and mystic at the same time in Rogerson, *W. M. L. de Wette*, p. 66.

9. Rogerson, *W. M. L. de Wette*, pp. 267-68.

plines and so connect up with the larger issues that impact their scholarship. De Wette's work is a reminder that, like it or not, our view of the world and our understanding of reason, religion, language, and so on, will shape the way we work with the Bible. The great merit of de Wette is his consciousness of these influences.

Second, de Wette recognized the fundamental role of philosophy in academic analysis. He saw, as it were, that philosophical scaffolding is always in place when academic construction is being done, even if scholars are not aware of it. Always an epistemology is assumed, always some ontology is taken for granted, always some view of the human person is in mind. De Wette is remarkably contemporary in this respect, for he was alert to the philosophical subtext of his work that Derrida insists upon (see below), but which many contemporary scholars seem blissfully unaware of. As Thiselton notes, biblical scholars tend to remain philosophically illiterate and thus destined to work within outworn paradigms.[10] De Wette's work is a salutary reminder of *all* the ingredients involved in biblical interpretation.

Third, de Wette believed that the true philosophy was that done in the tradition of Kant, Schelling, and Fries, and his life's work is devoted to rethinking religion and the Bible and theology within that framework. Especially in our late modern moment this commitment to Kantian philosophy is controversial. But whatever one thinks of de Wette's Kantianism, his candor is refreshing as is his quest for integration of his philosophy with his scholarship and his theology.

Scholars continue to work with philosophical paradigms shaping their work, of course, but generally they ignore these paradigms with the result that they are hidden from view and their scholarship has the appearance of neutral, objective analysis. De Wette's openness about his paradigm enables us to get a look at the total picture that makes up his work, and this puts us in a position to examine and evaluate his work in its totality.

Rogerson agrees with de Wette that philosophy is unavoidable in theoreti-

---

10. Anthony C. Thiselton, "Communicative Action and Promise in Interdisciplinary, Biblical, and Theological Hermeneutics," in *The Promise of Hermeneutics*, ed. Roger Lundin, Clarence Walhout, and Anthony C. Thiselton (Grand Rapids: Eerdmans, 1999), p. 137, notes that, "Curiously, the limits of scientific method to explain all of reality seem to be appreciated more readily in the philosophy of religion than in biblical studies. Views and methods that students in philosophy of religion recognize as 'positivist,' 'reductionist,' or even 'materialist' are often embraced quite uncritically in issues of judgment about, for example, acts of God in biblical narrative. In place of the more rigorous and judicious exploration of these issues in philosophical theology, biblical studies seems too readily to become polarized."

cal analysis. But from there Rogerson makes some extraordinary moves. He asserts that Christian belief implies certain philosophical positions. And then, on *this* basis, de Wette is commended for adopting a *Kantian* framework and fitting religion within it! Does Christian belief imply the framework of Kant's secular city so that we then search for a place for religion within the limits of reason? The assumption that Kant's philosophy is compatible with Christian belief is not an unusual view, as the image of Kant as the "philosopher of Protestantism" reminds us.[11] There is a strong tradition in liberal Protestant theology of Kant's philosophy as a mediator between faith and modern culture. However, as Frederick Beiser shows, even in Kant's day his views were very controversial and the issues of theology and God in relation to Kant's theology were fiercely debated.[12] In recent decades Kant's anthropology has come in for strong criticism from liberation and feminist theologians and from post-liberals,[13] reminding us at the very least that "the Cartesian-Kantian model of the self is historically contingent, rather than the indispensable conceptual device for properly framing the issue of faith and transcendence."[14]

It is true that evaluation of Kant as a "Christian thinker" remains controversial today. Personally, I think Gordon Michalson is right to argue that Kant's immanentism and view of human autonomy subvert theism so that Kant, as much as Hegel, should be understood as facilitating the transformations in European culture that we associate with the rise of atheism rather than being foundational for a mediating theology.[15] From this perspective Kant is a key figure on the Kant-Feuerbach-Marx trajectory, and one of whom (as Buckley notes in his explorations of the origins of atheism) Christian thinkers should be cautious![16] The implications for theology and biblical interpretation are clear:

11. Gordon E. Michalson, *Kant and the Problem of God* (Oxford: Blackwell, 1999), p. 1.

12. Frederick C. Beiser, *The Fate of Reason: German Philosophy from Kant to Fichte* (Cambridge, MA: Harvard University Press, 1987).

13. Michalson, *Kant and the Problem of God,* pp. 128ff.

14. Michalson, *Kant and the Problem of God,* p. 136.

15. Michalson, *Kant and the Problem of God,* p. 127.

16. Michael J. Buckley, *At the Origins of Modern Atheism* (New Haven: Yale University Press, 1987), especially pp. 322-33. Buckley rightly notes that "The atheism evolved in the eighteenth century was thus not to be denied by the strategies elaborated in the revolutions of Kant and Schleiermacher: it was only to be transposed into a different key. Argue god as the presupposition or as the corollary of nature; eventually natural philosophy would dispose of god. Argue god as the presupposition or as the corollary of human nature; eventually the denial of god would become an absolute necessity for human existence" (pp. 332-33).

The consistent subordination of divine transcendence to the demands of autonomous rationality strongly suggests that Kant's own thought . . . is moving in a non-theistic direction rather than in a direction with obviously constructive possibilities for theology. . . . the religious feature may remain present, but that is not where the real life is, any more than the twitching body of a beheaded reptile indicates real life. As a result, Kant's own example is hardly a comforting model for those committed to holding divine transcendence and a modern sensibility in proper balance. In his case, the balancing act cannot be sustained; his particular way of endorsing modernity is finally too self-aggrandizing.[17]

One may — although I do not — wish to argue that Kant is a helpful mediating figure for biblical interpretation between faith and modern culture, but then the case has to be argued, and not assumed. As John Caputo perceptively notes, "So what you think about modernity lies at the root of many of the arguments you hear about philosophy and theology."[18] Alvin Plantinga, in my view, rightly claims that Kant's philosophy is incompatible with Christian theism. Kant replaces the older way of thinking, according to which God's knowledge was creative, with human knowledge as creative. Existence, for example, is a category of the understanding that *we* contribute to the world. The ultimate implication is that God, too, "in a stunning reversal of roles, would owe his existence to us."[19] Rogerson rightly notes that de Wette's lasting "achievement" was to apply historical criticism to the Bible so as to produce a history radically different to that of the Bible itself. Nicholson notes the indebtedness of Reuss, George, Vatke, and crucially Wellhausen to de Wette.[20] What tends to be forgotten is de Wette's indebtedness to Kant in moving Old Testament scholarship in this direction in the first place.

Wellhausen: A Watershed

The most thorough of recent studies of Julius Wellhausen and German philosophy is Lothar Perlitt's 1965 *Vatke und Wellhausen*. Perlitt notes the similarities

---

17. Michalson, *Kant and the Problem of God*, p. 137.

18. John D. Caputo, *Philosophy and Theology* (Nashville: Abingdon, 2006), p. 11; for a trenchant, accessible critique of Descartes and Kant, see pp. 21-34.

19. Alvin Plantinga in *The Analytic Theist: An Alvin Plantinga Reader*, ed. James F. Sennett (Grand Rapids: Eerdmans, 1998), p. 332.

20. Rogerson, *W. M. L. de Wette*, p. 4.

of Wellhausen to Vatke, but also their differences. For example, Wellhausen, unlike Vatke, does not see post-exilic Judaism as a positive development,[21] whereas a Hegelian view of history would push one in this direction. And, in his finding of a secure starting point for the history of Israel in the formation of Israel as a people, Wellhausen follows the organological method of the historical school *and* Hegel and Vatke.[22] Likewise with his view of progress, Perlitt points out that Wellhausen does not need Hegel or nineteenth-century evolutionism: "The concept of development stretching from Lessing via Herder, Goethe, Schleiermacher and idealistic philosophy to De Wette, Ranke and Wellhausen has, of course, a specific, common foundation and colouring in its application to history."[23] Perlitt argues later that Wellhausen's view of Israel's development is akin to "historicism's individualising concept of development" of which Herder is a prime example.[24] The relationship of Wellhausen to the philosophies of his day is complex and such areas of overlap with Vatke and Hegel do not demonstrate strong dependence.

Perlitt notes, furthermore, that Wellhausen, like the Dutch critic Abraham Kuenen, firmly rejected the imposition of alien philosophies upon the Bible: Wellhausen and Kuenen "agree completely at least in the rejection of pre- and alien philosophical determination."[25] In contrast to Vatke, Wellhausen began his work with philological and text-critical analysis of the biblical text. "Thus Wellhausen proceeded in a methodologically secure way from literary analysis to historical criticism."[26]

Wellhausen was aware that history writing is never a neutral, totally objective enterprise. However, despite this awareness, his response to Strauss's *Leben Jesu* manifests where his real sympathies lie with respect to philosophical influence on biblical study. Wellhausen writes:

> Because Strauss showed and acknowledged himself to be, a child of Hegel in his concept of myth, his book was judged simply as an extension of so-called Hegelianism. Biblical criticism, however, did not in general develop under the influence of philosophical ideas. . . . Philosophy does not precede,

---

21. Lothar Perlitt, *Vatke und Wellhausen* (Berlin: Verlag Alfred Töpelman, 1965), p. 177.

22. Perlitt, *Vatke und Wellhausen*, p. 172.

23. Perlitt, *Vatke und Wellhausen*, pp. 178-79.

24. Perlitt, *Vatke und Wellhausen*, p. 185. On the key role of "development" in nineteenth-century historiography see Maurice Mandelbaum, *History, Man, and Reason: A Study in Nineteenth-Century Thought* (Baltimore: Johns Hopkins University Press, 1971).

25. Perlitt, *Vatke und Wellhausen*, p. 160.

26. Perlitt, *Vatke und Wellhausen*, p. 168.

but follows [biblical criticism], in that it seeks to evaluate and to systematise that which it has not itself produced. The authors — who were friends — of the two great theological works of 1835 [Strauss's *Life of Jesus* and Vatke's *Biblical Theology*] were certainly Hegelian. But, that which is of scholarly significance in them, does not come from Hegel. As Vatke is the disciple of, and the one who brings to completion the work of, de Wette, so Strauss completes the work of the old rationalists. The true value of the *Life of Jesus* lies not in the philosophical introduction and concluding section, but in the main part which in terms of its extent exceeds the others by far.[27]

Perlitt and Rogerson note how this statement exemplifies Wellhausen's view of philosophy and biblical study: "Where Wellhausen positions his own work in this clear distinction between biblical criticism (as science) and philosophy (as an interpretation which follows criticism and merely systematizes it), can after all not be doubted."[28] And, "One must rather proceed from particular impulses which arise from the exegesis."[29]

With this statement we see the extent to which Wellhausen differed from Vatke and many of his other predecessors. Their extensive treatments of the nature of religion indicate a strong awareness of the influence of philosophical questions upon their work. Wellhausen has a different view of the relationship between Old Testament exegesis and philosophy. It is a view in which exegesis is relatively uncontaminated by philosophy; Old Testament research uncovers the facts, and philosophy can follow the facts but should not precede them!

Rogerson is alert to philosophical influence on biblical studies, and he acknowledges that biblical criticism has been more influenced by philosophy than Wellhausen allows. However, he quotes from Wellhausen's discussion of Strauss's *Leben Jesu* and then in agreement with Wellhausen argues that

> If biblical criticism is defined as the investigation of the literary processes which brought the books of the Bible to their extant form, together with a critical evaluation of the history and culture of ancient Israel and Judea so as to interpret biblical material in its original historical and cultural setting, *it is difficult to see how philosophy, even defined very broadly, can affect such investigations. Surely, the reconstruction of the history of Israel, or of the apostolic period, involves the use of an historical method unaffected by philosophy.*

27. Quoted in Perlitt, *Vatke und Wellhausen*, p. 204.
28. Perlitt, *Vatke und Wellhausen*, p. 204.
29. Perlitt, *Vatke und Wellhausen*, p. 205.

Further, the conclusion, based upon the alteration of the divine names and other criteria in the "Flood" narrative of Genesis 6-9, that this narrative is a combination of two originally separate written accounts, is something else that in *no way depends upon philosophy. . . . I am happy to agree that in many of its technical procedures, biblical criticism is not affected by philosophy.*[30]

Wellhausen — and Rogerson, and so many others — has thereby adopted a radically different understanding to de Wette and Vatke of how philosophy relates to biblical criticism. For de Wette biblical interpretation is shaped by one's view of religion and one's philosophy. For Wellhausen and for Rogerson, philosophy follows on from biblical interpretation and scholarship. The effect is dramatic! In one fell swoop, as it were, what Stephen Toulmin calls the standard account of modernity is entrenched in biblical criticism, thereby obscuring the tradition(s) in which this style of biblical interpretation is embedded. The observation of the text by Wellhausen and his followers now becomes objective and scientific, (relatively) unadulterated by philosophical perspectives.

The effect of this approach to biblical study is in a positivist direction in the sense that historical criticism is now understood to uncover the facts of Israel's history, and to be scientific, objective, and neutral in this regard. And since Wellhausen this view has come to dominate Old Testament studies. James Barr has been very influential on Old Testament studies, and in a recent publication, despite the emergence of postmodernism, he can still assert:

> The typical biblical scholarship of modern times has been rather little touched by philosophy — certainly much less than it has been touched by theology. Going back to the last century, one remembers Vatke and his Hegelianism, and it has long been customary to accuse Wellhausen of the same thing though the accusation has long been proved to be an empty one. And after that we do have an influence of philosophy, but mostly on the theological use of the Bible rather than on biblical scholarship in the narrower sense.[31]

This approach won the day in modern liberal and, to a significant extent, evangelical Old Testament studies. A common epistemological starting

---

30. John W. Rogerson, "Philosophy and the Rise of Biblical Criticism: England and Germany," in *England and Germany: Studies in Theological Diplomacy,* ed. Stephen W. Sykes (Frankfurt: Peter Lang, 1982), p. 63; emphasis mine.

31. James Barr, *History and Ideology in the Old Testament: Biblical Studies at the End of a Millennium* (New York: Oxford University Press, 2000), pp. 26-27; emphasis mine.

point was assumed, the difference generally being the conclusions reached. Thus there is some truth in Barr's critique of evangelicalism in his *Fundamentalism* that one generally knows which conclusions evangelicals are going to reach. Nowadays this common epistemological starting point often manifests itself in the noble guise of "going where the truth takes us" as if the questions we ask and our epistemology and unavoidable religious starting point have no influence on the "truth" at which we arrive.

Retrospect and Prospect

Retrospect

In the light of postmodernism's savaging of modernity it is far harder nowadays to defend the neutrality of Old Testament criticism. For example, we are aware in Old Testament study that the romantic historicism that underlies Wellhausen's and Hermann Gunkel's quest for the individual prophet detracts from the prophetic books in the shape we have received them.[32] One may still wish to pursue Wellhausen's approach and continue the endless search for, say, Ur-Amos, but nowadays it is harder to do this without being aware of the prejudices this embodies. And Wellhausen's profane-holy distinction is intensely troubling, as is his negative view of the Judaism that follows the Exile. His view of development may indeed not be that of Hegel and Darwin but it is historicist,[33] and it does shape his reading of the Old Testament in a major way. Wellhausen's discussion of *Volk* and *Blut* is hard to read in a post-Holocaust context without some sense of incipient anti-Semitism.[34]

It is easy to understand how the historicism that Wellhausen depended upon in the late nineteenth century might appear to be presuppositionless. The roots of this classical historicism are located in Leopold von Ranke's rejection of Hegelian *a priori* conceptualizations of history and attempt to ground history in *a posteriori* concern with particulars.[35] This emphasis, in the late-nineteenth-century context of "Wissenschaft for the sake of Wissen-

---

32. See Mark G. Brett, *Biblical Criticism in Crisis: The Impact of the Canonical Approach on Old Testament Studies* (Cambridge: Cambridge University Press, 1991), pp. 89-93.

33. See Mandelbaum, *History, Man, and Reason,* for the centrality of "development" in nineteenth-century historicism.

34. Perlitt, *Vatke und Wellhausen,* p. 219.

35. G. G. Iggers, "Historicism: The History and Meaning of the Term," *Journal of the History of Ideas* 56 (1995): 129-52.

schaft"[36] gave the aura of pure science to historicism and historical criticism. However, historicism's concern with facts "as they actually are" should not detract from the very real philosophy of history embodied in historicism and evident in Wellhausen's work.

Prospect

So where are we now in terms of Old Testament interpretation and philosophy? The effect of postmodernism or what Plantinga calls "creative anti-realism" has led to a wild pluralism in Old Testament studies in which an immense variety of approaches to the Old Testament are on display. Amid this smorgasbord historical criticism continues to thrive and its conclusions continue to be taken seriously by many scholars. The wild pluralism has certainly included a lot of philosophy; it is common to find Derrida, Habermas, Foucault, etc., cropping up in Old Testament books. Indeed there is hardly an area of Old Testament study where some form of postmodern approach is not in print. Another recent development has been the minority renewal of theological interpretation. Brevard Childs's canonical hermeneutic paved the way for this growing movement. In terms of philosophy, however, it should be noted that Childs's lifelong project emerged from his encounter with Barth, and an effect of this is that an antipathy for philosophy continues to typify much theological interpretation.

In our day no one has done more to point out the importance of philosophy for biblical interpretation than Anthony Thiselton. Amid the astonishing resurgence of Christian philosophy in North America, Nicholas Wolterstorff and Alvin Plantinga have attended closely and creatively to the relationship between philosophy and biblical interpretation. However, Barth's shadow is long, and many of the key proponents of theological interpretation continue to reject what they see as a needless and time-consuming detour through general hermeneutics.[37] Better, in their view, to get on with reading the Bible for the church.

36. This is Max Weber's description. See Howard, *Religion and the Rise of Historicism*, pp. 103-4, for this reference and a useful description of the priority of "Wissenschaft" in the second half of the nineteenth century in Germany.

37. A manifestation of this is the view that theological interpretation requires a *regional* hermeneutic rather than a *general* hermeneutics. See Francis Watson, *Church, Text and World: Biblical Interpretation in Theological Perspective* (Edinburgh: T&T Clark, 1994), p. 1: "The text in question is the biblical text; for the goal is a theological hermeneutic within

However, philosophy is not so easily put aside. I do not often invoke Derrida, but, in an interview with Richard Kearney, Derrida, rightly in my opinion, argues that

> In all the other disciplines you mention, there is philosophy. To say to oneself that one is going to study something that is not philosophy is to deceive oneself. It is not difficult to show that in political economy, for example, there is a philosophical discourse in operation. And the same applies to mathematics and the other sciences. Philosophy, as logocentrism, is present in every scientific discipline and the only justification for transforming philosophy into a specialized discipline is the necessity to render explicit and thematic the philosophical subtext in every discourse. The principal function which the teaching of philosophy serves is to enable people to become "conscious," to become aware of what exactly they are saying, what kind of discourse they are engaged in when they do mathematics, physics, political economy, and so on. There is no system of teaching or transmitting knowledge which can retain its coherence without, at one moment or another, interrogating itself philosophically, that is, without acknowledging its subtextual premises; and this may even include an interrogation of unspoken political interests or traditional values.[38]

Charles Taylor makes the same point when he notes that you get deeper and deeper into a question and finally you're into these really fundamental questions *that we usually take for granted.* And that's philosophy.

Questions of epistemology, ontology, and anthropology can be ignored or taken for granted but only at the expense of having them unconsciously at work in one's discourse. Take for example, the vital question of how the Old Testament speaks to present-day questions about the environment: Theodore Hiebert argues that Hegelian influence led many scholars to adopt a history-nature dichotomy that prevented the Old Testament's powerful message about nature and the creation from being attended to.[39] Meanwhile,

---

which an exegesis oriented primarily towards theological issues can come into being. This is therefore not an exercise in general hermeneutics. . . . [T]he hermeneutic or interpretative paradigm towards which the following chapters move is a theological rather than a literary one, and the idea that a literary perspective is, as such, already 'theological' seems to me to be without foundation."

38. Richard Kearney, "Jacques Derrida," in his *Dialogues with Contemporary Thinkers: The Phenomenological Heritage* (Manchester: Manchester University Press, 1984), pp. 114-15.

39. Theodore Hiebert, *The Yahwist's Landscape: Nature and Religion in Early Israel* (Oxford: Oxford University Press, 1996), pp. 3-22.

Barr rocked the boat of Old Testament scholarship by attending to the philosophies of language at work in Old Testament studies. In my own introduction to *After Pentecost* (2001) I attempted to show how a philosophy of language influences Jacob Milgrom's exegesis of Leviticus. It is surely time to acknowledge that philosophy is unavoidable in academic biblical interpretation so that we can be conscious of its influence.

Once the importance of philosophy for Old Testament interpretation is conceded, the critical question becomes *how* to construe the relationship between philosophy and Old Testament interpretation. For trinitarian Old Testament interpretation this will, I suggest, mean looking closely at the relationship between theology and philosophy and Old Testament exegesis.

Theology and Philosophy . . . and Old Testament Interpretation

Major progress has come about in philosophical epistemology through *meta-epistemology*, a process of standing back to attain a bird's-eye view of the major epistemologies in operation in philosophy. As Nicholas Wolterstorff notes, once scholars did this, the dominance of classical foundationalism became apparent. At the same time it became apparent that such a view tended to be assumed rather than argued for. As is well known, both Plantinga and Wolterstorff have played a major role in critiquing classical foundationalism and in proposing Christian alternatives. I suggest that a similar standing back to see what major paradigms are operative in Old Testament studies is very insightful in terms of locating our practice and developing a genuinely trinitarian Old Testament scholarship.

There are a variety of ways one could do this; for our purposes I will use the relationship between philosophy and theology to open up the main paradigms operative in Old Testament study today. By definition a trinitarian hermeneutic is theological; however, we have also argued that it is philosophical. Thus it becomes crucial to ask, how do philosophy and theology relate to each other[40] and how does our construal of this relationship relate to Old Testament interpretation?

40. Relevant sources are John Milbank, "Knowledge: The Theological Critique of Philosophy in Hamann and Jacobi," in *Radical Orthodoxy,* ed. John Milbank, Catherine Pickstock, and Graham Ward (London: Routledge, 1999), pp. 21-37; Caputo, *Philosophy and Theology;* Nicholas Wolterstorff, *Reason within the Bounds of Religion* (Grand Rapids: Eerdmans, 1984); James K. Beilby, ed., *For Faith and Clarity* (Grand Rapids: Baker Academic, 2006); Ingolf U. Dalferth, *Theology and Philosophy* (Eugene, OR: Wipf & Stock, 2001). The

I propose that we think in terms of the following main ways of philosophy being related to theology:

1. *Theology subservient to philosophy* (Christ of culture).[41] Kant and, as we have seen, much historical criticism embody this approach. If theology has a place here it is as a suburb of philosophy. De Wette's early hermeneutic typifies the implications of this type of approach for biblical interpretation, although as his hermeneutic develops the tensions in it drive it toward position two below. However, the overarching framework remains Kantian. Some of the postmodern work on the Bible fits firmly in this category. Often it lacks any theological interest and in a strongly secular way simply applies postmodern philosophy and critical theory to the Bible.

2. *Double truth* (Christ and culture in paradox and/or Christ above culture). Theology and philosophy are different but equally important ways of getting at truth and we need both. This approach takes diverse forms. Some argue that theology and philosophy have different *objects,* that is, theology deals with the events of faith while philosophy deals with concepts and interpretation. In my essay "Uncharted Waters" I suggest that Kevin Vanhoozer's typology of the philosophy-theology relationship, articulated in terms of the Christ (theology)–concept (philosophy) relationship, falls prey to this danger. Thiselton, too, argues along similar lines and sees philosophy as helping to provide a corrective to theological interpretation. He has also spoken of theology as dealing with event and philosophy with concept. Others argue that theology and philosophy may overlap in their objects but have different means (faith and revelation versus universal experience and reason) of studying these objects. This view manifests itself in John Paul II's *Faith and Reason.* The pope compares faith and reason (that is, theology and philosophy) to the two wings of a bird: in order for it to fly properly, both are required.[42]

---

latter is the most rigorous exploration, but Dalferth concludes — unsatisfactorily in my view — that "All we can (and must) do, therefore, is to secure harmony between the perspectives of Faith and Reason by designing rational means of translating between them" (p. ix).

41. It is helpful, I think, to connect these categories with H. Richard Niebuhr's Christ-culture categories in his *Christ and Culture* (New York: Harper Torchbooks, 1951). Niebuhr's categories are the ones in parentheses.

42. John Paul II, *Faith and Reason,* p. 3. There is a tension in *Faith and Reason,* I think, between the unity of truth and a nature-grace distinction between philosophy and theology. This is unfortunate because Catholic theology this century has made significant advances in overcoming this tension. See John Milbank, *Theology and Social Theory: Beyond Secular Reason* (Oxford: Blackwell, 1990), pp. 210-32.

John Milbank traces the separation of theology and philosophy back to Duns Scotus in particular,[43] arguing that it was he who first radically separated the two. The epistemological reason-revelation duality that stems from this "far from being an authentic Christian legacy, itself results from the rise of a questionably secular mode of knowledge."[44] It is, indeed, hard to see how one can consistently maintain that theology and philosophy deal with different *objects*, not least when the common focus is the Old Testament. Clearly (secular) philosophers might choose to reflect on the events of faith too. And the problem with seeing the means as different is that theology too is rational and philosophy is not exempt from a view of religion and an underlying worldview. Issues of epistemology, ontology and anthropology are present in theology as in philosophy.

The danger inherent in the double truth approach is that of eclecticism, in which conflicting perspectives sit in uneasy tension with each other. John Paul II warns in this respect of

> the approach of those who, in research, teaching and argumentation, even in theology, tend to use individual ideas drawn from different philosophies, without concern for their internal coherence, their place within a system or their historical context. They therefore run the risk of being unable to distinguish the part of truth of a given doctrine from elements of it which may be erroneous or ill-suited to the task at hand.[45]

Old Testament interpretation is riddled with double truth approaches to the philosophy-theology relationship. Jon Levenson discerns like few others the radical implications of historical criticism for the "Hebrew Bible" and the "Old Testament," but still holds out hope that somehow a literary and a historical critical approach will together lead to a larger truth![46] Plantinga shows, in his "Two (or More) Kinds of Scripture Scholarship," how readily biblical scholars — many of them Christian — work on the Old Testament with unchristian assumptions built into their interpretive methodologies.

3. *Theology alone* (Christ against culture). Tertullian — "What has Je-

---

43. Milbank, "Knowledge," p. 23. This is, however, a much contested view.

44. Milbank, "Knowledge," p. 24.

45. John Paul II, *Faith and Reason*, p. 127.

46. See Jon Levenson, *The Hebrew Bible, the Old Testament, and Historical Criticism* (Louisville: Westminster John Knox, 1993), pp. xiv-xv; Craig G. Bartholomew, "Review of J. D. Levenson, *The Hebrew Bible, the Old Testament and Historical Criticism*," *Calvin Theological Journal* 30, no. 2 (1995): 525-30.

rusalem to do with Athens?" — is the great early representative of this view. The effect of this approach is, of course, the Trojan horse syndrome. Despised and unacknowledged, philosophy remains at work in the discourse. Few of the contemporary proponents of a theological hermeneutic would argue for this understanding of the theology-philosophy relationship. However, the danger of a theological hermeneutic that fails to negotiate its relationship with philosophy will surely be similar. Philosophical subtexts will continue to shape the discourse but in a relatively unconscious way.

4. *Christ the clue to theology and philosophy* (Christ the transformer of culture). I am using here Lesslie Newbigin's seminal insight, argued from his exegesis of John 1, that Christ is the clue to all that is.[47] This does not mean that revelation delivers all we need in a kind of instant package, but it does insist that in our pursuit of (all) truth we go astray if we are not guided by that clue which is Christ. According to this view theology *and* philosophy are academic disciplines that are both traditioned; that is, they *both* depend on and presuppose views of who we are and the nature of our world, so that their rationalities are always particular. This approach insists that, if Christ is the clue to creation, then he is the clue to all of creation and not just to theology. It insists that "faith seeking understanding" is not the peculiar terrain of theology but should be true of all academic research.[48]

Nowhere have I seen the "autonomy" of philosophy challenged so strongly in recent days as in Milbank's "Knowledge." In his quest for a radical orthodoxy Milbank discerns the fundamental importance of subverting the autonomy of philosophy and he invokes the neglected "radical pietist" tradition of Hamann and Jacobi in this respect. "Hence there can be *no* reason/revelation duality: true reason anticipates revelation, while revelation simply is *of* true reason which must ceaselessly arrive, as an event, such that what Christ shows supremely is the world as really world, as creation."[49]

From this perspective, a biblical hermeneutic has theological and philosophical dimensions and both need to be informed by faith seeking under-

---

47. Lesslie Newbigin, *The Light Has Come: An Exposition of the Fourth Gospel* (Grand Rapids: Eerdmans, 1982), pp. 1-11.

48. I am not aware that Newbigin wrote about the relationship between philosophy and theology and biblical interpretation. However, his "The Word in the World," in his *Foolishness to the Greeks: The Gospel and Western Culture* (London: SPCK, 1986), pp. 42-64, and his attention to a theology of history in *The Gospel in a Pluralist Society* (Grand Rapids: Eerdmans, 1989), pp. 66-79, 103-15, are highly relevant to biblical hermeneutics.

49. Milbank, "Knowledge," p. 24.

standing.[50] "God has planted a head on our shoulders and put eyes in that head, and so the full job description of a believer is to be a thinking believer or a believing thinker. . . . God has given us revelation in the very widest sense. . . . That is why philosophy and theology have to learn to get along."[51] My argument is that they will only "get along" when both are informed at root by Christ the clue to all that is. Such an integrally trinitarian hermeneutic(s) will not solve all exegetical problems but will, as Stephen Neill said of a theology of history, hold the ring within which solutions may be found.[52] At the very least, it is worth noting that, had de Wette been open to such an integral model, and had he read a text like Wolterstorff's *Reason within the Bounds of Religion,* the direction of modern Old Testament studies might have been very different indeed!

Ways Forward

My suggestions for ways forward are as follows:

1. We need once and for all to reject the assumption that a neutral, autonomous reading of the Old Testament is possible or desirable. It serves merely to conceal hidden motives directing the reading. A trinitarian hermeneutic will insist that, ontologically and objectively, the Old Testament is best and rightly described as the *Old Testament,* the first half of the written Word of God that comes to fulfillment in Christ. Of course the Old Testament is "also" a collection of ancient Near Eastern texts in Hebrew and Aramaic that came into existence over a long period of time, but to stop there is reductionistic. *This* collection of ancient Near Eastern texts is different from any other; it is part of the inspired Word of the triune God.

2. Thus, a trinitarian hermeneutic must not only begin with this assumption, but its goal must be to listen for God's address in the Old Testament. A hermeneutic that stops short of this goal is inadequate.

3. A trinitarian hermeneutic alerts us to the fact that the Old Testament is a written text that came into existence in history and thus is subject to the dynamic but constant order of creation. Three crucial dimensions of the Old

---

50. I have attempted to outline the possible contours of such a hermeneutic in Craig G. Bartholomew, *Reading Ecclesiastes: Old Testament Exegesis and Hermeneutical Theory* (Rome: Editrice Pontificio Instituto Biblico, 1988), pp. 207-26.

51. Caputo, *Philosophy and Theology,* p. 36.

52. Stephen Neill and N. T. Wright, *The Interpretation of the New Testament, 1861-1986,* 2nd ed. (Oxford: Oxford University Press, 1988), p. 366.

Testament are the historical, the lingual and literary, and the kerygmatic/ theological. A non-reductionistic hermeneutic must take the organic interplay of all three into account. Neither history, nor language, nor kerygma is arbitrary; there is an order in creation that holds for them and in my view, this is precisely what philosophy tries to ascertain. Every Hebrew grammar and syntax works with a philosophy of language (or with several of them), whether it is Chomsky's generative linguistics or Saussure's structuralism, or a multitude of other possibilities. Similarly, postmodern readings of the Old Testament have alerted us to how strongly one's philosophy of literature can impact one's exegesis. Clearly philosophy impacts Old Testament interpretation in a multitude of ways, and a trinitarian — as opposed to a narrowly Christological — hermeneutic leads us to expect this with its explicit doctrine of creation. As Caputo notes, "We make no progress with God by beating up on the world God made."[53]

4. A trinitarian hermeneutic alerts us to the fact that the privileged place from which to know the order of creation is "in Christ." The dynamic order of creation holds for everyone and as Oliver O'Donovan has so creatively pointed out, the resurrection is the reaffirmation of creation. However, it is only "in Christ" that the order can be known aright. I know of no better exposition of an appropriate epistemology for reading this order than chapter four, "Knowledge in Christ," in O'Donovan's *Resurrection and Moral Order* (1994). It should be compulsory reading for every aspiring trinitarian Old Testament exegete.

5. Philosophy, as I understand it, endeavors, however inadequately, to discern and to describe logically the structures of creation, whether these are the structures of language, history, or literature. As we have noted, such philosophical insight is indispensable to Old Testament interpretation. However, a trinitarian hermeneutic alerts us to the need for contemporary, modern, *Christian* philosophical insight in these areas, and this is what makes the contemporary renaissance of Christian philosophy such an opportune time for trinitarian Old Testament interpretation. Apart from the rich historical tradition of Christian philosophy, Old Testament scholars have a growing smorgasbord of contemporary Christian philosophy available to them to draw on in their work. There is no need to reinvent the wheel!

In this respect it is important to note that I am not appealing for a return to pre-critical interpretation of the Old Testament, despite the fact

---

53. Caputo, *Philosophy and Theology*, p. 36.

that it was never "uncritical" and that we have much to gain from excavating it. Modernity has brought major advances, not least in Old Testament studies, and the challenge is to discern where real progress has indeed been made and to build on it. Modern philosophy, as Thiselton would not hesitate to remind us, is a complex phenomenon. While Descartes, Kant, and Hume may be distinctly unhelpful paths for a trinitarian hermeneutic they are by no means the only philosophical paths available. For those of us in the Augustinian tradition Pascal may offer resources still to be excavated.[54] Within the Lutheran tradition Paul Hinlicky argues the path from Luther through Leibniz is one that has not been taken but offers real possibilities for Christian thought today.[55] Within the Lutheran tradition there is, of course, also Kierkegaard, whose philosophy is full of Scripture and whose perspective, in my view, is pregnant with possibilities for philosophy and biblical interpretation today.[56] Johann Georg Hamann, a contemporary and major critic of Kant, is finally starting to receive the attention he deserves in the English-speaking world, and he certainly presents a Christian alternative to Kantianism.[57]

Alasdair MacIntyre has made a major philosophical contribution in his recent works *After Virtue* and *Whose Justice? Which Rationality?*, in which he has rightly argued that rationality is always traditioned and that we need to become aware of the tradition in which we operate as scholars.[58] Roy Clouser in his *The Myth of Religious Neutrality* argues that "religion" is unavoidable in the work of theorizing; there are always some beliefs at the root of theories which count as that on which all else depends. Thomas Reid's common-sense realism provides a very different version of foundationalism to that of many of his Enlightenment contemporaries; and Reformed epistemology, most notably represented by Plantinga and Wolterstorff, has drawn

54. J. R. Peters, *The Logic of the Heart: Augustine, Pascal, and the Rationality of Faith* (Grand Rapids: Baker Academic, 2009).

55. P. R. Hinlicky, *Paths Not Taken: Fates of Theology from Luther through Leibniz* (Grand Rapids: Eerdmans, 2009), p. 294.

56. The best contemporary work on Kierkegaard, in my view, has been done by C. Stephen Evans. Amidst his many works see most recently *Kierkegaard: An Introduction* (Cambridge: Cambridge University Press, 2009).

57. See the excellent chapter in Beiser, *The Fate of Reason*, pp. 16-43; as well as James C. O'Flaherty, *Johann Georg Hamann* (Boston: Twayne, 1979); and W. M. Alexander, *Johann Georg Hamann: Philosophy and Faith* (The Hague: Martinus Nijhoff, 1966).

58. For a useful work on MacIntyre on tradition and a good defense of the criticisms from Nagel and Nussbaum, see Christopher S. Lutz, *Tradition in the Ethics of Alasdair MacIntyre: Relativism, Thomism, and Philosophy* (Lanham, MD: Lexington, 2004).

on his work in an attempt to provide a viable Christian alternative to classical foundationalism.[59]

Modernity thus provides ample philosophical resources for Christian Old Testament scholars to draw upon in their development and practice of a trinitarian hermeneutic. Does this mean that other philosophical paradigms — secular or Islamic or Jewish — have nothing to offer? Absolutely not! In my view some of the most creative developments in Old Testament exegesis have come from Jewish scholars such as Meir Sternberg, Robert Alter, and Leon Kass. A trinitarian approach will affirm with Augustine that all truth is God's truth and be open to insights wherever they may issue from. Simultaneously, a trinitarian approach will be committed to the painstaking work of taking over insights without necessarily assuming their philosophical baggage and integrating them in a trinitarian framework.

6. This will mean that amid the demands of specialization Old Testament scholars will need to become philosophically literate and to draw consciously on the best (Christian) scholarship in their work. Iain Provan's work on Old Testament history;[60] Thiselton's work on speech act theory; and Gibson's work on Near Eastern archeology, philosophy, and the Old Testament[61] are notable examples in this respect.

7. A major help in this respect is a rich, nuanced understanding of the history of Old Testament interpretation, as I hope the discussions of de Wette and Wellhausen above indicate. Old Testament interpretation is not well served in this respect. We urgently need a retelling of the story of modern philosophy, a retelling in which philosophers such as those mentioned above receive deserved recognition. Such a re-narrating would be of great service in the task of re-narrating the story of modern Old Testament studies. Chapter 2 by Al Wolters in the present volume is thus vital for "hearing the Old Testament" today, and we urgently need rigorous histories of Old Testament interpretation from a trinitarian perspective.

---

59. See, e.g., Kelly James Clark, *Return to Reason: A Critique of Enlightenment Evidentialism and Defense of Reason and Belief in God* (Grand Rapids: Eerdmans, 1990), pp. 139-51; Nicholas Wolterstorff, *Thomas Reid and the Story of Epistemology* (Cambridge: Cambridge University Press, 2001).

60. See among others, chapters 1-3 in Iain Provan, V. Philips Long, and Tremper Longman III, *A Biblical History of Israel* (Louisville: Westminster John Knox, 2003).

61. Arthur Gibson, *Text and Tablet: Near Eastern Archeology, the Old Testament, and New Possibilities* (Aldershot: Ashgate, 2000). Gibson starts his book with an astonishing quote from the archeologist Ian Hodder: "there is almost no literature available on how archeologists come to their conclusions" (p. 3). Among others, Gibson works to fill this gap.

8. Trinitarian Old Testament interpretation will be informed by Christian philosophy and systematic theology. Theology I take to be systematic reflection on special revelation, ranging from biblical theology to the creeds and confessions to highly theoretical systematic theology. It is instructive to note that Calvin wrote his *Institutes* to enable Christians to read the Bible better, whereas we tend to think of the move *from* the Bible *to* systematic theology. The move needs, of course, to go both ways; indeed, the relationship of Old Testament, philosophy and theology will in practice form a complex ecology of interpretation. The precise relationship of theology and philosophy is complex; for the present what I wish to affirm strongly is that a trinitarian hermeneutic rules out taking Christ as the clue to theology while leaving philosophy as an autonomous discipline. That clue which is Christ needs to be pursued with rigor in both disciplines and only thus will they be able to serve Old Testament exegesis well. And in turn trinitarian Old Testament interpretation will be of great service to such philosophy and theology.

4 Literary Approaches and Old Testament Interpretation

David J. H. Beldman

To say that the Old Testament is literature is to state the obvious. After all, Scripture comes to us as narrative, poetry, riddle, parable, oracle, and the list goes on. So seeing the Old Testament as literature is not itself problematic. The problem, it seems, is how to apply literary tools in a way that honors (in fact, enhances our sense of) the sacred text as the Divine Word, and how to attend to the literary dimension of the Old Testament without neglecting other equally important dimensions (for example, the historical and kerygmatic). This chapter aims to discern what literary approaches to the Old Testament have to offer believing readers. In other words, how does reading the Old Testament with specific attention to literary features help us to hear God's address in the Old Testament? The first part of this chapter offers an overview of how literary approaches have been used and developed in the history of interpretation. The remainder identifies and describes some of the most important features of Hebrew biblical literature that, when we are aware of them, help us to hear the Old Testament as God's Word.

The trinitarian hermeneutic that provides the framework for this volume begins, appropriately, with a discussion of truth.[1] Many regard the result of the historical critical project as having undermined the "truth" of the Old Testament.[2] And indeed for some Old Testament readers the literary

---

1. See Chapter 1 by Craig Bartholomew in the present volume.

2. I put "truth" in quotation marks to indicate that the truth of the Old Testament cannot be reduced to historicity. It seems that some scholars think that if we can prove that modern biblical criticism is wrong (in, say, the denial of the Exodus or of the existence of a united

turn provides an excuse for avoiding the question of historical truth. However, what is at stake in neglecting the literary dimension of the Old Testament is the very truthfulness of these texts. If as believing readers we are convinced that "God imparts himself to [us,] his image bearers"[3] in the Old and New Testament, then attention to *how* he communicates to us (i.e., through historical narrative, poetry, wisdom sayings, etc.) is nonnegotiable.

History of Literary Appreciation of the Old Testament

Interpreters of the Old Testament have long been attuned to its aesthetic and literary power.[4] Many of the earliest Jewish methods of interpreting Scripture recognized the power of the words of Scripture in their literal meaning as well as in what they evoke metaphorically or allegorically. One medieval Jewish mystic regarded the Bible as an object of love and affection, communicating signals of adoration through the meaning and beauty of the text in its minutest detail.[5] Augustine appreciated the Scriptures' superiority of beauty and eloquence, which he regarded as intricately bound up with the meaning and wisdom of the text's message and ultimately with the beauty and eloquence of God.[6] David L. Jeffrey maintains that the church fathers and medieval scholars used "critical" literary theory, but that the telos of that use was ultimately nothing less than an encounter with the Author of the sacred text.[7]

Israelite monarchy) then we have adequately attended to the truth of the Old Testament. For a discussion of historicity see Chapter 5 by Tremper Longman and Chapter 11 by Iain Provan in the present volume.

3. Page 15 above.

4. See especially Leland Ryken, "The Bible as Literature: A Brief History," in *The Complete Literary Guide to the Bible*, ed. Leland Ryken and Tremper Longman III (Grand Rapids: Eerdmans, 1993), pp. 49-68; see also Tremper Longman III, *Literary Approaches to Biblical Interpretation*, Foundations of Contemporary Interpretation 3 (Grand Rapids: Zondervan, 1987), pp. 13-15; K. P. Bland, "The Rabbinic Method and Literary Criticism," in *Literary Interpretations of Biblical Narratives*, ed. Kenneth R. R. Gros Louis, James S. Ackerman, and Thayer S. Warshaw (Nashville: Abingdon, 1974), pp. 16-23.

5. Cited in Bland, "The Rabbinic Method," pp. 16, 23.

6. Augustine, *On Christian Doctrine* IV, cited in Ryken, "The Bible as Literature," p. 53.

7. David Lyle Jeffrey, *People of the Book: Christian Identity and Literary Culture* (Grand Rapids: Eerdmans, 1996), p. 95. This sketch runs counter to Nicholas Wolterstorff, *Divine Discourse: Philosophical Reflections on the Claim That God Speaks* (Cambridge: Cambridge University Press, 1995), p. 16, who maintains: "For millennia now it has been assumed that the biblical books in general, and the biblical narratives in particular, have little by way of admirable literary qualities. The categories and strategies of literary analysis available to the

During the Renaissance and Reformation, literary appreciation of the Bible gained new impetus.[8] However, in spite of significant progress that has been made through historical critical analysis of the Old Testament in the modern era, an unfortunate effect of this approach has been the reduction of the Old Testament to its historical dimension at the cost of its other essential dimensions, including the literary.[9] The literature of the Old Testament, according to historical critics, is in some cases stitched together from varied and sometimes contradictory sources, and the critic's task ought to be to strip back the layers in order to uncover the "original text."[10]

In the 1960s and 1970s a growing number of scholars began to articulate their unease with the state of Old Testament studies.[11] Pioneers in the guild advocated a reevaluation of the dominant interpretative methods. Important voices urged for the primacy of *reading* in Old Testament interpretation. Of course authorship, date, and provenance are important for the interpretation of Old Testament texts, but in the vast majority of cases these things are unknown and must be reconstructed *from the text itself.* Therefore, Meir Sternberg distinguishes between source-oriented inquiry, which focuses on some historical object behind the text (e.g., the history of Israelite religion or the process that generated a particular text), and discourse-oriented analysis, which is concerned with the text itself as a pattern of meaning and effect.[12]

---

readers of late antiquity yielded the conclusion that the bulk of the biblical writings were, if not uncouth, at least inept."

8. Ryken, "The Bible as Literature," pp. 53-54.

9. The literary was not the only casualty of this era. Wellhausen's evaluation of his own contribution to theology is most illuminating: "I became a theologian because I was interested in the scientific treatment of the Bible; it has only gradually dawned on me that a professor of theology likewise has the practical task of preparing students for service in the Evangelical Church, and that I was not fulfilling this practical task, but rather, in spite of all reserve on my part, was incapacitating my hearers for their office"; cited in Alfred Jepsen, "The Scientific Study of the Old Testament," in *Essays on Old Testament Hermeneutics,* ed. Claus Westermann, trans. J. Bright (Richmond: John Knox Press, 1971), p. 247. The fact that the marginalization of the literary and theological dimensions took place simultaneously is probably of significance.

10. Barton warns against the misconception that the original intent of source criticism was to chop up a unified, coherent work. See John Barton, *Reading the Old Testament: Method in Biblical Study,* rev. ed. (London: Darton, Longman, and Todd, 2003), p. 22.

11. Often regarded as a watershed is James Muilenburg's presidential address at the annual meeting of the Society of Biblical Literature in 1968, published as "Form Criticism and Beyond," *JBL* 88 (1969): 1-18.

12. Meir Sternberg, *The Poetics of Biblical Narrative: Ideological Literature and the Drama of Reading,* Indiana Studies in Biblical Literature (Bloomington: Indiana University Press, 1985), p. 15.

Sternberg exposes the false claim of objectivity in much source-oriented interpretation: "The knowledge we possess of the 'real world' behind the Bible remains absurdly meager. . . . For better or worse, most of our information is culled from the Bible itself, and culling information entails a process of interpretation, where source abjectly waits on discourse. . . . The movement from text to reality cannot but pass through interpretation."[13] Similarly, Robert Alter relegates historical and even textual criticism to a place of secondary importance in relation to literary analysis. He maintains,

> The application of properly literary analysis to the Bible is a necessary precondition to a sounder textual scholarship . . . before you can decide whether a text is defective, composite, or redundant, you have to determine to the best of your ability the formal principles on which the text is organized. . . . There is a distinctive poetics informing both biblical narrative and biblical poetry, and an understanding of it will help us in many instances to make plain sense of a puzzling text instead of exercising that loose and derivative mode of literary invention that goes under the scholarly name of emendation.[14]

Prominent voices within the guild of Old Testament studies have argued along similar lines. David Clines, for example, lists historical, source, and form criticism as third-order methods in Old Testament study, following the first-order methods of historical-grammatical exegesis, textual criticism, and methods in literary criticism; and the second-order methods, including ideological criticisms, reader-response criticism, and deconstruction.[15]

The tension between historical approaches and literary approaches is one of the most significant issues in Old Testament studies today. Paradoxically, both sides advocate reading the Old Testament like any other book. David Gunn picks up on this irony:

> The life-force of modern historical criticism was a determination to deal with the biblical text in the same way as secular texts were treated, even if that should lead to the shaking of some dearly held verities. And that as-

13. Sternberg, *Poetics,* p. 16.

14. Robert Alter, "Introduction to the Old Testament," in *The Literary Guide to the Bible,* ed. Robert Alter and Frank Kermode (Cambridge, MA: Harvard University Press, 1987), pp. 26-27.

15. See David J. A. Clines, "Methods in Old Testament Study," in *On the Way to the Postmodern: Old Testament Essays, 1967-1998,* ed. David J. A. Clines (Sheffield: Sheffield Academic Press, 1998), pp. 23-45.

sumption, ironically, is at the heart of the current challenge which histori-cal criticism faces — a challenge to both its notion of history and its no-tion of a text.[16]

Believing readers may at this point object and say that advocates of both his-torical and literary approaches are wrong to assume that the Bible is like any other book and hence should be read like any other book. However, one of the marvels of our God is that we hear his voice as it is mediated through hu-man writers, using the conventions of literary composition at their disposal. Thus, as we read the Bible *as any other book* we will recognize it as *unlike any other book*.[17] Essentially, the literary turn is advocating a return to the basic principles of reading, and this is good news for those of us who aim to hear God's address in the Old Testament.

The Literary (Re)turn

The literary turn in Old Testament studies received its impetus from a vari-ety of sources. The first is the discipline of English literary studies. The pub-lication of Richard Moulton's *Literary Study Bible* and *Modern Reader's Bible* in 1895 marks a landmark in the study of the Bible as literature. Up until the 1960s, interest among literary scholars in the Bible as literature was nurtured primarily through Bible-as-literature courses by English departments in sec-ular universities.[18] This movement, while important in the development of literary approaches to the Old Testament, dealt with the Old Testament in English translation and, according to Ryken, lacked sophistication.[19] It was not until the 1960s and 1970s that literary scholars published works on the Bible that, even if they received mixed reception, could not be ignored.

Erich Auerbach's *Mimesis* (1953) was also a landmark, comparing the storytelling technique in Homer's *Odyssey* with that of the book of Gene-sis. Similarly, in Northrop Frye's influential *Anatomy of Criticism* (1957), the Bible "emerges as the chief organizing framework for Western Litera-

16. David M. Gunn, "New Directions in the Study of Biblical Hebrew Narrative," *JSOT* 39 (1987): 66.

17. See Paul Ricoeur, *Philosophical Hermeneutics and Theological Hermeneutics: Ideol-ogy, Utopia, and Faith,* Center for Hermeneutical Studies in Hellenistic and Modern Culture 17 (Berkeley: Graduate Theological Union and the University of California Press, 1976), p. 4.

18. Ryken, "The Bible as Literature," pp. 57-58.

19. Ryken, "The Bible as Literature," p. 58.

ture."[20] The discipline of literary studies has been and remains an important impetus for literary approaches to the Old Testament, as literary scholars now publish in biblical studies journals and as biblical scholars look to literary theory in order to shed light on biblical texts.

Perhaps the most significant impetus for the development of literary approaches to Old Testament interpretation has come from some key Jewish literary scholars. Old Testament studies set down an irreversible track, with groundbreaking work toward a poetics of Hebrew narrative (preeminently the work of Alter and Sternberg,[21] but also of Adele Berlin, Shimeon Bar-Efrat, and others).[22] Poetics of biblical narrative aims to find the rules that govern biblical Hebrew storytelling. Berlin provides a helpful analogy: "If literature is likened to a cake, then poetics gives us the recipe and interpretation tells us how it tastes."[23] The difficulty, of course, is that the Old Testament was not passed down with a manual of poetics, and therefore such a manual must be deduced from the literature itself. To continue the metaphor, one must produce the recipe from the finished cake (through multiple tastings!). Thus, poetics is "an inductive science that seeks to abstract the general principles of literature from many different manifestations of those principles as they occur in actual literary texts."[24] Among the other important voices in the 1970s and 1980s along these lines are those of Jacob Licht, Michael Fishbane, Yairah Amit, Robert W. Funk, Jonathan Magonet, J. P. Fokkelman, Andrea L. Weiss, and Luis Alonso Schökel. The impact of the literary turn in Old Testament studies is evident in new journals (e.g., *Semeia*) and series (e.g., The Bible and Literature Series from JSOT Press) and in published monographs and commentaries (e.g., Berit Olam).[25] The features of these new literary approaches and the implications of the literary turn appear below, but first we must situate the literary turn within the larger philosophical and hermeneutical context in which it emerged.

20. Ryken, "The Bible as Literature," p. 58.

21. Incidentally, Alter and Sternberg are literary scholars, but their work on the Hebrew Bible has profoundly influenced the direction Old Testament studies has taken.

22. For the sake of simplicity I will continue to use the term "Old Testament" while recognizing that not all readers regard it as such.

23. Adele Berlin, *Poetics and Interpretation of Biblical Narrative* (Sheffield: Almond Press, 1983), p. 15.

24. Berlin, *Poetics*, p. 15.

25. For a thorough and detailed survey of literary-critical studies of Hebrew narrative, complete with references, see David M. Gunn, "Narrative Criticism," in *To Each Its Own Meaning: An Introduction to Biblical Criticisms and Their Application,* ed. Steven L. McKenzie and Stephen R. Haynes (Louisville: Westminster John Knox, 1999), pp. 201-29.

Interpretation of the Old Testament has followed an overall trend in general hermeneutics from a focus on the author, to a focus on the text, and finally to a focus on the reader.[26] The literary turn emerged at a time when many questioned the legitimacy of author-oriented interpretation and when critics were applying methods like New Criticism and structuralism, which focus on the text as a self-sufficient work. The methodological pluralism that characterizes Old Testament Studies today reflects that of hermeneutics in general. Ideological criticism, reader-response criticism, and deconstruction have taken their place alongside more traditional approaches to Old Testament interpretation.

The Postmodern Turn

Before the literary turn took hold in Old Testament studies another turn took place, complicating the full appropriation of the literary one. The turn to postmodernism itself (closely associated with the linguistic turn of Saussure and others — the idea that language constitutes reality) began in literary studies and the arts but quickly led to a reassessment of the foundations of the whole of modern Western culture. Whereas during the height of modernism nearly all scholars agreed that there was one respectable way to interpret the Old Testament in the academy, as postmodernism took hold in biblical studies in the 1990s a methodological pluralism emerged in which, as Bartholomew puts it, "all methods are equal on the hermeneutical smorgasbord, even if some are more equal than others!"[27] At the turn to the twenty-first century, interpreters of the Old Testament have subjected it to every kind of approach imaginable.

Perhaps even more significant than the new methods that postmodernism provides is the philosophical and hermeneutical challenge that it represents. The postmodern critique rightly foregrounds the various assumptions at work in all interpretation and exposes the false objectivity of modern critical approaches. It rightly confronts the views of history, language, and so

---

26. Of course this is a deliberate simplification. One can see, for example, how some older types of pietistic readings of the Bible closely resemble the principles of reader-response readings. On the other hand, in the history of Old Testament interpretation in the church there has perpetually been a determined focus on the text as such.

27. Craig G. Bartholomew, "Introduction," in *Renewing Biblical Interpretation*, ed. Craig G. Bartholomew, Colin Greene, and Karl Möller, Scripture and Hermeneutics Series 1 (Grand Rapids: Zondervan, 2000), p. xxv.

forth at work in modern biblical criticism, and we ought to pay attention to these critiques. Postmodernism has effectively deconstructed the modern Enlightenment project by exposing serious flaws in its foundation. However, it is far from clear that a new foundation of subjectivism and unrestrained pluralism will be any more sound. Christians need to (continue to) develop conceptions of literature and language that are consistent with a biblical view of God, humanity, and the world.[28]

The postmodern turn has some unexpected implications for a literary appropriation of the Old Testament. On the one hand, the postmodern turn seems to have cut short the full appropriation of the literary turn in Old Testament studies. What is more, historical criticism still holds sway in the guild, even though it does not enjoy the hegemony it once did. The result is that an uneasy relationship exists between literary and historical approaches. In addition, a multitude of new approaches has emerged in Old Testament studies. Whereas traditionally the dominant historical-critical voice silenced theological approaches like the trinitarian hermeneutic proposed in this volume, now the great effort is for theological approaches to be heard among the plurality of voices clamoring for a hearing.[29] Even so, for those of us interested in interpreting the Old Testament so as to hear God's address, the present climate is a time of opportunity: postmodernism "has loosened up the regnant paradigms and provides an opportunity to reassess the foundations of biblical interpretation in the academy."[30] The postmodern turn forces readers to account for their approach to interpretation. For a trinitarian approach this means making use of the best tools from literary criticism while at the same time not reducing the Old Testament to "mere" literature but honoring the other key dimensions of the text.

Characteristics of Old Testament Literature

The diversity of types of literature in the Old Testament requires a full-orbed poetics of legal, narrative, wisdom, lyric, and prophetic literature, and in-

---

28. In this regard see the seminal work in the eight volumes of the Scripture and Hermeneutics Seminar (Grand Rapids: Zondervan, 2000-2007).

29. Arguably, the present context of methodological pluralism in Old Testament studies is preferable, but as Bartholomew has pointed out the tendency in postmodernism is to embrace all methods *except* those which claim to be the right way to read Scripture; "Introduction," p. xxv.

30. Bartholomew, "Introduction," p. xxv.

deed fruitful work in most of these areas has emerged.[31] In the remainder of this chapter, however, I will limit myself to consideration of some of the basic elements of Old Testament narrative and poetry

Narrative

"Telling stories," says Richard Kearney, "is as basic to human being as eating. More so, in fact, for while food makes us live, stories are what make our lives worth living . . . what make our condition *human*."[32] Stories, both our individual and our communal stories, give us our identity.[33] This basic truth is evident in the Old Testament insofar as the texts recount the crucial identity-forming events in Israel's history. For example, God's rescue of the Israelites from their slavery in Egypt is the basis for his relationship with Israel. In the Old Testament, this Exodus becomes the foundation for the Mosaic Law (e.g., Exod. 20:2; Deut. 5:6), is to set them apart from the pagan nations as they go into the Promised Land (e.g., Josh. 24:5-6; cf. Judg. 2:7-10), and is the basis on which the prophets indicted God's people and called them to repentance (e.g., Ezek. 20:3-11; Mic. 6:4). Moreover, the story of the Exodus was ritualized in the yearly feast of the Passover and appears as a recurring theme in Israel's repertoire of song (e.g., Pss. 78, 106, 114, 136, etc.).[34] Indeed, the Old and New Testaments together tell what Michael Goheen and Craig Bartholomew call "the true story of the whole world." Starting with creation, through the fall and God's saving mission that culminates in the restored heavens and earth (Rev. 21:1-5), the full revelation of God in Scripture provides the answers to the most basic existential questions: Who are we? Where did we come from? What is wrong? What is the solution? We are

---

31. See the chapters in Part III of this volume.

32. Richard Kearney, *On Stories* (London: Routledge, 2001), p. 3; emphasis in original.

33. To say that the Bible is a story is not to diminish the historicity of the events recorded in it. Wright notes that history as well as fiction "involves the telling of a story, the gathering of data into significant plots. And the Christian claim is that one particular story, centered upon Christ, tells the universal truth about history"; T. R. Wright, *Theology and Literature* (Oxford: Blackwell, 1988), p. 84. See also in this volume Chapter 1 by Craig Bartholomew chapter on a trinitarian hermeneutic and Chapter 5 by Tremper Longman on history. On history and fiction see V. Philips Long, *Art of Biblical History,* Foundations of Contemporary Interpretation 5 (Grand Rapids: Zondervan, 1994).

34. For the significance of song for individual and community formation see Gordon J. Wenham, *Psalms as Torah: Reading Biblical Song Ethically* (Grand Rapids: Baker Academic, 2012).

invited to make the world that Scripture projects our own, to find our place in it, and to indwell it.[35]

Although Old Testament narrative shares characteristics that are universal to all narrative, it is worth attempting to uncover the distinct characteristics of Hebrew (biblical) narrative. V. Philips Long identifies three basic characteristics of Old Testament narratives: they are *scenic, subtle,* and *succinct.*[36] That is, they are *scenic* not in the sense of providing detailed descriptions of a given story's physical setting; in fact, in most cases that kind of description is absent. The scenic character has to do instead with the way in which the narratives unfold as dramatic scenes. In this regard, Old Testament narrative involves much more "showing" than "telling." The narrator appears to remain at a critical distance from the events and characters of the story, keeping overt evaluation to a minimum and allowing readers to make judgments based upon their observations. The characterization of Old Testament personalities is mediated most often through their actions and speech rather than by direct evaluation from the narrator.[37] Likewise, judgment of events must be inferred from the way the narrator recounts them.

This relates to the *subtle* character of Old Testament narrative. Occasionally, the narrator's voice becomes overt, providing explanations, judgments or interpretations of people or events. For example, "Now the earth was corrupt in God's sight, and the earth was filled with violence" (Gen. 6:11); "For the LORD had ordained to defeat the good council of Ahithophel, so that the LORD might bring evil upon Absalom" (2 Sam. 17:14); "But the thing that David had done was evil in the eyes of the LORD" (2 Sam. 11:27); "And it was good in the Lord's eyes that Solomon requested this thing" (1 Kgs. 3:10).[38] More often, though, the narrator resists these kinds of overt statements, preferring to guide the reader much more indirectly. The characterization of the patriarch Jacob as a deceiver is a case in point. The narrator resists commenting on Jacob's deceptive tactics to obtain Isaac's blessing; instead, as Robert Alter notes, the narrator chooses a much more cunning way

35. Craig G. Bartholomew and Michael W. Goheen, *The Drama of Scripture: Finding Our Place in the Biblical Story* (Grand Rapids: Baker Academic, 2004).

36. See V. Philips Long, "Reading the Old Testament as Literature," in *Interpreting the Old Testament: A Guide for Exegesis*, ed. C. C. Broyles (Grand Rapids: Baker Academic, 2001), pp. 105-9; Iain Provan, V. Philips Long, and Tremper Longman III, *A Biblical History of Israel* (Louisville: Westminster John Knox, 2003), pp. 91-92.

37. The book of Esther is perhaps the most extreme example of this phenomenon.

38. For the distinction between the overt and covert narrator see Shimeon Bar-Efrat, *Narrative Art in the Bible*, Bible and Literature Series (Sheffield: Almond Press, 1989), pp. 23-45.

to show readers his disapproval: "The *only* commentary made on Jacob's getting the firstborn's blessing from his blind father through deception occurs several chapters later in an analogy with a reversal — when he is deceived in the dark and given Leah instead of Rachel, then chided that it is not the law of the land to marry the younger sister before the firstborn."[39] Other such examples of narrative subtlety could be multiplied exponentially.

Finally, Long notes that Old Testament narratives are *succinct:* biblical narrators "accomplish the greatest degree of definition and color with the fewest brushstrokes."[40]

These three characteristics of Hebrew narrative often result in the presence of ambiguity, making it difficult to answer some fundamental questions about the nature and purpose of the narrative or the causal relationship of events. As Sternberg puts it, "From the viewpoint of what is directly given in the language, the literary work consists of bits and fragments to be linked and pieced together in the process of reading: it establishes a system of gaps that must be filled in."[41] Reading Old Testament narratives, therefore, is a dynamic process of active interaction with what is (and is not) given in the text. On the other hand, although Hebrew narrative is typically scenic, subtle and succinct, it is not always so. Deviations from this characteristic way of narration require close attention. For example, why does the account of the Danite conquest of Laish repeatedly describe Laish as quiet and unsuspecting (Judg. 18:7, 10, 27)? What is the purpose of the lengthy and detailed instructions for the building of the tabernacle and its furnishings (Exod. 26–31) and then the account of the actual construction of the tabernacle and its furnishings (Exod. 35–40)?

I want now to consider four major elements of Hebrew narrative, namely, plot, narrator, character, and style. Although it is helpful to treat these distinctives of Old Testament narrative separately, it is important to bear in mind that they are intricately interconnected, and to separate them is somewhat artificial.

Plot

In narrative literature, plot is what gives an otherwise random chronicle of events its essential narrative quality. Yairah Amit defines plot as "a selection

---

39. Robert Alter, *The Art of Biblical Narrative* (New York: Basic, 1981), p. 180.
40. Provan, Long, and Longman, *A Biblical History of Israel,* p. 92.
41. Sternberg, *Poetics of Biblical Narrative,* p. 186.

and organization of events in a particular order of time."[42] Most basically, narratives have a beginning, middle, and end, and a basic plot line unfolds along the lines of (1) exposition, (2) complication, (3) change, (4) unraveling, and (5) ending. So, for instance, the story in the book of Esther begins with the events surrounding Queen Vashti's descent from the king's grace and Esther's ascent to the king's harem. The reader is also informed about how Esther's uncle Mordecai had uncovered a conspiracy to assassinate the king. All this constitutes the exposition. Chapter 3 introduces the complication or conflict, namely, Haman's hatred of the Jewish people and his successful plot to pass a law to completely annihilate the Jews in Xerxes' kingdom. As the plot unfolds and Mordecai and Esther attempt to circumvent Haman's plans, other events unfold that heighten the tension (e.g., Esther's anxiety over intervention and her tactic of stalling, the increased tension between Haman and Mordecai, etc.). The story comes to a climax at Esther's second feast with the king and Haman. There Esther exposes Haman's destructive hatred for her people, and the king orders Haman hanged on his own gallows and determines to do what he can to help the Jews. Chapter 9 contains the unraveling stage of the plot, in which the events of the preservation of the Jews unfold. The concluding chapters are a kind of epilogue, showing the contemporary significance of the events of the book for subsequent generations of Jews. On the surface, the book of Esther seems in some ways out of place in the biblical canon. Yet some attention to the book's plot reveals that the structure of the book undergirds its theme, namely, the salvation of God's people in the face of imminent and certain disaster.

Not all narratives of the Old Testament have the kind of clear linear plotline evident in Esther. The book of Judges, for example, is made up of a number of individual narratives. Each of these can be analyzed according to plot development; however, taken as a whole the book presents a cyclical rather than a linear pattern: (1) Israel rebels; (2) the Lord's anger is aroused and he uses foreign domination as a scourge; (3) the Israelites cry to the Lord; (4) the Lord raises up a deliverer; (5) the land remains in peace as long as the deliverer lives; and (6) the cycle begins again with Israel's rebellion. On top of this cyclical pattern the book follows a degenerative trajectory, so that the circularity of the plot might better be characterized as a downward spiral. This progressively degenerative plot of the book manifests itself, among other ways, in characterization (from the sure leadership of Othniel

42. Yairah Amit, *Reading Biblical Narratives: Literary Criticism and the Hebrew Bible*, trans. Y. Lotan (Minneapolis: Fortress, 2001), p. 47.

to the morally dubious escapades of Samson), in the actions of the Israelites (from their military solidarity in the Ehud account to the increasing reluctance on the part of some of the tribes to join the battle and finally to the people's desire to deliver up Samson to the Philistines), and in variations on the six elements of the cycle (so, for example, the Lord raises up Samson in spite of the fact that Israel *fails* to cry out for deliverance, Samson only *begins* to deliver Israel, and the land *does not* experience rest). The ending of Judges (chs. 17–21) represents the ultimate spiritual and moral decline of a nation that has cast off the rule of Yahweh in order to pursue their own (destructive) self-interest. Thus the fact that the book of Judges lacks resolution is itself significant for an understanding of Judges.

Attention to the plot helps to focus the theme and purpose of a narrative. As these brief sketches of Esther and Judges suggest, the plots of individual books as well as plots of single narratives or narrative cycles are designed to help readers see not randomness in the events of history, but rather God's sovereign ordering of events for his redemptive purposes. What is more, a trinitarian hermeneutic acknowledges that the Old Testament is part of a dramatic plot whose arc is often articulated as creation — fall — redemption — consummation. Old Testament plot renders to us the character of the God who addresses us: not distant or detached, but immersed in the life of Israel and also in our lives.

Narrator

The narrator is the figure in whose voice and from whose perspective a story is told. In the Western tradition narrative perspective tends to be either first-person or third-person; in the Old Testament only the book of Nehemiah is told from a first-person perspective.[43] The rest, we might reasonably assume, are third-person accounts, but recently philosopher Eleonore Stump has demonstrated the importance of what she calls "second-person accounts" in biblical narrative. She argues that acknowledging the significance of second-person perspectives is essential for making sense of the book of Job, for example:

> There is an intricate set of nested second-person accounts in the book of Job. The description of God's personal relations with the non-human parts of his creation is contained within an account of God's conversation with

---

43. Ecclesiastes appears to be a first-person narrative since Qohelet's voice dominates the book, but in fact the voice of the third-person narrator emerges in 1:1 and 2; 7:27; 12:8-14.

Job, which is part of the dialogues commenting on God's relations with Job, which relations are themselves the subject of the story of God's relations with Job, which is in turn part of the framing story about God's exchanges with Satan. All of this taken together constitutes the book of Job.[44]

Stump's reading of Job is intriguing and creative, and alerts us to an important dimension of Old Testament narrative. Certainly a hermeneutic that aims to hear God's address in the Old Testament will give serious attention to places in the Old Testament where God actually does address his people directly. Several features of Old Testament narration are important for appropriating Old Testament narrative as God's address.

While scholars of literature often have to draw distinctions between omniscient and limited narrative perspectives, in biblical narratives the narrator is always omniscient.[45] The narrator reports details of times and places where no human has been, like the creation of the world (Gen. 1) or the encounters between the accuser and God in the heavenly council (Job 1:6-12; 2:1-6). The narrator is privy to information that happens behind closed doors, as in the case of Ehud's assassination of Eglon in his private chambers after the latter dismisses his attendants (Judg. 3:12-25), or Amnon's rape of his sister Tamar when the two are alone in his chambers (2 Sam. 13:8-19). The narrator's omniscience is perhaps never as obvious as when the narrator reports the inner thoughts and intentions of Old Testament characters, and even those of God (Gen. 6:6, 8; Exod. 2:25; 2 Sam. 17:14).

Sternberg sees an association in literature between models of narration and models of reality, and so for him the omniscience of the narrator in Hebrew narrative reflects the reality of an omniscient God.[46] Thus the narrator is afforded the status of authority equaled to God. An implication of the prophetic/divine character of the biblical narrators is that they are reliable, and though they may choose to withhold information, they never deceive. The reliability of the biblical narrator has been articulated in different ways by many different commentators. Amit notes that "Doubting the narrator of the Pentateuch . . . means doubting the Pentateuch's authority and its laws, which is tantamount to breaking the contract."[47] Thus, while we may (in-

44. Eleonore Stump, *Wandering in Darkness: Narrative and the Problem of Suffering* (Oxford: Clarendon, 2010), p. 183 (see especially chapter 9).

45. Sternberg, *Poetics of Biblical Narrative*, pp. 84-128. See the critique of Sternberg's view in Wolterstorff, *Divine Discourse*, pp. 245-52.

46. Sternberg, *Poetics of Biblical Narrative*, pp. 84-128.

47. Amit, *Reading Biblical Narratives*, p. 95.

deed, we must!) question the motivation and reliability of any character's speech, we should hear the voice of the narrator as authoritative.

However, a key characteristic of Hebrew narration is its overall lack of evaluative statements. Most typically, the narrator allows scenes to unfold with a minimum of description and evaluation.[48] We can distinguish between the narrator "showing" rather than "telling," though a given narrative will typically represent a combination of both. So, for example, the account of Othniel in Judges 3:7-11 is an example of strict telling, while the story of Abraham's acquisition of the Cave of Machpelah in Genesis 23 is almost entirely a dramatic showing.[49] In the bulk of the book of Job, the narrator allows the speech of Job and his friends to dominate and intervenes only to introduce a new speaker; by contrast, in the succession accounts in the books of Kings, the narrator plays a much more dominant role.

In all cases, we do well to attend not only to *what* is being narrated but also *how* the narrative is told. Through the point of view of the narrator we see the world of the Old Testament through divine eyes, and in the narrator's voice we hear the voice of God.

Characters and Characterization

In comparison to modern literature, descriptive characterization in Hebrew narratives is extremely rare. This absence has caused some to regard Hebrew narrative as primitive and unsophisticated; more recently, however, literary critics have come to appreciate characterization in the Old Testament as anything but shallow and transparent. Alter asks, "How does the Bible manage to evoke such a sense of depth and complexity in its representation of characters with what would seem to be such sparse, even rudimentary means?"[50] Description is indeed sparse, and when present it is almost always in order to relay information that is crucial to the plot: Esau's hairiness, Goliath's stature, Bathsheba's beauty, Job's righteousness, and so on.

Berlin distinguishes between three types of characters in Hebrew narrative: the full-fledged, the type, and the agent,[51] examples of which can be seen in the women in David's life. Full-fledged characters are realistically represented, and readers can discern their motivations explicitly or implic-

48. For a valuable discussion of point of view see Berlin, *Poetics*, pp. 43-82.

49. Amit, *Reading Biblical Narratives*, pp. 50-51.

50. Alter, *Art of Biblical Narrative*, p. 114.

51. Berlin, *Poetics*, p. 23. The first and second correspond to the more common distinction in literary criticism between "round" and "flat" characters respectively.

itly. We can know them intimately, and even though they may be antagonistic characters we can to some extent identify with them. Full-fledged characters are multi-dimensional, and we receive more information about them than is necessary for the plot.[52] So Michal emerges in the books of Samuel as a full-fledged character, as does Bathsheba in the narrative of Solomon's succession in the first chapters of 1 Kings. Abigail, by contrast, is a character type. The narrator describes her in some detail, but she lacks the depth of a full-fledged character. According to Berlin, the characterization of Abigail brings depth to the biography of David, and serves the purpose of endorsing David's destiny as God's chosen king. Finally, Bathsheba in 1 Samuel 11–12 and Abishag in 1 Kings 1–2 function as mere agents, important insofar as they have an effect on plot or other characters. Berlin traces a connection between characterization and plot, noting that David's attitude toward these women corresponds to his public/political characterization. The cold, calculating rise to power corresponds to the cool attitude of David toward Michal and his use of her for political leverage. His self-assurance and popularity correspond to his eager but charming response to Abigail. His hunger for imperial expansion relates to his lust for Bathsheba and his grasping what is not his. Finally, his loss of control of the monarchy corresponds to his impotence in the embrace of the virgin Abishag.[53]

The art of reticence in characterization means that how we ought to regard and judge characters is not always immediately apparent. Alter has helpfully catalogued the various means by which the biblical narrators convey information about the motives, attitudes, and moral nature of characters, and has mapped them on a scale from inference to explicitness and certainty.[54] At the low end of the scale is characterization through an individual's actions or appearance. One can speculate only so far about Job's character through his practice of sacrifice alone (Job 1:5), or about Saul by the fact that he stood a head taller than all the other Israelites (1 Sam. 9:2), or about Ehud by his left-handedness (Judg. 3:15). In the middle are characterization indirectly through the comments of another character and characterization through the individual's own voiced or inward speech. Amit notes that in the characterization of Nabal, we must balance comments made by Nabal himself, those made by David, and those made by Nabal's servants in order to make sense of Nabal's initial affront. The reported speech of Nabal's servants, confirming the truth

---

52. Berlin, *Poetics*, p. 32.
53. Berlin, *Poetics*, p. 33.
54. Alter, *Art of Biblical Narrative*, pp. 116-17.

of David's claim, validates that Nabal is indeed acting as a scoundrel.[55] Returning to an earlier example, we gain deeper insight into the psyche of Job by the motivation for his sacrifices reported as interior speech: "Perhaps my children have sinned and cursed God in their hearts" (Job 1:5). At the top of the scale are comments made explicitly about the characters by the narrator, such as the narrator's comment that Job was upright and blameless, a God-fearer and an evil-shunner (Job 1:1), or that Nabal was harsh and his deeds were evil (1 Sam. 25:3).[56]

These are just some of the ways in which the biblical narrators portray their characters, and often several techniques combine to reflect the complexity of character. A danger, of course, is that readers who are very familiar with the narratives of the Old Testament may preempt the reading process, so that the villains and heroes are already predetermined. However, as Alter maintains, the complexity of human nature is brilliantly reflected in Hebrew narratives:

> [E]very person is . . . made in God's likeness as a matter of cosmogonic principle but almost never as a matter of ethical fact; and each individual instance of this bundle of paradoxes, encompassing the zenith and the nadir of the created world, requires a special cunning attentiveness in literary representation. The purposeful selectivity of means, the repeatedly contrastive or comparative technical strategies used in the rendering of biblical characters, are in a sense dictated by the biblical view of man.[57]

In the Old Testament we rarely encounter unequivocally good or unequivocally bad people. Rather, we encounter many-layered individuals — wretched and lovable, rebellious yet chosen, pitiless and pitiable, wounded but healing — just like the individuals we come across daily and whom we see in the mirror. And on every page we encounter the triune God, the One Character who is most complex of all but whose redemptive purposes for the world are apparent.

Style

Style refers to such characteristics of literature as repetition, gapping, irony, intertextuality, and so on. Among these, repetition is a particularly signifi-

---

55. Amit, *Reading Biblical Narratives*, p. 76.
56. At the top of the scale I would add explicit statements made by God.
57. Alter, *Art of Biblical Narrative*, p. 115.

cant feature of Old Testament literature. While this may initially seem at odds with the succinctness that characterizes Old Testament narratives, in fact it becomes an extremely powerful literary device. In the books of the Old Testament we find repetition of any number of elements: themes, scenes, sequences, motifs, and individual words. A *Leitwort* is a recurring word, word-root, or pattern of words whose significance Alter describes thus: "Through abundant repetition, the semantic range of the root-word is explored, different forms of the root are deployed, branching off at times into phonetic relatives (that is, word-play), synonymity, and antonymity; by virtue of its verbal status, the *Leitwort* refers immediately to meaning and thus to theme as well."[58]

As significant as this is to the Old Testament writers, the modern tendency to avoid verbatim repetition has the unfortunate result that often for the sake of fluency English translations will render the same Hebrew word with different English words.[59] Yet even in translation the repetition of key words can emerge.[60] For instance, in 2 Samuel 7, David's palace, the (future) temple, and the Davidic dynasty are all represented by the *Leitwort* בית ("house"), which appears fifteen times in the chapter. The function of the *Leitwort* is to emphasize the fact that although David had completed building his "house" (i.e., the palace) and now desires to build a "house" (i.e., a temple) for God, in actual fact God, who cannot be contained in a material house, would build and establish an everlasting "house" (i.e., a dynasty) for David. Other examples of this kind of word repetition abound.[61]

A motif is a "concrete image, sensory quality, action, or object [that] recurs though a particular narrative."[62] Some key examples of the use of motif in Old Testament narratives are fire in the Samson narrative; stones and the

---

58. Alter, *Art of Biblical Narrative*, p. 95.

59. Alter, *Art of Biblical Narrative*, p. 93.

60. Alternatively, Alter has translated large portions of Hebrew narrative and poetry, translations that are highly recommended. He has tried to provide a translation that reflects the style of Hebrew literature, including, among other things, the techniques of repetition. See Robert Alter, *Genesis: Translation and Commentary* (New York: Norton, 1997); *The Five Books of Moses: Translation and Commentary* (New York: Norton, 2008); *The David Story: A Translation with Commentary of 1 and 2 Samuel* (New York: Norton, 2000); *The Book of Psalms: A Translation with Commentary* (New York: Norton, 2007); R. Alter, *The Wisdom Books: Job, Proverbs and Ecclesiastes; A Translation with Commentary* (New York: Norton, 2010).

61. See, for example, Bar-Efrat, *Narrative Art in the Bible*, pp. 211-15; Alter, *Art of Biblical Narrative*, pp. 92-95.

62. Alter, *Art of Biblical Narrative*, p. 95.

colors white and red in the Jacob cycle; and dreams, prisons, and silver in the Joseph story.[63]

Sometimes the technique of repeating a sequence of action will appear, frequently with a threefold or a three-plus-one repetition that ends with a climax or reversal.[64] Job's four servants announcing in similar fashion the destruction of his possessions and children (Job 1:13-19), Esther's strategy of inviting the king and Haman to her banquets (Esth. 5:1-8), and Samuel's confusion of God's and Eli's voices (1 Sam 3:4-10) are all examples of a recurring sequence of action.

A type-scene is a recurring episode consisting of a set sequence of motifs, frequently related to a recurring theme. Alter has done groundbreaking work on the nature and use of type-scenes.[65] The most common type-scenes in the Old Testament are the birth announcement of a hero, betrothal at a well, and trials in the wilderness.[66]

On a much broader level, themes transcend individual narratives. According to Alter, a theme is an "idea that is part of the value-system of the narrative — it may be moral, psychological, legal, political, historiographical, theological — [and] is made evident in some recurring pattern. . . . (For example, the reversal of primogeniture in Genesis; obedience versus rebellion in the Wilderness stories; knowledge in the Joseph story; exile and promised land; the rejection and election of the monarch in Samuel and Kings.)"[67] Clines has argued that the theme of the Pentateuch is the partial fulfillment of the patriarchal promises.[68]

Alter identifies another type of repetition that is important for understanding the art of biblical narrative. This type of repetition occurs when entire statements are quoted by distinct characters, by the narrator, or by both the narrator and one of the characters. In these cases, and indeed with all uses of repetition, seemingly small changes in the repetition are almost always extremely significant. The classic example is Eve's additional fencing ("and you must not touch it, or you will die") of God's original command not to eat of the tree of the knowledge of good and evil. Likewise, the subtle differences between what Nathan instructs Bathsheba to say in 1 Kings 1:13

---

63. Alter, *Art of Biblical Narrative*, p. 95.

64. Alter, *Art of Biblical Narrative*, p. 95.

65. Alter, *Art of Biblical Narrative*, pp. 47-62.

66. Alter, *Art of Biblical Narrative*, p. 96.

67. Alter, *Art of Biblical Narrative*, p. 120.

68. David J. A. Clines, *The Theme of the Pentateuch*, 2nd ed., JSOTSup 10 (Sheffield: Sheffield Academic Press, 2007).

and what she actually says in 1:17-21 suggest that Bathsheba expands and embellishes Nathan's version for persuasive purposes.

Clearly, then, repetition — whether of a *Leitwort* in an individual narrative or of themes and motifs across whole books — is a significant and powerful tool for the Old Testament writers.[69] Wherever we encounter it, we need to bear in mind a number of questions:

What kind of repetition appears (*Leitwort*, motif, etc.)? What is being emphasized or brought into focus by the use of repetition? Are there deviations from the expected pattern and, if so, to what purpose?

Hearing God's address in Old Testament literature requires listening attentively to what is being emphasized or drawn out through the use of repetition. In addition, a trinitarian hermeneutic alerts us to themes that span the overarching story of Scripture. Being aware of these themes helps us to hear God's voice in the various parts of the Old Testament as harmonious and of one purpose, rather than as discordant.

Poetry

Recent years have seen a good deal of helpful work being produced on biblical poetry, and yet it seems rare to find scholars going beyond the aesthetics, technique, or analysis of Old Testament poetry to ask the more fundamental questions about its significance. A notable exception is Patrick Miller, who has encouraged us to ask the more basic questions: "What does poetry mean *theologically,* or what does it mean theologically that we have poetry in the Bible? What does poetry do or not do as part of the Bible's claim to speak about God?"[70] To these questions I would add: What does biblical poetry do or not do as part of the Bible's nature as "God-speaking" literature?[71]

Like other forms of literary art, poetry projects a world, one that we ex-

---

69. For more on intertextuality and biblical theology see Chapter 6 by Mark Boda in the present volume.

70. Patrick D. Miller, "The Theological Significance of Poetry," in *Israelite Religion and Biblical Theology: Collected Essays,* ed. Patrick D. Miller, JSOTSup 237 (Sheffield: Sheffield Academic Press, 2000), p. 234; emphasis in original. At the 2010 annual meeting of the Society of Biblical Literature in Atlanta, the Theology of the Hebrew Scriptures group and the Biblical Hebrew Poetry group held a joint session in which they considered together the theological significance of biblical poetry under the theme "Poetics as a Vehicle for Theology: The Medium, the Message," using Miller's essay as a jumping-off point.

71. The Bible as "God-speaking literature" derives from Calvin Seerveld, *Rainbows for a Fallen World* (Toronto: Tuppence Press, 1980).

perience, which we can evaluate and, ultimately, to which we are invited to re-orient our lives.[72] Poetry speaks to us in pictures that often capture the world in ways more poignant than other forms of writing can. As Miller puts it,

> One can talk much about human pain but hardly hear it as sharply as in the voices of those who cry out in the Psalms. Chapter 2 of the Westminster Confessions of Faith is very good on the attributes of God. I use it with some regularity in my teaching of the Old Testament. But I am confident that neither my mother nor Karl Barth — to take two quite different theologians — turned to that chapter as often as they did to Psalm 103 to hear and think about the God who made them.[73]

Poetry provokes us to see the world through the poets' eyes, and through biblical poetry the Divine Poet proffers us glimpses of the world from his perspective — not only the depths of the world's brokenness but also the glorious wonder of what it was meant to be and what it has the potential to be. Poetry does not merely aim at the level of the intellect but rather provokes our emotions, passions, and imaginations. The biblical poets invite us to perceive a strange and wonderful world in which infants, animals, and inanimate objects are vouchsafed voices, singing the praises of the Creator, a world in which the most terrifying creatures are docile pets before the Almighty — but also a world in which the Deliverer not only speaks but also listens to those in the most destitute of human predicaments.

Poetry is what we might call heightened speech.[74] It is far more compressed than prose, and the basic unit of poetry is a simple image or figure of speech. Hebrew poetry abounds not only in the poetical books like Psalms, Proverbs, Job, and Song of Songs, but prevails in the prophetic books and appears in various places in the narrative sections of the Old Testament.[75]

---

72. See the excellent chapter "A Plea for Poems" in Craig G. Bartholomew and Ryan P. O'Dowd, *Old Testament Wisdom Literature: A Theological Introduction* (Downers Grove: IVP Academic, 2011). The authors survey the history of poetry, explore the nature and function of poetry in general and then focus on the nature and function of Old Testament poetry in particular (especially Old Testament wisdom).

73. Patrick D. Miller, "Poetry and Theology," in *Theology Today: Reflections on the Bible and Contemporary Life*, ed. Patrick D. Miller (Louisville: Westminster John Knox, 2006), p. 10.

74. Alter, *Art of Biblical Narrative*, p. 4; Miller, "The Theological Significance of Poetry," p. 249; Leland Ryken, *Words of Delight: A Literary Introduction to the Bible* (Grand Rapids: Baker, 1992), p. 159.

75. For example, the Song of the Sea (of Moses, Exod. 15:1-18), the Song of Hannah (1 Sam. 2:1-10), the Psalm of Jonah (Jon. 2:2-9), and the Song of Hezekiah (Isa. 38:10-20).

Furthermore, various poetic genres appear in the Old Testament, including but not limited to hymns of praise, lament psalms, wisdom sayings, and so on, and each of these genres has unique characteristics. There are several distinct characteristics of Hebrew poetry, some of which are not immediately present to those reading the Old Testament in translation.

Terseness

The first characteristic of Hebrew poetry, a feature it shares with much poetry throughout history, is its terseness.[76] Even in translation the lines of poetry are shorter than those of prose, and in Hebrew this economy of words is even more pronounced. Often absent from poetry are the definite article, the relative particle (אשר), and the direct object marker; and conjunctions, temporal markers, and causal markers appear infrequently.[77] Furthermore, often nouns, verbs, or prepositions appear in the first half of a line (or cola) and are understood but not present in the second line, a feature called ellipsis. So, for example, Job 28:26:

> When he made a decree for the rain,
> A way for the thunderstorm.

Far from unsophisticated, this is a powerful means of heightening the power of language,[78] conveying profound insights with an economy of expression.

Parallelism

The second and most distinctive characteristic of Hebrew poetry is parallelism. Over the history of interpretation our understanding of parallelism in Hebrew poetry has undergone a number of subtle but significant shifts. Some of the earliest commentators were convinced that in Holy Writ God does not repeat himself and they therefore maintained that in Hebrew poetry parallel lines must not be saying the same thing. Of course this conviction prompted some creative exegesis by these early commentators.

Robert Lowth's groundbreaking work on parallelism, *Lectures on the Sacred Poetry of the Hebrews,* was a standard for analyzing Hebrew poetry until

---

76. James L. Kugel, *The Idea of Biblical Poetry: Parallelism and Its History* (New Haven: Yale University Press, 1981), pp. 87-92.

77. Longman, *Literary Approaches to Biblical Interpretation,* p. 122.

78. Kugel, *Idea of Biblical Poetry,* p. 87.

well into the twentieth century.[79] Lowth perceived two main categories of parallelism, the synonymous (in which the second line says the exact same thing as the first line; A = B) and the antithetical (in which the second line says the exact opposite of the first; A ≠ B).

For instances of parallelism that did not fit into these types, Lowth proposed the catchall category of "synthetic parallelism." Yet Ryken is perhaps correct when he says that categorizing types of parallelism in Hebrew poetry can degenerate into mere distraction.[80] More recent work by Kugel, Alter, and Berlin emphasizes that parallelism never involves a static equivalence between lines, but that there is always a dynamic movement from the first line to the second. This progression or intensification is most significant on the semantic level, increasing the impact of a statement.

Figurative Language

"Images are the glory, perhaps the essence of poetry," notes Luis Alonso Schökel, "the enchanted planet of the imagination, a limitless galaxy, ever alive and ever changing."[81] The paradox of poetry is that nonliteral (i.e., metaphorical) language can help us see God, the world, and the human condition as they truly are. Rather than conveying truth through propositions, poetry uses evocative images to stimulate the imagination. What poetic imagery loses in precision it gains in clarity.[82] While Old Testament poetry contains a wide variety of figures of speech — hyperbole, apostrophe, and personification, among others[83] — perhaps it is most powerful in its use of simile and metaphor. Of course, God is not a literal shepherd and his people are not literal sheep, but Psalm 23 conveys profound insight into God's providence and protection and humanity's utter dependence.

Ryken emphasizes that "metaphor and simile are not 'poetic devices'; they are a way of thinking and formulating reality. They are an important way in which the human race expresses meaning."[84] As William P. Brown rightfully notes, poetry is not merely expressive, but aims at instruction; biblical poetry

---

79. Robert Lowth, *Lectures on the Sacred Poetry of the Hebrews* (London: T. Tegg & Sons, 1835 [1753]).

80. Ryken, *Words of Delight*, p. 183.

81. Luis Alonso Schökel, *A Manual of Hebrew Poetics*, Subsidia Biblica 11 (Rome: Pontifical Biblical Institute, 1988), p. 95.

82. Longman, *Literary Approaches to Biblical Interpretation*, pp. 131-32.

83. See Ryken, *Words of Delight*, pp. 177-79.

84. Ryken, *Words of Delight*, p. 169.

is "poetry with a purpose."[85] And yet, in the words of Miller, "The images of poetry speak to startle and puzzle us, to provoke us and cause us to think. They set the imagination free, opening the reader to theological possibilities that might be less acceptable or even unthinkable in the essay mode."[86]

Patterns

Hebrew poetry is most often organized according to patterns. Groundbreaking work on the book of Proverbs suggests that even the individual sayings that make up the bulk of the book have been consciously arranged into fundamentally coherent patterns.[87] The following are some of the more common patterns in Old Testament poetry.[88] An acrostic is a poem in which each line begins with succeeding letters of the alphabet (in this case, the Hebrew alphabet). Acrostics give a sense of orderliness and completeness, and may have originally been used as mnemonic devices. Several acrostics appear in the Old Testament, with notable examples being Psalm 119, Lamentations 1, and Proverbs 31:10-31. A chiasm (or palistrophe) is a structural pattern in which the poet arranges words or themes in inverted order. The basic pattern of a chiasm is *A B B′ A′* but they can also be more elaborate, including a pivot point in the centre of the chiasm. Psalm 124 is an example of chiasm:

A vv. 1-2a: Yahweh's presence
  B vv. 2b-5: Protection from dangers
    C v. 6a: Praise to Yahweh
  B′ vv. 6b-7: Protection from dangers
A′ v. 8: Yahweh's presence

The structure is thus circular, with a clear sense of closure, and the emphasis is often on the element at the center of the chiasm. An inclusio is the repetition at the end of a poem of a word, phrase, or concept that appears at the beginning. The repetition of the phrase "Give thanks to the LORD, for he is good; his love endures forever" in the first and last verse of Psalm 118 is an

---

85. William P. Brown, *Seeing the Psalms: A Theology of Metaphor* (Louisville: Westminster John Knox, 2002), p. 2.

86. Miller, *Theology Today*, p. 11.

87. For example, R. Van Leeuwen, *Context and Meaning in Proverbs 25–27* (Atlanta: Scholars Press, 1984), pp. 16-17.

88. For more details on the following patterns of Hebrew poetry see the very helpful work by Wilfred G. E. Watson, *Classical Hebrew Poetry: A Guide to Its Techniques*, JSOT 26 (Sheffield: JSOT, 1984), pp. 190-221.

example of an inclusio. Often these "bookend" phrases or concepts represent the guiding principle of the poem as a whole. Anadiplosis, or terrace pattern, is a structure in which terminology in one line is repeated in the next. Song of Songs 2:15 offers one instance:

Catch for us foxes,
Small foxes ruining vineyards,
[For] our vineyards are blossoming.

Depending on the context, anadiplosis serves any number of functions — heightening tension, creating a sense of movement, and so on.

The preceding patterns are formal; however, conceptual patterns also appear in Old Testament poetry. Some of the most promising work on the books of Proverbs and Psalms has uncovered conceptual and formal patterns that span the entirety of each of these books. Several scholars have argued persuasively, for example, that the book of Proverbs is not a patchwork of individual sayings thrown together helter-skelter but that the book reveals deliberate design at the compositional level.[89] Proverbs 26:1-12 provide good evidence for this argument. With the exception of verses 4 and 5, all the proverbs are sayings, all begin in their first line with a figurative comment (which is negative) that elaborates on the topic in the second line (also negative), and all of the verses except 2 contain the Hebrew word for "fool." Verses 4 and 5 are not sayings but admonitions, but like the sayings they relate by way of opposition — "do not answer" (26:4), "answer" (26:5).[90] Furthermore, the content of these blatantly contradictory admonitions ties in with a theme of the whole passage: all the sayings in 26:1-12 have to do with what is fitting/appropriate (see 26:1).[91] Examples of this kind of compositional design in Proverbs abound.

---

89. For an easy entry into this way of reading Proverbs see especially Raymond C. Van Leeuwen, "Proverbs," in *A Complete Literary Guide to the Bible*, ed. Leland Ryken and Tremper Longman III (Grand Rapids: Zondervan, 1993), pp. 256-67; and the booklet by Bartholomew, *Reading Proverbs with Integrity*, Grove Biblical Series B22 (Cambridge: Grove Books, 2001). See also Raymond C. Van Leeuwen's accessible commentary "The Book of Proverbs," in *The New Interpreter's Bible*, vol. 5 (Nashville: Abingdon, 1997), pp. 17-264; and Bruce K. Waltke, *The Book of Proverbs*, 2 vols., NICOT (Grand Rapids: Eerdmans, 2004, 2005). For the theoretical foundation for this way of reading Proverbs see Van Leeuwen, *Context and Meaning;* Knut M. Heim, *Like Grapes of Gold Set in Silver: An Interpretation of Proverbial Clusters in Proverbs 10:1–22:16*, BZAW 273 (Berlin: de Gruyter, 2001).

90. Van Leeuwen, *Context and Meaning*, p. 94.

91. Van Leeuwen, *Context and Meaning*, p. 94.

Taking his cue from the headings of the various collections in the book, Raymond Van Leeuwen perceives the following structure:[92]

1. Title, Introduction, and Basic Principle (1:1-7)
2. Parental Instructions on Wisdom and Folly (1:8–9:18)
3. First Solomonic Collection of Sayings (10:1–22:16)
4. "Sayings of the Wise" (Admonitions) (22:17–24:22)
5. Further "Sayings of the Wise" (24:23-34)
6. Second Solomonic Collection of Sayings (25:1–29:27)
7. Sayings of Agur and Numerical Sayings (30:1-33)
8. Sayings of King Lemuel (31:1-9)
9. Heroic Hymn to the Valiant Woman (31:10-31)

These collections each show evidence of design within them and, at least to some extent, in their relation to one another. Chapters 1–9 and chapter 31 provide the structural and conceptual framework. They combine to form

> an "envelope construction" surrounding the shorter sayings, admonitions, and poems of chapters 10–30. Whereas Proverbs 1–9 invited young men to a love affair with cosmic Wisdom, Proverbs in its end presents a woman/wife — active and glorious in her own right — as wisdom, a divine gift (cf. 18:22) without whom life would seem incomplete. Wisdom's standing in relation to humankind as woman to man, and Yahweh's standing over against humankind/Israel as husband/wife, are metaphoric representations of reality whose depths remain unplumbed.[93]

The benefit of such an approach to Proverbs is that it requires that the individual sayings be *heard* within the context of the whole teaching of the book.[94] Two significant implications of this are, first, wisdom in Proverbs is anything but secular (as many believe) but is worked out before the face of Yahweh, the Creator and Redeemer. In such a reading chapters 1–9 become the vital key to understanding the individual sayings that make up the bulk of the book, so that living according to wisdom's way is akin to fearing the Lord and living for him in a good but fallen world. Second, reading Proverbs holistically guards against reading a kind of retribution theology into the book. Van Leeuwen puts it well when he notes, "*In general,* the sages clearly

92. Van Leeuwen, "The Book of Proverbs," pp. 257-58.
93. Van Leeuwen, "The Book of Proverbs," p. 263.
94. See Peter T. H. Hatton, *Contradiction in the Book of Proverbs: The Deep Waters of Council,* Society for Old Testament Study Series (Hampshire: Ashgate, 2008).

believed that wise and righteous behaviour did make life better and richer, though virtue did not *guarantee* those consequences."[95] Thus, the sayings that seem to suggest a mechanical relationship between virtue and blessing must be taken together with statements about the limits of wisdom and about discipline and along with the "better-than" sayings.[96] To come back to the analogy of hearing, when we appropriate the whole teaching of Proverbs, reading the individual parts in the context of the whole, we are much less likely to mute or amplify one aspect of God's instruction over the other.

Similarly, much good work has been done to discern the overall shape of the Psalter and the theological implications of that shape.[97] The book divides into five books, with a doxology marking out the ending of each book.[98] Psalms 1 and 2 combine as the introduction to the Psalter as a whole, and invite attention to divine instruction (i.e., *torah*) and justice and righteousness through the enthronement of God's anointed. Although it would be a stretch to regard the Psalter as a narrative, nevertheless over the course of its 150 chapters it does display narrative movement. Perhaps the best example of this is how the theme of kingship weaves from the enthronement psalm in the introduction (Ps. 2), to the great hope for shalom and justice as a result of the divinely chosen king at the end of Book Two (Ps. 72), the promise and hope for and then rejection of the anointed one of David at the end of Book Three (Ps. 89:1-37 and 89:38-52 respectively), and then the psalms in the 90s that announce with wonder and praise the reign of Yahweh, which many regard as the theological centre of the Psalter. The general tenor of the rest of Book Four and Book Five is one of praise and adoration to the Lord.

Obviously we can read the individual psalms that make up the Psalter separately, but if it is possible to discern design in the compilation of the

95. R. C. Van Leeuwen, "Wealth and Poverty: System and Contradiction in Proverbs," *Hebrew Studies* 33 (1992): 32, cited in Craig G. Bartholomew, *Reading Ecclesiastes: Old Testament Exegesis and Hermeneutical Theory,* Analecta Biblica 139 (Rome: Pontificio Instituto Biblico, 1998), p. 256.

96. For example, 3:9-10 states that if one gives the Lord the first fruits one's barns will be full and one's wine vats will overflow. It is no doubt by design that the following statement has to do with the Lord disciplining the child that he loves.

97. See J. Clinton McCann Jr., "Psalms, Book of," in *Dictionary for Theological Interpretation of the Bible,* ed. Kevin J. Vanhoozer et al. (Grand Rapids: Baker Academic, 2005), pp. 645-52; *A Theological Introduction to the Book of Psalms: The Psalms as Torah* (Nashville: Abingdon, 1993); "The Book of Psalms," in *The New Interpreter's Bible,* vol. 4 (Nashville: Abingdon, 1996), pp. 639-1280.

98. Book One (Pss. 1–41); Book Two (42–72); Book Three (73–89); Book Four (90–106); and Book Five (107–150).

Psalter then this should affect the way we interpret (and hear) the psalms. In this vein, Gordon Wenham advocates four guidelines for this kind of literary (or canonical) reading of the Psalms.[99] He urges readers to (1) pay attention to the connection between one psalm and its neighbors, (2) be attentive to the position of a psalm within its redactional unit, (3) regard the titles of the psalms as an interpretative horizon, and (4) take into consideration the connections and repetitions of psalms within the collection.

Approaching Old Testament Poetry

Of course, hearing God's address in Old Testament poetry (or narrative for that matter) is never a matter of getting the technique right. S. E. Gillingham rightly notes that analytical study can reduce poetry to a mere object; instead, she calls for an approach in which "the poem becomes the subject, so that as we allow ourselves to be addressed, the poetry is the active element and we are the recipients."[100] Old Testament poetry evokes the whole range of human experience and meaning. Brown captures something of this vast sweep when he notes,

> The public and private spheres, corporate worship and inner devotion, find their nexus in the Psalms. From anger to adulation, the various psalms cover the gamut of human emotion and response to God's presence in the world, or lack thereof. All that is humanly experienced is related to God. . . . The Psalms at once caress and assault the soul. They orient, disorient, and reorient; they scale the heights of praise as well as plumb the depths of despair. The anguished cry, "My God, my God, why have you forsaken me?" (22:1a) is matched by the joyful summons, "Make a joyful noise to God, all the earth!" (66:1). The poetry oscillates between anguish and joy, righteous protest and personal confession. Rife with the pathos of praise and the ethos of agony, the book of Psalms captures better than any other corpus of Scripture the "bi-polar" life of faith.[101]

Brown is referring specifically to the book of Psalms, but if we include the poetry found elsewhere in the Bible (for example, Job, Proverbs, Ecclesiastes, Song of Songs, the prophets) we would be hard-pressed to find a single hu-

99. Gordon J. Wenham, "Toward a Canonical Reading of the Psalms," in *Canon and Biblical Interpretation,* ed. Craig G. Bartholomew et al., SAHS 7 (Grand Rapids: Zondervan, 2006), p. 344, leveraging Erich Zenger's work on the Psalter.

100. S. E. Gillingham, *The Poems and Psalms of the Hebrew Bible,* Oxford Bible Series (Oxford: Oxford University Press, 1994), p. 4; cited in Brown, *Seeing the Psalms,* p. 9.

101. Brown, *Seeing the Psalms,* p. 2.

man experience or a dimension of public or private life that biblical poets did not touch upon. Listening to God's address in Old Testament poetry involves heeding his summons to reimage radically our notions of suffering, human labor, political power, sexuality, consumption, justice, family life, agriculture, economics, beauty, and so on.

Conclusion

A trinitarian hermeneutics for hearing the Old Testament affirms that the Creator of the cosmos and Redeemer of Israel came to us in human form and dwelt among us. This God communicated to his people via the many forms of ancient Hebrew literature we find in the Old Testament. By giving attention to the literary dimension of the Old Testament we affirm that *our* Creator and *our* Redeemer speaks *to us* through these literary forms.

To be sure, the kind of trinitarian hermeneutics that this volume is advocating acknowledges that the literary is only one of several dimensions of Old Testament interpretation, and thus this chapter should be read in harmony with the other chapters in this section of the volume. The Old Testament is not mere literature after all. The reduction of the Bible to mere literature was George Steiner's major critique of Alter and Frank Kermode's *Literary Guide to the Bible:*

> Does this "Literary Guide" help us to come to sensible grips with the singularity and the overwhelming provocations of the Bible — singularity and a summons altogether independent of the reach of current literary-critical fashions? Does it help us to understand in what ways the Bible and the demands of answerability it puts upon us are like no others?[102]

And yet, to by-pass the literary aspect of these texts would be to the detriment of hearing the Old Testament. Attention to the literary dimension is a vital component of hearing the kerygma of the Old Testament: to experience its overwhelming provocations and to heed its summons — in other words, to *hear God's address* in the Old Testament.

102. George Steiner, "The Good Books," *The New Yorker* (January 11, 1988): 95. Steiner continues: "I can — just — come to imagine for myself that a man of more or less my own biological and social composition could have written *Hamlet* or *Lear* and gone home to lunch and found a normal answer to the question 'How did it go today?' I cannot conceive the author of the Speech Out of the Whirlwind in Job writing or dictating that text and dwelling within common existence."

5 History and Old Testament Interpretation

Tremper Longman III

Even a superficial reading of the Old Testament shows the importance of coming to grips with its relationship to history in order to hear God's word in it. Much of the Old Testament purports to narrate past events. Genesis through Ezra-Nehemiah and Esther present narrative accounts of a time period that stretches from creation to the late postexilic period.[1] The prophetic books often begin with superscriptions that associate oracles with specific moments in Israel's history. Even the poetic and wisdom books relate their contents to particular kings (most often David and Solomon).[2] The focus of this chapter, though, will be on the first group, the narrative texts.

The biblical concern with history is further affirmed by the frequent call that God's people "remember" *(zākar)* God's acts in the past. Such remembrance is not simply for antiquarian reasons, but to engender confidence during a difficult present and hope for an uncertain future. In Deuteronomy,

---

1. Of course, the extent to which these books accurately reflect past events is contested, as will become clear in our later discussion of different schools of thought within the guild of Old Testament studies (see below on minimalist, maximalist, and centrist perspectives). There is, however, no question that these books narrate past events; the debate is over whether these events actually happened or are invented. As Baruch Halpern says, "Whether a text is history, then, depends on what its author meant to do" (*The First Historians: The Hebrew Bible and History* [San Francisco: Harper and Row, 1988], p. 8).

2. Though of course it remains a debated question whether there is an actual historical connection between, say, Ecclesiastes and Solomon; see Tremper Longman III, *Ecclesiastes*, NICOT (Grand Rapids: Eerdmans, 1998), pp. 2-9, and Craig G. Bartholomew, *Ecclesiastes*, BCOTWP (Grand Rapids: Baker Academic, 2009), pp. 43-54.

Moses encourages Israel to "remember what the LORD your God did to Pharaoh and to all Egypt" (Deut. 7:18) on the eve of their conflict with "nations more numerous" (7:17) than they were. In Psalm 77, the petitioner turns from anguish to joy as he remembers the time God brought his people through the Sea. On at least one occasion, the biblical text more generally calls on Israel to "remember the days of old" (Deut. 32:7).

The biblical texts themselves raise the question of historical reference in two senses. In the first place, what is the relationship between the Old Testament and past events? Do some or all of the Old Testament books make ostensive reference to past events? What is the importance of the historical veracity of biblical texts to the message of the Old Testament? In the second place, what is the history of composition of the various books of the Old Testament? Do they have a history of composition? How important is it to know the process that brought these books to their present form in the canonical text?

Of course, these two issues are closely connected and cannot be treated separately. Indeed, the historical critical methods (source, form, redaction, tradition-historical, etc.) that explore the history of composition of a biblical book affect scholars' understanding of that book's presentation of history. For example, the Old Testament associates the law with Moses, a figure who precedes prophets like Isaiah, Jeremiah, and Ezekiel. Traditional source criticism challenges that idea by arguing that much of the law (P) is post-exilic, thus placing the prophets before the law (more on this below).

These questions raise the further question of the appropriate presuppositions and methods to adopt and utilize in the study of the Old Testament. As we will see, the history of the field in the past two centuries has been preoccupied with the question of history.[3] The past thirty years have seen dramatic shifts in the attention that biblical scholars have given to these issues. Indeed, at the present moment, the question of history and the Old Testament divides scholars more than any other issue.

This chapter intends to delineate the field of study and describe the various perspectives. Even so, it will advocate for a certain approach to these questions that are in keeping with the perspective that the Old Testament is the Word of God.

---

3. Craig G. Bartholomew, "Introduction," in *"Behind" the Text: History and Biblical Interpretation,* ed. Craig G. Bartholomew et al., SAHS 4 (Grand Rapids: Zondervan, 2003), p. 3, citing Anthony Thiselton, "New Testament Interpretation in Historical Perspective," in *Hearing the New Testament: Strategies for Interpretation,* ed. Joel B. Green (Grand Rapids: Eerdmans, 1995), p. 10.

Is History Important?

"If Jericho was not razed, is our faith in vain?" With this clever play on Paul's statement about the resurrection of Christ in 1 Corinthians 15:14 ("If Christ has not been raised, then our proclamation has been in vain and your faith has been in vain"), George W. Ramsey poses a crucial question concerning the significance of history in the Old Testament.[4] Ramsey answers his question negatively. The destruction of Jericho obviously does not have the same redemptive significance as the death and resurrection of Christ. Thus, if the events narrated in Joshua 6 did not happen, then there is no harm to the faith, and he points out that this is a good thing, too, since the evidence for Joshua's taking and burning of the city is flimsy at best.

Ramsey uses Jericho to make a general point about Old Testament history. He could have just as easily (though not as cleverly) posed this question about the patriarchs, the Exodus, wilderness wanderings, the period of the monarchy, the Exile, and the post-exilic period. None of these events are on a redemptive par with the resurrection of Christ; thus if they did not take place, then, according to Ramsey and many others, no harm is done to the theological significance of the Old Testament.

Ramsey's viewpoint has been bolstered in subsequent decades by a renewed appreciation of the power of story (fiction). Story does not have to be historical in order to be true. Indeed, the Yale theologian Hans Frei has described the "eclipse of biblical narrative" and expresses appreciation for the history-like character of biblical stories.[5] Nothing like the Exodus may have happened, such a view suggests, but the account of the Exodus and the crossing of the Red Sea may still teach its readers that Yahweh is a God who saves his people when they are in distress.

But can it? One cannot doubt that fictional stories are able to teach important lessons to readers. New Testament parables provide examples that most readers happily concur are fictions that serve important theological and didactic purposes. There is, however, a difference between a parable and the account of the Exodus. The latter presents a verbal description of God's intrusion into space and time in order to rescue his enslaved people. The message of the Exodus is that God saves even when human resources run out.

But what if it did not happen? The theological message would have no foundation. In other words, the Exodus account establishes a track record

---

4. See George W. Ramsey, *The Quest for the Historical Israel* (London: SCM, 1984).

5. Hans Frei, *The Eclipse of Biblical Narrative* (New Haven: Yale University Press, 1974).

for God. The Israelites gain confidence for the present and hope for the future in the midst of their own struggles because God has done it before. He has rescued his people when it seemed impossible (see Psalm 77).

To question the importance of the historical nature of the Old Testament is to challenge the fundamental nature of Old (and New) Testament religion and thus Judaism and Christianity. These are historical religions. Their claim is that God has not withdrawn from human history but is integrally involved in it for its redemption.

But why hesitate to affirm the history presented in the Old Testament? The following section discusses some of the leading challenges to the historicity of the Old Testament. Each challenge will be followed by a response from a perspective that affirms the value of the historical presentation of the biblical text.

Challenges to the Historicity of the Old Testament

Historical Criticism

The Challenge

Questions concerning the Old Testament's presentation of history and traditional ascriptions of the authorship of the various books did not arise until the second part of the seventeenth century. While the philosopher Baruch Spinoza (1632-1677) raised provocative questions about Mosaic authorship of the Pentateuch,[6] Jean Astruc (1684-1766) was the first to propose sources as a solution to what was perceived as problems (double stories, double namings, tensions) in the Pentateuch. While he did so in an attempt to defend Mosaic authorship, others (notably W. G. Eichhorn, professor at Göttingen from 1788 to 1827) not only continued the search for sources, but divorced the sources from any connection to Moses. Even so, his work did not lead to a radical rewriting of the history of Israel. This task was accomplished by W. M. L. de Wette (1780-1849), beginning with his *Contributions to Old Testament Introduction*.[7] In this work, de Wette argued that the post-

---

6. Levenson calls Spinoza "a great pioneer of the historical criticism of the Christian Bible"; see Jon Levenson, *The Hebrew Bible, the Old Testament, and Historical Criticism* (Louisville: Westminster John Knox, 1993), p. 5. See also Chapter 2 by Al Wolters in the preesent volume, esp. pp. 37-38.

7. W. M. L. de Wette, *Beiträge zur Einleitung in das Alte Testament*, 2 vols. (Halle, 1806-

exilic Chronicles projected its own legal and ritual systems back into earlier times. He also presented the view that the Pentateuch was late, the earliest parts from Josiah's reign. Thus, according to de Wette, Moses did not play the pivotal role assigned to him in the biblical text.

We turn next to that landmark scholar of the Old Testament, who continues to cast his long shadow on the field of Old Testament study and in particular the study of Old Testament history, Julius Wellhausen (1844-1918). More detailed studies of the history of Old Testament criticism narrate the many lesser but still important scholars that worked between the time of de Wette and Wellhausen,[8] but the latter's conclusions succeeded in winning over doubters (like Franz Delitzsch) and became the dominant view of the nature of the Pentateuch and more broadly of the history of the development of Israelite religion.

Wellhausen's "triumph"[9] followed the publication of his magnum opus *Prolegomena zur Geschichte Israels* (published in German in 1883, in English in 1885). Wellhausen here argued that the Pentateuch was composed of four sources: J (Yahwist or Jahwist, tenth century B.C.), E (Elohist, ninth century), D (Deuteronomist, associated with the Josianic reform in the last quarter of the seventh century), and P (Priestly, post-exilic). Since Wellhausen, there have been many variations on his basic schema, but his work, perhaps more than any other, has led to serious scholarly suspicion concerning traditional views of the composition of biblical books as well as the Old Testament's presentation of history.

While Wellhausen's influence was widespread not only in Germany but eventually also in England and the United States, some scholars resisted his ideas (O. T. Allis, E. J. Young, and Umberto Cassuto, to name a few), but they were often marginalized by the mainstream of the guild. The most successful attempt to marshal a defense against Wellhausen's skepticism regarding the Old Testament's historical presentation was that of the American mid-twentieth-century scholar W. F. Albright and his disciples (including G. E. Wright and J. Bright).[10] They used archaeology and ancient Near Eastern

---

1807). See the insightful description and analysis by John Rogerson, *Old Testament Criticism in the Nineteenth Century: England and Germany* (Philadelphia: Fortress, 1984), pp. 28-49, as well as the comments of Craig G. Bartholomew in Chapter 3 in the present volume.

8. See Rogerson, *Old Testament Criticism*, pp. 50-272; and Chapter 3 in the present volume.

9. Rogerson, *Old Testament Criticism*, p. 273.

10. According to J. Maxwell Miller, "Israelite History," in *The Hebrew Bible and Its Modern Interpreters*, ed. D. A. Knight and G. M. Tucker (Philadelphia: Fortress, 1985), p. 20,

sources to argue for the essential historicity of biblical events beginning with the patriarchs. For example, when tablets were discovered at the ancient sites of Mari and Nuzi that dated to the mid-second millennium, these and other scholars compared the social customs described in these tablets to the social customs of the patriarchs. Since, it was suggested, the Mari and Nuzi tablets dated to the patriarchal era (or near enough to be relevant) and came from a place (the region between Mesopotamia and Syria-Palestine) relatively near the action described in Genesis 12–26, the similarities in customs were taken as evidence that the patriarchal narratives authentically reflected this early time period.

The Albright school's optimism about history carried the day at least in America from the 1930s into the 1960s, but came under the withering examination of John van Seters and Thomas L. Thompson, who showed that many of the supposed similarities were superficial or false and that those that were legitimate were not unique to the first half of the second millennium, and so the patriarchal narratives, in their estimation, were not historically accurate, but were the literary-theological creation of much later writers.[11] In a word, after the 1960s the historical skepticism of Wellhausen returned to the field.

Of course, historical criticism is broader than simply source criticism, and each of the critical methods have provided their own challenge to using the Old Testament for historical reconstruction. Form criticism, for instance, as developed by Hermann Gunkel and others, examined textual units according to their literary pattern in order to discover their original pre-literary form and to establish the texts' connection to their original setting-in-life *(Sitz im Leben)*. The assumption is that the text's present form includes later accretions to the text and that there is value in recovering its original oral form. Like source criticism, therefore, it is a type of textual archaeology that is interested in getting behind the text as it now appears in its final form. Redaction criticism builds on form criticism in that this method examines the ideological interests of the editor(s) of a biblical book as they take their source material and shape it into a final form.

Albright and his followers tended to ignore the conclusions of historical criticism in their reconstruction of Israelite history in contrast to the German school of Albrecht, Alt, and Martin Noth, who felt it was important to first subject the text to criticism. Thus it is not surprising the latter were more skeptical about the biblical presentation of history.

11. John Van Seters, *Abraham in History and Tradition* (New Haven: Yale University Press, 1975); Thomas L. Thompson, *The Historicity of the Patriarchal Narratives*, BZAW 133 (Berlin: de Gruyter, 1974).

The Response

Historical criticism is an attempt to deal with legitimate issues in the biblical text and often leads to helpful insights into the biblical text. While one might not accept Wellhausen's approach to the issues, the Pentateuch has a history of composition and was not written at one sitting by Moses or any single author.[12] Gunkel's form criticism drew attention to the importance of genre.[13] Redaction criticism is perhaps the most helpful of the historical critical methods because it asks questions about the theological motivations of those who produced the final form of the text.

Historical criticism, however, arises from a set of presuppositions that are in conflict with a Christian worldview. John J. Collins gives a clear presentation of these presuppositions. He points out that historical criticism is founded on typical principles of modernist historiography most associated with the late-nineteenth-century theorist Ernst Troeltsch.[14] The first principle, autonomy, represents a dramatic break from premodern ideas concerning tradition. Rather than confidence, the historian must exercise doubt toward sources of the past. Second, the historian must operate with a principle of criticism that always treats conclusions as provisional and open to change. Finally, and perhaps most devastating to the discipline of biblical history, is the principle of analogy, which suggests that the historian can treat as plausible in the past only those events that conform with present experience. If seas do not split today, then we may not presume that they split at the time of the Exodus from Egypt.

Collins rightly points out that historical criticism with its Troeltschian presuppositions made its "impact . . . felt mainly in connection with the his-

12. Most conservative scholars concede this when they speak of post- and a-Mosaica in the text. Granted there are only a handful of texts (though the narrative voice in Deuteronomy that speaks of events in the Transjordan as "beyond the river [Jordan]" betrays a significant part of that book which could not be Mosaic), these may be only the tip of the iceberg. For a recent and intelligent look at the authorship of the Pentateuch, see T. Desmond Alexander, *Abraham in the Negev: A Source-Critical Investigation of Genesis 20:1–22:19* (Carlisle: Paternoster, 1997).

13. Tremper Longman III, "Form Criticism, Recent Developments in Genre Theory, and the Evangelical," *WTJ* 47 (1985): 46-67, though it is precisely in form criticism's diachronic analysis of a biblical text (getting behind the final form to its putative original oral form) that we believe the method goes wrong.

14. Ernst Troeltsch, "Über historische und dogmatische Methode in der Theologie," in *Gesammelte Schriften* (Tübingen: Mohr, 1913). In English, consult, "Historiography," in *Encyclopedia of Religion and Ethics*, ed. James Hastings et al., vol. 6 (New York: Scribner, 1914), pp. 716-23.

torical reliability of the biblical text." In one sense, this approach in particular leads to suspicion concerning the early history of Israel (most often from Genesis through the Conquest and sometimes Judges), but Collins expresses a different attitude toward what he calls the later history of Israel. He points out that "there are obvious differences in literary genre between the legendary, miracle-filled book of Exodus, the sober prose fiction of 1 and 2 Samuel, and some rather annalistic passages in the book of Kings."[15]

While we do not have the space to interact with Troeltsch's principles of historiography, which form the background of historical criticism, we immediately recognize how they might conflict with scholars who want to study the Bible from a position of faith.[16] Collins objects to those who do[17] on the basis of the fact that such a position does not provide reasons for someone who does not share his presuppositions to accept his position. Jon Levenson, though, effectively undermines Collins' point by saying that Collins' perspective is no different. One has to accept Troeltsch's principles to fully embrace historical criticism and therefore to be convinced of its critique and rewriting of Israelite history.[18] Scholars and others who do not ac-

---

15. John J. Collins, *The Bible after Babel: Historical Criticism in a Postmodern Age* (Grand Rapids: Eerdmans, 2005), p. 47, though he goes on to qualify his comments by saying that this later history combines authentic historical remembrance with story-like elaborations.

16. For a recent attempt to argue that historical criticism is compatible with faith, see Kenton L. Sparks, *God's Word in Human Words: An Evangelical Appropriation of Critical Biblical Scholarship* (Grand Rapids: Baker Academic, 2008). Sparks's work deserves a thoroughgoing analysis, but here we will point out that the criticism he develops is a non-Troeltschian form, which would not be recognized by scholars like Collins. It is true, however, that he is willing to sacrifice the historical nature of much of the Old Testament in his belief that there is not enough extrabiblical evidence to substantiate events like the patriarchs or the Exodus. Critical to him, though, is the historical basis of the resurrection of Christ, which he tries to support by appeal to the after-the-fact influence of this event (the Church). My own sense is that Sparks is inconsistent in his embrace of historical criticism and will fail to convince many on either side of his position.

17. And in particular he criticizes the work of Brevard Childs on this count since Childs wants to argue that "the status of canonicity is not an objectively demonstrable claim but a statement of Christian belief" (quoted in Levenson, *The Hebrew Bible*, p. 120). Childs did not reject historical criticism, as his Exodus commentary (*The Book of Exodus* [Philadelphia: Westminster, 1974]) aptly illustrates and as Christopher Seitz reminds us ("What Lesson Will History Teach? The Book of the Twelve as History," in *"Behind" the Text*, pp. 450-51), but his canonical method does, in the words of Levenson, "relativize" it.

18. Levenson, *The Hebrew Bible*, p. 120. Levenson later (p. 124) points out that historical criticism has an "essentially secular character, which derives its origins from Enlightenment rationalism." See the incisive critique of Alvin Plantinga, *Warranted Christian Belief* (Oxford: Oxford University Press, 2000), particularly pp. 374-421; see also Alvin Plantinga, "Two

cept these principles do not recognize the need to follow the conclusions of historical criticism.

Archaeology

The Challenge

Of course, the ebb and flow of skepticism surrounding Old Testament history is not only connected to historical criticism, but also, as intimated above, to archaeological research. The modern era of archaeology in the ancient Near East began in the aftermath of Napoleon's invasion of Egypt in the early nineteenth century. For much of the rest of that century, archaeology was little more than sophisticated plundering, but it still resulted in the recovery of ancient cultures, literatures, and languages.

The twentieth century saw the development of methods and interpretive principles for the survey and excavation of ancient tels that attempted to yield more objective interpretations of sites. Not surprisingly, archaeologists, biblical scholars, and their audiences were most interested not only in how excavations informed and enlarged the biblical picture but also in whether they confirmed the history as presented in the texts. The results have been mixed at best, and more often disappointing.

For instance, archaeology has not confirmed and has even presented evidence against the biblical description of the Exodus, wilderness wanderings, and conquest. A full description of archaeological research that touches this question is well beyond the scope of this chapter. The discussion is complex for many reasons, including debate over when the biblical text situates these events chronologically (typically Late Bronze [fifteenth century] or Early Iron [thirteenth century] Age). Even so, the tenor of the present assessment can be summarized by saying that there is no direct evidence of a large number of Israelites in Egypt at either of these times, no indication of their presence in the wilderness, and many of the cities said to be destroyed or captured by Joshua (most notably Jericho and Ai) show no sign of habitation during the time period involved. Needless to say, such conclusions have fed both scholarly and popular skepticism, or at least confusion, about the historical veracity of the Old Testament history.

(or More) Kinds of Scripture Scholarship," in *"Behind" the Text: History and Biblical Interpretation,* pp. 19-57. Also insightful is C. Stephen Evans, *The Historical Christ and the Jesus of Faith: The Incarnational Narrative as History* (Oxford: Oxford University Press, 1996).

The Response

Archaeology is not a hard science that presents objective facts. The material remains that are uncovered through archaeological excavation must be interpreted, and, not surprisingly, the interpretation of archaeological materials that bear on the question of the historicity of the Old Testament is passionately contested.[19] The same data examined by two or more archaeologists can lead to radically different conclusions. Fundamental principles of approach affect these variant interpretations. They are too numerous to be developed here, but one example will suffice. Should archaeological interpretation happen apart from textual witnesses (including the Bible) or in their light? As we will later see (on minimalism, below), some scholars believe that the Bible should not be a factor in the interpretation of archaeological materials, while others (see below on maximalism) take the opposite approach and proceed by analyzing the mute material remains in the light of the rich testimony provided by the text. Regardless of whether he is ultimately correct, the work of John Bimson, who argues that archaeology in fact supports a fifteenth-century Exodus, illustrates how the same archaeological data can be interpreted in more than one way.[20]

Literary Approaches

The Challenge

Preoccupation with the history of composition and the reconstruction of Israel's history continued until around 1980. At that time, a radical shift in focus took place in the guild of Old Testament studies that was associated primarily with the new (synchronic) literary approach[21] but also with a new

19. For an interesting example, see the description of the debate between Israel Finkelstein and Amihai Mazar concerning evidence for the existence of the United Monarchy provided by Paul Davies, *Memories of Ancient Israel: An Introduction to Biblical History — Ancient and Modern* (Louisville: Westminster John Knox, 2008), pp. 74-76. Note his correct acknowledgement of the "huge uncertainty that archaeological interpretation can involve."

20. See John J. Bimson, *Redating the Exodus and Conquest,* JSOTSup 5 (Sheffield: University of Sheffield Press, 1978). For a full and accessible discussion of the issue of the archaeology and historicity of the Exodus, see Tremper Longman III, *How to Read Exodus* (Downers Grove: IVP, 2009).

21. See Chapter 4 by David Beldman in the present volume for a fuller exposition of the literary approach to the Old Testament.

interest in the study of the Old Testament as canon. The shift to literary study found its trigger in Robert Alter's *The Art of Biblical Narrative*,[22] while the originator and main advocate of the canonical approach was Brevard S. Childs.[23] Perhaps this shift can be explained in part by the skepticism that resulted from the research described above. Old Testament scholars tired of debating over the contours of the Pentateuchal sources, for instance, and so turned to an analysis of its literary (not authorial) unity.[24] Further, once it was concluded that the biblical text did not authentically represent real events (or at least such could not be proven to an objective observer), questions of historicity could be bracketed by a turn to a literary study.

The literary approach dominated biblical scholarship from the time of Alter's watershed book through the mid-1990s. Indeed, during this time, few books on the Old Testament lacked the term "literary" in their title. Biblical scholars resourced their interest in literary analysis by turning to literary theory. Initially, these scholars tended to practice the kind of close reading advocated by the New Critics of the mid-twentieth century, mimicking the kind of analysis done by Alter and others. The rupture between the literary and the referential was an axiom of this type of literary theory[25] (and others such as structuralism and deconstruction), and it is not surprising that such an attitude was imported to the study of the Bible. In other words, recognition of the literary characteristics of the Bible led scholars to equate the Bible and literature, with the corollary that the Bible as a literary text does not refer outside of itself and, in particular, makes no reference to history.[26] This position led some scholars to a substantial denial of a historical approach to the text, often taking the form of denying or denigrating traditional historical-critical methods. Source and form criticism particularly were attacked. The following quotation represents the views of some who adopted the literary approach and exposes belief that the truth of the story is inde-

22. Robert Alter, *The Art of Biblical Narrative* (New York: Basic Books, 1981).

23. See Brevard S. Childs, *Introduction to the Old Testament as Scripture* (Philadelphia: Fortress, 1979).

24. Not that most literary scholars denied the presence of sources, as witnessed by Alter's phrase "the composite unity" of the Pentateuch.

25. Frank Lentricchia, *After the New Criticism* (London: Methuen, 1980).

26. In this way the literary approach not only threatened the use of the Bible for historical reconstruction but also raised questions about the historical critical approach. See Leander Keck, "Will the Historical-Critical Method Survive?" in *Orientation by Disorientation: Studies in Literary Criticism and Biblical Literary Criticism, Presented in Honor of William A. Beardslee,* ed. Richard A. Spencer (Pittsburgh: Pickwick, 1980), pp. 115-27.

pendent of any historical information: "Above all, we must keep in mind that narrative is a *form of representation*. Abraham in Genesis is not a real person any more than the painting of an apple is real fruit."[27]

Similar evaluation may be seen in the hermeneutics of Hans Frei, who pinpoints the major error in both traditional critical and conservative exegesis in the loss of understanding that biblical narrative is history-like and not true history with an ostensive, or external reference.[28] In addition, Alter's brilliant analysis of Old Testament narrative is coupled with the assumption that the nature of the narrative is "historicized fiction" or "fictional history."[29]

The Response

Not all early advocates of the literary study of the Bible turned away from history with such monolithic abandon. Meir Sternberg advocated an approach that proved to be a precursor to the return to history that took place in the mid-1990s. In *The Poetics of Biblical Narrative,* published in 1984, Sternberg spoke against the idea that literature has no ostensive reference. He exposed the "antihistorical bias" of much literary criticism,[30] and in response he addressed the issue of the relationship between history and fiction. He did not deny that history writing involved literary artifice. As he pointed out, "History writing is not a record of fact — of what 'really happened' — but a discourse that claims to be a record of fact."[31] However, he carefully and persuasively differentiated the artifice that was part and parcel of any literary representation of an actual event from the free-wheeling invention of fiction. In other words, history writing is constrained by an "allegiance . . . binding on a historical equivalent."[32] As a result, Sternberg refused to reduce the function of biblical literature to only a literary one. Rather he argued that we should speak of its "ideological, historiographic, and aesthetic" functions.[33] To do otherwise would have

---

27. Adele Berlin, *Poetics and Interpretation of Biblical Narrative* (Sheffield: Almond Press, 1983), p. 13.

28. Frei, *The Eclipse of Biblical Narrative.*

29. Alter, *The Art of Biblical Narrative,* pp. 24-25.

30. Meir Sternberg, *The Poetics of Biblical Narrative: Ideological Literature and the Drama of Reading,* Indiana Studies in Biblical Literature (Bloomington: Indiana University Press, 1985), p. 8.

31. Sternberg, *The Poetics of Biblical Narrative,* p. 25.

32. Sternberg, *The Poetics of Biblical Narrative,* p. 29.

33. Sternberg, *The Poetics of Biblical Narrative,* p. 41.

devastating results turning God "from the lord of history into a creature of the imagination."[34]

Sternberg's perspective has significantly won the day. Not everyone would agree with his entire position, but it is telling that the view that the Bible is a literary object and that issues of history of composition and ostensive reference should thereby be bracketed is hard to find these days. On the other hand, a lasting benefit of the literary approach of the 1980s and early 1990s is a renewed appreciation for the literary shaping and the conventions of Old Testament narrative that need to be taken into account when talking about the sources that lead to the final form of a biblical book[35] or for a study of its depiction of historical events.[36]

The Present State of the Field

The challenges to the Old Testament's depiction of the past have been formidable and have provoked responses from those who affirm the value of the biblical text as a witness to the past. At an earlier period (roughly pre-1980), the academic guild of Old Testament studies was dominated by scholars who presented a monolithic view. In the area of history, for instance, one might fairly describe the mainstream of Old Testament scholarship as concluding that the early history of the Old Testament was not historically accurate, but at a later point the narrative did reflect actual events (though not in all its details). The debate was over where the shift from myth and legend to history occurred, with some arguing it began with the patriarchs, others the Exodus, and perhaps the largest group with the United Monarchy. Scholars who disagreed with this "consensus" were relegated to the sidelines by the guild. Those so marginalized included scholars who took a more radically skeptical view as well as those who expressed more confidence in the Old Testament's depiction of the past.

The situation is quite different at the beginning of the twenty-first cen-

---

34. Sternberg, *The Poetics of Biblical Narrative*, p. 32.

35. For an example of a source-critical study done in the light of developments in literary methods, see David Carr, *Reading the Fractures of Genesis: Historical and Literary Approaches* (Louisville: Westminster John Knox, 1996).

36. See V. Philips Long, *The Art of Biblical History*, Foundations of Contemporary Interpretation 5 (Grand Rapids: Zondervan, 1994), as well as Iain Provan, V. Philips Long, and Tremper Longman III, *The Biblical History of Israel* (Louisville: Westminster John Knox, 2003), to be discussed below.

tury. While many scholars continue to espouse the consensus that dominated until the 1970s, today the field is filled with competing views on history. It would be impossible to represent every perspective on the topic, but we will content ourselves by describing three different viewpoints. One view has been called minimalist and another, its counterpart, maximalist, though those labels are often heard as pejorative by their advocates. The middle view is the one most in continuity with the earlier consensus and we will refer to it as centrist.

Centrist Histories

We begin with a consideration of the centrist position because today (and at least since the end of the nineteenth century) this viewpoint dominates in the academy.[37]

As we see below, the minimalists' radical proposal is that the Old Testament provides little if any authentic historical information. The Old Testament was composed very late (Persian or Hellenistic period) and serves the political interests of its authors. Centrists back away from the radical claims of the minimalists, but without embracing the more optimistic approach to history represented by maximalist histories (see below). Instead they adopt a middle road, suggesting that while some of the history is invented, there comes a point in time when the Old Testament contains authentic memory of the past. Indeed, we call this perspective centrist because today it is common for its advocates to situate their approach as a moderate (and to them reasonable) middle way between minimalism and maximalism.[38] To represent this view, we will consider recent works by John J. Collins and Mario Liverani. The former articulates and defends the approach and the latter writes a history of Israel utilizing it.

Collins begins by describing a historical-critical approach (including source, form, redaction, and other methods) to the biblical text in contrast

37. Such judgments are difficult to make. Indeed, the argument can be made that the maximalist perspective is dominant, if one simply counts those Old Testament professors who hold doctorates and teach at colleges, universities, and seminaries. However, such pronouncements typically are made in regard to mainline universities, particularly research universities. The prevalence of the centrist position in these schools is not surprising since hiring practices typically involve the weeding out of those who hold a maximalist (or in the United States, even a minimalist) viewpoint.

38. See the discussion in Collins, *The Bible after Babel*, pp. 27-39.

to the more radical approach of minimalism and the more conservative (and to Collins, apologetic) approach of the maximalists. We have already cited Collins' description of the Troeltschian principles backing the historical-critical enterprise as well as his assessment that its conclusions require a re-assessment and rewriting of biblical history.

Collins nicely describes the position that we here call centrist. A historical-critical approach leads to a skeptical attitude toward the Old Testament's depiction of history. Nevertheless, a distinction can be discerned between texts that concern early history, which are fictional, and later history, which contains valuable historical tradition. The transition is not absolute, however. There are legendary elements to the later history as well. Differences exist between scholars who can be called centrist concerning where the transition between legend and history takes place as well as precisely to what extent and in what way the later history is authentically depicted. J. Alberto Soggin, for example, argued that true history begins with the United Monarchy,[39] and J. Maxwell Miller and John Hayes start with the period of the Judges.[40]

Our main example of a centrist history comes from Mario Liverani, though he is difficult to categorize.[41] However, in the final analysis, it is best to think of him as a centrist rather than a minimalist, even though he argues the Old Testament's representation of the past was largely elaborated at a late point in history, the post-exilic period. He refers to all pre-monarchical history as "invented," though even here he allows for some residual memory of the past. He does differentiate this completely invented history from the texts that describe the period of the monarchy and after. Even here, he believes that these materials have been rewritten by post-exilic theologians for a political purpose. It is in this way that he is perhaps most like a minimalist in that he believes that the ideological shaping of the Old Testament narrative is a result of those who returned from exile as they sought to justify their

39. J. Alberto Soggin, *History of Israel: From the Beginning to the Bar Kochba Revolt*, A.D. 135 (London: SCM, 1984).

40. J. Maxwell Miller and John H. Hayes, *A History of Ancient Israel and Judah*, 2nd ed. (Louisville: Westminster John Knox, 2006).

41. Mario Liverani, *Israel's History and the History of Israel* (London: Equinox, 2005). Liverani is difficult to categorize in part because he provides little reflection on his method and, in addition, writes without citations of other scholars, but Nils Lemche (*The Old Testament between Theology and History* [Louisville: Westminster John Knox, 2008]) appears to share the judgment that he is not minimalist when he says (with apparent disappointment) that his history "is still, when it comes to the historical part, 'biblical' in essence" (p. xix).

societal dominance and territorial right to the land over against those who had remained in the land. Liverani, in the final analysis, represents a position that straddles the centrist and minimalist position and thus leads to a discussion of full-blown minimalism.

Minimalist Histories

Minimalism describes a perspective on biblical history that is shared by a group of prolific scholars, mostly from Europe and England. There are clear differences between advocates of this approach, but one also gets the impression from their writings that they participate in a common cause.

Advocates of this perspective are labeled minimalists because they hold that the Old Testament contains very little reliable history. Differences exist between minimalists. Indeed, individual authors themselves have changed their perspective over the years. For instance, Nils Peter Lemche in the preface of his book *The Old Testament between Theology and History* (2008) describes how his conclusions have become increasingly skeptical since the publication of his earlier book *Ancient History: A New History of Israelite Society* (1984).

Our brief presentation of minimalism will simply describe the general themes that are shared by minimalists and only occasionally indicate the differences between them. These themes are:

(1) Archaeology and extrabiblical documentation are the primary sources for the reconstruction of ancient Palestinian history.

(2) The Old Testament is a secondary source, but not for the events it narrates, but rather for the historical context in which they were written.

(3) The Old Testament writings are much younger than other scholars suggest. Here the minimalists diverge among themselves. Israel Finkelstein and Neil Silberman believe that many of the writings are from the late seventh century B.C. and associated with the reign of Josiah.[42] Most, though, believe that the biblical texts were written later, during the Persian period[43] or the Hellenistic period.[44] Even so, Thomas L. Thompson has adopted the

---

42. Israel Finkelstein and Neil A. Silberman, *The Bible Unearthed: Archaeology's New Vision of Ancient Israel and the Origin of the Sacred Texts* (New York: Free Press, 2001).

43. See Paul Davies, *In Search of Ancient Israel*, JSOTSup 148 (Sheffield: Sheffield Academic Press, 1992).

44. Lemche, *The Old Testament between Theology and History*.

most radical stance in regard to the Old Testament as a historical source, concluding that it has no value whatsoever for the purpose of historical reconstruction.[45]

(4) The Old Testament writings are thus far removed from the events they purport to describe and they report past events with an ideological bias that distorts them. Accordingly for any biblical tradition to be affirmed, historians require collaboration from other sources. Due to its nature, much of the biblical narrative is unverifiable by means of archaeology or extrabiblical attestation.

Maximalist Histories

The third and last school of thought will be illustrated by a description of the approach to the history of Israel presented by Iain Provan, V. Philips Long, and Tremper Longman III.[46] Their approach is sometimes characterized as maximalist because of its optimistic attitude toward the historical veracity of the Old Testament and because it is the polar opposite of the minimalist approach described above. The label "maximalist" is often applied pejoratively, though, as if this view is anti-critical. It is true that these authors have clear differences with the historical-critical perspective advocated by Collins and others, but it would be wrong to characterize their approach as anti-critical since its advocates are sensitive to issues of genre, literary convention, history of composition, archaeology, extrabiblical evidence, and so on in its reconstruction of the history of Israel. It is misleading to suggest, as some of their critics have, that their history is a simple paraphrase of the biblical storyline.

It is a sign that the issue of biblical historiography is highly contested that *A Biblical History of Israel* begins with over one hundred pages of prolegomenon before the book presents an accounting of the period of the patri-

45. Thomas L. Thompson, *The Mythic Past: Biblical Archaeology and the Myth of History* (New York: Basic Books, 1999).

46. Provan, Long, and Longman, *A Biblical History.* For other, likeminded scholarly approaches to the history of Israel, see the collection of essays (and bibliography) found in A. R. Millard, J. K. Hoffmeier, and D. W. Baker, eds., *Faith, Tradition, and History: Old Testament Historiography in Its Near Eastern Context* (Winona Lake, IN: Eisenbrauns, 1994). See also Jens Bruun Kofoed, *Text History: Historiography and the Study of the Biblical Text* (Winona Lake, IN: Eisenbrauns, 2005), and Kenneth Kitchen, *The Reliability of the Old Testament* (Grand Rapids: Eerdmans, 2003).

archs.[47] Most of the discussion in this introduction is polemical toward the minimalists, but it also points out that scholars who find their confidence in the midpoint of the biblical narrative (e.g., Miller and Hayes; Soggin) are simply inconsistent in the application of their principles.

At the heart of their claim that the Old Testament preserves viable history is a defense of testimony as the bulwark of remembrance of the past. All history, not just biblical history, is based solely on past testimony.[48] The Old Testament is the most obvious and expansive testimony of Israel in antiquity, and to discount it, as the minimalists do, is simply to concede that we cannot know anything of substance about the past. It has really only been recently that the onus has been put on the side of proving the value of a tradition that contains ancient testimony. The authors of *A Biblical History of Israel* counter by saying that the onus should really be on falsification rather than on verification.[49] For one thing, if we must wait to have confidence in the biblical witness to the past until there is some type of extrabiblical corroboration, then we will be paralyzed (like the minimalists) from saying anything positive about the history of Israel during the Old Testament period since such extrabiblical sources are few and far between. In addition, we would hardly expect that extrabiblical texts or archaeology would directly attest many of the events recorded in the Old Testament since they often concern individuals or families and not large nation states.[50] Thus, Provan and his coauthors advocate a falsification rather than a verification principle. Historical judgments are further enhanced when there is evidence from archaeology and epigraphic materials that distinctly support the historicity of elements of a biblical story. But, rather than waiting for every element of the story to be specifically verified, those elements that can be corroborated lend confidence to the story as a whole.[51]

---

47. The authors are presenting a history of Israel, which explains, at least in part, why they start with Gen. 12 and do not include any discussion of Gen. 1–11.

48. Provan, Long, and Longman, *Biblical History*, p. 37.

49. In this, they find themselves in agreement with Kitchen, *Reliability of the Old Testament*, though Kitchen does not show awareness of the philosophical, theological, or literary issues involved in the question of Old Testament historiography.

50. Provan, Long, and Longman, *Biblical History*, pp. 54-56.

51. An example might be seen in the discussion of the patriarchal period on pp. 112-17 in Provan, Long, and Longman, *Biblical History*. In spite of telling and persuasive criticism of overblown comparison with contemporary social customs as revealed by the tablets at Mari and Nuzi, some of these comparisons continue to be relevant. In addition, certain of the behaviors of the patriarchs would not only have been anachronistic to a later period (which some believe is the period in which the patriarchs were "invented"), but would have

The authors of *A Biblical History of Israel* address the issue of the ideology of the text head-on by acknowledging that the texts do have a clear ideology that shapes the presentation of the history. They deny that ideology necessarily distorts the events. Below we will give an example (the reign of Abijah) that will show that the biblical text gives us two presentations of a period of time and make the argument that their different ideologies do not distort the events but rather apply the events to their own contemporary audiences.

Provan, Long, and Longman also utilize the results of archaeological research, including extra-biblical texts, in their reconstruction of ancient Israel's history. They too are testimonies of the past. However, contrary to the minimalists (and some centrist historians), they do not take precedence over the biblical testimony.

Though many issues place the maximalist school of thought at odds with the minimalist and centrist approaches, none is larger than the principle of analogy, most famously formulated by Troeltsch as described above.[52] Provan and his coauthors present a spirited attack on the principle of analogy.[53] We might pointedly ask, "Whose experience?" Troeltsch and his disciples would likely think of a modern, Western intellectual who does not acknowledge a supernatural reality, but these are not the only experiences available. Countless millions experience what they would call the intrusion of the divine into their life experience every day — even though few have had experiences on the scale of the crossing of the Red Sea or the raising of a cadaver.

In the final analysis, in spite of legitimate attempts to speak to the minimalist and centrist objections to our approach, we must recognize that different presuppositions and worldviews are ultimately what clash in this debate. If there were numerous documents attesting Israel's enslavement in Egypt as well as extensive and undisputed archaeological attestation of their journey through the wilderness as well as their defeat and partial settlement of Canaan, this evidence would not convince a historian committed to a sec-

---

been distasteful, thus providing an argument that the patriarchal narratives are testimonies that reflect ancient realities; see also Gordon J. Wenham, *Genesis 16–50*, WBC 2 (Dallas: Word Publishing, 1994), pp. xx-xxv, xxx-xxxv.

52. This attitude was expressed to me by a scholarly friend who heard I was working on a history of Israel and commented, "You cannot believe in God and write history." Davies asserts the same sentiment when he writes: "if we choose to include miracles, then we shall end up not writing history" (*Memories of Ancient Israel*, p. 141).

53. Provan, Long, and Longman, *Biblical History*, pp. 70-73.

ularist paradigm of the most important point of the story: God graciously intruded into history to rescue his people from slavery.

What Kind of Historiography? The Art of Biblical History

Interacting with critical theory is important and illuminating, but we turn now to a more positive assessment to understand how to hear God's word in the historical materials in the Old Testament.

"All history is created."[54] With this sentence, Marc Brettler begins his insightful and often provocative book on biblical historiography. His point is indisputable. Writings about past events are not the same as the events themselves; they are a representation of the events and thus involve literary artifice.

V. Philips Long, a visual artist as well as a specialist in Old Testament history, offers an analogy between writing history and painting a portrait. The latter is "visual representational art," while the former is "verbal representation art."[55] Thus, "biblical narrative, as verbal representation . . . does not duplicate but, rather, depicts the past."[56] Long goes on to explain that the past can be represented in different ways and still be viable as accurate to the events it describes, just as portrait painters can represent the same individual in two styles and still accurately capture an authentic depiction of their subject.

History writing must be representational by the nature of the case. After all, historians must select events to be included from the past out of the myriad of events that have occurred. They must choose which events should be emphasized. Their selection and emphasis are driven by the questions that they are attempting to answer by their look to the past, and their questions and their interpretation of the events are shaped by their point of view (or ideology). This can be illustrated with a look at the account of the reign of Abijah (1 Kings 15:1-8; 2 Chron. 13); the synoptic presentation of his reign allows the representational nature of the biblical picture to stand out in bold relief.

First, all history writing, biblical history writing included, must be selec-

54. Marc Brettler, *The Creation of History in Ancient Israel* (New York: Routledge, 1995), p. 1.

55. See his comments in Provan, Long, and Longman, *A Biblical History,* p. 82, as well as Long's earlier book, *The Art of Biblical History.*

56. Provan, Long, and Longman, *A Biblical History,* p. 85.

tive. An exhaustive account of the past is simply impossible, so only certain events can be narrated. The last verse of the Gospel of John expresses the obvious in regard to the life of Jesus: "But there are many other things that Jesus did; if every one of them were written down, I suppose that the world itself could not contain the books that would be written" (John 21:25). In regard to Abijah, the account in Kings makes the selective nature of its representation obvious when it says "The rest of the acts of Abijah, and all that he did, are they not written in the Book of the Annals of the Kings of Judah?" (15:7). For its part, Chronicles appeals to the "story of the prophet Iddo" for the "rest of the acts of Abijah" (13:22). We can only speculate about the nature of these references, but the point is that the Kings and Chronicles accounts of Abijah's reign are only partial and extremely selective.

As we examine the accounts of Abijah's reign in Kings and Chronicles, the contrast is quite striking. They do not select the same material from his life. The account in Chronicles is consistently positive; that is, we hear about a king who is devout and confident in Yahweh, whereas in Kings, "his heart was not true to the LORD his God" (15:3).

Further, the historians not only select events for inclusion in their accounts, they also choose to emphasize some more than others. To illustrate this, we might point to the lengthy treatment given by the Chronicles account to Abijah's speech on the eve of a battle with King Jeroboam of the Northern Kingdom, a speech that emphasizes the former's piety and confidence in God (13:4-12). Or, examining the Abijah accounts in their broader book-length treatment, we might note that Abijah's reign is not considered worthy of as much emphasis as, say, David's reign.

Certainly the most interesting factor that determines the shape of the presentation of the past has to do with the historian's point of view or ideology as the historian attempts to present the past to a present audience. Historians, and certainly biblical historians, are not interested in writing about the past for no reason. We, their readers, are interested in history for what it tells us about the present. Kings and Chronicles were written to address issues that concerned the audience at the time of their writing (or final redaction), and the events of the past are selected, emphasized, and interpreted in such a fashion as to provide answers to the questions of the present. It is here that we are likely to find the answer to why the presentation of Abijah's reign is so different between Kings and Chronicles.

In Kings, Abijah's reign is characterized as evil. This depiction fits with a consistent emphasis throughout the book on the negative acts of the kings of Israel and Judah. It seems clear that the author is surveying the monarchy and choosing stories that illustrate their dark side. What point of view motivates this perspective? We might begin by noting the evidence that Kings (and Samuel) reached their final redaction at the time of the Exile.[57] We might further surmise that the defeated and exiled people of God might be asking, "What did we do to deserve this?" Thus, an important question driving the representation of Israel in Kings would encourage the author to select accounts that showed that Israel and its kings had a history of faithlessness toward God. Further study might convince a modern reader that the lens through which the historian looked at the history of Israel was provided by the book of Deuteronomy. After all, among other distinctive Deuteronomic laws, Kings seems concerned to evaluate whether Judah and Israel obeyed the law of centralization (Deuteronomy 12). So to answer this question, Kings recounts negative stories and provides a negative evaluation of Abijah's reign. The author's point of view also explains why he slightly changes the king's name from Abijah ("My father is Yah") to Abijam ("My Father is Yam/the Sea," the god of chaos) as well as the fact that he associates the king through genealogy with Abishalom/Absalom, a negative figure in earlier Israelite history.

On the other hand, the Chronicler is writing at a later period of time, after the Persians had defeated Babylon and allowed the Jewish people to return to Jerusalem.[58] Different questions are in the historian's mind as well as in the minds of the audience. The Jewish people are returning to the land, but their lives have been disrupted. Their questions were "What is our connection to the past?" and "How do we now behave?" There is less interest in the dark stories of the past and more concern to provide a positive model of behavior. The Chronicler's picture of Abijah thus fits in with the general trend of that book to narrate positive stories and give positive evaluations of the kings. The interesting and subtle change in Abijah's genealogy where his mother Maacah is no longer connected with Abishalom but rather with an unknown Uriel of Gibeah seems to affirm this positive strategy of the historian.

The accounts of Abijah well illustrate the representational nature of (biblical) history, accounts that are highly selective and are clearly presented

57. Note that the last recorded event, the release of Jehoiachin from prison, took place during the reign of Evil-Merodach (the Babylonian king Amel-Marduk), who reigned 562-560 b.c. (2 Kings 24:27-30) and there is no awareness of the Persian defeat of Babylon.

58. After all, the last recorded event is the Cyrus Decree, permitting the return (2 Chron. 36:22-23), and some of the genealogies of 1 Chron. 1–9 extend into the post-exilic period.

from specific (and different) perspectives. They illustrate the nature of all biblical history, but the synoptic presentation makes these characteristics stand out all the more clearly.

Of course, such radically different presentations raise the question of the veracity of the accounts. Would it really be fair to say that both accounts are true since they are so radically different? Was Abijah a faithful man and king or not? We have no third source about this king that might settle that question. The "Annals of the Kings of Judah" and the "story of the prophet Iddo" are no longer available to us. We have to content ourselves with the question, is it possible that they are both true or are they by necessity mutually contradictory?

This question raises the viability of harmonization, or devising an explanation that suggests how two historical sources in tension might be reconciled. Harmonization has hit on hard times as a method in biblical studies and for good reasons. A previous generation of evangelical scholars harmonized too quickly in order to provide an apologetic for the biblical text. Embarrassed by seeming contradiction, they did everything they could to cover it up. Harmonizations became increasingly fanciful and unbelievable, doing more harm than good. They also served to obscure the intentional differences of the synoptic accounts that express important theological emphases to which the reader needs to attend. That said, however, harmonization is a strategy used by historians of any period as they deal with different sources that bear on a given event or period.

We return now to the question of the Abijam of Kings and Abijah of Chronicles. Can these accounts be reconciled? I believe they can be. After all, we know from kings like Solomon that they can be devout at one point in their life and rebellious in another. Perhaps the same is true for Abijah. Neither historian is interested in being "fair" to Abijah. They have other interests, as we have seen, and they chose those parts of Abijah's life that made their point.

History as Theology

Again, there is no such thing as objective, in the sense of disinterested, history. All history involves selection and emphasis of some events over others and these events must be interpreted in order to be narrated. In other words, all history writing is ideologically driven. Yet the assumption that ideology inherently distorts history is not self-evident. To view history through faulty lenses will obviously distort it. To take an obvious example, histories that attempt to deny the Holocaust are ideological in a false and dangerous way.

The ideology of the Old Testament might better be called theological,[59] as demonstrated by the example of Kings' and Chronicles' accounts of Abijah's reign above. The biblical text is interested not primarily in politics or economics but in God and in his relationship with his creatures. Events are selected and interpreted in a way that reveals God in his relationship with his people. Indeed, it might be said that the purpose of the Old Testament is to give glory to God. So it reports events showing how God is working in the world with the purpose of leading its readers to worship God. Thus, we may see just how important it is to read Old Testament history in order to hear God's word.

Such a purpose may be seen in the account of the crossing of the Red Sea in Exodus 14 and 15. The purpose of the event that is represented by this selective and interpreted account is stated by God himself in anticipation of the event: "I will gain glory for myself over Pharaoh and all his army, his chariots, and his chariot drivers. And the Egyptians shall know that I am the LORD" (Exod. 14:17-18).

The biblical writers see God's hand throughout their history. God's actions in space and time are not isolated events but rather part of a history of redemption in which God pursues humanity to restore with them the harmonious relationship that they experienced in the beginning (Gen. 2:4b-25) before the fall.[60] The biblical writers express the coherence of God's actions by seeing later events as reactualizations of earlier events. Again, we will consider the example of the Exodus and in particular the crossing of the Red Sea. Forty years after the Exodus as Israel enters the land, the waters of the Jordan River stop, allowing the Israelites to cross on dry ground (Josh. 3). This event calls to mind the earlier event, demonstrating to Joshua and the people that the God of power who rescued them from Egypt is with them as they go into hostile territory. Later, God will show that his power is with the

---

59. See the helpful essay by Murray A. Rae, "Creation and Promise: Towards a Theology of History," in *"Behind" the Text,* pp. 267-99: "We may say, therefore, that the Bible is a theological account of history" (p. 283).

60. Craig Bartholomew in Chapter 1 in the present volume notes that a trinitarian hermeneutic "alerts us to the fact that the Old Testament is part of a larger whole" and "provides the basis for typological and figural analysis" (principle 2 of a trinitarian hermeneutic); p. 11 above. Of course, such an analysis begins with an appreciation of the Old Testament's "discrete witness" to God (Bartholomew's principle 3). See also Chapter 6 by Mark Boda in the present volume.

prophet Elijah (2 Kings 2:8) and then with Elisha (2:14) as God again dries up the waters of the Jordan to let them cross on dry ground.

Turning to the prophets, they too speak of a future Exodus and return to the land that will follow God's judgment (e.g., Isa. 40:1-5; Hos. 2:14-16). This second Exodus theme echoes in Ezra as God's people under Shesh-bazzar and Zerubbabel return from Babylonian exile. And here we even see a dramatic connection with the New Testament. In the Gospels, as is well known, Jesus' life and ministry are depicted as reflecting the events of the Exodus, beginning with his baptism and forty days and nights in the wilderness and concluding with his crucifixion on the eve of the Passover. The author of the book of Hebrews in the New Testament utilizes the Exodus tradition in yet a different way when he likens his Christian readers to those who were in the wilderness in order to encourage them to faith in the midst of difficulties.

In conclusion, history cannot be divorced from theology, nor theology from history. It is in history that God reveals himself to his people as a God who judges and who redeems, and it is in biblical historiography that later audiences can read, remember, and praise the God who involves himself with his creation. We read history in order to hear God's word therein.

A Way Forward

The Old Testament's connection to history is thus both important as well as passionately contested. This chapter attempts to describe the issues and the debate, but goes further in delineating an approach that is consistent with a view of the Old Testament as Scripture that intends to reveal God to humanity. The following summarize the leading points of such a way forward.

(1) The genre of Old Testament books needs to be evaluated before using them for historical reconstruction. Not all narrative intends to describe actual events of the past.

(2) A written account of a past event is not the event itself, but is a verbal representation of the event and as such involves literary artifice. It is right to consider Old Testament narrative as story-like histories.[61] The interpreter of biblical history must be competent in the literary conventions of Hebrew storytelling. It is important to remember that, though it is often important

---

61. Reversing Frei's formulation (in *The Eclipse of Biblical Narrative*) that Old Testament narrative presents history-like stories.

that the text reflect an actual event, it is the text and not the event that is important to the church as Scripture.

(3) The biblical accounts of past events are traditions that present testimony of these events. Affirmation of their veracity should not depend on external collaboration (by extrabiblical texts or archaeology, for instance), but they should be presumed to be true unless falsified.

(4) Archaeology and extrabiblical texts are important to provide a broader understanding of Israelite history. It is, however, a misuse of these materials to either prove or disprove the biblical testimony since they themselves require interpretation. They can, however, provide evidence that corroborates or works against the biblical depiction of history.

(5) All history is ideological, in that it involves interpretation and perspective, though in the case of the Old Testament, it is better to speak of the ideology as theology. The purpose of Old Testament historiography is to describe God's actions in space and time for the purpose of leading readers to worship him.

(6) Biblical histories address the concerns of their contemporary audiences (see the above example concerning Abijah's reign). Even when synoptic accounts are absent, it is incumbent on the interpreter to ask what theological purposes are behind a text's presentation of history.

(7) The Old Testament's theological history presents God's redemptive actions in a coherent fashion. Later writers, for instance, describe God's redemptive acts in the light of his earlier acts (see the example of the Exodus above).

6 Biblical Theology and Old Testament Interpretation

Mark J. Boda

Biblical theology is an essential discipline for releasing the Bible's theological treasures for the contemporary church, academy, and culture. By placing the message of individual biblical passages into the broader context of the message of the Bible as a whole, the biblical witness has greater potential to speak to the theological issues of the day. Christian biblical theological analysis is by nature trinitarian, not because it finds within the Old Testament a fully developed trinitarian theology, but rather because it takes seriously the inseparable link between the Old and New Testaments. The presupposition that makes the message of the Old Testament relevant for Christians is that the trinitarian God of the New Testament is the same Creator and Redeemer revealed in the Old Testament. And Christian interpretation of the Old Testament revelation not only begins with this trinitarian foundation, but also takes into account that Jesus Christ represents the climax of the redemptive and revelatory activity of this trinitarian God and that the Holy Spirit is the One responsible to form a covenant community with the potential to transform all of creation. A Christian biblical theology will thus place the message of the Old Testament within these broader redemptive and revelatory realities.

Definition

Biblical theology is a theological discipline that reflects on the theological witness of the Bible in its own idiom with attention to both its unity and diversity.[1] In partnership with sound exegetical theology, understood as disciplined reading of the individual pericopae and books of the Bible that seeks after their theological messages to their historical audiences, biblical theology discerns macro level connections within the biblical witness without ignoring disconnections between these various texts and books. The emphasis in biblical theology is on the messages of whole books, canonical sections, entire testaments, and the Bible as a collection and the connections between individual texts and these larger literary-canonical units. By ascertaining "inner points of coherence and development"[2] it seeks for a "comprehensive presentation of the theological character of the biblical literature."[3]

History of Biblical Theology

Biblical Theology as an Academic Discipline

The origin of biblical theology as an academic discipline is often traced to Johann Philipp Gabler's late-eighteenth-century inaugural lecture, delivered originally in Latin, whose title translates into English as "Address about the Correct Distinction of Biblical and Dogmatic Theology and the Right Definition of Their Goals."[4] As the title suggests, Gabler's concern was to delineate

---

1. See especially Craig G. Bartholomew, "Biblical Theology and Biblical Interpretation: Introduction," in *Out of Egypt: Biblical Theology and Biblical Interpretation,* ed. Craig Bartholomew, Mary Healy, Karl Möller, and Robin Parry, SAHS 5 (Grand Rapids: Zondervan, 2004), p. 1, who defines biblical theology as "the attempt to grasp the Scripture in its totality according to its own, rather than imposed, categories." Also Graeme L. Goldsworthy, "Relationship of Old Testament and New Testament," in *New Dictionary of Biblical Theology,* ed. T. Desmond Alexander and Brian S. Rosner (Downers Grove: IVP, 2000), p. 81: "Biblical theology as a discipline presupposes that the Bible, notwithstanding its great diversity, has some kind of perceptible unity"; cf. Gerhard F. Hasel, *Old Testament Theology: Basic Issues in the Current Debate,* 4th ed. (Grand Rapids: Eerdmans, 1991), p. 112; James Barr, *The Concept of Biblical Theology: An Old Testament Perspective* (Minneapolis: Fortress, 1999), p. 7.

2. Scott Hafemann, "Biblical Theology: Retrospect and Prospect," in *Biblical Theology: Retrospect and Prospect,* ed. Scott Hafemann (Downers Grove: IVP, 2002), p. 16.

3. Patrick D. Miller, "Theology from Below: The Theological Interpretation of Scripture," in *Reconsidering the Boundaries between Theological Disciplines (Zur Neubestimmung der Grenzen zwischen den theologischen Disziplinen),* ed. Michael Welker and Friedrich Schweitzer, Theology, Research, and Science 8 (Münster: Lit Verlag, 2005), p. 3.

4. John Sandys-Wunsch and Laurence Eldredge, "J. P. Gabler and the Distinction between Biblical and Dogmatic Theology: Translation, Commentary, and Discussion of His Originality," *Scottish Journal of Theology* 33 (1980): 133-58.

two theological disciplines within the academy. Such "correct distinction" was needed, according to Gabler, so that the Bible could be understood as a document with a message rooted in history before it was used for constructing normative and abstract theology for the church. Gabler, however, was not innovative in expressing this concern to distinguish between the theology of the Bible and that of the church.[5] Pietistic leaders like Philipp Jakob Spener in the century before Gabler's appearance had already outlined an agenda to distinguish between biblical and dogmatic theology in order to stimulate a biblically based godliness within the church by avoiding the theological controversies of their day. Interestingly, in the period before Gabler scholars like Johann Semler had called for a similar distinction but for a different reason, that is, in order that rationalist scholars might be freed from the constraints of creed in order to investigate Scripture. Unlike these earlier movements, however, Gabler saw an enduring role for systematic theology, but argued that biblical theology served as a foundation for dogmatics.

These two interpretive streams that gave rise to the delineation of biblical theology as an academic discipline separate from systematic theology can be discerned throughout the centuries after Gabler's address.[6] Some, rejecting the divine origins of the Scriptures, used this freedom from systematic theology to investigate the message of the Bible as history of religion, while others, embracing the Bible's divine origins, used this freedom to highlight the theological content of the Bible using its own idiom and categories. Most produced works that represented a combination of these two streams, but at times the discipline would be dominated by one or the other hermeneutical agenda. The late nineteenth and early twentieth centuries were dominated by the agenda of history of religion. However, in the second half of the twentieth century there was a resurgence of biblical theology as a discipline, with a variety of approaches represented among the many books produced in this period. In general one can see how the reigning hermeneutical approach of a particular decade influenced the various approaches to biblical theology, ranging from traditio-historical to literary to ideological approaches.

In general the history of the academic discipline of biblical theology has been one driven by an agenda to bring greater focus to the meaning of the

5. See further Christine Helmer, "Biblical Theology: Reality, Interpretation, and Interdisciplinarity," in *Biblical Interpretation: History, Context, and Reality*, ed. Christine Helmer and Taylor G. Petrey (Atlanta: Society of Biblical Literature, 2005), pp. 1-16.

6. On this history see Hasel, *Old Testament Theology: Basic Issues;* Helmer, "Reality, Interpretation," pp. 1-16; Elmer Martens, "Old Testament Theology since Walter Kaiser," *JETS* 50 (2007): 673-92.

biblical texts within their original contexts, without regard to the alignment of that meaning with creedal expressions of the Christian faith associated with systematic theology. On the positive side this agenda has provided theological space for the biblical texts in general and the Old Testament in particular to speak in their own idiom without concern to force the meaning of these texts into a particular individual's or community's confessional theological grid. There is great opportunity for the biblical text to reassert its authority within ecclesial communities if this discipline takes this as its ultimate goal. On the negative side, however, this agenda has often led to an abandonment of the theological enterprise, resisting any contribution to creedal development and ethical formation. Furthermore, distinguishing biblical theology from systematics has led to an abandonment of creedal direction for understanding the character of the texts in view and often an embrace of an a-theological and at times anti-theological hermeneutic for reading Scripture. It is essential at this present juncture in history to bring biblical theology back into conversation with systematic theology.[7] These two disciplines should be practiced in dialogue, both functioning as foundational for the other. Biblical theology needs some measure of systematic theology to function,[8] but systematic theology must be based upon and constantly challenged by biblical theology.[9]

---

7. Christine Helmer speaks of biblical theology as "a bridge-building discipline" that "is wonderfully poised to address both the historical and the theological dimensions of biblical texts"; Christine Helmer, "Introduction: Multivalence in Biblical Theology," in *The Multivalence of Biblical Texts and Theological Meanings*, ed. Christine Helmer and Charlene T. Higbe (Atlanta: Society of Biblical Literature, 2006), p. 7. See further Ben C. Ollenburger, ed., *So Wide a Sea: Essays on Biblical and Systematic Theology* (Elkhart, IN: Institute of Mennonite Studies, 1991); D. A. Carson, "Systematic Theology and Biblical Theology," in *New Dictionary of Biblical Theology*, pp. 89-104; Kevin J. Vanhoozer, "Exegesis and Hermeneutics," in *New Dictionary of Biblical Theology*, pp. 52-64; Joel B. Green and Max Turner, *Between Two Horizons: Spanning New Testament Studies and Systematic Theology* (Grand Rapids: Eerdmans, 2000); Bartholomew et al., eds., *Out of Egypt*, especially the essays by Trevor Hart (pp. 341-51) and R. R. Reno (pp. 385-408); Welker and Schweitzer, eds., *Reconsidering the Boundaries between Theological Disciplines*.

8. See Graeme Goldsworthy, "'Thus Says the Lord': The Dogmatic Basis for Biblical Theology," in *God Who Is Rich in Mercy*, ed. Peter T. O'Brien and David Peterson (Homebush, Australia: Lancer Books, 1986), pp. 25-40.

9. See especially the interaction between Warfield and Vos, noted in Richard Lints, "Two Theologies or One? Warfield and Vos on the Nature of Theology," *WTJ* 54 (1992): 235-53.

Biblical Theology as a Scriptural Impulse

While the origin of the academic discipline of biblical theology is often traced to the eighteenth century, it is important to note that the ecclesial practice of biblical theology is evident in the church from its inception, inherited from its Jewish forebears.[10] One discovers within the Old Testament itself various reflective summaries and rehearsals of what lay at the core of Israelite theology. Of note in this regard are the theological rehearsals of the core of Yahweh's character of mercy and justice revealed in Exodus 34:6-7 (Num. 14:18; Joel 2:13; Jon. 4:2; Nah. 1:2-3; Pss. 86:5, 15; 103:8; 111:4; 112:4; 145:8; Neh. 1:5; 9:17, 19, 27, 28, 31; cf. Exod. 20:5-6; Deut. 5:9-10; 7:9-10; Jer. 32:18)[11] or the theological rehearsals of the story of Yahweh's acts of mercy and justice reflected in what Gerhard Von Rad called the "kleine geschichtliche Credo" ("short historical creed," Deut. 6:20-24; 26:5-9; Josh. 24:2b-13; 1 Sam. 12; Pss. 78, 105, 106, 135, 136; Neh. 9; Jer. 32; Ezek. 20).[12] A good portion of the book of Deuteronomy is presented as a rehearsal of the core narrative and legal traditions found in Exodus-Numbers. Zechariah 1:3 and 7:7-10 offer what is explicitly called a summary of the heart of the "earlier prophets," that is, "Return to me, and I will return to you." The book of Chronicles represents a re-presentation of the earlier inscripturated traditions in Genesis-2 Kings, both in terms of its genealogies and narratives. Besides such summaries and large-scale re-presentations there is significant evidence of inner-biblical allusion and exegesis within individual verses and passages, especially in later books in the Old Testament.

---

10. Because evidence of this ecclesial practice in the post-apostolic era has been documented in Craig Bartholomew's contribution at the outset of this volume, the present article will develop the biblical theological evidence for this impulse of biblical theology; cf. Bartholomew, "Biblical Theology and Biblical Interpretation," pp. 1-19.

11. See J. Scharbert, "Formgeschichte und Exegese von Ex 34,6f und Seiner Parallelen," *Biblica* 38 (1959): 130-50; R. C. Dentan, "The Literary Affinities of Exodus xxxiv 6f," *VT* 13 (1963): 34-51; Phyllis Trible, *God and the Rhetoric of Sexuality*, OBT 2 (Philadelphia: Fortress, 1978), pp. 1-5; Michael A. Fishbane, *Biblical Interpretation in Ancient Israel* (Oxford: Clarendon, 1985), pp. 335-50; Gordon R. Clark, *The Word Hesed in the Hebrew Bible*, JSOTSup 157 (Sheffield: JSOT, 1993), pp. 247-52.

12. See Gerhard von Rad, *Gesammelte Studien zum Alten Testament*, Theologische Bücherei 8 (Munich: Chr. Kaiser, 1958), pp. 9-86; Gerhard von Rad, *Old Testament Theology* (Edinburgh: Oliver and Boyd, 1962); Gerhard von Rad, *The Problem of the Hexateuch and Other Essays* (London: Oliver and Boyd, 1966), pp. 1-78; cf. G. E. Wright, *God Who Acts*, Studies in Biblical Theology 1/8 (London: SCM, 1952), pp. 11, 13.

This impulse toward theological reflection and summary, re-presentation, and inner-biblical allusion can be discerned as well within the New Testament. The theological rehearsal of Yahweh's character can be discerned at several points (e.g., John 1:14-18; 1 John 1:9; Rev. 19:11-12). So also the practice of theologically rehearsing the story of Yahweh's acts of mercy before and through Jesus continues in the New Testament witness (e.g., Acts 2:14-36; 3:12-26; 7:2-53; 13:16-41; Heb. 11–12; cf. Luke 24:45-47; Phil. 2:6-11; 1 Cor. 15:1-11; 1 Tim. 3:16). In the Gospels Jesus provides a theological summary of the heart of what he calls the Law and the Prophets (Matt. 7:12; 22:37-40), a reference to the Hebrew Scriptures. After his resurrection Luke tells us that Jesus was concerned to trace the revelation of himself throughout the Old Testament canon (Luke 24:27, 44). The witness of the early church found in the epistles follows this practice of Christ. This witness consists largely of theological reflection on key broader themes (for example, the theme of sin in Romans 3:9-20 or that of faith in Hebrews 11) and ubiquitous inner-biblical citation and allusion to earlier Old Testament passages.[13]

What we see, then, in the foundational canonical witness of the church is a consistent impulse towards summary, re-presentation, and inner-biblical allusion,[14] which represents reflection on the theology of the Bible in whole or in part and this is what can be identified as biblical theology.

A Hermeneutical Agenda for Biblical Theology: The Character of Old Testament Revelation

Since the impulse for biblical theology can be discerned in the Old and New Testaments it is helpful to look more carefully at the hermeneutical framework that underlies this impulse in the biblical witness. For Christian biblical theology that means giving attention to those New Testament texts which describe the character of revelation and which express a more global agenda

---

13. See G. K. Beale and D. A. Carson, *Commentary on the New Testament Use of the Old Testament* (Grand Rapids: Baker Academic, 2007).

14. See further the thoughtful voicing by Möller on the typical concern of biblical scholars that theological abstraction is by nature "alien to the biblical material" and even if so "inherently distorting and unsuitable"; Karl Möller, "The Nature and Genre of Biblical Theology," in *Out of Egypt*, p. 55. He is wise to challenge the second concern by noting that academic discourse itself is by nature "second-level discourse." My review here questions the first concern that somehow denies the biblical tradition the ability to engage in theological abstraction.

for reading the biblical witness. It will be seen that New Testament reflection on the character of this revelation is not foreign to the Old Testament, but rather an echo of the Old Testament's witness to its own character. These characteristics of Old Testament Scripture must impact the discipline of biblical theology.[15]

Communicative

First, it is clear that the New Testament teaches the communicative character of Old Testament revelation. The New Testament makes the claim that in the Old Testament God has successfully communicated himself to humanity, not only through the oral proclamations of his servants (e.g., Heb. 1:1-3; 2 Pet. 1:21), but also through the Scriptural witness formed from such proclamations (e.g., Acts 1:16). This echoes the witness of the Old Testament itself, which consistently portrays a God seeking to communicate with humanity, whether directly or through the agency of created figures (e.g., Exod. 20:1-18). That this communication was successful is obvious in the rehearsal of these words within the biblical text itself.

It is this communicative character of revelation that makes possible a biblical theology rather than merely a history of religion. The Scriptures represent God's successful communication of his character and ways. Such a claim also runs counter to the prevailing notions of a postfoundational age in which the efficacy of all communication is called into question. But attempts to thwart the communicative efficacy of the biblical witness run against the grain of the text. This claim that God speaks successfully through Scripture encourages us to approach Scripture to hear God's address. It is not merely the record of human attempts at religion, but a theological witness of divine origin.

Incarnational

Second, the New Testament teaches the incarnational character of revelation, that is, that divine revelation is communicated through created

---

15. For a superb review of the key hermeneutical issues related to developing biblical theological method see John Sailhamer, *An Introduction to Old Testament Theology: A Canonical Approach* (Grand Rapids: Zondervan, 1995).

means.[16] This is seen in the foundational oral proclamations of the prophets through whom God spoke "at many times and in various ways" (Heb. 1:1). This revelation was delivered at times through a fully human personality embedded within a particular era of history, as Acts 1:16 reminds us, "long ago through the mouth of David." Although "carried along by the Holy Spirit," it was still "people" who "spoke from God" (2 Pet. 1:20-21). Even when communicated directly from God's mouth, this revelation was delivered by necessity through human language that is historically conditioned. That this is foundational for the character of Scripture is made clear in 2 Timothy 3:15-16, which reveals that the "human writings" (Scripture) are "God-breathed" and "holy." Such a view of revelation is not unique to the New Testament. The Torah and Latter Prophets in particular emphasize the way in which Divine Words are delivered in human language and most often through human figures. Although these words are contained in a physical book in human language, the people in Ezra's day respond to this book with reverence akin to that reserved for God himself (Neh. 8).

The incarnational nature of revelation reminds us that, although divine in origin and character, Old Testament revelation is at the same time fully human in its communicative form. This revelation is not presented in timeless form, but rather is particularized to unique historical situations in languages and forms understandable to that audience. It is the divine dimension that infuses unity and timelessness into this theological witness, and yet the human dimension that simultaneously infuses it with diversity and timeboundedness. Attention, then, must be given to both these dimensions since they are inextricably linked. This will mean attention to the historical

---

16. See, for example, Goldsworthy, "Relationship," pp. 82-83; Peter Enns, *Inspiration and Incarnation: Evangelicals and the Problem of the Old Testament* (Grand Rapids: Baker Academic, 2005); Kenton L. Sparks, *God's Word in Human Words: An Evangelical Appropriation of Critical Biblical Scholarship* (Grand Rapids: Baker Academic, 2008). Some have expressed concerns over utilizing incarnation as a model for Scripture, especially because debates over incarnation were not originally focused on Scripture but rather on the nature of Christ, and links to incarnation can easily lead to bibliolatry (see the superb review in Stephen B. Chapman, "Reclaiming Inspiration for the Bible," in *Canon and Biblical Interpretation,* ed. Craig G. Bartholomew, Scott Hahn, Robin Parry, Christopher Seitz, and Al Wolters, SAHS 7 [Grand Rapids: Zondervan, 2006], pp. 190-93). However, one cannot deny a close relationship between revelation and incarnation in the New Testament witness (see Heb. 1:1-3); and, as is argued here, one cannot deny the simultaneous divine-human character of the Scriptures. The link to incarnation is not necessarily the first step towards bibliolatry any more than links between the relational character of the Trinity and the character of the church or the image of God in humanity are a necessary step toward deification of the church or humans.

and literary aspects of texts without losing sight of their theological and spiritual aspects.

One of the greatest challenges in the modern development of the discipline of biblical theology has been the tension between whether the discipline is concerned with reflection on the shape of the theology of the Old Testament or delineation of the history of the religion depicted in the Old Testament text. The former is typically considered a category more closely associated with the belief that the Old Testament is a record of divine revelation, while the latter with the assumption that the Old Testament is a record of human religion.[17]

That these two categories need not be juxtaposed is seen in the explicit assertions in the New Testament that divine revelation is communicated through human means, that is, through human personalities (e.g., 2 Pet. 1:10; Heb. 1:1-3) and human language (e.g., 2 Tim. 3:14-17). While all forms of revelation found within the biblical canon are communicated through an inseparable and mysterious combination of divine origin and human agency, the expression of some forms is dominated more by the divine side of this combination with explicit claims of divine origin, while the expression of others by the human side with explicit claims of human origin.[18] For instance, the Psalms in the main constitute human speech to God, although at times one does hear God's direct voice. And yet early on this was considered a normative text (some would suggest Psalm 1 makes this clear),[19] that is, these human speeches were considered as revelatory and normative, prompted by God to shape faith and reveal God. Furthermore, prophecy in the main constitutes divine speech to humanity, although it is clear that this divine speech is being delivered through human characters who speak "about" Yahweh and even challenge this God at times. However, all such text is recognized as normative. For those reflecting on the character of these various forms of revelation, there is no difference in authority.

17. See such juxtaposition in Willem VanGemeren, *Interpreting the Prophetic Word* (Grand Rapids: Zondervan, 1996), pp. 19-27; also Bruce K. Waltke and Charles Yu, *An Old Testament Theology: A Canonical and Thematic Approach* (Grand Rapids: Zondervan, 2006), pp. 30, 64-65, although I understand that much depends on the definition of "religion" (cf. 1 Tim. 5:4; James 1:26-27).

18. On this see further John Goldingay, *Theological Diversity and the Authority of the Old Testament* (Grand Rapids: Eerdmans, 1987).

19. See J. Clinton McCann Jr., *A Theological Introduction to the Book of Psalms: The Psalms as Torah* (Nashville: Abingdon, 1993); cf. Brevard S. Childs, *Introduction to the Old Testament as Scripture* (Philadelphia: Fortress, 1979), pp. 513-14.

All forms are considered Scripture, authoritative for the development of Christian doctrine.

In this way one can truly speak of the Old Testament as simultaneously a depiction of the "faith of Israel" and the "revelation of God." It is both religion (if understood as a record of human interaction with God) and revelation (a record of divine interaction with humanity). At all times revelation takes the form of human religious interaction, whether that is in the prophets' records of their revelatory experiences or the psalmists' rehearsals of the cry of their souls. The biblical witness, and so by extension biblical theology, has both anthropological and theological dimensions that are inseparable, and in that way it is incarnational.

Inscripturated

Thirdly, the New Testament teaches the inscripturated character of revelation, that is, that while the oral proclamations of those ancient servants who delivered God's word to generations long past is considered divine revelation, such revelation is now preserved in the inscripturated witness. Even 2 Peter 1:20-21, which focuses on how men and women moved by the Holy Spirit spoke orally within their generation, identifies such proclamations as "prophecy *of Scripture*," that is, prioritizing its inscripturated form (cf. Rom. 16:26). It is this inscripturated form that, according to 2 Timothy 3:15-16, is "God-breathed" and "holy" and, according to Romans 15:4, is authoritative to instruct. For this reason we find throughout the New Testament nearly monotonous employment of the phrase "it is written" and the term "Scripture(s)" to introduce uses of the Old Testament as authoritative witness for theological reflection. This fixation with the text is reflected in Christ's statement that "not one jot or tittle" would disappear from the Law (Matt. 5:18). At times Scripture takes on a life of its own as it functions as an active subject that, Paul tells us, foresaw God's future actions (e.g., Gal. 3:8).

Such focus on the inscripturated character of Old Testament revelation is not restricted to the New Testament. It is evident throughout the Torah (Exod. 31:18; 34:28-29; 40:20; Lev. 26:46; 27:34; Num. 36:13; Deut. 31:9). The Former Prophets emphasize the "Book of the Law" both at the outset in Joshua's commission (Josh. 1:8) and near its close in the Josianic renewal of 2 Kings 22. The Latter Prophets allude to the written character of their prophetic witness at several points: Isaiah 8:1-2, 16; Jeremiah 36:1-32; 51:59-64; Ezekiel 2:9–3:3; 43:10-11; Nahum 1:1. The Writings witness to this at several points, especially Psalms (Pss. 1, 19, 119) and Nehemiah 8–9, which highlight the Torah as authoritative inscripturated tradition, and Daniel 9:2, which highlights the importance of the Prophets as authoritative inscripturated tradition (cf. Dan. 7:1).

The inscripturated nature of revelation reminds the biblical theologian that the source of biblical theological reflection is first and foremost the biblical text in its canonical form.[20] It is not the experiences or traditions that underlie the biblical text, but rather the biblical text itself, that is the defined corpus in view.[21]

A biblical theological reading of the Old Testament means primarily a reading of the text within the broader canonical witness of that text. It seeks to discern the ways in which an individual text or biblical book contributes to and participates within the broader theological witness of the Bible. One may understand this broader witness in various ways, but for it to be truly a "biblical" theological reading it must focus on the witness of the canonical text, that is, that final literary form of books which now constitute an authoritative collection.[22] This, then, lays bare a key presupposition for biblical theological study of the Old Testament: the form of the text in view as well as the context for reading this text is one identified as canonical within a community of faith. Christian communities have identified the form and extent of this text in a variety of ways, but it is this text that is in view in biblical theology.

What this means is that pre-canonical forms or collections of the text are not the primary context in view in biblical theology, although they may provide insights into our understanding of that final form. For instance, an understanding of the theology of the Deuteronomic or Priestly traditions, often seen as underlying the Torah or Former Prophets, may be helpful for delineating the meaning of particular words or concepts, but ultimately biblical theology is focused on the meaning of the text in its present form. Thus, while some may use the identification of tradition streams within a text as a point of departure for insights into those traditions, the direction is reversed

---

20. See Brevard S. Childs, *Old Testament Theology in a Canonical Context* (Philadelphia: Fortress, 1985), p. 6.

21. See further Hafemann, "Retrospect," p. 20.

22. On the implications of the canonical shape of the biblical text for biblical theology see Chapter 7 by Stephen Dempster in the present volume, as well as Craig G. Bartholomew et al., eds., *Canon and Biblical Interpretation;* and Mark J. Boda, *A Severe Mercy: Sin and Its Remedy in the Old Testament,* Siphrut: Literature and Theology of the Hebrew Scriptures 1 (Winona Lake, IN: Eisenbrauns, 2009).

in biblical theology: insights from those tradition streams may be helpful for interpreting the text in its present shape. So also non-canonical forms or collections of the text are not the primary focus in a biblical theological reading of the text. In the end the theology in view is that articulated by texts within the canon under consideration. This, however, does not render non-canonical texts irrelevant for the interpretation of the text in its present shape. For those embracing what is often called the Protestant canon (excluding the Apocrypha), the broader ancient Near Eastern, Mediterranean, and Second Temple Jewish literary traditions may provide insights into the meaning of the biblical text, but it is the interpretation of the biblical text that drives the agenda of biblical theology.

Authoritative

Fourthly, the New Testament teaches the authoritative character of this written revelation. The inscripturated revelation is normative for the believer and not to be resisted. It is for this reason that Timothy was to give close attention to the Scriptures (2 Tim. 3:14-17), that Paul could declare that he believes all that agrees with the Law and is written in the Prophets (Acts 24:14), and that Jesus prohibited the breaking of the Law's demands (Matt. 5:17-20). That the Old Testament was treated as normative for the early church is seen in the constant appeals to the Old Testament for the establishment of foundational doctrine (e.g., Rom. 3:9-18).

This focus on the authoritative character of written revelation is seen also in the Old Testament itself. Passages like 2 Kings 22 reveal how the Book of the Torah was considered authoritative, prompting a penitential response and adherence to its demands communicated in written form. It is the Book of the Law that brackets the book of Joshua and is connected with the demand for obedience to Yahweh (Josh. 1:8; 24:25-26). It is the Book of the Law raised high in Nehemiah 8 that prompts the submissive and penitential responses of the people and the reading of the Book of the Law that precedes the penitential response of the community in Nehemiah 9 (see vv. 3-4).

The authoritative nature of revelation reminds biblical theologians that the agenda of biblical theology is not merely descriptive, that is, to merely describe what the Bible states, but is also prescriptive, that is, to respond to the Scriptures as a normative voice that speaks to interpreters, making demands upon them even as they articulate its claims. The Bible "draws its readers into transformative discourse" and challenges their "willingness . . .

to inhabit Scripture's own story."[23] As a result biblical theology "aims at Christian formation rather than historical reconstruction."[24] Biblical theology is not just a foundation for systematic theology or ethics, but functions as a key component of these two normative disciplines. Furthermore, those engaged in biblical theology are, because of the authoritative character of the canon they study, involved in these other theological exercises.

Cumulative and Progressive

Fifthly, the New Testament teaches the cumulative and progressive character of revelation.[25] After highlighting the revelation of God through the prophets "long ago," Hebrews 1:1-3 is careful to note that "in these last days" revelation has now come "by a Son." 2 Peter 1:19-21 speaks of "the prophetic message more fully confirmed." Revelation must not be treated all on the same level, but rather as that which accumulates and progresses in significance as history unfolds. Such a view of revelation is evident in the Old Testament witness itself as Yahweh transcends his self-revelation to the patriarchs of Israel in Genesis, by revealing himself in heightened ways through the Exodus and Sinai accounts (Exod. 6:2-8; cf. 34:6-7).

The cumulative and progressive character of revelation helps the biblical theologian arrange and prioritize the variety and diversity found within the biblical witness. It helps the biblical theologian deal with the diversity within the biblical witness, not only in terms of the historico-cultural particularity of the witness (see above on the incarnational nature), but also in terms of its historico-theological particularity. What this highlights is the need for sensitivity to the accumulation and progression of God's redemptive and revelatory acts throughout history. Redemption was not fully accomplished, nor was revelation fully disclosed, in a single moment in history. Rather, there were a progressive accomplishment of redemption and a

23. Joel Green, "Scripture and Theology: Uniting the Two So Long Divided," in *Between Two Horizons*, p. 42.

24. Robert W. Wall, "Canonical Context and Canonical Conversations," in *Between Two Horizons*, p. 175.

25. The word "cumulative" is a reminder of the fact that in the New Testament witness the progressive character of later phases of the biblical witness did not eliminate the enduring role of earlier phases of this witness, with thanks to Elmer Martens, "Reaching for a Biblical Theology of the Whole Bible," in *Reclaiming the Old Testament: Essays in Honour of Waldemar Janzen*, ed. Gordon Zerbe (Winnipeg: CMBC Publications, 2001), pp. 93-95.

progressive unfolding of revelation in history and this explains some of the diversity within the Bible's theological witness.

The Cohesion of the Biblical Witness:
Inner-Biblical Use of Scripture

This hermeneutical agenda for biblical theology, which arises from the self-witness of Scripture, explains the ubiquitous interconnections between the various parts of the canon. The Old Testament canon itself displays inner cohesion through the regular use of quotations, allusions, and echoes of earlier Old Testament passages. This trend, which is observable in the Old Testament, only increases in the New Testament.[26] It is important to take a closer look at this phenomenon of inner-biblical connectivity by looking at the ways the New Testament writers used the Old Testament and the ways Old Testament writers used other parts of the Old Testament.[27] The biblical witness itself lays the foundation hermeneutically for Christian biblical theologians to follow as they seek to read the Old Testament as Christian Scripture.[28]

If one were to speak of the various connections between the Old and New Testaments using the image of roads built between two distant locations, one could think of the different levels in the construction of a road, the different routes each road may take to its destination, and the place at which each road intersects on its way to the New Testament and the life of the church.

26. See further Mark J. Boda, *Haggai/Zechariah*, NIVAC (Grand Rapids: Zondervan, 2004), pp. 48-65; Mark J. Boda, *After God's Own Heart: The Gospel According to David* (Phillipsburg, NJ: Presbyterian and Reformed, 2007).

27. The realization that New Testament approaches to appropriating the Old Testament can also be discerned in the Old Testament itself calls into question the dismissal of John Goldingay, *Old Testament Theology*, vol. 1: *Israel's Gospel* (Downers Grove: IVP, 2003), pp. 25-27, regarding these New Testament approaches.

28. In his earlier work, Childs proposed doing biblical theology based on the New Testament use of the Old Testament, but later abandoned this. Compare Brevard S. Childs, *Biblical Theology in Crisis* (Philadelphia: Westminster Press, 1970), with Brevard S. Childs, *Biblical Theology of the Old and New Testaments: Theological Reflection on the Christian Bible* (Minneapolis: Fortress Press, 1993), p. 76. The present chapter advocates a recovery of Childs's original project, although carefully nuanced to include a greater variety of ways in which the biblical witness is interlinked (see below, Level and Routes) and without restriction to the explicit links made in the biblical witness (see below, Conclusion).

Level

First, using the imagery of the building of roads (connections) between the Old and New Testaments, instances of the New Testament use of the Old Testament can be discerned at several levels in the structure of the road. Some connections are obvious on the road's surface, painted on the pavement (explicit), while others are hidden below the surface in the deeper substructure of the road (implicit). The most explicit are those cases where there is an overt claim of connection with an Old Testament expectation, event or figure (e.g., Heb. 12:15-17: Esau) or there is a formal citation of an Old Testament passage in the New Testament (e.g., Acts 2:16-21: Joel 3:1-5 [Engl. 2:28-32]). The most implicit are those that assume a foundational Old Testament theological theme (e.g., James 3: the tongue) or narrative structure (Matt. 11:14: Elijah tradition). Between these two extremes lie a range of levels of connection through allusions employing common vocabulary and imagery.[29] These various levels are not restricted to the New Testament use of the Old Testament, but are also displayed in the reuse of the Old Testament within the Old Testament itself.[30] One can find everything from overt connections (e.g., Hos. 11:1-4) and formal citations (e.g., Lev. 23:42 in Neh. 8:14) to implicit development of themes (e.g., Deuteronomic themes in Joshua–2 Kings) and narrative structures (e.g., Exod. 25–40 in 2 Chron. 1–10),[31] and all levels in between.

Routes

Second, that the New Testament speakers and writers connect their message to the Old Testament does not mean that each part of the Old Testament is related in an identical way to the New Testament. Some elements

---

29. One needs to be sensitive to the diversity of ways in which biblical texts reference other biblical texts, since, for example, as Kaiser notes, "the book of Revelation, which probably contains more Old Testament imagery and phrases than any other New Testament writing . . . does not contain a single formal quotation from the Old Testament!"; Walter C. Kaiser, *The Uses of the Old Testament in the New* (Chicago: Moody, 1985), p. 3.

30. See Fishbane, *Biblical Interpretation*.

31. See Mark J. Boda, "Legitimizing the Temple: The Chronicler's Temple Building Account," in *From the Foundations to the Crenellations: Essays on Temple Building in the Ancient Near East and Hebrew Bible*, ed. Mark J. Boda and Jamie R. Novotny, Alter Orient und Altes Testament 366 (Münster: Ugarit-Verlag, 2010), pp. 303-18.

in the Old Testament are related nearly directly to the New Testament while others are transformed significantly. Returning to the analogy of roads connecting two locations, these ways of relating the message of the Old Testament to the New Testament could be described as the variety of routes through which Christ and his early followers connected the witness of the Old Testament with that of the New Testament.[32] Some of these routes are very direct and close (continuity) while others are very indirect and distant (discontinuity).

The Old Testament Initiates what the New Testament Continues

The closest and most direct "route" between the Old and New Testaments is the one in which the Old Testament initiates what the New Testament continues. This route represents the greatest continuity between the testaments. In Matthew 22:36-40 Jesus cites Deuteronomy 6:5 and Leviticus 19:18 and identifies them as the two greatest commandments on which hang the Law and the Prophets, that is, loving the Lord your God with all your heart, soul, and mind and loving your neighbor as yourself. Paul follows Jesus in citing Leviticus 19:18 in Romans 13:8-10 as the foundation for Christian ethics. For Jesus and Paul these Old Testament commandments had enduring relevance for the Christian community. Admittedly, there remains some element of discontinuity since the fulfillment of this is only possible through the work of Christ and the Spirit (see below), but here the content of the law is identical, even though the process by which it is fulfilled has shifted (precisely as indicated in Jer. 31:31-34; Ezek. 36:26-27; cf. 2 Cor. 3:1-18; Heb. 8:7-12). Paul follows this route in Romans 12:20 as he draws on Deuteronomy 32:35 and Proverbs 25:21-22 to teach the church how to treat one's enemy. So also 1 Peter 2:9-10 applies titles connected to Israel of old (Exod. 19:5-6; Hos. 1:8-9) to the church today in order to teach them how to walk within an often hostile world. At times the New Testament draws on examples from the Old Testament both positive (James 5:11, 17-18: Job, Elijah) and negative (1 Cor. 10:6-14: Israel in the wilderness) in order to encourage positive and discourage negative behavior. The emphasis in all these instances is on continuity.

32. On such a multiplex approach see Hasel, *Old Testament Theology: Basic Issues,* p. 183; David L. Baker, *Two Testaments, One Bible: A Study of the Theological Relationship between the Old and New Testaments,* rev. ed. (Leicester: Apollos, 1991); cf. overview in Nicholas Perrin, "Dialogic Conceptions of Language and the Problem of Biblical Unity," in *Biblical Theology: Retrospect and Prospect,* pp. 212-14. I am unconvinced by James D. G. Dunn, "The Problem of 'Biblical Theology,'" in *Out of Egypt,* p. 182, that these are "superimposed paradigms."

This route between Old and New Testaments can also be discerned in the Old Testament itself. For example, one can see how legislation initiated in the Torah is carried on throughout the Old Testament witness, whether it is shaping the renewal under Josiah (see close connections between Deuteronomy and 2 Kings 22–23) or the restoration in Ezra-Nehemiah (see references to the Torah in Ezra 3:2; 6:18; 7:6; Neh. 1:7, 8; 8:1, 14; 9:14; 10:29; 13:1).[33]

The Old Testament Falls Short of the New Testament, Which Surpasses It

The longest and most indirect "route" between the Old and New Testament is the one in which the Old Testament falls short of the New Testament, which surpasses it. This route represents the greatest discontinuity between the testaments. Passages that reflect this route include Galatians 3:23-25, which speaks of the function of the law to lead us to Christ, or Romans 10:5, which cites Leviticus 18:5 in order to describe a righteousness that comes through the law, rather than through faith.[34] The New Testament makes much of the "new covenant" promises of Jeremiah, which spoke of the divine work of writing the law on the hearts of believers. The difference between old and new covenants was not the content of ethics, but rather the mode by which this ethic would be realized. This "route" may also be discerned in Christ's statements in Matthew 5:21-22, where he first cites Exodus 20:13, "Do not murder," and then challenges his followers not to disregard this law, but to understand its spirit and eschew even anger and hatred toward one's brother or sister. This helps us understand Christ's statement that he did not come to abolish the law but to fulfill it (Matt. 5:17-20). New Testament treatment of the ceremonial law (food, festal) is related to this category (e.g., Matt. 15:11; Mark 7:19; Acts 10:9-15; Rom. 14; Col. 2:16-17), but even so it is important to note that this was legitimate revelation that was operative for a time and thus does have theological significance as a revelatory witness as understood within its own phase of redemptive history (see Matt. 23:23; Luke 11:37-42).

The Old Testament itself also reflects this "route" between Old and New Testaments. The failure of the Sinai covenant and the prophetic agenda of

33. On this phenomenon in the Old Testament see Fishbane, *Biblical Interpretation*, pp. 91-277.

34. Of course, for Paul this does not eliminate the law as a source for the gospel, as the very next verses in Rom. 10:6-8 reveal, citing Deut. 30:14. Also Paul did not eliminate the law as a key source for Christian ethics, as is obvious from passages like Rom. 13:8-10; cf. Dunn, "Problem," p. 182.

repentance due to hardness of human hearts opens the way for the promise of a new covenantal approach (Jer. 31:31-34).[35] The failure of non-dynastic leadership in the book of Judges leads to the rise of royal leadership (Judges–Samuel).[36]

The Old Testament Promises That Which Is Fulfilled in the New Testament

Between these two extremes of routes between the Old and New Testaments are a variety of routes with relatively similar directness and length, representing a balance between continuity and discontinuity. Some passages reveal that the Old Testament promises someone or something that is fulfilled in the New Testament. This is one of the most common approaches taken by Christian interpreters. Thus, the Old Testament promised a messianic royal figure and that figure is identified as Jesus the Christ (e.g., Matt. 1:1; Rom. 1:2-3). The Old Testament promised a new covenant and Christ establishes this covenant through his redemptive acts (e.g., Luke 22:20; 1 Cor. 11:25; 2 Cor. 3:6; Heb. 8:8, 13; 9:15; 12:24). The Old Testament promised a restoration community that would return from the nations and receive of the Spirit, and this community is identified with those Jewish festal pilgrims at Pentecost in Acts 2.

These promises of old are not always treated as fulfilled in a single figure. Thus, while the Abrahamic hope of seed (Gen. 12:7; 13:15; 24:7) is fulfilled in Israel (Exodus, Joshua) in the Old Testament, it is linked by Paul ultimately to the appearance of Jesus functioning as Israel in Galatians 3:16, and this hope is subsequently linked to all those who "belong to Christ" in Galatians 3:29. The Davidic hope (2 Sam. 7:14) is considered fulfilled in Solomon (1 Kings 8:19) in the Old Testament and in the New Testament in Jesus Christ (Heb. 1:5), and yet in 2 Corinthians 6:18 the apostle Paul considers this Davidic hope fulfilled in the Christian community as a whole. The hope of an ultimate prophet (Deut. 34) is fulfilled in Christ (Acts 3:21-26) and yet the community that bears his name is identified as a prophetic community (Acts 2:17-21). While the Servant of Yahweh figure in Isaiah (Isa. 40–66) is linked to exilic Israel (e.g., Isa. 41:8-10; 42:18-19; 44:1-5), Jesus is identified as the fulfillment of this figure whose suffering would bring salvation for Israel (e.g., Matt. 8:17; Luke 22:37) and light to the Gentiles (e.g., Luke 2:32), and yet the early church

35. Cf. Boda, *A Severe Mercy*, pp. 246-52, 289-93, 355-56.
36. Cf. Mark J. Boda, "Judges," in *Expositor's Bible Commentary*, vol. 4, ed. David Garland and Tremper Longman III (Grand Rapids: Zondervan, forthcoming).

linked their suffering to that of this suffering servant (1 Pet. 2:21-25) and considered the role of bringing light to the Gentiles their own (Acts 13:46-48).

This "route" between Old and New Testaments is seen in the Old Testament itself, as already noted in relation to the hoped-for descendant(s) of Abraham and David above, as well as in Jeremiah's promised royal ṣemaḥ figure (traditionally, "branch," Jer. 23:5-7; 33:14-18) is fulfilled in Zerubbabel (Zech. 3; 6:9-15).[37]

The Old Testament Is Reactualized in the New Testament in Order to Complete It

Other passages reveal that the Old Testament is reactualized in the New Testament in order to complete it. Falling under this category is that approach referred to as typology, which "seeks to discover a correspondence between people and events of the past and of the future or present."[38] Typological connections may exist between persons (Adam), institutions (sacrifices), offices (priesthood), events (exodus), actions (lifting up the bronze serpent), and things (tabernacle).[39] Thus, for example, the Gospel of John creates a close link between Jesus Christ and the tabernacle/temple in the Old Testament. John 1:14 speaks of the Word "tabernacling" among humanity and Jesus links his own body to the "temple" (2:19-22). What this reveals is that, through the incarnation, the manifest presence of God that filled the tabernacle/temple of old once again was made manifest on earth. Later in the Gospel of John, the lifting up of Christ on the cross is connected to the lifting up of the bronze serpent in the wilderness in order to save the rebellious nation from death (John 3:14-15). Here the focus is not only on the action of lifting up, but on the common call to faith in Yahweh's provision for salvation.

It is important to distinguish between typological exegesis and allegory. The key difference is that in typology the significance of the elements in the Old Testament person, institution, office, event, action, thing is derived from the function of those elements within their original context and phase of re-

37. Mark J. Boda, "Oil, Crowns and Thrones: Prophet, Priest and King in Zechariah 1:7–6:15," in *Perspectives on Hebrew Scriptures,* ed. Ehud ben Zvi (Piscataway, NJ: Gorgias Press, 2006), pp. 379-404.

38. David S. Dockery, "Typological Exegesis: Moving beyond Abuse and Neglect," in *Reclaiming the Prophetic Mantle: Preaching the Old Testament Faithfully,* ed. George L. Klein (Nashville: Broadman, 1992), p. 166. Possibly the term "trajectory" is better than "typology"; cf. Steve Motyer, "Two Testaments, One Biblical Theology," in *Between Two Horizons,* p. 159.

39. See Jack Weir, "Analogous Fulfillment," *Perspectives in Religious Studies* 9 (1982): 68.

demptive history.[40] Thus, typological exegesis does not justify linking, for instance, anything red within a passage to the blood of Christ, or any wood within a passage to the cross of Christ. However, if that red or wood element functions in a similar way to the blood or cross of Christ it may be legitimate in typological exegesis.

What is happening in typology is that the Old Testament is being relived in the New Testament. There are instances where the mission of figures in the Old Testament is brought to completion by the mission of New Testament figures. This explains the connection between Jesus and Israel using Hosea 11 in Matthew 2:13-15. Hosea 11 does not promise a future figure, but rather traces God's past work for Israel. For the gospel writer Jesus' journey during his infancy into and out of Egypt represents a reliving of the experience of Israel. In contrast to Israel, however, Jesus would fully realize all of Yahweh's hopes for Israel. This category may make sense of many passages in the New Testament that identify in Christ a fulfillment of a hope that appears to have been fulfilled already in the Old Testament. For instance, while the Emmanuel prophecy in Isaiah 7–8 appears to be linked to an event in Isaiah's own generation, the Gospel of Matthew links this prophecy to the birth of Jesus. One may understand this as a reliving of an Old Testament hope to bring it to a new level.[41] It is also important not to collapse all the significance of what are often seen as "types" into one typological connection nor to restrict one to its function only as a type. What this means is that while the tabernacle is clearly seen as a type of Christ, it also has theological significance beyond the specific connections to Jesus. Thus the sacrificial system is a type of Christ (Heb. 9:11-15), but also has theological significance as to its

---

40. Edmund P. Clowney, "Preaching Christ from All the Scriptures," in *The Preacher and Preaching: Reviving the Art in the Twentieth Century,* ed. Samuel T. Logan (Phillipsburg, NJ: Presbyterian and Reformed, 1986), pp. 163-91, wisely identifies two key steps in typological analysis. The first step is "to relate the text to its immediate theological horizon," the second, "to relate the event of the text, by way of its proper interpretation in its own period, to the whole structure of redemptive history; and in that way to us upon whom the ends of the earth have come." Furthermore, he stresses "that this second step is valid and fruitful only when it does come second. All manner of arbitrariness and irresponsibility enter in when we seek to make a direct and practical reference to ourselves without considering the passage in its own biblical and theological setting."

41. See Rikki E. Watts, "Emmanuel: Virgin Birth Proof Text or Programmatic Warning of Things to Come (Isa 7:14 in Matt 1:23)?" in *From Prophecy to Testament: The Function of the Old Testament in the New,* ed. Craig A. Evans (Peabody, MA: Hendrickson, 2004), p. 113, who in dealing with Isa. 7:14 in Matt. 1:23 writes: "'fulfillment' seems best understood in paradigmatic terms: as Yahweh had acted in the past, so he would act again."

function within its own phase of redemptive history, let alone for worship within the New Testament era (see Heb. 13:15-16).

This "route" between Old and New Testaments can be seen in the Old Testament,[42] for instance, as the Exodus motif reappears in texts like Isaiah 40 and Ezra 1,[43] and as the tabernacle building account of Exodus 25–40 functions in relationship to the temple account in Chronicles.[44] It is also seen in the "reliving" of the Saul traditions from Samuel in the book of Esther as Mordecai redeems the Saulide family and shows how this preserves the exilic community,[45] or the "reliving" of the Moab/Judah traditions in the book of Ruth as Ruth and Boaz redeem their two family lines and show how they preserve and contribute to the royal line.[46]

The Old Testament Participates in the
New Testament by Progressing the Redemptive Story

Another closely related route is seen in those instances where the Old Testament participates in the New Testament by progressing the redemptive story.[47] Several passages in the New Testament remind the Christian community that their experience is inextricably linked with Old Testament figures. 1 Peter 1:10-12 declares that their actions in the past "served" the New Testament community and Hebrews 11:39-40 that only together with us are they made "perfect." Hebrews 12 presents Christ as author and perfecter of faith,

42. On typology (figural representation) in the Old Testament see Fishbane, *Biblical Interpretation*, pp. 350-79; Baker, *Two Testaments*, p. 181; M. Jay Wells, "Figural Representation and Canonical Unity," in *Biblical Theology: Retrospect and Prospect*, pp. 111-25.

43. For Isaiah, see Rikki E. Watts, *Isaiah's New Exodus and Mark*, WUNT (Tübingen: Mohr Siebeck, 1997), and for Ezra, see Mark A. Throntveit, *Ezra-Nehemiah*, Interpretation (Louisville: John Knox, 1992), pp. 15-18.

44. See Raymond B. Dillard, *2 Chronicles*, WBC 15 (Waco: Word, 1987), p. 4; Boda, "Legitimizing the Temple," pp. 303-18.

45. Elliott S. Horowitz, *Reckless Rites: Purim and the Legacy of Jewish Violence*, Jews, Christians, and Muslims from the Ancient to the Modern World (Princeton: Princeton University Press, 2006), p. 69; Christopher Nihan, "Saul among the Prophets (1 Sam. 10:10-12 and 19:18-24): The Reworking of Saul's Figure in the Context of the Debate on 'Charismatic Prophecy' in the Persian Era," in *Saul in Story and Tradition*, ed. Carl S. Ehrlich and Marsha C. White, FAT 47 (Tübingen: Mohr Siebeck, 2006), p. 114, n. 115.

46. Harold Fisch, "Ruth and the Structure of Covenant History," *VT* 32 (1982): 425-37.

47. For a recent articulation of the redemptive story as biblical theology see Craig G. Bartholomew and Mike W. Goheen, "Story and Biblical Theology," in *Out of Egypt*, pp. 144-71; Craig G. Bartholomew and Michael W. Goheen, *The Drama of Scripture: Finding Our Place in the Biblical Story* (Grand Rapids: Baker Academic, 2004).

upon whom Christians must look as that host of Old Testament saints watch from heaven expectant that the Christian community will bring to completion all the hopes of that community of old. This means that as Christians read the redemptive story in the Old Testament they are reading their own story and they are offered a vision for the kind of activity that is essential to bring the kingdom of God into reality in this world. This makes sense of the use of Job and Elijah as exemplars of perseverance and prayer in James 5:11, 17-18. This is also true for negative examples such as Paul's warning using the disobedience of Israel in the wilderness in 1 Corinthians 10:1-13.

This "route" between Old and New Testaments can also be discerned in the Old Testament, for example, in the rehearsal of the Torah narrative traditions in Psalms 78, 104-106, and 135-136, which show how these earlier texts progress or regress the redemptive story in which the psalmists participate.

Implications

These various routes for connecting the biblical witness reflect varying degrees of continuity and discontinuity and yet all contribute to the understanding that the Scriptures are interconnected. These routes provide well-worn interpretive paths for Christian interpreters to traverse as they continue to reflect on the endless connections between passages and sections of the canonical witness, whether that is between Old and New Testaments or various parts of the Old Testament.[48]

Intersection

While there is diversity in terms of the level (from explicit to implicit) at which connections between canonical sections are made and diversity in the route (from continuity to discontinuity) used for such connections, thirdly, there is unity in a single intersection through which these various roads must pass. While one should resist the temptation to collapse all biblical theology into a single "center," but rather remain open to the multiplex character of the theological expression of the biblical witness,[49]

---

48. See Martens, "Biblical Theology," pp. 90-93, for his wise observations on this issue.

49. On the problem of identifying a limited centre or creating simplistic and rigid systems when expressing biblical theology, see Hasel, *Old Testament Theology: Basic Issues*, pp. 139-71; Möller, "Nature and Genre," pp. 56-59.

there are certain core theological values that function as an intersection through which all thematic connections on their various routes do run as they move between canonical witnesses. As the revelatory character of the Bible is both divine and human, so also is the revelatory content of this intersection.

Focus on Creator and Redeemer

First of all, the Old and New Testament alike make clear that the Scriptures are focused on the revelation of the one true God, revealed as Yahweh in the Old Testament and then as the Triune God in the New Testament. Interpretation of these Scriptures must then be theocentric in focus.[50] Ultimately the biblical witness points to God, his character, and his ways in this world as both creator and redeemer.

Secondly, the New Testament makes clear that the Scriptures have as their goal the redemption of all creation through the Son, Jesus the Christ (2 Tim. 3:14-17; Luke 24). Interpretation of these Scriptures must then be Christotelic in character, that is, that which has been revealed is by definition part of a larger story that has the revelation of and redemption through the Son as its goal. As William Caven once wrote, "They were wont to say in Europe that every road led to Rome; and so we may affirm that every line of Scripture truth leads to Christ,"[51] or Willem VanGemeren, "Christian students of the Old Testament must pass by the cross of Jesus Christ on their return to the Old Testament, and as such they can never lose their identity as a Christian" since "the center of the Bible is the incarnate and glorified Christ, by whom all things will be renewed."[52] To read the Old Testament (and the New Testament) as if Jesus did not show up at the turn of the ages and change the course of history would not be Christian.

Thirdly, the New Testament makes clear that the realization of this Christotelic redemption of all creation, witness of which is articulated throughout the canon, is only possible through the agency of the Holy Spirit (Rom. 8; Eph. 3:14-21). Interpretation of these Scriptures must then be Pneumamorphic in character, that is, the realization of the redemption and

---

50. See Hasel, *Old Testament Theology: Basic Issues*, pp. 168-73, for God as the center of Old Testament theology and Christ as the center of New Testament theology.

51. William Caven, *Christ's Teaching Concerning the Last Things and Other Papers* (Toronto: The Westminster Co., 1908).

52. Willem VanGemeren, *The Progress of Redemption: From Creation to the New Jerusalem* (Grand Rapids: Zondervan, 1988), pp. 21, 27.

its associated ethic is by definition only possible through the active work of the Holy Spirit within individual, community, culture, and creation.[53] To read the Old Testament as if the Spirit were not active would not be Christian. For Christians the ethical demands of the Old Testament are not rendered irrelevant, but rather achievable through the indwelling Spirit who writes the law upon the heart.[54]

These Christotelic and Pneumamorphic values do not mean that one finds Jesus or the Spirit "behind every bush" in the Old Testament, somehow symbolically placed in every passage, for example, through an element with the color red (for Christ's blood) or a bird (for the Spirit's descent). But it does mean, since Jesus inaugurates the age that brings redemption and revelation to its climax, that any Old Testament redemptive act or revelatory insight will contribute toward and/or receive greater clarity in and through Jesus Christ and the Holy Spirit. After the Christian interpreter has discerned the theological significance of an Old Testament passage and/or an Old Testament theological theme, she or he must reflect on the significance the Christ-event makes for this passage and/or theme.

These Christotelic and Pneumamorphic values also do not mean that one should avoid reflection on the unique aspects of biblical revelation prior to the arrival of Christ and the Spirit in the New Testament.[55] This is an essential element in biblical theological reflection that takes seriously the diversity in Scripture.[56] But the Christian interpreter does understand that the ultimate significance of what has been called the "untamed witness of the

---

53. These Christotelic and Pneumamorphic aspects can be discerned in Paul's epistles in Romans and Ephesians. The ethical demands presented in the latter sections of these books (Rom. 12–15; Eph. 4–6) are clearly predicated on what is developed in the earlier sections of these books (see esp. the transitional verses in Rom. 12:1 and Eph. 4:1). These earlier sections are focused on the impact of the redemptive work of Christ, and yet both end with focused attention on the role of the Spirit as the one who empowers the people of God (see Rom. 8 and Eph. 3:14-21).

54. On the role of the Spirit in interpretation see Mark J. Boda, "Word and Spirit, Scribe and Prophet in Old Testament Hermeneutics," in *Spirit and Scripture: Examining a Pneumatic Hermeneutic,* ed. Kevin L. Spawn and Archie T. Wright (London: T&T Clark, 2011), pp. 25-45.

55. In this I am trying to take seriously the later concern of Childs that the discrete witness of the Old Testament has an enduring role and should not be reduced to New Testament use of the Old Testament; Childs, *Biblical Theology,* p. 76.

56. See Wall, "Canonical Context," p. 180, for a creative approach to diversity within the canon in which the tension between traditions "commends these same controversies to its current readers."

Old Testament"[57] is only realized in Christ and through the Spirit in the new age inaugurated by the gospel witness.

At the heart of this intersection, which provides cohesion to the biblical witness as a whole, is the assumption that all Scripture witnesses to one God who has revealed himself and enacted a plan of salvation in progressive ways throughout history.

Focus on Created and Redeemed

This central intersection, however, also contains a focus on that which God has created and redeemed. The biblical drama begins with the description of the origins of all creation through the actions of Yahweh God. From the outset of redemptive history it is clear that God is forming a community through whom he will bring redemption into the world. That community emerges from a single family identified with the descendants of Abraham who are called by the name Israel in the Old Testament and by the name of the son of Israel, Jesus Christ in the New Testament.[58] God enters into relationship with this community through a series of interrelated covenants that reach their climax in the new covenant enacted in and through Jesus Christ. God's desire is to transform all of culture and the cosmos through this covenant community redeemed by the redemptive act of Jesus the Christ and the agency of the Holy Spirit.[59] To read the Old Testament without these broader redemptive goals in mind would not be Christian.

At this intersection, which brings cohesion to the biblical witness as a

57. Walter Brueggemann, *Theology of the Old Testament: Testimony, Dispute, Advocacy* (Minneapolis: Fortress, 1997), p. 107.

58. On the relationship between the church and Israel see my *Haggai/Zechariah*, pp. 51-57. There is a legitimate discipline called Jewish Hebrew Bible theology and opportunity for enrichment in dialogue between this discipline and Christian biblical theology, even though the latter is by necessity different due to variation in canonical shape, worshiping communities, and theological convictions. See Benjamin D. Sommer, "Dialogical Biblical Theology: A Jewish Approach to Reading Scripture Theologically," in *Biblical Theology: Introducing the Conversation*, ed. Leo D. Perdue, Robert Morgan, and Bejamin D. Sommer (Nashville: Abingdon, 2009), pp. 1-53; Marvin A. Sweeney, *TANAK: A Theological and Critical Introduction to the Jewish Bible* (Minneapolis: Fortress, 2012).

59. The transformation of this community, culture, and creation involves what Scott W. Hahn, "Canon, Cult and Covenant," in *Canon and Biblical Interpretation*, p. 225, has identified as the "clear liturgical *trajectory* and *teleology.*" See also the missional matrix of biblical theology espoused by Christopher J. H. Wright, "Mission as a Matrix for Hermeneutics and Biblical Theology," in *Out of Egypt*, pp. 102-43; cf. Christopher J. H. Wright, *The Mission of God: Unlocking the Bible's Grand Narrative* (Downers Grove: IVP, 2006).

whole, is the assumption that all Scripture describes one story of redemption that moves from creation (Gen. 1–2) to new creation (Rev. 21–22) and is enacted through an enduring single redemptive community. This means that the interpretation of the Scriptures provides resources for living in fellowship within this redemptive community, but also for transforming the broader creational context in which this redemptive community lives. Biblical theology thus offers perspectives for realms such as politics, education, law, environment, immigration, and economics.[60]

Implications

This central intersection that brings cohesion to the biblical witness should inform Christians desirous to hear the Old Testament. Keeping in mind the convictions that God is the focus of the Old Testament, that Christ is the goal of the redemptive drama depicted throughout the Old Testament, and that the Spirit is the one who makes possible adherence to the demands of the Old Testament, one should listen to the theological witness of individual pericopae of Scripture in order to determine how the particular passage relates to the broader canonical development of a redeemed community and transformed culture and cosmos. It is important to remember that the Old Testament endures as a scriptural witness that makes demands upon our lives as it did upon the early church. That early church lived after Christ's death, resurrection, ascension, and giving of the Spirit and yet the New Testament makes clear that the Old Testament did not only testify to the coming of Christ and the Spirit, but also continued to inform the church theologically and make demands upon it ethically.

Conclusion

This consideration of inner-biblical connections within Scripture highlights some of the key methods by which biblical writers linked the various parts of the canon. This clearly authorizes biblical theological reflection and shapes Christian approaches to such reflection. It sensitizes the Christian in-

60. For example, see Oliver O'Donovan, *The Desire of the Nations: Rediscovering the Roots of Political Theology* (Cambridge: Cambridge University Press, 1996), on politics; Sandra L. Richter, "A Biblical Theology of Creation Care," *Asbury Journal* 62 (2007): 67-76, on environment; and M. Daniel Carroll R., *Christians at the Border: Immigration, the Church, and the Bible* (Grand Rapids: Baker Academic, 2008), on immigration.

terpreter to the diverse levels (from explicit to implicit) at which connections are made, the diverse routes (from continuity to discontinuity) through which connections are made, but the singular intersection (divine and human) through which all connections must pass.

This evidence provides examples that should inspire the Christian interpreter. One does not need to have a citation of the Old Testament in the New Testament for that Old Testament passage to have legitimacy as Scripture.[61] Nor does one have to limit one's reading of the Old Testament to only the nuance given to the reading in a New Testament citation of a particular Old Testament Scripture. The Old Testament is truly Christian Scripture and continues its role now in a new age inaugurated by the work of Christ and empowered by the work of the Spirit.

Hearing the Old Testament with Sensitivity to Biblical Theology

How, then, does one hear the Old Testament with sensitivity to its biblical theological character and context? It should shape our reading of the Old Testament whether that reading is focused on individual pericopae or broader canonical sections.

Disciplined Exegesis

First of all, this demands disciplined exegesis of individual texts within their historical and literary contexts in order to discern wisely their core theological themes. As Hebrews 1:1-3 makes clear, Old Testament revelation has been communicated at various times through diverse means and thus its theological witness cannot be divorced from the historical setting in which and literary forms through which this revelation has come. However, the focus of such exegesis should remain on the theological witness of the text, that is, what the text revealed at particular historical moments and through particular literary forms has to say about God, his character and ways in relation to his people and all of creation.

---

61. Christopher R. Seitz, *Word without End: The Old Testament as Abiding Theological Witness* (Grand Rapids: Eerdmans, 1998), pp. 213-28.

Biblical Theological Reflection

But, secondly, this particular theological witness needs to be placed within the broader trajectory of the theological witness of the canon as a whole. Important in this is to avoid suppressing the unique witness of particular passages and books while bringing this witness into dialogue with other voices within the canon. A dual focus is necessary as one seeks to connect the particular text to the broader canonical witness. Attention should be given to both continuity and discontinuity. Continuity refers to the ways the theological witness of the particular passage echoes the theological witness of other passages within the canon, while discontinuity refers to the ways the theological witness of particular passages contrasts the theological witness of other passages. In most cases one discerns points of continuity and discontinuity simultaneously.

One should begin by attending to continuity, reflecting on other passages in Scripture (both Old and New Testaments) that develop the theme(s) of a particular passage. Past approaches to biblical theology often focused too much on "word studies" for investigating theological themes in the biblical corpus. While words are very important for biblical theological analysis, it is important that one neither equate a single word or few words with a biblical theological theme nor consider these words apart from their broader linguistic context, in terms of the language as a whole as well as the passages in which they appear.[62] While words may be helpful for identifying passages relevant to a biblical theological analysis, so also are collocations and images.[63] Thus, for instance, while one may investigate the theme of repentance in the Psalms by searching for passages that employ the term שׁוּב (return), the contrastive image of the two ways in Psalm 1 subtly encourages repentance without employing explicit vocabulary. The key is to focus on passages that develop a particular theme both in positive and negative ways.

Focus, then, should shift to discontinuity, reflecting on how these many passages contrast the witness of one another, and on other passages that have themes contrasting with that of a particular passage. This entails being sensi-

---

62. On earlier excesses see James Barr, *The Semantics of Biblical Language* (Oxford: Oxford University Press, 1961); James Barr, "Semantics and Biblical Theology: A Contribution to the Discussion," in *Congress Volume: Uppsala 1971*, ed. Henrik Samuel Nyberg (Leiden: Brill, 1972); D. A. Carson, *Exegetical Fallacies*, 2nd ed. (Grand Rapids: Baker, 1996).

63. For an excellent example of Old Testament theological analysis with attention to images see John Goldingay, *Old Testament Theology: Israel's Faith* (Downers Grove: IVP, 2006).

tive to the socio-historical, redemptive-historical and revelatory-historical context of individual passages. As incarnational, the biblical witness is embedded within history, which means the particular socio-historical moment of a people who lived in vastly different places. For instance, references to servants and masters in different parts of the Old and New Testaments may not signify an identical social relation, and so one must remain sensitive to this dynamic. The Bible bears witness to a God who has acted in a variety of ways throughout redemptive history as he has unfolded the mystery that has reached its climax in Jesus Christ. Thus, how God acts at a certain phase of redemptive history may not be relevant to how he acts at a later phase. For example, the sacrificial system laid out in Leviticus 1–7 was relevant for the covenant community after Sinai, but not so for the Patriarchs described in the book of Genesis, the Israelites living in exile, or Christians after Christ's death. The Bible also bears witness to a God who has revealed himself in progressive ways throughout history.[64] Thus, as the biblical witness unfolds, readers are given more and more details about the character of this God and the constitution of the spiritual and physical world he has created. For example, while the New Testament offers much insight into the afterlife, such is not the case in the Old Testament. This is a feature of progressive revelation.

Example

How does this practically impact our reading of a text?[65] A close look at the rhetorical flow of 1 Samuel 16 reveals that the anointing of David by Samuel prompted a transfer of the Spirit of God from Saul (16:14a) to David (16:13) and a simultaneous divine commissioning of an injurious spirit to torment Saul (16:14b).[66] The association of the Spirit with royal anointing is not surprising in light of the earlier account of Saul's rise to power in 1 Samuel 10,

64. Sensitivity to the impact of the canonical shape to this revelatory history should also be taken into account; see further Chapter 7 by Stephen Dempster in the present volume and Boda, *A Severe Mercy*, pp. 31-39.

65. See further Boda, *After God's Own Heart*.

66. David M. Howard, "The Transfer of Power from Saul to David in 1 Sam. 16:13-14," *JETS* 32 (1989): 477: "The transfer in the immediate context is related to the empowerment by YHWH's Spirit, but it is symbolic of the transfer of political power as well." Later also: "It is not that the Spirit could not have maintained a special presence with both but rather that this appears to be the pattern of his activity in the Old Testament. Particularly in this section of 1 Samuel the presence of YHWH's Spirit symbolizes, among other things, his favor on his chosen king" (p. 480).

where Saul was endued with power by the Spirit of the LORD (10:6) that would enable him to carry out the great feat (ch. 11) that in turn would qualify him publicly as royal leader (cf. ch. 17).[67] A biblical theological perspective provides an important caution for Christian readers well aware of the role of the Spirit of God according to New Testament and Christian systematic theology.[68] Focusing on continuity rather than discontinuity, one may be tempted to see here a text relevant to the role of the Spirit within New Testament soteriology, a role that is articulated first in the Old Testament by the prophet Ezekiel who presaged the enlivening Spirit who would transform the inner motivations of the community of God to obey Yahweh. While one cannot deny a relationship between 1 Samuel 16 and New Testament soteriology, attention to the role of the Spirit within the textual and theological context of 1 Samuel 16 helps nuance this considerably.

The role of the Spirit here is one related to the execution of covenantal leadership for the people of God. The dominant feature of Old Testament pneumatology is that the Spirit of God appears to be restricted to covenantal leaders, whether leader (Deut. 34:9), elder (Num. 11:25), judge (Judg. 3:10), king (1 Sam. 10:6), or prophet (Zech. 7:12), but does not appear to indwell the community as a whole (Num. 11:29). The significance of the promises of the new age (last days) according to Joel 3:1-5 [Engl. 2:28-32] is that the Spirit would indwell the entire covenant community, something that had implications for the gifting of the New Testament community (1 Cor. 12–14), but also for its union with Christ (Rom. 8:9), regeneration (John 3:5), and transformation (Rom. 8:1-17). It is interesting that the move of the Spirit from Moses to the seventy elders in Numbers 11 presages the ultimate move of the Spirit from the covenant head Jesus to the church as a whole. As Jesus teaches in John 14:17, the Spirit who "lives with you" (that is, in Christ who

67. William J. Dumbrell, *Covenant and Creation: A Theology of the Old Testament Covenants* (Nashville: Thomas Nelson, 1984), p. 140.

68. See the superb treatment of Old Testament pneumatology in Christopher J. H. Wright, *Knowing the Holy Spirit through the Old Testament* (Downers Grove: IVP Academic, 2006), esp. pp. 87-120; cf. George T. Montague, *The Holy Spirit: Growth of a Biblical Tradition* (New York: Paulist Press, 1976); Leon J. Wood, *The Holy Spirit in the Old Testament* (Grand Rapids: Zondervan, 1976); Gordon D. Fee, *God's Empowering Presence: The Holy Spirit in the Letters of Paul* (Peabody, MA: Hendrickson, 1994), pp. 905-10; Wilf Hildebrandt, *An Old Testament Theology of the Spirit of God* (Peabody, MA: Hendrickson Publishers, 1995); F. A. Gosling, "An Unresolved Problem of Old Testament Theology," *The Expository Times* 106 (1995): 234-37. Also note the sensitivity to the Old Testament theology of the Spirit in the systematic theology of Stanley J. Grenz, *Theology for the Community of God* (Grand Rapids: Eerdmans, 2000), pp. 361-65.

had received the Spirit at his baptism) will soon be "in you" (cf. John 20:22). It is Jesus who asks of the Father and grants this community the Spirit who takes up residence within them.

This reality, however, is not yet true in the phase of redemptive history depicted in 1 Samuel 16. What is not in view here is the Spirit's role in regeneration. This passage is not then concerned with the fate of Saul in terms of salvation, but rather with his fate in terms of his role within salvation history. The Spirit's role in this era is focused on empowerment for covenantal service, in particular on dynamic endowment for royal leadership within the nation.[69] This role of the Spirit relates, first and foremost, to the function of Jesus Christ as the covenantal leader whose ministry was marked by the power of the Holy Spirit in word and deed.[70] But this same Spirit also continued and continues to endow leaders of the covenant community, whether they serve within the church or more broadly within society. 1 Samuel 16 reminds redeemed leaders of the necessity of the Spirit's endowment as they seek to transform all of creation.

Conclusion

Biblical theology is an important resource for the broader theological and religious discourse of church and society today. However, there is a risk that this resource will not be fully appreciated or utilized if greater attention is not given today to dialogue among the various theological disciplines. With the increasing specialization of the academic world Old Testament theology has largely been written with attention to discussions within the discipline of Old Testament and Hebrew studies. What is needed today are daring attempts to move outside these disciplinary walls and write and reflect on Old Testament theology within the broader canon (biblical theology), the broader Christian theological tradition (historical, systematic theology), and the broader contemporary context (ethics, pastoral theology, worldview studies, political theology, etc.).[71] This interdisciplinary sensitivity is prac-

---

69. On the "royal" or "princely Spirit" see J. H. Eaton, *Kingship and the Psalms,* 2nd ed., The Biblical Seminar 3 (Sheffield: JSOT, 1986), pp. 71, 157; cf. Ps. 51:12. Most likely this role of the Spirit is related to dynasty.

70. See especially the emphasis on this Spirit endowment in Luke 3–4; cf. Boda, "Word and Spirit."

71. See further Mark J. Boda, "Theological Commentary: A Review and Reflective Essay," *McMaster Journal of Theology and Ministry* 11 (2010): 139-50.

ticed regularly by those involved in church ministry and, interestingly, by those in broader cultural institutions. Such an approach demands hospitality, a willingness to dialogue in community across the theological disciplines and life experiences, but also courage to venture outside one's expertise. In this way, then, Old Testament exegetical and biblical theology has the potential to impact the church's preaching and worship[72] as well as the church's reflection on creational activities ranging from politics to education to law. It is through such reflection that the redeemed community has the potential to fully realize its role as transformative agents within creation.

Biblical theology is an essential discipline that enables Christians to hear the Old Testament. While highlighting the unique voice of the Old Testament, it provides the theological perspective and interpretive discipline for reading Old Testament texts within their ultimate theological context, that of the canon as a whole, the community gathered around it, and the culture and creation longing for the redemptive work of the Creator revealed within these Scriptures.

72. See Chapter 16 by Aubrey Spears in the present volume.

7 Canon and Old Testament Interpretation

Stephen G. Dempster

Canon in Contemporary Old Testament Study

A recent book on the formation of the Old Testament begins with these words: "The canon is in. The canon of the Bible has been the focus of interest ever since the American exegetes J. A. Sanders and B. S. Childs launched biblical criticism at the end of the 1970s. It was the subject of publications nearly too numerous to survey."[1] Far from an exaggeration, the quote could qualify for the understatement of the decade, as amply attested by that book's own voluminous bibliography.[2] Brevard Childs in particular has been responsible for this resurgence, especially as it applies to canon and theology. His program, as evidenced in numerous articles and books, has shown the failure of a strictly historical understanding of the contents of the Bible.[3] The historical approach tends to reduce the biblical message to its ancient Near Eastern context. But this misunderstands fundamentally the nature of the biblical text and its distinctive genre as Holy Scripture — that is, canon. As the Word of the Living God, it cannot be reduced to any one context but speaks to every context. Thus Childs shows his indebted-

---

1. Luc Zaman, *The Bible and Canon: A Modern Historical Inquiry*, Studia Semitica Neerlandica 50 (Leiden: Brill, 2008), p. 1.

2. Zaman, *The Bible and Canon*, pp. 599-685.

3. For an appreciation and critical assessment of the work of Brevard Childs along with exhaustive bibliography see Craig G. Bartholomew et al., eds., *Canon and Biblical Interpretation*, SAHS 7 (Grand Rapids: Zondervan, 2006).

ness to Karl Barth,[4] who dropped the bombshell of the implications of canon on the academic world of his day with the publication of his commentary on Romans.[5] But Barth simply claimed that he was following the much earlier mentors Luther and Calvin, for whom the Bible was first of all the Word of the Living God.

The canonical approach has had a number of hermeneutical implications for the study of the Old Testament. First, the authors, editors and tradents of the biblical message treated this literature in a sacred way; it was distinguished from all other literature and it made ultimate claims on the community. Second, exegesis is practiced on the final form of the book — and not, for example, on all of the various stages of the book's prehistory — and the place of each book in the larger authoritative collection, the canon. Thus the "Book of Adam" (Gen. 5:1-32) may have been an earlier source in Genesis providing a genealogy for ancient humanity, but now it functions to indicate the spread of divine blessing and hope for a world that has been cursed. Similarly, although many Old Testament surveys begin with the story of Exodus,[6] stressing the beginning of Israel as a nation, the fact that this book follows the more global Genesis in the canon shows that the calling of Israel to be a kingdom of priests has universal implications. Finally, all the books of the Old Testament canon find their ultimate context in the Christian Bible. While the Old Testament has its own discrete witness, it points in a New Testament direction and has as its goal the final Word of God in Jesus Christ.[7] As Karl Barth observed, "the name Jesus Christ, concealed under the name Israel in the Old Testament, [is] revealed under his own name in the New Testament."[8]

---

4. For the dependence of Childs on Barth see, e.g., Charles J. Scalise, *From Scripture to Theology: A Canonical Journey into Hermeneutics* (Downers Grove: IVP, 1996), pp. 47-55.

5. Note Barth's comments in the preface to his commentary: "The historical-critical method of biblical investigation has its rightful place: it is concerned with the preparation of the intelligence — and this can never be superfluous. But were I driven to choose between it and the venerable doctrine of Inspiration, I should without hesitation adopt the latter, which has a broader, deeper, more important justification. The doctrine of Inspiration is concerned with the labour of apprehending, *without which no technical equipment, however complete, is of any use whatever*" (emphasis added). See Karl Barth, *The Epistle to the Romans* (New York: Oxford University Press, 1968), p. 1.

6. Bernard Anderson, *Understanding the Old Testament* (Englewood Cliffs, NJ: Prentice-Hall, 1986).

7. For an exploration of the significance of some of these hermeneutical implications see Ellen F. Davis and Richard B. Hays, eds., *The Art of Reading Scripture* (Grand Rapids: Eerdmans, 2003).

8. Karl Barth, *Church Dogmatics* I/2, *The Doctrine of the Word of God, Part 2*, ed. G. W.

Some scholars have decried the hermeneutical implications of the genre of canon, suggesting that this new emphasis is a sophisticated type of fundamentalism, certainly not reflecting an ancient Israelite understanding of the biblical text.[9] But the fact of the matter is that the ancient Jews and early Christians were both "peoples of the Book" for good reason. The Book was no ordinary one.[10] To read the Bible as canon is to be addressed by God.[11] The Creator brought the world into being through words, announced Israel's salvation through words, and provided the divine part of a dialogue through a host of literary means: promise, commandment, curse, blessing, instruction, genealogy, history and finally in an ultimate Word expressed in a human life.[12]

The Idea of "Canon"

The Christian church hears in the Old Testament the voice of the living God and has used a special word to denote this collection of books: "canon." This word is derived from a Hebrew word signifying "reed" (qāneh) and by extension "measuring stick."[13] It enters into the Greek language as "canon" (kanōn) with a wider semantic range, signifying exemplary standards ranging from literary works, grammatical rules and even certain human beings.[14] The word was deployed in the early church to indicate an absolutely authoritative, complete list of God-inspired books, which was the standard of truth,

---

Bromiley, trans. G. Th. Thomson and H. Knight (Edinburgh: T&T Clark, 1956), p. 720. I am indebted for this reference to an unpublished paper by David Gibson, "The Answering Speech of Men: Karl Barth on Holy Scripture."

9. See, among others, e.g., James Barr, *Holy Scripture: Canon, Authority, Criticism* (Oxford: Oxford University Press, 1983).

10. See, e.g., Deut. 8:3; Matt. 4:4; John 5:39.

11. See Chapter 1 by Craig Bartholomew in the present volume.

12. Heb. 1:1-3; John 1:14.

13. For "reed" see, e.g., 1 Kings 14:15; Isa. 19:6. For "measuring stick" see Ezek. 40:3, 5; 42:16-19.

14. For example, Aristotle writes of a good man being "a canon and measure of the truth"; in grammar and rhetoric a canon was "a general rule or principle," and collections of old Greek authors were viewed as "canons" or "models of excellence." See the entry under "canon" in Henry G. Liddell and Robert Scott, *Greek and English Lexicon* (Oxford: Clarendon, 1869), p. 775. The word is used four times in the New Testament: three times to indicate the boundaries of a sphere of influence (2 Cor. 10:13-16) and once to refer to a standard or principle (Gal. 6:16).

as early as A.D. 350. Athanasius uses this definition in his *39th Festal Letter.* Consequently it is often regarded as anachronistic in modern scholarship to use the term to describe collections of books the church or synagogue had in their possessions at earlier times.[15] While there is a certain truth to this observation, it is clear that the concept of a closed collection of absolutely authoritative books was not new with the early church.[16] Nor is it true that this authoritative collection was created in an instant of time; it had a long and complex history that is difficult to trace. The Jewish historian Josephus (A.D. 95) describes a closed list of inspired books that had been authoritative for all Jews for centuries (*Against Apion* 1:37-42) and this view is also reflected in another document contemporary with the Jewish historian (2 Esdras 14). This is as clear and coherent a doctrine of canon as can be imagined.[17] Jews themselves did not use the term "canon" to designate their books, but rather the expression "books which defiled the hands." This enigmatic idiom is probably meant to be understood paradoxically.[18]

Scholars frequently distinguish between two senses of canon: material and formal. "Material" refers to a *collection of authoritative books* that is in the process of formation — an evolving or open canon. Sometimes this is termed Canon 1, or proto-canon. "Formal," on the other hand, signifies an *authoritative collection of books,* or Canon 2 — a closed canon.[19] Until the

---

15. Eugene Ulrich, "The Notion and Definition of Canon," in *The Canon Debate,* ed. Lee M. McDonald and James A. Sanders (Peabody, MA: Hendrickson, 2002), pp. 21-30; Robert Kraft, "Para-Mania: Beside, Before, and Beyond Bible Studies," *Journal of Biblical Literature* 126 (2007): 3-27.

16. See, e.g., my comments in "Canons on the Left and Canons on the Right: Finding a Resolution in the Canon Debate," *Journal of the Evangelical Theological Society* 52 (2009): 47-77.

17. "Thinly concealed behind Josephus' Greek apologetics is a clear and coherent theological doctrine of canon that must stem, we believe, from the canonical doctrine of Hillel and his school." Frank Moore Cross, "The Text Behind the Text of the Hebrew Bible," in *Understanding the Dead Sea Scrolls,* ed. Herschel Shanks (New York: Vintage, 1993), pp. 153-54.

18. In *Mishna Yadayim* 4:6-8 there is a debate recorded as to why documents that defile the hands are more worthy and precious than those, like the writings of Homer, that do not pollute. Human bones are regarded as precious and pure and therefore impossible to be used for profane purposes such as being made into spoons, while this is not true of animal bones. Thus, although the former are impure from a ritual point of view and the latter are not, the human bones are holy and precious from another point of view. Practically, it may have been the case that these writings were designated as unclean in order to discourage individuals who would engage in reading in the temple from bringing food with them. Such practices would have attracted rodents that would damage the scrolls.

19. For the distinction see Gerald T. Sheppard, "Canon," in *Encyclopedia of Religion,* ed. Mircea Eliade, vol. 3 (New York: Macmillan, 1987), pp. 62-69.

Old Testament was complete, then, it would have been an "open canon" (proto-canon). The attempt to explain an open canon as simply an arbitrary collection of sacred documents ("scripture") or valued religious literature as opposed to "canon" fails to understand the nature of its content.[20]

The Formation of the Old Testament Canon in Modern Scholarship

Old Testament canonical studies were dominated in the late nineteenth and twentieth centuries by a theory of formation that took the tripartite form of the Hebrew Bible as the clue to its historical evolution. The Torah was regarded as canonized around 400 B.C., the Prophets around 200 B.C., and the third division of the Writings around A.D. 90 at a rabbinic council at Jabneh. Daniel's place among the Writings was thus accounted for. Since it was a prophecy but was written after the prophetic division was closed, it was relegated to the Writings.

Another theory conveniently explained the wider canon of the Christian church. It simply represented the wider canon of the Septuagint, which represented the canon of the Jewish community living in Alexandria, which was larger than the narrower Palestinian canon.

Both these theories started to unravel in the latter third of the twentieth century. First, it was shown that there was no evidence at all for a rabbinic "canonizing" council at Jabneh.[21] Second, since the evidence for a wider canon came from demonstrably late and Christian sources, it did not reveal anything about an earlier Alexandrian canon.[22]

Contemporary theories for canon formation fall into two basic classes. One pushes the endpoint of the formation backward into the Maccabean

20. See Andrew Plaks, "Afterword: Canonization in the Ancient World: The View from Farther East," in *Homer, the Bible, and Beyond: Literary and Religious Canons in the Ancient World*, ed. Margalit Finkelberg and Gedaliahu A. G. Stroumsa, Jerusalem Studies in Religion and Culture 2 (Leiden: Brill, 2003), p. 270; Christopher Seitz, *The Goodly Fellowship of the Prophets: The Achievement of Association in Canon Formation* (Grand Rapids: Baker Academic, 2009). But cf. also others like Sundberg, Barton, and MacDonald, for whom the distinction between "scripture" and "canon" is fundamental. See Albert Sundberg, *The Old Testament of the Early Church* (Cambridge, MA: Harvard University Press, 1964); John Barton, *Holy Writings, Sacred Text: The Canon of Early Christianity* (Louisville: Westminster John Knox, 1997); Lee Martin McDonald, *The Biblical Canon* (Peabody, MA: Hendrickson, 2007).

21. J. P. Lewis, "What Do We Mean by Jabneh?" *Journal of Bible and Religion* 32 (1964): 125-32.

22. Sundberg, *The Old Testament*.

period at the latest, and the other basically modifies the standard theory by pushing the endpoint of canonization forward into the second century A.D. or later. Yet the latter position fails to explain satisfactorily important external witnesses to a B.C. canon and does not really come to terms with the unique status of the scriptural material.[23]

The Old Testament: The Bible of the Early Church, the Hermeneutical Key, and Early Trinitarian Interpretation

The Christian church was born with a Bible in its hands.[24] That Bible was certainly not the New Testament, which was in the process of being written; rather, it was an authoritative collection of sacred books that was eventually to be called the Old Testament. In Luke 24, the recently resurrected Christ instructed his disciples on the Emmaus Road that he was the hermeneutical key to the entire gamut of the Scriptures (Law, Prophets, and Psalms).[25] Indeed, as Richard Hays remarks, "The whole story of Israel builds to its narrative climax in Jesus, the Messiah, who had to suffer before entering into his glory. That is what Jesus tries to teach them on the Road."[26]

Even in the church's infancy it was in grave danger of losing the precious treasure of the Old Testament. Objecting to the content of this revelation, the heretic Marcion (ca. A.D. 150) rejected it entirely as the product of an inferior, wrathful deity who was totally different from the merciful God revealed in Christ.[27] In repudiating Marcion, the church affirmed the foundation and basis of Christian faith, and the fact that in the Old Testament and

23. For example, see Josephus, *Against Apion* 1.37-42; 2 Esdras 14; Prologue to Ben Sira; *Baba Bathra* 14b. Also there is the evidence of Greek translations being revised toward a Hebrew prototype of the Masoretic Text in the late first century B.C. For a consideration of both points of view and an attempt at resolution see Dempster, "Canons on the Left."

24. Although there are many scholars who question the extent of the Old Testament canon at this time, the fact of the church having a Bible in its hands is indisputable. Much of the New Testament consists in quotations, allusions, and images drawn from the Old Testament. For a recent survey of the state of the field of Old Testament canonical studies see Dempster, "Canons on the Left."

25. Luke 24:13-53.

26. Richard B. Hays, "Reading Scripture in the Light of the Resurrection," in *The Art of Reading Scripture,* p. 229.

27. For the classic nineteenth-century study of Marcion, see Adolf von Harnack, *Marcion: The Gospel of the Alien God,* trans. John H. Seeley and Lyle D. Bierma (Durham: Labyrinth, 1990).

the emerging New Testament the people of God hear unmistakably the voice of the same God. The God of Abraham, Isaac, and Jacob *is* the God of Jesus of Nazareth. The ghost of Marcion has reappeared in the history of the church from time to time, the contemporary period being no exception.[28] But without the Old Testament the New Testament is simply a brute fact appearing as it were out of nowhere, a climax without a plot. Likewise, without the New Testament the Old Testament is a plot without a climax.

In opposition to Marcion's dualistic hermeneutical approach to the Scriptures, which effectively decanonized the Old Testament and pitted an inferior Old Testament god against a superior New Testament one, the early church fathers discerned the outlines of the Trinity in the Old Testament. In other words, the interpersonal triune God did not just appear in the New Testament but Father, Son, and Holy Spirit all played a role in the Old Testament canon. For example, Irenaeus saw not only the Father and the Holy Spirit present at creation in Genesis 1:1-3 but also the Word, and therefore the Son as well. Similarly, the Father made humanity in the image of his Son by the Spirit, and the Son was sent by the Father and prophesied by the Spirit to restore humanity to its pristine glory of communion with God.[29]

Although the church inherited its Bible from Judaism, as it expanded there was some confusion about the exact boundaries of its original Bible. Within contemporary Christendom it might be more accurate to speak of the *canons* of the Old Testament rather than one canon. The Old Testament canon consists of thirty-nine books in Protestantism, forty-six books in Roman Catholicism (adding Tobit, Judith, Baruch, Ben Sira, Wisdom, 1 and 2 Maccabees, with additions to Daniel and Esther) and forty-eight books in the Orthodox Church (adding 1 Esdras and 3 Maccabees).[30] The Jewish Bible, which is identical with the content of the Protestant Old Testament, con-

---

28. See examples in Dempster, "Adolf von Harnack," in *Encyclopedia of the Historical Jesus*, ed. Craig A. Evans (New York: Routledge, 2008), pp. 273-75; Erich Zenger, *Das Erste Testament. Die jüdische Bibel und die Christen* (Düsseldorf: Patmos Verlag, 1998). For an implicit popular Marcionistic work see Jack Miles, *Christ: A Crisis in the Life of God* (New York: Vintage, 2002), who claims that the Old Testament is not to be rejected, but it contains the history of God's errors for which he needs to apologize, that apology being the cross.

29. See, e.g., Irenaeus, *Demonstration of the Apostolic Preaching*, 5, 22, 26, 29, 44.

30. There are minor variations in other traditions. Ethiopic Bibles add Jubilees, Enoch, 3-4 Ezra and 4 Baruch. The Syriac Peshitta adds the Letter of Baruch. For a comprehensive survey of canonical lists in the early church see Roger T. Beckwith, *The Old Testament Canon of the New Testament Church and Its Background in Early Judaism* (Grand Rapids: Eerdmans, 1984), and Peter Brandt, *Endgestalten des Kanons. Das Arrangement der Schriften Israels in der judischen und christlichen Bibel* (Berlin: Philo, 2001).

sists of twenty-four books, being divided and arranged differently. Christian Old Testaments, as they end with the prophets, emphasize eschatology;[31] Jewish Bibles have three divisions arranged concentrically around the Torah, thus stressing ethics.[32] In essence, the Jewish Bible and Protestant Old Testament constitute an irreducible core to which a few books have been added in the other Christian denominations. These wider "canons" represented expansions of an original narrower one inherited by the church; the additional books' popularity and usefulness within various Christian communities resulted in their inclusion within the scriptural canon. At the same time, in the early church there was a sharp distinction made between the status of these books and the "canonical" ones.[33]

The Evolution of the Old Testament Canon

Writing, Books, Literacy, and Canons

When the word "Bible" is used in contemporary culture, it refers to a single book. The first time, however, the word was used to designate sacred literature in antiquity, it referred to some of the *books (ta biblia)* of the Old Testament (*Letter of Aristeas* 316). The Bible did not become a book in the modern sense until probably the third and fourth centuries A.D., after the codex (the modern book) was invented.[34] Before that time it was a series of scrolls forming a collection. Greek manuscripts from Christian sources in the fourth and fifth centuries A.D. were the first complete books (pandects) to contain all the writings of the Old Testament (e.g., *Codex Vaticanus, Sinaiticus*). In Judaism, the first attested Bible containing all the Jewish sa-

31. Although this is sometimes viewed as somewhat of a hackneyed cliché (Brandt, *Endgestalten*), there is an element of truth in it. A significant number of early Christian lists conclude the Old Testament with eschatological material.

32. See, e.g., Stephen G. Dempster, "The Prophets, the Canon, and the Canonical Approach: No Empty Word," in *Canon and Biblical Interpretation*, ed. Craig G. Bartholomew et al., SAHS 7 (Grand Rapids: Zondervan, 2008), pp. 293-96. It is nonetheless true that there is a significant eschatological element to certain forms of the Jewish Bible.

33. The clear demarcation between the two types of books became blurred as the church grew away from its roots in Judaism as evidenced in the lists of the Western church and the great Greek codices.

34. Colin H. Roberts and T. C. Skeat, *The Birth of the Codex* (London: British Academy, 1987). The codex was probably invented in the first century A.D. Remarkably, it was the Christian church that popularized and adapted the codex to meet its religious needs.

cred writings is dated to the early eleventh century A.D. *(Codex Leningradensis)*. Jews were far more reluctant than Christians to adopt the codex, since they venerated the scroll.

The first words of the Bible depict God speaking (Gen. 1:3), and it is also true that the Bible was first experienced as oral proclamation, which was subsequently made permanent in writing because of its importance. The Hebrew word used to indicate the activity of proclamation is the word "to call," "to call out," and "to read aloud" *(qārā')*. Later Jewish tradition refers to the Bible as not that which primarily is written but that which is called out *(miqrā')*.[35] Of course, this assumes that there is written material to be read aloud. The biblical literature, then, was preeminently that which was proclaimed, frequently in public gatherings. The New Testament shares this focus as there are explicit directives to read aloud some of the letters in a public gathering of believers (Col. 4:16; 1 Thess. 5:27; Rev. 1:3). It was not until the invention of the printing press and the proliferation of literacy that the emphasis upon private reading by an individual supplanted the largely public and social context of *miqrā'*.

Nevertheless, the Bible consisted of *writings*. In the ancient world, particularly before the invention of the alphabet, writing and reading were the prerogative of an elite group of scribes.[36] Writing systems were complex and ponderous, requiring the memorization of hundreds of signs. Accordingly, only a small cadre of professionally trained scribes would be literate, employed in administrative tasks such as recordkeeping and accounting as well as political and cultural ones like the production of royal propaganda, legal documents, and culturally significant texts (which would often be the basis for oral performance). With the dawn of the alphabet at the turn of the second millennium B.C., this all changed. Now, at least potentially, there could be a democratization of literacy because of the dramatic reduction of writing symbols to a few dozen signs. Semitic alphabets begin to appear in the ancient Near East in the second half of the second millennium B.C. (Ugarit, Izbet Sartah). One has recently been found in Tel Zayit, dating to the tenth

35. M. J. Mulder and Harry Sysling, eds., *Mikra: Text, Translation, Reading, and Interpretation of the Hebrew Bible in Ancient Judaism and Early Christianity* (Minneapolis: Fortress, 2005), p. xxiii.

36. See, e.g., Piotr Bienkowski et al., eds., *Writing and Ancient Near East Society: Papers in Honor of Alan R. Millard* (Edinburgh: T&T Clark, 2005); David M. Carr, *Writing on the Tablet of the Heart: Origins of Scripture and Literature* (New York: Oxford University Press, 2005); William M. Schniedewind, *How the Bible Became a Book: The Textualization of Ancient Israel* (Cambridge: Cambridge University Press, 2005).

century b.c.[37] The beginnings of the Bible take place, then, in the midst of an epistemological and social revolution as well as a religious one — the God of the universe begins to make himself known in texts! "The gods of all the other nations revealed themselves in images, but Israel found her God in the Text."[38] This surely provided an additional theological motivation for literacy in Israel (Deut. 6:9).

If literacy did not become pervasive in Israel, it surely was not rare. It quickly diffused outward from professional circles. In the book of Judges, for instance, a young man is able to write out the ancient version of a "hit list" when he is captured (Judg. 8:14); Isaiah can divide people equally into literate and illiterate classes (Isa. 29:11). In extrabiblical documents, a common soldier thinks it demeaning that his superior officer considers him illiterate (Lachish letter 3); an ordinary laborer commemorates the completion of a building project in writing (Siloam Inscription). In addition, the ending of Ecclesiastes (12:12) assumes a great deal of literacy among its audience, not to mention that it was — ideally at least — important for the head of each Israelite household to write some of the Torah on the doorposts and gates of his homestead (Deut. 6:9).

The formation of the Old Testament evolved gradually over a long period of time. The earliest writer to appear in its pages is Moses (Exod. 17:14) and the last is Ezra (8:1), a distinguished scribe who is patterned after the great Moses.[39] Between this first and second Moses, there is a potpourri of writings, spanning centuries, that became part of the Old Testament: legal collections, poetry, narratives, stories, fables, prophecies, apocalypses, proverbs, lamentations, hymns, riddles, protests, curses, chronicles, lists, letters, and love songs. All this diversity has been arranged in such a fashion that it is seen to be part of a larger story, which begins with creation (Genesis) and ends with Israel's return from exile (Ezra-Nehemiah).

Significantly, the Hebrew Bible reflects an arrangement of books that is older and different from the Christian Old Testament, which is largely based on the Greek practice of concluding with the prophetic books. The Hebrew order is designated by the acronym *Tanakh*, which refers to its three major divisions: Torah (Law, Instruction), Nevi'im (Prophets), and Ketuvim (Writ-

---

37. Ron E. Tappy and P. Kyle McCarter Jr., eds., *Literate Culture and Tenth-Century Canaan: The Tel Zayit Abecedary in Context* (Winona Lake, IN: Eisenbrauns, 2008).

38. Paul Dion, personal communication, 2009.

39. For a study of these two figures see G. J. Venema, *Reading Scripture in the Old Testament: Deuteronomy 9–10, 31, 2 Kings 22–23, Jeremiah 36, Nehemiah 8*, trans. C. E. Smit (Leiden: Brill, 2004).

ings). The Torah contains the books of Genesis through Deuteronomy, and is identical in arrangement to the Old Testament. The Nevi'im consists of eight books, eventually grouped into four books of Former Prophets (Joshua, Judges, Samuel, and Kings) and four books of Latter Prophets (Jeremiah, Ezekiel, Isaiah, and the Twelve). The Ketuvim consists of a number of books whose sequence is not fixed. Probably the earliest order was as follows: Ruth, Psalms, Job, Proverbs, Ecclesiastes, Song of Songs, Lamentations, Daniel, Esther, Ezra-Nehemiah, Chronicles.[40]

An alternate Jewish order of twenty-two books can be traced back to antiquity as well. This order was based on the Hebrew alphabet and probably annexed Ruth to Judges and Lamentations to Jeremiah. In addition, it transferred all the historical books to the second section to provide a history from the beginning of creation to the Persian period (Esther), and its third section consisted of the non-historical books of Psalms, Proverbs, Ecclesiastes, and Song of Songs. This order is first attested in Josephus[41] and may well be a reflection of an early Septuagint.[42] It is not coincidental that both Jewish orders are early and both have a tripartite signature.

In the early church there were lists of books and manuscripts that contained additional writings. As the church moved away from Judaism, there was confusion about its canon, and some religious books that became extremely popular made their way into various Christian lists and manuscripts. In order to clarify some of this confusion, Melito, a bishop from Sardis, left his city in Asia Minor around A.D. 170 to go to Palestine, to determine the original order and number of the books of the "Old Covenant." Origen (A.D. 230) was also aware of books that had been added. Later, individuals like Athanasius and particularly Jerome recognized the differences between the canon of Hebrew "truth" and its Christian counterparts. However, the force of tradition was so strong that it was not until the Reformation that there was a concerted attempt within the new Protestant Christian movement to return to the narrower canon. This was probably an influence of the Renaissance, which stressed the importance of cutting through the "logjam" of tradition to get back to the original sources. For various reasons, this path was not followed by the Roman Catholic and Orthodox Churches.

---

40. This is the order found in the Talmud (*Baba Bathra* 14b). This text is a *baraita*, an oral tradition dating to the period of the Mishna (A.D. 1-200), which was not included in the latter document when it was codified in writing (A.D. 200).

41. *Against Apion* 1.37-42.

42. P. Katz, "The Old Testament Canon in Palestine," *Zeitschrift für die neuttestament-liche Wissenschaft* 47 (1956): 191-217.

Their additional books are often called "deutero-canonical" to indicate their distinction from the earlier "proto-canonical" books.[43]

The Beginning of the Old Testament Canon

If there was an event that can be regarded as providing the impetus and nucleus for the canonical process, it was the Sinai covenant. The content of the covenant was largely the giving of the Ten Words (Commandments), which reflected the will of the Creator for Israel, which was regarded as having a divine mission to the world (Exod. 19:5-6; 20:1-17). In this public event, God spoke directly to Israel in the thunder of Sinai. This oral proclamation was then made permanent in stone tablets written with the very finger of God.

The climax of the covenant at Sinai indicated again the importance of the written word. The experience of being confronted with the unmediated presence of God traumatized the Israelites, who wanted Moses to be a mediator (Exod. 20:18-20). Acting in this capacity, Moses wrote down the words of God in "a book of the covenant," which was an application of the Ten Words to the daily life of the people (21–23).[44] This "book," which was probably written on papyrus, became part of a sacrificial blood ritual in which the Israelites affirmed obedience to God (24:1-8). They were consecrated and cleansed to accomplish a priestly mission to the world. The ritual of the word and blood led to communion: Moses, Aaron, and seventy elders ascended Sinai and experienced a unique encounter with God (24:10ff.). But its basis was not only God's grace but the desire to obey the words written in a book.[45]

One of the consequences of the Sinai covenant was the realization of the

43. The distinction between proto- and deuterocanonical works is first made by Sixtus of Siena (ca. 1520-1569).

44. This text raises many literary-critical questions. Many modern scholars are skeptical of Moses' role in the formation of the book of the covenant and view this text as a retrojection of a later point of view. Others have argued that Moses would have played only an oral role, not a textual one, and that when literacy became important at a later time (the Deuteronomistic period) his early role was transformed. Against these positions, it can be observed that there is an inextricable link in the early traditions of Israel with Moses and the formation of Israel's scriptures. The most economic explanation is a historical one. For further reading see Brevard Childs, *The Book of Exodus: A Critical, Theological Commentary* (Philadelphia: Westminster, 1974), pp. 497-511; Schniedewind, *How the Bible Became a Book*, pp. 121-34.

45. Exod. 24:4-7.

presence of God with the people, housed in a tent in the centre of the Israelite camp (Exod. 25–31). In the heart of this tabernacle God's invisible presence hovered above the Ark of the Covenant — a footstool for the divine throne. The ten words written on two stone tablets were placed in the Ark. Presumably the book of the covenant was placed nearby. The idea of canon began here and it is intimately related to covenant and communion, as Meredith Kline has keenly observed.[46] Unique content and conspicuous setting demarcate these writings and ensure their privileged authoritative status among a people with whom God has chosen to dwell. Their written form serves to ensure their relevance transcends their historical context.

Canonical Expansion

The development of this covenant relationship coincided with an expansion of the canon. A number of other texts suggest this growth. Moses is depicted involved in writing other texts: a memorial (Exod. 17:14), a travel log (Num. 33), and a poem (Deut. 31:22), which all would likely have been added to the nuclear canon. After his death, there was provision for a prophetic institution that continued the oral proclamation of the will of God (Deut. 18:15ff.). The authority of the members of this institution was ultimately authorized by their adherence to the nuclear canon and not to dramatic, charismatic qualities (Deut. 13:1-6). This opened the way for the integration of future prophetic texts into the nuclear canon of Moses. At the end of the Pentateuch, Moses is depicted writing a copy of this Torah, a form of the book of Deuteronomy, and placing it beside the Ark, where it was to be read publicly every sabbatical year (Deut. 31:9-13, 24-26).

Two other laws in Deuteronomy stress the importance of this new text. Future rulers had to make a copy from one in the possession of the Levites, who alone had access to sacred space, and who were entrusted with the scribal task of textual preservation and transmission. The royal copy was to govern completely the thinking of the king in order that his rule incarnated the divine will. The ordinary king — not the ideal one — is envisioned as truly literate (Deut. 17:14-20). Literacy is not primarily about learning letters but about doing the will of God.[47] Secondly, this type of thinking was to perco-

---

46. Meredith Kline, "The Correlation of the Concepts of Canon and Covenant," in *New Perspectives on the Old Testament,* ed. J. Barton Payne (Waco: Word, 1970), pp. 265-79.

47. See further Carr, *Writing on the Tablet of the Heart.*

late down to the head of every Israelite household, who was to inscribe Torah words on his doorposts and gates. This suggests an ideal of at least functional literacy for many members of Israelite society (Deut. 6:4-9). The fact that kings and commoners were to be involved in the same literary activity suggests a democratization of kingship. All — at least theoretically — could obtain access to the word of the Living God. It was not a magical, esoteric formula to 'which only an elite few had access.[48]

During the conquest, Joshua functioned as an exemplary leader by writing part of the Torah on a newly made altar at Shechem (Josh. 8:30-35). There it was read in the presence of all Israel, the blessing and the curse (cf. Deut. 27). This was the "doorposts and gates" of the new, national "house" of Israel. After the conquest, Joshua renewed the covenant with Israel at Shechem, after which he wrote the words of the covenant down in "a book of the Torah of God" (24:26) that was placed near a stone in a sanctuary. Later, immediately preceding the rise of kingship, Samuel wrote down the responsibilities of a king in a book, placing it in a sanctuary (1 Sam. 10:25). The nuclear canon was clearly expanding and at its heart was communion with the living God. Other literature dealing with the history of the nation would have been added to this collection.

Hearing the Old Testament: Varieties of Divine Address

As the canon was expanding and was contained in sacred space under the supervision of priestly scribes, there came to be three types of literature in which Israel recognized authoritative revelation: Torah, Prophecy, and Wisdom (Jer. 18:18; Ezek. 7:26; cf. 1 Sam. 28:6).[49]

In the biblical tradition, the Torah was associated with Moses, who was regarded as the ultimate prophet. Priests interpreted the relevance of this Torah for the people, and the locus of this revelation was the sacred space of the sanctuary. Meanwhile, the word was associated with prophets, and prophetic literature was a complement to the Torah. Its locus would often transcend the sanctuary, as the inspiration of the prophet and a circle of disciples who recorded, preserved, and transmitted the oral communication, was not

48. For example, as seen in the seventh-century B.C. amulet that contains abridged and slightly altered forms of the Aaronic blessing.

49. For the use of these three streams to account for the making of the Hebrew Bible see the following insightful study: Max Leopold Margolis, *The Hebrew Scriptures in the Making*, 1st ed. (Philadelphia: Jewish Publication Society of America, 1922).

confined to the sacred space of the priest (Isa. 8:16-20; Jer. 36). Wisdom literature, by contrast, was more of a human word from below — a form of immanent revelation, or the ability to discern through enlightened reason the divine will in nature and human experience. This type of revelation transcended the sanctuary to encompass the limits of creation itself and came to be associated with the sage, who had the powers of observation and insight, with Solomon memorialized as the sage par excellence. The locus for this revelation in Israel would have been everyday life, anywhere, and the place for the dissemination of this wisdom would have been particularly the city gate where the elders gathered and the home where values were inculcated by parents.[50] The major locale for the transcription and transmission of wisdom would have been the royal court (Prov. 25:1), where professional scribes would have been responsible for it. The court or the sanctuary may have been the locus for musical compositions that reflected human address to God in prayer, protest, and praise — that is, the psalms. David and various musicians were associated with many of these, and later texts show that written materials provided the basis for such worship (e.g., 2 Chron. 29:30). The authority for such compositions would have been linked to the most venerable kings in Israel, David and Solomon, God's chosen instruments to lead his people.

The architecture of the temple itself can help provide an analogy for the origins and loci of the various streams of revelation. The temple building proper would be the main locus of the Torah, the temple courts and surrounding environment within Israelite culture would be the place for prophecy, and wisdom would move out to the limits of creation itself.

Torah and Prophecy

When prophets arose in Israel, they were in fact the "mouthpiece of God" (Exod. 6:29–7:2) who enforced the covenant, and called the people back to the will of God expressed in the Torah. When David sinned against Uriah and Bathsheba, he was confronted by Nathan because of the violation of the sixth and seventh commandments, which was regarded as despising "the word of Yahweh" (2 Sam. 12:9). During Ahab's reign, Naboth was "framed"

---

50. The social origin for wisdom is disputed. For a list of the main possibilities and critical discussion see particularly the work of James Crenshaw, *Education in Ancient Israel: Across the Deafening Silence* (New York: Doubleday, 1998), pp. 85-114.

by being accused of "cursing God and the king" (1 Kings 21:10), both prohibitions in the book of the Covenant (Exod. 22:28). The prophetic reaction to the apostasy in the Northern Kingdom can only be understood against the background of an authoritative word that had been violated.

When prophets began to record their words to preserve them as evidence of their truthfulness, many of their condemnations are comprehensible only with the assumption of a body of earlier, authoritative texts — the Torah — and many of their promises are clothed with the language of previous descriptions of pivotal salvific events in Israel's early history. For example, Hosea upbraided the people for their violations of the Ten Words (4:1-3) and condemned them with the worst form of judgment: they were disowned by the covenant God (1:9, cf. Exod. 3:12). When he envisioned salvation, he projected the ancient Exodus into the future (1:10-11 [2:1-3 Heb.]). Prophetic words were probably written down by disciples of the prophets (Jer. 36) and preserved and treasured in circles associated with them (Isa. 8:16-20, Jer. 36), their authority increasing with the passage of time. Ezekiel's (ch. 3) and Jeremiah's prophecies (ch. 36) were specifically linked to written scrolls.

The authority of a prophetic scroll is shown in a striking example from the seventh century B.C. During a period of reform in Judah after a long period of apostasy in which the Torah was lost, it was found during a renovation of the temple (2 Kings 22–23). This book of the Torah, which probably represents at least the core of the book of Deuteronomy,[51] was read to King Josiah, who then radicalized his reform by renewing the ancient covenant with the people. The Torah scroll had absolute authority. During the same general period, the prophet Jeremiah had a scroll of his prophecies destroyed by Josiah's successor and son (Jer. 36). The text implies that the son should have showed the same respect for the prophetic scroll as his father did for the Torah scroll. These positive and negative examples of Josiah and his son demonstrate that Torah and prophecy functioned on the same "canonical" level even if they did not share the same geographic space.

---

51. The literature on the identification of this book is voluminous. Most scholars understand the book of the covenant to be a form of Deuteronomy. Beginning with Jerome (*Against Jovianus* 5), the consensus of scholarship has come to this position. For the main reasons, see Moshe Weinfeld, *Deuteronomy 1–11*, AB (New York: Doubleday, 1991), pp. 111-14.

Torah and Wisdom

The authority of the sage in Israelite thought was grounded in the gift of divine wisdom (1 Kings 3), which also required patient study and observation. Even though there are few specific allusions to early authoritative texts in wisdom literature, the presence and authority of those texts are assumed.[52] At strategic points, there is the recognition that the first step to wisdom is acknowledging the God of Israel's Sinaitic covenant, Yahweh (Prov. 1:7; 9:10; Job 1–2; 12:9; 28:28; 38–42; cf. Eccles. 12:13). Moreover, the wisdom literature is saturated at various points with the language of creation, implying that a robust doctrine of creation is the raison d'être for the literature (Prov. 3:19-20; 8:22-31; Job 3; 9:4-10; 38–42). The conclusion to Ecclesiastes recognizes that there is a stream of wisdom literature ("the sayings of the wise" 12:11) whose ultimate source is the One Shepherd, who defines what it means to be human in Torah terms (12:13).

That the written wisdom material was connected with the literary craft of the royal court can be seen in Proverbs 25:1, where Hezekiah's scribes were responsible for copying an edition of Solomonic proverbs. Presumably such scribes edited Solomon's proverbs and added sayings of other sages, even non-Israelite ones (Prov. 22:17–23:21; 24:23-34; 30:1-33; 31:1-31; Eccles. 12:9-14). The authority of such wisdom can be seen in not only the message of the various books, but in their appended editorial statements. For example, Ecclesiastes warns about reading works outside a certain collection (12:12).

Exile and Canon

The Exile had a profound impact on the nation, calling its very existence into question. Although the temple was destroyed, the literature housed in it would have been saved, and literature from prophetic and wisdom sources, including psalms, would have been gathered. In the absence of sacred space, sacred texts became all the more important.[53] A sustained effort was made to make sense of the Exile in historical narrative, and the result was largely a four-volume work that used many older sources to narrate Israel's history

52. See especially Chapter 13 by Craig Bartholomew in the present volume.

53. This is a point made in the stimulating work by Donald Akenson, *Surpassing Wonder: The Invention of the Bible and the Talmuds* (Chicago: University of Chicago Press, 2001). See also Andrew Steinmann, *The Oracles of God* (St. Louis: Concordia Academic Press, 1999), p. 118.

from the conquest to the middle of the Exile. Combined with the Torah, this history would have extended from creation to the Exile. At the end of both the Torah and this new history, Israel is outside the Promised Land (Deut. 34; 2 Kings 25:27-30). The extension of the Torah's history with that of Joshua–2 Kings (excluding Ruth) represented the outworking of the predictions of the last book of the Torah, Deuteronomy — blessing for obedience and curse for disobedience — in the life of the nation. It began with a celebration of Passover in the land (Josh. 5) and ended with one during Josiah's reformation (2 Kings 23). The history was completed with the release of the exiled Davidic king, Jehoiachin, from a Babylonian prison (2 Kings 25:27-30).

The language used to edit this history was also used to provide titles to the major prophetic works, and there are crucial repetitions that link the Former and Latter Prophets (2 Kings 25 = Jer. 52; 2 Kings 18–20 = Isa. 36–39). These works complemented one another as the history leading to the Exile is matched by the prophetic words that predicted the doom of the nation. But the literature was not only gathered and edited to explain disaster; it also offered hope. In the Former Prophets (Joshua–2 Kings) there is a covenant with David, that he would have an everlasting dynasty (2 Sam. 7); Jehoiachin's release from prison shows that this promise has not been forgotten. In the Latter Prophets (Jeremiah, Ezekiel, Isaiah, the Twelve), there are also many announcements of future salvation that cluster around the resurrection of the Davidic house. The fact that the Twelve, in particular, contains prophets who were post-exilic (Haggai, Zechariah, Malachi) indicates that the last prophetic scroll was not completed in the Exile.

Post-Exilic Canonical Synthesis and Closure

After the return of the exiles from Babylon to Judah, another reform occurred that was inspired by the written word. Reforms instituted by Ezra and Nehemiah culminated with a dramatic reading of the Torah before a large assembly of Jews (Neh. 8). In a public square in one of the main areas of the city, a large wooden podium was erected upon which Ezra, the latter-day Moses, stood to read this book. When he opened the scroll, his audience stood, and as he read in the Hebrew of the Torah, the priests helped the people understand it by paraphrasing it in Aramaic. The people learned about various issues and festivals, and they enacted what they could immediately. It is clear that the Torah consisted of Genesis-Deuteronomy, since the prayer of Nehemiah in the next chapter rehearses the history of Israel in sequence through the Pentateuch and beyond. The importance of the written word is symbolized not only by its physical elevation, but by its importance for governing the life of the people. During this time, there probably was a library in the rebuilt temple, where all the holy writings would have been placed, as the rebuilt temple would have become the major locus for the holy books.[54]

Jewish tradition indicates that sometime during the latest period in the Old Testament, revelation ceased. Prophecy was waning (Zech. 1:5; 7:7, 12). In 1 Maccabees, written in the second century B.C., there is an awareness that prophecy has ceased (4:46; 9:27; 14:41). Writing toward the end of the first century A.D., Josephus states categorically that the Jewish Bible for all Jews has been a finished product since the Persian period because of "the failure of the exact succession of the prophets" (*Against Apion* 1.37-42; cf. 2 Esdras 14). Later Jewish tradition is unanimous in confirming this picture. Any later book that tried to present itself as "canonical" was written under the guise of an ancient biblical figure in order "to make the canonical cut" (e.g., Enoch, Eldad and Moded, Joseph and Asenath, Baruch).[55]

Since revelation ceased at the end of the biblical period, a decision was made, probably in temple circles, to synthesize all the authoritative writings into an integrated unity, stitching the various collections together into a completed whole. The various media of revelation resulted in bringing together the three distinct sections we have already mentioned: Torah, Prophets, and Wisdom. The latter category became more of a generic one to which later more diverse genres could be added. This became the basis for the later threefold designation known by Ben-Sira as "the Law of the Most High, the wisdom of the ancients and . . . prophecies" (39:1), and by his grandson as "Torah, Prophets and the Rest of the Books." It was not until the second century A.D. that the third division became known as "the Writings."

Probably during the latest period of the Old Testament under "the second Moses," Ezra (and/or Nehemiah), the literature was edited and synthesized into a complete whole. Much of the Torah and the Prophets — both Former and Latter — were substantially shaped, as were other documents outside these categories. A final redaction probably took place that imparted to the material a definitive canonical stamp, its distinctive eschatological message, as well as the importance of study and meditation leading to wis-

---

54. Beckwith, *The Old Testament Canon of the New Testament Church*, pp. 80-86.
55. It is telling that only Daniel "fooled" everyone.

dom in the meantime.[56] The focus was on becoming spiritually literate while waiting for God to act in the future.[57]

The Torah, Prophets, and Writings are stitched together with significant canonical seams that stress the importance of wisdom and study. At the beginning of the Torah, there is the creation of light by the Word of God, which establishes the rhythm of the day and night (Gen. 1:3). At the beginning of the Prophets, there is a call for the wise Joshua to meditate on the Torah day and night and thus prosper in his way (Josh. 1:8-9). And at the beginning of the Writings, there is an identical exhortation to each Israelite (Ps. 1:2-3). As if to ensure the importance of Torah, the Psalms are divided into five "books." The great words of life that lit up the world can now light up one's life with wisdom as one meditates on them day and night and speaks them back to God.[58]

This suggests an editorial activity that united the whole and that has a number of implications: there is an awareness that a great era of revelation has come to an end, and the call is to meditate on the Torah day and night, and to be wise. Thus it is probably not an accident that many of the last books of the Tanakh are wisdom books, and stress the importance of the sage, the student. Chronicles may well have been written as a way to close the entire sequence, as it is clearly a book of reflection, which constantly reinforces through its stories the importance of obeying the divine word and prospering (2 Chron. 20:20; 31:21; 32:30). It is not just a recapitulation of the biblical Story from beginning to end, but one long meditation on that Story. Its focus on the story of David shows what surely has become the main locus of biblical hope — the Davidic covenant. That the third division of the Tanakh closes with this emphasis on David, when it is remembered that it begins with David, the book of Ruth essentially functioning as an introduction to the Psalms, it would be appropriate to show the locus of biblical hope with the designations: Moses (Torah), Elijah (Prophets), and David (Psalms, Wisdom).[59]

---

56. Gerald T. Sheppard, *Wisdom as a Hermeneutical Construct: A Study in the Sapientializing of the Old Testament*, BZAW 151 (Berlin: De Gruyter, 1980).

57. See, e.g., John H. Sailhamer, *Introduction to Old Testament Theology: A Canonical Approach* (Grand Rapids: Zondervan, 1995); Stephen G. Dempster, "An Extraordinary Fact: Torah and Temple and the Contours of the Hebrew Canon, Part 1," *Tyndale Bulletin* 48 (1997): 23-54.

58. For further discussion see Dempster, "Canons on the Left."

59. For further considerations of Chronicles as a conclusion to the canon see Georg Steins, *Die Chronik als kanonisches Abschlussphänomen. Studien zur Entstehung und Theologie von 1/2 Chronik* (Weinheim: Beltz Athenäum, 1995); Hendrik J. Koorevaar, "Die

From another perspective the entire canon becomes one comprehensive Story from Genesis to Nehemiah, whose narrative movement is suspended with prophetic commentary and wisdom literature before being resumed again in Daniel, Esther, Ezra-Nehemiah, and being completed with a recapitulation in Chronicles.

External evidence for a process like this is not lacking but it is scarce. The two earliest canonical lists (Josephus, *Baba Bathra* 14b), while differing, reflect this tripartite structure of Torah, Prophets and Psalms. One probably reflects an original Palestinian order and the other the Greek order of the Septuagint, which stressed genre categorization. In the book of 2 Maccabees, there is a reference to Nehemiah gathering books to form a library, which could represent books from the second and third divisions of the canon (2 Macc. 2:13-14). A later text dating to the end of the first century A.D. indicates that Ezra was involved in producing ninety-four books, twenty-four of which were to be used in public and seventy in private by the enlightened (2 Esdras 14). The first collection probably refers to canonical books and identifies Ezra as having an important part to play in their production. Similar comments are made in later Jewish sources. The fact that the canonical process is not explicitly described probably is the result of the canonical editors or tradents obscuring their tracks in order to stress the uniqueness of the resulting canonical collection: "The shape of the canon directs the reader's attention to the sacred writings rather than to their editors."[60] The Old Testament is thus "the book of God."[61]

The New Testament Era and Beyond

One common reference to designate the scriptures in the New Testament is the bipartite formula, "the Law and the Prophets" (Matt. 7:12; John 1:45; Rom. 3:21). However, in two texts Jesus refers to the vast canonical sweep of revelation either in promise or judgment. In Luke 24 Jesus states that his death and resurrection fulfilled all the predictions in *all* of the scriptures, which he calls not only "Moses and the prophets," but also "the law of Moses, the prophets and the psalms" (Luke 24:27, 44). The "psalms" may have

---

Chronik als intendierter Abschluss des alttestamentlichen Kanons," *Jahrbuch für evangelikale Theologie* 11 (1997): 42-76.

60. Brevard S. Childs, *Introduction to the Old Testament as Scripture* (Philadelphia: Fortress, 1979), p. 59.

61. Philo, *Quod Deterius*, 139.

been an abbreviated reference to the third part of the canon. Moreover, in Luke 11:49-51, Jesus predicts the completeness of judgment that is going to come upon the present generation for rejecting him. He accuses religious leaders of belonging to a chain of murderers who killed prophets from Abel to Zechariah the priest, whose respective martyrdoms both called out for vengeance (Gen. 4:10; 2 Chron. 24:22). It is probably not accidental that these individuals are found in the first and last books, respectively, of the canon noted above. Thus Jesus is attacking the religious leaders for their scriptural piety, but it is a piety that has killed the prophets, from the first book of the Bible to the last — and all those in between. This completeness in judgment is particularly effective if there is completeness to the entire canonical range of Scripture.

As mentioned before, Josephus indicates that for all Jews the canon was closed. The evidence from Qumran strongly points in the direction of an authoritative canon that was virtually, if not completely, identical to the later rabbinic canon. There is evidence of the presence of every book from this collection among the Qumran sect except Esther, whose absence may be simply due to chance. Although there is evidence of many other books that were used, virtually the only books that were cited authoritatively are "canonical" books.[62] Moreover, the same terms used to describe the Jewish Bible are found, such as "Moses and the Prophets."[63] There also may be a reference to a tripartite designation of the collection: "the book of Moses, the words of Moses and David."[64] There is even reference to a book that is to be studied day and night called the "Book of Meditation," a possible reference to the Torah, or to the entire collection of Scripture.[65]

---

62. See the list of James VanderKam in Eugene Ulrich, "Qumran and the Canon of the Old Testament," in *The Biblical Canons*, ed. J. M. Auwers and H. J. De Jonge (Leuven: Leuven University Press), p. 80. It is interesting in the list of forty-three citations that there is only possibly one from an extra-biblical book (Jubilees). VanderKam himself puts a question mark beside it. See also the study by Johan Lust, who takes the position that this is not a citation: "Quotation Formulae and Canon in Qumran," in *Canonization and Decanonization*, ed. A. van der Kooij and K. van der Toorn, Studies in the History of Religions 82 (Leiden: Brill, 1988), pp. 67-77. The reference in question is CD 16:2-4.

63. 1QS 1:1ff; 8:15-16; CD 7:15-17; 4QMMT 16.

64. 4QMMT 10.

65. CD 10:6; 13:2; 1QS 1:7. It may also be a reference to a "book of sighs," perhaps like Ezekiel or the book of Haggai, but it is probably too important to refer to only one book of Scripture. See Moshe Goshen-Gottstein, "'Sefer Hagu' — the End of a Puzzle," *Vetus Testamentum* 8 (1958): 286-88; Lawrence H. Schiffman, *The Halakhah at Qumran* (Leiden: Brill Archive, 1975), pp. 44-45.

Another enumeration from the late first century testifies to an order of twenty-four books (2 Esdras 14). Later tradition (Origen, 230 A.D.) suggested that the numbers twenty-two and twenty-four were alternate orders, the smaller number resulting from books being combined with each other (Ruth with Judges and Lamentations with Jeremiah). A list dating to the late first century and possibly early second century A.D. identifies twenty-seven books.[66] This probably comes from Christian sources and places the prophets at the end. The different number is reached by dividing the books differently. The first explicit Christian list (by Melito of Sardis) claiming Jewish influence identifies twenty-five books. Missing from Melito of Sardis's canon is Esther, which had been a controversial book in both Christianity and Judaism. Nevertheless, there is a remarkable continuity with the numbering of Josephus and 2 Esdras 14. One source dating from the Mishnaic period (A.D. 1-200) presents a canon of twenty-four books that is tripartite, beginning with Genesis and concluding with Chronicles (*Baba Bathra* 14b).

Text and Hermeneutics

After Christianity separated from Judaism because of the events surrounding the destruction of the temple and the influx of Gentiles into the church, the Greek Bible (the Septuagint) was quickly adopted for Christian use. Paul used it widely in the developing church of the first century, as his citations from the Old Testament clearly indicate. As the rift between Judaism and Christianity widened, it was inevitable that there would be confusion within Christianity regarding the exact limit and contours of their Jewish scriptures. As the geographical distance increased between the church and the centre of Judaism, Christian "canons" reflected this difference. Early Latin translations were almost always based on the Greek of the Septuagint rather than the Hebrew. Resulting confusion led to attempts to distinguish between canonical and noncanonical books. Reformation Christianity returned to its Jewish sources for the Old Testament, but with a different arrangement and numbering system based on Christian antecedents. It is thus in some ways a compromise.[67]

Within Judaism, there are remarkable stability and continuity, not only in the numbering of the books but also in their texts. The content of the

---

66. Jean-Paul Audet, "A Hebrew-Aramaic List of Books of the Old Testament in Greek Transcription," *Journal of Theological Studies* 1 (1950): 135-54.

67. See Koorevaar, "Die Chronik."

Tanakh is remarkably stable over time, which suggests that an archetype produced in Second Temple circles would have been preserved after the destruction of the Second Temple to provide the basis for transmission for the next millennium. The scrupulous care that this process demonstrates is enough to demonstrate the practical authority of this single corpus of books. The fact that, shortly before the first century A.D., Greek translations of Hebrew texts were being revised to this particular archetype further demonstrates canonical authority.[68]

The structure of the Hebrew Bible stresses the importance of internalizing the divine Word, and meditating on it while waiting for the great future act of God. Perhaps there is even an allusion to the trinitarian dimension in the Hebrew canonical structure, although we cannot state this conclusively. We might say that the Father is involved in Creation in the Torah and in the giving of the Law at Sinai; and the Son in redemption in the Prophets, where the prophets incarnate the divine word in history and announce the coming Messiah. In the Writings there is a focus on the Holy Spirit as Woman Wisdom moves in the structure of Creation and in the lives of all peoples, preparing the way for the future salvation, when all creation — everything that has breath — will praise the Lord (Ps. 150:6). Of course, at the beginning of the New Testament, when Jesus is baptized at the Jordan River and begins his ministry, the trinitarian dimension is conspicuous: the Father announces his good pleasure in his beloved Son while the Spirit hovers over the Son as he emerges from the waters (Matt. 3:16-17). Yet it is interesting that the Father's pronouncement consists of statements laced together from all three parts of the Hebrew Bible: "This is my beloved son [Gen. 22:2; Ps. 2:7] in whom I am well pleased [Isa. 42:1]."

It is sometimes said that the Hebrew Bible, by concluding with the Writings, effectively diminishes the eschatological force of the first three-quarters of the Christian Bible.[69] Concluding with Chronicles rather than Malachi blunts the prophetic thrust of the Old Testament. While this may be partly true, it is not the whole truth. Chronicles sums up the entire story of the Hebrew Bible. In many ways it is a genealogy in search of an ending, concluding

---

68. Albert Wolters, "The Text of the Old Testament," in *The Face of Old Testament Studies: A Survey of Contemporary Approaches*, ed. David W. Baker and Bill T. Arnold (Grand Rapids: Baker Academic, 2004), pp. 28-31; E. Tov, *Textual Criticism of the Hebrew Bible* (Leiden: Brill, 2005), p. 28.

69. Hartmut Gese, *Vom Sinai zum Zion: Alttestamentliche Beiträge zur biblischen Theologie*, Beiträge zur evangelischen Theologie 64 (Munich: Chr. Kaiser, 1974), p. 17; James A. Sanders, "Spinning the Bible," *Bible Review* 14 (1998): 23-29, 44-45.

with an eschatological hope for a Davidic descendant. It concludes with the ruler of the then-known world, Cyrus — the anointed of the Lord — declaring that all the kingdoms of the world have been given to him so that he can now issue the summons for the Jewish exiles to return home to rebuild the temple.[70] The first book of the New Testament begins with a long genealogy clearly ordered in three groups of fourteen descendants to highlight the Davidic theme, and concluding with Jesus as the ultimate Son of David.[71] The book of Matthew concludes with this same Jesus, now resurrected from death, declaring to his disciples that all authority has been given to him so that they can now be summoned to "rebuild the temple," i.e., make disciples of all nations.[72]

Conclusion: Two Testaments, One Bible

The fundamental structure of the Hebrew Bible has even left its stamp on the structure of the New Testament canon: the four gospels function as a Torah-like foundation. Jesus sends his disciples into the world conquering and to conquer; so Acts functions like the Former Prophets, describing the young church's growth and conquest over darkness, to reach the whole world. The Pauline letters function as a complement to Acts, with Paul's pastoral and prophetic addresses, expounding the essential meaning of the Torah of Christ's life, rebuking, encouraging, and advising many of the converts to whom he preached in Acts. The Catholic Letters complete this structure with a more diverse, apostolic collection. The Book of Revelation effectively brings closure to the canon with its triadic seven-fold structure indicating completion and with its prolific Old Testament allusions recalling but surpassing the primal Edenic paradise. Heaven has now joined earth, and the long-hoped-for fulfillment of all the Old Testament hopes for creation is now a reality. While the canonical formula at the end of Revelation not to add or subtract from "this book" probably originally referred specifically to that book (Rev. 22:18), it now serves as a fitting conclusion to the entire Christian canon.

The Old Testament is absolutely crucial to the church's Bible; without it

---

70. 2 Chron. 36:22-23.

71. Matt. 1:1-18. The numerical value of the name David in Hebrew is 14!

72. Matt. 28:18-20. I am indebted to Hendrik Koorevaar for this insight: Koorevaar, "Die Chronik," p. 74.

the New Testament is incomprehensible. It is not just an antiquated relic, to be viewed but no longer used, as beautiful furniture for a building. Rather, it is an integral part of the architecture of the scriptural building. Or to change the metaphor, it is not an outmoded vehicle no longer to be used since it has served its purpose by carrying its passengers to a new destination — like a booster rocket that lifts its missile into the sky, sending it into orbit.[73] Rather, in the striking image of Al Wolters,[74] it is like a rocket that carries a payload of fireworks up into the dark night sky. When it finally reaches its summit, it explodes into a dazzling display of color and light, illuminating the entire landscape. The stunning resulting vision would be impossible without the long ascent into the blackness of the night.

73. For this example, see Seitz, *The Goodly Fellowship of the Prophets.*
74. Al Wolters, "The Centre and the Circumference," *Vanguard* (April 1980): 5-6.

8 Mission and Old Testament Interpretation

Christopher J. H. Wright

Hearing the Old Testament from the angle of mission presupposes the possibility and validity of a missional hermeneutic of the Bible as a whole. That is a relatively recent quest in the academy, even though those of us engaged in it would want to say that it is a way of reading Scripture that goes back to the Bible itself. Perhaps some account of my own personal journey in this direction may be forgiven and will set the context for the discussion below.

My doctoral work in Cambridge in the 1970s was in the field of Old Testament economic ethics. That led to a few early lectures and publications in Old Testament ethics (which at that time was also a relatively uncultivated field). After some years of ordained pastoral ministry, I taught at All Nations Christian College (a training institution near London for people involved in cross-cultural Christian mission) for a year prior to going to teach in India. During that year I heard Martin Goldsmith talking about the missiological context out of which New Testament texts had arisen. That is to say — he urged us (as staff and students) to see that it was not enough merely to exegete the biblical text and then ask "what are the missiological implications?" Rather, we needed to take into account that the circumstances that had led to the writing of the text in the first place were missional. Mission was intrinsic to the texts at the point of origin — not merely an extrinsic implication or application that we derive later. I was struck by that insight and began to apply it to Old Testament texts, finding the results interesting and hermeneutically fruitful.

I then went to teach the Old Testament in India for five years and found enormous stimulation in reading these texts with students who were going to be engaged in ministry and mission in that cultural and religious context. The ethical and spiritual challenges for God's people living in the midst of a polytheistic context seemed to step off the pages of the Old Testament straight onto the streets of India in remarkably relevant ways. Missional reading of the Bible seemed very appropriate in that environment, and my combination of ethical and missiological appropriation of the texts continued to develop.

Back in the United Kingdom in 1988, and teaching again at All Nations, I inherited Martin Goldsmith's course, The Biblical Basis of Mission. I applied the hermeneutical approach I had first learned from him and tried to read the whole Bible from a missional perspective. I used to tell the students that I would like to change the title of the course to "The Missional Basis of the Bible" — that I wanted to help them read the whole Bible for mission, not just to collect a few "missionary texts" like beads on a string. At the same time, I encouraged a number of our M.A. students to explore a missiological reading of Old Testament books. Some interesting master's-level dissertations emerged — on Deuteronomy, the Deuteronomic history, wisdom literature, the Book of the Twelve, and Ezekiel. In my own writing of commentaries on Deuteronomy[1] and Ezekiel,[2] I sought to apply some missiological reflection, with sections in the introductions devoted to the hermeneutical challenge that involved.

Eventually all this came together in my book *The Mission of God: Unlocking the Bible's Grand Narrative*.[3] This was the culmination of all those years of reflection and teaching, and an attempt to argue for the validity of a missional hermeneutic of Scripture in principle, and to offer some outline of what it might look like in practice.

Then, just as that was coming to completion, I was introduced to a group of biblical and missiological scholars, mostly from Canada and the United States, who had been meeting annually since 2002 in the context of the annual convention of the Society of Biblical Literature to wrestle with a missional hermeneutic of Scripture. I found even more encouragement and stimulation in that group of cheerfully encouraging fellow-travelers who welcomed my own contribution to the task.

---

1. Christopher J. H. Wright, *Deuteronomy*, NIBCOT (Peabody, MA: Hendrickson, 1996).

2. Christopher J. H. Wright, *The Message of Ezekiel*, The Bible Speaks Today (Downers Grove: IVP, 2001).

3. Christopher J. H. Wright, *The Mission of God: Unlocking the Bible's Grand Narrative* (Downers Grove: IVP, 2006).

In the 2008 meeting of that group, George Hunsberger offered a most helpful summarizing paper, "Proposals for a Missional Hermeneutic: Mapping the Conversation,"[4] analyzing some key ways that the contributors to the group's reflection over seven years had developed. Referring to articles and books published by the group over the previous six years, Hunsberger suggested that the term "missional hermeneutics" was being used in four distinct, though obviously related, ways. In the hands of different scholars it could mean the missional direction or framework of the biblical narrative; the missional purpose of the biblical texts; the missional locatedness of readers of the Bible; and the missional engagement of the gospel with cultures.

In this chapter we will first survey these four dimensions of a missional reading suggested by Hunsberger. Then we shall outline what seem to me to be five primary contributions that the Old Testament has made to the theological underpinning of Christian mission, ever since its origins in the New Testament. We will observe how these theological themes cohere with several of the dimensions of missional reading identified by Hunsberger's article.

The first part of our chapter, then, is an attempt to survey some current thinking on what a missional approach to the Bible as a whole involves, while the second part focuses on the challenge that this present volume addresses — hearing the Old Testament in particular — and asking what such a missional approach enables us to hear when we do so.

The Shape of a Missional Hermeneutic

The four headings below and the quotes that follow them are drawn from Hunsberger's article. The authors I refer to are all contributors to the group's deliberations.

The Missional Direction of the Story

The *framework* for biblical interpretation is the story it tells of the mission of God and the formation of a community sent to participate in it.

---

4. George R. Hunsberger, "Proposals for a Missional Hermeneutic: Mapping the Conversation," presented at the annual meeting of AAR/SBL (2008). The full paper and its bibliographical references can be read at http://www.gocn.org/resources/articles/proposals-missional-hermeneutic-mapping-conversation.

This is the approach that aligns most closely with my own work; it constitutes the major argument of my book *The Mission of God.* The Bible as a whole renders to us the narrative of God's mission, through God's people, in God's world, for God's purpose — the redemption of all of God's creation. This grand overarching narrative, from creation to new creation, constitutes what Paul called "the whole counsel of God," or the whole will, plan, purpose, mission of God (Acts 20:27). Specifically, it is the narrative that takes us from Genesis 10–11, to Revelation 21–22; from the nations scattered in rebellion as the climax of the escalation of sin since Genesis 3, to the nations gathered in worship of God and the Lamb who was slain. Or indeed, it is the narrative that takes us from the creation that was good in Genesis 1–2 but spoiled by our sin in Genesis 3, to the new creation, redeemed and reconciled by the blood of Christ in Colossians 1:20 and Revelation 20–21. The whole Bible narrative in between is the mission of God to get from the one to the other.

Mission is often thought of as a New Testament and post–New Testament phenomenon. Is it possible to read the Old Testament also as a missional text? The clearest justification for doing so is that Jesus himself told his disciples to read it that way. In Luke 24 he twice surveys the whole canon of Old Testament Scripture and claims that "this is what is written": both that the Messiah would come, suffer, die, and rise again; and that repentance and forgiveness of sins would be preached in his name to the nations (vv. 45-47). The first claim reads Scripture messianically; the second reads Scripture missiologically — and Jesus urges this double hermeneutical strategy on those who read the Old Testament in conscious relation to himself.

This sets the Old Testament canon in continuity with the New, the beginning with the climax. Thus, God's election of Abraham and gift of a land is instrumental in God's plan for the blessing of all nations and the whole earth. The sequence of election, redemption, covenant, and land-gift is thus paradigmatic for the wider story of God's multinational people, redeemed to inhabit the earth. This, according to Paul, is the narrative heart of the gospel promise (cf. Gal. 3:6-8; Rom. 4). The universality that is of the essence of the New Testament gospel is the outworking of the genetic code already embedded in the DNA of Old Testament Israel.

But the failure of Old Testament Israel, and the broken covenant, led to both judgment (in the immediate history of Old Testament Israel — i.e., the Exile), and also to future hope (the eschatology of restoration for Israel and ingathering of the nations). This is a theme that is found in poetic anticipation in Deuteronomy 32, but gathers clarity and emphasis in the prophets, especially during and after the Exile itself. All this prepares the way for the New Testament proclamation of the embodiment and fulfillment of God's mission through Israel in the person and accomplishment of Jesus of Nazareth, and the New Testament mission of the church in the power of the Spirit to accomplish the ingathering of the nations by going to them with the message of the gospel.

Starting in this way with Jesus' theocentric and teleological use of Scripture also reminds us that handling the Bible in relation to mission is not merely a matter of identifying themes within it that justify and shape *our* engagement in mission. For behind all human mission stands the mission of God. And the Bible itself (including of course the Old Testament), by its very existence, is a dimension of the mission of God. The whole canon of Scripture is a missional phenomenon in the sense that it witnesses to the self-giving movement of this God, in revelation and redemption, towards his creation and towards us, human beings made in God's own image, but wayward and rebellious. The writings, which now comprise our Bible, are themselves the product of, and witness to, the ultimate mission of God for the redemption of humanity and creation.

This is the great overarching framework of the biblical narrative, which renders to us the mission of God. We shall return to some of these key features below. But for the moment, these observations mean that a missional hermeneutic will work hard to read any text in the Old Testament canon within this overarching narrative framework, discerning its place within that framework, assessing how the shape of the grand narrative is reflected in the text in question, and conversely, how the particular text contributes to and moves forward the grand narrative itself.

Obviously not all features of the story will be discernable in every text. But, for example, it is not difficult to see how many of the psalmists and prophets clearly see the purpose of Israel's election and redemption (not just for their own sake but for God's wider plans among the nations of the world — e.g., Pss. 22:27-28; 47:9; 67:1-2; Isa. 48:1-4, 18-19; Jer. 13:1-11; 4:1-2); how they expose the reality of Israel's failure and God's covenant judgment (Pss. 74; 78; 106; Amos 2:8–3:2; Hos. 4–5; Isa. 5:1-7; Jer. 2:1–3:5; 11:1-3; Ezek. 5:5-17; and *passim*); how they hold out hope of future restoration beyond that judgment (Amos 9:11-15; Hos. 2; Isa. 40–55; Jer. 33:8-9; Ezek. 34–37); and how they anticipate the resultant blessing among the nations when God acts to redeem his people (Deut. 32:43; Ps. 102:13, 15-16, 21-22; Isa. 19:24-25; Isa. 60; Jer. 3:17; 12:14-17; Zech. 2:10-11). This is just a tiny selection of a much wider range of texts that I have tried to explicate in *The Mission of God* (particularly chapter 14).

The Missional Purpose of the Writings

The *aim* of biblical interpretation is to fulfill the equipping purpose of the biblical writings.

Darrell Guder, referring primarily to the documents of the New Testament, argues that the purpose of the written word was the same as that of the teaching and preaching of Jesus and the apostles, namely for the formation of a missional community of disciples. The texts arose with the purpose of equipping the church for witness, for carrying on the mission of God in the world.[5] Michael Barram sees this as an important element in the mission strategy of the Apostle Paul, and hence argues for a missional understanding of Paul's letters.[6]

My own work on the purpose of the law in Old Testament Israel includes the observation that it was given in order to "shape" Israel into a community that would reflect the character of Yahweh, enabling them to be the public, visible exemplar of God's intention for a redeemed community of people.[7] So the legal texts can be interpreted with this sense of their "mission" within Israel's society. The mission of Israel was to be a light and blessing to the nations. The "mission" of the law was to shape Israel for that task.

The same shaping function can be discerned in other texts, however, even if more implicitly than the explicit statements of such purpose in the law. Narratives, for example, functioned with powerful ethical impact, shaping the self-perception of Israel and their understanding of the norms and paradigms of what was "done" or "not done" in Israel.[8] The prophets spoke to generations of Israelites that had gotten badly "out of shape" and needed to be called back to radical repentance and conformity with the covenant requirements. The wisdom literature is most explicitly didactic in this direction, while the poetry of worship inculcates the kind of behavior, attitudes, and relationships that fit with the claims and promises of the covenant. At

5. Darrell Guder, "Biblical Formation and Discipleship," in *Treasure in Clay Jars: Patterns in Missional Faithfulness,* ed. Lois Barrett et al. (Grand Rapids: Eerdmans, 2004), pp. 59-73.

6. Michael Barram, *Mission and Moral Reflection in Paul* (Berlin: Peter Lang, 2005).

7. Christopher J. H. Wright, *Old Testament Ethics for the People of God* (Downers Grove: IVP, 2004), especially chapters 2 and 9.

8. See, e.g., Waldemar Janzen, *Old Testament Ethics: A Paradigmatic Approach* (Louisville: Westminster John Knox, 1994); and Gordon J. Wenham, *Story as Torah: Reading the Old Testament Ethically* (Edinburgh: T&T Clark, 2000).

the same time, some psalms also lament and protest when God, Israel and the world seem to be so out of joint and those who are trying to live in the ways of God get nothing but suffering and oppression.

So a missional hermeneutic asks: How did this or that particular text function to equip and shape God's people for their missional witness, and how does it continue to shape us today? The answer may include negative as well as positive dimensions, but the point is to see how Scripture, including Old Testament Scripture, functioned to enable the people of God to live out that identity and role in the midst of the world of surrounding nations. We will give more attention to this angle in the section below on the missional relevance of Old Testament ethics.

The Missional Locatedness of the Readers

The *approach* required for a faithful reading of the Bible is from the missional location of the Christian community.

Michael Barram, arguing in support of the perspective mentioned above, shifts the perspective from the text itself to the community reading it.[9] That community of God's people has its own located context in history and culture, within which it must work out its own missional life and witness. Every generation of God's people in every human context is called upon to respond to these given scriptural texts in and for the location of their missional existence. So a missional hermeneutic arises when the believing community searches the Scriptures intentionally in order to discern the shape and demands of the mission God has for them in their particular context. Every community of God's people shares in the "sent" nature of God's people as a whole. They have a missional reality and calling, and they read the scriptural texts in relation to that. Such a reading calls for *both* serious attention to the original contexts of the texts, with the exegetical discipline needed to ascertain what was being said to those who first heard or read them, *and* serious questioning of the contemporary reader's own context to discern the missional opportunities and challenges that arise when the text is read in the light of it.

Now this has considerable similarity to the hermeneutics long associ-

9. Michael Barram, "The Bible, Mission, and Social Location: Toward a Missional Hermeneutic," *Interpretation* 61 (January 2007): 42-59.

ated with the various models of liberation theology. A major contribution that liberation theology made to the hermeneutical task was to perceive the importance of the historical, social, and cultural location of the reader(s) of the biblical text. To read the text from a position of poverty, exclusion, or oppression will generate questions and answers in the process of reading and responding to the text that will be different from those that may arise when reading from positions of relative wealth or sociopolitical dominance. Contexts count. And theology must be done in the process of missional engagement with each context, seeking to be both faithful to the text and the doctrinal tradition it embodies, and relevant to the context and the committed praxis for which it calls.

However, we can take this perspective further back. It is not merely the context of contemporary readers that is missional. The processes by which these texts came to be written were themselves often profoundly missional in nature — as I noted above in referring to the insight I first encountered from Martin Goldsmith at All Nations Christian College. Many of them emerged out of events, or struggles, or crises, or conflicts, in which the people of God engaged with the constantly changing and challenging task of articulating and living out their understanding of God's revelation and redemptive action in the world. Sometimes these were struggles internal to the people of God themselves; sometimes they were highly polemical struggles with competing religious claims and worldviews that surrounded them. Biblical texts often have their origin in some issue, need, controversy or threat, which the people of God needed to address in the context of their mission. The text in itself is a product of mission in action.

This is readily apparent in the New Testament. Most of Paul's letters were written in the heat of his missionary efforts: wrestling with the theological basis of the inclusion of the Gentiles; affirming the need for Jew and Gentile to accept one another in Christ and in the church; tackling the baffling range of new problems that assailed young churches as the gospel took root in the world of Greek polytheism; confronting incipient heresies with clear affirmations of the supremacy and sufficiency of Jesus Christ, and so on. Similarly, the Gospels were written to explain the significance of the good news about Jesus of Nazareth, especially his death and resurrection. Confidence in these things was essential to the missionary task of the expanding church.

But if we look carefully we can see that many Old Testament texts emerged out of the engagement of Israel with the surrounding world in the light of the God they knew in their history and in covenantal relationship.

People produced texts in relation to what they believed God had done, was doing, or would do, in their world. The Torah records the Exodus as an act of Yahweh that comprehensively confronted and defeated the power of Pharaoh and all his rival claims to deity and allegiance. It presents a theology of creation that stands in sharp contrast to the polytheistic creation myths of Mesopotamia. The historical narratives portray the long and sorry story of Israel's struggle with the culture and religion of Canaan, a struggle reflected also in the pre-exilic prophets. Exilic and postexilic texts emerge out of the task that the small remnant community of Israel faced to define their continuing identity as a community of faith in successive empires of varying hostility or tolerance. Wisdom texts interact with international wisdom traditions in the surrounding cultures, but do so with staunch monotheistic disinfectant. And in worship and prophecy, Israelites reflect on the relationship between their God, Yahweh, and the rest of the nations — sometimes negatively, sometimes positively — and on the nature of their own role as Yahweh's elect priesthood in their midst.

This observation that the canon of Scripture, including the Old Testament, is missional in its origin (in the purpose of God), and in its formation (in the multiple contexts of cultural engagement), means that so-called contextualization is not something we add to "the real meaning" of biblical texts, but is intrinsic to them. The task of recontextualizing the word of God is a missional project that has its basis in Scripture itself and has been part of the mission of God's people all through the centuries of their existence. The finality of the canon refers to the completion of God's work of revelation and redemption, not to a foreclosure on the necessary continuation of the inculturated witness to that completed work in every culture.

So, then, we should take into account not only the missional locatedness of today's readers, but also the missional locatedness of the very first readers of the canonical texts. The Scriptures, after all, are not disembodied pronouncements dropped from heaven, but collections of texts that addressed living people in specific contexts, who were therefore called upon to respond to them, in faith and action. What can we know about those original contexts, and how can we discern the missional drive and energy that the texts injected into them?

An interesting case in point would be the canonical book of Jeremiah. Thinking first of all about the way Jeremiah addresses modern readers, we are not short of illustrations. There are so many ways in which the world into which Jeremiah spoke is paralleled in today's international world, and the message that Jeremiah brought has continuing sharpness. So our missional reading of Jeremiah engages the text from the perspective of the many concerns of our own contexts, which find matching concerns in the text.

We might think, for example, of the following aspects of Jeremiah's context that have missional relevance to our own in ways that are not difficult to articulate:

- *the international scene* — collapse of the old world order (the Assyrian empire), fear over new threats
- *religious confusion among God's own people* — all the changes of Josiah's reformation, but continuing idolatry, and misplaced nationalism posturing as patriotism
- *social evils* — inequality, cheating, injustice, immorality, and so on
- *abuse of political power to stifle dissent* — the murder of prophets, the suffering of Jeremiah
- *abuse of religious power* — false prophets and corrupt priests, and collusion in social evils and immorality
- *the message of God's sovereignty in history* — including contemporary events, and seeing his hand even in the attack upon the homeland; the necessity of judgment
- *the mission of God's people* — even in exile
- *grace in the end* — after judgment, and the unquenchable forward-looking hope

However, moving to my second point above, a missional hermeneutic will take into account not only the missional locatedness of contemporary readers of the book, but the missional locatedness even of the original readers. And who were they?

Note the opening and closing editorial sections: Jeremiah 1:1-3; 52:27-34. The book has been put together for those who had experienced the ending of it — i.e., the Exile. Thus, when we read the text of Jeremiah, we need to engage in "double listening." We need to listen through the ears of those who first heard Jeremiah in the forty years of his ministry before 587 B.C. (and failed to respond); and also, we must read the collected text through the eyes of those who would read these words in the circumstances that Jeremiah had predicted for those forty years. The poignant calls to repentance, for example, must have sounded different, as between those who first heard them preached but refused to heed them, and those who heard them or read them as they sat under the judgment that had finally fallen on such refusal.

Did the exiles have a "missional location" as they read the text of Jeremiah? They probably didn't think so. Psalm 137 and Lamentations reflect their mood, at least in the early years of exile.

But see Jeremiah 29:1-14, Jeremiah's letter to the exiles. Here surely is a powerful piece of "located missiology"! It is full of surprises. Indeed, it must have sounded shocking to those who were languishing in the first traumatic experience of exile. It offered them a new perspective on their situation, to see it as the work of their God, not just the work of Nebuchadnezzar (vv. 1, 4), thus turning them from temporary refugees into residents who needed to settle down with God for at least two generations. It also called them, secondly, to a surprising new mission — to seek the shalom of Babylon and to pray for it (v. 7). This was an astounding piece of advice to give to people reduced to singing Psalm 137 and knowing only the instruction to seek the shalom of Jerusalem (Ps. 122). But it turned their mourning into mission — the mission of fulfilling the Abrahamic role of being a blessing to the nations even in the midst of their enemies. And thirdly, it gave them a surprising new hope (vv. 10-14), that the Exile was not in fact (as some of them feared) the end of all God's plans for Israel and the world. The story would go on. Their was hope for their future — not in the short-term optimism of some of the false prophets, but in the long term faithfulness of God for coming generations. This turned victims into visionaries, able to live in Babylon knowing that it was not their final destination but a transit lounge for God's ongoing mission.

One can go on to read the rest of the book of Jeremiah with that question in mind: in what ways would this or that text in the book have spoken to the exiles — negatively and positively, with challenge and encouragement, in relation to what it *now* meant to be the people of God in a foreign land facing a present and a future that looked so bleak? The so-called Book of Consolation (chs. 30–33) would enable them to see that the promise of restoration for Israel would ultimately extend the knowledge of God among the nations, so that the hope of God for his people first expressed in 13:11, but so sadly frustrated by their sin, would eventually be fulfilled.

> I will cleanse them from all the sin they have committed against me and will forgive all their sins of rebellion against me. Then this city will bring me renown, joy, praise and honour before all nations on earth that hear of all the good things I do for it; and they will be in awe and will tremble at the abundant prosperity and peace I provide for it. (Jer. 33:8-9)

The Missional Engagement with Cultures

> The gospel functions as the interpretive matrix within which the received biblical tradition is brought into critical conversation with a particular human context.

Jim Brownson (whom Hunsberger credits with the first use of the term "missional hermeneutic") observes how New Testament authors used Old Testament texts in addressing the new situations that they faced in the expanding missionary work of the church, but did so according to a gospel-shaped framework. The Scriptures were "given"; the new situations were fluid and changing. The hermeneutical task meant relating the former to the latter in a way that remained faithful to the essential core of the gospel.[10]

Once again, it would be possible to transfer this method back to the Old Testament itself. For there too we find later authors and texts addressing new situations on the basis of received tradition — namely the great historic pillars of Israel's faith: election, redemption, and covenant (which we shall explore in a moment). That is certainly how we find the prophets using Israel's history in order to challenge successive generations of Israelites over their unfaithfulness to the covenantal obligations that that history had laid upon them.

Or, conversely, we may find a text anticipating a new situation that lies ahead, and articulating what Israel's missional response to it needs to be. This is one of the dimensions of a missional reading of Deuteronomy that I discussed in the introduction to my commentary on that book.[11] Whatever one's critical view of its date and authorship, the presenting argument of the book is that the Israelites would face a seductive and dangerous culture of polytheism and related social evils in the land of Canaan, and they needed therefore to fortify their resolve to remain loyal to their one covenant Lord, in order to be a model to the watching nations and ultimately (and mysteriously in ch. 32), to be the means of the nations coming to praise Yahweh the God of Israel.

Or we might explore the missional relevance of the way Israel's wisdom tradition was able to absorb and adapt the wisdom of surrounding cultures, but to do so through the filter of their own monotheistic faith. I have explored this both in my books *Old Testament Ethics* (chapter 10) and *The Mission of God* (chapter 13).

---

10. James V. Brownson, *Speaking the Truth in Love: New Testament Resources for a Missional Hermeneutic* (Harrisburg: Trinity Press International, 1998).

11. Wright, *Deuteronomy.*

Pillars of Old Testament Faith That Support Christian Mission

What follows is a brief survey of some of the key Old Testament themes that undergird a biblical theology of Christian mission. This is not a search for odd verses of the Old Testament that might say something relevant to a narrow concept of sending missionaries or "going on missions," but rather a sketch of some of the great trajectories of Israel's understanding of their God and of God's mission through Israel for all the nations. We are not concerned about how the Old Testament gives incidental support to what we already do in "missions," but about the scriptural theology that undergirds the whole worldview that Christian mission presupposes. That is, we are seeking to "hear the Old Testament" as it speaks its great claims and affirmations in relation to the mission of God's people as a whole.

Yet I would not want the above comment about the nature of the following discussion to suggest any negative reflection on the work of cross-cultural missions and the core element of "sending" that is implicit in Christian mission. On the contrary, the concept of being called and sent by God is deeply rooted in the Old Testament itself, and there are indeed rich resources for exploring the "sending" dimension of mission. Most of us will have heard "missionary sermons" on the call of Moses, Isaiah, Jeremiah, and even (especially) Jonah. Hearing the Old Testament for missional purposes from these texts is not inappropriate. We could reflect further (in line with my reference above to a missional hermeneutic of Jeremiah) on the missional cost to the messengers whom God chose to send. All of this has valid and fruitful scope for reflection. However, in what follows I am concentrating on the theological dimensions of Old Testament faith, rather than the specific examples of people whom God "sent."[12]

We will survey briefly the missiological implications of five major pillars of Old Testament faith — monotheism, election, redemption, ethics, and eschatology.

---

12. I have explored in some depth the biblical concept of sending and being sent, in relation to the mission of the church, in Christopher J. H. Wright, *The Mission of God's People: A Biblical Theology of the Church's Mission*, Biblical Theology for Life (Grand Rapids: Zondervan, 2010), chapter 12.

The Uniqueness and Universality of Yahweh as Against All the Gods of the Nations: The Missiological Implications of Biblical Monotheism

Yahweh is God and there is no other (Deut. 4:32-39). Israel made remarkable affirmations about Yahweh, affirmations which had a polemical edge in their own context and still stand as distinctive claims. Among them was the monotheistic declaration that Yahweh alone is God and there is no other (e.g., Deut. 4:35, 39). This is not the place to do an extended critical survey of the vast literature on Old Testament monotheism. Suffice it to say that I am convinced by the arguments of Richard Bauckham[13] and others that there was a categorical distinctiveness about the claims made by Israel concerning the transcendent uniqueness of Yahweh as only true and living God. I have explored in detail the missiological dimensions of Old Testament monotheism in *The Mission of God,* Part 2.

As sole deity, it is Yahweh, therefore, who owns the world and rules the world (Deut. 10:14; Ps. 24:1; Jer. 27:1-12; 1 Chron. 29:11). This ultimately means the radical displacement of all other rival gods and that Yahweh must be acknowledged as God over the whole earth and all nations (e.g., Ps. 96; Jer. 10:1-16; Isa. 43:9-13; 44:6-20). The impact of these claims is felt in such widely varying contexts as the struggle against idolatry, the language of worship, and the response to other nations, both in their own contemporary international history, and in eschatological vision. Monotheism, in other words, is inevitably and intrinsically missional. For this one true living God wills to be known throughout his whole creation and to all nations.

There is no doubt that the strength of these Old Testament affirmations about the uniqueness and universality of Yahweh as God underlies, and indeed provides some of the vocabulary for, the New Testament affirmations about the uniqueness and universality of Jesus (cf. Phil. 2:9-11, based on Isa. 45:23; and 1 Cor. 8:5-6, based on Deut. 6:4). The amazing fact is that the earliest followers of Jesus recognized in him all of the major identities and functions of Yahweh in the Old Testament. The essence of Old Testament mono-

---

13. Richard Bauckham, "Biblical Theology and the Problems of Monotheism," in *Out of Egypt: Biblical Theology and Biblical Interpretation,* ed. Craig Bartholomew et al., SAHS 5 (Grand Rapids: Zondervan, 2004), pp. 187-232. Several of Bauckham's seminal contributions in this whole field of a Christian understanding of Old Testament monotheism are now collected in his monograph *Jesus and the God of Israel: God Crucified and Other Studies on the New Testament's Christology of Divine Identity* (Grand Rapids: Eerdmans, 2008). Cf. also Nathan Macdonald, "Whose Monotheism? Which Rationality?" in *The Old Testament in Its World,* ed. R. P. Gordon and J. C. de Moor (Leiden: Brill, 2005), pp. 45-67.

theism is to say that Yahweh alone is Creator, Sovereign, Judge, and Savior.[14] The New Testament affirms these very same things about Jesus of Nazareth. It is also noteworthy that these early Christian affirmations were equally polemical in their own historical context as those of ancient Israel and in turn provided the primary rationale and motivation for Christian mission.

If Yahweh alone is God and if Jesus alone is Lord, and if it is God's will (as it manifestly is in the Bible) that these truths be known throughout the whole creation, then there is a missional mandate intrinsic to such convictions. A fully biblical understanding of the universality and uniqueness of Yahweh and of Jesus Christ stands in the frontline of a missional response to the relativism at the heart of religious pluralism and some forms of postmodernist philosophy. Biblical monotheism in both its New Testament, Christocentric, richness, and in its Old Testament foundations, is one of the key pillars of all Christian mission.

This point strongly connects with the trinitarian perspective of Chapter 1 in the present volume. In terms of our overarching biblical theology, the God whom we have come to know in the fullness of his self-revelation as God the Holy Trinity is clearly identical with Yahweh, the unique covenant God of Old Testament Israel. That is to say, Yahweh "includes" within himself all three persons we now speak of as Father, Son, and Holy Spirit, even though Old Testament Israelites did not think or speak in those terms. Ever since the second verse of Genesis we meet the Spirit of God, creating, empowering, anointing, transforming. And through the Old Testament era there are theophanies that anticipate, in their anthropomorphic descriptions of encounters with God in human form, the ultimate incarnation of God the Son in Jesus of Nazareth. However, it is probably right most often to have God the Father in mind when we read of Yahweh in Old Testament texts. The most compelling argument for this view is the prayer life of Jesus himself. Here is what I have written elsewhere on this point:

> Jesus was fully human. He grew up in a devout and believing Jewish home, and was without doubt a worshiping, praying child, young man, and adult. The daily habit of prayer that we read of in the Gospels must have been ingrained in him from childhood. So when Jesus worshiped and prayed, in his home or in the synagogue in Nazareth, to whom was his worship directed? Who was the God whose name he read in all the Scriptures he recited and all the songs he sang? To whom did Jesus pray at the

14. See Wright, *The Mission of God,* pp. 105-35.

knees of Mary and then through all his life? The answer is, of course, to the LORD, Yahweh (though he would have said *Adonai*). Jesus would have recited the Shema' daily with his fellow Jews, and he knew the "LORD our God" of that text to be the God of his people, his human parents and himself. So Jesus' whole perception of God was entirely shaped by the Scriptures that we call the Old Testament. When Jesus thought of God, spoke of God, reflected on the words and will of God, set out to obey God — it was *this* God, Yahweh God, that was in his mind. "God" for Jesus was the named, biographied, character-rich, self-revealed God Yahweh, the Holy One of Israel. When Jesus and his disciples talked together of God, this is the name they would have used (or would have known but piously avoided pronouncing). When Jesus read Isaiah 61 in the synagogue in Nazareth, he claimed that the Spirit of the LORD was upon him "Today" — the Spirit of Yahweh, God of the Old Testament prophets.

But of course, Jesus also knew this God of his Scriptures in the depth of his self-consciousness as *Abba,* as his own intimate personal Father. Luke tells us that this awareness was developing even in his childhood, and it was sealed at his baptism, when he heard the voice of his Father, accompanied by the Holy Spirit, confirming his identity as God's beloved Son. So in the consciousness of Jesus the *scriptural* identity of God as Yahweh and his *personal* intimacy with God as his Father must have blended together. The God he knew from his Bible as Yahweh was the God he knew in prayer as his Father. When Jesus took the Psalms on his lips on the cross, the God he was calling out to in the agony of abandonment was the God addressed in Psalm 22:1 as Elohim, but throughout the Psalm as Yahweh. The Psalmist was calling out to Yahweh. Jesus uses his words to call out to his Father.

Now since all our understanding of God as Father must start out from knowing Jesus, it makes sense for us also to think of Yahweh, the God of Old Testament Israel and the God of the one true faithful Israelite Jesus, as God the Father, for that is who Yahweh primarily was in the consciousness of Jesus himself.[15]

---

15. Christopher J. H. Wright, *Knowing God the Father Through the Old Testament* (Oxford: Monarch Press, 2007), pp. 18-20; and (Downers Grove: IVP, 2007), pp. 16-18. This is part of a trilogy exploring the persons of God from an Old Testament perspective that is often lacking in systematic theologies, and even more so in popular Christian consciousness. See also Christopher J. H. Wright, *Knowing Jesus Through the Old Testament* (Oxford: Monarch Press; Downers Grove: IVP, 1995); Christopher J. H. Wright, *Knowing the Holy Spirit Through the Old Testament* (Oxford: Monarch Press; Downers Grove: IVP, 2006).

The Universality of Yahweh's Plan through Israel for the Blessing of the Nations: The Missiological Implications of Election

The Old Testament begins on the stage of universal history. After the accounts of creation we read the story of God's dealings with fallen humanity and the problem and challenge of the world of the nations (Gen. 1–11). After the stories of the Flood and of the Tower of Babel, could there be any future for the nations in relation to God? Or would judgment have to be God's final word? The narrative from Genesis 3–11 presents the double problem of humanity — the universality of sin (in every human person and in every dimension of human personhood, spiritual, mental, physical, and social), and the dividedness and strife of the nations.

The story of Abraham, beginning in Genesis 12, is the launch of God's solution to both problems, a solution that will take the rest of the Bible to unfold.[16] God's declared commitment is that he intends to bring blessing to the nations, "all the families of the earth will be blessed through you" (Gen. 12:3). Repeated five times in Genesis alone, this key affirmation is the foundation of biblical mission, inasmuch as it declares the mission of God. The creator God's mission is nothing less than blessing the nations of humanity.

So fundamental is this divine agenda that Paul defines the Genesis declaration as "the gospel in advance" (Gal. 3:8). And the concluding vision of the whole Bible signifies the fulfillment of the Abrahamic promise, as people from every nation, tribe, language and people are gathered among the redeemed in the new creation (Rev. 7:9). The gospel and mission both begin in Genesis, then, and both are located in the redemptive intention of the Creator to bless the nations. Mission is God's address to the problem of fractured humanity and is universal in its ultimate goal and scope.

The same Genesis texts which affirm the universality of God's mission to bless the nations also, and with equal strength, affirm the particularity of God's election of Abraham and his descendants to be the vehicle of that mission. The election of Israel is one of the most fundamental pillars of the biblical worldview and of Israel's historical sense of identity. It is vital to insist that although the belief in their election could be (and was) distorted into a narrow doctrine of national superiority, that move was resisted in Israel's own literature (e.g., Deut. 7:7ff.). The affirmation is that Yahweh, the God who had chosen Israel, was also the creator, owner, and Lord of the whole world and all

---

16. On the missiological significance of the Abrahamic covenant, in both its universality and particularity, see Wright, *Mission of God,* chapters 6 and 7.

nations (Deut. 10:14f., cf. Exod. 19:4-6). That is, Yahweh was not just "the national God of Israel" — he was God of all nations. This is what Paul saw so clearly (e.g., in Rom. 4). Yahweh had chosen Israel in relation to his purpose for the world, not just for Israel. The election of Israel was not tantamount to a rejection of the nations, but explicitly for their ultimate benefit. Election is not an exclusive privilege but an inclusive responsibility. If we might paraphrase John, "God so loved the world that he chose Israel."

Thus, rather than asking if Israel itself "had a mission," in the sense of being "sent" anywhere (anachronistically injecting again our assumption that mission is only about "sending missionaries"), we need to see the missional nature of Israel's existence in relation to the mission of God in the world. Israel's mission was to *be* something, not to *go* somewhere. This perspective is clearly focused in the person of the Servant of Yahweh in Isaiah 40–55, who both embodies the election of Israel (identical things are said about Israel and the Servant), and also is charged with the mission (like Israel's) of bringing the blessing of Yahweh's justice, salvation, and glory to the ends of the earth.

From this we can see much more clearly the dynamic theology that underpinned Paul's understanding and practice of mission. He saw his task as taking the gospel to the Gentile nations and assuring them that, by trusting in the Messiah Jesus (who embodied the identity and mission of Israel but had been faithful where Israel had been rebellious, and had died to take upon himself their sin and the sin of the world), they were included in the family of God, members of the covenant people of God. The nations too, like Israel, were now being called, as he put it twice in Romans, to "faith's obedience" (Rom. 1:5; 16:26), that is to the status and the responsibility of covenant membership. In other words, through Christ God solved the problem of Genesis 3 and Genesis 11 — the root of sin, and the dividedness of humanity, seen most sharply in the separation of Jew and Gentile.

Two other implications of this point may be briefly mentioned. First, it indicates that in biblical theology, election is fundamentally missional, not merely soteriological. That is to say, God's choice of Abraham and Israel was instrumental, not preferential. The election of Israel was not into some singularly saved status from which all other nations would be excluded and rejected. Rather it was the election of Israel into a servant status to be the means by which God would enable all other nations to have the opportunity of being included and accepted — as so many Old Testament texts point out (which we will sketch in the final point below).

And second, it highlights the very close connection between missiology and ecclesiology. God's redemptive mission began by creating a community of blessing, to be a blessing, so that all nations would come to praise the living God (cf. Ps. 67's universalizing of the Aaronic blessing). Salvation would not be a matter of whisking individual souls out of the earth and "up" to heaven. Rather it would be a long-term project of creating a people for God, initially the descendants of one man, Abraham, but with the intention (emphatically built in from the very beginning) of becoming a multinational community (cf. Ps. 87). Not only, then, is it correct to say that mission is the primary reason for the church's existence in history, it is also true that the church itself — the people of God from Abraham to the "great multitude whom no-one could count from every nation, tribe, people and language" (Rev. 7:9) — is the creation of the mission of God, and the demonstration of the gospel (Eph. 3:6-10).

The phrase "missional church" is therefore virtually tautologous. What other kind of church is there? As a friend said to me recently, "Talk about 'missional church' sounds to me like talking about 'female women.' If it's not missional, it's not church."

The Comprehensiveness of God's Work of Redemption for Israel: The Missiological Dimension of the Old Testament Story of Salvation

Mission (from a human point of view) might be defined as sharing the good news of God's redemptive work with all nations. But what is our understanding of "redemption"? The temptation in some Christian traditions is to confine it to the "spiritual" dimension — forgiveness of personal sin and release from its bondage. While this is undoubtedly a precious biblical truth, it fails to grasp the comprehensiveness of the biblical understanding of God's redeeming work, as portrayed in the Old Testament (which of course provided the foundational source of meaning for the metaphor in the New Testament also).

The primary model of redemption in the Old Testament (primary both chronologically as well as theologically), is of course the Exodus. It is the event to which the language of redemption is first applied. It is therefore vitally important to attend to all the dimensions of what God actually accomplished in that event. At least four dimensions are clearly highlighted in the key narratives at the beginning of Exodus, and in the later texts that celebrate the event (e.g., in the Psalms or prophets).

- *Political.* The Hebrews were not a free people. They found themselves in Egypt as the descendants of people who had migrated there as famine refugees and found a welcome (a fact that was not forgotten: Deut. 23:7). But under the current government, they were being oppressed as an ethnic minority and viewed with suspicion and state-generated fear.

- *Economic.* The Hebrews were being exploited as a source of cheap labor for the economic benefit of their host nation — in construction projects and agriculture (things haven't changed much). They were not enjoying the fruit of their own work but suffering the harsh slavery of working for a hostile state.

- *Social.* The policy of that state progressed from economic exploitation to outright genocidal fury. The interference in the family life of the Hebrews, by the government mandate to all the citizens of Egypt to make sure that newborn Hebrew boys were killed at birth, must have inspired fear in every pregnant mother and despair among the whole community whose very survival into the next generation was threatened.

- *Spiritual.* The play on the word ʿăbōdâ highlights this point. The word can mean slavery, but also worship. While the Hebrews were under slavery to Pharaoh (the self-asserting member of the gods of Egypt) they were not free to worship their true God and Lord. This explains Yahweh's insistence, "Let my people go that they may serve/worship *me*" (that is, not Pharaoh). Israel's problem in Egypt was not that they were in slavery and needed to be liberated, but that they were being forced to serve the wrong master. The point of the Exodus was not merely the gift of freedom, but to bring Israel back to their true Lord and to enter into covenant relationship with him.

As we reflect on all these dimensions of the great redemptive event of the Old Testament, and the first great model of God acting as redeemer in the Bible, we need to see the holistic, integrated nature of the whole accomplishment. It is missiologically deficient *either* to use the Exodus only as biblical support for political, economic or social action for liberation (without reference to the spiritual dimensions of redemption usually included in the work of evangelism), *or* to spiritualize the Exodus into nothing more than a picture-story of which the real message is to do with forgiveness of personal sin and release from the personal bondage to sin. Once again, these are issues in mission that I have explored in much greater depth, and with reference to much wider biblical resources in *The Mission of God*.[17]

It should also be added that the Old Testament's vision of the mission of

17. Particularly in chapters 8 and 9.

God extends even beyond the ultimate redemption of people from all nations and includes the redemption of the whole creation — a "new heavens and new earth." The cosmic universality of this vision is affirmed by Paul in his understanding of "all things in heaven and on earth," which have been created by Christ, are sustained by Christ, and have been reconciled to God through the blood of Christ shed on the cross (Col. 1:15-20).

The Ethical Distinctiveness of Israel, a Light to the Nations: The Missiological Dimension of Old Testament Ethics, or of Israel's Holiness

Israel was called to be distinctive from the surrounding world in ways that were not merely religious but also ethical. In Genesis 18:19 this is expressed as the very purpose of Israel's election in relation to God's promise to bless the nations. In stark contrast to the world of Sodom and Gomorrah (the focus of the narrative in Genesis 18–19), Yahweh says of Abraham: "I have chosen him *so that* he will direct his children and his household after him to keep the way of the LORD by doing what is right and just, *so that* the LORD will bring about for Abraham what he has promised him [i.e., the blessing of all nations, specified in the preceding verse]" (emphasis mine). This verse, in a remarkably tight syntax, binds together election, ethics and mission as three interlocking aspects of God's purpose. His choice of Abraham is for the sake of his promise (to bless the nations); but the accomplishment of God's mission demands the ethical obedience of God's community — the fulcrum in the middle of the verse. In other words, God binds the accomplishment of his missional agenda to the ethical quality of life of the community he is creating through Abraham. If they will be committed to walking in the way of the Lord (rather than the way of Sodom), by doing righteousness and justice (rather than the wickedness that was producing the "cry for help" coming up to God out of Sodom), then God will be able to fulfill his mission of bringing all nations into the sphere of his blessing.

In Exodus 19:4-6 Israel's ethical distinctiveness is also linked to their identity and role as a priestly and holy people in the midst of the nations. As Yahweh's priesthood, Israel would be the means by which God would be known to the nations and the means of bringing the nations to God (performing a function analogous to the role of Israel's own priests between God and the rest of the people). As a holy people, they would be ethically (as well as ritually) distinctive from the practices of surrounding nations. The moral and practical dimensions of such holy distinctiveness are spelled out in Leviticus 18–19.

In Deuteronomy 4:6-8, we find that such visibility would be a matter of observation and comment among the nations. This expectation in itself was a strong motivation for keeping the law — a point which I have also expanded in seeking a missional hermeneutic of Deuteronomy. The question of Israel's ethical obedience or ethical failure was not merely a matter between themselves and Yahweh, but was of major significance in relation to Yahweh's agenda for the nations (cf. Jer. 4:1-2), and indeed to Yahweh's reputation ("name") among the nations (Ezek. 36). And that means that Old Testament ethics is inseparably linked to God's mission as the Old Testament declares it.[18]

This missiological perspective on Old Testament ethics seems to me a fruitful approach to the age-old hermeneutical debate over whether and how the moral teaching given to Israel in the Old Testament (especially the law) has any authority or relevance to Christians. If the law was given in order to shape Israel to be what they were called to be — a light to the nations, a holy priesthood — then it has a paradigmatic relevance to those who, in Christ, have inherited the same role in relation to the nations. In the Old as well as the New Testament, the ethical demand on those who claim to be God's people is determined by the mission with which they have been entrusted. There is no biblical mission without biblical ethics.

The Universality of Israel's Vision of the Future Ingathering of the Nations: The Missiological Dimension of Old Testament Eschatology

Israel saw the nations (including themselves) as being subject to the sovereign rule of God in history — whether in judgment or in mercy (cf. Jer. 18:1-10; Jonah). But Israel also thought of the nations as spectators ("witnesses," in Old Testament terms) of all God's dealings with Israel, whether positive or negative. That is to say, whether on the receiving end of God's deliverance, or of the blows of God's judgment, Israel lived on an open stage and the nations would draw their conclusions (Exod. 15:15; Deut. 9:28; Ezek. 36:16-23).

Eventually, however, and in a rather mysterious way, the nations could

---

18. For extended exegesis and discussion of these three texts in Genesis, Exodus, and Deuteronomy, in relation to the missional dimension of Old Testament ethics, see Wright, *The Mission of God*, pp. 358-87.

be portrayed as the beneficiaries of all that God had done in and for Israel, and even invited to rejoice, applaud, and praise Yahweh the God of Israel for the history of Israel and the prayer-answering presence of God in the midst of Israel (Ps. 47; 1 Kings 8:41-43; Ps. 67).

Most remarkable of all, Israel came to entertain the eschatological vision that there would be those of the nations who would not merely be joined to Israel, but would come to be identified as Israel, with the same names, privileges, and responsibilities before God (Ps. 47:9; Isa. 19:19-25; 56:2-8; 66:19-21; Zech. 2:10-11; Amos 9:11-12). Psalmists and prophets envisaged a future in which the nations could be

- registered in God's city (Ps. 87)
- blessed with God's salvation (Isa. 19:19-25 — with its clear echoes of exodus and Abraham)
- called by God's name (Amos 9:11-12)
- accepted in God's house (Isa. 56:2-8)
- joined with God's people (Zech. 2:10-11)

These texts are quite breathtaking in their universal scope. This is the dimension of Israel's prophetic heritage that most profoundly influenced the theological explanation and motivation of the Gentile mission in the New Testament. It certainly underlies James's interpretation of the Christ-event and the success of the Gentile mission in Acts 15:16-18 (quoting Amos 9:12). And it likewise inspired Paul's efforts as a practitioner and theologian of mission (e.g., Rom. 15:7-16; Eph. 2:11–3:6). Indeed, Paul saw the fulfillment of this great scriptural hope and vision as nothing less than the very essence of the gospel itself, now that it had been made possible through the coming of the Messiah, Jesus, and his death and resurrection. And it provided the theological shape for the gospels, all of which conclude with their various forms of the great commission — the sending of Jesus' disciples into the world of nations.

And finally, we cannot omit the even wider vision that not only the nations, but also the whole creation will be included in God's purposes of redemption. For this God of Israel, of the nations, and of the world, declares himself to be creating a new heavens and a new earth, with redeemed humanity living in safety, harmony and environmental peace within a renewed creation. Again, this is a portrait enthusiastically endorsed in the New Testament (Ps. 96:11-13; Isa. 65:17-25; Rom. 8:18-21; 2 Pet. 3:13; Rev. 21:1-5), and so not only sustains our hope today, but also enables us to see Christian concern and action in relation to the environment and care of creation as an essential part of our holistic biblical mission.

Conclusion

I trust it is sufficiently clear from the above survey that a missional approach can provide a fruitful way of "hearing the Old Testament." There are, as we saw in the first part, a variety of complementary ways that such a missional hermeneutic may operate. But there can be no doubt, it seems to me, that the great pillars of the faith of Old Testament Israel not only supported their identity as a people of memory and hope, but also continue to support the mission of God's people — believing Jews and Gentiles united in the Messiah Jesus — since the New Testament times until the return of Christ.

My hope is that there will be more fruitful interaction between Old Testament scholars and missiologists in the task of reading these texts in this way. I am certain that a close missional reading of specific books and texts in the canon (using all four of the senses of that phrase identified by Hunsberger) will yield fresh insights for the church in mission.

9 Ethics and Old Testament Interpretation

M. Daniel Carroll R.

Introduction

Twenty-five years ago there was a comparative dearth of material in the field of Old Testament ethics. Not much had been published in the preceding decades, and no new, full-length works appeared to be forthcoming. In the ensuing years interest would explode. Now one can draw from volumes covering the entire Old Testament[1] to studies of different sections, books, genres, and ethical themes. The approaches are diverse, as are the evaluations of the potential of the Old Testament to contribute constructively to contemporary ethical discourse. What once was a sparsely populated area of research is now richly inhabited by many voices.

To review the literature is to become aware that "Old Testament ethics" is a broad label, which can refer to several objects of study. In a seminal essay, John Barton differentiates three foci that those interested in Old Testament

---

1. E.g., Bruce C. Birch, *Let Justice Roll Down: The Old Testament, Ethics, and the Christian Life* (Louisville: Westminster John Knox, 1991); Waldemar Janzen, *Old Testament Ethics: A Paradigmatic Approach* (Louisville: Westminster John Knox, 1994); Eckart Otto, *Theologische Ethik des Alten Testaments,* Theologische Wissenschaft 3/2 (Stuttgart: W. Kohlhammer, 1994); J. David Pleins, *The Social Visions of the Hebrew Bible: A Theological Introduction* (Louisville: Westminster John Knox, 2001); Christopher J. H. Wright, *Old Testament Ethics for the People of God* (Downers Grove: IVP, 2004); Andrew Sloane, *At Home in a Strange Land: Using the Old Testament in Christian Ethics* (Peabody, MA: Hendrickson, 2008); John Goldingay, *Old Testament Theology,* vol. 3: *Israel's Life* (Downers Grove: IVP, 2009).

ethics have sought to discover within the text. "We must distinguish," he says, "three types of assertions about ethics: (a) all or most ancient Israelites held that X; (b) certain Old Testament authors held that X; (c) the Old Testament taken as a canonical text may be taken to support the view that X."[2] The first category refers to attempts to explain the moral tenets and behavior of Israelite society; the second deals with the biblical authors' evaluation of those matters, while the third spans the Old Testament to establish its views on diverse topics. For example, one could analyze, in turn, the socioeconomic convictions and realities in the Northern Kingdom during the eighth century, the critique in the book of Amos, or the Old Testament's perspective on injustice.

Barton's classifications concentrate on the world "behind the text" and on what the Old Testament says to that ancient world. The application of social-scientific theories, coupled with the growing fund of archaeological data, renders reconstructions of the dynamics of Israelite society more complex, and ideally more accurate.[3] Some scholars concentrate on the ethics of particular books as the products of their time and place.[4] Others compare and contrast elements of the Old Testament's ethical thinking, such as the sensitivity toward the vulnerable in the law codes and the prophetic and wisdom literature, with that of surrounding cultures.[5]

Barton's methodological distinctions are useful, and the data from these approaches are indispensable for a fuller grasp of the ethical material within the Old Testament. Nevertheless, this information is not sufficient for those whose goal ultimately is "hearing the Old Testament" as Christian Scripture. Not included among Barton's three categories is (to borrow his formulation) what Christians and Christian communities do with what the Old Testament has to say about X. Christopher Wright has this as his goal, and also employs three categories. These include, first, "The descriptive question: What ethical behaviors characterized ancient Israel?"; second, "The canoni-

---

2. John Barton, "Understanding Old Testament Ethics," in *Understanding Old Testament Ethics: Approaches and Explanations* (Louisville: Westminster John Knox, 2003), p. 16.

3. Pleins, *Social Visions;* Walter J. Houston, *Contending for Justice: Ideologies and Theologies of Justice in the Old Testament,* LHB/OTS 428 (London: T&T Clark, 2006).

4. E.g., Andrew Mein, *Ezekiel and the Ethics of Exile,* OTM (Oxford: Oxford University Press, 2001); Olof Bäckersten, *Isaiah's Political Message: An Appraisal of His Alleged Social Critique,* FAT 2/29 (Tübingen: Mohr Siebeck, 2008).

5. Moshe Weinfeld, *Social Justice in Ancient Israel and in the Ancient Near East* (Minneapolis: Fortress, 1995); Joshua A. Berman, *Created Equal: How the Bible Broke with Ancient Political Thought* (Oxford: Oxford University Press, 2008).

cal question: What do Old Testament texts tell us about how the Israelites should have behaved?"; and third, "The normative question: What do Old Testament texts tell us about how we ought to behave?"[6] Wright's two initial groupings encompass Barton's, but his third classification points in the direction that is the concern of this chapter.

The movement from the Old Testament to the present requires making decisions on a series of methodological issues. This chapter introduces in summary fashion some of these key matters related to Christian appropriation[7] of the Old Testament for ethics from the particular viewpoint that today is being called the theological interpretation of Scripture.

The Authority of the Old Testament for Ethics

The first questions to be decided are whether the Old Testament can serve as a viable authority in ethical discourse, and, if so, how this should be understood. There are several ways to approach the issue of authority. One is historical: de facto, the Old Testament has been taken as having divine authority in the past. Awareness of how the Old Testament has been utilized — for good or ill — to deal with topics such as government, war, slavery, the role of women, and sexuality, and the influence of contextual realities in its appropriation is essential to inform contemporary discussions.[8]

This input is needful, but to investigate the role of the Old Testament in the moral life of the church in its various contexts in the past is quite different from contending that it has worth for the present. Today the claim of the Old Testament's authority for ethics is a point of contention. There are those who reject it wholesale or at least have serious misgivings. Critiques take aim at what are thought to be the harmful ideologies intrinsic to its message —

6. Wright, *Old Testament Ethics*, pp. 442-45.

7. For differences between Jewish and Christian approaches, see Gershom M. H. Ratheiser, *Mitzvoth Ethics and the Jewish Bible: The End of Old Testament Theology*, LHB/OTS 460 (London: T&T Clark, 2007).

8. See diverse surveys in, e.g., Ernest R. Sandeen, ed., *The Bible and Social Reform*, The Bible in American Culture (Philadelphia: Fortress, 1982); Mark A. Noll, *The Civil War as a Theological Crisis* (Chapel Hill: University of North Carolina Press, 2006); John Rogerson, *According to the Scriptures? The Challenge of Using the Bible in Social, Moral, and Political Questions*, Biblical Challenges in the Contemporary World (London: Equinox, 2007); Mark G. Brett, *Decolonizing God: The Bible in the Tides of Empire*, The Bible in the Modern World 16 (Sheffield: Sheffield Phoenix, 2008).

those contextually conditioned beliefs embedded in the text which, it is asserted, have been ignored or not properly understood. The issue is not just that passages have been misinterpreted (which everyone recognizes); the problem lies with the Old Testament itself.

Some voices of this "hermeneutics of suspicion" come from feminist scholarship. The Old Testament is said to be inherently patriarchal in its portrayal of women as of lesser value than men, with their social roles limited to marriage and bearing children; what is worse, it contains accounts, without comment or condemnation, of the exploitation of women. As a sacred text, this view maintains, the Old Testament sanctions similar attitudes toward women by its readers and, therefore, is problematic as a resource for ethics.[9] This feminist disapproval has been combined with condemnation of what is perceived to be the pervasive violence of the Old Testament.[10]

Postcolonial studies decry how the Bible has been used to oppress peoples around the world.[11] Those of ecological convictions fault the Old Testament for being insensitive to the environment and believe it is responsible to some degree for the neglect of nature in Western societies.[12] The Old Testament is criticized, too, for stigmatizing the physically disabled in its narratives, the blessings and curses of the law codes, and prophetic metaphors.[13]

No part of the Old Testament has escaped censure. What were once considered texts of great moral import have lost their ethical capital. David Clines, for instance, argues that the Ten Commandments reflect the point of view of the elite, who would have been married urban males with property.[14] Harold Bennett believes that legislation in Deuteronomy, which ap-

---

9. For a survey of feminist approaches, see Alice Ogden Bellis, *Helpmates, Harlots, and Heroes: Women's Stories in the Hebrew Bible*, 2nd ed. (Louisville: Westminster John Knox, 2007).

10. Carol J. Dempsey, *Hope amid the Ruins: The Ethics of Israel's Prophets* (St. Louis: Chalice, 2000); Julie M. O'Brien, *Challenging Prophetic Metaphor: Theology and Ideology in the Prophets* (Louisville: Westminster John Knox, 2008).

11. R. S. Sugirtharajah, *The Bible and the Third World: Precolonial, Colonial, and Postcolonial Encounters* (Oxford: Clarendon, 2001).

12. For a survey, see David G. Horrell, Cherryl Hunt, and Christopher Southgate, "Appeals to the Bible in Ecotheology and Environmental Ethics: A Typology of Hermeneutical Stances," *SCE* 21, no. 2 (2008): 219-38.

13. Jeremy Schipper, *Disability Studies and the Hebrew Bible: Figuring Mephibosheth in the David Story*, LHB/OTS 441 (London: T&T Clark, 2006); Rebecca Raphael, *Biblical Corpora: Representations of Disability in Hebrew Biblical Literature*, LHB/OTS 445 (London: T&T Clark, 2008).

14. David J. A. Clines, "The Ten Commandments, Reading from Left to Right," in *Inter-*

pears to have as its purpose to help the needy (14:22-29; 16:9-12; 24:17-18, 19-22; 26:12-15), in reality represents measures promulgated by the Yahweh-alone movement that were designed to secure its material advantage and to prevent a possible uprising of the poor.[15] Others maintain that the Law is not as ethically responsive as some think.[16] Even the eighth-century prophets, whom nineteenth-century Old Testament scholars lauded for their "ethical monotheism," are targets. The book of Isaiah is presented as ethically inconsistent,[17] and commentators are reprimanded for assuming as correct the moral highhandedness and exaggerations of Amos.[18]

The most comprehensive questioning of the value of the Old Testament is found in Cyril Rodd's *Glimpses of a Strange Land*.[19] The title derives from the metaphor of looking at the countryside through the slits of a medieval castle. Only snippets of what lies beyond the walls are visible. This word picture holds, Rodd contends, for the Old Testament. It contains only hints of the convictions of its authors (some of whose concerns do not match ours), and these were deeply influenced by their ancient settings. What is more, the multiplicity of authors and settings of the literature contains diverse opinions on ethical topics.

These negative appraisals stand in contrast to those who insist on the continuing authority of the Old Testament for ethics. Even here, however, there are differences of opinion concerning the nature and extent of this authority. Most opinions can be divided in heuristic fashion into three groups, which can be designated the functional, ontological, and theological views. These are not necessarily mutually exclusive.

The first position makes the case for the role of the Old Testament in moral life on the basis of literary theory and philosophical hermeneutics, in particular notions about the capacity of certain texts — above all, religious ones — to shape perspectives on human reality and empower a particular

---

ested Parties: The Ideology of the Writers and Readers of the Hebrew Bible, JSOTSup 205; Gender, Culture, Theory 1 (Sheffield: Sheffield Academic Press, 1995), pp. 26-45.

15. Harold V. Bennett, *Injustice Made Legal: Deuteronomic Law and the Plight of Widows, Strangers, and Orphans in Ancient Israel* (Grand Rapids: Eerdmans, 2002).

16. Cheryl Anderson, *Ancient Laws and Contemporary Controversies: The Need for Inclusive Biblical Interpretation* (New York: Oxford University Press, 2009).

17. Andrew Davies, *Double Standards in Isaiah: Re-evaluating Prophetic Ethics and Divine Justice*, Biblical Interpretation Series 46 (Leiden: Brill, 2000); Mark Gray, *Rhetoric and Social Justice in Isaiah*, LHB/OTS 432 (London: T&T Clark, 2006).

18. Clines, "Metacommentating Amos," in *Interested Parties*, pp. 76-93.

19. Cyril S. Rodd, *Glimpses of a Strange Land: Studies in Old Testament Ethics*, OTS (London: T&T Clark, 2001), pp. 1-4.

way of life through its rhetoric. The world depicted within the Bible is offered to readers (especially in narrative) as a compelling alternative to the reality that modern society propagates and legitimizes. Biblical texts, as the canon of Christians, disclose the truth about human life and serve as a moral compass for individuals and the believing community.

This notion of textual potential, joined with the fact that the Old Testament has proven its worth over the centuries, yields a functional definition: The authority of the Old Testament is the judgment and confession of the church of its power to orient and transform those who embrace it as Scripture; it is not a divine quality intrinsic to the Bible. Some allow for problematic sections or concepts within the Old Testament that must be resisted, or at least qualified to a greater or lesser degree.[20]

A second position defines the authority of the Old Testament in relationship to the doctrine of divine inspiration (which occasionally is connected to a propositional theory of revelation and inerrancy). Authority, in this case, is essentially ontological, a property of the text.[21]

A third way finds merit in both the previous views. It appreciates that the Old Testament is a persuasive text and has a high view of biblical authority.[22] Yet, this perspective is more reluctant than the functional view to cede that the text contains insurmountable limitations, and, in contradistinction to the ontological persuasion, desires to move beyond debates about properties of a particular kind (such as inerrancy) toward a "thicker" appreciation of authority. It interacts with contemporary debates about the nature of language,[23] values the missional character of the Old Testament,[24] and locates the topic within a theological interpretation of the Old and New Testaments.[25] In the

---

20. Birch, *Let Justice Roll Down*, pp. 29-68; cf. Bruce C. Birch and Larry L. Rasmussen, *The Bible and Ethics in the Christian Life*, rev. ed. (Minneapolis: Augsburg, 1989), pp. 141-88. Jacqueline E. Lapsley describes her stance as a hermeneutics of "informed trust" in *Whispering the Word: Hearing Women's Stories in the Old Testament* (Louisville: Westminster John Knox, 2005), pp. 18-19. Cf. Johanna W. H. van Wijk-Bos, *Making Wise the Simple: The Torah in Christian Faith and Practice* (Grand Rapids: Eerdmans, 2005), pp. xix-xxi.

21. Walter C. Kaiser, *Toward Old Testament Ethics* (Grand Rapids: Zondervan, 1983), pp. 1-13, 24-29, 39-48.

22. Wright, *Old Testament Ethics*, pp. 454-70; cf. John Goldingay, *Models for Scripture* (Grand Rapids: Eerdmans, 1994).

23. C. Bartholomew, C. Greene, and K. Möller, eds., *After Pentecost: Language and Biblical Interpretation*, SAHS 2 (Grand Rapids: Zondervan, 2001).

24. Christopher J. H. Wright, *The Mission of God: Unlocking the Bible's Grand Narrative* (Downers Grove: IVP, 2006), pp. 48-69; and Chapter 8 by Wright in the present volume.

25. E.g., Stephen E. Fowl, *Engaging Scripture: A Model for Theological Interpretation*,

opening chapter of this volume, Craig Bartholomew grounds the authority of the Old Testament within a discussion of the Trinity. In it is revealed the God of our Lord Jesus Christ; within it the Spirit announces the coming Messiah; from it themes developed in the New Testament form part of a unified story.

The Appropriate Context for Old Testament Ethics

Once it is granted that the Old Testament has authority for ethics, the next matter to decide is what might be the best social and institutional setting within which to engage Old Testament ethics from a theological interpretation perspective.

Research into Old Testament ethics is a scholarly discipline within the academy. In that arena, it is not uncommon to look at it without faith or ecclesial commitments. Over the last two hundred and fifty years the relationship between critical scholarship and the church and its view of the relevance of the Bible often has been contentious.[26] Those who do hold the Old Testament to be the word of God in a significant way sometimes feel obligated to bracket their beliefs.[27] Indeed, there are those who criticize academic institutions for allowing too much commingling of non-confessional research and those approaches with acknowledged theological concerns.[28]

While it would be easy to make the generalization that the predominant scholarly culture consistently operates according to a set of empirical methods severed from creed and community, this is not the case. There are schol-

---

Challenges in Contemporary Theology (Malden: Blackwell, 1998); Stephen E. Fowl, *Theological Interpretation of Scripture*, Cascade Companions (Eugene, OR: Cascade, 2009); Kevin J. Vanhoozer, *The Drama of Scripture: A Canonical-Linguistic Approach to Christian Theology* (Louisville: Westminster John Knox, 2005); Brian Brock, *Singing the Ethos of God: On the Place of Christian Ethics in Scripture* (Grand Rapids: Eerdmans, 2007).

26. Note, e.g., John W. Rogerson, *Old Testament Criticism in Nineteenth-Century England and Germany* (London: SPCK, 1984); John W. Rogerson, *W. M. L. de Wette, Founder of Biblical Criticism: An Intellectual Biography*, JSOTSup 126 (Sheffield: Sheffield Academic Press, 1992); John W. Rogerson, *The Bible and Criticism in Victorian Britain: Profiles of F. D. Maurice and William Robertson Smith*, JSOTSup 201 (Sheffield: Sheffield Academic Press, 1995).

27. E.g., Walter Moberly, *The Bible, Theology, and Faith: A Study of Abraham and Jesus*, Cambridge Studies in Christian Doctrine (Cambridge: Cambridge University Press, 2000), pp. 1-37.

28. Philip Davies, *Whose Bible Is It Anyway?* JSOTSup 204 (Sheffield: Sheffield Academic Press, 1995).

ars within the academy who claim to be Christians and proceed with their tasks using these methods in ways that they feel do not contradict their religious convictions. There is a spectrum of views regarding to what degree critical biblical studies are incompatible with the interpretation of the Bible as Scripture. Even among those who espouse theological approaches opinions differ.[29]

The tension about "place" needs to be framed differently. The most basic issue concerns what milieu is most suited to Old Testament ethics done from the theological commitments that inform this book. For that perspective, the church or larger Christian community is the most helpful setting — a point also made in Bartholomew's introduction. This does not imply that there are no other viable settings for Old Testament ethics. The contention is that the enterprise of Old Testament ethics will proceed differently when situated within confessional environs. *How* the text is approached, *why* it is mined, and *for whom* and *among whom* this work is done take on meanings different from those within the academy. Accountability now must be rendered to the Christian community to see whether these studies contribute to fulfilling its mission in the world.

Situating Old Testament ethics within the Christian community means that the concern is to nurture people with a certain kind of character that will guide their reading and living out of Scripture in a manner commensurate with that character. What is essential is a practical wisdom, or *phronēsis*, which brings Christian convictions to bear on interacting with the text and embodying it in the Christian community and larger society.[30] In other words, the interpretation and embodiment of Scripture require, theologically speaking, an anthropology of the reader. Engaging Old Testament ethics is not just about discovering ethical material within the text (the descriptive exercise) or ascertaining correct ethical advice (prescription); it also is about the ethical character of those doing Old Testament ethics.

This focus will influence the tone and strategies employed to deal with disagreements in opinions and applications. Stephen Fowl speaks of charity and patience in interpretation, John Burgess of a "piety of the Word," and

29. Craig G. Bartholomew et al., eds., *"Behind" the Text: History and Biblical Interpretation,* SAHS 4 (Grand Rapids: Zondervan, 2003); John Goldingay, *Models for Interpretation of Scripture* (Grand Rapids: Eerdmans, 1995), pp. 167-99, 236-38; Fowl, *Engaging Scripture,* pp. 179-91; Brock, *Singing the Ethos,* pp. 3-18.

30. Fowl, *Engaging Scripture,* pp. 8-9, 12-13, 188-202; Vanhoozer, *Drama of Scripture,* pp. 324-54; Richard S. Briggs, *The Virtuous Reader: Old Testament Narrative and Interpretive Virtue,* Studies in Theological Interpretation (Grand Rapids: Baker Academic, 2010).

Brian Brock of becoming sensitive to the voice of God through prayer and praise.[31] Attention to character also can alert readers to views that may be self-deceiving or self-serving.[32] This leads quite naturally to the importance of considering exemplars of interpretation, past and present, who have proved to be virtuous readers. For this reason, within theological approaches to the Bible there is a return to cases of the Old and New Testaments,[33] the church fathers, early theologians (e.g., Augustine, Aquinas), and the Reformers; in the modern period, Dietrich Bonhoeffer has garnered much interest.[34]

The second item to highlight is the role of Christian communities. It is in the church that moral identity is informed by the Word and developed in communal activities like preaching, baptism, and the Lord's Table, as well as in any number of informal gatherings. There the Old Testament text is recited, explained, and exemplified, and its ethics take on flesh in the multiple social relationships through which Christians fulfill their calling to be a blessing to the nations. These activities take on added significance as contributors to the formation of a moral people.[35] Old Testament ethics involves the imitation of God, obedience to his will, and awareness of the divine moral order in life and nature.[36] The Christian community should be oriented toward learning to live an ethical life as the people of God.

To speak of particular Christian communities or the Christian church also should take into account ethical reflection by the global communion of saints, especially vulnerable groups on the margins. These people have lived the issues with which Old Testament ethics grapples — poverty, war, and

31. Fowl, *Engaging Scripture*, pp. 86-96, 161-77; Fowl, *Theological Interpretation*, pp. 64-70; John P. Burgess, *Why Scripture Matters: Reading the Bible in a Time of Church Conflict* (Louisville: Westminster John Knox, 1998); Brock, *Singing the Ethos*, pp. 241-363.

32. Fowl, *Engaging Scripture*, pp. 62-86.

33. Note the examples explored in Briggs, *The Virtuous Reader*.

34. Stephen E. Fowl and L. Gregory Jones, *Reading in Communion* (Grand Rapids: Eerdmans, 1991), pp. 62-65, 135-64; Brock, *Singing the Ethos*, pp. 71-95.

35. Burgess, *Why Scripture Matters*.

36. John Barton, "The Imitation of God in the Old Testament," in *The God of Israel*, ed. R. P. Gordon, University of Cambridge Oriental Publications 64 (Cambridge: Cambridge University Press, 2007), pp. 35-46; B. C. Birch, "Divine Character and the Formation of Moral Community in the Book of Exodus," in *The Bible in Ethics: The Second Sheffield Colloquium*, ed. J. W. Rogerson, M. Davies, and M. D. Carroll R., JSOTSup 207 (Sheffield: Sheffield Academic Press, 1995), pp. 119-35; cf. E. W. Davies, "Walking in God's Ways: The Concept of *Imitatio Dei* in the Old Testament," in *In Search of True Wisdom: Essays in Old Testament Interpretation in Honor of Ronald E. Clements*, ed. E. Ball, JSOTSup 300 (Sheffield: Sheffield Academic Press, 1999), pp. 99-115.

natural disasters. Various liberation theologies come to mind, but there also are significant contributions from evangelical and Pentecostal circles.[37] For a long time within these contexts there also has been a call for scholars to walk alongside the suffering in the pilgrimage of faith. Daniel Carroll R. speaks of "the responsible reader" and Gerald West of "socially engaged biblical scholars" who work among "ordinary readers"; Bob Ekblad relates his experiences of reading "with the damned," and Clodovis Boff analyzes three levels of interpreters all pledged to their context.[38] Old Testament ethics cannot be looked at as an academic exercise divorced from socio-ethical commitments; it requires appropriate involvement in and for the faith community as well as society in general.

This emphasis on the community of the people of God reflects its prominence within the Old Testament. Ethics in the Old Testament has a decidedly communitarian orientation. Wright is correct to have two parts of his triangular paradigm be economic and social (therefore, communal) concerns and deliberately places individual ethics against the backdrop of the covenant community.[39] The Old Testament is eminently about the people of God organized into communities — ranging from the families, clans, and tribes in Genesis, to the nation states of the monarchical period, the remnant left in the land after the defeat of Judah, the minority diaspora enclaves in Babylon (and then Persia), onto the arrangements of the post-exilic era — and the moral behavior that God expects in each setting.[40]

There is much textual data to corroborate this community-ethical framework. A few examples will substantiate the argument.[41]

---

37. Philip Jenkins, *The New Face of Christianity: Believing the Bible in the Global South* (Oxford: Oxford University Press, 2006). For Latin America, see M. Daniel Carroll R., "Liberation Theology: Latin America," in *The Oxford Illustrated History of the Bible*, ed. J. Rogerson (Oxford: Oxford University Press, 2001), pp. 316-29.

38. M. Daniel Carroll R., *Contexts for Amos: Prophetic Poetics in Latin American Perspective*, JSOTSup 132 (Sheffield: Sheffield Academic Press, 1992), pp. 162-73; Gerald O. West, *The Academy of the Poor: Towards a Dialogical Reading of the Bible*, Interventions 2 (Sheffield: Sheffield Academic Press, 1999); Bob Ekblad, *Reading the Bible with the Damned* (Louisville: Westminster John Knox, 2007); Clodovis Boff, "Epistemología y método en la teología de la liberación," in *Mysterium liberationis: Conceptos fundamentals de la teología de la liberación*, ed. I. Ellacuría and J. Sobrino (San Salvador: UCA, 1993), pp. 79-113.

39. Wright, *Old Testament Ethics*, pp. 48-99, 363-67.

40. John Goldingay, *Theological Diversity and the Authority of the Old Testament* (Grand Rapids: Eerdmans, 1987), pp. 59-96.

41. Cf. Wright, *Old Testament Ethics, Mission of God*, and Chapter 8 in the present volume.

a. One element of the call of Abram in Genesis 12 is the divine promise that from him would come a "great nation" (v. 2). The following narratives present the growth of this family, but these narratives also are about "being a blessing" to others (v. 3).[42] This task is accomplished as the patriarchs and their kin exhibit worthy character and confess their dependence on Yahweh (e.g., 14:17-24; 22:15-19), but it is put in peril by harmful actions (e.g., 12:14-20; chs. 20, 34). Genesis portrays the birth of a people, whose ethics are to be a testimony of the God of all the earth.[43] The narratives of this people are set against the background of creation, the fall, and the flood (chs. 1–9), the Table of Nations and Tower of Babel (chs. 10–11), and the engagement with neighbors and Egypt (chs. 12–50).[44]

b. With the Exodus, Israel is founded as a covenantal society. From the start, ethical obligations are core to its identity as a "priestly kingdom and a holy nation" (Exod. 19:1-6). The experience of the Exodus was to be a powerful memory, an important motivation to be compassionate and just towards the needy (e.g., Exod. 22:21 [Heb. 22:20]; 23:9; Lev. 25:38, 42, 55; Deut. 15:15; 24:18, 22). At Sinai the people received the Law. In a wonderful turn of phrase, Patrick Miller styles this Law as the foundation of the "good neighborhood."[45] It contains ethical material applicable to the various communities of Israel: families, "cities," and the people as a whole. Familial and the larger periodic ritual gatherings were occasions for teaching the foundational stories and this new way of life (e.g., Deut. 6:1-9; 31:9-13).

The narrative context also anticipates the monarchy. It presents guidelines for a distinct kind of politics, unlike what was common in the ancient world, where the size of armies and harems and quantities of precious goods were the measure of greatness. Instead, humility was to

42. M. Daniel Carroll R., "Blessing the Nations: Toward a Biblical Theology of Mission from Genesis," *BBR* 10, no. 1 (2000): 17-34; Wright, *Mission of God*, pp. 191-221; cf. Goldingay, *Old Testament Theology*, vol. 1: *Israel's Gospel*, pp. 213-41.

43. Janzen, *Old Testament Ethics*, pp. 26-54; Gordon J. Wenham, *Story as Torah: Reading the Old Testament Ethically*, OTS (Edinburgh: T&T Clark, 2000), pp. 17-43, 73-107; Robin Parry, *Old Testament Story and Christian Ethics: The Rape of Dinah as a Case Study*, PBM (Milton Keynes: Paternoster, 2004), pp. 123-78.

44. William P. Brown, *The Ethos of the Cosmos: The Genesis of Moral Imagination in the Bible* (Grand Rapids: Eerdmans, 1999); J. G. McConville, *God and Earthly Power — An Old Testament Political Theology: Genesis-Kings*, LHB/OTS 454 (London: T&T Clark, 2006), pp. 30-49.

45. Patrick D. Miller, "The Good Neighborhood: Identity and Community through the Commandments," in *Character and Scripture: Moral Formation, Community, and Biblical Interpretation*, ed. W. P. Brown (Grand Rapids: Eerdmans, 2002), pp. 55-72.

mark the rule of the king (Deut. 17:14-20).[46] Ultimately, the God of the Exodus himself is the moral standard — in his actions, words, and commitments (Exod. 34:5-7).

The Law and the demand for an obedient Israel are hinted at already in Genesis (18:19).[47] The Law echoes, too, God's ethical order in creation,[48] even as it offers lessons for the nations (Deut. 4:5-8).[49]

c. The historical narratives focus on societal concerns, as they track the rise and demise of the monarchy and the return from exile.[50] Accounts of individuals (primarily of kings and other leaders) and their character and actions are intertwined with the ethos and fate of the nation. No thought is given to isolated individuals disconnected from the life of the larger community.

d. The condemnation of sin in the prophetic literature has Israel and Judah's societies in view in its censure of socioeconomic abuses, political miscalculations, and worship at the sanctuaries. The proclamation of restoration is eminently communal, too, in the descriptions of rebuilding cities, replanting crops, participating in worship in a more glorious temple, and living in peace under a Spirit-filled king.

e. The wisdom and poetic literature, which many think reflect an individualistic ethic, can be placed within a communal framework.[51] Job's losses are experienced at the level of family, but then he sets his hurt within a wider setting. He defends his uprightness by detailing how he cared for the needy (chs. 29, 31), and explains his sufferings and shame within his community (12:1-6; 19:13-22; 30:1-15). In the Psalms, those who come before the Lord must demonstrate their good character in their treatment of others (Pss. 15, 24). In Proverbs, Wisdom cries out in the streets of the city (1:20-21; 9:1-3), the "son" is schooled to function well within society, and the virtuous woman of chapter 31 makes her mark in the community

---

46. McConville, *God and Earthly Power*, pp. 81-98.

47. James K. Bruckner, *Implied Law in the Abrahamic Narrative: A Literary and Theological Analysis*, JSOTSup 335 (Sheffield: Sheffield Academic Press, 2001).

48. Brown, *Ethos of the Cosmos*, pp. 71-132; Wright, *Old Testament Ethics*, pp. 103-81; McConville, *God and Earthly Power*, pp. 30-81.

49. Wright, *Old Testament Ethics*, pp. 61-74, 182-211.

50. Wright, *Old Testament Ethics*, pp. 212-45, 269-79; McConville, *God and Earthly Power*, pp. 118-67.

51. William P. Brown, *Character in Crisis: A Fresh Approach to the Wisdom Literature of the Old Testament* (Grand Rapids: Eerdmans, 1996); Brown, *Ethos*, pp. 271-380; Wright, *Old Testament Ethics*, pp. 363-83.

(31:10-31). The search for meaning by the "Preacher" in Ecclesiastes is set within a society: the contradictions of wealth (2:1-11; 5:13-17; 6:1-6), the enigmas of work (2:18-26), the paradoxes of communal gatherings (7:2-4), the life of the destitute (4:1-8; 5:8, 12), the challenges of politics (8:2-9; 9:13-18; 10:16-20), and the intimacies of the home (5:18-20; 9:7-10).

This very brief survey underscores that the Old Testament places ethical life within a broader social setting and envisions moral training within the home and cult, which are themselves types of community.

Which Form of the Text for Old Testament Ethics?

If the Old Testament is authoritative for the community of faith, then another important issue to decide is what form of that text is most suitable for doing ethics. We would argue that the final, or canonical, form is the best option for our theological orientation. Not all would agree, of course. Several scholars with an interest in Old Testament ethics make the case that reconstructions of the redactional history of the text are essential to that enterprise.

John Rogerson, for example, explores the dynamic relationship between the ethics of Israel (and, by extension, Christians) at any given moment and what he calls the "natural morality" of that time and place.[52] To discover those moral engagements recounted in Scripture requires the critical tools to retrieve the historical processes reflected in the redaction of the text. The ethics of the people of God have always interacted with these consensuses. Overlap is expected, but the motivations of God's people are distinct because of the "imperatives of redemption." These are the ethical demands generated by the gracious acts of God. In the Old Testament, the redemption of Israel from Egypt is key; in the New Testament, the imperatives spring from the cross of Jesus. These should take concrete form in "structures of grace," tangible measures that embody that redemption and fit the context. Despite a different moral reasoning, God's people can collaborate with projects of their context that approximate divine ideals (of human worth and flourishing) and that, in some measure, are structures of grace.

On the other hand, David Pleins looks primarily at the debates internal to Israel. Pleins holds that the Hebrew Bible is "an anthology of theological

---

52. John Rogerson, *Theory and Practice in Old Testament Ethics,* ed. M. D. Carroll R., JSOTSup 405 (London: T&T Clark, 2004).

diversity, radical political dissent, and conservative resurgence."[53] The composite history of the text is a window into the back-and-forth ethical discourse within ancient Israel. That complexity also is found in the intricacy of social reality and the theological density of moral problems today.

For other scholars, to burrow down to the original text is to retrieve the moral core that has been muted or distorted by accretions added by subsequent redactors. Examples of this view include Norman Gottwald's hypothesis of an initial revolutionary peasant account of the Exodus that was later modified by monarchical and priestly interests.[54] Liberation scholars applied his work to their contexts to rally their people to seek social change.[55] José Miranda uses critical theory to discount as late the notion of covenant as the reason for divine intervention at the Exodus or the prophetic critiques of oppression. Eliminating the covenant allows recovery of the earliest message of universal "interhuman justice."[56] In the South African context, Itumeleng Mosala's studies of the Cain and Abel story and Micah also attempt to recapture their original liberating word.[57]

Clearly these scholars have an investment in the ethical value of the Old Testament. Why then the turn to the canonical form as the most appropriate shape of the text? There are several reasons. One is that efforts at reconstruction are only as viable as their social and/or literary theory, the availability of archaeological data, and the interpretation of those data that sustain them. Shifts in any of these areas can call a hypothesis (and, therefore, its ethical implications) into question. Interest in the final form reflects, too, the trend over the last couple of decades in literary theory and postmodernism to focus on the reader and the creation of meaning.

There are at least two other grounds for the choice of the canonical form that are more directly connected to ethics. The first is pragmatic and pastoral. To build an Old Testament ethics on critical theory is to take the Bible out of the hands of the "ordinary reader" and limit its use for ethics to ex-

---

53. Pleins, *Social Visions*, p. 21.

54. Norman K. Gottwald, "Theological Education as a Theory-Praxis Loop: Situating the Book of Joshua in a Cultural, Social Ethical, and Theological Matrix," in *The Bible in Ethics: The Second Sheffield Colloquium,* ed. Rogerson, Davies, and Carroll R., pp. 107-18.

55. Jorge V. Pixley, *On Exodus: A Liberation Perspective,* trans. R. R. Barr (Maryknoll: Orbis, 1987).

56. José Porfirio Miranda, *Marx and the Bible: A Critique of the Philosophy of Oppression,* trans. J. Eagleson (Maryknoll: Orbis, 1974).

57. Itumeleng J. Mosala, *Biblical Hermeneutics and Black Theology in South Africa* (Grand Rapids: Eerdmans, 1989).

perts. This call for the text of the people is especially important in the Majority World, where literacy rates can be low and access to scholarship difficult. The canonical text is the only available form of the Bible.[58]

The second reason is pastoral as well, but has a specific theological basis: the canon of the Old Testament is part of the Scripture of the Christian church. Assenting to the Spirit's witness and affirming its experience over those years, the church confesses that the Old Testament testifies to God and to his Christ and is unique revelation about human reality and history (Chapter 1 by Craig Bartholomew and Chapter 7 by Stephen Dempsey in the present volume are pertinent here). Contemporary theologians such as Stephen Fowl, Francis Watson, Kevin Vanhoozer, and Brian Brock[59] are exploring the meaning of the Bible as scripture for the faith, life, and worship of the Christian community.

Significant voices among Old Testament scholars also highlight the priority of the final form of the text for Christian communities. A pioneer of this approach was Brevard Childs.[60] Critiques of his work have been strident,[61] but he rightly turned attention to the Old Testament as Scripture in its received form as the foundational locus of Christian theological deliberation. Although he was interested in possible stages of redaction, this was subordinated to the ecclesial role of the canon. Others construe their appreciation of the canon in ways that differ from Childs's work.[62] There is no single exegetical methodology that defines the theological interpretation of the Old Testament, but there is a shared commitment to the final form and its centrality for Christians individually and the church corporately.

Recent volumes on the ethics of the Old Testament are based on the received text as Scripture. This is plainly stated in the works of Bruce Birch,

---

58. Carroll R., *Contexts*, pp. 153-56; Jenkins, *New Face of Christianity;* cf. n. 38 above.

59. Fowl, *Engaging Scripture* and *Theological Interpretation;* Francis Watson, *Text, Church, and World: Biblical Interpretation in Theological Perspective* (Grand Rapids: Eerdmans, 1994), and *Text and Truth: Redefining Biblical Theology* (Grand Rapids: Eerdmans, 1997); Vanhoozer, *Drama of Scripture;* Brock, *Singing the Ethos.*

60. Brevard S. Childs, *Introduction to the Old Testament as Scripture* (Philadelphia: Fortress, 1979); Brevard S. Childs, *Biblical Theology of the Old and New Testaments: Theological Reflection on the Christian Bible* (Minneapolis: Fortress, 1992).

61. James Barr, *The Concept of Biblical Theology* (Minneapolis: Fortress, 1999), pp. 401-38; John Barton, *The Old Testament: Canon, Literature, and Theology,* SOTSMS (Aldershot: Ashgate, 2007).

62. E.g., Christopher R. Seitz, *Word without End: The Old Testament as Abiding Theological Witness* (Grand Rapids: Eerdmans, 1998); Christopher R. Seitz, *Figured Out: Typology and Providence in Christian Scripture* (Louisville: Westminster John Knox, 2001).

Waldemar Janzen, Christopher Wright, and John Goldingay,[63] as well as in more circumscribed studies, like J. Gordon McConville's political theology of Genesis–2 Kings, Jacqueline Lapsley's work in Ezekiel, or studies on Deuteronomy.[64] Literary approaches and interest in virtue ethics encourage this concentration on the final form.[65] Working with the canon does not mean that these authors do not use critical methodologies. Their appropriation varies, yet the ultimate goal always is to grapple with the canonical shape.

The option for the canon raises at least three methodological issues for ethics. The first is the correlation of these final form approaches with history — more specifically, the historical referents as reconstructed by modern research. The second concerns how this perspective deals with the ethical diversity within the Old Testament. Does it not flatten the multiple points of view within the text and impose a foreign uniformity? The third issue that surfaces is the connection with the New Testament. We will comment briefly on the first topic here. The next two are dealt with in the following sections.

Chapter 5 by Tremper Longman in the present volume presents key points of contemporary debate on historicity and the text, so there is no need to rehearse those here. Historical referents themselves, though, are relevant for our discussion. The biblical text is not an autonomous, self-referring literary work without connections to the world beyond its pages. Opinions vary about the importance of historical reconstructions for ethics and what sort of data is most pertinent. Interest can center on more long-lasting social realities and structures reflected in a text — that is, those items that constitute the *longue durée*.[66] This information grounds the ethical material in the text in the concreteness of social life. Thus, some Old Testament ethicists who use the canonical form of the text use social science approaches.[67]

---

63. Birch, *Let Justice Roll Down*, pp. 21, 43-46, 60-65; Janzen, *Old Testament Ethics*, pp. 3-6; Wright, *Old Testament Ethics*; Goldingay, *Israel's Life*.

64. McConville, *God and Earthly Power*, pp. 6-11; Jacqueline E. Lapsley, *Can These Bones Live? The Problem of the Moral Self in the Book of Ezekiel*, BZAW 301 (Berlin: de Gruyter, 2000); Terence E. Fretheim, "Law in the Service of Life: A Dynamic Understanding of Law in Deuteronomy," in *A God So Near: Essays on Old Testament Theology in Honor of Patrick D. Miller*, ed. B. A. Strawn and N. R. Bowen (Winona Lake, IN: Eisenbrauns, 2003), pp. 183-200; Miller, "The Good Neighborhood."

65. E.g., Carroll R., *Contexts*, pp. 143-53; Wenham, *Story*, pp. 1-15; Brown, *Character and Scripture*; Parry, *Old Testament Story*; Briggs, *The Virtuous Reader*.

66. F. Braudel, *On History*, trans. S. Matthews (Chicago: University of Chicago Press, 1980), pp. 25-54.

67. Wright, *Old Testament Ethics*; McConville, *God and Earthly Power*, pp. 6-8; van Wijk-Bos, *Making Wise*, pp. 40-78; cf. Berman, *Created Equal*.

The Old Testament also is perennially socially and historically *realistic;* it rings true regarding the experiences of human beings. The complexity of its narratives mirrors and illuminates the complications of life itself,[68] even as it confronts its readers with alternative views of existence. Its narratives and the overarching story from creation to the coming of God's kingdom are the stories of the people of God and, ultimately, of all of humanity.

The text draws readers in through the analogous experiences of its characters, the force of its language, and the vividness of its scenes. It invites ethical engagement. Note, for instance, the type characters in Proverbs whose counterparts readers can recognize in their own lives (the wise person, the fool, the sluggard, the mocker), and the anonymity of those condemned by the prophets ("woe to those who . . ."), who are like corresponding oppressive individuals in modern society. Other texts address readers directly (e.g., Hos. 14:9 [Heb 14:10]), and the use of the first person plural ("we") and the second person singular and plural ("you") communicates advice and admonitions to readers.

On the basis of the insights of theorists such as Hans-Georg Gadamer and Paul Ricoeur, Old Testament ethicists who use narrative or poetic approaches[69] speak of the "world in front of the text," of that compelling interaction of the world of readers with the world depicted in the Old Testament that yields a "fusion of horizons." This also is expressed as the text's impact on the moral imagination, or as the power of its mimesis (the relationship of its vision of reality to the reader's life) to produce a new configuration of existence. Wright speaks of the fourfold reality engendered by the Old Testament: that of God, of the Old Testament story, of this revelatory and performative word, and of the people of God.[70] All this gives it tremendous ethical authority.

In Old Testament ethics done from a theological and canonical perspective, then, the treatment of historical referents moves in several directions. It can be concerned with those that lie behind the text and that are accessible by research. How this data is applied depends on the ethicist. Reflection on referents also must include the relationship to the historical and existential realities of the community that embraces it as Scripture.

68. Wenham, *Story;* Mary E. Mills, *Biblical Morality: Moral Perspectives in Old Testament Narratives,* Heythrop Series in Contemporary Philosophy, Religion, and Theology (Aldershot: Ashgate, 2001).

69. Carroll R., *Contexts,* pp. 156-62; Birch, *Let Justice Roll Down,* pp. 51-68; Wenham, *Story,* pp. 8-15; Parry, *Old Testament Story,* pp. 3-84.

70. Wright, *Old Testament Ethics,* pp. 457-69.

Ethical Diversity and Coherence in Old Testament Ethics

An approach that seeks to read the Old Testament canon theologically for ethics can raise doubts about its ability to reflect adequately its different, and seemingly contradictory, stances toward issues and its diverse theological frameworks. Does this position require forcing a false unity of ethical perspective upon the text?

The query is a legitimate one. In response, it must be recognized that "unity" is not a helpful term. Other descriptors, like "compatibility," "complementarity," or "coherence," are better, because the conviction is not that the ethics of the Old Testament is homogeneous, but rather that variety does not produce irresolvable tensions. Belief in the Old Testament as Scripture suggests that its array of viewpoints can fit together within broader boundaries to make ethical sense. This diversity is actually a rich ethical fund.

One manner of handling the ethical diversity is organizational: one genre is prioritized, and other Old Testament material is subordinated to it. Historically, the Law has held this privileged position. This is the option of Walter Kaiser, who bases his work on the law codes: the Ten Commandments (Exod. 20:1-17; Deut. 5:6-21), the book of the Covenant (Exod. 20:22–23:33), the Holiness Code (Lev. 18–20), and Deuteronomy. Kaiser conjoins his accent on the Law with the theme of the holiness of God.[71] Others choose different themes under which to subsume the variety of ethical material.[72] Recently, narrative has become the primary genre for Old Testament ethics. This is the option of Birch and Wenham. Even Johanna van Wijk-Bos, who highlights the Torah, places it within its narrative context. Janzen's is the most focused presentation of the narrative approach. He offers five "model stories" that reflect the good life that God desires — the familial, priestly, wisdom, royal, and prophetic. Coherence is found in the supremacy and comprehensiveness of the familial paradigm.[73]

Wright, like Janzen, proposes a paradigm approach, although he means something quite different by this term.[74] "Paradigm" for Wright refers to a set of beliefs and a worldview that define the life of individuals and societies. The three components of his basic paradigm are God (the theological an-

71. Kaiser, *Toward Old Testament Ethics*.

72. In *Text, Church, and World*, Watson argues for a Law/Gospel hermeneutic to gauge the viability of certain material.

73. Van Wijk-Bos, *Making Wise*; Janzen, *Old Testament Ethics*.

74. Wright, *Old Testament Ethics*, pp. 62-74, 182-211.

gle), Israel (the social angle), and the land (the economic angle). This triangular paradigm is extrapolated from Israel to encompass all of humanity
and creation, and is applied typologically to New Testament parallels and eschatologically to the hope of a redeemed world. This construct allows
Wright to respect cultural particulars and various genres (diversity) within a
larger three-part scheme that embraces the entire Bible (coherence).

A second way to engage the ethical diversity is to see the various ethical
views as contributions to a fuller appreciation of the ethical topic at hand. A
case in point is the issue of poverty. This was an acute problem in ancient Israel, and its importance is evident in the prominence given to it across the
Old Testament. Narratives offer glimpses of life under threat by the lack of
food and powerlessness (e.g., Gen. 42–43; 47; Ruth; 2 Kings 4:1-7); the Law
recognizes the need for structural measures to meet the needs of the poor
(e.g., sabbatical and jubilee years, gleaning and tithing laws); the prophets
denounce the systemic injustices that cause suffering and expose the callous-
ness of the elite (e.g., Isa. 3:16-23; 5:8-25; Amos 2:6-8; 4:1; 6:4-6; 8:4-6; Mic.
3:1-4); sensitivity to the poor is presented as an expression of wisdom (Job
29–31; Prov. 14:31; 19:17; 22:9) and as a requisite for acceptable worship and
responsible leadership (Pss. 15; 72; cf. Isa. 1:10-20; Amos 5:21-24; Jer. 7:1-11).
God cares for the poor, and this theological fact is constantly repeated (e.g.,
Deut. 10:17-19; Ps. 140:12). In sum, a canonical approach grounds its moral
demands in God, while surfacing the many dimensions of the realities of
poverty and the responses to it: the personal and the societal, the existential
and the concrete, individual charity and community legislation. This
breadth exposes the reader to the scope of issues related to the issue and reveals the corresponding need to act on a variety of fronts to reflect the heart
of God.

A third strategy involves discerning canonical trajectories. These can be
of several kinds. One trajectory model moves through the Old Testament
and into the New. Topics such as the role of women, the institution of slavery, and war have been dealt with in book-length studies.[75]

Another kind of trajectory focuses on the final form of particular books
and genres. To track entire books or sections from beginning to end can
yield ethical insights. For instance, the opening verses (1:1-2) and the closing

75. Willard M. Swartley, *Slavery, Sabbath, War, and Women: Case Issues in Biblical Interpretation* (Scottdale, PA: Herald, 1983); Willard M. Swartley, *Homosexuality: Biblical Interpretation and Moral Discernment* (Scottdale, PA: Herald, 2003); William J. Webb, *Slaves,
Women and Homosexuals: Exploring the Hermeneutics of Cultural Analysis* (Downers Grove:
IVP, 2001).

lines of Amos (9:11-15), which critical scholars routinely deem later additions, acquire ethical power as one moves across the length of the book. Consistent with other prophetic literature, in Amos judgment is not the final word of Yahweh; restoration and the reestablishment of a relationship with God lie beyond the chastisement. That future of plenty and peace will reverse harsh present realities (2:6-8; 3:10; 4:6-11; 5:7-13; 6:3) and the suffering to be born in an imminent invasion (3:11–4:3; 5:1-3; 6:8-14; 8:8–9:4). In addition, from the very start of the book, the regime and religion are discredited: Yahweh roars from Jerusalem and Zion, not Samaria and Bethel (1:2; cf. 7:9-17). The picture of the end time underscores their illegitimacy. True political hope lies not with the Northern dynasty of Jeroboam, but with the Davidic line (9:11). As a canonical word, Amos becomes a lens for the ideological suspicion of corrupt economic, political, and military hegemonies and for a realistic appraisal of nationalistic religion at the service of the state.[76]

The value of this sort of approach is evident, too, in Isaiah.[77] The descriptions of a coming Spirit-led ruler empowered by King Yahweh are a stark contrast to the kings of Judah (9:2-7 [Heb 9:1-6]; 11:1-11; 32:1). The royal figure of the first part of the book is linked later to the person of the Servant, who exercises the kingly prerogative of establishing justice (42:1-9; cf. 61:1-11). The portrayals of this individual (42:1-9; 49:1-7; 50:4-9; 52:13–53:12), the ethical hope of his coming reign, and the call to respond to the divinely appointed mission and self-sacrifice of this person (50:8-11; 53:1-6) generate a strong moral stance. Toward the end of Isaiah appear the "servants" (56:6; 65:8-9, 13-15; 66:14), who continue the work of that Servant in contrast to the nation, the rebellious "servant" (41:8-9; 42:19; 43:10; 44:1-2, 21; 45:4; 48:20). Like Amos, this book can serve as a tool for evaluating politics and raising hopes for a future unlike the injustices of contemporary society. It also points toward the Servant-King, whose character becomes a standard to follow in the crucibles of life.

---

76. M. Daniel Carroll R., "The Prophetic Text and the Literature of Dissent in Latin America: Amos, García Márquez, and Cabrera Infante Dismantle Militarism," *BibInt* 4, no. 1 (1996): 76-100; M. Daniel Carroll R., "Imagining the Unthinkable: Exposing the Idolatry of National Security in Amos," *Ex Auditu* 24 (2008): 37-54.

77. See Richard L. Schultz, "The King in the Book of Isaiah," in *The Lord's Anointed: Interpretation of Old Testament Messianic Texts*, ed. P. E. Satterthwaite, R. S. Hess, and G. J. Wenham (Grand Rapids: Baker, 1995), pp. 141-65; Christopher Seitz, "How Is the Prophet Isaiah Present in the Latter Half of the Book? The Logic of Isaiah 40–66 within the Book of Isaiah," in *World without End: The Old Testament as Abiding Theological Witness* (Grand Rapids: Eerdmans, 1998), pp. 168-93.

This sort of trajectory-type readings of canonical texts can be multiplied. For example, it is possible to trace development in the content and goals of moral training in Proverbs 10:1–31:9,[78] to appreciate the rhetorical power of Jeremiah and Lamentations to grapple with faith in times of personal and communal disaster,[79] and to see the probing of moral anthropology in Ezekiel.[80] Attention also can be given to genres, such as divergences between law codes or developments along the course of the Book of the Twelve, which in its present order could demonstrate didactic intent and ethical significance.

These several means of dealing with ethical diversity in the Old Testament require what one might call canonical competence — that is, knowledge of what the entire Old Testament says about ethical matters and the ability to be able to coordinate inter- and intratextual information in appropriate fashion. Texts can be engaged and brought together in multiple ways, which respect both diversity and interconnectedness.

Relating Old Testament Ethics to the New Testament

A final area that requires attention for Old Testament ethics done from a theological-canonical perspective concerns the relationship between the two Testaments. Defining the relationship between the testaments has been a perennial problem.[81] Discussions concern whether the Old Testament can or should be used and the exegetical method and theological controls to be employed if that possibility is granted. These topics, of course, were a source of problems from the very beginning of the Christian faith, as the New Testament amply demonstrates. Surveys demonstrate how many different solutions have been proposed over the centuries.[82] Even those who champion a theological understanding of the Bible do not agree on the topic. Witness, for instance, the exchange between Old Testament scholar Christopher Seitz

78. Brown, *Character in Crisis*, pp. 22-49.

79. Kathleen O'Connor, "The Book of Jeremiah: Reconstructing Community after Disaster," in *Character Ethics*, ed. Carroll R. and Lapsley, pp. 81-92.

80. Lapsley, *Can These Bones Live;* Lapsley, "A Feeling for God: Emotions and Moral Formation in Ezekiel 24:15-27," in *Character Ethics and the Old Testament*, ed. M. Daniel Carroll R. and Jacqueline E. Lapsley (Louisville: Westminster John Knox, 2007), pp. 93-102.

81. See Chapter 6 by Mark Boda in the present volume.

82. A. H. J. Gunneweg, *Understanding the Old Testament*, trans. J. Bowden, OTL (Philadelphia: Westminster, 1978); David L. Baker, *Two Testaments, One Bible: The Theological Relationship between the Old and New Testaments*, 3rd ed. (Downers Grove: IVP, 2010).

and theologian Francis Watson.[83] The historical, hermeneutical, and theological reasoning of each is profound, but Seitz's concern to allow for the Old Testament to have its own voice disagrees with Watson's construal of the meaning of a Christological reading.

The New Testament invites Christians to utilize the Old Testament for their moral life (e.g., Matt. 22:34-40; 1 Cor. 10:11-13; 2 Tim. 3:16-17; Heb. 3:12-19; 11:1–12:1), but what is not specified is *how* the Old Testament is to be appropriated.[84] The scholarly field dealing with the use of the Old Testament in the New, of which the ethical connection is a subset, is huge. The goal of what follows is to point out how various Old Testament ethicists, who hold a view of the text and the kind of theological and ecclesial commitments akin to those of this book, deal with this conundrum.

Because of the specialized nature of biblical ethics, the treatment in volumes on Old Testament ethics of how it relates to that of the New is usually brief. Authors concentrate on establishing the contributions of the former and, as Christians, take the link between the testaments as a working assumption. Birch is particularly brief, presenting in just two pages that there is continuity in divine grace, of the people of God, and of God's word and work.[85]

Discussions by others are more extensive, and, not surprisingly, these aim to demonstrate how their approaches extend into the New Testament. Kaiser appeals to Paul to prove that the principles of the "weightier" demands of Old Testament law have an abiding relevance for the Christian (Rom. 3:31; 7:12-14, 22, 25; 8:7; cf. Matt. 5:17-20; 23:23).[86] Van Wijk-Bos carefully exposits the correlation between the teaching of the Torah and that of Jesus and Paul (both Jews), the latter making sense only with the former as their background. These connections are grounded in the eternal character of God.[87]

Janzen sees parallels between the offices of Jesus as priest, sage, king, and prophet and the paradigmatic models of the Old Testament and echoes of

---

83. Christopher Seitz, "Christological Interpretation of Texts and Trinitarian Claims to Truth: An Engagement with Francis Watson's *Text and Truth*," *SJT* 52.2 (1999): 209-26; Seitz, *Figured Out*, pp. 42-44; Francis Watson, "The Old Testament as Scripture: A Response to Professor Seitz," *SJT* 52, no. 2 (1999): 227-32.

84. Of course, this was a topic of contention in the early church, which struggled with ascertaining the significance of the Law (see, e.g., Matt. 5:17; Acts 15; Gal. 3–4).

85. Birch, *Let Justice Roll Down*, pp. 356-57.

86. Kaiser, *Toward Old Testament Ethics*, pp. 24-29, 64-67, 307-14; cf. Joe M. Sprinkle, *Biblical Law and Its Relevance: A Christian Understanding and Ethical Implications of the Mosaic Regulations* (Lanham, MD: University Press of America, 2006), pp. 20-27.

87. Van Wijk-Bos, *Making Wise*, pp. 263-305.

the familial paradigm as well.[88] Wright argues that the church has a spiritual organic continuity with Old Testament Israel. On this basis, he works to show the typological connections with Old Testament concerns and their reshaping in the New, using the jubilee as a test case.[89] Wenham points to the assumption of the New Testament writers that their readers were well acquainted with Old Testament narratives and ethical teaching, thus their constant appeal to that material. They also believed that they were part of that larger story of redemption of the people of God. This continuity went hand in hand with the certainty of the transformation of that earlier revelation because of the inauguration of the eschatological reign of God by Jesus (he gives the examples of the dietary and marriage laws and violence).[90]

These authors argue that the Old Testament has a valuable contribution to make to Christian ethics *as the Old Testament*. It is a discrete witness to the revelation and will of God, as Chapter 1 by Craig Bartholomew in the present volume makes clear, and is fundamental to shaping the moral life of the people of God. It must be taken seriously on its own even as it looks to and interacts with the New (although, as has been shown, they interpret that relationship in different ways).[91] In addition, the Old Testament offers material that is not covered in as detailed fashion (e.g., creation, politics) or from the same angles as in the New by its sheer volume, chronological span, and links to a particular history. In other words, the direction of biblical moral reasoning is forward and dialectical, not simply retrospective with New Testament ethics overriding or negating the Old.

Several New Testament ethicists recognize the importance of the Old Testament. Yoder frames his study of the message of Jesus around the Jubilee;[92] Glen Stassen and David Gushee propose that the background for Jesus' teaching of the kingdom lies in the prophet Isaiah;[93] and Hays sees roots of his three-pronged approach (community, cross, new creation) in the Old Testament.[94]

88. Janzen, *Old Testament Ethics*, pp. 187-216.

89. Wright, *Old Testament Ethics*, pp. 182-211, 469-70.

90. Wenham, *Story*, pp. 129-49.

91. E.g., Childs presents the ethics of each testament before discussing biblical ethics as a whole; see *Biblical Theology*, pp. 658-716.

92. John Howard Yoder, *The Politics of Jesus*, 2nd ed. (Grand Rapids: Eerdmans, 1994).

93. Glen H. Stassen and David P. Gushee, *Kingdom Ethics: Following Jesus in Contemporary Context* (Downers Grove: IVP, 2003).

94. Richard B. Hays, *The Moral Vision of the New Testament: A Contemporary Introduction to New Testament Ethics* (New York: Harper Collins, 1996).

Concluding Remarks

This chapter has attempted to introduce the reader to some of the key areas to consider in doing Old Testament ethics from the set of theological and canonical commitments that inform this volume. These have to do with the authority of the Old Testament for ethics, the significance of an ecclesial setting, the option for the final form of the text, the treatment of ethical diversity in the Old Testament, and the relationship of Old Testament ethics to the New Testament. Each demands methodological choices, and one must be aware that holding broadly shared convictions does not mean that these beliefs are understood in the same way or that there will be uniformity in appropriating the Old Testament for moral life today.

Other challenges for Old Testament ethics remain. One is to interact more at length with systematic theology categories — Lutheran, Reformed/ Calvinist, Anabaptist, Dispensational, and Roman Catholic — that can determine in large measure what from the Old Testament is applicable to Christians and how that material is to be processed.[95] Another rich arena for reflection would be for biblical ethicists to engage those theological ethics (such as those by Barth and Bonhoeffer)[96] that have made creative use of the Old Testament. Two recent efforts demonstrate the value of this kind of interchange: the consultation dealing with the political ethics of Oliver O'Donovan,[97] and William Brown's volume on the Ten Commandments.[98]

To believe that the Old Testament is Scripture is to hold that it is relevant for Christian living. As such, it must be taken seriously as "useful for teaching, for reproof, for correction, and for training in righteousness, so that everyone who belongs to God may be proficient, equipped for every good work" (2 Tim. 3:16-17). There are disagreements as to how this is to be accomplished, but the responsibility remains to hear the voice of God in its pages and to be shaped by its revelation.

95. See surveys in Wright, *Old Testament Ethics*, pp. 387-414; Sprinkle, *Biblical Law*, pp. 1-20.

96. Karl Barth, *Church Dogmatics*, II/2, *The Doctrine of God, Part 2*, trans. G. W. Bromiley (New York: Charles Scribner's Sons, 1957), ch. 8; III/4, *The Doctrine of Creation, Part 4*, trans. G. W. Bromiley (New York: Charles Scribner's Sons, 1961), ch. 12; Dietrich Bonhoeffer, *Ethics*, trans. R. Krauss, C. C. West, and D. W. Stott, Dietrich Bonhoeffer Works 6 (Minneapolis: Fortress, 2005).

97. Craig Bartholomew et al., eds., *A Royal Priesthood? The Use of the Bible Ethically and Politically*, SAHS 3 (Grand Rapids: Zondervan, 2002).

98. William P. Brown, ed., *The Ten Commandments: The Reciprocity of Faithfulness*, Library of Theological Ethics (Louisville: Westminster John Knox, 2004).

PART III HEARING THE OLD TESTAMENT

10 Hearing the Pentateuch

Gordon J. Wenham

Recent work on the Pentateuch has transformed its study. Long-established critical theories — the "assured results of criticism" — have been widely abandoned and new paradigms have been proposed that make a theological if not a trinitarian reading much more acceptable.

For many years the documentary theory dominated pentateuchal study. Pioneered by W. M. L. de Wette at the beginning of the nineteenth century, made mainstream by Julius Wellhausen in the late nineteenth century, and popularized in the English-speaking world by S. R. Driver, the documentary theory held that the Pentateuch was composed of four major sources ranging in date from the tenth to fifth centuries B.C. This late dating cast doubt on the historical worth of the Pentateuch, and much scholarship was devoted to attempting to determine what nuggets of historical information could be mined from these sources, especially as they were held to contradict each other at many points. These preoccupations prevented much attention being given to theological interpretation.

Historical concerns continued to dominate the early twentieth century. The form-critical works of Hermann Gunkel and Albrecht Alt were primarily interested in identifying earlier traditions underlying the four written sources postulated by the documentary theory. However, there was a theological edge to these researches. This was the era of Karl Barth and the biblical theology movement, and these developments seem to have influenced Alt's pupils Martin Noth and Gerhard von Rad. They endeavored to show that the patriarchal promises and the covenant were ancient. These institutions may not go back to the patriarchs or Moses, but they were considerably older than the age of the pentateuchal sources might have suggested.

It is with von Rad's *Old Testament Theology*[1] and his commentaries on Genesis[2] and Deuteronomy[3] that we see a new concern for theological interpretation. These works presuppose the findings of source criticism, so they do not offer an interpretation of the canonical text but rather a series of studies of the theology of the postulated sources. Thus von Rad's *Theology* has a section on the theology of the hexateuch, which is largely an exposition of the material assigned to J, the Yahwistic source, but throughout there are comparisons made with P and E versions and also subsections on the Priestly Document and on Deuteronomy. A movement toward a canonical approach is, therefore, apparent. This becomes explicit in his Genesis commentary, where he states his preference for reading the Joseph story as a unity and calls for a comprehensive review of the whole documentary theory.[4]

This review came in the next decade. An array of alternatives were put forward by scholars from a variety of countries. John Van Seters[5] from Canada argued in favor of a supplementary hypothesis; i.e., an originally short account was subsequently expanded by a succession of supplementers. An alternative supplementary approach was advocated in Germany by Rolf Rendtorff[6] and his disciple Erhard Blum.[7] This approach is now commonly accepted in the German-speaking world. But in Britain Norman Whybray,[8] renowned for his work on wisdom literature, attacked both the documentary approach and the supplementary models, arguing instead for a fragmentary approach. Whybray's view holds that the Pentateuch was composed by a single author at a particular time, using a variety of older sources. Whybray suggested that this author acted in the sixth century, though I prefer to think that the author worked in the united monarchy period.[9]

1. Gerhard von Rad, *Old Testament Theology,* vol. 1 (Edinburgh: Oliver & Boyd, 1962).

2. Gerhard von Rad, *Genesis: A Commentary* (London: SCM, 1972).

3. Gerhard von Rad, *Deuteronomy: A Commentary* (London: SCM, 1966).

4. Von Rad, *Genesis,* p. 440.

5. John van Seters, *Abraham in History and Tradition* (New Haven: Yale University Press, 1975).

6. Rolf Rendtorff, *The Problem of the Process of Transmission in the Pentateuch* (Sheffield: JSOT Press, 1990).

7. Erhard Blum, *Die Komposition der Vätergeschichte* (Neukirchen: Neukirchener Verlag, 1984).

8. R. Norman Whybray, *The Making of the Pentateuch,* JSOTSup 53 (Sheffield: JSOT Press, 1987).

9. Gordon J. Wenham, *Genesis 1–15,* WBC 1 (Waco: Word, 1987).

In the subsequent decades scholars devoted to historical criticism have continued to debate these proposals, but no agreed theory has emerged. Many still favor the classic documentary hypothesis, often with a number of minor changes, while others back some form of supplementary hypothesis. Still others, recognizing the limited contribution such theories make to understanding of the canonical text, prefer to ignore the debates and adopt approaches which focus on the final form of the text. The church and synagogue have always seen the final form as authoritative and as that in which they hear the divine word. It is to these approaches we shall now turn.

In 1974 Brevard Childs published his commentary on Exodus,[10] a volume that illustrated his conception of canonical criticism. Instead of merely focusing on source criticism and historical issues, Childs sets the interpretation of Exodus within the long history of commentaries on its text and concludes each section with theological reflection on its final form. The year 1978 saw the publication of David Clines's *The Theme of the Pentateuch*,[11] a fairly compact volume sketching out what the Pentateuch in its final form is trying to communicate: he defines it as "the partial fulfilment . . . of the promise to . . . the patriarchs."[12] Clines builds on the Old Testament theology of von Rad, but whereas von Rad gave an exposition of the individual sources, particularly J, Clines looks at the overall picture given by the final form of the Pentateuch, incorporating all its putative sources.

These two works anticipated a wave of studies by Jewish literary scholars exploring Old Testament narratives using the insights and methods current in modern literary studies. These works include Jacob Licht's *Storytelling in the Bible*, Adele Berlin's *Poetics and Interpretation of Biblical Narrative*, and Shimon Bar-Efrat's *Narrative Art in the Bible*.[13] But the two most influential works in this genre have been the more popular *The Art of Biblical Narrative* by Robert Alter and the more detailed *The Poetics of Biblical Narrative* by Meir Sternberg, published in 1981 and 1985 respectively.[14] While

10. Brevard S. Childs, *Exodus: A Commentary* (London: SCM, 1974).

11. David J. A. Clines, *The Theme of the Pentateuch* (Sheffield: JSOT Press, 1978).

12. Clines, *Theme of the Pentateuch*, p. 29.

13. Jacob Licht, *Storytelling in the Bible* (Jerusalem: Magnes, 1978); Adele Berlin, *Poetics and Interpretation of Biblical Narrative* (Sheffield: Almond Press, 1983); and Shimon Bar-Efrat, *Narrative Art in the Bible*, Bible and Literature Series (Sheffield: Almond Press, 1989). See Chapter 4 by David Beldman in the present volume.

14. Robert Alter, *The Art of Biblical Narrative* (New York: Basic, 1981); Meir Sternberg, *The Poetics of Biblical Narrative: Ideological Literature and the Drama of Reading*, Indiana Studies in Biblical Literature (Bloomington: Indiana University Press, 1985).

these writers insist that their methods do not rule out the insights of source criticism, they do challenge its principles from time to time, and certainly tend to make it redundant in many instances.

These two impulses, the canonical criticism of Childs and the literary criticism of Jewish scholars, have flowed together in subsequent decades to spawn many a doctoral thesis and a multitude of monographs exploring the theological and ethical messages of different parts of the Old Testament. To give a comprehensive list of these studies would be a large task, and so just a few examples will be mentioned: some of the most innovative are Walter Moberly, *At the Mountain of God* (1983); *The Old Testament of the Old Testament* (1992); Joe M. Sprinkle, *The Book of the Covenant* (1994); Dennis T. Olson, *The Death of the Old and the Birth of the New* (1985); Robin A. Parry, *Old Testament Story and Christian Ethics* (2004).[15]

Though the canonical and literary impulses have had the most impact on pentateuchal study, other methods employing the tools of cultural anthropology and the law have also shed light on the sense of the ritual and penal laws in the Pentateuch. In this area the works of Mary Douglas,[16] Raymond Westbrook,[17] and Christopher Wright[18] have been most influential.

These and other developments have meant that the last three decades have seen more fluidity and innovative study of the Pentateuch than in the previous century.[19] And most significantly these new approaches have in

15. R. Walter L. Moberly, *At the Mountain of God* (Sheffield: JSOT Press, 1983); *The Old Testament of the Old Testament* (Minneapolis: Fortress, 1992); Joe M. Sprinkle, *"The Book of the Covenant": A Literary Approach* (Sheffield: JSOT Press, 1994); Dennis T. Olson, *The Death of the Old and the Birth of the New: The Framework of the Book of Numbers and the Pentateuch* (Chico: Scholars, 1985); Robin A. Parry, *Old Testament Story and Christian Ethics* (Milton Keynes: Paternoster, 2004).

16. Mary Douglas, *Purity and Danger: An Analysis of Concepts of Pollution and Taboo* (London: Routledge, 1966); *In the Wilderness: The Doctrine of Defilement in the Book of Numbers* (Sheffield: Sheffield Academic Press, 1993); *Leviticus as Literature* (Oxford: Oxford University Press, 1999).

17. Raymond Westbrook, *Studies in Biblical and Cuneiform Law* (Paris: Gabalda, 1988); *Property and the Family in Biblical Law* (Sheffield: JSOT Press, 1991).

18. Christopher J. H. Wright, *Living as the People of God: The Relevance of Old Testament Ethics* (Downers Grove: IVP, 1983); *God's People in God's Land: Family, Land, and Property in the Old Testament* (Carlisle: Paternoster, 1990); *Old Testament Ethics for the People of God* (Downers Grove: IVP, 2004).

19. For a fuller survey of developments in pentateuchal criticism see Gordon J. Wenham, "Pondering the Pentateuch: The Search for a New Paradigm," in *The Face of Old Testament Studies: A Survey of Contemporary Approaches*, ed. David W. Baker and Bill T. Arnold (Grand Rapids: Baker, 1999), pp. 116-44.

many instances led to a much richer and more nuanced understanding of the text, which enables those with ears to hear to appreciate the divine word the text enshrines. In what follows I shall try to show how these approaches illuminate the message of the Pentateuch. But the interpretation of the opening chapters of the Pentateuch is not clarified by these methods so much as by comparing them with other oriental texts of a similar genre.

Genesis 1

As an account of creation Genesis 1 invites comparison with other texts from the ancient Near East, most obviously the Atrahasis epic, *Enuma Elish,* and the Sumerian flood story.[20] There are many allusions to the gods' creative activity in other texts. Modern Western readers are often struck by the similarities between the biblical version and the contemporary oriental tales, but those immersed in those ancient cultures would have been more struck by the differences. They would have noted the absence of a multitude of gods and goddesses in the biblical account: instead there is only a single deity in total control. The sun and moon are no longer gods in their own right, but simply light-givers called into being by the one God. The fighting between gods that characterizes *Enuma Elish* is again conspicuous by its absence in Genesis. The sky, land, and waters are simply called into existence by divine fiat. When it comes to the creation of humans, the discrepancy in thinking is again marked. Atrahasis sees the creation of human beings as the great gods' answer to a strike by the lesser gods, who had downed tools and refused to cultivate the land and supply the great gods with food. Similarly, *Enuma Elish* sees mankind as created to take on the duties of the minor gods.

But in Genesis the emphases are quite different. Humanity is no afterthought but rather the climax of a creative program that covers six days. The whole account in Genesis 1 builds up to God's work on the sixth day. Indeed, on the previous five days most attention is devoted to those aspects of the cosmos that impact human life the most. Dry land, the platform for human life and the source of its food, is the focus of day three (Gen. 1:9-13). The cre-

---

20. Stephanie Dalley, *Myths from Mesopotamia* (Oxford: Oxford University Press, 1989), offers a useful compendium of the main texts. See also Andrew George, ed., *The Epic of Gilgamesh* (New York: Barnes and Noble, 1999); John H. Walton, *The Lost World of Genesis One: Ancient Cosmology and the Origins Debate* (Downers Grove: IVP, 2009); Richard S. Hess and David T. Tsumura, *I Studied Inscriptions from Before the Flood* (Winona Lake, IN: Eisenbrauns, 1994).

ation of the sun and moon, whose movements determine the seasons and the calendar, are described relatively fully in Genesis 1:14-19. Then on the fifth day the birds and sea creatures are created. Finally, on the sixth day, after the creation of the land animals, there is a great flourish as God speaks in the plural: "Let us make man in our image," and his role is announced, to "have dominion over the fish . . . the birds . . . the livestock and over all the earth" (Gen. 1:26). The fulfillment of this decree follows: "So God created man in his own image, in the image of God he created them; male and female he created them" (1:27). Then the dominion mandate is reaffirmed and humankind is told to be fruitful and multiply.

The importance of man in the divine scheme could hardly be made clearer. God's goodwill toward the human race is reinforced by the command to be fruitful. This contrasts with the attitude of the gods of the Atrahasis epic, who try to curb human population growth by sending drought, plague, flood, infertility, and premature death. Not only does the God of Genesis commend human propagation, he also enables it by granting man and beast every plant for food. Again this contrasts with other ancient Near Eastern thinking, which saw one of mankind's fundamental roles as supplying the gods with food. The God of Genesis takes care of his creatures — he does not use and exploit them like other contemporary deities.

In this way Genesis 1 sets the scene for the rest of Scripture. It provides a theological framework for understanding the unfolding grand narrative that follows. It discloses the nature of the God whose providential dealings control history. It offers a pair of spectacles through which the subsequent narratives, law, and poetry must be read. It sets out some of the fundamental assumptions of biblical theology and ethics.[21] It declares the unity of God: unlike other ancient religions Israel's God has no rivals, which is not to say there are no other spiritual or supernatural beings, but that none of them can challenge his sovereignty. This implies that none of them are worth worshiping. In the words of Exodus: "You shall have no other gods before me" (20:3).

Genesis 1 clearly demonstrates divine sovereignty. God has only to speak and something is created: light, sun, stars, the sea and dry land, birds, fishes, animals, and man. Nothing created by the divine word is outside his purpose and control. There are no struggles with other gods to impede the fulfillment of the divine commands.

---

21. Most obviously on the image of God, sexuality (1:27-28), non-violence (1:29-30), and the Sabbath (2:1-3).

Finally, the creation of human beings attests the special place of humanity within the divine plan. Human beings are created in the image of God,[22] which means that they are God's representatives on earth, appointed to manage creation on God's behalf. Other cultures saw their kings as representing the divine, thus legitimating their rule, but Genesis democratizes this outlook, making every human an image of the divine. This gives man a unique status within creation and makes every individual special and bestows on each one the responsibility of acting in a godly manner. On the other hand, the Genesis account highlights God's care for man. As we have seen, other cultures saw humans supplying the gods with food and other necessities. Genesis, however, sees God as providing food for man and the animals. Only plants and fruit trees are assigned to be eaten, indicating a vegetarian diet for both. Neither humans nor animals are to eat meat; in other words, the created world knew no violence on the sixth day.

These themes — the unity, sovereignty, and benevolence of God, and the unique status of man in creation — are constantly underlined and reaffirmed in the rest of Scripture. Indeed, they reach their ultimate fulfillment in the incarnation, which demonstrates at once God's love for the human race and makes visible his true image. It would, however, be anachronistic to ascribe these fuller insights to the author of Genesis. Nevertheless, there are hints of the richer picture of God that appears in later books of the canon. The second verse of the Bible mentions the Spirit of God hovering over the face of the waters, while the third records God's almighty word declaring, "Let there be light." "The Spirit of God" may of course be translated "Wind of God," in which case it is a vivid and powerful image of the divine Spirit hovering over the waters of chaos. While it is unjustified to suppose that the author of this text was envisaging the Trinity, it does open that possibility. For why, one might ask, does not the text say simply, "God was hovering over the water," if an undifferentiated monotheism is meant?

Similarly, the repeated mention that God spoke and it happened affirms his total sovereignty over all his works. But again one might ask, Who is supposed to hear his commands? Is it just the part of creation addressed or are other listeners envisaged? The question becomes more insistent in 1:26 when God says, "Let us make man in our image." Who is referred to by "us" and

---

22. For further discussion see Wenham, *Genesis 1–15*, pp. 27-28; Claus Westermann, *Genesis 1–11* (Minneapolis: Augsburg, 1984), pp. 147-61. Gunnlaugur A. Jónsson, *The Image of God: Genesis 1, 26–28 in a Century of Old Testament Research* (Stockholm: Almqvist & Wiksell International, 1988).

"our"? Over the centuries a variety of suggestions have been made. It is a plural of majesty like the royal "we." It expresses self-deliberation: God is exhorting himself to act. It is the remnant of a polytheistic account. It expresses plurality in the godhead: God is addressing his spirit. But the two oldest interpretations are, first, that God is addressing the heavenly court, that is, the angels. This is the Jewish interpretation. Alternatively, early Christian exegesis understands this as witnessing to the Trinity; the Father invites the Son and the Spirit to be involved in the creation of mankind. Though I think the angelic understanding was that of the original human writer, the doctrine of inspiration legitimates a trinitarian interpretation as the *sensus plenior* of this passage.[23]

Genesis 2–11

If Genesis 1:1–2:3 is the overture to the Bible, Genesis 2:4–4:26 constitutes the first act. It opens with the heading, found another ten times in Genesis, "These are the generations of . . ." This heading introduces both long narrative sequences (2:4; 6:9 [the flood]; 11:27 [Abraham]; 25:19 [Jacob]; 37:2 [Joseph]) and short genealogies (5:1; 10:1; 11:10; 25:12; 36:1; 36:9). These links with subsequent accounts indicate that the author understood these early stories in a similar light to those of the patriarchs. The patriarchal stories trace the origin of Israel and its twelve tribes: the earlier chapters set the origin of Israel into world history and anticipate many of the themes in the rest of the Pentateuch in a clear and vivid way.

To put it simply, Genesis 1–2 describes life as it ought to be: fruitful, peaceful, and endued with the presence of God. Meanwhile Genesis 3–11 describes human life as it often is: difficult, violent, and under divine judgment. Genesis 2 reinforces the picture of a creation that is very good. Though the order of creative acts is different, a similar message is conveyed about God and his relationship with mankind. Man's central place in the divine schema is again apparent by the focus of the narrative on the creation of Adam and then Eve. God's solicitude for man is also very apparent. He puts man in a garden full of beautiful fruit trees, encouraging him to eat from all but one of them. He creates the animals as potential companions and allows the man to exercise authority over them by naming them, a role implicit in creating humans in the divine image. Finally, the woman is formed out of

23. Wenham, *Genesis 1–15*, pp. 79-81.

the man to demonstrate the strength of the marriage bond, alluded to but not spelled out in 1:27-28.

Implied but hardly commented on is the fact that God is present with the creatures he has made. He places man in the garden, brings the animals and birds to him to name, and introduces Eve to Adam. The next chapter implies that the Lord God used to walk in the garden in the cool of the day. This terminology of "walking" anticipates later comments in Leviticus 26:11-12, which say that in his tabernacle God will walk among his people. Many other features of Eden anticipate later sanctuaries such as the tabernacle and temple: they are entered from the east, guarded by cherubim, adorned with gold and precious stones, with a tree of knowledge and a tree of life. They draw on ideas of the cosmic mountain where the gods dwell and from which abundant waters flow. Placed in the garden, man is told to till it and guard it, prefiguring the duties of the later Levites in the tabernacle. But a trinitarian hermeneutic allows us to see these features that speak of God's presence in the garden as anticipating the incarnation and the heavenly Jerusalem.

Genesis 1–2 pictures human life as it ought to be. The next chapter describes life as it is. Mankind disobeys and is separated from God. Man and wife fall out. The animals intended to be man's companions now threaten him, and instead of living in an orchard of fruit trees Adam has an endless struggle with thorns and thistles to produce his food. Chapter 4 shows things disintegrating further with Cain murdering his brother and Lamech threatening seventy-seven-fold vengeance. And in 6:13 God observes that "the earth is filled with violence." Genesis 6:5 sees the root of the problem as deep-seated: "every intention of the thoughts of his heart was only evil continually." This prompts God's decision to send a flood to wipe out all mankind, save the one perfect righteous man Noah and his family.

The flood story constitutes the third main section of Genesis (6:9–9:29). The flood is seen not simply as an archetypal act of judgment on human sin (many of its motifs recur in the destruction of Sodom and the cities of the plain in Genesis 18–19), but as a return to the watery chaos that characterized the world of Genesis 1:2. This implies that the waters subsiding after the flood are an act of new creation, as first the mountaintops appear, then the olive trees, then the birds and the animals. Finally Noah is told to leave the ark and then is urged like Adam before him to "be fruitful and multiply," not once but three times (8:17; 9:1, 7). Noah is thus recognized as the second father of the human race: all the nations in chapter 10 are descended from him. He fulfills the role of second Adam in yet another respect: consuming too much fruit of the vine, like the first Adam he sins. And then, like Adam's son Cain, Noah's son Ham sins even more gravely (9:20-27).

The new creation thus faces the same problems as the old: God himself remarks that "the intention of man's heart is evil from his youth" (Gen. 8:21). So what is to be done to prevent creation disintegrating again and prompting another universal judgment? Genesis offers two remedies: sacrifice and law. We shall discuss the place of sacrifice later. But here we must simply comment on the role of law. The first case law prescribing a penalty for wrongdoing is found in Genesis 9:6:

> Whoever sheds the blood of man,
> by a man shall his blood be shed,
> for God made man in his own image.

The prescription of the death penalty for murder is paradoxical, for it involves killing a second human being who bears the image of God. But the reason for punishing murder so severely in the first place is that it is an assault on the divine image. Though it might be thought better not to exact the death penalty, Genesis sees it as preferable to execute the murderer than to see men like Lamech practicing multiple vengeance, and violence spiraling out of control. This rationale for the penal law may be seen to govern many of the penalties prescribed in Exodus to Deuteronomy. They set limits as to the type and extent of compensation that may be demanded in many situations. Though idealists may hope for forgiveness for every fault, the realistic Pentateuch is aware that the much greater danger is excessive revenge, and so the penal law prescribes what it sees as just and proportionate punishment for a variety of offenses.[24]

As already noted, the new creation with the fall of the second Adam does not start well. However, the decline does not appear to be so catastrophic as the first. The ultimate act of hubris is punished not by annihilation but by the confusion of language and the scattering of the human race. This is the prelude to the second divine attempt to redeem the situation, the call of Abraham.

---

24. The much-maligned *lex talionis*, "an eye for an eye, and a tooth for a tooth," is a vivid way of insisting that the punishment should fit the crime. One should not demand two or three eyes in revenge for the loss of one eye. Wright, *Old Testament Ethics*, p. 310; Westbrook, *Studies in Biblical and Cuneiform Law*, pp. 39-88.

Genesis 12–50: The Patriarchal History

The call of Abraham, "Go from your country . . . to the land that I will show you," initiates the main plot of the Pentateuch, the story of the patriarchs and their descendants and their journey to the promised land of Canaan. It must be remembered that all the laws, sermons, songs, and so on in Genesis to Deuteronomy are essentially part of a narrative about the formation of Israel before they settled in the land. We must interpret these subgenres within the framework of the overarching genre of historical narrative. Though historically minded scholars have argued and do argue that the patriarchal narratives are fictional, there can be little doubt that the author(s) of the Pentateuch understood them to be about real people in real places and intended them to be read as history. Even should the historical skeptics be right, a theological reading must respect the intention of the author.

Four promises are made to Abraham in Genesis 12:1-3 and developed subsequently. He is promised that he will inherit a land, that his descendants will become a nation, that he will be blessed and protected, and that through him all the families of the earth will find blessing. Clines has helpfully defined the theme of the Pentateuch as "the partial fulfillment — which implies also the partial non-fulfillment — of the promise to or blessing of the patriarchs."[25] It should be noted that Clines follows von Rad in not seeing the blessing of the nations as part of the theme, although it does form the climax of the promises. But if we are to appreciate the theology of the Pentateuch correctly we need to read every section of it in the light of the theme.

Perhaps the simplest element of the theme concerns the land. It is first promised to Abraham in vague terms, "the land that I will show you" (12:1). The next time it is "this land" (12:7), which still leaves its extent undetermined. The third promise of land defines it as "all the land that you see" and promises it "forever" (13:15). In 17:8 the promise is even more emphatic and precise: "I will give to you and your offspring after you . . . all the land of Canaan, for an everlasting possession." But the fulfillment of these promises is quite slow. Abraham in his lifetime acquires only a burial plot for his wife in Canaan, and Isaac adds just a few wells (23:1-20; 26:26-33). Jacob purchases some land near Shechem (33:19), but by the end of Genesis his whole family has migrated to Egypt.

The books of Exodus to Deuteronomy tell the story of the return to the Promised Land. The plagues demonstrate God's sovereign power cowing the

---

25. Clines, *Theme of the Pentateuch*, p. 29.

might of Egypt, and one might expect the Exodus from Egypt to be followed by immediate entry into Canaan. But instead, the people of God are sent on a lengthy detour to avoid the land of the Philistines (Exod. 13:17), a route that Deuteronomy describes as "the great and terrifying wilderness." Exodus and Numbers recount many episodes of grumbling on the way, which threaten to undo the whole enterprise. The worst of these takes place on the very border of the land, when the spies bring back a discouraging report on the prospects for conquest. This sets back the entry to the land by forty years (Num. 13–14). The Pentateuch ends with the people waiting to cross the Jordan, and Moses seeing the land but dying outside it. It is therefore quite correct to describe the promises of land as only partially fulfilled within the Pentateuch: Deuteronomy 34 leaves the reader waiting for the people to take possession of the land.

The same is true of the final promise, that in Abraham and his offspring shall all the nations of the earth be blessed. We see partial adumbrations of this in Abraham's rescue of the cities of the plain (Gen. 14), praying for Sodom and Abimelech (Gen. 18:23-33; 20:17), and most obviously Joseph's management of the famine, which led to "all the earth" coming to Egypt to buy grain (Gen. 41:57). But then this aspect of the theme fades out in the Pentateuch, and it is left to the psalmists and prophets to reawaken the expectation that through Israel the nations will be blessed. This illustrates Clines's point that the theme is the partial fulfillment of the promises, not their complete fulfillment.

The promises often mention Abraham's offspring (Hebrew zera'), literally "seed," affirming that they will see the fulfillment of the different promises. They seem to be echoes of Genesis 3:15, which promises that the woman's offspring will bruise the serpent's head. This glance back to the opening chapters of Genesis is not an isolated one. The patriarchal promises are "a reaffirmation of the primal divine intentions for man,"[26] that is, what is set out as given to humanity in Genesis 1 and 2 is promised to the patriarchs in the future. Mankind is given dominion over the earth, and Eden is theirs to care for: the patriarchs are promised the land. Man is told to be fruitful and multiply: the patriarchs are going to become a great nation. The ultimate blessing is the presence of God, realized in Eden and in the lives of the patriarchs. The whole human race enjoyed the blessing of Eden: all families of the earth will be blessed through Abraham's offspring.

The Pentateuch needs to be read with the ideals of its opening chapters

---

26. Clines, *Theme of the Pentateuch*, p. 29.

in mind. From these initial stories we pick up hints as to how humans ought to behave toward God and toward each other. And as we read the accounts of the patriarchs, of the deeds of Moses and the other Israelites, we are encouraged to ask how far the ideals of the implied author are being realized. There are great acts demonstrating courage and faith, but there are plenty of examples of cowardice (e.g., 12:10-20; 20:1-7), deceit (27:1-29), violence (34:1-31), and so on. The bulk of Genesis revolves round two dramas of intense family jealousy and discord: Esau versus Jacob and Joseph versus his brothers. Both stories climax in beautiful scenes of reconciliation, showing that the violence that triggered the destruction of the original creation in the flood can be overcome. They point to the possibility of the promises of blessing being fulfilled in the present, if not in their totality, at least enough to transform strife into peace.

The Book of Exodus

With the book of Exodus the Pentateuch hits its stride. Without the book of Genesis the remaining four books could be best characterized as a biography of Moses, as they begin with his birth (Exod. 2:1-10) and end with his death (Deut. 34). Indeed, many motifs in Genesis seem to prefigure Mosaic experiences — for example, his sojourn in a foreign land, finding his future wife at a well, receiving the offer to be made a great nation (Exod. 2:11–4:30; 2:16-22; 32:10). But this should probably be described as a subplot rather than as the main storyline. For Exodus tells how the theme of the Pentateuch develops further.

It begins by noting that the people of Israel were fruitful and multiplied greatly (Exod. 1:1-7). In so doing they fulfilled the mandate given to mankind in Genesis 1:28, and the fulfillment of the promise that Abraham would become a great nation was brought much nearer. But the Pharaoh, the narrative's incarnation of anti-God forces, attempts to block Israel's expansion by drowning all the Hebrews' baby boys. Nevertheless, at the burning bush God assures Moses that he has not forgotten his promise to the patriarchs and that he will rescue his people from Egyptian oppression. The revelation of his name, *Yahweh*, paraphrased in 3:14 as "I am who I am," is a pledge of divine victory over opposing powers.

The plagues demonstrate the power of the Lord over the supposedly divine king of Egypt. He is forced to confess that he has sinned against the Lord (Exod. 10:16), but then he refuses to let Israel go, so that the final plague, the death of the firstborn, a fitting retribution for Egyptian infanti-cide of Israelite boys, is sent. The Israelites flee from Egypt, and like the sin-ful flood generation the Egyptian army drowns in the waters of the Red Sea. This paves the way for the creation of a new redeemed Israel, which will journey to the new Garden of Eden on the holy mountain of Sinai.

The covenant made at Sinai is indeed Israel's constitution. Its function is succinctly described in Exodus 19:5-6: "You shall be my treasured possession among all peoples . . . a kingdom of priests and a holy nation." Three elements of the covenant relationship are here noted: God's unique choice of Israel ("treasured position"), their mediating role between God and the other na-tions ("kingdom of priests"), and their calling to be holy, manifesting God's character in their lifestyle ("holy nation"). The Decalogue reinforces this vi-sion of Israel's role. It opens with a reminder that the Lord has brought them out of Egyptian slavery. Its injunctions clarify the moral dimension of holi-ness, while their observance of the Sabbath mirrors God's pattern of activity. As I have already argued, the laws in the book of the covenant (Exod. 21–23) show what must be done to those who fail to live up to the divine standard: offenders are punished with penalties proportionate to their offense (lex talionis) to prevent society from disintegrating as it did in Noah's time.

Unfortunately, all Israel is caught up in a sin so heinous that God threat-ens to destroy them as he did all humanity in the flood. There are many allu-sions to the flood in Exodus 32–34, which show that the making of the golden calf, a violation of the first two commandments, was seen as equally serious as the pre-flood violence. In both cases only two individuals deserve to survive, namely, Noah and Moses. Noah preserves the world from future floods by his sacrifice; Moses saves Israel by his intercession.

It is not easy to persuade God to relent. Moses' first prayer leads to the Lord agreeing not to destroy all Israel, but he says he will not accompany them into Canaan. It takes further pleading from Moses for him to agree that he will be with them on the journey into the land promised to the patri-archs. The building of the tabernacle is the visible pledge of God's presence with Israel, and its importance is indicated by the amount of space given to describing its design and then its creation. Symbolically the tabernacle is both a miniature garden of Eden and also a portable Sinai. We have already noted the Eden/tabernacle parallels, but the parallels with Sinai are just as striking.[27] Both have three zones. The top of the mountain, accessed only by Moses, matches the Holy of Holies entered only by the high priest. The

---

27. Nahum J. Sarna, *Exodus*, JPS Torah Commentary (Philadelphia: JPS, 1991), p. 105.

slopes of the mountain, which the priests and elders ascend, correspond to the Holy Place, and the base of the mountain, open to ordinary Israelites, corresponds to the court of the tabernacle. Finally one should note that when the tabernacle is consecrated, the cloud, the glory of the Lord, fills it, recalling the thick cloud and fire which covered Mount Sinai when God delivered the Ten Commandments (Exod. 19:16-20; 40:34-38). This demonstrates that the tabernacle is a tented version of Sinai in which the Lord fulfills his promise to walk with Israel.

The Book of Leviticus

Leviticus opens with the Lord speaking to Moses from the newly consecrated tabernacle, reinforcing the message that his presence there is as real as it was on Mount Sinai. Traditional critics split the book into two halves, chapters 1–16, which give prescriptions about worship and the priesthood, are ascribed to the P source, while chapters 17–27, which are more concerned with ethical and social issues, are said to derive from the holiness code. But it is difficult to sustain this division clearly, for example, when language typical of the second section occurs in the first (e.g., Lev. 11:44-45).[28] Nevertheless, there are differences of topic and emphasis between the first and second halves of the book.

The first half of Leviticus is primarily concerned with the worship to be conducted in the tabernacle. Chapters 1–7 are regulations on sacrifice, 8–10 on the ordination of the priests, 11–15 on conditions that prevent participation in worship, called uncleanness, and chapter 16 tells of the most sacred rituals of the day of atonement.

Leviticus spells out the procedures for five different types of sacrifice and gives some hints as to the occasions for their use and what they achieve in the way of atonement. These hints need to be read in the light of the three most significant sacrifices described in Genesis, which give general principles applicable to all sacrifices. First, Abel's sacrifice was preferred to Cain's because he offered firstlings and their fat pieces, i.e., the best of his flock, whereas Cain only brought *some* of the fruit of the ground. Leviticus repeatedly insists that only unblemished animals may be offered in sacrifice (e.g., 1:3, 10; 3:1, 6; 4:3).

---

28. See further Leigh M. Trevaskis, *Holiness, Ethics, and Ritual in Leviticus* (Sheffield: Sheffield Phoenix, 2011).

Second, Noah's sacrifice turned away God's anger at mankind's inbuilt tendency to sin, which had originally prompted the flood: "When the LORD smelled the pleasing aroma, the LORD said . . . 'I will never again curse the ground because of man'" (Gen. 8:21; cf. 6:5). Most of the sacrifices in Leviticus are said to make a "pleasing aroma," or better "a soothing aroma" (Lev. 1:9; 2:9; 3:5; 4:31), and they endorse the idea illustrated in Genesis that sacrifices offered by the righteous can atone for the sins of other people.

Third, Abraham's offering of Isaac (Gen. 22:1-19) acted out another principle of sacrifice, namely that an approved animal, such as a ram, is an acceptable substitute for the human whose life is symbolically offered to God in sacrifice. Every sacrifice in Leviticus requires the worshiper to press his hand down on the offering, thereby expressing his identification with the animal about to be offered on his behalf.[29]

As already mentioned, at Sinai and in the tabernacle the laity may only enter the outer zone or tabernacle courtyard, and they are dependent on the priests to bring their sacrifices to the altar, which represents the presence of God. So the ordination of the priests is the next step in implementing true worship. This involves a variety of sacrifices and climaxes with the glory of God filling the tabernacle (Lev. 9:23-24).

The erection of the tabernacle and the ordination of the priests mean that God, who dwells in the tabernacle, can now be approached — but with caution. Two newly ordained priests die offering unauthorized incense (Lev. 10:1-7), and this introduces the uncleanness rules that specify what conditions are an obstacle to worship. Skin diseases, menstruation, sexual discharges, and childbirth seem a strange set of bodily conditions to impede worship. Various explanations have been offered for these rules. But the most likely are that these conditions somehow are abnormal, and only whole and unblemished people should enter God's presence, just as only unblemished animals may be sacrificed.[30] An alternative explanation is that these conditions, such as rotting skin and loss of blood, speak of death, whereas God is the source of perfect life, so those bearing the marks of death should not contradict this truth by coming close to him.[31]

29. For further discussion see Jacob Milgrom, *Leviticus 1–16* (New York: Doubleday, 1991), pp. 151-55; Rolf Rendtorff, *Leviticus 1–10* (Neukirchen: Neukirchener Verlag, 2004), pp. 40-48.

30. Douglas, *Purity and Danger*, pp. 53-55.

31. Gordon J. Wenham, "Purity," in *The Biblical World*, vol. 2, ed. John Barton (New York: Routledge, 2002), pp. 378-94.

An associated type of uncleanness is found in the food laws.[32] Dead animals are unclean and pollute water supplies and containers. Carrion-eating birds of prey and carnivorous animals are themselves unclean and must not be eaten by humans. Thus these laws reinforce the principles stated in Genesis 9 forbidding the consumption of blood. Genesis 9 views meat-eating as a concession, as Genesis 1 envisages that animals and humans should eat only plants. The restrictions of Leviticus 11 reaffirm these principles. They also act as a reminder to Israel of their election. The clean (edible) birds and animals symbolize Israel, whereas the unclean creatures represent the Gentiles. By insisting that Israelites eat only clean types of food, Leviticus does more than remind them of their elect status; it encourages the separation of Israel from the nations, who are not so discriminating about their diet. The abrogation of these rules in Acts 10 is linked to the proclamation of the gospel to Gentiles.

Leviticus 16 describes the climax of Israel's liturgical year, the Day of Atonement, the one day in the year when the high priest could enter the Holy of Holies in the tabernacle, i.e., the very throne room of God himself. In so doing he reenacts Moses' ascent to the summit of Mount Sinai and Adam's entry into the Garden of Eden. Like Moses on Sinai the high priest is not permitted to see God's face, but he has to shroud himself in protective incense. Incense, like sacrifice, had a propitiatory effect. Atonement for the sins of the nation is completed by the high priest, confessing them over a goat, which was then dispatched into the wilderness, symbolically carrying all the guilt of the people away.

The second half of Leviticus expands more fully on the moral and social dimensions of holiness, explaining further what it means to be a "holy nation." It involves more than offering sacrifice and abstaining from unclean food. Leviticus 18 and 20 place great emphasis on chaste behavior and threaten Israel with the same fate as the Canaanites: "the land will vomit [them] out" if Israel copies their mores. But holiness involves many other dimensions, some of which are spelled out in the commandments: Sabbath-keeping, honoring parents, avoiding theft, and so on. Another prominent emphasis in these chapters is a concern for the poor. Twice the Israelites are told to leave the edges of their fields unreaped so that the poor and sojourner may have some grain to eat (19:9; 23:22). Provision for the poor reaches a climax with the regulations for the Jubilee in chapter 25. These are

---

32. For a full discussion see Walter J. Houston, *Purity and Monotheism: Clean and Unclean Animals in Biblical Law* (Sheffield: Sheffield Academic, 2003).

designed to prevent the poor from being permanently trapped in slavery or landlessness. Every fiftieth year all slaves are released, and all land reverts to its original owner. The Promised Land was eventually allocated to the tribes by Joshua, and every extended family was supposed to be given a plot. But when drought and crop failure led to famine and bankruptcy, the bankrupt might be forced to sell off their family members or their land to richer, more successful neighbors. The Jubilee law would ensure that those who fell on such misfortune eventually received back their land and freedom. All these motives are summed up in Leviticus 19:18: "You shall love your neighbor as yourself."

The Book of Numbers

The book of Numbers carries the story of the nation from Sinai to the borders of Canaan. Many of the same motifs that characterize Exodus and Leviticus recur in Numbers, but whereas it takes only a year from leaving Egypt to the erection of the tabernacle on Mount Sinai, it takes another forty to cross the Jordan and enter the land. The cause is national unbelief and disobedience, problems already encountered on the way to Sinai and at the mount itself.

There are two main ways of reading the structure of Numbers. Dennis Olson has argued that the book is essentially the tale of two generations: "One generation ends in failure and death in the wilderness (Numbers 1–25). A second arises, whose end is not yet determined but whose perspective is one which is poised on the edge of the promised land (Numbers 26–36)."[33] There are a number of striking parallels between these two halves of the book. Both begin with censuses (Num. 1–4 // 26); follow with laws about women (5:11-31 / / 27:1-11); vows (6 // 30); offerings (15 // 28–29), lists of spies/land distributors (13:4-16 // 34:17-29). The sinful generation of chapters 1–25 dies in the wilderness, leaving the next generation to enter the land (chapter 26–36).

But most commentators[34] prefer to see the book as divided into three main sections determined by the geographical notes: (1) Israel at Sinai (chs. 1–10); (2) Israel at Kadesh (11–21); (3) Israel in the Plains of Moab (22–36). Between these main blocks of material come two itineraries: the journey

---

33. Olson, *Death of the Old,* p. 83.

34. For a fuller review see Gordon J. Wenham, *Numbers* (Sheffield: Sheffield Academic, 1997), pp. 15-25.

from Sinai to Kadesh (10:11–12:16) and from Kadesh to Moab (20:1–22:1). In the course of each journey, victory songs are sung (10:35-36; 21:14-15), Miriam is mentioned (12:1-15; 20:1), the people grumble and Moses intercedes (11:1-2; 21:5-7), and on each journey there is miraculous provision of food and water (11:4-35; 20:2-13). In these respects the journeys in Numbers echo the journey from Egypt to Sinai (Exod. 13–19). Clearly history repeats itself: the general message is that Israel does not learn much from its mistakes, but the Lord remains faithful to his promise. Despite Israel's unbelief, the fulfillment of the land promise draws near and the Israelites are protected from unfriendly neighbors.

At each main center (Sinai, Kadesh, and Moab) laws are given dealing with similar topics, but these centers also witness rebellion, plague, and atonement made by priests and Levites. The most serious of these rebellions occurs on the very borders of Canaan. From Kadesh twelve spies are sent out to view the land, and they traverse it from south to north and bring back a huge branch of grapes, visible proof of the fertility of the land. But their gloomy assessment of the military might of the Canaanites persuades the people that conquest is impossible. In other words, the people believed that God's promises made to the patriarchs in the very places the spies visited were untrustworthy. This fundamental act of unbelief leads to God's threat to wipe them out as he threatened to do at Sinai. Once again Moses' intercession saves the day, but the unbelievers are sentenced to die in the wilderness, which led to the long delay in the occupation of the land (Num. 13–14).

This is not the only act of unbelief recorded in Numbers. A rebellion led by Korah, Dathan, and Abiram against the authority of Moses and Aaron leads to them perishing in spectacular fashion (Num. 16). On the banks of the Jordan, the people commit apostasy with the local deity of Baal-Peor (Num. 25). Even Moses fails to carry out God's commands exactly, as he strikes the rock instead of speaking to it,[35] and in consequence he is banned from entering the land.

The book of Numbers thus illustrates the theme of the Pentateuch, that is, the partial fulfillment of the promises, which also implies their partial non-fulfillment. But in no way are the promises abrogated: in fact, they are reaffirmed and elaborated by a most unexpected character. Balaam, a heathen prophet from distant Amaw, declares in glorious colors Israel's bright future of dwelling in the land under a triumphant king (Num. 22–24). When some-

---

35. So Johnson L. T. Kok, *The Sin of Moses and the Staff of God: A Narrative Approach* (Assen: Van Gorcum, 1997).

one hired to curse Israel instead blesses them, that blessing must be valid. And the book itself ends on a positive note, with Moses promising in a legal judgment that each tribe "shall hold on to its own inheritance" (Num. 36:9).

The Book of Deuteronomy

The last book of the Pentateuch, Deuteronomy, is of a different character from its predecessors. It does complete the biography of Moses that began in Exodus: in Deuteronomy 34 he climbs Mount Nebo, has a vision of the Promised Land, and dies. But the book mainly consists of three farewell sermons delivered to the nation before his death: chapters 1–4, 5–28, and 29–30. They are described as Moses' exposition of the law in 1:5, and that is apt. They take up several of the laws found in the previous books and explain how they may be applied in the land of Canaan. More than that, in these sermons Moses recalls various episodes from the past, notably the making and worship of the golden calf and the fiasco with the spies (1:19-46; 9:6–10:11). He urges Israel to remember their past mistakes, so that they may flourish in the land. One could describe the whole of chapters 1–11 as a command to live the Shema: "Hear, O Israel: . . . you shall love the LORD your God with all your heart and with all your soul and with all your might" (6:4-5).

But Deuteronomy is more than an exposition of law and theology. Moses' epitaph in 34:10-12 describes him as the greatest of the prophets, and canonically Deuteronomy is the first great prophetic book of the Old Testament. Moses' calling as a prophet is illustrated in a variety of ways. He is a great intercessor whose prayers save Israel from annihilation (Deut. 9:18-19; 10:10; cf. 1:35-39). Like other prophets, he suffers on behalf of the nation (1:37; 3:26; 4:21; 32:50). But his prophetic role is most clearly seen in his preaching. It is both expository and monitory. He applies the old law to the new situation, and he gives dire warnings of the likely consequences of not observing his advice. Indeed, past experience leads him to expect that Israel will break the law and suffer as a result. He foresees the covenant curses (28:15-68) being fulfilled and the nation being deported to foreign lands (29:2-28). But, as previous apostasies have proved, that will not be the end of the story: if they repent and return to the Lord with all their heart, he will restore their fortunes and bring them back to the land.[36] These messages are

36. See Paul A. Barker, *The Triumph of Grace in Deuteronomy: Faithless Israel, Faithful Yahweh in Deuteronomy* (Carlisle: Paternoster, 2004).

reiterated by the two poems that conclude his instruction of Israel: the Song of Moses warns the nation of the dire effects of faithlessness, while the Blessing of Moses is much more upbeat, concluding with, "Happy are you, O Israel! Who is like you, a people saved by the LORD" (33:29). These Mosaic prophecies thus set a pattern followed by later prophets: they are gloomy about the nation's immediate prospects, but through the darkness they still retain hope.

Critical scholarship of the last two centuries has not taken Deuteronomy's claim to Mosaic authorship seriously, preferring instead to see it as the work of late-seventh-century scribes, priests, prophets, or Levites intent on legitimating the reforms of Josiah (2 Kings 22–23). More recent dissent has failed to overturn this critical consensus. But once again uncertainty about the exact origins of a book need not disturb canonical or final-form reading. Conjectures about date and authorship must take second place to the data presented in the text.

Deuteronomy presents the last sermons of Moses in the form typical of a second-millennium legal document, such as a treaty or law code. And it is striking that Deuteronomy could be classed as a hybrid between a treaty and a law code. Treaties typically begin with a historical prologue detailing the benevolent deeds of the suzerain toward his vassal since the last treaty was made. So Deuteronomy 1–11 reflects on God's dealings with Israel since the previous covenant was made at Sinai. Its retelling of the history is more didactic than the account in Exodus to Numbers: it draws out more explicitly the lessons to be learned from past events than Exodus and Numbers do. In this regard Deuteronomy has been compared to John's Gospel, whereas the straight telling of Exodus-Numbers resembles the Synoptic Gospels.

Like ancient legal documents, Deuteronomy 12–25 then introduces a selection of laws, most of which have been broached in earlier parts of the Pentateuch. Now they are explicitly reoriented toward life in the Promised Land, showing how old legislation may be applied in new situations. The sequence of the laws in Deuteronomy seems to be based on the Decalogue, which gives further insight into the principles enshrined in the book.

But probably the most significant section is chapter 28, which corresponds to the blessings and curses often attached to treaties and law codes. Israel is promised prosperity at home, good harvests and health, security, and children if they keep the law. On the other hand, if they do not observe the law, they will suffer a terrible series of calamities — drought, famine, disease, defeat by their enemies, and deportation from the land. This cause-and-effect theology is often termed deuteronomic, as it is most clearly spelled out in Deuteronomy. It informs the ideology of the historical books from Joshua to Kings, and also the thinking of the later prophets. But though it is put most clearly in Deuteronomy, similar principles are found in other books both inside and outside the Bible. That God rewards righteous individuals and nations and allows the wicked to suffer is fundamental to a religious ethic.

So Deuteronomy both concludes the Pentateuch and serves as an overture to the following parts of the canon. The death of Moses marked the end of an era: "There has not arisen since a prophet like Moses." His message that Israel must remember the laws of the covenant if the nation is to prosper reverberates down the succeeding centuries and biblical books. Regrettably, his warnings are too often ignored and his gloomy predictions, not his encouraging promises, are fulfilled. Droughts and famine, war and exile are the nation's fate because of its persistent sinfulness. Yet Deuteronomy does not despair of God's ultimate mercy, and it holds out the hope of restoration, a hope reaffirmed in various ways by the latter prophets and the New Testament.

The Pentateuch and the New Testament

Deuteronomy is one of the most quoted books in the New Testament, especially by Jesus, who appeals to it more than he does to any other book. In his temptation in the wilderness he quotes it three times to refute the devil's suggestions. His forty-day fast is a reenactment of Israel's wilderness experience. He sees himself and his disciples as the new Israel, and his mission is recapitulating the experiences of the old Israel. Thus he can apply Deuteronomy's texts to himself.

Asked by a scribe which is the greatest command in the law, Jesus combines Deuteronomy 6:5 with Leviticus 19:18 to identify love for God and love for one's neighbor as the central demands of the law. Challenged by the Sadducees about the resurrection, Jesus cites Exodus 3:6 ("I am the God of Abraham, the God of Isaac, and the God of Jacob") as demonstrating that he is the God of the living not the dead (Mark 12:26-27). Confronted by the Pharisees over his teaching on marriage, Jesus appeals to Genesis 1:27 and 2:24: "Have you not read that he who created them from the beginning made them male and female, and said, 'Therefore a man shall leave his father and his mother and hold fast to his wife, and they shall become one flesh'?" (Matt. 19:4-5). He goes on to expound the difference between God's intentions revealed in the opening chapters of Genesis and his accommodation to human sinfulness in the provisions of the Law in Deuteronomy 24:1-4, a vital hermeneutical principle that we have already addressed above.

Finally, of course, Luke tells us that, after the resurrection, "beginning with Moses . . . he interpreted to them in all the scriptures the things concerning himself" (Luke 24:27). This gives all the theological interpretation of the Pentateuch found in the rest of the New Testament the stamp of dominical authority, for evangelists and apostles claim to have been taught their hermeneutic by Christ.

Conclusion

This attempt at a trinitarian reading of the Pentateuch indicates how central its ideas are to a theology that tries to embrace the whole Bible. It portrays a God who is almighty and omniscient, concerned with human well-being, compassionate, and forgiving. In it are set out divine ideals for human behavior and guideline legislation for serious infractions of those ideals. A trinitarian reading of rules on uncleanness or talion, for example, cannot be simply transposed into an urban, post-Christian culture, but such rules still can act as signposts for the people of God in the third millennium.

We have argued that different approaches are required to elucidate different parts of the Pentateuch. Ancient Near Eastern epic literature illuminates the distinctiveness of Genesis 1–11 and its vision of God and man. By contrast, social anthropology offers the most penetrating insights into the significance of the ritual procedures set out in Leviticus and Numbers. It must not be forgotten that the collections of law are set within the framework of a history that runs from creation to the death of Moses, and that in grasping the significance of these stories the insights of literary theorists have been invaluable. But helpful as these different approaches are, they must not obscure that the overriding concern of the Pentateuch is to teach us about God and his will. This is the essential contribution of a trinitarian hermeneutic.

11 Hearing the Historical Books

Iain Provan

Introduction

It is as well to begin with a definition. By the term "historical books" I mean to refer to the literature of the Christian Old Testament that lies between Joshua and Esther inclusive. This literature is dispersed throughout different parts of the Old Testament canon in the Jewish tradition.[1] Joshua, Judges, 1-2 Samuel, and 1-2 Kings are found in the Prophets, while the remaining books are found in the Writings. In the Christian Old Testament, however, all these books are drawn together into one place to form a single, continuous story. The story begins in Joshua, with an account of the initial entry of the people of Israel into the Promised Land. It continues through Judges, which describes the eventual failure of Israel to live in this land without a king; and Ruth, which tells the story of one faithful family living during this same time, from which an important king will one day arise. This is King David, whom we meet in 1-2 Samuel, first in the context of the reign of King Saul and of the prophetic ministry of Samuel. The ups and downs of the monarchy in Israel after David are documented in 1-2 Kings, in a story that comes to its end with the fall of northern Israel to the Assyrians in the eighth century B.C. and the fall of Judah to the Babylonians in the seventh century B.C., and the beginning of Israel's exile from the land. The future of the monarchy is uncertain as this part of the story concludes, although the way in which 1-2 Chronicles retells the account of most of its past (from David

1. See further Chapter 7 by Stephen Dempster in the present volume.

onwards) suggests that it does *have* a future. Israelite kings are nowhere to be found, however, in the narratives about Israel that bring the story told in the historical books to its end. These are narratives of Israelite life within empires ruled by foreign kings, whether those Israelites are still living in exile (Esther) or have returned to Palestine (Ezra and Nehemiah).

History and the Historical Books

What are some of the challenges that face us when as Christians we seek to hear the address of God to the church through these texts? Perhaps the first is hinted at even in the title of this chapter, which refers to "historical" books. The adjective implies that these are books about the past — the past of a particular people in a particular period of history. These books might be interesting, therefore, to those who are interested in the history of Israel, or even in the ancient world more generally. They might even be somewhat important in terms of understanding what happened afterwards, in the period of the New Testament; perhaps we need to know something about these books so that we have the appropriate background for our reading of later biblical literature (e.g., so that we know, when Jesus is called "son of David," who David was). All of this might be true; but how are these texts to *address* us? As modern people we do not normally expect historical texts to *address* us. We expect them to provide us with facts. This is no doubt one of the main reasons why in so much of the modern Christian church the Old Testament is not much preached, but functions only as a depository of facts — facts about the ancient Israelites that may or may not be useful, illustratively, in Christian preaching. It is no doubt one of the main reasons, also, why commentaries on the Old Testament's historical books in the modern period have so often focused on establishing what the facts are and arguing that the texts do or do not provide us with facts. So the first challenge we must think about has to do with how these *historical* texts can be said to address *anyone.*

Here it will be helpful to reflect for a moment on *why* we normally expect historical texts, not to address us, but instead to provide us with facts. We have this expectation precisely because we are modern. We stand as the inheritors, in fact, of a quite novel tradition arising in relatively recent times as to how we should think about accounts of the past. Prior to the late eighteenth century, historiography was valued, when it was valued at all, precisely because it addressed the reader. It was valued as an art that had close links to the ancient art of rhetoric, an art that had as its purpose to teach (as well as to delight) the reader. The ancient words of Dionysius of Halicarnassus, writing during the reign of the Roman emperor Augustus, capture this reality well: "History is philosophy teaching by examples." It is only in the late eighteenth and nineteenth centuries that we find a general move away from this position, as an allegedly *scientific* approach to historical reality was widely adopted, in which penetrating behind the art and ideology of pre-modern sources of historical information in search of brute facts became the historian's main task. The search was on, utilizing proper empirical scientific method, for what the important German thinker Leopold von Ranke would refer to as *wie es eigentlich gewesen ist* — "the way it really was." For most of the nineteenth century Ranke himself presided in Germany over the vast scholarly enterprise of searching out such facts and presenting them in an objectively scientific form, allegedly free from bias and presupposition — and certainly free from any intention to teach or to delight. History-as-science had been born, history in pursuit merely of facts. Insofar as art was to be found in ancient accounts of the past, including rhetorical art in pursuit of education, this was now a problem that needed to be overcome by the historian. It was not of the essence of the text; it was indeed an obstacle requiring to be removed in pursuit of the facts that were the essence of the text. Indeed, history itself needed to be thoroughly rewritten; for accounts of the past written prior to the nineteenth century had not been produced by authors who possessed proper scientific methods. Everything now had to be done again in the proper manner by those who did now employ such proper methods. The ancient texts were useful now only as mines out of which "facts" that could be ascertained empirically might be quarried by the discerning miner.[2]

My interest in this development, in the present context, lies not in what it has ultimately spawned in the world of academic biblical studies, where many scholars have now come to believe, for remarkably poor reasons, in a "real" history of Israel that has remarkably little to do with the traditional history of Israel as described in the Old Testament. The ancient *biblical* tradition, among many others, apparently cannot be trusted in this new world; we must invent our own. My interest lies in what has happened, as a result of this development, to Christian attitudes toward the historical books of the

---

2. See further on the true nature of history and of historiography Iain Provan, V. Philips Long, and Tremper Longman III, *A Biblical History of Israel* (Louisville: Westminster John Knox, 2003), pp. 3-104; and Chapter 5 by Tremper Longman III in the present volume. Another volume that repays careful attention on the theme of Scripture and history is Craig Bartholomew, C. Stephen Evans, Mary Healy, and Murray Rae, eds., *"Behind" the Text: History and Biblical Interpretation*, SAHS 4 (Grand Rapids: Zondervan, 2003).

Old Testament. The effect of it has precisely been to focus much of our modern Christian discourse about these books on this question of facts. If it has been questioned by some whether these historical books provide us with facts (e.g., whether the conquest of Canaan under Joshua "really happened"), then we have responded by insisting that they do, and that we can show that they do (e.g., by arguing that "archaeology proves the Bible"). But all are agreed that the important thing is the facts — and apparently only the facts. Having established at least to our own satisfaction that the facts are the facts, we have then retired, as it were, to our intellectual and devotional beds for the night. The biblical historical books are safe for another day. We feel better; but we are none the wiser as to what to *do* with these books that our efforts have made so safe. We have won the argument, we think; but the argument itself has distracted us from the larger issue, which was always about hearing God speak to the church through these texts. We have won the battle for the facts, perhaps; but we have lost the war, which was always about what the facts *mean.*

The fundamental mistake here was ever, even for a moment, to allow modern scholars to get away with claiming that proper historiography is about the discovery of brute facts somewhere beneath or behind tradition, and about the dispassionate, unbiased, and presuppositionless presentation of the same to others. This is simply nonsense. We have no access to brute historical facts. To the extent that we know about the past at all, we know about it *primarily* through the testimony of other people. There is no way of writing historiography that does not involve such testimony or "story-telling." Because this is so, *interpretation* is integral to all historiography as well. All testimony about the past is also interpretation of the past. It has its ideology or theology; it has its presuppositions and its point of view; it has its narrative structure; and (if at all interesting to read or listen to) it has its narrative art, its rhetoric.[3] It is intrinsically embroiled in advocacy, even if it may go out of its way to try to disguise this fact and appear neutral. There is no true neutrality, however; no dispassionate, unbiased, and presuppositionless presentation of the facts is possible. People always write about the past because they wish to communicate some kind of truth to their readers or to advocate some kind of virtue. It has always been so; it will always remain so. All historiography is ideological narrative about the past that involves, among other things, the selection of material and its interpretation by authors who are intent on persuading themselves or their readership of certain truths. This selection and

3. See further Chapter 4 by David Beldman in the present volume.

interpretation are always made by people with a particular perspective on the world — a particular set of presuppositions and beliefs that do not derive from the facts of history with which they are working, but are already in existence before the narration begins. All historiography is like this, whether we are thinking of the ancient Greek Thucydides or the medieval English Bede, or of the modern Gibbon, Macaulay, Michelet, or Marx.[4] It is just the way things are, as a matter of fact and regardless of the attempts of modern rhetoricians to persuade us otherwise. All historiography *addresses* its readers through its rhetorical art. Historians tell their story of the past always with an eye to what is to be believed and carried out in the present.

The historical books of the Old Testament likewise *address* their readers through their rhetorical art. They are of course profoundly *interested* in the past — alone among the literature of ancient peoples, biblical literature "addresses a people defined in terms of their past and commanded to keep its memory alive . . . a people 'more obsessed with history than any other nation that has ever existed'"[5] — but they are not interested in it for its own sake. They tell the story of the past, selecting their material and interpreting it, in order to persuade their readership of certain truths and to advocate certain ways of living. We miss the point if we dwell on the facts themselves — no matter how important it may be to defend the idea that these texts are indeed rooted in real events. We shall only get the point if we are able to overcome false modern notions about the nature of historiography that lead to false expectations as to what our biblical historical texts should be able to do for us. We shall only get the point if we pay attention to the story itself that our biblical authors have woven out of the facts, which is also the story (interpreted properly within the context of the whole biblical story) through which God addresses the church. That should be the focus of our attention: the story itself, in all of its artfulness, through which God speaks.

Rhetoric and the Historical Books

This brings us naturally to the second challenge, then, bound up with seeking to hear the address of God to the church through the historical books of the

4. These and other historians are discussed by J. Clive, *Not by Fact Alone: Essays on the Writing and Reading of History* (London: Collins Harvill, 1990).

5. Meir Sternberg, *The Poetics of Biblical Narrative: Ideological Literature and the Drama of Reading* (Bloomington: Indiana University Press, 1985), p. 31, depending partially on H. Butterfield, *The Origins of History* (New York: Basic, 1981), pp. 80-95.

Old Testament: the challenge of their artfulness — of their rhetoric. What is the structure of each book, and why might a particular book be structured in precisely the way it is and not in some other way? What has the author chosen to write about, and what has he not? Which literary conventions govern its composition, in whole and in part? Why is that particular language chosen in that particular passage within the work? These are some of the questions that arise as we try to understand, in the first instance, how the form in which each individual book is written communicates the message that the author is seeking to get across.[6] If God's Word comes to us embodied in artistic form, then we must surely try to read the art well in pursuit of that Word — or we may well mishear it. Some examples will help us to see why this is important.

Selection and Interpretation

I take as my first example 1-2 Chronicles, because these books illustrate so well what I have just been saying about historiography in general: that it is always ideological narrative about the past that involves the selection of material and its interpretation by authors who are intent on persuading themselves or their readership of certain truths. 1 Chronicles opens with multiple genealogical lists (1 Chron. 1–9), which take the history of Israel in the briefest form from the beginning of the world down to the return from exile. It is brief because the author is not particularly interested in this *whole* story; he is much more interested in the period of the Israelite monarchy, the description of which takes up the remainder of the space. His story of the monarchy is, however, rather different from the one we find in Samuel and Kings, which date from an earlier time period than 1-2 Chronicles and were clearly used as a source by the Chronicler. In 1 Samuel we read extensively of the first king, Saul; however, the Chronicler begins his story only with the death of Saul (1 Chron. 10). The remainder of 1 Chronicles is given over to an account of the reign of David, much of which parallels closely material found in 2 Samuel.[7] We also find new material, however (e.g., a new list of those who supported David before his accession to the throne, 1 Chron. 12; and a new description in 1 Chron. 22–29 of various cultic arrangements made by David). There are, in

---

6. On the generalities of literary reading of the Old Testament, see Chapter 4 by David Beldman in the present volume; and specifically on the rhetorical art of the historical books, see V. Philips Long, *The Art of Biblical History,* Foundations for Contemporary Interpretation 5 (Grand Rapids: Zondervan, 1994).

7. Cf., e.g., 1 Chron. 11:1-9 and 2 Sam. 5:1-10; 1 Chron. 11:10-14 and 2 Sam. 23:8-10.

addition, notable omissions.[8] The careful reader will further notice certain differences of detail and ordering between passages in 1 Chronicles and 2 Samuel, even where the passages are substantially the same. This same pattern of addition to, omission of, and close reproduction of earlier material (albeit with changes in detail and ordering) is also found when we compare 2 Chronicles to 1-2 Kings. For example, Hezekiah has three chapters devoted to him in 2 Chronicles that are virtually unparalleled in 2 Kings (2 Chron. 29–31), while the Chronicler's Solomon story omits the Kings account of his fall into idolatry at the end of his reign (cf. 1 Kings 10–12 with 2 Chron. 9–10).

What does all this signify? The Chronicler is clearly telling a story of his own, not simply repeating a story from the past — which, indeed, there would be no point in doing. He is not even merely supplementing that prior story, as the Septuagint title for Chronicles, *Paraleipomenon* ("the things omitted") would suggest. He is in fact telling a new version of an older story to an audience that now inhabits a different context from the original audience — an audience of the third century B.C., perhaps, rather than an audience of the sixth or fifth century B.C.[9] As we compare his work with that of his forebears, it is possible to describe what are the main themes that he wishes his readers/hearers to dwell upon. There is in 1-2 Chronicles, first of all, a marked interest in the unity of the people of Israel as a twelve-tribe entity. The Chronicler passes over, in his accounts of David and Solomon, those hints that are found in 2 Samuel and 1 Kings 1–11 of the later division between northern and southern kingdoms in his accounts, stressing the participation of "all" Israel in the major events of the time. After the division of the kingdoms, he shows that the northern tribes did not forfeit their position as Israelites. He also suggests that a kind of unity was restored between north and south toward the end of the monarchy (e.g., Hezekiah is portrayed as a second Solomon, uniting the whole population in worship at Jerusalem). The Chronicler has a very broad and inclusive view of the people of God, and his story is told partly with the desire to communicate this. He also has a particular view of Davidic kingship in Israel, which is both equated essentially with the kingdom of God and also thought of as consultative (the king frequently consults with his people in 1-2 Chronicles, and the

---

8. Among the omissions: all the ground covered by 2 Sam. 1–4 (David's reign over Judah alone); 2 Sam. 9 (David's kindness to Mephibosheth); 2 Sam. 11–12 (David's sin with Bathsheba); and 2 Sam. 13–20 (the revolt of Absalom and its aftermath).

9. There is nothing in 1-2 Kings that compels us to think of a date for these books later than the sixth century B.C.; but various details in 1-2 Chron. imply a date during the fourth and third century B.C.

people are more visible as a result than they are in Samuel-Kings). The Chronicler emphasizes very much the Jerusalem Temple and the need to worship there, understanding the people of God more as a community of faith than as an ancient Near Eastern state. Finally, he is clearly anxious to explain to his audience how it is that God's blessing and judgment work themselves out in the world, and how they do not.

All this makes perfect sense in a post-exilic period in which the question "What does it mean to be a true Israelite?" was apparently very much a live question. The Chronicler's answer appears to be that everyone — northerner and southerner — has a place in the new Israel as long as they belong to the community of faith that is centered around the Jerusalem Temple. It is in fact participation in a worshiping community, rather than citizenship in a royal state, that is important — participation in the kingdom of God, which forebears such as David and Solomon modeled. It is no doubt this paradigmatic function of David, Solomon, and others that leads the Chronicler to omit much of the negative material on the Davidic kings that is found in Samuel-Kings (e.g., David's sin with Bathsheba; Solomon's eventual idolatry). He knows that his audience knows about such things; but it is not these aspects of the older stories that he wants to emphasize. He wants his audience to think on higher things. In an age without kings, what can be learned from them is not how to *disobey* God, but how to *obey* him. He also wants his readers to know that they are in fact free to obey God and to know God's blessing. They do not carry any burden on behalf of their ancestors. This fear of being "fated" by the past is reflected clearly in the books of Jeremiah and Ezekiel. The Chronicler addresses it by emphasizing in his retelling of the past that every generation suffers for its own sins, and indeed that even the most wicked (like King Manasseh, 2 Chronicles 33) are free to repent and thus avert the coming judgment of God. His contemporaries' fate, he implies, lies in their own hands. In all these various ways the Chronicler retells the past in order to make sense of his and his contemporaries' present and future. The tradition that he inherits is reshaped so that it can speak to the people in the present in a way that the earlier account, written at least two generations before, can presumably not do sufficiently clearly any longer.

Literary Convention

Careful attention to the selection of material and its interpretation by the authors of our historical books is crucial if we are to hear the address of God to the church through these books. So too is careful attention to literary convention. To illustrate this point, let us move our focus from 1-2 Chronicles to Joshua. For example, a first reading of the opening twelve chapters of the book of Joshua might lead the reader to believe that its author is claiming that the Israelites entered the land of Canaan, vanquished all its peoples, and killed all the inhabitants of the land. This is certainly the impression given by a passage like Joshua 10:40-42[10] (see also 11:16-23). Such a reading, however, comes into question when we proceed to the second half of the book and discover that, although the Promised Land has now been allotted to the various Israelite tribes (chapters 13–22), it has in fact not all yet been conquered. Joshua 14:6-12, for example, describes Caleb as announcing his *intention* of conquering the hill country. Toward the end of the book, in chapter 23, we are explicitly told that Joshua has allotted as an inheritance all the land of "those nations that remain," which the Israelites will one day possess if they remain obedient to God; but in Judges 2:3 God tells them that because of disobedience he "will not drive them out before you; they will be thorns in your sides and their gods will be a snare to you." Clearly, then, we must understand the words of Joshua 10 in a different way than we might first have thought. They are not intended to indicate literally and mathematically that Joshua "left no survivors" or "totally destroyed all who breathed." They must be taken as intending to tell us only, and hyperbolically, that Joshua won remarkable victories — which nonetheless then had to be repeated by the Israelites who came afterwards. *How* it is that such words can in fact mean something different from what first appears to be the case is clearer to us now than it was to those other modern readers who came before us; for we now possess non-biblical second- and first-millennium B.C. conquest accounts from Assyria and Egypt (for example), which make it plain that our Joshua conquest account is a fairly typical example of this ancient form of writing and uses commonly shared literary conventions to speak about its conquest. The use of hyperbolic language to indicate a very successful campaign is simply a feature of this kind of ancient writing.[11] Any reading of our

---

10. "So Joshua subdued the whole region, including the hill country, the Negev, the western foothills and the mountain slopes, together with all their kings. He left no survivors. He totally destroyed all who breathed, just as the LORD, the God of Israel had commanded. Joshua subdued them from Kadesh Barnea to Gaza and from the whole region of Goshen to Gibeon. All these kings and their lands Joshua conquered in one campaign because the LORD, the God of Israel, fought for Israel."

11. K. Lawson Younger Jr., *Ancient Conquest Accounts: A Study in Ancient Near Eastern and Biblical History Writing*, JSOTSup 98 (Sheffield: Sheffield Academic Press, 1990).

Old Testament historical texts in pursuit of the address of God to the church will need to take account of this kind of use of literary conventions in such texts; for God has clearly chosen to address the church through texts that are composed in line with such conventions.

Subtlety

A different kind of "art" in our biblical texts is evident in the story of Solomon in 1 Kings 1–11. A first reading of these chapters might lead the reader to understand that in the case of Solomon we are dealing with a king who was wise and virtuous, and therefore blessed by God, for most of his reign; yet who fell suddenly into idolatry late in his reign, with the result that his son Rehoboam lost the northern tribes (1 Kings 12). A more careful reading, however,[12] suggests that Solomon was a more questionable character right from the beginning of his reign. He begins it in 1 Kings 2 by enacting the advice of his father David and ridding himself of his enemies. He uses his "wisdom" to do this (1 Kings 2:6, 9), although what this wisdom consists in is open to question in a chapter that is highly ambiguous about the rights and wrongs of the executions and banishments described in it. 1 Kings 3 then presents Solomon as a king very much aware of the deficiency of his previous wisdom and addressing God about this fact. A "wise and discerning heart" is now granted by God, which will enable Solomon to govern his people and to distinguish between right and wrong (3:9) — as he immediately goes on to do in the latter part of chapter 3, in the story of the two women and the disputed child. In chapters 4–5, Solomon's wisdom then brings great blessing on his people more generally.

However, even as we read 1 Kings 3–5, we are struck by two curiosities. First, at the beginning of chapter 3 Solomon marries the daughter of the Pharaoh of Egypt. Egypt is, of course, a name that resonates throughout Old Testament tradition with negative connotations: oppressor, arch-enemy, source of temptation (e.g., Exod. 1–15, esp. 13:17-18). The book of Deuteronomy, in particular, warns against "a return to Egypt" (Deut. 17:16) in terms of too-close relations with that nation, and explicitly forbids intermarriage with foreigners, lest the Israelites be led into apostasy (Deut. 7:3). We are being shown right at the beginning of Solomon's reign what our authors per-

---

12. Iain W. Provan, *1 and 2 Kings*, NIBCOT (Peabody, MA: Hendrickson, 1995), pp. 41-98.

ceive to be the very root of his later apostasy — this first marriage to a foreign princess. He loves God, but already at the beginning of his reign he carries with him also the seeds of his own destruction. By the end of his reign he will have multiplied such wives, in direct contradiction of Deuteronomy 17:17, and they will have led him astray. Second, in the midst of chapter 4, we come across two references to Solomon's many horses (vv. 26, 28). With Deuteronomy 17 in our minds, we cannot see these as the harmless beasts they may at first appear to be; for Deuteronomy 17:16 forbids the king from acquiring "a great number of horses for himself" and forbids him further from making the people "return to Egypt to get more of them." The first part of this prohibition Solomon clearly infringes in 1 Kings 4:26. The second he will infringe in 1 Kings 10:26-29, just before we hear again of Pharaoh's daughter and of Solomon's apostasy. By this point in Solomon's story we are also reading of huge amounts of gold entering his kingdom. Deuteronomy 17 also forbids the king from acquiring for himself excessive silver and gold (v. 17). By the time we reach the end of Solomon's reign, the various instructions to the king in Deuteronomy 17 have all been transgressed; but they *began* to be transgressed at its beginning.

It is now easy to see that the authors of 1 Kings 1–11 are intent, even in passages that are otherwise positive about Solomon, to help the reader see his darker side — to see that Solomon, in breaking God's law early in his reign, was already storing up trouble for himself in the future. Ultimately, the Solomon story is exploring these questions: What is the source and the nature of true wisdom, and can wisdom truly be wisdom that does not issue in obedience to divine law? It does so by telling us the story of a very complex person, obedient and disobedient to God in turn — a story marked by the subtle juxtaposition and insertion of material whose significance is clear once one has paused to consider it, but all the same might easily be missed by the inattentive reader. It is the Solomon of a literary artist, even while it is the Solomon also of history. It is indeed a three-dimensional Solomon vastly more interesting and colorful, and much easier to connect with our own lives in all their own mixed nature, than the two-dimensional Solomon often created by the reader of the text who would like to have the history without the art. This true Solomon painted by our literary artist is a character in turn embedded in a larger story about wisdom that reaches all the way back into 2 Samuel.[13] In this story, David too is portrayed as an ambiguous and com-

13. See further Iain W. Provan, "On 'Seeing' the Trees While Missing the Forest: The Wisdom of Characters and Readers in 2 Samuel and 1 Kings," in *In Search of True Wisdom:*

plex character from whom the reader is invited to learn — a wise man after God's own heart for so much of his early reign, yet in the aftermath of the Bathsheba incident a king whose mind is darkened as he lives his life under divine judgment. Under these circumstances his wisdom is of no avail as he faces his troubles. He is no match for Jonadab in 2 Samuel 13, or the Tekoan woman in 2 Samuel 14; he comes off badly in comparison to Barzillai in 2 Samuel 19, and he fails to convince us of his wisdom in regard to Saul's family in the same chapter. On the one occasion in the story when the failure of another's wisdom rebounds to David's advantage (the case of the doomed counsellor Ahithophel in 2 Samuel 17), the narrator pointedly tells us that it was not David who truly engineered it, but God. In the end the king who had previously had the reputation of possessing "wisdom like that of the angel of God [to know] everything that happens on the earth" (2 Sam. 14:20) finds himself in old age unable to "know" a beautiful woman sexually (1 Kings 1:4) and lacking knowledge, too, of the coup that is unfolding around him (1 Kings 1:18). This is the fate of human wisdom when it seeks to function independently of the divine will.

The kind of literary art of which I am writing here often involves quite specific things like the choice of a particular word or phrase, as we have just seen. It is careful attention to such particular words and phrases, and how they are picked up (or not) in subsequent narrative, that helps us make the appropriate connections within texts that enable a correct reading. In the story of the beginnings of monarchy in Israel in 1 Samuel 8–12, for example, we encounter once again the problem first noted in Judges 2:19 — that a good "judge" or appointed military leader within Israel has no lasting influence. 1 Samuel 8 begins by describing how Samuel grew old, and how Samuel's sons were disqualified as leaders because of their dishonesty (8:1-3). The people therefore ask for a king. Chapter 9 introduces to us for the first time Saul, who is out looking for his father's lost donkeys, but finds the kingship of Israel instead. He is anointed king, and he is told that various events will take place as he returns home to confirm his choice as king (10:2-4). The last of these will be that when he reaches Gibeath-elohim, he will meet a band of prophets, God's spirit will come upon him, and he must "do whatever your hand finds to do, for God is with you." He is then to travel to Gilgal and wait seven days until Samuel arrives and shows him what to do next (10:5-8). The key phrase here is "do whatever your hand finds to do" (10:7).

Essays in Old Testament Interpretation in Honor of Ronald E. Clements, ed. E. Ball, JSOTSup 300 (Sheffield: Sheffield Academic Press, 2000), pp. 153-73.

at does this refer? Coming as it does after a significant reference to a
stine outpost near Gibeah (10:5), we are justified in thinking that Saul is
attack this outpost and, having provoked a Philistine response, muster the
Israelites at Gilgal for a full-scale battle. He is then to await Samuel's arrival.
What actually happens, however, is quite different. Saul does nothing about
the Philistines. The spirit of God does come upon him, but, in contrast to
what regularly happens in the book of Judges, there is no subsequent act of
deliverance. Instead Saul, when questioned by his uncle, hides the fact that
Samuel has even spoken to him about kingship (10:13-16). It is not until
1 Samuel 13:1-4 that Saul carries out the first part of Samuel's earlier instructions, and only when his son Jonathan, in fact, provokes the Philistines. It is
then that Saul summons the Israelites to Gilgal. The Philistines respond in
force, however, and many of Saul's men desert him, while the rest become
afraid (13:5-7). Saul does wait seven days for Samuel, but when Samuel does
not appear he offers the sacrifices that Samuel is supposed to offer. Samuel
arrives just as he has finished (vv. 8-10) and tells Saul that he has failed to
keep God's commandment. God will not establish his kingdom; instead, he
will seek out "a man after his own heart" (vv. 13-14).[14]

The underlying issue here is the one highlighted by Samuel in 1 Samuel
12: will Saul uphold or undermine God's rule, as expressed through the prophetic voice? It is not just his failure to wait seven days that suggests he will
not uphold it; it is his failure right from the start to obey Samuel by doing, at
the God-ordained moment, "whatever your hand finds to do" and fight
God's battles. The contrast between Saul and the early David in this respect
is stark, and it is embodied in David's words to Goliath in 1 Samuel 17:45-47:
"You come to me with sword and spear and javelin; but I come to you in the
name of the LORD of hosts, the God of the armies of Israel, whom you have
defied. This very day the LORD will deliver you into my hand . . . so that all
the earth may know that there is a God in Israel, and that all this assembly
may know that the LORD does not save by sword and spear; for the battle is
the LORD's and he will give you into our hand." This is not the kind of thing
we find Saul saying. Here is someone (David) who understands God's power
and his purposes for Israel; and in the chapters that follow he demonstrates
time and again what a "man after [God's] own heart" (13:14) looks like, just
as Saul shows what it means to have forfeited God's favor. David fights the
battles of the Lord, not his own (1 Sam. 18:17; 25:28; 30:26); he fights these

14. See further V. Philips Long, *The Reign and Rejection of King Saul: A Case for Literary
and Theological Coherence*, SBLDS 118 (Atlanta: Scholars, 1989).

battles while Saul stays at home (18:12-16). He treats Saul and his family properly at all times (24:1-7; 26; 2 Sam. 1; and later, 2 Sam. 4; 9), whereas Saul treats him very badly (18:10-30; 19:8-10). He never tries to "take" the kingship, as Saul is said to have done in 1 Samuel 14:47; he does not grasp hold of it, as Saul continues to do throughout 1 Samuel 16–31. He simply waits on God, and it is delivered into his hand. After he is crowned, David dances all the way to Jerusalem in front of the Ark of the Covenant (2 Samuel 6). It is not regal behavior, and it attracts the contempt of Saul's daughter Michal; but David has no time for a Saulide view of kingship. He is quintessentially one who humbles himself before the Lord. This is indicated equally clearly in 2 Samuel 7, where he piously asks the prophet if he can build God a house, but acquiesces when God speaks through the same prophet to say that *God* will build *David* a house instead. It is such ready obedience to the prophetic voice that was beyond Saul.

The Problem of Translation

It is probably worth mentioning here one of the sub-challenges within the challenge to deal well with literary art in the historical books, since it is a sub-challenge relating to this matter of paying careful attention to particular words and phrases. It is the sub-challenge presented by the fact that translators of the Hebrew text sometimes do not themselves pay sufficiently careful attention to particular words and phrases. Their translations therefore fail to communicate the artfulness of the Hebrew text. The average Bible reader who does not have direct access to the Hebrew is thereby disabled from grasping important connections and signposts in the text. One example will suffice, taken from 1 Kings. I made a connection above between 1 Kings 1:4, in which we are told that David did not "know" a beautiful woman sexually, and 1 Kings 1:18, in which David is told that he lacks knowledge of the coup that is unfolding around him. This connection undoubtedly exists in the Hebrew of those verses, but it is obscured in the NIV by the translator's decision to render the Hebrew *lo' yd'*, "did not know," as "had no intimate relations with." The translation is well-intentioned; the translator wishes the modern reader to understand which kind of "knowing" is involved. It is also misguided, however, on two counts. First of all, it does not really help many modern readers to understand which kind of "knowing" is involved, because they do not know what the quaint "having intimate relations" means; if clarity is the main concern, better just to say that the couple did not have sex (or some such straightforward phrase) and be done with it. Second, however, this "clarity" on the particular verse removes all possibility for the non-Hebrew reader to gain clarity on the whole movement of 1 Kings 1 with respect to the "knowing" theme. Translators as much as interpreters really must take seriously the art of the biblical story as well as its facts, and try to communicate both to others.[15]

The Canon and the Historical Books

The historical books of the Old Testament *address* their readers through their rhetorical art, one by one; and taking account of this rhetorical art is crucial for their correct understanding. It is central to the development of what Craig Bartholomew describes in the opening chapter of this volume as an "integrated theological hermeneutic that retains critical rigor while aiming throughout to hear God's address."[16] The address of God to the church through these books is not heard, however, in these books one by one. It is heard as these books are read together, as a corpus, and as this corpus is read within the whole canon of the Old Testament and then of the Christian Bible. So now we must finally come to this larger question: How are the historical books to be read *together*, within the context of the biblical canon? We have clarified through attention to literary art that the book of Joshua does not mean to be read as indicating the wholesale slaughter of Canaanite peoples by the Israelites under Joshua; but what does any book about Israelite military conquest have to do with the church? We have clarified that both David and Solomon are presented to us in Samuel-Kings as flawed heroes of their faith; but what does their faith have to do with ours? And what does it mean for us that they are portrayed somewhat differently in 1-2 Chronicles? And how are we supposed to imagine that God is addressing *us* through the story of disobedient Saul — or, for that matter, through the often horrendous stories of the book of Judges?[17]

---

15. On the challenges of negotiating "the difficult tension between faithfulness to the original text and the requirement to 'make sense' in the target language," see further Raymond C. Van Leeuwen, "On Bible Translation and Hermeneutics," in *After Pentecost: Language and Biblical Interpretation,* ed. Craig Bartholomew, Colin Greene, and Karl Moeller (Grand Rapids: Zondervan, 2001), pp. 284-311 (quotation from p. 285).

16. Chapter 1 by Craig Bartholomew, p. 3 above.

17. The importance of this question of how we read the Old Testament texts *together* is well illustrated in Craig Bartholomew, Jonathan Chaplin, Robert Song, and Al Wolters, eds.,

To know how to hear God's Word to us now through the Old Testament historical books we must know first where they fit into the great story of the Bible that reaches from Genesis to Revelation. Who are these people whose history is told in such a way? They are people who are characters in what Chris Wright calls in Chapter 8 in the present volume "the narrative of God's mission, through God's people, in God's world, for God's purpose — the redemption of all of God's creation."[18] God calls Abraham out of Mesopotamia and makes a covenant with him, so that a people of Israel may come into being who are central to God's plan to bless all nations (Gen. 12). This people is given a law (Exod. 20–23), "in order to 'shape' Israel into a community that would reflect the character of Yahweh, enabling them to be the public, visible exemplar of God's intention for a redeemed community of people."[19] Our historical books themselves open with a reference to this law, in Joshua 1:7-8, where Joshua is told by God: "Be careful to obey all the law my servant Moses gave you; do not turn from it to the right or to the left, that you may be successful wherever you go. Do not let this Book of the Law depart from your mouth; meditate on it day and night, so that you may be careful to do everything written in it. Then you will be prosperous and successful." These are books, it quickly becomes clear, that are to be about Israel's successes and failures in obeying God and thus channeling God's blessing to the nations; that is, being a "kingdom of priests" (Exod. 19:6). They explore those successes and failures both before the Exile, portraying "the long and sorry story of Israel's struggle with the culture and religion of Canaan,"[20] and during and after the Exile, as the Israelites seek to "define their continuing identity as a community of faith in successive empires of varying hostility or tolerance."[21] They document them in terms of the Israelites' ability to affirm and to adhere to the uniqueness and universality of Yahweh as against all the gods of the nations.[22] They document them at the level of the Israelites' ability to pursue God's universal plan for the blessing of the nations and ultimately the whole of creation through Israel, remembering that they have

---

A Royal Priesthood? The Use of the Bible Ethically and Politically; A Dialogue with Oliver O'Donovan, SAHS 3 (Grand Rapids: Zondervan, 2002), where the issue of which kinds of praxis flow from which kinds of reading of Scripture is very much to the fore.

18. Christopher J. H. Wright, "Mission and Old Testament Interpretation," p. 83 above.

19. Page 185 above.

20. Page 188 above.

21. Page 188 above.

22. Page 193-94 above.

been chosen not for themselves but for the world ("God's choice of Abraham and Israel was instrumental, not preferential"[23]). And they document these successes and failures in terms of the Israelites' ability to embody God's call on their lives in terms of politics, economics, justice, worship, and personal holiness — the call to be a "light to the nations."

Our task in seeking God's address to us is to strive to position each particular text correctly within this overarching narrative context, "assessing how the shape of the grand narrative is reflected in the text in question, and conversely, how the particular text contributes to and moves forward the grand narrative itself,"[24] moving toward judgments as to what the text also has to say concerning the shape and demands of the mission God has for us in our particular contexts. The church is not Israel; Christians are not Israelites. Yet it is still the case that God's people are called to affirm and to adhere to the uniqueness and universality of Yahweh as against all the gods of the nations. God has not changed, nor has the call to worship this one true God. It is still the case that God's people are called to pursue God's universal plan for the blessing of the nations and ultimately the whole of creation, remembering that we have been chosen not for ourselves but for the world. God's choice of the church is also instrumental, not preferential. It was because God so loved the world that he chose Israel, and sent his only Son, whose body we are. It is still the case that God's people are called to embody God's call on their lives in terms of politics, economics, justice, worship, and personal holiness — to be a "light to the nations." It is still the case that we find ourselves characters in "the narrative of God's mission, through God's people, in God's world, for God's purpose — the redemption of all of God's creation" — albeit that we, too (like the Israelites), struggle with the cultures and religions of our own "Canaans" and still face "empires of varying hostility or tolerance."[25] Since these things are still the case, we may hope for comfort and rebuke, as well as instruction, as we read our historical books, listening for the address of God to us, sure of the continuities between our Testaments as much as we are aware of the discontinuities.

As we read the book of Joshua, for example, we should not make the mistake made by many Christians of times past of identifying the church so closely with Israel that we think it to be one of the tasks of godly Christians in the present to subdue their enemies by force and indeed to deal with them

---

23. Page 197 above.
24. Page 184 above.
25. Pages 183, 188 above.

much as Joshua dealt with the Canaanites.[26] In the Old Testament itself the conquest of the land is not understood as paradigmatic for Israel's relationships with the surrounding nations; that moment in Israel's history is clearly understood as an unusual moment. God's people after the resurrection are in any case no longer one nation distinguished from other nations, but a global people. Yet there *is* an address of God to the church in the book of Joshua with respect to such themes as faithfulness to God in the midst of idolatry and wickedness and the necessity of struggle with dark forces as we seek to walk in God's light. The book of Judges then makes clear that these dark forces can be as much in evidence inside the boundaries of the people of God as outside; but the book of Ruth tells us that capitulating to them is not inevitable, and that a godly, virtuous life is possible even in the worst of times — in fact, that such a life contributes to the saving plan of God in the world. There are discontinuities, to be sure, as we read these texts as Scripture; but the continuities are significant and important, as we seek to work out what it means that these Scriptures are "useful for teaching, rebuking, correcting, and training in righteousness" (2 Tim. 3:16). Wisdom is required, as we discern this "usefulness" — not least the wisdom to discern which aspects of the life of an Old Testament hero of the faith are given to us for imitation and which are not. For something may be right and proper for Joshua to believe and to do that is not right for a Christian to believe and to do; and although David's faith and virtue in the early part of his story are exemplary in many ways for us, we are certainly not supposed to imitate him closely at all in the later part of that story.

This need for discernment is perhaps particularly required in respect of three historical books I have not yet discussed: Ezra, Nehemiah, and Esther. These are stories of exile and return. In the case of Esther we are dealing with a people of Israel that has not returned to the land of Israel, but has chosen to remain where they were settled in Persia. In the case of Ezra and Nehemiah, we are dealing with a people of Israel that has returned to the land of Israel, but remains in a broader sense "in exile," since they are still "slaves" (Ezra 9:9) in bondage to the king of Persia. We are connected to these books, then, by the theme of exile, since Christians too are addressed in 1 Peter as exiles in this world,[27] and are indeed instructed to "live your lives as strang-

26. We have a long history behind us of Christians identifying with Israel and identifying their enemies as the Canaanites; note, for example, A. Abbot, "Traits of Resemblance in the People of the United States of America to Ancient Israel," in *The American Republic and Ancient Israel,* ed. J. Cellini (New York: Arno Press, 1977), pp. 5-25.

27. "God's elect, strangers in the world, scattered throughout Pontus, Galatia, Cappadocia, Asia, and Bithynia," 1 Peter 1:1.

ers here in reverent fear" (1:17). It might well be expected, then, that Christians have much to learn from Ezra, Nehemiah, and Esther about "living in exile"; and no doubt there *are* things to learn (about courage in the face of adversity, for example, and about the importance of putting God first in our lives).

Yet these three books are also filled with curiosities. To begin with Ezra and Nehemiah: the book of Isaiah had prophesied (chapters 40–55) that the return of the exiles to Palestine would be like a new exodus out of Egypt, leading on to a glorious future in the land in line with the promise to Abraham that occupies a central role in the story from Genesis to 2 Kings. Yet, as we have just seen, the "Exodus" that is reflected in Ezra-Nehemiah is not really an exodus *out of* slavery at all, and the promise of the Promised Land is far from fulfilled by the Israelites' presence there. It seems a disappointing end to Israel's story in Palestine; and indeed the *behavior* of the Israelites in the land is surprising in the *context* of that story. There is certainly no trace of the Abrahamic notion of Israel *blessing* other nations. What we find in Ezra and Nehemiah instead is a rather narrow idea of what the people of God are supposed to be: they repel and aggravate others rather than blessing them (Ezra 4:1-4; 10:9-12). People on the outside are not accepted into community with them, even though they claim that "we seek your God and have been sacrificing to him since the time of Esarhaddon king of Assyria" (Ezra 4:2);[28] and even those who are on the inside, having married into the people of God, and having borne children, are not considered truly a part of the community (Ezra 9–10; Neh. 13). The narrative reports that the leaders of the people claim to Ezra (9:1) that these marriages have led to apostasy; but that is not in fact clearly established by the narrator himself. It is in fact the mere foreignness of the marriages that is the focal point of the narrative that follows in Ezra 10; no distinction is made between foreign marriages that have not led to apostasy, on the one hand, and those that have, on the other hand. All foreign marriages are simply annulled; and the same is true in Nehemiah 13, where there is not even a hint that the issue is one of apostasy — it is simply that the people have intermarried with other races. We are a long way here from the mixed multitude that came out of Egypt, and from Moses, who married a Cushite. We are a long way from the story of Ruth, the Moabite ancestor of King David, and a very long way from Isaiah 56:4-8,

28. Some of these people may well be part of the group that eventually celebrates Passover with the returned exiles (6:21) — "all who had separated themselves from the unclean practices of their Gentile neighbors in order to seek the LORD, the God of Israel."

which envisages a time after the Exile in which the law of Deuteronomy 23:1-8 will no longer apply — precisely the section of Old Testament law cited in Ezra-Nehemiah regarding mixed marriages. We are, finally, a long way from Chronicles, with its "inclusive" view of Israel's community of faith, that all who want to belong to the worshiping community may do so.

All in all, Ezra and Nehemiah present us with a very puzzling story — a rather sorry sort of conclusion to the story of Israel inside the land. Nothing has been resolved as expected. The promise of redemption for and through Israel that is held out in Genesis 12 has certainly not been fulfilled: there is no nation; there is no real possession of the land; and there is no blessing for the world. The law of God is applied in an apparently literal way without any thought being given to whether it is now appropriate to apply it in this way, especially given the very real ethical questions that arise (what about the poor women and their children, when they are sent away by their husbands?). And throughout the whole story, God himself does not speak; and the narrator is himself entirely non-directive in how he tells this story — he simply *describes* what is happening. We must always take note of this kind of thing in seeking for the address of God in our biblical texts — precisely because (as discussed above) what the characters in a biblical text say and do is not always intended to be taken as a model for our own behavior.[29] There are things for Christians to learn from Ezra and Nehemiah, then; but they include negatives as well as positives, and perhaps the negatives predominate. As we read these books within the larger biblical context, we must surely read them as indicating mainly that people of God fell short of their calling in the Promised Land in the postexilic period, just as much as they did in the preexilic period. As such, they have nothing to teach us about a number of matters: for example, how to handle mixed marriages within the church, or how to exercise church discipline more generally. Indeed, they represent a disappointing cul-de-sac within the biblical story, in which story the main stream of theology is running elsewhere from now on. In Ezra and Nehemiah, the great onward movement of the redemptive history is stalled, as it were; and when it gets going again, it will not be the inheritors of the Ezra-Nehemiah tradition who move it onwards, but the great inheritor of the prophetic tradition, Jesus of Nazareth. It is Jesus who picks up the same Abrahamic (and indeed Isaianic) vision that Ezra-Nehemiah ignores and calls out a people in which there is neither Jew nor Gentile, male nor female, slave nor free; in which all distinctions of such kinds, maintained in God's Old Testament Law for particular reasons,

---

29. See further Chapter 4 by David Beldman in the present volume.

are now seen to belong to an age that is past and to have served their various purposes (whatever those may have been).

Much the same kind of puzzlement is experienced by the thoughtful reader of the book of Esther — the final part of the story about Israel *outside* the land, just as Ezra-Nehemiah is the final part of the story of Israel *inside* the land. The main theme of the book of Esther seems to be similar to the theme of the book of Ruth: that God looks after his people, providentially moving in subtle ways to ensure their well-being. It is an understated theme, though, to put it mildly. In fact, Esther is the only book in the Bible in its Hebrew form that makes no mention of the name of God.[30] We see providence in the book of Esther; but we see it in veiled form, not in terms of extraordinary divine intervention, as in a book such as Daniel.[31] In Esther, providence and normal human activity seem to go hand in hand. God is understood as working through such things as political intrigue, intellectual endeavor, and courage — through the actions of his people. But not all of these actions are beyond moral question, as we set them in the context of the remainder of Scripture. What are we supposed to think of Esther's presence in the king's harem, for example, or the more general fact that she merges into the scenery of Persia, her Jewishness concealed (2:10, 20)?[32] What are we supposed to think of the revenge taken by the Jews on their enemies (8:11-12; 9:5-10, 16)? The way the story is told reminds us of the conquest narratives in Joshua, but the situation is really not the same. It is very difficult, in fact, to read the book of Esther as anything other than a parody of the concept of peoplehood that the book of Genesis has in mind. This is how it has all ended, in our Old Testament narrative tradition. The people called to come out from among the nations in order that they should bless them — called to be a special and distinctive people dependent upon God in all things — this people has decided to *stay* in exile, to *merge* into the fabric of existence with no special identity, to *survive* through dependence upon their own resources, and to hold on to a narrow and nationalistic (rather than a particularly religious) view of peoplehood, which brings only destruction to others rather than blessing. These are people who are not really waiting for the pro-

30. It looks as if the Greek translators of the Bible were rather nervous about this, since they have introduced numerous passages into the book of Esther that make the story more explicitly theological.

31. For an interesting discussion of the differences between Daniel and Esther (comparing both to the Joseph story in Genesis), see W. L. Humphreys, "Life-Style for Diaspora: A Study of the Tales of Esther and Daniel," *JBL* 92 (1973): 211-23.

32. Contrast the very different stance adopted by Daniel and his friends.

phetic vision in any real sense at all. Like the people in the books of Ezra-Nehemiah, then, these people, too, point beyond themselves into the future, looking for a community to inherit God's promises.

The New Testament and the Historical Books

To know how to hear God's Word to us now through the Old Testament historical books we must know first where they fit into the great story of the Bible that reaches from Genesis to Revelation. We are helped to do this, finally, by paying particular attention to what we might call intertextual connections between the Old Testament and the New Testament, the way in which the New Testament tells its story in part by reminding us in its telling of aspects of the Old Testament story. For example, the stories of Simon the sorcerer and the Ethiopian eunuch in Acts 8:9-40 are modeled largely on the Old Testament story of Naaman and Gehazi in 2 Kings 5. Naaman's status as "great" and his misguided preference for actions and objects that are great have been used in characterizing the negative figure of Simon; Naaman's status as a "foreign royal official" has been used to depict the Ethiopian. Naaman arrives in Israel with royal backing, money, and a scroll, but initially fails to do the one thing necessary — establish appropriate communication with God's prophet. The Ethiopian arrives in a similar way and, like Naaman, in a chariot. In both texts the foreign official washes and is renewed. In both texts the question arises as to whether the gift of God can be exchanged for money. Elisha refuses Naaman's attempt to pay him, but Gehazi is happy to cash in on the miracle. Simon thinks that he can buy spiritual power. Both are confronted about their attempt to commercialize the gift; both are described in their wrongdoing as being (or fated to be) in the grip of a powerful negative force. 2 Kings 5 is not the only Old Testament text lying behind Luke's story at this point;[33] but it has clearly provided its foundation.[34] The general influence of the Elisha stories on the New Testament is, in fact, well recognized and provides the larger context in which to assess the

33. Note Deut. 23:1-2; 29:17; Isa. 58:6. The story has been told in such a way as to retain fairly close narrative continuity also with the earlier Gospel narrative of Jesus' meeting with the men on the road to Emmaus (Luke 24:13-35).

34. Another good example of this kind of phenomenon in the book of Acts is found in Acts 10, where the story of Peter and Cornelius has been significantly shaped by the Old Testament story of Jonah; see Robert Wall, "Peter, 'Son' of Jonah: The Conversion of Cornelius in the Context of Canon," *JSNT* 29 (1987): 79-90.

significance of individual examples. Jesus' mission is explicitly paralleled with that of Elisha in Luke 4:27 (what Jesus will do is analogous to what Elisha did when healing Naaman), and the implicit connections are numerous. For example, Jesus heals lepers, just like Elisha. He transforms water and suspends the laws of gravity in relation to it. He raises the dead and multiplies food. It seems that some effort has been expended by the New Testament authors in presenting Elisha as a "type" (prefigurement) of Christ, perhaps spurred on in particular by the fact that the names "Elisha" and "Jesus" have essentially the same meaning ("God saves").[35] Paying attention to such intertextual connections between the Old Testament and the New Testament is a critical part of the endeavor to hear the Old Testament correctly in relation to the New Testament.

Conclusion

It is this kind of discerning reading of individual parts of Old Testament Scripture that arises (I believe) from the proper attempt to take seriously the whole "narrative of God's mission, through God's people, in God's world, for God's purpose — the redemption of all God's creation," and to assess "how the shape of the grand narrative is reflected in the text in question, and conversely, how the particular text contributes to and moves forward the grand narrative itself." It is this kind of discerning reading of individual parts of Old Testament Scripture that arises from an overall intention to read the Old Testament *missionally* and *canonically,* and which results in Christians hearing the address of the Triune God in our Old Testament historical books in particular.

35. See further on all this Iain W. Provan, *1 and 2 Kings*, Old Testament Guides (Sheffield: JSOT Press, 1997), pp. 99-118.

12 Hearing the Psalter

J. Clinton McCann Jr.

Applying a Trinitarian Hermeneutic to the Psalter: The Psalms as *Torah*

Of all the many books or portions of the Old Testament, it might seem that the Psalms would be the least likely candidate to which to apply reasonably and constructively a trinitarian hermeneutic — that is, the least likely place in the Old Testament for "listening for God's address."[1] After all, it is the virtually unanimous consensus of contemporary Psalms scholarship that the book of Psalms originated out of Israel's *response* to God's address, and that it was transmitted as a record of that response and as a means to provide future generations of God's people with materials so that they could continue to respond faithfully to God (as opposed to hearing themselves addressed by God in the Psalms).

Given the prevalence of this understanding of the Psalms, it is not surprising that many Old Testament scholars and homileticians conclude that it is not appropriate to preach on the Psalms. Rather, they should be used in worship as songs and prayers, in keeping with their origin as a record of faithful response to God's address.[2] Many pastors over the years have told

---

1. See Chapter 1 by Craig Bartholomew in the present volume.

2. See, for instance, Donald E. Gowan, *Reclaiming the Old Testament for the Christian Pulpit* (Atlanta: John Knox, 1980), p. 146; David Buttrick, *Homiletic: Moves and Structures* (Philadelphia: Fortress, 1987), p. 478. This situation has begun to change in recent years; see, for instance, *Psalms for Preaching and Worship: A Lectionary Commentary*, ed. Roger E. Van Harn and Brent A. Strawn (Grand Rapids: Eerdmans, 2009).

me that it has never occurred to them to preach on the Psalms, and that even if it had occurred to them, they would not have known how to proceed. In this same direction, the ecumenical liturgical consensus is that the psalm assigned for each Lord's Day or holy day by the Revised Common Lectionary is to be understood not as one of the day's Scripture lessons, but rather as a means of responding to the Old Testament lesson, which is understood as at least capable of addressing God's people with the divine Word. As *The Book of Common Worship* of the Presbyterian Church (U.S.A.) and the Cumberland Presbyterian Church puts it:

> The singing of a psalm is appropriate at any place in the order of worship. However, the psalm appointed in the lectionary . . . is intended to be sung following the first reading [the Old Testament lesson], where it serves as a congregational meditation and *response* to the reading. The psalm is not intended as another reading.[3]

Again, note well — the clear implication is that the Psalms enable, facilitate, or constitute a *response* to being addressed by God, and thus the Psalms are not suitable material for listening for God's address.

What both the academic and the ecumenical liturgical consensus miss is an awareness of and appreciation for the canonical process of collecting, shaping, and transmitting the book of Psalms.[4] When the shape of the Psalter is taken seriously, as Klaus Seybold points out, the book "takes on the character of a documentation of divine revelation, to be used in a way analogous to the Torah, the first part of the canon, and becomes an instruction manual for the theological study of the divine order of salvation, and for meditation."[5] If the Psalter is anything like "a documentation of divine revelation," then it is certainly suitable material in which to listen for God's address.

To put it most plainly perhaps, the material in the Psalter that originated from, and is a record of, human response to God was ultimately received and transmitted as God's address to humankind — that is, as Scripture. The words of Brevard Childs are apt in this regard:

---

3. *The Book of Common Worship* (Louisville: Westminster John Knox, 1993), p. 37; emphasis added.

4. See Chapter 4 by David Beldman and Chapter 7 by Stephen Dempster in the present volume.

5. Klaus Seybold, *Introducing the Psalms*, trans. R. G. Dunphy (Edinburgh: T&T Clark, 1990), p. 24. See also J. Clinton McCann Jr., "The Psalms as Instruction," *Interpretation* 46 (1992): 117-28.

I would argue that the need for taking seriously the canonical form of the Psalter would greatly aid in making use of the Psalms in the life of the Christian Church. Such a move would not disregard the historical dimensions of the Psalter, but would attempt to profit from the shaping which the final redactors gave the older material in order to transform traditional poetry into Sacred Scripture for the later generations of the faithful.[6]

Because the Psalms are Scripture, even functioning "in a way analogous to the Torah," we can, and indeed we should, approach the Psalms not only as a record of and means of facilitating the human response to God, but also as a primary source for "listening for God's address."

As suggested above by both Seybold and Childs, the canonical shaping and shape of the Psalter are crucial, in terms of indicating to its readers that the Psalms are to be received as Scripture in which God addresses humankind. One of the most prominent aspects of the shape of the Psalter in its final form is the placement of Psalms 1–2 at the beginning. There is nearly unanimous agreement among scholars that Psalm 1 was either written or explicitly chosen to introduce the collection; and there is a healthy consensus that Psalms 1–2 together form a paired introduction, given the fact that neither psalm has a title and that the word "happy" in 1:1 and 2:12 forms an envelope-structure for the pair (see also the repetition of "way" and "perish" in 1:6 and 2:12).

In any case, one of the major accomplishments of Psalm 1 as part of the paired introduction is to orient the reader from the beginning to hear the Psalms as *torah*, "instruction" (twice in v. 2; NRSV and NIV "law"). To be sure, it is possible to interpret *torah* here as a reference to the Pentateuch (the Torah); but given the five-book arrangement of the Psalter (Psalms 1–41; 42–72; 73–89; 90–106; 107–150) that parallels the Pentateuch, it is more likely that *torah* here is meant to be understood more broadly as any divine instruction or address, including the Psalms themselves. The importance of *torah* in the Psalter is manifest in other ways as well. As James L. Mays argues, the placement of Psalm 1 at the beginning of the Psalter, the imposing presence of Psalm 119 (in which the word *torah* occurs twenty-five times) at the heart of Book V, and the scattering of references to *torah* and/or its synonyms throughout the Psalter (see Psalms 18, 25, 33, 78, 89, 93, 94, 99, 103, 105, 111, 112, 147, 148) have the following effect: "Taken together, this harvest of texts con-

---

6. Brevard Childs, "Reflections on the Modern Study of the Psalms," in *Magnalia Dei, the Mighty Acts of God: Essays in Memory of G. Ernest Wright,* ed. F. M. Cross, W. E. Lemke, and P. D. Miller Jr. (Garden City: Doubleday, 1976), p. 385.

tains a profile of an understanding of the Lord's way with people and the world that is organized around Torah. Torah applies to everything."[7] Indeed, so important is *torah* in the Psalter that Jerome Creach even concludes that "torah has become a surrogate for the Lord himself."[8] To attend to *torah,* God's "instruction," is to be addressed by God; and the Psalms are to be received and heard as *torah.*

In short, as suggested above, material that originated as human address to God is now to be received as God's address to humanity. Thus, the canonical shaping and shape of the Psalter invite the application of what this volume calls a trinitarian hermeneutic — that is, listening for God's address. As it turns out, Psalms 1 and 2 not only orient the reader of the Psalter to listen for God's address, but they also anticipate the *content* of what God intends for the faithful to hear. To the content of God's address in the Psalter we now turn.

The Reign of God

In the ancient Near East, the prerogative and responsibility of promulgating *torah* belonged to kings. Thus, the pervasive importance of *torah* in the Psalter is at least an implicit affirmation that God reigns. Walter Brueggemann summarizes the Psalter's fundamental portrayal of God and God's presence in the world like this: "YHWH is the key player . . . Lord of the nations and the Savior of Israel."[9] Other features of Psalms 1–2 reinforce this interpretive direction. For instance, there is an abundance of royal terminology in Psalm 2. To be sure, the title "king" is applied not to God, but to "kings of the earth" (v. 2) and God's own "king on Zion" (v. 6). But clearly God is the kingmaker. God is directly responsible for installing "my king on Zion," and God's laughter (v. 4) at the "kings of the earth" is an indication of God's ultimate sovereignty. The NIV's translation of the Hebrew participle of *yšb* as "The One enthroned" (v. 4) is appropriate. The root does mean basically "to sit" (see NRSV), but it is used elsewhere of kings in their ruling capacity. Again, the affirmation is that God reigns.

Even more explicit in this regard is the invitation in Psalm 2:11, "Serve the LORD with fear." The verb invites submission to a sovereign master, and

7. James L. Mays, "The Place of the Torah-Psalms in the Psalter," *JBL* 106, no. 1 (1987): 8.

8. Jerome F. D. Creach, *The Destiny of the Righteous in the Psalms* (St. Louis: Chalice, 2008), p. 143.

9. Walter Brueggemann, *An Introduction to the Old Testament: The Canon and Christian Imagination* (Louisville: Westminster John Knox, 2003), p. 288.

the only other occurrence in the Psalter of the invitation to "Serve the LORD" is found in Psalm 100:2 (NIV and NRSV "Worship the LORD"). This verbal link between Psalms 2 and 100 is significant, since Psalm 100 immediately follows a collection of enthronement psalms (Psalms 93, 95–99) that employs the Hebrew root *mlk* either to name God as "King" (95:3; 98:6) or to assert that God "reigns" (93:1; 96:10; 97:1; 99:1, NIV). As it turns out, this collection is also highlighted by the shape of the Psalter. The placement of royal psalms (psalms about the earthly king — see below) at the "seams" of the Psalter appears to be intentional — Psalm 2 near the beginning, Psalm 72 at the end of Book II, and Psalm 89 at the end of Book III.[10] In particular, Psalm 89 and its poignant lament by the "rejected" (Ps. 89:38) Davidic king (vv. 38-51) seem to mark a major break, concluding Book III "with the anguished cry of the Davidic descendants,"[11] and offering up images of rejection and destruction that recall the Exile and its losses — land, temple, and monarchy. In turn, Book IV gives every appearance of responding to Psalm 89 and the crisis of exile. The book starts with Psalm 90, which offers "A Prayer of Moses," who led the people before they had a land, a temple, or a king. And continuing the Mosaic perspective of Book IV, the enthronement collection responds to the crisis of exile with the explicit affirmation of God's reign, thus recalling the conclusion of the Song of the Sea in Exodus 15:18: "The LORD will reign forever and ever." Because of the pivotal position and function of Book IV, and of the enthronement psalms in particular, Gerald Wilson concludes that Book IV is "the editorial 'center' of the final form of the Hebrew Psalter,"[12] and that the enthronement psalms form the Psalter's "theological 'heart.'"[13] Frank-Lothar Hossfeld and Eric Zenger concur; as they see it, the enthronement psalms (Psalms 93–100, in their view) actually formed the conclusion of an earlier edition of the Psalter that consisted of Psalms 2–100, thus giving them an even more emphatic position.[14] In any case, Psalm 2 seems to be performing its introductory function by anticipating the Psalter's theological heart and the message that the enthronement collection will make explicit: God reigns.

---

10. See Gerald H. Wilson, "The Use of Royal Psalms at the 'Seams' of the Hebrew Psalter," *JSOT* 35 (1986): 85-94.

11. Gerald H. Wilson, *The Editing of the Hebrew Psalter,* SBLDS 76 (Chico: Scholars Press, 1985), p. 213.

12. Wilson, *Editing of the Hebrew Psalter,* p. 215.

13. Wilson, "Use of Royal Psalms," p. 92.

14. Frank-Lothar Hossfeld and Eric Zenger, *Psalms 2,* Hermeneia (Minneapolis: Fortress, 2005), p. 7.

In a perhaps less obvious but no less important way, Psalm 1 also anticipates the Psalter's theological heart. In Psalms 96 and 98, what God "comes" (96:13; 98:9, NIV) into the world to do is to "establish justice on the earth . . . with righteousness" (96:13; 98:9, my translation; NIV and NRSV "judge the earth . . . with righteousness"). In short, as we shall discuss in more detail below, justice and righteousness constitute a summary of God's *torah*, "instruction" — that is, God's will. Not coincidentally, both the Hebrew roots for justice and righteousness are present in Psalm 1. Those who delight in and attend constantly to God's *torah* are called "the righteous" (vv. 5-6). Conversely, "the wicked" are those who "will not stand up for justice" (v. 5, my translation; NIV and NRSV "The wicked will not stand in the judgment"), because they are "scoffers" (v. 1), a word that describes people who refuse to be taught. Because "the wicked" refuse to listen to God, they do not know, or do not care (or both), that the sovereign God wills justice and righteousness in and for the world.

To be sure, the translation and interpretation of Psalm 1:5 are contested. But even if the NIV and NRSV are correct, it is still the case that Psalm 1 contains the two key Hebrew roots that will be emphasized by the enthronement psalms as they proclaim what God wills in and for the world. Thus, like Psalm 2, Psalm 1 seems to be performing its introductory function by anticipating the Psalter's theological heart and the message that the enthronement psalms make explicit: God reigns, and God wills justice and righteousness. The message that God reigns is, above all, what the Psalter wants us to hear, according to Mays:

> The declaration of *yhwh malak* ["the LORD reigns"] involves a vision of reality that is the theological center of the Psalter. . . . The psalmic understanding of the people of God, the city of God, the king of God, and the law of God depend on its validity and implications. . . . The organizing role of the declaration does not ignore or obviate the variety and plurality of thought about God in the psalms. It does announce a metaphor that transcends and lies behind the variety. It is what every reader and user of the psalms may know as the code for understanding all of them.[15]

As Mays suggests, the affirmation that God reigns is related to all the psalms, but there seems to be a special relationship between this affirmation and the psalms that feature the reign of the earthly king. In short, the reign of God is

---

15. James L. Mays, *The Lord Reigns: A Theological Handbook to the Psalms* (Louisville: Westminster John Knox, 1994), p. 22.

inextricably related to the reign of God's chosen earthly agent, who, not surprisingly, is mentioned already in Psalm 2 — God's "anointed" (v. 2).

The Rule and Role of God's Anointed and God's Faithful

As noted above, the royal language in Psalm 2 is applied, not to God, but rather to earthly monarchs. Of particular interest and importance perhaps for a trinitarian hermeneutic is that God does speak in Psalm 2, both to the "kings of the earth" in verse 6 and to God's own "king on Zion" in verses 7-9. If the "kings of the earth" heard God's address, it is not reported in the psalm. But it is clear that "my king on Zion" has listened for and heard God's address, for it is he who reports in verses 7-9 what God "said to me" (v. 7).

The substance of God's address is an affirmation: "You are my son; today I have begotten you" (v. 7), and a promise in verses 8-9 of world-encompassing sovereignty. This promise corresponds to God's world-encompassing sovereignty that is implied in verse 4 and that will be articulated explicitly throughout the Psalter, especially in the enthronement collection (see above). This sweeping promise to the king at the beginning of the Psalter, along with the description of the king as "his [God's] anointed" (v. 2; the Hebrew is usually transliterated as *messiah*) and "my [God's] son" (v. 7; see 2 Sam. 7:14), is certainly sufficient to indicate the profoundly important relationship between God's reign and the reign of the earthly king. But there is much more in this regard. As noted above, royal psalms occur in strategic positions in the Psalter, especially Psalms 2, 72, and 89. So significant are the royal psalms in the view of Hossfeld and Zenger that they conclude that the developing Psalter would have consisted at some point of Psalms 2–89 — that is, a collection bounded by two royal psalms that Hossfeld and Zenger call "The Messianic Psalter."[16]

Beyond the significance of the placement of royal psalms, the overlap in content between the royal psalms and the enthronement psalms indicates the inseparable relationship between the reign of God and the rule and role of the earthly king. Most important in this regard is Psalm 72, which is a prayer for the king. What is desired and fervently prayed for is that the earthly king possess and do exactly what God, the heavenly king, "comes" into the world to do — namely, justice and righteousness (see Ps. 72:1-7, especially vv. 1-2; and see above on Psalms 96 and 98, and the next section on

16. Hossfeld and Zenger, *Psalms 2*, pp. 5-6.

God's will). The earthly agency of the king is crucial for the implementation of the divine will.

This relationship between God and God's messiah explains why the Exile, which included the loss of the institution of the monarchy, was such a profound theological crisis. The pained lament of the "rejected" Davidic descendants (see above) pointedly raised the question: Who will do on earth what the heavenly God wills? As suggested above, the response to Psalm 89 and its articulation of the crisis of exile is Book IV of the Psalter, especially the enthronement collection and its affirmation that God reigns. But it is noteworthy that immediately following the enthronement collection (especially if one views Psalms 93-100 as the extent of the collection, as do Hossfeld and Zenger), there is another psalm that is almost universally categorized as a royal psalm (Psalm 101), as if to press the question: But who is responsible for the earthly implementation of the will of God, the heavenly king?

The answer to this question is not clear. It is possible that the appearance in Books IV-V of Psalm 101 and several other royal psalms (Psalms 110, 132, 144) expresses the Psalter's hope for the eventual restoration of the Davidic monarchy. This is a reasonable conclusion; and it may be correct, but not necessarily. It is more likely that the royal psalms in Books IV-V (along with those in Books I-III) express the conviction that God will provide some sort of agency to effect concrete, earthly implementation of God's will for justice and righteousness, just as the Davidic messiahs were supposed to have done in the past. An answer to the question — Who? — is at least suggested by Psalm 149, especially by way of its allusion to Psalm 2. In Psalm 149:6-9, it is "the faithful" (vv. 1, 5; see v. 9) who exercise a world-encompassing sovereignty that is described in a manner that is very similar to the way that the earthly king's sovereignty is described in Psalm 2:8-9. The implication is that in the absence of the monarchy, the people as a whole become God's earthly agents. The language in both Psalms 2 and 149 is disturbingly violent, but the purpose of the exercise of sovereignty by "the faithful" is suggestive — "to enact among them ['the nations' and 'the peoples'] the justice decreed" (Ps. 149:9, my translation; NRSV "to execute on them the judgment decreed"). By enacting *mišpāt,* "justice," the people of God are doing what the kings were supposed to have done (Psalm 72) as agents of God's royal will (Psalms 96 and 98).

We shall deal further with the importance of justice and righteousness in the next section. But first we need to consider the questions: What do contemporary Christians listen for when we recognize the Psalter's messianic orientation? How does God address us? A traditional approach has been to view the Psalms as predictions of Jesus Messiah (or Jesus Christ; the Hebrew *messiah* came into Greek as *christos*), but a trinitarian hermeneutic insists that the Old Testament be "heard on its own terms."[17] Thus, the Psalms are not to be understood as predictions of Jesus' messiahship, but rather as testimony that the same God was at work in and through the monarchy, in and through the people of Israel, and in and through Jesus of Nazareth. The relationship between the Psalms and Jesus moves in both directions. We Christians appreciate more fully the shape of the justice and righteousness that God wills because we know Jesus, and we appreciate more fully what it means that Jesus is Messiah/Christ because we know the Psalms.

In particular, we hear in the Psalms the claim that to be God's "anointed"/Messiah/Christ is to have a mission that has everything to do with the enactment and embodiment of God's justice and righteousness in and for the world. When we Christians profess Jesus as *the* Messiah or *the* Christ, we profess that Jesus is the perfect embodiment of this divine mission. As suggested above, the Psalter seems to suggest that this mission is shared by God's people; and Jesus himself points in the same direction when he says of his followers: "so I have sent them into the world" (John 17:18 ; see Matt. 28:16-20; Luke 24:44-49). Because discerning the Psalter's messianic orientation is ultimately to be addressed with a divine call to mission, we turn now to a more detailed consideration of what the Psalms say that God "comes" into the world to do.

The Will of God: Justice, Righteousness, and Peace

The topic of justice and righteousness is inevitably related to the topics of the three preceding sections — God's "instruction" or will *(torah)*, God's reign, and the rule and role of God's "anointed" and "the faithful." Because God, the universal king, "comes" to do justice on earth and to set things right (Psalms 96 and 98) by way of the agency of the earthly king (Psalms 2, 72) and/or "the faithful" (Psalm 149), the words "justice" and "righteousness" function as a summary of what God wills in and for the world *(torah)*.

To be sure, every portion of the Old Testament participates in proclaiming the pivotal importance of justice and righteousness — the Torah, beginning in Genesis 18:19 (see also Deut. 16:18-20);[18] the Prophets, who

---

17. See Chapter 1 by Craig Bartholomew in the present volume.
18. See Chapter 8 by Christopher J. H. Wright in the present volume.

called the kings and the people to account for failing to enact and embody God's will (see Isa. 1:16-17; 5:1-7; 32:1, 16-17; 56:1-2; 58:2; Jer. 22:16-17; Amos 5:7, 15, 21-24; Micah 3:1, 8-9, 11; 6:8; Zeph. 3:3-5; Zech. 7:8-10); and the Writings (see Prov. 1:3; 2:8-9; 8:15-16, 20); but it is especially important that the theological heart of the Psalter is explicit and emphatic about presenting justice and righteousness as the fundamental platforms of God's royal policy in and for the world (in addition to Ps. 96:13 and 98:9 where, as mentioned above, "establish justice" is preferable to "judge," see also 97:2, 6, 8; 99:4).

Like the prophets in particular, the Psalms also make it very clear that justice and righteousness are more than slogans or high-sounding principles. They have a very specific content that is articulated unambiguously in Psalm 72, which also adds a third word/concept that belongs inextricably with justice and righteousness — that is, *shalom,* "peace" or "well-being" (v. 3, NIV and NRSV "prosperity"; v. 7, NIV "prosperity" and NRSV "peace"). Verses 12-14 of Psalm 72 amount to something like a job description for the earthly king in his role as the agent entrusted with the enactment and embodiment of God's will. These verses also make it clear that justice, righteousness, and shalom can be observed and even measured. The fundamental criterion for determining whether justice, righteousness, and shalom exist is whether "the needy" (v. 12 and twice in v. 13), "the poor and those who have no helper" (v. 12), and "the weak" (v. 13) are being attended to, valued, and provided for. If they are not, justice is not being served, righteousness is absent, and even though some people may say otherwise, "there is no peace" (Jer. 6:14; see Mic. 3:5).

What all this means is that discernment of God's will — justice, righteousness, and shalom — inevitably involves what we today call "economic indicators." Poverty and need in the human community are simply unacceptable to God; they indicate the presence of "oppression and violence" (Ps. 72:14), in the face of which God's chosen agents are called upon to deliver (v. 12), save (v. 13), and redeem or rescue (v. 14). Deliverance, salvation, redemption, and rescue are usually thought of as divine actions in the Old Testament; and they are. Thus, the call of Psalm 72 is for God's chosen agents to join God at God's work in and for the world — ending "oppression and violence" in the human community.

That it is indeed the *human* community that is in view in Psalm 72 is indicated by the cosmic language and imagery — "the sun" (vv. 5, 17), "the moon" (vv. 5, 7), "rain" (v. 6), "sea to sea" (v. 8), "the mountains" (v. 16) — and even more clearly by the allusion to Genesis 12:3 in verse 17, "May all nations be blessed in him."[19] In Genesis 12, when the narrative focus narrows from creation and humankind to Abram, the promise of blessing to Abram and his descendants is accompanied by a promise to the human community that also functions as a commission to Abram and his descendants: "and in you all the families of the earth shall be blessed" (Gen. 12:3). Reading Genesis 12 and Psalm 72 in view of their intertextual connection leads to a conclusion that the contemporary human community desperately needs to hear — that is, the future flourishing of the earth and all of its peoples is dependent upon the enactment and embodiment of the justice, righteousness, and shalom that God wills in and for the world.

The same conclusion is offered dramatically in Psalm 82, which is reminiscent of both Psalm 72 and the enthronement collection, since it contains the Hebrew root underlying "righteousness" (see "maintain the right," v. 3) and features a fourfold repetition of the root *špṭ* ("holds judgment," v. 1; "judge," v. 2; "Give justice," v. 3; and "judge," v. 8, another case in which "establish justice" would be preferable). It is probably coincidental, but Psalm 82 stands almost exactly halfway between Psalm 72 and the beginning of the enthronement collection (Psalm 93). In any case, God's sovereignty is strongly implied, since God has the ability to "pursue justice among the gods" (v. 1, my translation). And the admonition to the gods in verses 3-4 is essentially the same as the job description of God's chosen agent in Psalm 72 (see "deliver" in v. 12 and in 82:4). Verse 5 is crucial. It offers essentially the same timely conclusion reached above in reading Genesis 12 and Psalm 72 together — that is, in the absence of justice and righteousness, "all the foundations of the earth are shaken." In other words, the failure to enact and embody God's will threatens nothing short of the undoing of creation.

The gods are dethroned in verses 6-7 precisely because their misadministration of justice threatens the world with destruction. Granted, a scenario in which the God of Israel sentences the Canaanite gods and goddesses to death — "you will fall like every other ruler" (v. 7, NIV) — might sound dangerously imperialistic in our pluralistic world. However, we must recognize that very shortly following Psalm 82 in the Psalter, Psalm 89 will offer the anguished lament of God's own "anointed," who has fallen "like every other ruler." The message is clear. Unlike the gods, the God of Israel shows no partiality, *except* to justice and righteousness. When God's own "anointed," God's own "son," fails to embody God's will, he too falls.

19. Again, see Chapter 8 by Christopher J. H. Wright and Chapter 10 by Gordon Wenham in the present volume.

In essence, Psalm 82 offers the fundamental biblical criterion for divinity (as well as the fundamental biblical criterion for faithful earthly agency of God's will) — the enactment and embodiment of justice and righteousness that establishes the world on its proper foundation (see Ps. 96:10 where the proclamation of God's reign means that "The world is firmly established; it cannot be moved," NIV; "moved" in this verse is the same Hebrew word as "shaken" in Ps. 82:5). Because Psalm 82 claims that what it means to be divine involves the establishment of justice and righteousness in the human community, John Dominic Crossan concludes that Psalm 82 is "the single most important text in the entire Christian Bible."[20]

Psalm 82 concludes in verse 8 with a prayer for God to do precisely what the gods have failed to do (and, anticipating Psalm 89, what God's "anointed" also failed to do) — namely, "establish justice on earth" (my translation). As in Psalm 72 and Genesis 12, the perspective is world-encompassing: "for all the nations are your inheritance" (NIV). Indeed, beyond world-encompassing, the perspective is universe-encompassing, since God's ultimate goal is to achieve the stability and security of the whole creation (v. 5). In this regard, Psalm 82 again is similar to the enthronement collection, in which God's coming into the world to secure the earth by establishing justice is greeted enthusiastically by "the heavens," "the earth," "the sea and all that fills it," "the field . . . and everything in it," and "all the trees of the forest" (Ps. 96:11-13).

Actually, the universe-encompassing perspective of Psalms 72 and 82 means that they are related not only to the songs of praise that compose the enthronement collection, but also to virtually all of the Psalter's songs of praise. The songs of praise regularly invite a world-encompassing congregation to praise God (see Pss. 66:1; 67:3-5; 100:1; 117:1; 148:11-13), and they sometimes invite a universe-encompassing congregation to praise God, culminating in the Psalter's final verse: "Let everything that breathes praise the LORD!" (Ps. 150:6; see 148:1-10, which is even more expansive!).

While the enthronement collection and the Psalter's other songs of praise can be understood as responses to God, as can be the prayers of Psalm 72 and portions of Psalm 82, these psalms also function as Scripture that addresses us with God's Word and invites us to listen. If we do, we shall be im-

20. John Dominic Crossan, *The Birth of Christianity: Discovering What Happened in the Years after the Execution of Jesus* (San Francisco: HarperSanFrancisco, 1998), p. 595. See also J. Clinton McCann Jr., "The Single Most Important Text in the Entire Bible: Toward a Theology of the Psalms," in *Soundings in the Theology of the Psalms: Perspectives and Methods in Contemporary Scholarship*, ed. Rolf A. Jacobson (Minneapolis: Fortress, 2011), pp. 63-75.

pelled into the world as participants in God's mission of establishing world-encompassing, universe-encompassing justice, righteousness, and shalom. In a world characterized by "oppression and violence" (Ps. 72:14), in a world where literally billions of people are poor, weak, and needy, in a world where the creation itself is under duress and the foundations often seem to be shaking, our participation in God's mission is constitutive of our very identity as the people of God.[21]

The Opposition to God's Will, God's Reign, and God's Earthly Agents

The name of the Psalter in Hebrew means "Praises." As we have seen, the theological heart of the Psalter consists of songs of praise that directly proclaim God's universal reign, that clearly articulate God's will for the world, and that are closely related to other psalms that indicate the divine arrangement for agents who will enact and embody on earth what the heavenly sovereign wills. Given all this, there is every reason to praise God! And it would seem that the chorus of praise from God's people, from the nations, and from the creation should be uninterrupted and unending.

But not so! Somewhat unexpectedly (although not without anticipation, as we shall see), the first psalm beyond the paired introduction is not a song of praise, but rather a prayer for help that begins with an emphatic acknowledgment of pervasive opposition to God's faithful (see the threefold repetition of "many" in Ps. 3:1-2), and that continues by quoting the psalmist's opponents, who make it unmistakably clear that they are also enemies of God, when they say of or to the psalmist: "God will not deliver him" (v. 2, NIV). Really, however, we should not be surprised, since Psalms 1–2, again performing their introductory function, have already introduced us to the opposition

---

21. Again, see Chapter 8 by Christopher Wright in the present volume, especially where he quotes one of his friends as saying, "If it's not missional, it's not church" (p. 198). Also see his conclusion where he identifies "Christian concern and action in relation to the environment and care of creation as an essential part of our holistic biblical mission," citing Ps. 96:11-13 at this point (pp. 202-3). See also Arthur Walker-Jones, *The Green Psalter: Resources for an Ecological Spirituality* (Minneapolis: Fortress, 2009); the treatment of Psalm 148 in J. Clinton McCann Jr., *Great Psalms of the Bible* (Louisville: Westminster John Knox, 2009), pp. 133-43; and the treatment of Psalm 104 in McCann, "The Book of Psalms: Introduction, Commentary, and Reflections," in *The New Interpreter's Bible*, vol. 4 (Nashville: Abingdon, 1996), pp. 1096-1101.

— "the wicked" (1:1, 4-6), who have no intention of listening to or obeying God's *torah*, along with "the nations," "the peoples," "the kings," and "the rulers," who collaborate "against the LORD and his anointed" (2:1-2).

As it turns out, the enemies of God's will, God's reign, God's "anointed," and God's people (the latter usually called "the righteous" in Books I-II of the Psalter, as in 1:5-6) are omnipresent in the prayers for help, which explains why the traditional scholarly labels for these prayers are so apt — that is, laments, complaints, or protests. Indeed, at least according to one scholar, the pervasive presence of enemies in the Psalter is the most significant interpretive datum in dealing with the prayers for help:

> The absolutely most important motif in the individual complaint psalms' interpretation of suffering is the *enemy motif*. The motif is the most important in the sense that it is found in and throughout the psalms in question.[22]

To illustrate the interpretive significance of the enemies, we shall suggest how their pervasive presence affects the understanding of the aspects of the Psalms covered in the previous sections of this chapter: (1) God's *torah* or will, (2) God's reign, and (3) the rule and role of God's "anointed" and God's "faithful."

1. God's Torah or Will

In short, as Psalms 1–2 already make abundantly clear, God's *torah* or will is regularly *not* done. While Psalm 1 affirms that "the way of the wicked will perish" (1:6; see 2:12), and Psalm 2 suggests that the rebellious behavior of the nations and peoples is "in vain" (v. 1), this simply does not seem to be the case in the rest of the Psalter. The enemies never disappear; and indeed, they seem to do quite well for themselves, often at the expense of the righteous (see Psalms 73–74). The enemies are there at the beginning of the Psalter, and they are there at the end (see Psalms 138–144).

In fact, if anyone or anything seems to "perish" in the Psalter, it is God's "anointed" and other representations of God's sovereignty — the temple and the land (see above on Psalm 89, which concludes Book III, and which is

---

22. Fredrik Lindström, *Suffering and Sin: Interpretations of Illness in the Individual Complaint Psalms*, Coniectanea Biblica Old Testament Series 37 (Stockholm: Almqvist & Wiksell International, 1994), p. 6, as quoted in Brueggemann, *An Introduction*, p. 289.

preceded in Book III by several poignant communal laments that seem to mourn the destruction of Jerusalem and the temple: Psalms 74, 79, 80). This aspect of the Psalter is rather astonishing, but it serves as dramatic reinforcement of the conclusion suggested above — that is, God's will is regularly *not* done.

Given the fact that even God's "anointed" is rejected for failing to enact and embody God's justice and righteousness, it is not surprising that the Psalter contains psalms like Psalms 32, 51, and 130 that honestly acknowledge and confess that God's will is not done, even by God's own people. To be sure, these psalms ultimately celebrate God's willingness to forgive; and it is not coincidental that the crucial word *ḥesed,* "steadfast love," occurs in each one (see 32:10; 51:1; 130:7). These psalms perform the important function in the Psalter of demonstrating that "the righteous" are not those who are sinless, but rather those who live in fundamental dependence upon the faithfully loving and forgiving God. No wonder that one of the Psalter's standard invitations to praise celebrates God's gracious character: "O give thanks to the LORD, for he is good; for his steadfast love endures forever" (106:1; 107:1; 118:1, 29; see 100:5). Although the Psalter makes it clear that there are destructive and painful consequences for failing to do God's will, it ultimately portrays God as gracious, merciful, steadfastly loving, and faithful (see Exod. 34:6-7; Pss. 86:5, 15; 103:8; 111:4). There is a future for God's people and for the world, because God is faithfully loving and forgiving when God's people and humankind in general fail to do God's will.[23]

2. God's Reign

The fact that God's will is regularly opposed and not done has remarkable implications for understanding God's reign. In short, God's sovereignty or power does not take the form of coercion. In contrast to the way kings generally operate, God apparently chooses to be different and refuses to be an enforcer. This seems odd to many people, since they tend to define God in terms of the ability or power to do whatever God wants — in classical terms, omnipotence.

---

23. See Rolf A. Jacobson, "'The Faithfulness of the Lord Endures Forever': The Central Theological Witness of the Psalter," in *Soundings in the Theology of Psalms: Perspectives and Methods in Contemporary Scholarship,* ed. Rolf A. Jacobson (Minneapolis: Fortress, 2011), pp. 111-37.

But if God is an enforcer, there should be no enemies, at least not for long. But there always are! Again, the pervasive presence of the enemies in the Psalms is significant. More significant, however, is the character of God — that is, God's *ḥesed* again. If God is essentially loving, then human beings must have the freedom to choose (as they clearly do in Genesis 3). Otherwise, love is a charade; or as Douglas John Hall puts it, "A being programmed to love would be no lover."[24]

As the constant opposition to God in the Psalms demonstrates, God's omnipotence is not the all-powerfulness of force, but rather the all-powerfulness of love. And what an incredible power! Because God's reign is characterized by omnipotent love, God will not give up on sinful humankind, and God will not be crushed by the staggering burden of human failure to enact and embody God's will.

As the psalmists recognize, anything less than an omnipotently loving God would mean the demise of humankind: "If you, O LORD, should mark iniquities, Lord, who could stand?" (Ps. 130:3). But this question is followed by the affirmation that God forgives, and the following is the concluding invitation (v. 7):

> O Israel, hope in the LORD!
>   For with the LORD there is steadfast love,
> and with him is great power to redeem.

God's "great power" — God's omnipotence, we might say — is not about coercion or enforcement, but rather about redemption, grounded in faithful, forgiving love — *ḥesed*, "steadfast love," again. The hope of Israel and the hope of the world is that God reigns in omnipotent love.

3. The Rule and Role of God's Anointed and God's Faithful

As pointed out above, the pivotal Psalm 89 recounts the rejection of God's "anointed." If the appearance of royal psalms in Books IV-V indicates the postexilic hope for the restoration of the monarchy, it would seem that any future king would have shared "all the hardships he [David] endured" (Ps. 132:1) — that is, messianism and suffering would be inseparable realities (see "enemies" in Ps. 132:18, and note the setbacks articulated in vv. 9-14 of Psalm

---

24. Douglas John Hall, *God and Human Suffering: An Exercise in the Theology of the Cross* (Minneapolis: Augsburg, 1986), p. 70.

144, the final royal psalm in the Psalter). If, as seems more likely, the royal psalms in Books IV-V are testimony to God's commitment to provide some earthly agent to enact God's will, and if Psalm 149 suggests that "the faithful" have inherited the responsibility that formerly belonged to the kings (see above), there is still the unmistakable connection between suffering and being the earthly agent of the heavenly king. In short, as the pervasive presence of the enemies in the Psalms again suggests, "the faithful" or "the righteous" are always opposed. Suffering is the norm.

To be sure, the psalmists often identify God as their opponent, as in Psalm 13:1:

> How long, O LORD? Will you forget me forever?
>   How long will you hide your face from me?

And as in the well-known Psalm 22:1:

> My God, my God, why have you forsaken me?

But such conclusions are only preliminary. With one exception, Psalm 88, the psalmists accompany their laments/complaints/protests with expressions of trust, assurance, and/or praise, as in the conclusion of Psalm 13 (vv. 5-6):

> But I trust in your steadfast love;
>   my heart shall rejoice in your salvation.
> I will sing to the LORD,
>   because he has dealt bountifully with me.

The celebration in Psalm 22:21-31 is even more elaborate and extended, matching the length and intensity of the preceding lament. Not only does the psalmist praise God (v. 22), but he or she also envisions the gathering of a world-encompassing congregation to worship the God "who rules over the nations" (v. 28). Even the dead show up in verse 29 to join the celebration! And verses 30-31 conclude the psalm with the conviction that even "people yet unborn" will somehow join the celebration as well.

Scholars have struggled over the years to try to understand the coherence between the painful questions that open Psalms 13 and 22 and the effusive celebrations that conclude them — that is, the regular juxtaposition of pain and praise in the prayers for help is a crucial interpretive issue. Was the praise elicited by a cultic intervention of some sort, perhaps an oracle of salvation delivered by a priest that has not been preserved in the text? Is the praise an act of faith, anticipating that God will surely deliver? Were the concluding praises added later, only after some act of deliverance had occurred? No one knows for sure. What we do know is that the prayers for help regularly juxtapose complaint and celebration, protest and praise, hurt and hope; and the juxtaposition itself can be seen as important and instructive. As Mays concludes concerning Psalm 13:

> So in taking up the Psalm as our prayer, we are shown who we are when we pray. We are taught our true identity as mortals who stand on the earth and speak to a God who is ours but never owned. Agony and adoration hung together by a cry for life — this is the truth about us as people of faith. . . .
>
> . . . The Psalm is not given to us to use on the rare occasions when some trouble seems to make it appropriate. It is forever appropriate as long as life shall last. We do not begin at one end and come out at the other. The agony and the ecstasy belong together as the secret of our identity.[25]

For those who are earthly agents of the divine will — "the faithful" or "the righteous" — suffering, or the agony, will be the norm. But so will the ecstasy, what the Psalms name with words like "happiness," "refuge," and "salvation" (see below).

At this point, we should remind ourselves that the prayers for help — human words to God — have been received and transmitted as Scripture in which God addresses us. In Mays's words, we are "shown" and "taught"; and in the case of the lesson that "the agony and the ecstasy belong together," we are being taught something concerning an issue that lies at the heart of our faith — that is, the issue of theodicy, which many suggest is the fundamental theological issue. The word "theodicy" means literally "the justice of God"; and as usually defined, the issue is why the righteous or the innocent suffer while the wicked prosper. Without pretending to deal fully with this fundamental issue, suffice it to say that the Psalms, like the book of Job, demolish the traditional doctrine of retribution that would lead one to conclude that suffering represents divine punishment, and thus that "the righteous" should not suffer. The faithful psalmists, just like the faithful prophets and later the faithful Jesus, were always suffering. In short, the Psalter turns the traditional statement of theodicy upside down. In what Gerald Wilson (in

25. James L. Mays, "Psalm 13," *Interpretation* 34 (1980): 281-82.

commenting on Psalm 63) calls "our comfortable society,"[26] the primary question of faithfulness for most of us is almost certainly not, "Why am I suffering?" but rather, "Why am I *not* suffering?"

To be sure, we must be sensitive and careful at this point, and we must say clearly that suffering itself is neither good nor redemptive. But love is good and redemptive; and the biblical reality is that those who have faithfully committed themselves to God and the embodiment of God's loving purposes in the world — justice, righteousness, and peace — have regularly suffered precisely as a result of such a commitment. Insofar as they committed themselves to be the earthly agents of God's purposes, "the faithful" in the Psalter suffered in solidarity with the prophets and, in an anticipatory way, in solidarity with Jesus Messiah/Christ. As we shall see below, the Gospel writers could not tell the story of Jesus' passion without the Psalms, especially the prayers for help. Thus the Psalms teach us a lesson that should clearly be construed as one that is addressed to us by God — that is, in the words of John Calvin, the Psalms "principally teach and train us to bear the cross."[27]

Before considering the ecstasy dimension of the identity of the faithful, it is necessary to address a final aspect of the prayers for help that does not sound very cruciform or Christ-like. Just as, or perhaps just because, the enemies are a pervasive presence in the prayers for help, so are the psalmists' requests that God dispose of the enemies, or their affirmations that God will surely dispose of the enemies. These requests or affirmations are quite violently expressed, and they begin with the very first prayer for help: "For you strike all my enemies on the cheek; you break the teeth of the wicked" (Ps. 3:7). Actually, this one is quite mild compared to the infamous Psalm 137:9: "Happy shall they be who take your [the Babylonians'] little ones and dash them against the rock"! Almost inevitably such requests or affirmations sound as if they involve personal revenge; however, they serve the more positive function of naming victimization and entrusting the situation to God in prayer, thus in actuality surrendering the prerogative of seeking personal revenge. In other words, what may sound like a plea for personal revenge is better understood as a protest against the injustice of the enemies and a request for God to set things right, to establish justice: "thy will be done." Re-

---

26. Gerald H. Wilson, *Psalms,* vol. 1, NIV Application Commentary (Grand Rapids: Zondervan, 2002), p. 895.

27. John Calvin, *Commentary on the Book of Psalms,* vol. 1 (Edinburgh: Calvin Translation Society, 1845), p. xxxix.

fusing to act out of personal revenge and entrusting the situation to God mean that these violent-sounding requests and affirmations actually break the cycle of violence, and so are more Christ-like than they first appear.[28]

Happiness, Refuge, and Salvation

The very first word in the Psalter is "Happy" (NIV "Blessed"), and the final line of Psalm 2 begins with the same word, thus signaling a key word/concept as Psalms 1–2 perform their introductory function. As Mays concludes, the effect is "to invite us to read and use the entire book as a guide to a blessed life."[29] "Happy" will occur twenty-three more times, including several key points in the Psalter. From the beginning, it is clear that happiness has everything to do with *torah,* which occurs twice in Psalm 1:2. As Psalm 1 itself begins to suggest (see above on the translation of 1:5), and as the theological heart of the Psalter makes explicit, God's *torah* or will involves justice, righteousness, and peace. Genuine happiness consists of constant attention to, delight in, and conformity to the will of God.

Given that Psalm 72 defines justice and righteousness as provision for the poor, weak, and needy (see Ps. 72:12-14), it is not surprising that the final psalm of Book I, Psalm 41, begins with a happy-saying that provides an envelope structure for Book I and that reinforces the perspective of Psalm 1: "Happy are those who consider the poor." Again, not surprisingly, the word "happy" recurs in Psalm 72, which expresses the desire that "all nations" will respond to God's earthly king this way: "may they pronounce him happy" (v. 17). Presumably, this will happen insofar as the king does what God wants him to do — namely, to enact and embody justice, righteousness, and peace (see vv. 1-7). Again, happiness consists essentially of conformity to God's will. The final happy-saying in the Psalter is verse 5 of Psalm 146, which initiates a collection of hallelujah psalms (see "Praise the LORD!" at the beginning and end of each of Psalms 146–150) that concludes the Psalter and that also recalls the theological heart of the Psalter by way of its affirmation that "The LORD will reign forever" (v. 10). After a warning not to put trust in human princes

---

28. See Erich Zenger, *A God of Vengeance? Understanding the Psalms of Enmity,* trans. Linda Maloney (Louisville: Westminster John Knox, 1995), and J. Clinton McCann Jr., "Toward a Non-Retaliatory Lifestyle: The Psalms, the Cross, and the Gospel," in *Character Ethics and the New Testament: Moral Dimensions of Scripture,* ed. Robert Brawley (Louisville: Westminster John Knox, 2007), pp. 159-67.

29. James L. Mays, *Psalms,* Interpretation (Louisville: John Knox, 1994), p. 40.

(v. 3; recall Psalm 89, in which even God's "anointed" is rejected) or any human source, the affirmation of verse 5 is, "Happy are those whose help is the God of Jacob." The implication is clear: genuine and enduring happiness derives from dependence upon and submission to God and God's will (see vv. 7-9, which describe God's work and God's will, including the key term "justice" in v. 7 that again recalls the theological heart of the Psalter).[30]

The shape of the Psalter, especially the pervasive presence of the enemies, makes it abundantly clear that the happiness or prosperity (see "prosper" in 1:3) of "the righteous" is not a care-free cheeriness that derives from getting their own way. Rather, as suggested above, suffering is the norm for "the righteous." Thus, their happiness or prosperity consists of their connectedness to God, their constant attentiveness to God's *torah* that results in conformity to God's will. Because happiness and suffering are not mutually exclusive, happiness will ultimately involve "refuge" in God, as the concluding line of Psalm 2 affirms. At this point, Psalm 2 is again performing its introductory function. The word "refuge" occurs frequently in the prayers for help (see Pss. 5:11; 7:1; 11:1; 16:1; and more), and it is likely that it played a role in the shaping of the Psalter.[31] In any case, "the righteous" find safety, security, and stability in God; and Psalms 1–2 establish an inextricable relationship among the three key terms "happy," *torah*, and "refuge." As Creach concludes, *torah* becomes what he calls "The Ultimate Refuge . . . a source of God's presence and protection for the righteous."[32] In essence, conformity to God's will is its own reward, offering enduring happiness and genuine prosperity that the psalmists experience even in the midst of persistent opposition and suffering. The massive Psalm 119 at the heart of Book V solidifies the central significance of *torah*; and Psalm 119:92, which recalls Psalm 1, expresses well the role of *torah* in relation to happiness and refuge:

> If your law [*torah*] had not been my delight,
>   I would have perished in my misery.

So *torah*, as a source of happiness and refuge, equips the psalmist to resist the claim of "the wicked" that "There is no help for you in God" (Ps. 3:2).

---

30. See J. Clinton McCann Jr., "The Shape of Book I of the Psalter and the Shape of Human Happiness," in *The Book of Psalms: Composition and Reception*, ed. Peter W. Flint and Patrick D. Miller, VTSup 99 (Leiden: Brill, 2005), pp. 340-48.

31. See Jerome F. D. Creach, *Yahweh as Refuge and the Editing of the Hebrew Psalter*, JSOTSup 217 (Sheffield: Sheffield Academic Press, 1996), pp. 122-26.

32. Creach, *Destiny of the Righteous*, p. 135.

The Hebrew root translated "help" is often translated elsewhere as "deliverance" or "salvation," and it recurs in verses 7-8 in a petition and an affirmation. Despite being surrounded by opposition, the psalmist prays in verse 7, "Save me, O my God!" (my translation) and affirms in verse 8 that "Salvation comes from the LORD" (my translation), thus directly contradicting what the enemies had said in verse 2. Salvation is the experience of life as God intends it — that is, a life constantly oriented to God, lived in fundamental dependence upon God, and shaped in conformity to God's will.

Presence and Waiting

Because *torah* became "The Ultimate Refuge," a means of experiencing God's "presence and protection," it began to perform a function associated with Zion and the temple — that is, it became a "place" to meet God. In Creach's words, "Moreover, torah became a source of security for the righteous that fulfills the role once reserved for Mount Zion and its temple."[33] Psalm 46, a Zion song, demonstrates in verses 1 and 7 the association of refuge and divine presence with Zion:

> God is our refuge and strength,
>> a very present help in trouble . . .
> The LORD of hosts is with us;
>> the God of Jacob is our refuge [a different Hebrew root than
>> "refuge" above].

To be sure, throughout the Old Testament period and into the New Testament period, Zion and the temple remained places to experience God's presence, as Psalm 24, an entrance liturgy, also demonstrates. The pilgrims entering the temple precincts are those "who seek the face of the God of Jacob" (v. 6; see also Ps. 27:4, 8-9). Clearly, the temple is a place to meet God, to experience the divine presence, but it is not the only place. The Psalms are also evidence of a broadening understanding of God's presence, including how and where God's presence is experienced. For Creach, the key verse is Psalm 1:3, and this would be another instance of Psalm 1 performing its introductory function. Those who are constantly oriented to *torah*, God's will, "are like trees planted by streams of water." The language and imagery here are

---

33. Creach, *Destiny of the Righteous*, p. 135.

similar to that in Psalms 52 and 92, which describe the psalmist as a tree that is "planted in the house of the LORD" (92:13; see 52:8). Like a visit to the temple, a grounding in *torah* is a real experience of the presence of God, yielding happiness and refuge.

But beyond the association of *torah* with divine presence, in other psalms there appears to be an even further broadening of the understanding of the experience of God's presence. In Psalm 23, the psalmist affirms that God is "with me" even in "the valley of the shadow of death" (v. 4; NIV); and in Psalm 73, the psalmist is aware that "I am continually with you" (v. 23; the Hebrew preposition and suffix translated "with you" occurs also in v. 22, "toward you," and v. 25, "but you," and the repeated phrase with varying nuance has the effect of emphasizing the constancy of the experience of divine presence). Psalm 139:7-12 is an eloquent portrayal of an inescapable divine presence that, contrary to the usual Old Testament view, reaches even to Sheol (v. 8). Such expansive understandings of the experience of God's presence would prepare Judaism for the crisis of A.D. 70, when the Second Temple was destroyed. Such understandings would also provide resources for emerging Christianity in the first century A.D. to articulate the conviction that Jesus was the new and ultimate locus of God's presence in and for the world.

At the same time that they experience God's presence, the psalmists continue to be surrounded by the enemies. And so they continue to pray, "the ultimate act of faith in the face of the assault on the soul."[34] There is an "already–not yet" character to the psalmists' experience of God and the world. The divine presence is real; but the justice, righteousness, and peace that God wills have not been accomplished. So, as they pray, the psalmists wait, as in Psalm 40:1: "I waited patiently for the LORD" (see also Pss. 25:3, 5, 21; 27:14; 31:24). Both NIV and NRSV employ the adverb "patiently" in this line, but Ellen Davis suggests that the line is better understood like this: "I waited tensely for the LORD."[35] Given the tone of the psalmist's request — "do not delay, O my God" (v. 17; see v. 13) — and given the many "evils" besetting him (v. 12), along with his own "iniquities" (v. 12) and the people "who seek to snatch away my life" (v. 14), "tensely" works better than "patiently" to capture the urgency of the situation. In any case, at the same time that they experience God's presence (note that the psalmist affirms in v. 8 that God's "law [*torah*] is in my heart"), the psalmists are constantly op-

34. Mays, *Psalms*, p. 53.

35. Ellen F. Davis, "Demanding Deliverance," in *Preaching from Psalms, Oracles, and Parables,* ed. R. Alling and D. J. Schlafer (Harrisburg: Morehouse, 2006), p. 4.

posed and thus find themselves in the position of, in Davis's words, "Demanding Deliverance."[36]

So do we. From the Christian perspective, the world that Jesus saved is still pervaded by injustice, unrighteousness, "oppression and violence" (Ps. 72:14). And so, like the psalmists, we pray urgent, hope-filled prayers, demanding deliverance. With the will of God in our hearts, impelling us to join God at God's work in the world, we await the fulfillment of God's purposes for us and for all creation.

Listening for God's Address: The Psalms and the New Testament

The preceding sections have suggested that God does address us in the Psalms, and they have also identified illustratively the content of God's address to us in the Psalter. Much will sound familiar to Christian readers. The message of the theological heart of the Psalter — God reigns — is essentially what Jesus proclaimed: "the kingdom of God is at hand" (Mark 1:15, NRSV margin). God's provision for an earthly agency to carry out the divine will — God's "anointed" and/or "the faithful" — continues in the New Testament by way of Jesus Messiah/Christ and by way of the church, "the body of Christ" (Eph. 4:12). Not only did Jesus proclaim and embody God's will for justice, righteousness, and peace in a ministry of compassion, but he also invited his followers into this great co-mission. And Jesus invited us to pray, "thy will be done," which, if we know the Psalms, we recognize as a prayer for the establishment of justice, righteousness, and peace on a universe-encompassing scale.

Just as God's will was pervasively opposed in the Psalms, so Jesus' proclamation and embodiment of God's reign and God's will resulted in pervasive opposition — a cross. Not coincidentally, of course, the Gospel writers could not narrate the events of Jesus' passion without frequent reference and allusion to the psalms, especially Psalm 22, but also Psalms 31, 69, and 88, all long and intense prayers for help. But Psalm 22 not only anticipates Jesus' passion but also portrays a world-encompassing celebration of God's sovereignty in which even the dead participate.[37] The agony and the ecstasy belong together, or, in New Testament terms, the cross and the resurrection belong together as the secret of our identity.

36. Davis, "Demanding Deliverance," p. 1.
37. See Ellen F. Davis, "Exploding the Limits: Form and Function in Psalm 22," *JSOT* 53 (1992): 103.

So, even as we bear the cross at Jesus' invitation (see Mark 8:34), Jesus pronounces us "happy" or "blessed." The Beatitudes (Matt. 5:3-12), employing the language of Psalms 1–2, proclaim as happy the very sort of persons that "the righteous" were as they prayed the prayers for help — poor, grieving, afflicted, oppressed, and persecuted even as they committed themselves to the pursuit of righteousness and peace. To live in fundamental dependence upon God and submission to God promises genuine happiness. Like the psalmists, we simultaneously pray and praise, demanding deliverance even as we sing, and invite others to sing, a new song (see Pss. 33:3; 40:3; 96:1; 98:1; 149:1).

None of this is to say that the Psalms are predictions of Jesus, but it all goes to say that, in the Psalms, we encounter and are addressed by the same God who was and is at work in Israel, in Jesus Messiah/Christ, and in us.[38] Even though the Psalms originated out of Israel's response to God, they have been received and transmitted for centuries as Scripture, God's Word to humankind. And even as the Psalms retain their character and usefulness as means of responding to God in praise and prayer, they simultaneously confront the reader or pray-er with the divine Word. Even though he emphasizes that the Psalms are means of responding to God, Eugene Peterson also suggests, for instance, that the Psalter's "five-book arrangement is quietly but insistently provided to protect us against a presumption, whether inadvertent or willful, to pray in any other way than by *listening* and answering to God's word."[39] Because they simultaneously address us with God's Word and facilitate our faithful response, the Psalms remain a — indeed, perhaps *the* — primary locus of Christian spirituality.

38. See Chapter 6 by Mark Boda in the present volume.
39. Eugene H. Peterson, *Answering God: The Psalms as Tools for Prayer* (San Francisco: Harper and Row, 1989), pp. 54-55.

13 Hearing the Old Testament Wisdom Literature: The Wit of Many and the Wisdom of One

Craig G. Bartholomew

The subtitle of this chapter is an adaptation of the famous definition of a proverb by Lord John Russell (1792-1878): "A proverb is the wit of one, and the wisdom of many." Individual proverbs and much of Old Testament wisdom have their origins in individuals, from whence they achieved age and social currency and became part of tradition, which is an essential ingredient of a proverb.[1] The sources of Old Testament wisdom are many, but, as Ecclesiastes reminds us in its canonical note, "they are given by one Shepherd," namely God (Eccles. 12:11). A trinitarian hermeneutic will attend closely to the diversity of voices heard in the Old Testament wisdom literature[2] but will have as its goal to listen for the voice of that one Shepherd. Amid the wit of many it will listen for the voice of One.

Serious engagement with Old Testament wisdom literature was late on the historical-critical scene, but the twentieth century witnessed a welcome recovery of Old Testament wisdom once the similarities to Egyptian wisdom were noticed,[3] along with wisdom's overtly religious theology of cre-

---

1. Wolfgang Mieder, *Proverbs Are Never Out of Season: Popular Wisdom in the Modern Age* (New York: Oxford University Press, 1993), pp. 13, 6.

2. Song of Songs is usually included in Old Testament wisdom literature. However, within the limits of this chapter, I have focused on Proverbs, Job, and Ecclesiastes. A literary approach is, in my view, most fecund in relation to Song of Songs. Nor have I attended to Ben Sira and the Wisdom of Solomon.

3. Erman argued that the original of Proverbs 22:17–23:11 is to be found in the Wisdom book of Amenemope. But see Kenneth A. Kitchen, "Proverbs 2: Ancient Near Eastern Back-

ation.[4] However, it has remained difficult for scholars to see how wisdom fits into Old Testament theology, and it is still common for Job and Ecclesiastes to be seen as symptomatic of a crisis of wisdom, reflecting very different approaches to that of Proverbs. The unity of all three books remains contentious, so that the very possibility of hearing the Old Testament wisdom books as God's address might appear untenable.

The fragmentation of the Old Testament at the hands of historical criticism is no new problem, and scholars concerned with theological interpretation deal with it in different ways. Barth's approach was to acknowledge its legitimacy but to position it in the context of a larger theological hermeneutic. The problem with such an approach is that a nature/grace (historical criticism/theological interpretation) dichotomy remains uneasily at work in such scholarship.[5] The most serious challenge to the fragmentation of historical criticism has come from literary readings, but before this could be fully appropriated the postmodern turn was upon us with its wild pluralism. A curious result is that much of the historical-critical paradigm lingers as a sort of lowest common denominator for academic biblical studies.[6]

In my opinion the sort of trinitarian hermeneutic I articulate in Chapter 1 in the present volume provides a helpful barometer for measuring the extent to which historical criticism has helped us attend to the voice (or voices) of Old Testament wisdom. While there are many things to be grateful for in terms of the historical legacy in Old Testament wisdom studies, when it comes to attending to these books for God's address one is generally confronted with the aridity of historical criticism.[7] On all accounts books like

---

ground," in *Dictionary of the Old Testament: Wisdom, Poetry and Writings,* ed. Tremper Longman III and Peter Enns (Downers Grove: IVP Academic, 2008), pp. 552-66, 562-63.

4. W. Zimmerli, "Zur Struktur der alttestamentlichen Weisheit," *ZAW* 51 (1933): 177-204. Cf. W. Zimmerli, "Place and Limit of Wisdom in the Framework of the Old Testament Theology," *SJT* 17 (1964): 146-58.

5. This comment should not detract from the fact that Barth's rich and detailed theological exegesis is virtually unparalleled. See Craig G. Bartholomew, "Calvin, Barth, and Theological Interpretation," in *Calvin, Barth, and Reformed Theology,* ed. Neil B. MacDonald and Carl Trueman (Milton Keynes: Paternoster, 2008), pp. 163-77.

6. Carol Newsom ("Job and Ecclesiastes," in *Old Testament Interpretation: Past, Present, and Future; Essays in Honor of Gene M. Tucker,* ed. James Mays, David Petersen, and Kent Richards [Nashville: Abingdon, 1995], p. 184) notes that "Scholarly work on Ecclesiastes has remained, with very few exceptions, the province of traditional historical criticism."

7. An important exception in this respect is Gerhard von Rad's work on Old Testament wisdom in his *Old Testament Theology,* vol. 1: *The Theology of Israel's Historical Tradition,*

Job[8] and Ecclesiastes are great literature, but in Old Testament studies our energy is directed toward speculative determination as to whether the earliest Israelite wisdom was secular, the different layers in Proverbs, whether Job 28 is original to Job,[9] how many different voices there are in the epilogue of Ecclesiastes, and so on. Academic rigor is nonnegotiable, but there is a real sense in which a consistent historical-critical reading and a literary, final-form, theological reading are incommensurate paradigms. Each needs to tell its stories of these Old Testament books as best it can, and then the results can be compared and, perhaps, real discussions begin. In favor of the latter paradigm it should be noted that all historical criticism depends upon an initial reading of the text as we receive it, even if the conclusion is that the text does not make sense as it stands and that speculative critical reconstruction is therefore essential. Surprisingly, this initial reading is rarely foregrounded in historical criticism, a move one would think essential in the light of literary readings.

In a short chapter like this it is not possible to engage historical-critical issues at every point or to continually point out their important contributions.[10] Undoubtedly all three major Old Testament wisdom books have long histories underlying their final form. However, theologically the most fertile approach is to concentrate on the world opened up in front of the texts as we have received them.[11] While the variety of approaches to Old Testament interpretation contributes to this, approaching the Old Testament wisdom books as literary wholes is particularly fertile since such an approach opens up the world in front of the text. Thus, as I will argue below, the most helpful methods for reading the Old Testament wisdom books in order to listen for God's address are the following: literary reading; reading for spiritual formation; psychological readings (especially with respect to Job and Ecclesiastes); reception history;[12] and the comparative approach with respect to both the

trans. D. M. G. Stalker (New York: Harper, 1985); and *Wisdom in Israel,* trans. J. D. Martin (Nashville: Abingdon, 1972; repr. Harrisburg: Trinity International Press, 1993).

8. See Jon D. Levenson, *The Book of Job in Its Time and in the Twentieth Century* (Cambridge, MA: Harvard University Press, 1972).

9. On this issue see Alison Lo, *Job 28 as Rhetoric: An Analysis of Job 28 in the Context of Job 22–31* (Leiden: Brill, 2003).

10. An important source in this respect is Leo G. Perdue, *Wisdom Literature: A Theological History* (Louisville: Westminster John Knox, 2007).

11. See Paul Ricoeur, *Essays on Biblical Interpretation,* ed. Lewis S. Mudge (Philadelphia: Fortress Press, 1980).

12. The interpretive potential of reception history is demonstrated in Albert M. Wolters, *The Song of the Valiant Woman: Studies in the Interpretation of Proverbs 31:10-31* (Carlisle: Paternoster, 2001). In terms of my own work on Ecclesiastes I have found reception history in-

ancient Near East[13] and contemporary paremiology.[14] According to the New Testament, Christ is Lady Wisdom incarnate, and thus, while it is vital to attend to the discrete witness of the Old Testament wisdom books, a trinitarian reading is inadequate if it does not take the canon as a whole into account. Thus biblical theology and intertextuality will be a constituent part of reading these books to hear God's address. A trinitarian hermeneutic predisposes one to listen for the unified witness of the canon, whereas much historical criticism seems predisposed toward the fragmentation of the canon. Close attention to intertextuality is an important remedy in this respect. Even this limited range of interpretive approaches is too vast for a short chapter of this nature, and the reader is alerted to sources referenced in the footnotes to pursue some of these methods.

The Primacy of Proverbs

There is consensus that Proverbs is the foundational wisdom book in the Old Testament. Disagreement emerges on the interpretation of Proverbs and the relation of Proverbs to Job and Ecclesiastes. Much is at stake, therefore,

---

valuable, especially in terms of the contribution of the Lutheran Reformers (see Craig G. Bartholomew, *Reading Ecclesiastes: Old Testament Exegesis and Hermeneutical Theory*, Analecta Biblica 139 [Rome: Editrice Pontificio Istituto Biblico, 1998], pp. 31-205; C. G. Bartholomew, *Ecclesiastes*, Baker Commentary on the Old Testament Wisdom and Psalms [Grand Rapids: Baker Academic, 2009], pp. 21-43). One is also struck by the extensive use of Old Testament wisdom by the early church fathers. Amid the aridity of much contemporary biblical interpretation, those of us concerned with theological interpretation will often need to find fertile nodes in the history of interpretation and transfuse them into the present in genuinely post-critical mode. For example, Herder's work contains fruitful resources for study of Proverbs, Job, and Song of Songs.

13. Much depends on *how* one conducts comparative ancient Near Eastern investigations. In my view such studies should generally follow on from and be in dialogue with thorough literary analyses of texts. See Bartholomew, *Reading Ecclesiastes*, pp. 139-71. I have also found the sort of comparative work — albeit dated — done by Henri Frankfort, H. A. Groenewegen-Frankfort, John A. Wilson, Thorkild Jacobsen, and William A. Irwin in *The Intellectual Adventure of Ancient Man* (Chicago: University of Chicago Press, 1946), very stimulating and insightful.

14. "Paremiology" is the name for contemporary study of proverbs. Important work continues to be done in this area, and it offers significant comparative insight for Old Testament wisdom. See, e.g., Mieder, *Proverbs Are Never Out of Season;* Wolfgang Mieder and Alan Dundes, eds., *The Wisdom of Many: Essays on the Proverb* (Madison: University of Wisconsin Press, 1994).

in how we read Proverbs. In my view Raymond Van Leeuwen has done definitive work in making the case for reading Proverbs as a literary whole. Chapters 1–9 form a unity, and 1:7 and 31:30 provide an inclusio to the book, highlighting the fear of the Lord as the main theme. Proverbs moves from its motif in 1:7 to its climax in the example of the valiant woman in chapter 31.

The more challenging aspect in terms of Proverbs' literary unity comes in the collections in chapters 10–29. Most proverbs have their *Sitz im Leben* in oral tradition, and it is debated as to what happens to a proverb when it is reduced to writing in a collection and also as to whether the collections are haphazard or manifest a deeper unity. Reduction of a proverb to writing in a collection does not end its life; indeed, entry into a written collection forms an important part of its wider dissemination and marks a change into a new, literary life. Even if the proverbs are lumped together haphazardly, their juxtaposition inevitably sets up a myriad of intertextual links so that a close reading should discern connections between them rather than isolating them. Van Leeuwen's work on Proverbs 25–27 is exemplary in this respect, revealing the network of connections in these chapters.[15]

Van Leeuwen's work on poverty and wealth in Proverbs is also instructive in alerting us to the book's pedagogy. Proverbs 1–9, with its admonitions of a parent to a son and its speeches from Lady Wisdom, provides the hermeneutical key to the book as a whole by setting out the fundamentals of wisdom. In the latter parts of Proverbs greater nuance is given to these basic contours of wisdom.[16]

The basics of wisdom as portrayed in chapters 1–9 are as follows:

1. The great value of wisdom. This is rooted in a doctrine of creation order (3:19-20; 8:22-31).[17] It is by wisdom that God created the heavens and the earth, and it is this same wisdom which he makes available to human beings.

2. The character-consequence structure. It follows from point 1 that living according to the grain of the universe will lead to blessing whereas folly will lead to disaster.

3. A doctrine of two ways. Old Testament wisdom offers no explicit doc-

---

15. Raymond C. Van Leeuwen, *Context and Meaning in Proverbs 25–27*, SBLDS 96 (Atlanta: Scholars, 1988).

16. Raymond C. Van Leeuwen, "Wealth and Poverty: System and Contradiction in Proverbs," *Hebrew Studies* 33 (1992): 25-36.

17. See Rolf P. Knierim, *The Task of Old Testament Theology: Method and Cases* (Grand Rapids: Eerdmans, 1995), pp. 171-224, an important work in this respect.

trine of the fall but it is intensely aware that in all areas of life humans are faced with two ways, either wisdom or folly.

4. The fear of the Lord as the starting point and foundation of wisdom. This is a profound recognition that a false step at the beginning can skew the quest for wisdom and knowledge. As Rolf Knierim notes, "Ultimately the world cannot explain itself. This is the last word Israel's epistemology can say, inasmuch as that epistemology is based on empirical understanding."[18] This motif functions as an inclusio for Proverbs and recurs throughout the book.

With much of the ancient Near East, Israelite wisdom shares a doctrine of creation order. A comparative approach is helpful in highlighting the distinctiveness of Israelite wisdom in its *ethical monotheism*. Proverbs is clear that the creation and its order have their origin in one God, Yahweh, a perspective that is unique in the ancient Near East.[19]

Wisdom and the Particular: Proverbs 10–29

The genre of chapters 1–9 and 30–31 is very different from that of 10–29, in which we find the characteristic aphoristic form of the proverb. Chapters 1–9 use parental admonitions to "my son" and speeches by Lady Wisdom to evoke the value of wisdom and the importance of seeking it. Proverbs 1:1-6 makes it clear that this book is not only for the adolescent male; it certainly includes him, but the stress is rather on liminal stages[20] as ones in which wisdom or folly manifests itself with the greatest consequences (cf. Eccles. 12:1-7: "in the days of your youth . . . before . . . before . . . before . . .").

Proverbs deal with *particular* situations, and the change in form from 1–9 to 10–29 marks the shift from the basic contours of wisdom to the discernment of wisdom in life's situations. In terms of the character-consequence structure, the particularity of the proverbs of 10–29 is important because key proverbs alert us to the fact that we should not construe the character-consequence structure simplistically. Even in 1–9 we find the recognition that the quest for wisdom involves attending to God's discipline and reproof as

18. Knierem, *Task of Old Testament Theology*, p. 204. See also von Rad, *Wisdom in Israel*, for insightful comments about the epistemology of wisdom.

19. See Frankfort et al., *The Intellectual Adventure of Ancient Man*.

20. See Raymond C. Van Leeuwen, "Liminality and Worldview in Proverbs 1–9," *Semeia* 50 (1990): 111-44.

signs of God's love and delight (3:11-12; cf. 17:3). In terms of wealth and poverty, the "better than" proverbs are significant, indicating as they do that amid the complexity of reality wisdom does not guarantee prosperity (15:16, 17; 16:8; 21:9). Such proverbs are examples of what Jerry Gladson calls "retributive paradoxes,"[21] and they indicate a nuanced understanding of the character-consequence motif.

The proverbs of 10–29 immerse us in the rough-and-tumble of daily experience and account for the experiential nature of Old Testament wisdom. But "experiential" should not be equated with "empirical," as is so often the case. We would expect Israelite experience to be deeply informed by faith, and certainly in their final form the proverbs of 10–29 are intended to be read against the backdrop of 1–9. The unit 1–9 itself manifests a commitment to values that are far from empirical. James Crenshaw regards 7:6-20 as an example of the empirical nature of Old Testament wisdom,[22] but it is informed throughout by the view that adultery and prostitution are unwise. In our late modern context one could tell the same story from very different perspectives! If one inquires as to where the author acquired this view of sexuality, the obvious answer is Israel's *torah*. Observation and experience clearly play a constitutive role in wisdom, but never uninterpreted observation or experience, but rather experience read through the glasses of the fear of the Lord. Chapters 10–29, for example, have much to say about politics and government, but all of this material must be read against the background of the pivotal text in 8:15-16.

Retributive paradox is one kind of paradox in 10–29; another is the juxtaposition of apparent contradictions of which 26:4-5 and 17:27-28 are examples. Von Rad sees these as examples of wisdom's willingness to formulate antinomies and leave them unresolved.[23] This is, however, a misunderstanding of the function of such "antinomies." Wisdom has to do with what is fitting in a particular situation, and these contradictory juxtapositions alert us to the fact that wisdom has to be worked out in different and often novel situations. Herder perceptively notes that we do not have to learn "from" such proverbs but "with their help."[24]

21. Jerry A. Gladson, *Retributive Paradoxes in Proverbs 10–29* (Ph.D. diss., Vanderbilt University, 1978).

22. James L. Crenshaw, "Qohelet's Understanding of Intellectual Inquiry," in *Qohelet in the Context of Wisdom*, ed. A. Schoors, Bibliotheca Ephemeridum Theologicarum Lovaniensium 136 (Leuven: Leuven University Press, 1998), pp. 204-24.

23. Von Rad, *Old Testament Theology*, p. 422.

24. Johan Georg Herder, "Spruch und Bild, insonderheit bei den Morgenländern," in *Werke*, vol. XV, 11 (Munich: Hanser, 1953).

Old Testament wisdom is often labeled as unhistorical, and while it is true that it makes few explicit references to Israel's history — the question is whether this is assumed or ignored — wisdom's hermeneutical dimension is implicitly historical. Wisdom establishes itself as a tradition[25] and is implicitly aware that new and different situations will arise and that these will require insight if one is to act wisely.

Proverbs deals with an immense range of human experience, and this relates to its creational roots; the whole of life comes from God, and humans are called to act wisely in all areas of life, so that the content of Proverbs fits every aspect of life. All life, we might say, is religious, and it is not a choice of whether one acts in the different areas; the only choice is that between wisdom and folly. In the Reformed tradition this distinction is known as the antithesis. Indeed, Proverbs concludes with a rich portrait of the valiant woman. Historically scholars have struggled to know why she is so exemplary of the fear of the Lord when her activities are secular rather than religious. Of course this misses the point that her wisdom manifests itself in all areas of her life, ranging from homemaking and charity to viticulture, trading in fabrics, and so on.

Wisdom and the Furnace of Formation: Job and Ecclesiastes

The crucible is for silver, and the furnace is for gold,
but the LORD tests the heart.

Proverbs 17:3

Brevard Childs was once asked by a student how to become a better exegete of the Bible. "Become a deeper person!" replied Childs. There are few biblical books of which this is so true as Job and Ecclesiastes. Job and Ecclesiastes are acknowledged as great literature, but in Old Testament studies they are widely understood to represent a crisis for the act-consequence theology (or traditional wisdom) of Proverbs, and the unity of both books is contested. Yet I will argue that Job and Ecclesiastes do not represent a crisis in Proverbial wisdom, and that reading them as literature accounts for the characteristics that historical critics use to discern different sources.

---

25. Raymond C. Van Leeuwen, "Wisdom Literature," in *Dictionary for Theological Interpretation of the Bible,* ed. Kevin J. Vanhoozer et al. (Grand Rapids: Baker Academic, 2005), pp. 847-50.

Take a proverb such as 17:3. Literally it reads: "A crucible for the silver and a furnace for the gold; and testing for the heart, Yahweh." The metal-working imagery evokes rigorous formation; silver and gold have to be exposed to high temperatures and smelted down in order to be re-formed into jewelry. Proverbs is well aware that the path to wisdom might take one through the furnace. In the anthropology of Proverbs "the heart" is repeatedly referred to as the center of the human person. Thus, what is in view here is formation of the human person at the deepest levels of being. Far from having a simplistic view of wisdom as easily acquired technique that automatically leads to blessing, Proverbs is aware that the road to wisdom may be through intense testing, suffering, and purification.

And this, in my view, is precisely what we find in Job and Ecclesiastes. I used to hold the view that these books dealt with exceptions to the character-consequence structure of Proverbs, but I have come to believe that they do not deal with exceptions so much as the formation involved in the production of truly wise people.

Intellectual Crisis: Ecclesiastes[26]

Ecclesiastes sets before us the dilemma of one Qohelet. We do not know how, but he has found himself in an existential crisis of the first order: on a journey of an autonomous epistemology — the signposts on which he depends are observation, reason, and experience — he runs up against the utter enigma *(hebel)* of life no matter what area of life he explores. At the same time, as a believing Israelite he knows that life is good and a gift of God — articulated in the so-called "carpe diem" passages. The result of the contradictory juxtaposition of these views is an excruciating, irreconcilable tension in his life. He cannot live with the tension, but neither can he surrender either view.

As we would expect, resolution comes gradually and in fits and starts. Six stages of growing insight can be discerned in Ecclesiastes:

1. Qohelet goes out of his way to portray his epistemology as one of "wisdom" (1:13, 16; 2:3), but from 1:2 the reader is shocked into the realization that this type of "Solomonic" wisdom is very different from that found in Proverbs, whose starting point is the fear of the Lord. The reader is compelled to wonder how "Solomon" could come to such a radical conclusion.

26. See Bartholomew, *Ecclesiastes*, for exegetical support for positions taken below.

2. Ecclesiastes 5:1-7, which Norbert Lohfink regards as the center of the book,[27] articulates a very different approach to that of the autonomous Qohelet. Here one must approach God in the temple with care to listen, and one's words must be few. This is quite different from the loquacious Qohelet and strikes a theme common in Proverbs, namely, readiness to listen. The imagery is that of being instructed by Yahweh through the teaching of the Torah by the priests. There is even the recognition that *hebel* — Qohelet's major problem — arises from many dreams and words, and the section concludes with an alternative approach, namely, "Fear God"! The perspective here is that of Proverbs, but the difficulty Qohelet faces is of finding his way back to that starting point from where he is experientially.

3. Ecclesiastes 7:23-29 is a key passage in which Qohelet reflects on his journey. The passage is pregnant with irony: Qohelet thought he was searching by wisdom, but he has ended up in the arms of Dame Folly and, try as he may, he cannot find Lady Wisdom. Whereas previously he has argued that God has made the world crooked and there is nothing humans can do to make it straight, now in 7:29 he declares that God made humans straightforward but they have devised many schemes.

4. Another key passage is 11:7. "Under the sun" is a recurring expression in Ecclesiastes and always has negative connotations of despair and *hebel*. This passage stands out like a firefly on a dark night, signaling a turning point in Qohelet's journey. Whereas so much of the book thus far has found life under the sun distinctly unpleasant, here we find hope and optimism: it is pleasant for the eyes to see the sun! Prior to this observation, the world "under the sun" has been a source of darkness and despair for Qohelet; now seeing is good! What has enabled such a transformation?

5. The answer is found in the two imperatives that govern 11:7–12:8, namely "remember" and "rejoice." "Young man" and "in the days of your youth" should not be confined to youth and young men but are part of the liminal rhetoric of Old Testament wisdom (cf. Prov. 1:1-6), as the threefold "before" in 12:1-8 indicates. Qohelet mentions God's judgment in 11:9, and then in 12:1-8 cosmic judgment is evoked in prophetic eschatological terms. The liminal rhetoric alerts the reader to the significance of the choices made at formative stages in one's life, and the reader is urged to remember his or her creator before such times strike. "Remember your creator" is Ecclesiastes' equivalent to "the fear of the Lord"; it is diametrically opposite to the au-

27. Norbert Lohfink, *Qohelet: A Continental Commentary,* trans. Sean E. McEvenue, Continental Commentaries (Minneapolis: Fortress, 2003).

tonomy that Qohelet espoused previously and involves an embrace of one's creatureliness and thus the limitations of one's knowledge.

6. In 12:9-14 the narrator sums up Qohelet's message with the exhortation to fear God and obey his commandments, for this is the "whole person." This is a profound reflection upon what it means to be human. As Barth rightly notes, "As the being of man is being in responsibility before God, it has the character of obedience to God."[28] The stress in the epilogue on law has been a major reason for assigning it to a different source, but, as we will note below, there are multiple references to the law in the body of Ecclesiastes, and the stress on creaturely obedience fits with approaching carefully to listen to God, fearing God, and remembering one's creator. It involves nothing less than an embrace of one's humanity *coram deo*.

A literary approach to Ecclesiastes is illuminating in terms of the contradictory juxtapositions and organic logic of the book, opening onto the *experience* represented by the book's shape. There was a time when psychological readings of Ecclesiastes were common, but that time is past. Perhaps Frank Zimmerman is the most recent to attempt this, but in a highly speculative manner.[29] As I have argued elsewhere, the works of Carl Jung contain rich resources for understanding the sort of experience embodied in Ecclesiastes.[30]

The pervasive use of the first person "I" is the great characteristic of Qohelet's journey. Psychologically this is significant, focusing as it does on the ego and its relation to the self. This is territory that Jung explored in detail. For Jung the self is the center of the total person, conscious and unconscious, whereas the ego is the center of conscious personality. The ego is the center of subjective identity, while the self is the locale of objective identity. The self is identified by Jung with the *imago dei;* it is the creative center where God and humankind meet, what Old Testament wisdom calls "the heart."

Psychologically the relationship between the ego and the self is vitally

---

28. Karl Barth, *Church Dogmatics* III/1, *The Doctrine of Creation, Part 1,* ed. G. W. Bromiley and T. F. Torrance (Edinburgh: T&T Clark, 1958), p. 170 (see pp. 170-86). Qohelet never uses the name "Yahweh," but he is clearly an Israelite, interacting with Israelite religion, and the positive side of his theology equates with Proverbs' Yahwism.

29. Frank Zimmerman, *The Inner World of Qohelet* (New York: Ktav, 1973).

30. Bartholomew, *Ecclesiastes,* pp. 377-82. For a useful overview of psychological readings of the Bible see Wayne G. Rollins, "The Bible and Psychology: New Directions in Biblical Scholarship," in *Hearing Visions and Seeing Voices: Psychological Aspects of Biblical Concepts and Personalities,* ed. Gerrit Glas, M. H. Spero, P. J. Verhagen, and H. M. van Praag (Dordrecht: Springer, 2007), pp. 279-94.

important. Many psychological problems are illuminated in terms of the ego-self relationship. Jung distinguishes between the inflated ego, the alienated ego, and the encounter with the self leading to a healthy relationship between the ego and the self. Inflation refers to the identification of the ego with the self. "It is a state in which something small (the ego) has arrogated to itself the qualities of something larger (the Self) and hence is blown up beyond the limits of its proper size."[31] However, this state cannot perdure because the experiences of life frustrate the expectations of the inflated ego and result in an estrangement between the ego and the self. "This estrangement is symbolized by such images as a fall, an exile, an unhealing wound, a perpetual torture."[32] This experience of alienation is a necessary stage en route to awareness of and a healthy relationship to the self.

According to Jung, "The Self, in its efforts at self-realization, reaches out beyond the ego-personality on all sides; because of its all-encompassing nature it is brighter and darker than the ego, and accordingly confronts it with problems which it would like to avoid. . . . For this reason the experience of the Self is always a defeat for the ego."[33] The inflation of the ego is from this perspective symptomatic of idolatry with the "I" as the center of one's existence. The journey toward health involves a decentering of the ego, the "I," as *part of* the self and as *constituted by* the self, but not *as* the self. For Kierkegaard as for Jung, the process of moving from an inflated ego through an alienated ego to a healthy ego-self relationship is wrought by pain and struggle, for it is a journey that the ego instinctively resists.[34] Maturity or inner transformation is thus nothing less than an encounter with the self.

With Job we know what events catalyze his crisis of meaning, but with Qohelet we do not. This is instructive in itself, because the experience of confrontation with the unconscious takes a variety of forms. Qohelet's sort of struggle is commonly associated with the midlife crisis or "creative ill-

---

31. Edward F. Edinger, *Ego and Archetype: Individuation and the Religious Formation of the Psyche* (Boston: Shambhala, 1992), p. 7.

32. Edinger, *Ego and Archetype*, p. 37.

33. Carl G. Jung, *Mysterium Coniunctionis*, Collected Works, vol. 14 (Princeton: Princeton University Press, 1966-1979), p. 778.

34. David Bakan (*Disease, Pain, and Sacrifice: Toward a Theology of Suffering* [Chicago: University of Chicago Press, 1968], p. 72) argues that "pain is the demand on the conscious ego to work to bring the decentralized part back into the unity of the organism. Pain is the imperative to the ego to assume the responsibility of telic centralization, the ego itself having emerged as a result of telic decentralization."

ness" that occurs when one moves into the second half of life.[35] Chapter 2 of Ecclesiastes is a fine description of what Jung refers to as the two stages of life. The first involves establishing oneself in the world through accumulation of wealth and status, while the second arises from the crisis of wealth and status losing meaning. Ecclesiastes 5:3, 7 hint at the source of Qohelet's conflict, namely that dreams come through much work and with many dreams come enigmas. Jung would of course pounce on this, with his insistence, following Freud, that the unconscious manifests itself through dreams. For Freud dreams are the "royal road" to knowledge of the self.[36] Disturbing dreams are often a sign of the self, the unconscious, demanding to be heard above the inflated ego. Qohelet's association of dreams with overwork is intriguing in this respect, for it appears to indicate from his own experience that working very hard to achieve wealth and status, an approach characteristic of the first stage of life, results in the unconscious clamoring to be heard via disturbing dreams. As Jung warns, "there is more to our meaning than the ego would have us believe."[37]

Although we can only speculate about what triggers Qohelet's profound struggle with the meaning of life, this warning from Jung hits the nail on the head with respect to Qohelet's journey. His Greek epistemology confines him to what his ego knows, and his painful journey is one toward a growing awareness of the self of which the ego is only a part. Qohelet finds himself confronted in an unavoidable way with the utter enigma of life.

For Jung, the greatest sin is to live unconsciously, and Qohelet is exemplary in his refusal of that option, although he does not know what the root of the problem is that he is facing. For Jung to live consciously is to embrace the journey of alienation and pain through which the ego becomes properly aligned with the self. Ironically, Qohelet continually refers to his autonomous observation of life as "turning his heart" toward the different areas of life he explores. I say "ironically" because his epistemology is very much an egocentric one, one of the head rather than the heart. From a Jungian perspective Qohelet's struggle exposes the misalignment between his ego and his self, but by surrendering to the excruciating journey he embarks on, he opens the way toward realignment of the ego with the self.

Qohelet's constant bumping up against everything being *hebel* is thus a

---

35. A fine work on midlife transformation is Sue M. Kidd, *When the Heart Waits: Spiritual Direction for Life's Sacred Questions* (San Francisco: Harper and Row, 1990).

36. See Sigmund Freud, *Interpretation of Dreams* (New York: Basic Books, 1955).

37. John Welch, *Spiritual Pilgrims: Carl Jung and Teresa of Ávila* (New York: Paulist Press, 1982), p. 81.

painful confrontation with the limitation of his ego because of its inflation and its need to be repositioned in relation to his self. Qohelet's strong emotions, the extremity of the positions he articulates, are a sign of the inner turmoil as well as the fact that a lot of inner, transforming work is going on. But the transformation is not quick, and that is why narrative is so helpful in expressing this sort of journey. As Jung notes, there is a complexity involved in the hearing of and telling of one's story.[38] This is certainly true of Qohelet. The "carpe diem" passages grow stronger as the book progresses, but so too does the despair and darkness, until the two threaten to tear each other to pieces. In 5:3, 7 there is some indication of insight into the source of the enigmas Qohelet is struggling with: disturbing dreams resulting from overwork. The points of insight emerge slowly: in 7:23-29 the growing sense that "wisdom" is not what it seems reaches a high point when Qohelet finds that his egocentric "wisdom" has led him right into the arms of Dame Folly, who is more bitter than death.

But the real indication of a change comes in the proverb of 11:7, "Truly, the light is sweet and it is good for the eyes to see the sun." This proverb has always struck me as somehow the turning point in Qohelet's journey, and once again Jung is helpful in illuminating it. Jung notes that when the ego begins to approach the center of the self and thus moves toward realignment, the experience can be very powerful. The contrary pole of the self "represents a new life and would allow more of the self to come to *light*."[39] This, it seems to me, is what has happened to Qohelet in 11:7. At an experiential level something has shifted, a sign of the ego reaching toward a healthy alignment with the self. However, this emergence into realignment takes time, so that Qohelet's journey is not yet over at this point. "Jung speaks of two steps in the process of coming to terms with the unconscious. The first step requires hearing the unconscious; the second step involves consciousness relating to this content from the unconscious."[40] Ecclesiastes 11:7 seems to me to be akin to step one; Qohelet becomes aware of the self at an intuitive level, and this generates hope and life. What follows after 11:7 to 12:7 is Qohelet gradually unpacking the content of the unconscious.

Ecclesiastes 12:1, with its "remember your creator," is highly significant from a Jungian perspective, for it represents a profound realization that the ego is not God, but is limited in a creaturely way so that it is dependent on much more than its capacities for observation and experience and reason to

---

38. Welch, *Spiritual Pilgrims*, p. 81.
39. Welch, *Spiritual Pilgrims*, p. 151. Italics mine.
40. Welch, *Spiritual Pilgrims*, p. 154.

find resolution to life's enigmas. "Remember your creator" represents a decentering of the ego and thus a realignment with the self, which is the place where the human communes with God. The mysteries of life do not disappear; 12:1-7 contains Qohelet's strongest evocation of death in all its dimensions, but they are now contained within a remembering of one's creator and the spirit returning to God who gave it.

Qohelet has found a resolution to his quest, but it is deeply existential and not just academic. Little wonder the narrator warns that much study wearies the flesh. Qohelet's "wisdom" has been revealed as folly, but through that painful process of relentlessly interrogating his previous certainties he has arrived at the beginning — but now to understand it more fully and as a more integrated person.

As a literary reading leads on to a psychological reading, so a psychological reading leads on to a spiritual one. The description of Qohelet as "wise" in 12:9 is as surprising as God's statement in Job 42:7 that Job, unlike his friends, has spoken right of God. In this way Qohelet's excruciating struggle for meaning is affirmed. His sayings are associated with those of the wise, inspired by one shepherd, namely God. The reason for this, I suggest, is that Qohelet has faced up to his existential crisis and allowed it to do its work in him. The tension between autonomy and belief cannot be sustained indefinitely, but autonomy is far harder to relinquish than we imagine; hence the creativity of the psychological conflict at work in Qohelet. Eventually the autonomy yields to creatureliness, but now at a much deeper level than ever before. Wisdom involves depth transformation, a journey of the heart through the furnace, and this is what we witness in Ecclesiastes. This is more than character formation; it is transformation at the deepest levels of the person. In this way a psychological reading of Ecclesiastes alerts us to the powerful spiritual formation at work.

Existential Chaos: Job

Job is an unusual book on several accounts: although Yahweh/God is the central character, all the human characters are non-Israelites.[41] Apart from a short prose framework, the vast majority of the book is poetic. And this is to

---

41. There is some debate as to whether Elihu was an Israelite. David J. A. Clines (*Job 21-37* [Nashville: Thomas Nelson, 2006], p. 713) argues that Job 32:2 portrays Elihu as an Edomite.

say nothing of the content of Job: the shuttling between heaven and earth in the opening chapters and the subsequent non-appearance of the Satan who catalyzes Job's suffering, the lengthy speeches of Job's friends, Job's collapse into anger and frustration after his profound initial response to his sufferings, the divine speeches that take Job on a tour of the creation, and finally the epilogue and Job's restoration.

The book of Job is narrative art at its best; hence the fecundity of a literary approach to the book. Let me note here just a few of the many insights a literary reading offers:

1. The reader is given access to the opening scenes in heaven, but Job is not. We are made aware of the challenge by the mysterious figure of the Satan as to the real motivation for Job's service of God: "Does Job fear God for no reason?" (1:9).[42] In terms of Proverbs' anthropology, the focus is placed on Job's *heart* and the deepest source of his motivations.

2. It is significant that the Satan is given permission to inflict suffering on Job, but, while the terrible suffering is authorized by God, it does not come directly from God. As Barth notes,

> He [God] can give Satan, within a limited but very large sphere, a free hand in relation to Job. He can do so to such an extent that God himself can and actually does appear to Job to be an enemy and persecutor. He did not owe him favor, nor will he do so. He can also allow disaster to fall upon him. On the other hand, he can also bring to an end the experiments of Satan and bring about a new turn in the fortunes of Job. . . . He can and does do all these things as the free God who is also as such the Liberator of Job.[43]

3. 1:1-5 presents a picture of Job as the quintessential wise man, but, as with the association of Qohelet with Solomon, there is irony at work here. One gets the sense that the portrait is almost too good to be true, and Job's excessive activity on behalf of his children (1:5) hints at his obsessive use of religion to prevent anything upsetting his family life. This is confirmed by

---

42. Gustavo Gutiérrez (*On Job: God-Talk and the Suffering of the Innocent* [Maryknoll: Orbis, 1987]) makes much of disinterested service of God. For a very different view see Peter J. Leithart, *Deep Comedy: Trinity, Tragedy, and Hope in Western Literature* (Moscow, ID: Canon, 2006), p. 32: "Pious as it sounds to 'desire God for God's sake,' it is utterly pagan and simply a pious gloss on the Satanic temptation to be as God."

43. Karl Barth, *Church Dogmatics* IV/3, *The Doctrine of Reconciliation, Part 1*, ed. G. W. Bromiley and T. F. Torrance (Edinburgh: T&T Clark, 1958), p. 387.

the contrast with Job's approach to sacrifice and his family in the epilogue, where "Job's attention has shifted from an unnecessarily controlling and anxiety-ridden care for his children to a God-ordained, entirely proper intercession for his friends who have in truth offended God."[44]

4. That most of the book of Job is verse is significant. Poetry is uniquely suited to plumb the depths of Job's suffering, to evoke his tragedy for the reader, and to alert the reader to the sterility of the friends' speeches. The friends' speeches, like the Psalter, resort to stereotypical images, but without the life of the psalms. "Eliphaz," says Robert Alter, "speaks smugly without suspecting that there might be a chasm between divine knowledge and the conventional knowledge of accepted wisdom."[45] Elihu's poetry is more powerful and sophisticated than that of the friends, though it does not, as Alter says, "soar like the Voice from the Whirlwind"[46] in chapters 38–41. Job is not afraid to protest. Alter notes that "Job's cosmic poetry, unlike that of the Friends, has a certain energy of vision, as though it proceeded from some immediate perception of the great things it reports."[47]

Poetry thus enables the book of Job to evoke the depth of the tragedy that struck Job. George Steiner argues, using Job as an example, that "tragedy is alien to the Judaic sense of the world";[48] tragedy, he contends, is essentially Greek and arises from a view of the world in which humans encounter blind necessity. Steiner's narrow definition of tragedy has been rightly contested,[49] and it remains valuable to see Job in the context of tragic vision. Martha Nussbaum uses Alcibiades' speech in Plato's *Symposium,* in which he describes his repeated attempts to seduce Socrates, to foreground the important role of narrative and image in moral learning: "Certain truths about human experience can best be learned by living them in their particularity. Nor can this particularity be grasped solely by

---

44. Kathryn Schifferdecker, *Out of the Whirlwind: Creation Theology in the Book of Job,* Harvard Theological Studies 61 (Cambridge, MA: Harvard Divinity School, 2008), p. 109. A point also noted by Ellen F. Davis, "Job and Jacob: The Integrity of Faith," in *The Whirlwind: Essays on Job, Hermeneutics and Theology in Memory of Jane Morse,* ed. S. L. Cooke, C. L. Patton, and J. W. Watts, JSOTSup 336 (Sheffield: Sheffield Academic Press, 2001), pp. 119-20; William P. Brown, *Ethos of the Cosmos: The Generation of Moral Imagination in the Bible* (Grand Rapids: Eerdmans, 1999), p. 379.

45. Robert Alter, *The Art of Biblical Poetry* (New York: Basic, 1985), p. 89.

46. Alter, *Art of Biblical Poetry,* p. 92.

47. Alter, *Art of Biblical Poetry,* p. 90.

48. George Steiner, *The Death of Tragedy* (New York: Oxford University Press, 1961), p. 4.

49. Leithart, *Deep Comedy,* pp. 39-44.

thought 'itself for itself.' "[50] This relates to her point that a contribution of tragedy is to explore the gap between what we are and how well we manage to live our lives.[51] The poetic language and imagery of Job evoke precisely such tragic particularity. As Henri Nouwen noted, often the most personal is the most universal.

For Aristotle, unlike his opponents, who held to an abstract view of virtue, the emotions of pity and fear are central to tragedy and valuable as sources of illumination and clarification.[52] Clearly Job presents a full range of human emotions, and the book expects its readers to be formed as they journey — not least emotionally — with Job through his tragedy and to resolution.

Peter Leithart refers to the Christian vision as one of "deep comedy." The ending it envisages is uncontaminated by any fear of future tragedy, and the characters progress to a fulfillment that exceeds their beginning; the move is from glory to glory. However, as Leithart rightly notes, such deep comedy does not erase tragedy but enables us to see it in all its painful depths as "deep tragedy." "Because the resurrection vindicates the Crucified, not the crucifixion, the gospel story undercuts any easy moralism or sentimental liberalism. . . . Thus the cross and resurrection intensify sadness and the sense of loss, and in a sense make tragedy more tragic."[53] As Alvin Plantinga notes, "there could be no such thing as genuinely horrifying evil if there were no God."[54] There is thus a sense in which Bernard Williams is right to criticize moral philosophy's attachment to serving up "good news" about our condition.[55] A role of tragedy, and not least that of Job, is to con-

---

50. Martha Nussbaum, *The Fragility of Goodness: Luck and Ethics in Greek Tragedy and Philosophy,* 2nd ed. (Cambridge: Cambridge University Press, 2001), p. 186.

51. Nussbaum, *Fragility of Goodness,* pp. 378-85.

52. Nussbaum, *Fragility of Goodness,* pp. 378-94.

53. Leithart, *Deep Comedy,* p. 25.

54. In James F. Sennett, ed., *The Analytic Theist: An Alvin Plantinga Reader* (Grand Rapids: Eerdmans, 1998), p. 339. Alvin Plantinga discusses Job in his *Warranted Christian Belief* (Oxford: Oxford University Press, 2000), pp. 494-98, as does philosopher Eleonore Stump, *Walking in Darkness: Narrative and the Problem of Suffering* (Oxford: Oxford University Press, 2010), pp. 177-226.

55. Bernard Williams, *Shame and Necessity* (Berkeley: University of California Press, 1993). Williams's realism leaves us, however, resigned to our lack of control over much of life. Nussbaum, *Fragility of Goodness,* attempts to move this in a more positive direction by arguing that such realism enables us to accept what we cannot change while actively engaging the ethical space in which we find ourselves. However, this is proposed in the context of her move to affirm the Enlightenment goal of "a social life grounded in reason" and her ac-

front us with the horrors inherent in fallen human life. The critical difference, of course, between Job and Greek tragedy, between Williams and Nussbaum is the central character of Job, God, and his providential ordering of
his good creation.

The divine speeches in Job are remarkable, as Robert Alter attests:

> If the poetry of Job . . . looms above all other biblical poetry in virtuosity
> and sheer expressive power, the culminating poem that God speaks out of
> the storm soars beyond everything that has preceded it in the book, the
> poet having wrought a poetic idiom even richer and more awesome than
> the one he gave Job.[56]

As Alter says elsewhere:

> When God finally answers Job out of the whirlwind, he responds with an
> order of poetry formally allied to Job's own remarkable poetry, but larger
> in scope and greater in power. . . . That is, God picks up many of Job's key
> images, especially from the death-wish poem with which Job began
> (Chapter 3), and his discourse is shaped by a powerful movement of in-
> tensification, coupled with an implicitly narrative sweep from the cre-
> ation to the play of natural forces to the teeming world of animal life.[57]

Scholars debate whether the divine speeches are in fact an answer to
Job's experience of suffering.[58] Carol Newsom argues that historical criticism never had an answer to "the problem of how such a multigenre,
multiauthor composition [as Job] was to be read as a whole," and she also
criticizes final form readings. Using Bakhtin's notion of polyphony, she discerns a multiplicity of voices in Job and argues that no voice, not even God's,
provides an answer to the questions raised in the book. Yet in his review of
Newsom's *The Book of Job: A Contest of Moral Imaginations*, Jon Levenson
perceptively notes that "Three centuries of secularization and historical criticism impel us to place God's words about himself on a plane with human

---

knowledgment that "few of us now believe that we live in a world that is providentially ordered for the sake of the overall good; few even believe in a teleology of human social life
moving toward greater perfection" (*Fragility of Goodness*, pp. xvi, xv). It is hard to see how
hopeful such a vision actually is, and one also wonders how Nussbaum can be so certain that
so "few" believe these things amid a worldwide resurgence of religion.

56. Alter, *Art of Biblical Poetry*, p. 87.

57. Robert Alter, *The World of Biblical Literature* (New York: Basic, 1992), pp. 188-89.

58. For a sample of modern views see Schifferdecker, *Out of the Whirlwind*, pp. 5-11.

speculations about him. There is ample reason to doubt that ancient Israelites felt the same agnostic impulse or evaluated interminable dialogue with no chance of resolution so highly."[59]

It is a truism that Job receives no direct answer as to why he suffered, but Job's confession that whereas previously he had only *heard* of God but now he *sees* him alerts us to a profound transformation that his suffering worked in him. The divine speeches are the answer to Job — but not to the questions he was asking. God's agenda is radically different from his, and the divine speeches facilitate this momentous shift in Job from knowing about God to deep, interpersonal relationship in which Job assumes and embraces his creaturely status. Hence the focus in the divine speeches on aspects of the creation distinct from humankind. Kathryn Schifferdecker is rightly alert to this non-anthropocentric emphasis but falsely, in my view, concludes that the divine speeches are unique in the Bible in this respect. Creation, and not covenant, she stresses, is where Job's answer is to be found. Yet the recurrence of Yahweh in chapter 42, plus the cultic aspects, undercut any noncovenantal reading. And in terms of the unique place of humankind in the creation, it needs to be remembered that it is Job who is taken on the tour of creation, not an ostrich or a donkey.[60] The divine speeches do not articulate a different creation theology but place the emphasis on the nonhuman in order to facilitate the decentering of Job that his transformation requires, as we will see below. Rolf Knierim perceptively notes that

> Job is told that his challenge to Yahweh's justice is evaluated on the basis of the universal order of Yahweh's created and sustained world and not on the basis of his own experience. To the extent that Job saw Yahweh withdrawing from the wholeness of his life he was correct. But he was wrong when challenging Yahweh's justice universally. For such a challenge, his experience was not universal enough. His experience cannot be the sum total of wisdom because it does not represent the structure of the whole world, just as he himself is not the creator and sustainer of this structure.[61]

5. Ordinary Bible readers are doubtless put off by the length of Job, the seemingly endless speeches, and Job's long journey back to rest in God. Here, as with Ecclesiastes, it is helpful to note the performative nature of Job. His

---

59. Jon D. Levenson, review of Carol A. Newsom, *The Book of Job: A Contest of Moral Imaginations,* in *JR* 84 (2004): 271-72.

60. Job parodies Psalm 8 in 7:17-21.

61. Knierim, *The Task of Old Testament Theology,* p. 202.

furnace experience is long and difficult.[62] His suffering makes him vulnerable and in need of friends; but, as often happens, his friends provide much advice that may be well meant but is unhelpful. Indeed, the speeches by the friends are a lesson in how *not* to apply the character-consequence structure to a situation like that of Job.

6. After a long wait, God addresses Job. Michael Fox has rightly pointed out the extent to which questions dominate God's speeches; there are some eighty, which can be categorized into three types: who? what? and "Have you ever?"[63] Rhetorically, the questions alert Job and the reader to God's power, the limits of human knowledge, and God's compassion with his creation.

7. Through his suffering and ultimate encounter with God, Job is transformed. He describes his transformation as the move from hearing about to seeing God (42:5). His fortunes are restored twofold, but the major transformation has taken place within him. Job is thus above all a narrative of spiritual formation through terrible suffering.

8. In the epilogue, Job, in his suffering and his struggle to come to grips with that suffering, is affirmed by God as speaking rightly of/to him,[64] whereas the friends are castigated. There is no mention of Elihu in the epilogue, and from a literary perspective this opens up a gap in the storytelling that the reader has to fill. Some see Elihu as a prophetic figure, preparing the way for Job's encounter with God, but in my view Elihu represents a more sophisticated version of the three friends, and he is simply ignored. In contrast to the three friends, Job is referred to as "my servant" four times in 42:7-9.

A literary reading of Job alerts us to its central theme of formation through suffering. An experience such as that of Job is ripe for psychological analysis, and in this section we will again use insights from Jung to explore Job's experience.[65] Susannah Ticciati rightly notes that the self and its trans-

---

62. Although in Job the breakthrough comes after his encounter with God, one should not ignore the progress worked by his suffering prior to this encounter. Gutiérrez, *On Job*, notes how Job's self-centeredness opens out into a critique of injustice in general, in chapter 24 in particular.

63. Michael V. Fox, "Job 38 and God's Rhetoric," *Semeia* 19 (1981): 53-61.

64. Both meanings probably apply. See Kenneth N. Ngwa, *The Hermeneutics of the "Happy" Ending in Job 42:7-17*, BZAW 354 (Berlin: De Gruyter, 2005), pp. 11-14. However, it is notable how Job so often speaks to God, unlike his friends.

65. Analysis of the stages in the grief process are another helpful means of analyzing Job, but they lack the transformative element in Jung's psychology. M. H. Spero ("The Hidden *Subject* of Job: Mirroring and the Anguish of Interminable Desire," in *Hearing Visions and Seeing Voices*, ed. Glas et al., pp. 213-66) discerns mirroring as central to the experience

formation are central to Job.[66] In his *Answer to Job,* Jung treats the story of Job as a turning point in the development of Hebrew-Christian myth. Jung sees Job's encounter with God as a transition in humankind's awareness of God, which leads to God's humanization and then to the incarnation. Within the Jungian tradition, Edward Edinger proposes a more helpful reading of Job according to which Job gives a comprehensive account of the encounter with the self.[67]

When Job loses everything to which he attached value, he is plunged into despair and a state of alienation. If the self, from a Jungian perspective, is to be recognized as the supreme value, then all lesser attachments, those most closely connected with the inflation of the ego, must be loosened. Job evidently centers the meaning of his life in family, property, and health. The indications of this are found in his obsessive protection of his family in 1:5 and in his inflated vision of what should have happened to him at death in 3:14-15 (cf. 30:1), where he imagines himself at peace with the great and wise ones of the earth! When deprived of his attachments, he despairs and enters the dark night of the soul.[68] Job's life has shattered, and his response is to seek to cause the creation to shatter (Job 3).[69] Alter describes Job 3 as "a powerful, evocative, authentic expression of man's essential, virtually ineluctable egotism."[70] "Job's own world has descended into turmoil or chaos (רֹגֶז), and he attempts to inflict that chaos on creation itself; first by cursing creation, then by ascribing chaotic tendencies to God."[71] For Edinger, Job remains convinced of his innocence, thereby demonstrating that he is unconscious of his "shadow." The repetitiveness of the dialogue relates to such an experi-

---

of Job. Spero's analysis is detailed and sophisticated but, in my view, not nearly as compelling as Edinger's.

66. Susannah Ticciati, *Job and the Disruption of Identity: Reading beyond Barth* (London: T&T Clark, 2005).

67. Edinger, *Ego and Archetype,* pp. 76-96. In terms of the historicity of Job it is intriguing to note that Edinger regards Job as likely reflecting the actual experience of an individual. He sees the friends as an example of active imagination by the individual and suggests that the three-plus-one friends implies resolution so that Elihu's contribution should be read as an anticipation of the resolution of Job's suffering. On the role of the three and the four see Edinger, *Ego and Archetype,* pp. 179-93.

68. St. John of the Cross refers repeatedly to Job in *The Dark Night of the Soul* (London: Burns and Oates, 1976).

69. See Perdue, *Wisdom Literature,* pp. 98-102; Michael Fishbane, "Jeremiah IV 23-26 and Job III 3-13: A Recovered Use of the Creation Pattern," *VT* 21 (1971): 151-67.

70. Alter, *The Art of Biblical Poetry,* p. 96.

71. Schifferdecker, *Out of the Whirlwind,* pp. 67-68.

ence, since the resistance of the ego involves returning again and again to the same issues.

From Edinger's perspective, the centrality of God in Job is deeply significant, since it provides the assurance that there is meaning in Job's suffering. Through his encounters with God, Job is brought to the realization that the ego is ignorant of the self in its totality. The Satan's suggestion that Job will curse God and the encouragement to do so by his wife highlight the issue of ego inflation. "Therefore the program is arranged to test the ego in the fire of tribulation and out of that ordeal comes Job's full encounter with the reality of God. . . . [W]e can say that it was God's purpose to make Job aware of Him."[72] Through his riveting encounter with God, "Job's questions have been answered, not rationally but by living experience. What he has been seeking, the meaning of his suffering, has been found. It is nothing less than the conscious realization of the autonomous archetypal psyche; and this realization could come to birth *only through an ordeal*."[73]

A literary and psychological reading illumines the fact that the book of Job, like Ecclesiastes, is about the transformative dimension essential to true wisdom. Wisdom is far from mere technique; it involves deep formation of the heart, and this will often involve a journey through the furnace. "The Book of Job is really a record of a divine initiation process, a testing by ordeal, which when successful leads to a new state of being."[74]

Old Testament Wisdom in the Canon

Wisdom and the Old Testament

It is commonly held that it is only late in the development of Old Testament wisdom that the connection was made with Old Testament law.[75] From this perspective, we are meant to imagine the two as relatively separate streams in the life of Israel only really coming together in the exilic and post-exilic periods. In my view this is mistaken. Clearly there is development in both Old Testament law and wisdom, and it is unhelpful to view either one stati-

72. Edinger, *Ego and Archetype*, p. 80.
73. Edinger, *Ego and Archetype*, p. 91. Italics added.
74. Edinger, *Ego and Archetype*, p. 91.
75. Perdue, *Wisdom Literature*, p. 160, concludes that "During the Persian period the Torah became the theological center of traditional Jewish wisdom. This became the means for associating creation theology with sapiential ethics."

cally. However, Old Testament wisdom is imbued with the ethos of Old Testament law.

An insight of postmodernism is the realization that observation is never neutral; in Karl Popper's evocative imagery, we do not collect facts in a bucket but observe in the light of a torchlight we shine on the world.[76] The torchlight, or what I like to call the worldview, plays a constituent part in what we observe. Clearly experience and observation are important elements in the wisdom we find in Proverbs. However, a raft of ethical judgments form part of the ethos within which Proverbs makes its assessments.

A good example of this is the observation reported in Proverbs 7:6-20. Undoubtedly the observation is imaginatively developed, but, for argument's sake, let us assume that this is an event actually observed of a young man going off to the house of an adulteress in the evening. The woman's husband is away, and she seduces the young man into a night of sex. It is important to note that there is nothing in the facts reported that compel one to conclude that the young man is a fool and that his actions will cost his life (7:23). In order to realize the extent to which this report is informed by the view that adultery is folly, one need only think how differently many in our culture might report a similar event. Many would relate the story with admiration; here is a young man acquiring necessary sexual experience. Others might shake their head and make some comment about sowing one's wild oats. But not Proverbs: the story is told as an example of extreme folly that has life-threatening consequences. Now from where, we must ask, would the author have arrived at such a view? In my opinion the answer is obvious: from Sinai. The seventh commandment makes clear that for the covenant people adultery is strictly forbidden, and the wisdom of avoiding adultery, whether as a woman or a young man, is expressed several times in Proverbs 1–9.[77]

This is strongly confirmed when Proverbs 7:6-20 is read in its larger context of 7:1-27, which is clearly a unity. In his evocative discussion of this section under the heading "The Educational Theatre of Proverbs,"[78] Levy

---

76. Karl R. Popper, "The Bucket and the Searchlight: Two Theories of Knowledge," in *Objective Knowledge: An Evolutionary Approach* (Oxford: Clarendon Press, 1972), pp. 341-61.

77. Intriguingly, Proverbs 2:17 refers to marriage as a "sacred covenant." Cf. Gordon P. Hugenberger, *Marriage as a Covenant: A Study of Biblical Law and Ethics Governing Marriage Developed from the Perspective of Malachi* (Leiden: Brill, 1994). It should be noted that Proverbs not only forbids adultery but also has a very positive view of marriage and sex within marriage; see 5:15-19.

78. Shimon Levy, *The Bible as Theatre* (Brighton: Sussex Academic Press, 2000), pp. 135-42.

notes the intertextual echoes of the Torah in verses 1-6 and rightly argues that the *shema* of Deuteronomy 6:1-4 is clearly alluded to: "The father reuses the original Pentateuch text in a sophisticated way."[79] According to the *shema*, God's commandments — cf. "my commandments" of Proverbs 7:2 — are to be discussed in the home, presumably the context for the instruction of Proverbs 7. They are to be bound on the fingers (cf. Prov. 3:3); in Deuteronomy 6 they are to be bound on the hand. Furthermore, "the tablet of your heart" alludes to the "heart" of Deuteronomy 6:6, and "tablet" evokes the tablets of the law.

Patrick Miller has rightly argued that the ten words of Sinai establish the good neighborhood.[80] In this respect it is illuminating to work through Proverbs identifying the ethical values assumed and argued for and to note how strongly they connect with the Decalogue. Here are some examples:

1. The first three commandments find expression in the central motif of Proverbs, the fear of the Lord (cf. Prov. 1:7, 29; 2:5; 8:13; 9:10; 10:27; 14:26, 27; etc.).

2. The fourth commandment is connected with the strong work ethic we find in Proverbs. The Sabbath commandment is not just about a day of rest but also about the six days on which "you shall labor and do all your work" (Exod. 20:9; cf. Prov. 6:6-11; 10:26; 12:11, 27; 13:4; etc.).

3. The fifth commandment is echoed throughout Proverbs. In Proverbs 1–9 there are repeated exhortations to a young man to listen to his parent's instruction (1:8; 2:1; 3:1; etc.). Multiple proverbs reflect on the relationship between children and parents, with a common theme being that of discipline (cf. 10:1; 13:1, 24; 15:20; 19:13, 18, 26, 27; 22:15; etc.).

4. The sixth commandment, forbidding murder, is presupposed in Proverbs 1:10-19 in particular (cf. also 6:17; 11:30).

5. The seventh commandment, dealing with adultery, is prevalent especially in Proverbs 1–9 but also found elsewhere in Proverbs (cf. 2:16-19; 5; 6:24-35; 23:27-28; 30:20).

6. The eighth commandment, about not stealing, informs many proverbs (1:13; 10:2; 11:1; 15:6, 27; 16:8; etc.).

7. The ninth commandment, dealing with false witness, is surprisingly common in Proverbs (6:19; 14:5, 25; 21:28; 24:28; etc.).

79. Levy, *The Bible as Theatre*, p. 136.
80. Patrick Miller, *The Way of the Lord: Essays in Old Testament Theology* (Grand Rapids: Eerdmans, 2007), pp. 51-67.

8. Finally, there are explicit references to the danger of coveting in Proverbs (6:25; 12:12). René Girard relates the tenth commandment to constraining "mimetic desire," which he argues is at the heart of violence.[81] While the verb "covet" (*ḥāmad*) does occur in Proverbs, it also has a broader vocabulary in relation to desire, both positive and negative (*ta'ăwâ; 'āwâ; ḥēpeṣ*).[82] Seen in this light, the tenth commandment has considerable overlap with the ethos of Proverbs.[83]

References to particular Old Testament laws in Proverbs should also be noted: to the tithe in 3:9; to the false balance in 11:1; 16:11; 20:10, 23; to sacrifice in 15:8 and 21:27; to the casting of lots in 16:33; to making vows in 20:25 (cf. Eccles. 5:1-7); to removing a boundary in 23:10.

It is clear from the above that the ethical ethos which Proverbs assumes is that of the good neighborhood called into being at Sinai. If the Sinai covenant was as central to the life of Israel as the Old Testament suggests, then this should not be surprising; it is precisely what we would expect. Indeed, in Proverbs 28:4, 7, 9 and 29:18 there are explicit references to keeping and listening to "the law" *(torah)*. One also needs to take into account the vocabulary of "the wicked," "the righteous," "the commandments," "evil," and "the sinner." Especially in the light of the above, it simply will not do to void such vocabulary of the sort of ethical content it has in legal literature. It may well be that Proverbs extends this content in relation to wisdom and folly, but the overlap is clear. Much the same can be said of Ecclesiastes. It is not true that the reference to law is a novum in the epilogue; as I have argued elsewhere, Qohelet manifests knowledge of the law and of the cultus.[84]

How then to account for the distinctiveness of Old Testament wisdom? Von Rad seems to me right when he notes that

The man whom wisdom instructed was a member of the cultic community, his life was subject to manifold cultic ties, in the Temple at the great

---

81. René Girard, *I See Satan Fall Like Lightning* (Maryknoll: Orbis, 2001).

82. See, for example, Prov. 3:15; 8:11; 10:24; 11:23; 13:2, 12, 19; 19:2, 22; 21:10; 23:3, 6; 24:1.

83. See Craig G. Bartholomew, "The Tenth Commandment, René Girard, and the Good Neighborhood of Proverbs," forthcoming.

84. Bartholomew, *Ecclesiastes*, pp. 87-92. A similar attempt is made to void the language of righteous/unrighteous, sinner, and evil of the ethical content it has elsewhere in Qohelet studies. In my view this does not stand up to scrutiny. Job, furthermore, is clearly Israelite literature, and its focus on the act-consequence motif and the problem of suffering means that it lacks the range of references to the law that we find in Proverbs and Ecclesiastes.

pilgrimage festivals he heard the peremptory or the comforting voice of Jahweh: to order a man's life in this — that is, the cultic — sphere lay completely outwith the jurisdiction of the teacher of wisdom. But of course a wide sphere still remained unconditioned and unregulated by the cult. . . . It is the sphere of the most common and ordinary in daily life, in which the question was not always of murder or adultery or theft, though it was brimful of questions of a different sort.[85]

It is this *wide sphere of daily experience* that is the focus of Old Testament wisdom. Von Rad thinks that the advice of the wise was "derived essentially from experience"; but, as we have shown above, this was experience always interpreted from a Yahwistic perspective, that is, one informed by and imbued with *torah*.

It is true that Old Testament wisdom makes little mention of the history of Israel; the question is, How do we interpret this silence? First, it should be noted that Proverbs does refer to "the land" (10:30; reference is implicit in verses like 22:28 with its reference to "your ancestors"). Second, the association of Proverbs with Solomon links it into Israel's history. Third, as noted above, Proverbs' rootedness in tradition manifests a historical awareness. Fourth, the centrality of Yahweh evokes the story of Israel as does the ethos of the good neighborhood of the ten words. This evidence inclines me to read the comparative silence of Old Testament wisdom about the history of Israel positively, as a silence that assumes the history, rather than negatively, as if Old Testament wisdom is unaware of the story of Israel or regards it as irrelevant.

In terms of the rest of the Old Testament, it should be noted that Proverbs, Ecclesiastes, and Job manifest close links with the Genesis creation stories. Proverbs refers several times to the/a tree of life (cf. 3:18; 11:30; 13:12; 15:4), an intertextual link to Genesis 2–3; evidences a strong doctrine of creation (3:19-20; 8:22-31; 22:2); and refers to Deuteronomy 6 in 7:1-3. And, as Hans Hertzberg notes, it appears as though Qohelet had the opening chapters of Genesis open in front of him as he wrote![86] Ecclesiastes 12 also manifests knowledge of prophetic eschatology. All this suggests a deeply organic relationship between the different genres in the life of Israel, which is, after all, what one would expect in a covenant nation.

---

85. Von Rad, *Old Testament Theology*, vol. 1, p. 433.

86. Hans W. Hertzberg, *Der Prediger*, Kommentar zum Alten Testament 17.4 (Gütersloh: Mohn, 1963), p. 230.

Wisdom in the Canon

To use the analogy of the drama of Scripture, we live in an act of the play different from that in which Old Testament wisdom was produced, so that we cannot always apply Old Testament wisdom directly to our situations today. The major difference is that Lady Wisdom became incarnate in Jesus of Nazareth[87] and we live in the age of the Spirit, the age of mission, between the coming of the kingdom and its final consummation. Intriguingly, Barth reads Job typologically in relation to Jesus as the "True Witness": "Already the free servant of God, he [Job] strides through the hell of affliction to his liberation by and for the free God. And as this free servant of the free God he is from the very first, formally considered, a type of the true Witness."[88] I do not find Barth's reading persuasive, but, as we will see below, it is hard not to connect Job with the cross.

Wisdom motifs play a larger role in Jesus' ministry than is often recognized. For example, he concludes the Sermon on the Mount in the story of two houses (Matt. 7:24-27) with imagery that appears to come directly from Proverbs (9; 12:7; 24:3-4). Of course, wisdom is now defined as obedience to Jesus' teaching. However, as Jesus himself teaches, he has not come to abolish the Old Testament but to fulfill it. Elsewhere I have suggested that the affirmation of ordinary, embodied life in the "carpe diem" passages in Ecclesiastes may be a neglected background to Jesus' feasting, especially as we find it in Luke.[89] A wonderful proverb associated with Martin Luther captures this spirit: "Who does not love wine, women, and song, will remain a fool his whole life long."[90] In the dawning of the new age, believers still require wisdom, and especially in his letters Paul not only locates wisdom in Jesus but also prays that believers may be filled with wisdom. The dynamic is the same as that in the Old Testament, but now in the fullness of time. How might we continue to follow the clues from Old Testament wisdom in our situation today?

First, Old Testament wisdom serves as a reminder of the *comprehensive scope* of what Paul calls the "obedience of faith." Von Rad rightly notes of Old Testament wisdom that it "had to do with the whole of life, and had to be occupied with all its departments."[91] The range of topics addressed by

---

87. A typological reading of Prov. 8:22-31 is common in patristic literature.

88. Barth, *Church Dogmatics* IV/3.1, p. 388. See Barth's forays into Job in IV/3.1, pp. 368-434.

89. Bartholomew, *Ecclesiastes*, pp. 96-97.

90. Mieder, *Proverbs Are Never Out of Season*, pp. 80-91.

91. Von Rad, *Old Testament Theology*, vol. 1, p. 428.

Old Testament wisdom is remarkable: acquisition of knowledge, epistemology, family, speech, politics, work, business, law, education, government, and so on. Ecclesiastes covers all of life "under the sun"; what is not always recognized is that, while Qohelet casts a question upon all of life, if — as I think he does — he reaches resolution, then all of life becomes meaningful! As Gordon Spykman has noted, nothing matters but the kingdom, but because of the kingdom everything matters![92] Wisdom serves as a reminder that kingdom life embraces every aspect of the creation as God has made it and that Christians are called to serve God in all areas of life, including farming, politics, architecture, winemaking, marriage, eating, etc. The Proverbs 31 woman is exemplary of this kind of embodied wisdom.

Second, Old Testament wisdom serves as a reminder of the *appropriate limits* of Scripture. Sinai does not provide us with all we need to know, nor does the canon of Scripture. The canon is the field in which we find Christ, and, as Lesslie Newbigin notes, "Christ is the clue to all that is." But this clue has to be pursued in all areas of life! Wisdom drives a bus through the nature-grace, sacred-secular dualism that is so prevalent in too much contemporary Christianity. Proverbs 1–9 in particular serves as a great encouragement to pursue that clue which is the Wisdom Christ in all areas of life, both practical and academic.

Third, Old Testament wisdom reminds us of the importance of *the ordinary*.[93] The daily stuff of our lives provides the raw materials for our worship, and a Christian spirituality will play itself out amid the day-to-day experiences of life. As with Old Testament wisdom, believers will need to learn to practice wisdom amid the old and new situations that confront them.

Fourth, as followers of the Christ, believers are called to *take up their cross and follow him.* If you take up a cross, there is only one destination in view: crucifixion. James, a book deeply shaped by Old Testament wisdom, refers to Job as an example of suffering, patience, and steadfastness (James 5:10-11). If in Hebrews 2:10 Jesus is described as "made perfect through suffering," how much more true will that be of his followers, and we need to fill our understanding of what suffering may entail with the sort of experience Job went through. The age of mission is also one of suffering, and in this context Ecclesiastes and Job will continue to be of inestimable value for be-

92. Gordon J. Spykman, *Reformational Theology: A New Paradigm for Doing Dogmatics* (Grand Rapids: Eerdmans, 1992), p. 478.

93. See Charles Taylor, *Sources of the Self: The Making of the Modern Identity* (Cambridge, MA: Harvard University Press, 1989), for the narrative of the recovery of the ordinary by the Reformers and its subsequent secularization.

lievers as they are shaped by the Spirit to become truly wise. Human autonomy is at the heart of modernity, and the decentering that is involved in both Job and Ecclesiastes is highly instructive today.

Fifth, proverbial wisdom has a contribution to make to us moderns in terms of *the primacy of lived experience* as opposed to theoretical abstraction being the royal road to truth. In past ages proverbial wisdom was highly valued for its sense of tradition and local, particular knowledge. A characteristic of modernity is the privileging of abstract theoretical knowledge over lived reality. The result is that proverbial wisdom as practical knowledge is marginalized in Western culture. This is a great loss, and a recovery of contemporary, biblical, proverbial wisdom is one way in which we can recover the primacy of lived experience.

14 Hearing the Major Prophets: "Your Ears Are Open, but You Hear Nothing" (Isa. 42:20)

Richard Schultz

The Tragedy of Not Hearing and the Challenge of Hearing the Major Prophets Today

Repeatedly, throughout the eighth through sixth centuries B.C.,[1] the Major Prophets challenged the people of Israel — and possibly also their neighbors[2] — to "Hear the word of the LORD."[3] Addressing a wide range of audiences — monarchs and "mountains," false prophets and "prostitutes," rulers and remnant (Isa. 1:10; 39:5; Jer. 22:2; 42:15; Ezek. 6:3; 13:2; 16:35) — these courageous individuals asserted that the message they proclaimed was not theirs but that of the God who sent them.

Tragically, then as now, the word of the Lord was often not heeded. Jeremiah 25 summarizes his people's refusal to listen and the sad consequences for the nation:

> though the LORD has sent all his servants the prophets to you again and again, you have not listened or paid any attention. . . . Therefore the LORD

1. This is assuming the traditional sixth-century date for the prophet Daniel. This issue will be discussed further below.

2. Surprisingly, the phrase "Hear the word of the LORD" occurs only once in the Major Prophets in an oracle addressing a foreign nation (Ezek. 25:3; cf. also Jer. 31:10). It is unclear, however, that the prophet Ezekiel delivered this message directly to the Ammonites.

3. This phrase occurs thirty times in the Major Prophets (four times in Isaiah; 15 in Jeremiah; 11 in Ezekiel).

All biblical quotations are taken from the NIV (1984) unless otherwise noted.

Almighty says this: ". . . I will summon all the peoples of the north and my servant Nebuchadnezzar king of Babylon," declares the LORD, "and I will bring them against this land and its inhabitants and against all the surrounding nations. I will completely destroy them and make them an object of horror and scorn, and an everlasting ruin." (Jer. 25:4, 8-9; cf. 2 Kings 17:13-20)

The failure to hear is related to a failure to believe God and metaphorically related to being "stiff-necked" — a chronic ailment of the Israelites (cf. Exod. 33:5; Jer. 7:25-26). Thus the people's ongoing refusal to heed Jeremiah's prophetic warning is anticipated: "When you tell them all this, they will not listen to you; when you call to them, they will not answer" (Jer. 7:27). More than a century earlier, the prophet Isaiah faced an even more daunting task: his proclamation would serve rather to reduce the people's receptivity to God's word (Isa. 6:9-10). Since God's paradoxical plan required the decimation of the "holy seed" *prior to* its restoration (6:11-13), Isaiah was to harden his audience by means of his proclamation.[4] And future audiences would respond similarly to an even greater prophet (cf. Matt. 13:13-15; John 12:39-40)!

Richard Briggs takes Isaiah 6 as a paradigmatic text illustrating the "virtue of receptivity" to "the summoning presence" of God, a virtue that should be cultivated by modern readers of Scripture.[5] He advocates a kind of "self-involvement," an engagement with the realities that the prophets address and a "willingness to be summoned by the God of Christian (or in a different framework, Jewish) faith."[6] Unlike Isaiah, notes Briggs, too few modern readers of Isaiah 6 come to a similar "appreciation (if not an experience) of the holiness of God."[7]

Unfortunately, when it comes to the Major Prophets, modern listeners are still rather hard of hearing. Evangelical author Philip Yancey suggests that the Bibles of most Christians, even committed believers, have "a telltale band of white on the paper edges just over halfway through, a mark of cleanness indicating how seldom fingers touch the Old Testament Prophets."[8]

---

4. See Torsten Uhlig, *The Theme of Hardening in the Book of Isaiah,* FAT 2, 39 (Tübingen: Mohr Siebeck, 2009), p. 317.

5. Richard S. Briggs, *The Virtuous Reader: Old Testament Narrative and Interpretive Virtue,* Studies in Theological Interpretation (Grand Rapids: Baker Academic, 2010), p. 167. Although Briggs is presenting reading virtues, the prophets and their first audiences exhibited "receptivity" (or the lack thereof) through listening, not reading.

6. Briggs, *Virtuous Reader,* pp. 191n.27 and 120.

7. Briggs, *Virtuous Reader,* p. 182.

8. Philip Yancey, *The Bible Jesus Read* (Grand Rapids: Zondervan, 1999), p. 171.

And even when heard, the prophets are heard rather selectively, as determined by the hearer's special interest, whether she is an "end-times" buff, a "Jesus on every page of the Old Testament" christocentrist, or a social justice advocate.

What are the major challenges in hearing the Major Prophets today? First of all, as just mentioned, the selective interests of some listeners may make them tone deaf to other prophetic themes, regardless of their prominence within the corpus. In fact, the popular exploitation of some prophetic features may lead others to avoid this genre completely. Second, the listener's lack of familiarity with the historical-cultural world into which the prophets are speaking can result in cognitive dissonance comparable to overhearing a conversation regarding an unfamiliar technical topic. Third, the profuse use of vivid figurative expressions to portray current and future events can lure the hearer into pondering the medium rather than the message. Finally, the anthology-like collections of prophetic oracles in the canonical books sometimes defy efforts to identify a logical or chronological development, making it difficult to determine precisely what the prophet is seeking to communicate. Some historical-critical scholars have taken this to an extreme, as exemplified by Robert Carroll's essay advocating "Dismantling the Book of Jeremiah and Deconstructing the Prophet."[9] As a result of this procedure, one can no longer hear the prophetic voice, much less the word of God!

Despite these difficulties, it would be a great loss if we were to fail today to hear the Major Prophets — constituting more than one-fifth of the Old Testament — as interpreters of *torah,* advocates of the oppressed, and predictors of the future.[10] The community of faith is inexcusably impoverished if it fails to heed the repeated canonical claim that "Thus says the LORD."[11]

9. Robert P. Carroll, "Dismantling the Book of Jeremiah and Deconstructing the Prophet," in *"Wünschet Jerusalem Frieden": Collected Communications to the XIIth Congress of the International Organization for the Study of the Old Testament, Jerusalem 1986,* ed. Matthias Augustin and Klaus-Dietrich Schunck, BEATAJ 13 (Frankfurt: Peter Lang, 1988), p. 291.

10. J. J. M. Roberts ("A Christian Perspective on Prophetic Prediction," in *The Bible and the Ancient Near East: Collected Essays,* ed. J. J. M. Roberts [Winona Lake, IN: Eisenbrauns, 2002], p. 406) defends the importance of "prediction" in biblical prophecy, claiming that the common pronouncement that "prophets are forthtellers, not foretellers" has gone "out of fashion."

11. According to Abraham Heschel, *The Prophets: An Introduction* (New York: Harper & Row, 1962), 1:xii, "[t]he situation of a person immersed in the prophets' words is one of being exposed to a ceaseless shattering of indifference, and one needs a skull of stone to remain callous to such blows."

Foundational Issues: "My Ears You Have Opened" (Psalm 40:6, TNIV)[12]

In the initial chapter of this book, Craig Bartholomew commends a trinitarian hermeneutic. The Major Prophets, perhaps more so than any other Old Testament corpus, readily accommodate such an approach. In a very real sense, the Major Prophets are strikingly trinitarian. First of all, their message is christocentric, repeatedly looking beyond the ongoing series of political and military crises and the spiritual malaise that marked the Israelite monarchy, as well as the devastating humiliation of exile, to the coming of a Davidic heir and just ruler who would succeed where his predecessors had failed and would therefore enable Israel to experience the covenantal blessings that they frequently forfeited through disobedience. Otfried Hofius includes among the messianic texts, which describe Israel's eschatological salvation-bringing king, Isaiah 9:1-6; 11:1-9, 10; Jeremiah 23:5-6; 30:8-9; 33:14-16; and Ezekiel 17:22-24; 34:22-23; 37:15-28; but he excludes Daniel 7:13-14 as a collective figure.[13] Klaus-Dietrich Schunck, however, presents the Messiah's status as apocalyptic "son of man" in Daniel 7 as his highest and climactic attribute: here one sees an exalted, eternal ruler representing YHWH himself.[14]

To be sure, the degree to which the New Testament authors' understandings of Jesus' earthly ministry correspond to — or expand upon and modify — the Old Testament's messianic anticipation is disputed. But they frequently cite such texts to explain Jesus' mission and, surprisingly, also attribute to him various activities associated with God himself in the Old Testament (compare Ezek. 34:11 with Luke 15:1-7; 19:10; Isa. 35:4-6 with Matt. 11:5; and Isa. 52:10 with Luke 2:30-31).

Second, the Major Prophets refer more frequently to God as "Father" than other sections of the Old Testament (e.g., Isa. 9:6; 63:16; 64:8; Jer. 3:4, 19; cf. Mal. 1:6; 2:10). Finally, the Spirit is instrumentally involved in the ministries of the prophets and the future Davidic king (e.g., Isa. 11:2; 32:15; 34:16; 42:1; 44:3; 48:16; 59:21; 61:1; 63:10, 11, 14; Ezek. 2:2; 3:12, 14, 24; 8:3; 11:1, 5, 24;

---

12. The Old Testament also speaks of God "uncovering" the prophet's ear; cf. 1 Sam. 9:15 and Isa. 22:14.

13. Otfried Hofius, "Ist Jesus der Messias? Thesen," in *Der Messias*, ed. Ingo Baldermann et al., Jahrbuch für biblische Theologie 8 (Neukirchen-Vluyn: Neukirchener, 1993), pp. 110-11.

14. Klaus-Dietrich Schunck, "Die Attribute des eschatologischen Messias: Strukturlinien in der Ausprägung des alttestamentlichen Messiasbildes," *Theologische Literaturzeitung* 111 (September 1986): 650.

36:27; 37:1, 14; 39:29; 43:5). The Major Prophets should be heard as a message regarding the triune God's will and plan for humanity — with a special focus on Israel.

Old Testament prophecy is the biblical genre that most explicitly claims divine inspiration. As John Goldingay expresses it: "It is the prophets who characteristically claim to speak under divine prompting and to speak words framed by God rather than by them. Paul begins 'I Paul . . .'; they begin 'thus says Yahweh.'"[15] In other words, when hearing the Major Prophets, one is hearing the God of Israel. It is worth noting how frequently the prophets shift between directly and indirectly proclaiming the divine message. For example, Isaiah 1 and 3 are marked by the use of first-person references to the deity and related introductory formulae (e.g., 1:2-3, 11-16, 18, 20, 24-26; 3:1, 15, 16), while Isaiah 2 relates the prophet's vision and his message to the people using third-person references to God, as well as his personal responses (vv. 5, 10-11, 21). But Isaiah 2 is no less the word of God than chapters 1 and 3. Gordon Fee and Douglas Stuart remind us that, even when fulfilling their characteristic role as "covenant enforcement mediators," the prophets "did not invent the blessings or curses they announced. . . . [T]hey reproduced *God's* Word, not their own."[16]

The preceding brief analysis of Isaiah 1–3 suggests that, unlike the ancient Israelites, we hear the Word of God today through the Major Prophets by attentively reading the canonical books associated with them. This is certainly a disputed claim. For more than a century, critical scholarship has employed various analytical tools to "dismantle" the prophetic books, not in order to "deconstruct" but in order to "discover" the genuine prophetic voices within them. Ever since some scholars concluded that the prophetic books contained much material that did not originate with the traditional prophets, a concerted effort has been made to separate the prophetic wheat from the redactional chaff.

The relative amount of "chaff" claimed in the individual Major Prophets varies. Although Bernhard Duhm at the end of the nineteenth century popularized the distinction between First, Second, and Third Isaiah, most critical scholars today consider most of "First" Isaiah (i.e., chs. 1–

---

15. John Goldingay, *Models for Scripture* (Grand Rapids: Eerdmans, 1994), p. 205.

16. Gordon D. Fee and Douglas Stuart, *How to Read the Bible for All Its Worth*, 3rd ed. (Grand Rapids: Zondervan, 2003), pp. 184-85. Nicholas Wolterstorff, *Divine Discourse: Philosophical Reflections on the Claim That God Speaks* (Cambridge: Cambridge University Press, 1995), pp. 42-51, refers to this as "deputized discourse," in which the biblical prophet plays a role comparable to a foreign ambassador.

39) to be secondary as well, some of them limiting the contribution of the eighth-century prophet to a few hundred verses or less. In the case of Jeremiah, scholars commonly distinguish between the poems, the prose sermons, and the prophetic narratives, locating the "voice" of Jeremiah only in some of the poems. Ezekiel has fared somewhat better, with most of the book being attributed to the prophet or his immediate circle of "disciples." In Daniel, however, the traditional prophet virtually vanishes amid fictional narratives and pseudo-prophecies composed after the events they supposedly predict.

How should one seek to hear the Major Prophets in light of this assessment? One option is to continue the quest for the historical prophet.[17] A second option is to argue that the traditional prophet could be the source of most of what is contained in the present canonical book by harmonizing divergent portrayals of the prophet, his message, and his audiences' attitudes and status.[18] Such an effort is likely to be dismissed by some as "both misleading and destructive of intelligible [*sic*] exegesis."[19] Furthermore, even demonstrating that a text could have originated with the traditional prophet does not prove that it actually did.

Rather than viewing the Minor Prophets merely as loosely edited anthologies of prophetic oracles, elaborative commentaries, and narratives, a third — and preferable — option is to read them as Scripture, hearing therein the divine address. Some scholars view such an approach as illegitimate[20] — despite the precedent of the practice of the community of faith for two millennia — or as comparable to reading the Major Prophets simply as a guide to the "end times." Adopting such a hermeneutical stance, however, is not arbitrary. For more than three decades, Brevard Childs and others have sought to demonstrate that those who shaped the final form of the prophetic books edited them with a view to their ongoing use by the community of faith. These so-called "canoniclers" deliberately kept these texts open to future appropriations rather than assigning them to the past as "archives" of Israel's religious

---

17. H. G. M. Williamson, "In Search of the Pre-Exilic Isaiah," in *In Search of Pre-Exilic Israel*, ed. John Day, JSOTSup 406 (London: T&T Clark, 2004), pp. 181-206.

18. See the discussion in Richard L. Schultz, "How Many Isaiahs Were There and What Does It Matter? Prophetic Inspiration in Recent Evangelical Scholarship," in *Scripture in the Evangelical Tradition: Tradition, Authority, and Hermeneutics*, ed. Vincent Bacote, Laura C. Miguelez, and Dennis L. Okholm (Downers Grove: IVP, 2004), pp. 150-70.

19. Carroll, "Dismantling the Book of Jeremiah," p. 297.

20. Carroll ("Dismantling the Book of Jeremiah," p. 302, n. 22) would probably dismiss this as "developing alien dogmatic positions inimical to sound scholarship"!

experiences.[21] This approach also prevents us from regarding the Major Prophets simply as a record of ancient divine "speech acts," instead facilitating our continued hearing of God's Word today.

In discussing how to read the Latter Prophets in accordance with what he calls "new canonical criticism," Edgar Conrad draws on Umberto Eco's semiotic theory.[22] He concludes that, "[w]hile we have no access to the real authors of prophetic books, we can imagine a Model Author who composed a text to communicate to readers."[23] Although this is not necessarily Conrad's approach, we can understand this "Model Author" as the canonical author/editor or, better yet, as the divine author who speaks to us through these books, not simply through the "genuine" words of the named prophets, but through the entire text of the Major Prophets taken as a whole.[24]

The problem with such a holistic "final form" canonical or Model Author approach, as Gordon McConville has noted, is that there is "a significant shift away from the authentic voice of the prophet to the way in which the prophet continued to be heard in the community that remembered his words as mediated by a tradition."[25] McConville is not opposed to a focus on

21. Brevard S. Childs, "The Canonical Shape of the Prophetic Literature," *Int* 32 (1978): 46-55, is one of the earliest efforts to describe this process. Editorial strategies that he notes include subordinating the original historical setting to a larger theological framework or reorienting an oracle toward an eschatological fulfillment.

22. Edgar W. Conrad, *Reading the Latter Prophets: Towards a New Canonical Criticism*, JSOTSup 376 (London: T&T Clark, 2003). See also his *Reading Isaiah*, OBT (Minneapolis: Fortress, 1991); Peter D. Quinn-Miscall, *Reading Isaiah: Poetry and Vision* (Louisville: Westminster John Knox, 2001); Christopher R. Seitz, ed., *Reading and Preaching the Book of Isaiah* (Philadelphia: Fortress, 1988). These works, however, offer divergent understandings of what "reading" the Prophets entails. Conrad's guidelines include reading the Latter Prophets "as a continuation of the Former Prophets" and "as literary wholes . . . compiled with the purpose of communicating," reading each individual book "according to its order and arrangement," and reading the entire corpus in its canonical order, reflecting on "the significance of that order for arriving at meaning," while drawing on assumed "intertextual knowledge" in the process (*Reading the Latter Prophets*, pp. 1, 3, 27-28).

23. Conrad, *Reading the Latter Prophets*, p. 30.

24. In reading the Prophets, it is methodologically problematic to be told by members of the scholarly guild that one *must* view divergent "voices" identified within the individual prophetic books as contradictory and irreconcilable rather than as contextually warranted and potentially complementary perspectives within the divine author's communicative intentions.

25. Gordon McConville, "Divine Speech and the Book of Jeremiah," in *The Trustworthiness of God: Perspectives on the Nature of Scripture*, ed. Paul Helm and Carl R. Trueman (Grand Rapids: Eerdmans, 2002), p. 20. The entire essay, pp. 18-38, offers an extended argu-

the prophetic book, as long as one keeps in mind that it was the authoritative ministry of the prophet that gave rise to the book; the very preservation and ultimate canonization of the record of that ministry bear testimony to that fact. Both the "messages"[26] and the narratives point back to that ministry, as do any later elaborative or explanatory additions, regardless of whose "interpretive" work these represent. Thus, according to McConville, the "original speech event of the prophet is now carried in the book, in full cognizance of the fact that the outcome of the first event was a failure to respond." Paradoxically, the Major Prophets continue to issue "prophetic calls for response, while being themselves records of nonresponse."[27]

A Brief Early History of Hearing the Major Prophets

A history of hearing the divine Word through the Major Prophets must begin within the Old Testament period itself. According to the canonical witness, the prophets' earliest audiences displayed varying degrees of receptivity. Furthermore, the Hebrew Bible indicates that the writing prophets were familiar with and interpreted or reapplied the work of their prophetic predecessors. For example, Daniel ponders Jeremiah's prophecy about the seventy years of Jerusalem's desolation and refers to this as an authoritative "word of the LORD" recorded "in the books" (NRSV; NIV: "Scriptures"; Dan. 9:2; cf. Eccles. 12:12). Interestingly, the LXX version of Jeremiah 25:11-12, which first mentions the "seventy years" of desolation, makes no mention of "Babylon" (likely reflecting a different Hebrew text). The LXX reading more readily facilitates the angelic messenger's symbolic (re)interpretation of this period of desolation. The author of Chronicles also refers to this prophecy in connection with the Babylonian Exile, referring to it as "the word of the LORD by the mouth of Jeremiah" (2 Chron. 36:21, NASB). Another striking example is found in the book of Zechariah, which begins with the warning not to repeat the ancestors' failure to heed the former prophets' call to repentance (Zech.

---

ment for how the divine Word first uttered through the prophet can be "heard" through reading the canonical book associated with him.

26. Form critics usually speak of prophetic "oracles." This designation is problematic in two respects: (1) the word "oracle" is associated with oral proclamation, but scholars believe that some prophecies existed only in written form; (2) we now have access only to written prophetic texts, in which it is often quite difficult to determine, even using established form-critical criteria, where a specific oracle begins and ends.

27. McConville, "Divine Speech," p. 27.

1:4). This text most likely echoes the words of Jeremiah 25:3-5, in which the prophet declares that the "word of the LORD" to him is consistent with the words of "all his servants the prophets."

Such texts reflect what John Barton describes as a remarkable shift in the perception of the prophets between the preexilic and postexilic eras: "For pre-exilic Israel, the classical prophets were eccentrics, strange and alarming figures. . . . For post-exilic Judaism . . . the prophets were characters in a book written by the finger of God."[28] Sirach's description of Isaiah's message clearly reflects this attitude: "By his dauntless spirit he saw the future, and comforted the mourners in Zion. He revealed what was to occur to the end of time and the hidden things before they happened" (Sir. 48:24-25, NRSV).[29] The appropriation of the Major Prophets by the New Testament authors, which is both extensive and diverse, also reflects this way of thinking. Isaiah (419 times) is the most frequently cited Old Testament book, while Ezekiel (141 times), Daniel (133 times), and Jeremiah (125 times) rank sixth through eighth, respectively. In terms of individual verses, Daniel 12:1 is the most frequently cited verse (13 times), followed by Isaiah 6:1 (12 times), with Isaiah 53:7 (10 times) tied for sixth.[30] And Jeremiah 31 is the source of the longest citation, in Hebrews 8:8-12; a shorter citation of the same text in Hebrews 10:15-17 is introduced by "The Holy Spirit also testifies to us about this. First he says: . . ."

It is certainly not the case that the New Testament authors simply employ the Major Prophets according to a narrow prophecy-fulfillment schema. For example, the explicit quotations of Isaiah fall into five categories: texts (1) presented as fulfilled in Jesus, (2) applied or transferred (usually from YHWH) to Jesus, (3) relating to the end of salvation history and the "last things," (4) applied to Christian life or doctrine, or (5) suggesting parallels between events or Israel's conduct in the Old Testament and in the New.[31] Vital to any systematic effort to hear the Major Prophets today is the careful examination of how the inspired New Testament authors and (according to their authoritative testi-

---

28. John Barton, *Oracles of God: Perceptions of Ancient Prophecy in Israel after the Exile* (New York: Oxford University Press, 1986), pp. 268-69.

29. Contra Barton, *Oracles of God,* pp. 132-33.

30. Andrew E. Hill, *Baker's Handbook of Bible Lists* (Grand Rapids: Baker, 1981), pp. 102-3. These numbers include both quotations and allusions. Frequency statistics cited in other sources may differ.

31. See Richard L. Schultz, "Isaiah," in *Theological Interpretation of the Old Testament: A Book-by-Book Survey,* ed. Kevin J. Vanhoozer (Grand Rapids: Baker, 2007), pp. 205-6, for a listing of the texts in these categories and a fuller discussion of Isaiah's impact on the New Testament.

mony) Jesus heard the Major Prophets — not as a place for mining isolated "prooftexts," but as offering the foundation and theological substructure of the New Testament gospel of Jesus Christ and its proclamation to the nations. The Major Prophets also help us to understand the earthly ministry of Jesus, since he is portrayed as the ultimate Israelite prophet.[32]

In his chapter on biblical theology and the Old Testament, Mark Boda traces the "inner-biblical connectivity" of the "routes" leading from the Old Testament to the New, noting various ways in which the former is affirmed, surpassed, fulfilled, re-actualized, and continued in the latter. (See Chapter 6 by Mark Boda in the present volume.) The New Testament writers identify Jesus as the promised Davidic ruler (Matt. 4:13-16; Luke 1:79) and the Isaianic servant (Matt. 8:17; 1 Pet. 2:21-25), whose followers continue the task of being "a light to the Gentiles" (Acts 13:46). The New Testament also associates Jesus with the Danielic Son of Man who will come in the clouds (Mark 13:36). With his arrival, a new exodus is announced (Isa. 40; cf. Mark 1); in his death and resurrection, the new covenant is initiated and an inner transformation through the Spirit is made possible (Jer. 31:31-34; cf. Heb. 8:7-12; Ezek. 36:25-27; cf. 2 Cor. 3:6). The book of Revelation appropriates the eschatological-apocalyptic vision of the Major Prophets, most notably in portraying the new heavens and new earth (from Isaiah), the doom of Babylon (from Jeremiah), the heavenly temple (from Ezekiel), and the vision of the beasts and the coming of the Son of Man (from Daniel). Although it may be useful hermeneutically to distinguish between the typological, figural, analogical, and prediction-fulfillment usages of the Major Prophets, the bottom line is the same: in the eyes of the New Testament authors, what the prophets envisioned at a distance was now coming to pass in and through Jesus Christ.

Cleaning Out the Wax: On Mishearing the Major Prophets

In the initial post-biblical centuries, the church followed in the footsteps of the New Testament authors as they sought to hear the Major Prophets. In the second century, for example, Justin Martyr offers this description of the Hebrew prophets: "There were, then, among the Jews certain men who were prophets of God, through whom the prophetic Spirit published beforehand

---

32. See especially N. T. Wright, *Jesus and the Victory of God: Christian Origins and the Question of God* (Minneapolis: Fortress, 1996), pp. 145-457, Part Two: "Profile of a Prophet"; and Ben Witherington III, *Jesus the Seer: The Progress of Prophecy* (Peabody, MA: Hendrickson, 1999), both of whom view Jesus *primarily* as a prophet.

things that were to come to pass, ere ever they happened."[33] As Brevard Childs ably demonstrates in his sweeping analysis of the reception history of the book of Isaiah, the hermeneutical "struggle" was not in hearing the voice of God in the prophetic writings; there was a broad consensus regarding the authoritative status of the words of these divinely inspired spokespersons. While there was considerable diversity of opinion with respect to how to understand the literal and spiritual senses of the text, the struggle primarily concerned how to understand the prophetic books "as Christian Scripture," ultimately "the question of how to do justice to the relationship between the two canonical portions of its scripture."[34]

In the modern era, however, idiosyncratic ways of hearing the prophets (or specific prophetic texts) have sometimes made those attending to them "hard of hearing" with respect to the central themes of this corpus, as well as to the primary emphases of individual texts. Not surprisingly, the peace movement, especially those working toward nuclear disarmament, has turned repeatedly to the "swords into plowshares" vision of Isaiah 2 (although sometimes ignoring the nearly identical parallel text, Micah 4). In the mid-1980s, several German theologians engaged in an exchange regarding the validity of the church's appropriation of this text. Trutz Rendtorff claims that theologians can support either disarmament (Isa. 2 // Mic. 4) or armament (Joel 4 [3] — plowshares into swords!) from the prophets. Hans Walter Wolff sees in Isaiah 2 // Micah 4 an unmistakable charge to the church to pursue peace. And Wolfhart Pannenberg charges both positions with ignoring the crucial role of God's instruction in justice and binding mediation between nations.[35] Neglecting the divine

---

33. Justin Martyr, "The First Apology of Justin Martyr," in *The Ante-Nicene Fathers,* ed. Alexander Roberts and James Donaldson (Grand Rapids: Eerdmans, 1973), 1:173 (= Ch. XXXI).

34. Brevard S. Childs, *The Struggle to Understand Isaiah as Christian Scripture* (Grand Rapids: Eerdmans, 2004), p. 308.

35. Hans Walter Wolff, "Schwerter zu Pflugscharen — Mißbrauch eines Prophetenwortes? Praktische Fragen und exegetische Klärungen zu Joël 4,9-12, Jes 2,2-5 und Mi 4,1-5," *Evangelische Theologie* 44 (1984): 280-92; Wolfhart Pannenberg, "Diskussionsbeitrag," *EvTh* 44 (1984): 293-97. For a summary of the reception history of these texts, see James Limburg, "Swords to Plowshares: Text and Contexts," in *Writing and Reading the Scroll of Isaiah: Studies of an Interpretive Tradition,* ed. Craig C. Broyles and Craig A. Evans, VTSup 70 (Leiden: Brill, 1997), 1:279-93. See also the papers from a 2005 colloquium, published as Raymond Cohen and Raymond Westbrook, eds., *Isaiah's Vision of Peace in Biblical and Modern International Relations: Swords into Plowshares,* Culture and Religion in International Relations (New York: Palgrave Macmillan, 2008).

involvement in this vision of Zion's future exaltation results in mishearing Isaiah.

One could easily multiply examples of how contemporary interpreters mishear the Major Prophets. Prohibitionists and teetotalers find in the Rechabites of Jeremiah 35 a divinely commended model for their stance; one temperance movement, the Independent Order of Rechabites, established in England in 1835, even derived its name from them. As Gerald Keown has correctly noted, however, "Jeremiah makes no attempt to hold up the lifestyle of the Rechabites as a model for Judah. He does not call for abstention from wine for the nation."[36] Rather, Jeremiah uses them to contrast their long-term loyalty to a human ancestor with Judah's unwillingness to hear and heed the prophets (Jer. 35:12-16). As another example, according to a UFO "expert," the initial vision of Ezekiel (Ezek. 1:1-28) "does fit in very well with descriptions of flying saucers," giving him "contact with the angels of God."[37]

Others have heard in Daniel 1 only a "biblical" fast promoting spiritual renewal,[38] although it is hardly clear that this outstanding exiled Israelite youth was personally in need of renewal. Those less inclined to adopt a vegan diet but still committed to "hearing" Daniel could choose instead to join the "Left Behind Prophecy Club" — if it had not been discontinued! One prophetic "fan club" may have died, but certainly not the tendency to mishear the Major Prophets as functioning primarily to predict the future, supplying the raw data for constructing "end times" charts. Paul Boyer has thoroughly documented how deeply entrenched prophecy belief is in modern American culture — and has been since the founding of the nation. After reading "some one hundred pre-1945 prophecy books and over two hundred published since 1945, Boyer concludes that, within 'the vast subculture of . . . U.S. evangelicalism, . . . the conviction that God's plan for human history lies encrypted in ancient biblical texts remains very much alive.'"[39]

---

36. Gerald L. Keown, Pamela J. Scalise, and Thomas G. Smothers, *Jeremiah 26–52*, WBC 27 (Dallas: Word, 1995), p. 198. Regarding the modern Rechabite movement, see Lilian Lewis Shiman, *Crusade against Drink in Victorian England* (London: Macmillan, 1998), pp. 175-78.

37. Barry H. Downing, *The Bible and Flying Saucers* (New York: Avon, 1968), pp. 105-6. Downing relates the UFO encountered by Ezekiel to the one by which God parted the Red Sea and led the Israelites throughout their wilderness years, pp. 67-100.

38. See especially Elmer E. Towns, *The Daniel Fast for Spiritual Breakthrough* (Ventura: Regal, 2010), and Grace Bass and Lynda Anderson, *The Daniel's Fast Cookbook* (Brooklyn: A&B Publishers, 2008).

39. Paul Boyer, *When Time Shall Be No More: Prophecy Belief in Modern American Culture* (Cambridge, MA: Harvard University Press, 1992), pp. xiii, 339.

This is unfortunate, for such an emphasis tends to ignore the comprehensive nature of the Major Prophets' proclamation as they castigate both political and religious leaders, accusing the former of trusting in military armaments and alliances rather than in God and the latter of promoting empty ritual while exhibiting self-aggrandizement. At the same time, the prophets criticize their fellow citizens for a wide range of sins, social abuses, and repugnant attitudes, including blatant idolatry, greedy land-grabbing, violence, drunkenness, oppression of widows and orphans, perversion of justice, and arrogant pride. The scope of these topics suggests that the prophetic rebuke may be applied to various social ills and human inclinations that plague society today, including excessive reliance on other humans (Isa. 2:22), hypocritical religious ceremony (Isa. 1:10-17; Jer. 7:1-15), sexual perversion (Ezek. 22:10-11), the self-exalting and God-defying attitudes of world rulers (Dan. 5:18-24), and even, though less directly, exploitation of the nonhuman creation.[40] The oracles condemning the actions and attitudes of foreign nations (i.e., Isa. 13–23; Jer. 46–51; and Ezek. 25–32) offer an intriguing resource for contemplating how we can hear God's ethical demands on secular nations today. Yet the contemporary community of faith would also do well to give attention to the biting rebukes of the Major Prophets, since we are just as plagued by arrogance, self-reliance, and complacency as the ancient Israelites were.[41]

40. See Hilary Marlow, *Biblical Prophets and Contemporary Environmental Ethics* (Oxford: Oxford University Press, 2009).

41. There are a number of valuable studies of prophetic ethics, exploring their grounding in both covenantal and natural law. See, for example, Olof Bäckerstein, *Isaiah's Political Message: An Appraisal of His Alleged Social Critique*, FAT 2, 29 (Tübingen: Mohr Siebeck, 2008); John Barton, *Understanding Old Testament Ethics: Approaches and Explorations* (London: Westminster John Knox, 2003); Andrew Davies, *Double Standards in Isaiah: Re-evaluating Prophetic Ethics and Divine Justice* (Leiden: Brill, 2000); Eryl W. Davies, *Prophecy and Ethics: Isaiah and the Ethical Traditions of Israel* (Sheffield: JSOT Press, 1981); Michael A. Lyons, *From Law to Prophecy: Ezekiel's Use of the Holiness Code*, Library of Hebrew Bible/Old Testament Studies 507 (New York: T&T Clark, 2009); Christl Maier, *Jeremia als Lehrer der Tora: Soziale Gebote des Deuteronomiums in Fortschreibungen des Jeremiabuches*, FRLANT 196 (Göttingen: Vandenhoeck & Ruprecht, 2002); and Andrew Mein, *Ezekiel and the Ethics of Exile*, Oxford Theological Monographs (Oxford: Oxford University Press, 2001). Bäckerstein and Andrew Davies question some fundamental ethical assumptions and conclusions of previous studies.

Two Canonical Quartets

In order to hear the prophets properly today, the reader must begin by understanding the canonical shape of the prophetic corpus. Here one encounters two canonical "quartets" — the Hebrew corpus, consisting of Isaiah, Jeremiah, Ezekiel, and the Book of the Twelve (although not always in that order),[42] and modern Bibles, which, like the earlier Greek and Latin versions, include Daniel as the fourth Major Prophet, followed by the Minor Prophets printed as twelve individual books. Those accustomed to modern Bibles, which separate the "historical" books from the "prophetic," may miss the significance of the Hebrew canon's use of the designation "Prophets" to refer to Joshua, Judges, Samuel, and Kings, as well as to Isaiah, Jeremiah, Ezekiel, and the Twelve (later distinguishing between "Former" and "Latter" Prophets). Thus the repeated expression "the Law and the Prophets" (Matt. 7:12; 11:13; 22:40; Luke 16:16; cf. 24:27, 44; John 1:45; Acts 13:15; 24:14; 28:23; Rom. 3:21)[43] serves to affirm the foundational nature of these two groups of books — and the integral relationship between them — within the Hebrew canon. The latter corpus serves to interpret and apply the former, and the covenantal commitments of the former are the source for most of the threats and promises in the latter.[44] Stephen Chapman suggests that, especially within Jeremiah, the divine "Law" and "words" as proclaimed by the prophets represent "twin sources of authority" and may even "refer to the emerging collections of scripture that later became" the Law and the Prophets.[45]

---

42. See the canonical lists in Roger Beckwith, *The Old Testament Canon of the New Testament Church and Its Background in Early Judaism* (Grand Rapids: Eerdmans, 1985), pp. 194, 450-51. We will say little about the relationship between the Major and Minor Prophets, since there is a separate chapter in this volume devoted to the latter; see Chapter 15 by Heath Thomas.

43. According to Christopher R. Seitz, *The Goodly Fellowship of the Prophets: The Achievement of Association in Canon Formation* (Grand Rapids: Baker Academic, 2009), p. 94, the same expression is found in Ben Sira's Prologue, Tertullian, and Qumran. Seitz acknowledges, however, that the designation "Prophets" here may also include the Old Testament "Writings."

44. See Fee and Stuart, *How to Read the Bible*, pp. 184-89. It is striking that the Latter Prophets (in their current ordering) begin with a reference to "the law of our God" in Isa. 1:10 and conclude with a reference to "the law of my servant Moses" in Mal. 4:4 (both Heb. *torah*).

45. Stephen B. Chapman, *The Law and the Prophets: A Study in Old Testament Canon Formation*, FAT 27 (Tübingen: Mohr Siebeck, 2000), pp. 204-5. According to Gene M. Tucker, "Prophetic Superscriptions and the Growth of a Canon," in *Canon and Authority: Essays in Old Testament Religion and Theology*, ed. George W. Coats and Burke O. Long

It is also important for us to hear the Former and Latter Prophets together, since there are striking intertextual connections between them. These include the parallel texts 2 Kings 18–20 // Isaiah 36–39 and 2 Kings 25 // Jeremiah 52, and the repeated references in the Latter Prophets to the Davidic covenant of 2 Samuel 7 and the future Davidic ruler, as well as the prophetic superscriptions that associate the prophets with the reigns of particular Israelite kings. According to Christopher Seitz, these superscriptions "clearly intend us to read the witness of the individual prophetic works in the light of the Prophetic History, and vice versa."[46]

Stephen Dempster indicates what hearing the Former and Latter Prophets together would sound like: "When these prophetic texts are used to help to interpret the narrative storyline that has led to the dead end of exile in Babylon, instead of being regarded as books of doom and gloom they inspire hope and comfort."[47] The prophetic history offers further illustrations of how the prophets interacted with Israelite leaders, the kinds of responses they encountered, and how their words were fulfilled. The Latter Prophets emphasize their continuity with the Former Prophets by their repeated phrase "my servants the prophets" (Jer. 7:25; 26:5; 29:19; 35:15; 44:4; Ezek. 38:17; Zech. 1:6; cf. 2 Kings 9:7; 17:13; also 17:23; 21:10; 24:2). These references to the prophets, as well as those in Kings and in the New Testament (e.g., Acts 3:18, 24; 1 Peter 1:10-12), regard the prophets "as having proclaimed a unified message," and the New Testament identifies this message "as one concerning the era of salvation which the New Testament writers now regard as having dawned."[48] It is not easy for the modern (or modernist) student who has been trained to listen for jarring theological diversity and discord within and between the two Testaments to hear such canonical harmony!

(Philadelphia: Fortress, 1977), p. 70, the prophetic superscriptions point in the same direction: "The collectors and redactors of the prophetic tradition — early and late — began to interpret the words attributed to the prophets as a written form of divine revelation."

46. Seitz, *Goodly Fellowship*, p. 28.

47. Stephen G. Dempster, *Dominion and Dynasty: A Theology of the Hebrew Bible,* New Studies in Biblical Theology (Downers Grove: IVP, 2003), p. 188. This thematic development emerges more clearly if one considers Jeremiah as coming immediately after Kings, following the order of the prophets in the Talmudic tractate *Baba Batra* 14b, as Dempster does (pp. 35, 159-89).

48. Ronald E. Clements, "Patterns in the Prophetic Canon," in *Canon and Authority: Essays in Old Testament Religion and Theology,* ed. George W. Coats and Burke O. Long (Philadelphia: Fortress, 1977), p. 43. Clements concedes, somewhat ironically, that "it is precisely these features which modern literary-critical scholarship has found most difficult to accept" (p. 43).

The prophetic "quartet" in modern Bibles includes Daniel. There have been a number of reasons suggested for Daniel's exclusion from the Hebrew canonical prophetic collection, although the most likely is his description as a sage rather than a prophet — and not its purported late origin. Daniel's later inclusion among the Major Prophets is more easily explained, especially in light of Daniel's interpretive efforts in response to reading Jeremiah's prophecy of the "seventy years" in Daniel 9. This gives us three prophetic perspectives on the exilic period: Jeremiah from Jerusalem and Egypt, Ezekiel from a location outside the capital of Babylon, and Daniel from the power centers of the Babylonian and Medo-Persian empires. Are these different canonical collections hermeneutically significant? Dempster suggests that the Christian Old Testament, ending with the prophets, emphasizes eschatology, while the three subdivisions of Jewish Bibles emphasize ethics.[49] Regardless of whether this is the purpose of placing the Latter Prophets last, the effect of juxtaposing Malachi's announcement of the coming of the prophet Elijah (Mal. 4:5-6) with John the Baptist's coming in the opening chapters of all four Gospels "in the spirit and power of Elijah" (Luke 1:17) cannot be overlooked.

Hearing Therapy

Otherwise they might . . . hear with their ears, understand with their hearts, and turn and be healed. (Isa. 6:10)

In that day the deaf will hear the words of the scroll. (Isa. 29:18)

Hear the word of the LORD, you who tremble at his word. (Isa. 66:5)

In the course of the past century or so, a wide variety of methodologies have been developed to assist the biblical interpreter in understanding texts, including those of the Major Prophets. Some are diachronic in orientation, probing the world *behind* the text, as interpreters seek to reconstruct a particular text's oral origins and compositional growth (i.e., the world of the authors and editors who produced it) or to explain the social and cultural dynamics of prophecy, including the various roles assumed by prophets as intermediaries between the divine and human spheres and the function of

---

49. Chapter 7 by Stephen Dempster in the present volume. See Seitz's critique of this common contrast between the two canonical collections in *Goodly Fellowship*, pp. 92-95.

RICHARD SCHULTZ

their support groups. Others are synchronic, analyzing the world *of* the text, including its genre and literary and rhetorical features. Still others critically examine the world *in front of* the text — the world of the readers — exposing their cultural and individual values, blind spots, and prejudices.[50]

The methods in these three categories may help to overcome the "problems inherent in language itself" — that is, that language is "linear" (essential information is progressively revealed), "selective" (gaps in detail may result from an author's assumed knowledge or intentionally provoke reader participation), "ambiguous" (it generates diverse readings, which must be assessed), and "culturally embedded" (it is best understood by those sharing the author's culture and values).[51] But none of these methods necessarily helps us to hear the voice of God in the Major Prophets with a view to moving us toward "revising previously held views, to attitudinal shifts, to hearing . . . differently in the future, to new forms of behavior, or the like."[52]

Arnold Stiglmair helpfully sets forth three aspects of understanding the prophetic word as the Word of God, that is, as the self-communication of God to the believer through the medium of the biblical text. (This is encumbered by the common — but non-demonstrable — claim of biblical criticism that the prophetic books consist predominantly not of the inspired words of the prophets but of later reinterpretations and additions by members of the Israelite community.) First, in the prophetic word, the original audience heard God's Word in the prophet's gripping diagnosis of their situation, which challenged their faith in God and pressed them toward an unavoidable decision before God. Second, in the interpreted prophetic word, the Israelite community acknowledged its divine character as they increasingly drew on its power to overcome the diverse challenges and problems they faced. Third, in the prophetic books within their canonical context as holy Scripture, the prophetic word proves to be the Word of God by forming the horizon of understanding *(Verstehenshorizont)* for the entire Christ event, so the church cannot proclaim the work of God accomplished in Jesus without it.[53]

50. See Richard N. Soulen and R. Kendall Soulen, *Handbook of Biblical Criticism,* 3rd ed. (Louisville: Westminster John Knox, 2001), pp. 233-36.

51. Joel B. Green, "The Challenge of Hearing the New Testament," in *Hearing the New Testament: Strategies for Interpretation,* ed. Joel B. Green (Grand Rapids: Eerdmans, 1995), pp. 4-6.

52. Green, "Challenge of Hearing," p. 2. Green has reformulated this statement somewhat in the 2010 edition, p. 2.

53. Arnold Stiglmair, "'. . . So spricht Jahwe . . .' — Prophetenwort als Wort Gottes," in

The interpreter of the Major Prophets faces some unique challenges. According to Goldingay, "[t]he words of the prophets thus claim more explicitly than any other parts of Scripture to be words deriving from God; they also draw as much systematic attention to their human and historical origins as any part of scripture."[54] Form and redaction critics sometimes downplay the significance of narrative texts within the Major Prophets, labeling them prophetic "legends" or dismissing them as late additions from the Deuteronomistic history. To the extent that Marshall McLuhan's dictum, "the medium is the message," applies to the biblical prophets, we must give particular attention to what we are told about their personal struggles. That is, in serving as divine spokespersons, the prophetic experience itself — the pathos and pain, the betrayal and bullying — constitutes an integral part of their message.

Unlike some of the Minor Prophets, about whom we know virtually nothing, we are amply supplied with narrative descriptions of all four Major Prophets; we get to see them in action. We learn of their unsought call, of being dragged reluctantly into divine service and warned in advance of the recalcitrance of the people to whom they are being sent (Isa. 6:9-13; Jer. 1:17-19; Ezek. 3:4-9), which evokes great sorrow from them. They boldly confront their foes but experience no joy upon condemning them (see Isa. 15:5; 16:9; Jer. 48:31-32), and only a few individuals are described as forming their loyal support group (see Isa. 8:16; Jer. 36:8-10; 38:7-12). Jeremiah is condemned as a traitor, threatened with death, and repeatedly imprisoned, while Daniel is thrown to the lions for his unwavering loyalty to God. The prophet is not free to do as he pleases. Isaiah relates being divinely warned not to conform to the people's ways "with his strong hand upon me" (Isa. 8:11) and is instructed to go about Jerusalem "stripped and barefoot" (Isa. 20:2). Jeremiah is forbidden to marry and procreate, to mourn, or to feast (Jer. 16:1-9); Ezekiel is shuttled to and fro by the Spirit (Ezek. 8:3); and Daniel is terrified and troubled by visions (Dan. 7:7, 15; 8:17). At times, as in Isaiah's naked stroll and Ezekiel's numerous symbolic actions, the man literally becomes the message.[55] As noted above, in addition to interpreting the proclamation of the Major Prophets in light of the prophetic narratives, we must also read them in light of the events

---

Die alttestamentliche Botschaft als Wegweisung: Festschrift für Heinze Reinelt, ed. Josef Zmijewski (Stuttgart: Katholisches Bibelwerk, 1990), pp. 345-57.

54. Goldingay, *Models for Scripture,* p. 208.

55. See Kelvin Friebel, "A Hermeneutical Paradigm for Interpreting Prophetic Sign-Actions," *Didaskalia* 12 (2001): 25-45.

related in the canonical book of Kings. In sum, we must never lose sight of the human agent, despite our focus on hearing the divine voice.

How can we hear the words of the ancient prophets as the Word of God today when they were apparently so ineffective when first proclaimed? In his study *Prophecy and Discernment,* Walter Moberly correctly rejects Robert Carroll's supposition that "success in eliciting response should be a mark of verification of prophecy."[56] (Jonah's very success in Nineveh is an ironic exception to the "rule of rejection." Because his message provoked mass repentance, the threatened judgment was withdrawn, and Jonah appeared to be a false prophet!) Walter Houston turns to speech act theory to probe the phenomenon of prophetic discourse. Contrary to earlier studies that suggest that prophetic speech is "preternaturally powerful" (i.e., "capable of itself of accomplishing the thing of which it speaks"),[57] he contends that "as long as the prophets' hearers understood that they were warning them, calling for repentance . . . and understood the content of the warning . . . then the prophets had *done* what they set out to do, even if they had not achieved the effect they had hoped for."[58] In Houston's opinion, the preservation of the prophets' message and the existence of the prophetic books bear undeniable witness to the fact that someone recognized in them the authoritative voice of God, a voice that accordingly can still be heard today.

Prophetic narratives help us to identify the range of possible responses to oracles of doom (or salvation); these also represent "the actual range of responses whenever the prophetic words have been re-actualized and applied to contemporary situations by preachers in all ages."[59] The German theologian and martyr Dietrich Bonhoeffer vividly illustrates how the prophetic message can be heard today. He not only shared Jeremiah's empathy for a suffering people and a suffering God amid his own spiritual struggles, but he was also personally challenged by Jeremiah 45:1-5 "not to seek great things" for himself but rather to long for the (national) destruction that precedes rebuilding.[60]

---

56. R. W. L. Moberly, *Prophecy and Discernment,* Cambridge Studies in Christian Doctrine (Cambridge: Cambridge University Press, 2006), p. 84.

57. Walter Houston, "What Did the Prophets Think They Were Doing? Speech Acts and Prophetic Discourse in the Old Testament," *BibInt* 1 (1993): 169. Prophetic texts such as Isa. 55:11; Jer. 1:10; 5:14; and Hos. 6:5 are cited as illustrations.

58. Houston, "What Did the Prophets Think," p. 177.

59. Houston, "What Did the Prophets Think," p. 186.

60. Ian Stockton, "Bonhoeffer's Wrestling with Jeremiah," *Modern Believing* 40 (1999): 50-58.

Although prophetic narratives make a major contribution to our hearing the Major Prophets as the Word of God, these books consist primarily of poetry. "Since poetry is our best human model of intricately rich communication, not only solemn, weighty, and forceful but also densely woven with complex internal connections, meanings, and implications, it makes sense that divine speech should be represented in poetry."[61] Accordingly, one of the greatest resources — and hermeneutical challenges — in hearing the Major Prophets today is their profuse, even profligate, use of metaphor,[62] a prominent feature of biblical poetry. Metaphorical language employed to express abstract concepts, such as God and his dealings with Israel and the nations, can both clarify and obscure. Brent Sandy notes the difficulties that an interpreter can have in determining whether a given prophetic description is (1) predictive or poetic, (2) literal or figurative, (3) exact or emotive, (4) conditional or unconditional, (5) real or surreal, (6) originally oral or written, and (7) fulfilled or unfulfilled.[63] These difficulties are real but can be overemphasized. For example, Isaiah 1:2-20 utilizes imagery "borrowed" from the court of justice, parental care and child rearing, animal wisdom, an injured body, the harvest field, and Israelite history, as well as anthropomorphisms and color symbolism, but the prophet's point is certainly not difficult to discern! As David Beldman points out, what "poetic imagery loses in precision it gains in clarity,"[64] stimulating the imagination and often portraying the unfamiliar through the familiar, so that one can "see" divine truths as well as hear them, thereby increasing the persuasive power of the prophetic word.

Ultimately, however, in seeking to hear the prophetic word today, we are not simply seeking to recapture the original prophetic moment. Although a prophetic book "rides on the speech of the prophet . . . the speech of the prophet is accessible only through the book, with all the mediation and interpretation that is implied in this."[65] Here one is confronted with the tension between particularity and universality. Brevard Childs, in developing his canonical approach, emphasizes how canonical editors reshaped the very "particular" proclamations of individual prophets in order to enable them to

61. Robert Alter, *The Art of Biblical Poetry* (New York: Basic, 1985), p. 141.

62. See, for example, Julia M. O'Brien, *Challenging Prophetic Metaphor: Theology and Ideology in the Prophets* (Louisville: Westminster John Knox, 2008).

63. D. Brent Sandy, *Plowshares and Pruning Hooks: Rethinking the Language of Biblical Prophecy and Apocalyptic* (Downers Grove: IVP, 2002), pp. 33-57.

64. Chapter 4 by David Beldman in the present volume.

65. McConville, "Divine Speech," p. 36.

continue to address future generations of the people of God.[66] But Stephen Dempster reminds us that "Word and Event are inextricably linked" — "Prophecy happened at a particular place and time and that is why it can be addressed to later generations. Its authority had been proven."[67]

A correlate of this emphasis on prophetic books is that we must seek to understand their message *as a whole* out of the conviction that the whole is greater than the sum of the parts and that there is an integral relationship between structure and message. Early redaction critics — and some contemporary ones — have little regard for the compositional "design" of prophetic books. One scholar describes Isaiah as "an enormous bran-tub, containing the most wonderful variety of goodies,"[68] while another compares a prophetic book to a snowball, "which expands by picking up and incorporating new material into itself as it goes on its way."[69] Recently, scholars have given more attention to identifying evidence of intentional editorial shaping, which served to promote the editors' rhetorical and theological ends.[70] It is hermeneutically illuminating to examine the way in which the literary deposits of the prophetic spokespersons and their reinterpretations have been ordered to present and develop key theological themes.[71] In the book of Isa-

66. See n. 21 above and the insightful summary and analysis of Childs's contribution to understanding the prophetic literature by Stephen G. Dempster, "The Prophets, the Canon and a Canonical Approach: No Empty Word," in *Canon and Biblical Interpretation*, ed. Craig G. Bartholomew et al., SHS 7 (Grand Rapids: Zondervan, 2006), pp. 293-329.

67. Dempster, "The Prophets," pp. 323-24.

68. Richard J. Coggins, "Do We Still Need Deutero-Isaiah?" *JSOT* 81 (1998): 91, referring to J. F. A. Sawyer's presentation of Isaiah in *The Fifth Gospel: Isaiah in the History of Christianity* (Cambridge: Cambridge University Press, 1996).

69. William McKane, *A Critical and Exegetical Commentary on Jeremiah*, vol. 1, ICC (Edinburgh: T&T Clark, 1986), as summarized by John Barton, *Isaiah 1–39*, OT Guides (Sheffield: Sheffield Academic Press, 1995), p. 24.

70. See Thomas Renz's lengthy treatment (74 pp.) of "the disposition and arrangement of the book" of Ezekiel, *The Rhetorical Function of the Book of Ezekiel*, VTSup 76 (Leiden: Brill, 1999), pp. 57-130. See also Karl Möller, "Words of (In-)evitable Certitude? Reflections on the Interpretation of Prophetic Oracles of Judgment," in *After Pentecost: Language and Biblical Interpretation*, ed. Craig Bartholomew, Colin Greene, and Karl Möller, SAHS 2 (Grand Rapids: Zondervan, 2001), pp. 352-86.

71. Helpful brief discussions of the relationship between the structure and message of the Major Prophets can be found in T. D. Alexander and Brian S. Rosner, eds., *New Dictionary of Biblical Theology* (Downers Grove: IVP, 2000); William J. Dumbrell, *The Faith of Israel: A Theological Survey of the Old Testament*, 2nd ed. (Grand Rapids: Baker Academic, 2002); and Kevin J. Vanhoozer, ed., *Theological Interpretation of the Old Testament: A Book-by-Book Survey* (Grand Rapids: Baker Academic, 2008).

iah, for example, we can note a focus on history and eschatology, on Zion's present and future states, on failed and passed tests of faith, on the future work of an effective Davidic king and servant, and on nationalistic and universalistic hopes.[72]

Seeking first to hear the message of the four Major Prophets *as a whole* is foundational to properly tracing and relating any of the themes that we find in these individual books, prompting us to discover — but not impose — unity amid diversity, to hear prophetic harmony rather than discord or merely solo voices. Thus three central theological concerns in the Major Prophets, as discussed in previous chapters in this volume — the ethical mandate (Carroll), eschatological hope (Boda), and mission to the nations (Wright, even if only prominent in Isaiah) — converge in Isaiah 2:1-5. The eschatological exaltation of the temple mount will result in a gathering of nations to Zion to seek divine instruction and the resolution of disputes between nations, prompting the prophet to challenge his fellow citizens to "walk in the light of the LORD," as the nations one day will also do. We, too, can heed the prophet's call to walk today according to the revelatory light of God's Word, in keeping with our present calling and ultimate destiny. But we must heed the full scope of divine *torah* (rather than focusing solely on military disarmament), noting that the following verses (vv. 6-22) condemn arrogant reliance upon false gods, wealth, and other humans. On the "day of the LORD," the Lord alone will be exalted (v. 17), while those who have not learned to receive humbly the prophetic word will be humbled by the divine word of judgment.

As noted earlier, there are two dominant ways in which modern interpreters hear the Major Prophets — as social reformers (i.e., ethics) or as end-times visionaries (i.e., eschatology). A better approach is to probe the interrelationship between the two. As the Major Prophets emphasize repeatedly, both idolatry and injustice toward fellow Israelites constitute spiritual infidelity toward God and a breach of the people's covenantal obligations. Such actions provoke a divine purging of evil through judgment but also prompt the divine promise of the people's complete spiritual fidelity and ethical uprightness in the future beyond exile under a righteous ruler (e.g., Isa. 33:5-6; 60:17b-22). In the meantime, not only is the moral fabric of Israel-

---

72. See Schultz, "Isaiah," pp. 197-204. After tracing these various themes through the book, I am puzzled by Seitz's lament in *Goodly Fellowship*, p. 89, that "we have nothing like the eleven seams between books [as in the Book of the Twelve] to help us better understand Isaiah's compositional history." Discovering those "seams" would not help us to hear the message of Isaiah more clearly.

ite society tattered but also the revelatory light of Israel's covenantal relationship with the Lord is hidden from the nations. Yet Jeremiah proclaims, "If you put your detestable idols out of my sight and no longer go astray, and if in a truthful, just, and righteous way you swear, . . . then the nations will be blessed by him and in him they will glory" (Jer. 4:1-2).

In response to the obsession with end-times prophecy in some conservative theological circles, biblical scholars have often tended to neglect prophetic eschatology, even reducing it to vague utopian wishes arising amid the gloom of destruction and exile.[73] J. J. M. Roberts, however, affirms that "prediction is an important element in biblical prophecy, and even those apparently 'timeless ethical elements' are normally framed within or given urgency by threatening predictions or encouraging promises based on what God is about to do."[74] Prophetic threats and promises directed toward both Israel and the surrounding nations are grounded in God's covenantal commitments[75] and frequently allude to his paradigmatic actions of judgment (flood, Sodom and Gomorrah), blessing (creation), and salvation (Exodus) in the past. As a result, prophetic depictions of the future are richly intertextual in nature and warrant close textual comparisons,[76] while offering a further illustration of the integral relationship and striking continuity between the Torah, the Former Prophets, the Latter Prophets, and the New Testament. In a time of economic downturn, traumatic urban crime, far-flung natural catastrophes, worldwide terrorism, and seemingly endless

73. See C. Marvin Pate and Calvin B. Haines Jr., *Doomsday Delusions: What's Wrong with Predictions about the End of the World* (Downers Grove: IVP, 1995).

74. Roberts, "A Christian Perspective," p. 406. He distinguishes four categories (pp. 406-19): (1) those already fulfilled, (2) those that will remain unfulfilled, (3) those yet to be fulfilled, especially in connection with Jesus' second coming, and (4) those (being) fulfilled in "a way that is less — or more — than literal," noting how Revelation, for example, transforms and transcends prophecy from Ezekiel.

75. Rikki Watts argues persuasively that the judgment and salvation of the nations announced in the prophets represent alternative conditional destinies that individual (survivors from the) nations will receive on the basis of their response to Yahweh's self-revelation and their treatment of Israel, as expressed in the Abrahamic, Exodus, Conquest, and Davidic-Solomonic traditions. See Rikki E. Watts, "Echoes from the Past: Israel's Ancient Traditions and the Destiny of the Nations in Isaiah 40–55," *JSOT* 28 (2004): 505-8.

76. For a recent discussion of methodology in this regard see Lyons, *From Law to Prophecy*, pp. 47-75. See also Richard L. Schultz, "The Ties That Bind: Intertextuality, the Identification of Verbal Parallels, and Reading Strategies in the Book of the Twelve," in *Thematic Threads in the Book of the Twelve*, ed. Paul L. Redditt and Aaron Schart, BZAW 325 (Berlin: de Gruyter, 2003), pp. 27-45; and "Intertextuality, Canon, and 'Undecidability': Understanding Isaiah's 'New Heavens and New Earth' (Isa 65:17-25)," *BBR* 20 (2010): 19-38.

wars, can we hear any more hopeful sound than the message that rings forth in Isaiah 65:17-25? "'Behold, I will create new heavens and a new earth. The former things will not be remembered, nor will they come to mind. . . . Before they call I will answer; while they are still speaking I will hear. . . . They will neither harm nor destroy on all my holy mountain,' says the LORD."

15 Hearing the Minor Prophets:
The Book of the Twelve and God's Address

Heath Thomas

Brevard Childs rightly argued that Scripture is more than the manufacture of human ingenuity, often a reductionist outcome of academic study of the Bible. It is the testimony of God about himself to creation.[1] Through the Scripture, God's Spirit facilitates spiritual transformation in the believer (2 Tim. 3:16-17; Rom. 12:1-2) and communion between the church and God. Although this position is "confessional," that term does not necessarily entail a subjectivity that can only be countered by academic biblical criticism.[2] Biblical criticism may advance our understanding of what the text may mean and correct distorted readings — true for some research on the Minor Prophets — but then one must press further to assess how God confronts the reader through this particular text with his particular message(s).

This chapter aims to provide a framework by which one can begin to hear God's address in the Minor Prophets, also known as the "Book of the Twelve." To do so, we must assess whether we should be listening for a series of discrete messages that arise from a random collection of prophetic books,[3] or, on the other hand, if there is within the corpus an overarching

1. Brevard S. Childs, *Biblical Theology of the Old and New Testaments: Theological Reflection on the Christian Bible* (Minneapolis: Fortress, 1993), pp. 8-9.

2. Cf. Chapter 1 by Craig Bartholomew in the present volume.

3. Ehud Ben Zvi, "Twelve Prophetic Books or 'The Twelve': A Few Preliminary Considerations," in *Forming Prophetic Literature: Essays on Isaiah and the Twelve in Honor of John D. W. Watts*, ed. James W. Watts and Paul R. House, JSOTSup 235 (Sheffield: Sheffield Academic Press, 1996), pp. 125-57.

message despite the persistence of twelve discrete voices.[4] Further, we must consider these books in their own light and then in light of Jesus and the New Testament to shape a biblical-theological reflection[5] on what God is saying through the full testimony of Scripture.

The framework offered here is just that. The hope is that the reader might engage the text through this general structure so as to read in effect beyond it, more deeply into the Twelve and closer to the heart of God. The basic trinitarian approach to the Old Testament advocated by Craig Bartholomew above is presupposed here. One can only hear the corpus fully if one embraces that it is a word from God that addresses the reader through the power of the Spirit.[6] With these caveats noted, it is appropriate to begin to construct the framework for hearing God's address through the Twelve.

Prophet or Book?

To hear the Twelve well one must distinguish clearly the focus of interpretation. Should one center upon the prophet or the book that bears his name? A common impulse is to emphasize the former. The prophet then becomes a paradigm of piety for the church.[7] These ancient spokesmen for God become flesh-and-blood historical figures that one looks to for inspiration and instruction.[8] Through their "breathless impatience for injustice" in their own times, God invites the church to exemplify the prophets' piety.[9]

This approach has benefits. It treats the prophets seriously as engaging particular contexts. The social critiques of Micah, Hosea, and Amos against land misuse and exploitation of the poor in the eighth century B.C. gain a

---

4. Paul R. House, *The Unity of the Twelve*, JSOTSup 77 (Sheffield: Sheffield Academic Press, 1990), argues that the theme of the Twelve is a cycle of sin-judgment-restoration.

5. Chapter 6 by Mark Boda in the present volume.

6. James Barr is opposed to such a view as it does not belong in the academic study of the Bible: Barr, *The Concept of Biblical Theology: An Old Testament Perspective* (London: SCM, 1999), pp. 196-221. For counterviews, see in this volume chapters 1 and 3 by Craig Bartholomew and Chapter 2 by Al Wolters.

7. Christopher R. Seitz, *Prophecy and Hermeneutics: Toward a New Introduction to the Prophets*, STI (Grand Rapids: Baker Academic, 2007), pp. 45-111.

8. Cf. Carolyn Sharp, *Old Testament Prophets for Today* (Louisville: Westminster John Knox, 2009).

9. The language is that of Abraham J. Heschel, *The Prophets* (San Francisco: Harper-Collins, 2001), p. 4.

currency that may be otherwise overlooked.[10] By focusing upon the lives of the prophets, one gets a sense of the vitality of the truth they convey. The words of the prophets are deemed true for the real world. Nowhere is the focus upon *reality* and *truth* more evident than in the Twelve. They speak God's word(s) over the span of approximately four centuries to audiences of different contexts and nationalities. Within their own times these prophets called their hearers to "an announcement of the imminent," a true word concerning what God was about to do.[11]

But this approach has limits. Some books in the Twelve are reticent to provide firm historical information, leaving the prophet, the book, and its message sitting looser to history.[12] The books themselves may discourage a strict demand for historical fixity. Even if the profile of the prophet may be constructed to a degree, the prophets are not designed to be exemplars first and foremost. The more "historically defined" books mentioned above still do not eventuate into "biographies" of the prophets. We do not see much of their personalities or their motivations.

These books focus upon their theological message(s) rather than on the lives of the prophets.[13] The prophets and the events surrounding them are embedded within the larger theological messages of the books that bear their names. Both the life of the prophet and his cultural milieu will inform God's message(s) from the text, but these should not overdetermine the theological meaning of the book *qua* book. So, for instance, Hosea the book advances the *message* of God, whereas Hosea's *life* is only part of that message.

As David Beldman argues in Chapter 4 in this volume, a literary-theological reading is well suited to hearing God's address, and this holds true for the Twelve. This approach avoids flat historical readings that focus upon little parts of the books divorced from their canonical whole. The history that lies behind the text is contextualized in the canonical presentation

10. Ellen F. Davis, *Scripture, Culture, and Agriculture: An Agrarian Reading of the Bible* (Cambridge: Cambridge University Press, 2009), pp. 120-38.

11. Walther Zimmerli, "Prophetic Proclamation and Reinterpretation," in *Tradition and Theology in the Old Testament*, ed. Douglas A. Knight (Philadelphia: Fortress, 1977), pp. 69-100. Zimmerli's analysis is typical of a tradition-historical approach that is unduly circumscribed by its own methodology, as shown by Brevard S. Childs, "Retrospective Reading of the Old Testament Prophets," *ZAW* 108, no. 3 (1996): 362-77.

12. While Hosea, Amos, Micah, and Zephaniah contextualize the prophets' ministries in the reigns of the Israelite/Judahite kings in their introductory formulae (Hos. 1:1; Amos 1:1; Mic. 1:1; Zeph. 1:1), Habakkuk lacks an introductory formula, as do Joel, Obadiah, and Jonah.

13. Seitz, *Prophecy and Hermeneutics*, p. 88.

that gives the meaning of history.[14] The history that gives rise to the book — such as when the prophet gave this or that oracle, when God spoke to the prophet in this or that vision, when this or that incident took place — remains vital but communicates properly as a component of God's word in the book as a whole.

Books or Book of the Twelve?

Stephen Dempster raises important canonical questions in Chapter 7 in this volume that impinge upon reading and hearing the Twelve. How does God speak in the Twelve: through a book, or through a series of books? From a variety of fronts, whether by historical,[15] literary/thematic,[16] or canonical[17] approaches, scholars have recognized that the Twelve indeed should be read in some way coherently as a *book*. It was perhaps finalized sometime in the postexilic period, but the specific time of its canonical composition is debated.[18]

If the Twelve is a coherent book, then there are implications for hearing God's address in it. One will not have heard God's address fully in, for example, Zephaniah until that book is heard within the larger canonical context

14. See Childs, "Retrospective Reading," pp. 362-77; see also Chapter 6 by Mark Boda in the present volume on the "inscripturated" nature of revelation.

15. James D. Nogalski, *Literary Precursors to the Book of the Twelve*, BZAW 217 (Berlin: de Gruyter, 1993); *Redactional Processes in the Book of the Twelve*, BZAW 218 (Berlin: de Gruyter, 1993); Aaron Schart, *Die Entstehung Des Zwölfprophetenbuchs: Neubearbeitungen von Amos im Rahmen schriftenübergreifender Redaktionsprozesse*, BZAW 260 (Berlin: de Gruyter, 1997).

16. House, *The Unity of the Twelve*; Rolf Rendtorff, "Alas for the Day! The 'Day of the LORD' in the Book of the Twelve," in *God in the Fray: A Tribute to Walter Brueggemann*, ed. Tod Linafelt and Timothy K. Beal (Minneapolis: Fortress, 1998), pp. 186-97.

17. Seitz, *Prophecy and Hermeneutics*; Michael B. Shepherd, "Compositional Analysis of the Twelve," *ZAW* 120 (2008): 184-93. Donald C. Collett, "Prophetic Intentionality and the Book of the Twelve: A Study in the Hermeneutics of Prophecy" (Ph.D. diss., University of St. Andrews, 2007). Note the variety of approaches on display in Paul L. Redditt and Aaron Schart, eds., *Thematic Threads in the Book of the Twelve*, BZAW 325 (Berlin: Walter de Gruyter, 2003).

18. Its final form appears perhaps between the fifth and fourth centuries B.C. For discussion, see Marvin Sweeney, *The Twelve Prophets*, vol. 1 (Berit Olam; Collegeville: Liturgical Press, 2000), pp. xxxv-xxxix; Paul L. Redditt, "The Production and Reading of the Book of the Twelve," in *Reading and Hearing the Book of the Twelve*, ed. James Nogalski and Marvin Sweeney (Atlanta: Society of Biblical Literature, 2000), pp. 11-33.

of the Twelve.[19] But if it holds together as an intentionally arranged book, then we must ask other questions as well. Are there a number of messages that should be heard in this book? Is there one overarching message that the Twelve advances? Or is the search for a unified message (or series of messages) just an outcome of a readerly desire for textual coherence, a desire that the editors of the Twelve did not share?[20]

It is one thing to argue for a *unified book* of the Twelve and another thing to argue that it leads to a *unitary reading*. P. Guillaume and Ehud Ben Zvi highlight the problems of both arguments.[21] And yet despite their impressive analysis, the Twelve appears to have been incorporated[22] and then read together as a whole from early times. Even if one contests ancient evidence from Qumran, other significant indicators point to a unified corpus of the Twelve. Sirach 49:10 (ca. 200 B.C.) speaks of the "bones" of the Twelve Prophets that comforted Jacob. This presumably implies that this coherent book (the bones serve as a framework for a body) and the message of that book were to instill hope.[23] Paul speaks of "the *book* of the prophets" (Acts 7:42) before quoting a section of Amos. He seems to recognize individual books (τῶν προφητῶν) within a unified, singular book (βίβλος). Further, apocryphal and pseudepigraphal sources (4 Ezra 1:39-40; Martyrdom and Ascension of Isaiah 4:22; Lives of the Prophets) demonstrate corporate understanding of the Twelve. This cumulative evidence suggests that from 200 B.C. onward the Twelve often was understood as a unified book.

And still twelve distinctive *books* comprise the whole. As such, each book needs to be heard in its own right. The individual books play their

---

19. Shepherd, "Compositional Analysis," p. 192.

20. For discussion on these questions see Kenneth H. Cuffey, "Remnant, Redactor, and Biblical Theologian: A Comparative Study of Coherence in Micah and the Twelve," in *Reading and Hearing the Book of the Twelve*, ed. Nogalski and Sweeney, pp. 185-208; Richard L. Shultz, "The Ties That Bind: Intertextuality, the Identification of Verbal Parallels, and Reading Strategies in the Book of the Twelve," in *Thematic Threads*, ed. Redditt and Schart, pp. 27-45.

21. P. Guillaume, "A Reconsideration of Manuscripts Classified as Scrolls of the Twelve Minor Prophets (XII)," *JHS* 7 (2007): 2-10; accessible online at: http://www.arts.ualberta.ca/JHS/Articles/article_77.pdf. Cf. Collett, "Prophetic Intentionality," pp. 176-81.

22. See the different models for incorporation in Aaron Schart, "Reconstructing the Redaction History of the Twelve Prophets: Problems and Models," in *Reading and Hearing the Book of the Twelve*, ed. Nogalski and Sweeney, pp. 34-48.

23. For translation and discussion, see P. W. Skehan and A. A. di Lella, *The Wisdom of Ben Sira*, AB (New York: Doubleday, 1986), pp. 540-45.

parts in the Twelve analogous to the way individual instruments play their parts in a symphony. One cannot understand and enjoy the full performance of the symphony without the individual instruments. Similarly one cannot understand the full symphonic performance of the Twelve without the parts played by each of its books.

At a corporate level, what does the Twelve proclaim? Francis Watson thinks it teaches primarily that God promises a hopeful future for his people and world. A kind of chronological ordering of the books advances this story of hope — from promises of judgment (preexilic prophets), to judgment (exilic prophets), to restoration (postexilic prophets).[24] For Watson, this understanding of history supposedly comports with the Septuagint's "chronological" thinking in its arrangement of the Twelve as well, which differs from the Masoretic text.[25] The outcome of this thinking is that the Twelve presents a message of history: the non-fulfillment of God's restoration in the past and the hope of his certain restoration in the future.

For Watson, Habakkuk's emphasis upon hope in God's eschatological salvation epitomizes the theological message of the Twelve. The reader who "waits" on the Lord (Hab. 2:3) exercises faith in God's coming salvation (Hab. 2:4). The certainty of this salvation enables strength to live in the present or "to run" as Habakkuk 2:2 suggests. Watson relates the meaning here to the language of Isaiah 40:31: "Those who wait on the LORD shall renew their strength; they shall mount up on wings of eagles; they shall run and not grow weary." Waiting on God's coming salvation is the fundament for hope and the paradigm for faith. "It is the entire Book of the Twelve that is written 'so that one who reads it may run.' The assurance that 'the righteous shall live by his faithfulness' lies at the heart of this book."[26]

Others find different messages for the Twelve, largely by assessing thematic ties, catchwords, and intertextual allusions.[27] A significant thematic

24. Francis Watson, *Paul and the Hermeneutics of Faith* (London: T&T Clark, 2004), pp. 130-36.

25. The supposed LXX order: Hosea, Amos, Micah, Joel, Obadiah, Jonah, Nahum, Habakkuk, Zephaniah, Haggai, Malachi. The MT order: Hosea, Joel, Amos, Obadiah, Jonah, Micah, Nahum, Habakkuk, Zephaniah, Haggai, Zechariah, Malachi. Watson, *Paul and the Hermeneutics of Faith*, pp. 78-112.

26. Watson, *Paul and the Hermeneutics of Faith*, pp. 125-57, p. 157; cf. the view of Shepherd, "Compositional Analysis."

27. Nogalski, *Literary Precursors*, p. 215; Aaron Schart, "Reconstructing the Redaction History of the Twelve Prophets," in *Reading and Hearing the Book of the Twelve*, ed. Nogalski and Sweeney, pp. 34-48, esp. pp. 35-36.

message concerns the "Day of the Lord," adduced via catchword chains.[28] In the Twelve, the Day of the Lord is a day of judgment and/or salvation, for Israel and/or the nations, in accordance with the justice and mercy of God. Despite the diversity of presentation in the individual books, owing in part to the historical diversity of the texts themselves, corporately the Day of the Lord enfolds each historical moment presented in the Twelve, from the time of the Divided Monarchy in the eighth century B.C. to the Persian period, relating these periods figurally through the activity of God. Somewhat differently, Raymond Van Leeuwen thinks that allusions to Exodus 34:6-7 in the Twelve emphasize God's mercy and justice, and so the book as a whole teaches theodicy.[29]

And yet the book of the Twelve may be a bit too unwieldy to be constrained to only one message. Terence Collins believes it stresses these interconnected themes: covenant-election, fidelity-infidelity, fertility-infertility, turning-returning, justice-mercy of God, the kingship of God, Temple-Zion, and nations as enemies-allies.[30] Christopher Seitz suggests the meaning of the Twelve is fuller as well. He thinks it teaches God's history as a providentially ordered whole, the relationship between Israel and the nations in God's economy, faithful models of obedience to God, a proper way to understand prophecy among books in the Twelve, and the very character of God as patient and just but judging iniquity.[31] These scholars argue for a thicker account of the meaning of the corpus, rather than just one major theme, motif, or singular message.

With Seitz, it is probably best to understand the Twelve as advancing a number of theological messages rather than just one. To understand it fully,

---

28. Rendtorff, "Alas for the Day!" and "How to Read"; James D. Nogalski, "The Day(s) of YHWH in the Book of the Twelve," in *Thematic Threads,* ed. Redditt and Schart, pp. 192-212; Paul R. House, "Endings as New Beginnings: Returning to the Lord, the Day of the Lord, and Renewal in the Book of the Twelve," in *Thematic Threads,* ed. Redditt and Schart, pp. 313-38.

29. Raymond C. van Leeuwen, "Scribal Wisdom and Theodicy in the Book of the Twelve," in *In Search of Wisdom: Essays in Memory of John G. Gammie,* ed. L. Perdue, B. B. Scott, and W. J. Wiseman (Louisville: Westminster John Knox, 1993), p. 32. Note the repetition of language: Hos. 1:6 (mercy of God no longer operative through wordplay); Joel 2:13 (recalls the verses as a call to repentance due to God's compassion); Jon. 3:9; 4:2 (cites the verses as a kind of lament over the compassion of God); Mic. 7:18-20 (cites the verses to display the compassion of God); Nah. 1:2-3a (cites the verses to display the justice/judgment of God).

30. Terence Collins, *The Mantle of Elijah: The Redaction Criticism of the Prophetical Books,* BS 20 (Sheffield: Sheffield Academic Press, 1993), p. 65.

31. Collins, *Mantle,* pp. 59-87, esp. p. 65; Seitz, *Prophecy and Hermeneutics,* pp. 189-219.

the interpreter should be disinclined to flatten the testimony of each book to focus on the message of the whole. Rather, the interpreter is best served by following the distinctive testimony of each book and then by relating these testimonies to the message of the Twelve as a whole.[32]

God's Address in the Twelve

The variety of lessons the Twelve teaches may be oriented around God's activity in the past as it is related to God's activity in the future. Further, the Twelve provides instruction on how God's people might live in light of his divine activity. This section highlights four theological themes in the Twelve, each of which highlights the theological connection between divine activity (often through the Day of the Lord) and human response: history and theodicy, Israel and the nations, the future hope, and life before God.

History and Theodicy

God calls readers of the Twelve to trust in his salvific plans because of his justice. This call is achieved both through the presentation of history in the Twelve and through a developed theodicy. In the Twelve, God orchestrates history so that it moves between judgment and redemption, from the monarchy in the eighth century B.C. to the Persian period in the fifth century B.C. In and through judgment, God works toward redemption.

God's intentions for this covenant people are both for judgment and for restoration, as seen in Hosea 1:6-11. The symbolism of Hosea's children (Lo-Ruhamah and Lo-Ammi) in Hosea 1:2-9 reinforces divine judgment. But this gives way to restoration in 1:10-11. The relation between judgment and restoration is textually close despite the fact that they are historically distant. "The various ingredients that lie at the base of Israel's historical experience from the eighth to the fifth centuries are brought into relationship with one another. Seen from the perspective of individual prophetic snapshots, history could appear episodic and disconnected; but Israel's grasp of and presentation of history in the Twelve is an organic whole."[33]

---

32. Rolf Rendtorff, *The Canonical Hebrew Bible: A Theology of the Old Testament*, trans. D. Orton, TBS 7 (Leiden: Deo, 2005), pp. 264-314, esp. pp. 265-66.

33. Seitz, *Prophecy and Hermeneutics*, p. 214.

In restoration after judgment, a king from God's people will lead them faithfully (Hos. 1:11; cf. 3:5). Interestingly, this future king theologically contextualizes the portrayal of poor leadership in the chronologically earlier ministry of Amos, providing ballast to Amos's picture of destruction and preparing one for the rather abrupt turn to restoration at the conclusion of the book (Amos 9:11-15). So the messianic theme is wrapped up in the story of God's redemption in the Twelve. In this way, the structural arrangement of the opening of the Twelve presents history proper as bending to the intentions of God. Judgment is a category of justice in which the creation-destroying realities of sin and impurity (cf. Hos. 4:1-3) are removed so that the creation-confirming realities of restoration (cf. Hos. 6:1-3; 14:4-8) might be realized.[34]

The thrust of this movement of history in the Twelve achieved through figural association is nothing less than the death and resurrection of Israel. God reminds his people that, although they may suffer in exile and even die there, his purposes with his son will be achieved: he will rise again from exile and death (cf. Hos. 5–6, 11).[35] In this, God is affirmed as a life-giving and death-defeating Lord.

For the post-exilic group reading or hearing the Twelve, the book would remind them that God is justified as righteous. Despite all that has happened, God will enact restoration. This restoration encompasses all of creation (cf. Mic. 4) because God is the Lord of creation itself. For Israel, divine judgment is shown to be only a step along the way to restoration. The recurrence of the language of Exodus 34:6-7 reinforces that, while God's judgment is in force, it still remains an extension of the "steadfast love of the Lord" so that his mercy and compassion might be demonstrated.[36] The destructions of the northern and southern kingdoms were justified because of sin, but God in his mercy will restore his people and land — even creation itself — because of his justice and righteousness (Mic. 4:1-7).

Despite this theodicy, tension persists. The restoration that so many

34. A number of examples reinforce this theological presentation of history. See J. D. Nogalski, "Intertextuality and the Twelve," in *Forming Prophetic Literature*, ed. Watts and House, pp. 105-8; "Joel as 'Literary Anchor' for the Book of the Twelve," in *Reading and Hearing the Book of the Twelve*, ed. Nogalski and Sweeney, pp. 91-109; Marvin A. Sweeney, *Form and Intertextuality* (Tübingen: Mohr Siebeck, 2005), pp. 202-3.

35. Jon D. Levenson, *Resurrection and the Restoration of Israel: The Ultimate Victory of the God of Life* (New Haven: Yale University Press, 2006).

36. Hos. 2:19-23; Joel 2:13-14, 18; Amos 9:9-15; Jon. 3:7-10; 4:2; Mic. 7:18-20; Nah. 1:3; Hab. 3:2; Zeph. 3:16-20; Zech. 1:15-17; 8:8, 13; 10:6. See Chapter 12 by J. Clinton McCann in this volume for a discussion of divine *ḥesed*.

texts envision still stands far off. Notwithstanding real historical returns to the land (as Haggai and Zechariah confirm), in the canonical presentation of the Twelve, God's "day" of vindication is pressed forward eschatologically, creating space between the "now" of suffering and the "not yet" of justice and restoration (Mal. 3:16–4:6 [3:16-24]). There still remains an existential challenge of waiting and watching for God's future redemption. This "now/ not yet" dimension leaves the reader of the Twelve sensing the certainty of God's salvation and judgment against sin. Yet its eschatological dimension leaves room both for waiting expectantly for that future hope and for prayer and honest questioning in the meantime (cf. Hab. 1; Mic. 1:8-9). Readers must persevere in faith.

Israel and the Nations

The Twelve particularly proclaims God to be Lord over Israel and all nations, who judges both but envisions ultimate restoration for them both. God's restoration of Israel *and* the nations reinforces his divine care for the entirety of creation. The Twelve proclaims this message through Israel's amorphous identity as well as the fate of the nations.

It is certainly true that firm identification of "Israel" diverges at places because of historical factors.[37] Nonetheless this point only takes one so far. "Israel" remains a multiform theological and political construct in the Twelve. It may be a corporate covenant people (Amos 9:7-10), the northern kingdom (Amos 5:1-3), the southern kingdom (Mal. 2:11), or an idealized future community of faith (Zech. 12:1–14:21).

This ambiguous presentation of Israel enables God's people to find their identity in their past as well as their future. They are "Israel" by their covenantal roots, related historically to the divided monarchy through the periods portrayed in the individual books in the Twelve, and yet envisioned rhetorically and theologically as a future people who will be restored and united before God. The effect of this presentation charges the wise reader of

---

37. For a detailed discussion, see H. G. M. Williamson, "The Concept of Israel in Transition," in *The World of Ancient Israel,* ed. R. E. Clements (Cambridge: Cambridge University Press, 1989), pp. 141-60. For a specific example, see J. G. McConville, "'How Can Jacob Stand? He Is So Small!' (Amos 7:2): The Prophetic Word and the Re-Imagining of Israel," in *Israel's Prophets and Israel's Past: Essays on the Relationship of Prophetic Texts and Israelite History in Honor of John H. Hayes,* ed. B. E. Kelle and M. B. Moore, LHB/OTS 446 (New York: T&T Clark, 2006), pp. 132-51.

the Twelve to identify with faithful "Israel," God's people who will devote themselves to God and his actions in the world. By identifying with this eschatological, faithful Israel, God's people anticipate their participation in the eschatological community.

The vision of a wayward people brought together before God as a future "restored Israel" is matched with a similar vision for the nations. The Twelve often portrays the nations as antagonistic toward God. Amos's opening prophecy circumnavigates around the Levant, pronouncing judgment on the sinful foreign nations before incriminating Israel and Judah for like sins (1:3–2:6). Nahum depicts God's judgment against the sinful nation of Assyria. Likewise, for Habakkuk, even though a foreign nation (Babylonia) is an instrument of God for punishing Israel, it nonetheless is idolatrous and prideful. As such, God will judge its inhabitants for sin (1:5-17; 2:5-20). Finally, for Obadiah Edom is a scourge to God's people; its activity is an affront to God that demands just punishment (vv. 2-4, 10-15). Indeed, God's judgment against Edom in Obadiah becomes a figure for divine judgment against all nations who sin against God: "For the Day of the LORD draws near over all nations; just as you (Edom) have done, it will be done to you" (v. 15b, cf. v. 16).

Yet following upon Obadiah's vision of judgment is the book of Jonah, which holds out the promise of God's mercy to the nations if they only repent. The speech of Assyria's king becomes typical for this hope for the nations in the Twelve. "Let everyone repent from his evil ways and from the violence of his hands. Who knows? God may turn and relent and turn back from his wrath so that we would not perish" (Jon. 3:8b-9). Ultimately, the destiny of the nations in the Twelve is salvation and incorporation into the worship of the Lord: "I will pour out my Spirit on all humanity" and "everyone who calls on the name of the LORD will be saved" (Joel 2:28, 32).[38] Here God speaks a word of ultimate and loving restoration for humanity (both Israel and the nations). Especially through the book of Jonah, the readers of the Twelve are encouraged to adopt God's compassion for the nations that derives from God's care for them.

The Future Hope

As king over his creation (Amos 4), God is presented as having a comprehensive concern for all of life: humans, nations (Mal. 1), land (Hos. 2:18-23),

---

38. Cf. Amos 9:12; Mic. 4:2-3; Zeph. 3:9; Zech. 2:11; 8:22-23.

and beasts (Joel 1:18). God's rule over his world is one that is just and re-demptive. God's reign leads to restoration. The Twelve instills hope within its readers that God will restore creation in the future. This future hope is portrayed in a variety of ways and with particular language in the Twelve.[39] Nonetheless, when they are taken together, one sees the future hope through a series of symbols in the Twelve.

The first has already been mentioned as a future ideal community. Ideal "Israel" is repeatedly highlighted in the Twelve and informs its eschatologi-cal hope. The future ideal "Israel" is a holy and worshipful community, sometimes identified as the "remnant"[40] who has come through God's judg-ment and been saved. They will be called "holy to the LORD" (Zech. 14:20) and united under his appointed priest-king.[41] This king will reign in the day of vindication and restoration of ideal Israel before their God. As in Psalm 72, the Davidic ruler will rule under the authority of the Lord, and the Lord will be king in their midst.[42] God's presence in their midst highlights his di-vine immanence in this future time as well as the tacit sanctity and holiness of the people. This is possible because ideal Israel has been purified on the Day of the Lord.

By presenting Israel's identity in this fashion, the Twelve provides the reader "who is wise" (Hos. 14:9) a means to understand Israel as a witness to the ways of the Lord. Further, the reader is invited to live into that history by becoming a faithful, penitent, and expectant follower of the Lord. This "ideal Israel" is to trust in the Lord and return to his ways and by doing so will par-ticipate faithfully in this grand (eschatological) restoration.

The future hope often is indicated by a picture of restoration, particu-larly with the language "restore fortunes" (שוב שבות).[43] Restoration of for-tunes is a symbol of future life before God in the land. Its imagery trades upon the repeated Hebrew root שוב.[44] In a future time God's people experi-

---

39. Note the careful study of Simon J. De Vries, "Futurism in the Preexilic Minor Prophets Compared with That of the Postexilic Minor Prophets," in *Thematic Threads*, ed. Redditt and Schart, pp. 252-72.

40. Amos 9:12; Mic. 2:12; 4:7; 5:7-8; 7:18; Zeph. 2:7-9; Hag. 1:12-14; 2:2; Zech. 8:6-12; 9:7.

41. "Joshua" in Zech. 3, but otherwise a future Davidic king in Hos. 3:5; Mic. 2:13; 5:1-8; Hab. 3:13; Zech. 9:9.

42. Zeph. 3:15; Zech. 14:9, 17; Mal. 1:14.

43. Hos. 6:11; Joel 3:1; Amos 9:14; Zeph. 2:7; 3:20.

44. Cf. Hos. 3:5; 5:4; 6:1, *2*, *11*; 7:10; 8:13; 9:3; 11:5; 12:6; 14:1-2; Joel 2:12-13; *3:1*, 4, 7; Amos 4:6, 8-11; *9:11*; Obad. 15; Mic. 2:8; *4:8*; 5:3; *Nah. 2:2*; Zeph. 2:7, 10; *3:20*; Zech. 1:3, 16; 4:1; 8:3; *9:12*; 10:6, 9; Mal. 3.7. Numbers in italics indicate the semantics of *šûb* as "restore," while the others indicate the semantics of *šûb* as "return/turn." Cf. Jason Lecureaux, "The Thematic Unity of

ence restoration of fortunes, twice identified as "the last days" (באחרית
הימים).[45] Restoration of fortunes cannot be construed as a blithe return to
the status quo, where God gives back to the ideal community the land, her
habitations, and her kingdom. Rather, restoration of fortunes links to the
past, exposing the sins of Israel (Hos. 6:1), but then moves beyond that past
and projects a reestablishment of God's people into their land (Joel 3:1),
where they will be productive and remain in their place of rest forever
(Amos 9:14). In this vision, sins of the past will no longer be operative in the
future. God will reign perfectly, Israel will be completely devoted to their
God, and the divinely appointed king will rule over them in peace, justice,
and righteousness (Zech. 9:9-10). This symbol instills hope and faith in God
for the reader.

Finally, Zion reveals God's plan for a future hope. Zion as a physical entity encapsulates both God's people and his holy dwelling (whether the sanctuary or holy city). In the Twelve Zion is introduced in Joel and associated
with the Day of the Lord (Joel 2–3). Like the Day of the Lord, the symbol of
Zion appears in the context of God's judgment against his people and city
(Joel 2:1-17) as well as God's salvation (Joel 2:23-32). Zion regularly appears
as a people/city judged (Amos 1:2; 6:1; Mic. 3:12) or saved (Obad. 17; Mic. 4:1-
10) by the activity of God. Zion is a symbol for future hope when God's
kingship will be exercised (Mic. 4:7; cf. Pss. 95–100).

But Zion is not relegated to Israel alone in the Twelve. Zion as a symbol
intertwines the destiny of Israel with that of the nations. As those who have
been judged and remain, the nations and Israel will find refuge in Zion under
God's protection, God's instruction, and God's appointed king.[46] The Twelve
proclaims God's final judgment and salvation for Israel and the nations. After
purification of sin, Israel and the nations are incorporated into a new humanity — ideal Israel, in Zion. Zion, then, is an important symbol because it
presses the future hope well beyond any former localization in the Twelve's
presentation of history. As a rich eschatological symbol, Zion provides the
implied reader of the Twelve a vision in which future life is portrayed. In
Zion, ideal Israel is restored before God, and war, death, and sin are no more.
Zion represents a renewed creation united under God's reign.

---

the Book of the Twelve: The Call to Return and the Nature of the Minor Prophets" (Ph.D.
diss., University of Gloucestershire, 2010).

45. Hos. 3:5; Mic. 4:1. Cf. Zech. 8:6, 10. Shepherd, "Compositional Analysis."

46. Mic. 4:1-2; Zeph. 3:9; Zech. 2:10-11; 8:1-23. See Chapter 8 by Christopher Wright in
the present volume.

Life before God

In light of the future hope, the Twelve invites its readers to trust God and live faithfully as his people in the present. God will bring the future hope to pass, but in the meantime the Twelve expects its readers to be formed and transformed by his word so that they might live well and rightly before God. This is an act of spiritual formation by the Holy Spirit (Mal. 2:15-16). The text calls the reader to three primary habits of life before God: cultivating wisdom, repenting, and waiting on God in perseverance.

In the first place, life before God begins with discerning the "ways of the LORD" (Hos. 14:9 [10]), which Hosea addresses in particular and the Twelve discloses in general.[47] The epilogue to Hosea closes that book but also serves as a functional prologue to the remainder of the Twelve and is a call to wisdom. The "wise" reader will attend to the ways of God demonstrated in the history and theology of the Twelve. The past sin of God's people as well as future hope in God's restoration serve as a frame within which the wise reader can orient his or her life. History is not meaningless but anticipates God's restoration in Zion through his justice with Israel and the nations. Wisdom is recognizing and embracing God's ways.

Second, the reader is called to return to God in repentance. "Return/repent" (שׁוּב) is reiterated to different groups (prophets, priests, kings, or Israel/Judah writ large) in the Twelve. But consistent throughout is the message that if people, who are placed in various historical periods and in different locations on the reckoning of the individual books, will but repent and return to the Lord, then God will heal them (Hos. 6:1; 14:1; Joel 2:12-13). "Return to me [שׁוּבוּ אלי] — says the LORD of the Armies — and I will turn back [ואשׁוּב אליכם] to you" (Zech. 1:3). Because the peoples' sin is prevalent, God's call for repentance remains necessary. If they will repent of sin, God will heal (Hos. 6:1).

The reader, like Israel in whatever time period depicted in the Twelve, has the choice to follow God. And yet the reader is faced with an uncomfortable reality. In the corporate presentation of the Twelve, God's people will *not* respond to his command (at least not fully), and God knows they will not.[48] On the heels of the call for repentance in Hosea 6:1-3 is the Lord's la-

---

47. Collett, "Prophetic Intentionality," pp. 199-247.

48. To argue that God's people were completely faithless and unrepentant in the presentation of the Twelve overstates the case. At the very least, the prophets of the Twelve are examples of faithfulness and return to the Lord. Yet these represent exceptions that prove the rule.

ment over Israel's waywardness and rebellion against him in 6:4–7:16. If God commands his people to repent and yet demonstrates that they will not, then how is his promise for restoration sincere?

In the face of Israel's recalcitrance, the sovereign Lord will act to save them despite their (lack of) response. He will circumcise their hearts, restore their devotion to him, and restore their fortunes (cf. Deut. 30:6; Mic. 4:1-5). God holds out the offer of salvation through repentance, but in the end the offer is rebuffed and he alone will act to provide salvation. He *will* restore his people in the future despite Israel's recalcitrance and inability fully to return to him.[49]

The reader of the Twelve is invited to embrace this divine love and salvation. Further, the reader of the Twelve is called to an interpretative decision. Will the reader submit to God in repentance and be healed by him, or not? The rhetoric of the Twelve then presses for a life of repentance and dependence upon God, recognizing Israel's rebellious nature but trusting in God's restoration and forgiveness coming out of his divine grace.

Third, the Twelve invites the reader to wait expectantly for the day of God's salvation. Habakkuk perhaps teaches this most clearly. In the face of coming disaster and future salvation, Habakkuk is instructed: "Even if it [the vision] tarries, wait for it still; for it will surely come and it will not delay" (2:3b-c). The vision pictures God's activity of judgment and salvation. The vision invites Habakkuk (and the reader) to trust God in "faith" (2:4).

The conclusion to the Twelve gives Habakkuk's expectant faith a particular shape that correlates with the cultivation of wisdom highlighted above. Malachi 4 teaches about the coming day in which God will judge the wicked and bring healing to those who "fear" the Lord's "name" (Mal. 4:1-3 [3:19-21]). This day awaits fulfillment. In the meantime, what is expected from the reader is to "remember the instruction of Moses" given at Horeb (Mal. 4:4 [3:22]). "Horeb" is language that recalls the second giving of the law in Deuteronomy. In so doing, the conclusion of Malachi rhetorically places the reader of the Twelve at Sinai once again, responsible for the "statutes" and "judgments" that the first generation failed to keep.[50] The second generation, too, failed to keep the instruction of Moses, detailed through the condemnation of Israel in Deuteronomy (Deut. 28:15-68; 30:1-4) and in the Twelve (Hos. 4; Amos 2:4; Zeph. 3:4; Zech. 7:12). Despite Israel's failure in the past, here once again they are charged to "remember" God's instruction.

---

49. Hos. 6:11; Joel 2:25; 3:1; Zeph. 2:7; Zech. 9:12.
50. Cf. Deut. 5:2-5.

Considering that they failed in the minimum base requirements of the law, much less the weightier issues of justice, compassion, faithful love, and devotion toward God and one another (Zech. 7:8-9; cf. Lev. 19:18 and Deut. 6:5), how could such a command be given and taken seriously in Malachi? How could Israel hope to respond well?

The proper stance to "remembering" God's instruction comes only when Israel recognizes their inability to keep the law and then rests in God's grace and love toward them despite their failure. The tension between the command to keep God's law and the realization of Israel's unwavering waywardness to God subsides nowhere else within the Old Testament. Nor does it do so in the Twelve. As such, although both Malachi 4:4 (3:22) and Deuteronomy require following the letter of God's law, these texts show that this is not enough, because Israel will fail in that obedience. Thus Malachi 4:4 (3:22) (no less Deuteronomy; cf. Deut. 30:1-10) requires God's people ultimately to depend upon the Lord's saving work with their whole being in faith *despite* their waywardness.

The command of God at Horeb (both in Deuteronomy and in Malachi) demands not obedience to the letter of the law alone but rather a deep and abiding love of God with all one's heart. Through the language of "remember" in Malachi 4:4 (3:22), the reader of the Twelve is enjoined to recall *all* of Moses' instructions and to reinforce the notion that obedience to God's law is something that cannot be achieved by human initiative but rather by trust in God's commitment to his people despite their sin. This is, at heart, cultivating wisdom, namely, the "fear of the LORD" (cf. Prov. 1:7; 9:10; 31:30; Deut. 31:12-13; Mal. 4:1-3 [3:19-21]).

This lesson shifts the focus from human obedience solely to a focus upon divine activity in the heart and life of Israel herself. This lesson is taught in the corporate presentation of Israel in the Twelve: a rebellious and broken, yet divinely restored people, who look to the Lord to enable faith, trust, and obedience to his *torah* (Mic. 4:1-5).[51] Thus the Twelve casts a vision of obedience, but more than obedience. Obedience to the law, reduced to the term "remember" in Malachi 4:4 (3:22), reveals for the reader God's command for obedience, admits for the reader Israel's (and the reader's) own sinfulness and inability to meet the demands of law, and yet invites the reader to trust that God will enact change within the very heart of Israel by his restorative act (Mic. 4:1-5). Obedience to God flows out of that divinely initiated change.

---

51. Thomas Renz, "Torah in the Minor Prophets," in *Reading the Law*, ed. J. G. McConville and Karl Möller, LHBOTS 461 (London: T&T Clark, 2006), pp. 73-94.

The Book of the Twelve as Christian Scripture

The New Testament provides a fuller context to hear the Twelve as Christian Scripture and reveals the cohesion of the biblical witness.[52] But some ground must be cleared to proceed. In the first place, the New Testament usually cites from Greek versions of the Old Testament (the LXX) but likely is aware of Hebrew tradition as well. Second, on the basis of how they employ the Twelve, one may conclude that New Testament writers understand the person and work of Christ to be central to their understanding of history, Israel, life, and future salvation. As such, the New Testament writers often read the Twelve theologically and figurally, relating the person and work of Jesus to God's work in history and his dealings with Israel in the past, the present, and the future. This is what Mark Boda in this volume identifies as the "reactualization" of the Old Testament in the New Testament. For the New Testament reading of the Twelve, Christ serves as the hinge to history and the clue to living in God's creation. Finally, New Testament usage of the Twelve should not be understood as exhausting its meaning. The Twelve has its own discrete voice as God's Word even while correlated with New Testament use of it, as Craig Bartholomew rightly notes.[53]

A biblical-theological account of the Twelve proclaims a number of messages, but Christ holds the clue to all of them. From a wide-angle perspective, the New Testament use of the Twelve affirms the inherent continuity of the narrative arc of Scripture, from creation to new creation. Christ is the key to unlocking the meaning of this narrative and to giving God's people a way to live into that story. The following discussion picks up on places where the Twelve are referred to in the New Testament even though explicit citation and allusion only tell part of the story. Jesus is the climax of Israel's story advanced in the Old Testament in general and the Twelve in particular. Jesus is the king of God's Kingdom anticipated in the Twelve. Jesus is the one about whom the Law and Prophets testify, conjoined in Malachi 4:1-6 (3:19-24) and conjoined once again in Jesus' transfiguration (Mark 9:2-8). Jesus makes it possible to understand both judgment and salvation on the Day of the Lord. Jesus, like Jonah, is a sign for God's activity of judgment and salva-

---

52. Cf. Chapter 6 by Mark Boda in the present volume. The most accessible resources on the Twelve in the New Testament are the works of Menken and Moyise as well as Beale and Carson: Maarten J. J. Menken and Steve Moyise, eds., *The Minor Prophets in the New Testament*, LNTS 377 (London: T&T Clark, 2009); G. K. Beale and D. A. Carson, eds., *Commentary on the New Testament Use of the Old Testament* (Grand Rapids: Baker Academic, 2007).

53. Cf. Chapter 1 by Craig Bartholomew in the present volume.

tion (Matt. 12:40-41; Luke 11:29-32). Finally, Jesus is the clue that God's people pursue to live rightly in his kingdom. This life under God's Son invites one into a spirituality of faith, perseverance, and waiting on God's restoration of all things in him.

The Story of Israel, the Story of Jesus

The story of Jesus serves as the climax to the story of Israel, as is apparent in the citation of Hosea 11:1 in Matthew 2:15: "Out of Egypt I have called my son." The meaning of this citation has been a source of great consternation.[54] And yet, as Clay Ham notes, the evangelist highlights the typological, figural association between Israel portrayed in Hosea as a rebellious son and Israel portrayed in Matthew as Jesus, the faithful son. Ham concludes that "the evangelist makes a striking portrayal of Jesus as the true Israel, whose sojourn in and departure from Egypt intimates a 'new exodus,' during which Jesus proves faithful where Israel has not been."[55] As Israel experienced the wilderness, Jesus too has his wilderness temptation (Matt. 4:1-11). But Jesus — as the faithful son of God (Matt. 4:3-6) and the true, obedient Israel — overcomes temptation and obeys the Father. Ultimately, Jesus as Israel is the Son in whom the Father is well pleased (Matt. 3:17).[56] Readers of the Gospels receive the identity of Jesus and are invited to have faith in the Son and be incorporated into faithful Israel as well. By following him, "Jesus' disciples constitute the nucleus of eschatological Israel, of which Jesus is king."[57]

The Once and Future King

As the quote above indicates, the anticipated king in the Twelve is none other than Jesus (cf. Mic. 5:2). As such, the expectation of judgment, peace, and cosmic renewal anticipated with the coming king is crystallized in the advent of Jesus. This messianic king comes from Bethlehem, as does Jesus (Matt.

---

54. See Peter Enns, *Inspiration and Incarnation* (Grand Rapids: Baker Academic, 2005), pp. 132-34.

55. Clay Alan Ham, "The Minor Prophets in Matthew's Gospel," in *The Minor Prophets in the New Testament,* ed. Menken and Moyise, p. 45.

56. See also Hos. 6:2 and Matt. 16:21; 17:23; 20:19; Luke 18:33; 24:7; 24:46.

57. Menken, "The Minor Prophets in John's Gospel," in *The Minor Prophets in the New Testament,* ed. Menken and Moyise, p. 92.

2:6; cf. John 7:42). The Gospels draw from Zechariah to reveal Jesus as the coming king depicted in the Twelve.[58] Although the Gospels' use of Zechariah 9:9 varies to a degree, uniform to each of them is the view that Jesus is the long-awaited Davidic king who will bring peace and salvation to the entire world (Matt. 21:5; John 12:15).[59] The Markan quotation of Zechariah 9:9 affirms that Jesus is not just the anticipated Davidic king of Israel, but rather he is king over the Kingdom of God. His reign extends over the whole of creation (cf. Mark 11:1-11; 12:35-37; 13:27; cf. Rev. 21:5).[60] This vision of the reign of the messianic king comports with the creation-restorative vision of the Twelve.[61] Implicitly, the reader is invited to live rightly under his reign.

Jesus, Judgment, and Salvation

New Testament citation of the Twelve reinforces the concept of judgment and salvation that comes in the Day of the Lord. The use of this concept from the Twelve is perhaps the most extensive theological theme explored. But, for the New Testament, the Day of the Lord is an extension of God's work in the Christ-event. A pertinent example is found in the quotation of Hosea 10:8 in Luke 23:26-32. The quotation implies coming destruction in a day of judgment, as in Hosea. The difference, however, is in their temporal distance. Clearly Hosea speaks to an ancient context far removed from the first century A.D. Yet, for Luke, the same deviant behavior that marked the ancient audience of Hosea is typified in the faithless Israel of Luke's audience. In response, Luke focuses Jesus' citation of Hosea 10:8 (with various resonances to Hos. 9–10) to emphasize both the person and work of Christ and faithless Israel's rejection of him. Thus a cruciform focus comes into view in the Lukan account where it was not present in Hosea. The judgment coming in Jesus' day indicates the rejection of the Son of God. This kind of

58. Iain Duguid, "Messianic Themes in Zechariah 9–14," in *The Lord's Anointed: Interpretation of Old Testament Messianic Texts,* ed. P. E. Satterthwaite, R. S. Hess, and G. J. Wenham (Grand Rapids: Baker, 1995), pp. 265-80.

59. Ham, "The Minor Prophets in Matthew's Gospel," pp. 52-53; Maarten J. J. Menken, "The Minor Prophets in John's Gospel," in *The Minor Prophets in the New Testament,* ed. Menken and Moyise, pp. 80-85.

60. L. Schenke, *Das Markusevangelium* (Stuttgart: Kohlhammer, 2005), p. 264; Cilliers Breytenbach, "The Minor Prophets in Mark's Gospel," in *The Minor Prophets in the New Testament,* ed. Menken and Moyise, pp. 33-34.

61. Cf. Amos 9:12; Mic. 4:2-3; Zech. 2:11; 8:22-23; 9:9-13.

figural relation is typical of New Testament interpretation. So the New Testament proclaims that the judgment anticipated in the Twelve comes in and through Jesus. Judgment particularly falls upon faithless Israel, but also on the nations, as the New Testament reads and cites the Twelve (Acts 7:38-43).

Yet salvation is linked to the work of Jesus as well. Peter's sermon in Acts 2 is a poignant example and crystallizes the relationship between the Day of the Lord, Jesus, and salvation. As the Spirit of God pours out upon those in Jerusalem at Pentecost, Peter identifies the activity as a fulfillment of prophecy from Joel. Peter quotes closely (but not exactly) LXX Joel 3:1-5 in Acts 2:17-21. The vision of the text in Joel is that of the "glorious" Day of the Lord when God's salvation will be apparent through various visible signs. It is a day of both judgment of the wicked and salvation for Israel in which "everyone who calls upon the name of the LORD will be saved" (LXX Joel 3:5). Throughout the book of Acts, those who call upon the name of *the Lord* in fact call upon the name of *Jesus* out of belief in his salvation. So Peter says in Acts 2:38, "Repent and be baptized every one of you in the name of Jesus Christ for the forgiveness of your sins, and you will receive the gift of the Holy Spirit." From Acts 2, the day of salvation depicted in Joel is met in the person and work of Jesus, who is in fact the Lord. Salvation comes through him just as judgment comes for those who reject him. Both judgment and salvation, however, are intricately linked to the Day of the Lord theme from the Twelve. Peter calls the nations that hear him to embrace this Son of God, the king in these last days. The divine compassion toward the nations that the book of Jonah teaches is taken up by Peter's sermon. Further, it is taken up by those who would embrace this salvation and would proclaim God's salvation in Christ is come.

Further, the New Testament takes the Twelve's future judgment-salvation theme as present in Jesus. The anticipated "the last days" (באחרית הימים)[62] of the Twelve have become present in and through the work of Jesus. Peter adapts LXX Joel 3:1 in Acts 2:17 by using the words "in the last days" instead of the Greek word "afterwards" from Joel. As Huub van de Sandt states, "[Luke] clearly provides Joel's message with an eschatological understanding, thus underscoring that the 'last days' had dawned in his time. Luke was truly convinced that he was living in the last days of the present age."[63] In Peter's sermon, the work of God that brings salvation and judgment is the life, death, resurrection, and ascension of Jesus. The last days have broken

---

62. Hos. 3:5; Mic. 4:1. Cf. Zech. 8:6, 10. Shepherd, "Compositional Analysis."

63. Huub van de Sandt, "The Minor Prophets in Luke-Acts," in *The Minor Prophets in the New Testament,* ed. Menken and Moyise, p. 63.

into the present in Christ. But as we shall see below in the Synoptics' use of Zechariah 9:11, these "last days" are now, but not yet fully consummated under the reign of God in Christ.

Life under the Son

Further, the New Testament usage of the Twelve delineates what life before God should look like in light of this messianic king and the salvation that he brings. If Jesus is the long-awaited king who brings both salvation and judgment, ushering in the "last days," as Peter's sermon implies, then it follows that his exercise of kingship carries with it implications for how those who believe in the king should live. As in the Twelve's depiction of life before God, the New Testament is not monotonous on this point but highlights a number of habits for life under the reign of the Son of God.

First, a Christ follower is to live expectantly for God's consummate reign in Christ. As Jesus enters into Jerusalem and does his work there in the last days of his life, Matthew and Luke deploy a variety of either quotations or allusions to Zechariah 9–14.[64] One of particular interest for our discussion is an allusion to LXX Zechariah 9:11 that emphasizes the ransom of Jesus as the covenant sacrifice for the world. The allusion is set within the context of Jesus' final supper with his disciples (Mark 14:22-25; Matt. 26:26-29; Luke 22:14-23). It is fairly clear that the Synoptics' presentation of the wine as the "blood of the covenant" reminds the reader of the day of God's salvation mentioned in Zechariah through the work of God, on the basis of his covenant with Israel (Zech. 9:11).[65] This day of salvation comes with God's installation of the coming king, who rules all nations in peace (Zech. 9:9-10). Through this allusion, the Gospel writers link Jesus to this eschatological vision. Yet they go further to link Jesus as the sacrifice who will ransom the "prisoners" of Zechariah 9:11 and set them free. It is through the blood of the "covenant" — the blood of Jesus' sacrifice — that this ransom will be enacted. Jesus' blood then is inextricably linked to the blood of the old cov-

---

64. Zech 2:10 // Mark 13:27; Zech. 9:11 // Mark 14:24; Zech. 13:7 // Mark 14:27; Zech. 9:9 // Matt. 21:5; Zech. 12:12 // Matt. 24:30; Zech. 13:7 // Matt. 26:31; Zech. 11:12-13 // Matt. 27:9-10. See the classic discussion by R. T. France, *Jesus and the Old Testament* (Vancouver: Regent College Publishing, 1998).

65. The citation may refer to Exod. 24:8, but in light of the intertexts to Zechariah throughout the passion narrative it is better to see Zech. 9:11 foregrounded, even if the passage from Exodus is not dropped from view.

enant that God established with Israel, and yet it is new in that it is the sacrifice of Jesus (e.g., the pouring out of the blood) that serves to fully establish the reign of the king and forgive the sins of many (Mark 14:24).

Following upon this allusion to Zechariah, Matthew and Mark both present Jesus speaking of a time in which he will again have a meal with his followers. Christ will die as a ransom, but that will not be the end of the story. Jesus will rise again and have a meal with his followers in his Father's future kingdom. Unique to Matthew, the phrase "with you" (Matt. 26:29) provides expectancy for his coming kingdom and builds upon the quotation of Zechariah 9:11. So a sense of expectancy is built into Jesus' meal, expectancy in what God will do after the pouring out of Jesus' blood. Thus the message of "expectant living" pronounced in the Twelve is matched in the New Testament reception, although with a Christological focus.

Likewise, the full testimony of the Twelve reinforces a spirituality of patient faith in God. The New Testament teaches this as it uses Habakkuk 2:4 in Romans 1:17. Rikki Watts demonstrates that Paul uses both thematic and lexical ties to the book of Habakkuk in Romans 1, which culminate in the (altered) citation of Habakkuk 2:4: "The righteous will live by faith."[66] The purpose of the citation is to advance a line of thought in Romans that parallels the situation of Habakkuk. Paul relates the stance of the faithful follower of God in Habakkuk's day to the stance of the faithful follower of God in light of what he has done in and through Christ. In both historical situations, God is vindicated as just and righteous in his salvation. Paul centralizes and proves God's work in Christ as the decisive act of salvation. Watts concludes, "The gospel, then, is the revelation of Yahweh's faithful exercise of his power in effecting salvation (Hab. 3:18-19; Rom. 1:16), but it is a salvation on the basis of faith in the revealed gospel (Rom. 1:17b; cf. the vision of Hab. 2:1-4)."[67] The faith on display in Habakkuk is reiterated in Paul, but with a crucial difference. Faith in God ultimately culminates in God's salvation in Christ, in whom one trusts.

But faith demands perseverance in the present time. For both Habakkuk and Paul, present suffering remained potent. The issue was how to live in

---

66. Rikki E. Watts, "For I Am Not Ashamed of the Gospel: Romans 1:16-17 and Habakkuk 2:4," in *Romans and the People of God*, ed. Sven K. Soderlund and N. T. Wright (Grand Rapids: Eerdmans, 1999), pp. 3-25. Paul does not directly quote the Hebrew or Greek and omits the pronoun — whether a third-person-singular masculine suffixed pronoun in the Hebrew, "his faith," or a first-person pronoun in the Greek, "my faith" — that otherwise accompanies the noun in Hab. 2:4.

67. Watts, "I Am Not Ashamed," p. 23.

light of the suffering. As with Habakkuk, who waited for salvation to be enacted in his days (Hab. 3:2), Paul calls for Christ's followers to endure and wait (Rom. 4:18-25; 5:1-5; 8:18-27). For Paul, perseverance produces something inwardly in the believer (it is soul-building), but it is certainly more than this. Faith perseveres through present suffering as it eagerly awaits the certainty of new creation and the consummation of God's reign over creation, in Christ (Rom. 8). This message of perseverance is not merely introspective, to see what might be gained in suffering; rather, it is fundamentally prospective, anticipating the work of God in Christ, which is new creation. Perseverance, then, is a key for life under the Son (cf. Heb. 10:37-39).

Finally, faith ushers in praise. For Habakkuk, knowledge of God's salvation from exile and defeat of the enemy culminates in a final poem of praise to God. Paul argues that God's salvation in Christ is the final defeat of exile, death, and sin. Recognizing this drives one to praise God. Watts finds interesting parallels between the praise language of Romans 1:16; 16:25-27 and Habakkuk 2:4; 3:18-19. "The *righteous* shall live by *faith*" (Hab. 2:4b); "I will rejoice in the God of my *salvation*. The Lord God is my *strength*" (Hab. 3:18-19). "For it [the gospel] is the power of God for *salvation* to everyone who *believes*" (Rom. 1:16); "Now to the one who is able to *strengthen* you . . . according to my gospel . . . and the revelation of the mystery . . . to bring about the obedience of faith" (Rom. 16:25-27). In light of the intertextuality, Watts states, "Just as God has dealt mysteriously with Israel in the past, so also now. The right response is to believe."[68] Belief leads forth into praise for what God has done in his salvation.

Conclusion

The above framework has aimed at elucidating the message(s) of the Twelve so as to hear God's address in and through this corpus. As one both hears the discrete voice of the individual books and the voice of the book of the Twelve as a whole, and then follows the reception of the Twelve in the New Testament, one notes a good deal of continuity and degrees of discontinuity in Scripture. The expectation built into the Twelve, anticipating God's work of salvation in which all of creation is renewed, is carried further in the New Testament. There, this expectation is met in the person of Christ, who makes all things new. God's Christ-work enables the outpouring of the Spirit of

---

68. Watts, "I Am Not Ashamed," p. 23.

God on those who believe (Joel 2; Acts 2). The reader is called to be liberated by this Jesus and the world of faith that he opens up. In so doing, the reader is incorporated into the story of Christ and, by extension, the story of faithful Israel delineated in the Twelve and the New Testament. Alternatively, the reader may respond in disbelief and rejection of this Christ, ultimately identifying with the judged and unfaithful Israel delineated in the Twelve.

PART IV HEARING AND PROCLAIMING THE OLD TESTAMENT

16 Preaching the Old Testament

Aubrey Spears

The fact of the Canon tells us simply that the church has regarded these Scriptures as the place where we can expect to hear the voice of God. The proper attitude of preachers [depends] . . . on whether or not they expect God to speak to them here.

Karl Barth, *Homiletics*

Finally Arriving at the Beginning

At the conclusion of his fascinating journey Qohelet ironically confesses: "The end of the matter, all has been heard. Fear God and keep his commandments, for this is the whole duty of humankind" (Eccles. 12:13). Old Testament wisdom teaches the fear of God as the only beginning that leads to true knowledge (for example, Prov. 1:7; 9:10). The irony is that Ecclesiastes ends at the beginning. "In a world which depends at every point upon its creator,"[1] Qohelet has led us on a turbulent journey that ultimately exposes the bankruptcy of any approach to the knowledge of truth which resists one's creatureliness before the Creator.

Hearing the Old Testament heeds this warning and places readers at the proper and fecund beginning by approaching the Old Testament, not with

---

1. Craig Bartholomew, "The Theology of Ecclesiastes," in *Fresh Perspectives on Ecclesiastes,* ed. Mark Boda, Tremper Longman III, and Cristian Rata (Winona Lake, IN: Eisenbrauns, forthcoming).

modernity's and postmodernity's faith in human autonomy, but with a profound submission to the "one God who is the God of Israel [and] is also the God and Father of Jesus Christ."[2] Such a trinitarian hermeneutic leads one to read the Old Testament, as the introductory chapter argues, in order to hear God's address. In this chapter I will assess the current state of Old Testament homiletics and offer three theses indicating what is required for homiletics to grasp as much as possible, in all its fullness and in all its concrete force, a trinitarian hermeneutic.

Strengths of Contemporary Old Testament Homiletics

Elizabeth Achtemeier identifies the years between 1875 and 1933 as a time in which "the church as a whole lost the Old Testament."[3] While she and others identify the roots of the loss in "Europe more than three centuries earlier, in the aftermath of the wars of religion and the rise of the Enlightenment project,"[4] Achtemeier's point is that by the last quarter of the nineteenth century there was an effective silencing of the Old Testament in the church in general and in the pulpit in particular. Toward the end of this period there were powerful overtures to a breaking of the silence, such as Karl Barth's address of 1916, "The Strange New World within the Bible," the publication in 1918 of his *Commentary on Romans,* and Wilhelm Vischer's important work *Das Christuszeugnis des Alten Testaments* (The Witness of the Old Testament to Christ), which, Sidney Greidanus argues, "reclaimed the Old Testament for the Christian church and pulpit."[5] Despite these efforts, however, it was not until John Bright published *The Authority of the Old Testament* in 1967 that the situation really began to change in homiletical literature. Six years later, with Elizabeth Achtemeier's *The Old Testament and the Proclamation of the Gospel* (1973), followed closely by F. R. McCurley Jr., *Proclaiming the Promise: Christian Preaching from the Old Testament* (1974), we began to see regular

---

2. James Barr, *Old and New in Interpretation: A Study of the Two Testaments* (London: SCM, 1962), p. 149.

3. Elizabeth Achtemeier, "The Canon as the Voice of the Living God," in *Reclaiming the Bible for the Church,* ed. Carl Braaten and Robert Jenson (Grand Rapids: Eerdmans, 1995), p. 123.

4. Scott Hahn, "Worship in the Word: Toward a Liturgical Hermeneutic," *Letter and Spirit* 1 (2005): 101.

5. Sidney Greidanus, *Preaching Christ from the Old Testament: A Contemporary Hermeneutical Method* (Grand Rapids: Eerdmans, 1999), p. 172.

book-length offerings specifically addressing and encouraging Christian preaching of the Old Testament. Over the past thirty-five years, a great deal of excellent and fruitful work has been done in this whole area.

First, while the Enlightenment once made it appear hopelessly anachronistic to say that the Old Testament can "preach Christ," the growing recognition that all reading of the Bible is perspectival has opened the door for a return to the traditional role of the Trinity as a condition of a right reading of the Old Testament in the discipline of homiletics.[6] Michael Pasquarello's *Christian Preaching: A Trinitarian Theology of Proclamation* and *Sacred Rhetoric: Preaching as a Theological and Pastoral Practice of the Church* are just two examples of homiletical literature that argue for a trinitarian rule of faith as key to a preacher's approach to all of Scripture, including the Old Testament. In a similar vein, Old Testament homiletics has been influenced by the canonical approach, which has impacted large sections of biblical studies over the course of the last fifty years.[7] With its inherent sensitivity to the theological relationship between the two Testaments, the canonical approach has been a significant force in the reconsideration of the role of doctrinal predisposition in biblical interpretation. This has resulted in, among many other benefits, a growing capacity to appreciate and penetrate to the abiding theological concerns of patristic exegesis with its understanding of the Old Testament witness to Christ.[8]

Second, confessing the unified nature of the two Testaments is leading homiletics into a deeper engagement with the Old Testament. Unfortu-

---

6. See Chapter 1 by Craig Bartholomew in the present volume.

7. See Chapter 6 by Mark Boda in the present volume, along with the important collection of essays in *Canon and Biblical Interpretation,* ed. Craig G. Bartholomew et al., SAHS 7 (Grand Rapids: Zondervan, 2006).

8. For example, Ellen Davis, *Imagination Shaped: Old Testament Preaching in the Anglican Tradition* (Valley Forge: Trinity Press International, 1995); Ellen Davis, *Wondrous Depth: Preaching the Old Testament* (Louisville: Westminster John Knox, 2005); Sidney Greidanus, *The Modern Preacher and the Ancient Text: Interpreting and Preaching Biblical Literature* (Grand Rapids: Eerdmans, 1988); Greidanus, *Preaching Christ from the Old Testament;* Sidney Greidanus, *Preaching Christ from Genesis: Foundations for Expository Sermons* (Grand Rapids: Eerdmans, 2007); Sidney Greidanus, *Preaching Christ from Ecclesiastes: Foundations for Expository Sermons* (Grand Rapids: Eerdmans, 2010); Walter Kaiser, *Preaching and Teaching from the Old Testament* (Grand Rapids: Baker Academic, 2003); Rein Bos, *We Have Heard That God Is with You: Preaching the Old Testament* (Grand Rapids: Eerdmans, 2008); and Paul Scott Wilson, *God Sense: Reading the Bible for Preaching* (Nashville: Abingdon, 2001). For patristic exegesis, see The Ancient Christian Commentary on Scripture: Old Testament series, vols. I-XIV (Downers Grove: IVP, 2001-2009).

nately, as a continuing result of the loss of the Old Testament in the late nineteenth and early twentieth centuries, many churches remain, in the words of Richard Hays, "naïvely Marcionite in their theology and practice: in their worship services they have no Old Testament reading, or if the Old Testament is read, it is rarely preached upon. Judaism is regarded as a legalistic foil from which Jesus has delivered us."[9] The problem is that "the full biblical import of our sinful predicament, of the call to conversion and sanctification, and of our future hope comes to its own only against the backdrop" of the work of God in the Old Testament.[10] In the opening chapters of two separate volumes, Achtemeier clearly and correctly identifies the Old Testament as essential for the distinctively biblical view (1) of God, (2) of God's relation to humanity, and (3) of God's relation to creation.[11] The reclamation of the Old Testament in preaching is therefore essential to the recovery of the Bible itself and of the creation-wide dimension of Scripture for all of life.[12] It is of inestimable value, then, that the current literature on preaching the Old Testament, generally speaking, resists Marcionism and its nineteenth- and early-twentieth-century modified iterations in the works of Friedrich Schleiermacher, Adolf von Harnack, Friedrich Delitzsch, and Rudolf Bultmann.[13]

Third, many homileticians across a diversity of theological positions are returning to the premodern view of the unitary nature of the Bible existing at the level of "a single coherent story — a story in which Old Testament and New Testament together bear complementary witness to the saving action of the one God, a *true* story into which we find ourselves taken up."[14] Biblical

9. Richard Hays, "Can the Gospels Teach Us How to Read the Old Testament?" *Pro Ecclesia* 11 (2002): 403. See also Craig Bartholomew et al., eds., *Out of Egypt: Biblical Theology and Biblical Interpretation*, SAHS 5 (Grand Rapids: Zondervan, 2004).

10. Gordon Spykman, *Reformational Theology: A New Paradigm for Doing Dogmatics* (Grand Rapids: Eerdmans, 1992), p. 176.

11. Elizabeth Achtemeier, *The Old Testament and the Proclamation of the Gospel* (Philadelphia: Westminster, 1973), p. 37. See also Elizabeth Achtemeier, *Preaching from the Old Testament* (Louisville: Westminster John Knox, 1989), ch. 2.

12. See the seminal work of Herman Bavinck and Abraham Kuyper. For example, Herman Bavinck, *The Philosophy of Revelation: The Stone Lectures for 1908-1909, Princeton Theological Seminary* (New York: Longmans, Green, and Co., 1909), pp. 27-28.

13. See Chapter 2 by Al Wolters in the present volume.

14. Hays, "Can the Gospels Teach Us How to Read the Old Testament?" p. 404. Hans Frei's *The Eclipse of Biblical Narrative: A Study in Eighteenth and Nineteenth Century Hermeneutics* (New Haven: Yale University Press, 1974) is an important analysis of the breakdown of this approach to Scripture over the course of the eighteenth and nineteenth centuries.

theology, with its careful sense of the whole of Scripture and careful understanding of Scripture's own categories, is playing an essential role in this recovery.[15] While biblical theology and theological interpretation are distinct, they are complementary. Moreover, the capacity of the former to act as a key ingredient in the latter is difficult to overestimate.[16] In a trilogy of works Greidanus demonstrates this for homiletics from the perspective of a redemptive-historical Christocentric method.[17]

Finally, the recognition of the literary qualities of the Old Testament has been particularly fruitful for preaching the Old Testament. Meir Sternberg's *The Poetics of Biblical Narrative* has helpfully broadened the focus of historical criticism by integrating the historical, ideological, and aesthetic aspects of the Old Testament.[18] Thomas Long's fine treatment of the relationship of literary form to exegesis in *Preaching and the Literary Forms of the Bible,* Steve Mathewson's *The Art of Preaching Old Testament Narrative,* and Alyce McKenzie's *Preaching Biblical Wisdom in a Self-Help Society* are just three examples of how the literary turn in biblical studies has borne ripe fruit for Old Testament preaching.

Toward a Trinitarian Hermeneutic in Old Testament Homiletics

Major progress has been made since the period of silence of which Achtemeier spoke. However, there is still critical work to be done. In the remainder of this essay I will present three theses that orient homiletics to a

---

15. In addition to Chapter 6 by Mark Boda in the present volume, see Bartholomew, *Out of Egypt;* Craig Bartholomew and Michael Goheen, *The Drama of Scripture: Finding Our Place in the Biblical Story* (Grand Rapids: Baker Academic, 2004); Christopher Wright, *The Mission of God: Unlocking the Bible's Grand Narrative* (Downers Grove: IVP Academic, 2006); N. T. Wright, *The New Testament and the People of God* (Minneapolis: Fortress, 1992).

16. For example, see Craig Bartholomew, "Introduction," in *A Royal Priesthood? The Use of the Bible Ethically and Politically,* ed. Craig Bartholomew et al. (Grand Rapids: Zondervan, 2002). Particularly insightful is his analysis of the role of biblical theology in the extraordinarily creative theological interpretation of the Bible on display in Oliver O'Donovan's *Resurrection and Moral Order: An Outline for Evangelical Ethics* (Grand Rapids: Eerdmans, 1994).

17. Greidanus, *Preaching Christ from the Old Testament;* Greidanus, *Preaching Christ from Genesis;* Greidanus, *Preaching Christ from Ecclesiastes.* See also Edmund Clowney, *Preaching and Biblical Theology* (Grand Rapids: Eerdmans, 1961); Greidanus, *Modern Preacher;* and Graeme Goldsworthy, *Preaching the Whole Bible as Christian Scripture* (Grand Rapids: Eerdmans, 2000).

18. See Chapter 4 by David Beldman in the present volume.

fuller appropriation of the riches of a trinitarian hermeneutic aimed at hearing the voice of God in the Old Testament.

Thesis 1: For the preaching of the Old Testament to fully appropriate the riches of a trinitarian hermeneutic that aims at hearing the voice of the living God, we must recover the relationship between biblical studies and homiletics.

Historically, the church has approached the Old Testament with a trinitarian hermeneutic, and in the Old Testament the church has expected to hear God speaking. Closely connected to this commitment and expectation has been an equally ancient and widespread commitment to the distinct yet inseparable nature of Scriptural exegesis and preaching. Such a view stands behind the first sentence of the most influential book ever written on homiletics, Augustine's *De Doctrina Christiana:* "There are two things on which all interpretation of Scripture depends: the process of discovering what we need to learn, and the process of presenting what we have learnt."[19]

The necessary union of Scripture and sermon, so long nourished, fell prey to the well-documented atomizing and fragmenting effects of the Enlightenment. Karl Barth's preaching experience is illustrative. At the end of his theological education Barth began to preach on a weekly basis between the years of 1911 and 1921 in the small industrial village of Safenwil. Laboring under the historicist approach to Scripture,[20] he experienced the bankruptcy of this disjuncture, famously abandoned his "youthful theological idealism,"[21] and turned back to "The Strange New World within the Bible."[22] Barth, like Qohelet, discovered the beginning at an end.

Neither Barth's radical critique and turn to Scripture, nor the influential work of Walther Eichrodt in his *Theologie des Alten Testaments* (1933-1939), nor Vischer's important work previously referenced was absorbed into Old Testament homiletics. Elizabeth Achtemeier has argued that the reason for

19. Augustine, *On Christian Teaching*, I.1.

20. Historicism means many things; in this case it refers to the view that the meaning of Scripture is procured through historical research into the origins and development of Scripture since it is the historicity of a phenomenon that affords the means of comprehending its essence and reality.

21. William Willimon, *Conversations with Barth on Preaching* (Nashville: Abingdon, 2006), p. 13.

22. First delivered as an address in the church at Lentwil in the autumn of 1916. Karl Barth, "The Strange New World within the Bible," in *The Word of God and the Word of Man* (London: Hodder and Stoughton, 1928), pp. 28-50.

this failure is that biblical scholarship and American mainline Protestantism in general continued along the lines of Wellhausian developmentalism.[23] For Old Testament preaching to appropriate fully a trinitarian hermeneutic, it must engage the dominant historical and critical theories, assumptions, and methodologies funding both biblical studies and homiletics. It will be helpful to consider this issue from both sides of the relationship.

As regards biblical studies, Joseph Cardinal Ratzinger, now Pope Benedict XVI, has argued that the value of critical methods "depends on the hermeneutical (philosophical) context in which they are applied. . . . Again and again, competent scholars have purged [historical-critical exegesis] . . . of these rationalistic intentions, and it has yielded very many important insights, enhancing our understanding of the biblical testimony and the saving history which it contains. However, where the Enlightenment line is pursued, new divorces follow."[24]

The point that must not be missed for preaching the Old Testament is that, while preaching and biblical exegesis naturally fit together, they have been separated *because* modern biblical exegesis abandoned a trinitarian grounding and the telos of hearing the address of God. Their reunion, therefore, will depend in large part upon a genuine pluralism in biblical studies. Such pluralism will allow for the trinitarian approach being advocated in this volume. As Ratzinger implies in the above quotation, this does not mean that other approaches have nothing to offer. The demanding task of Christian interpretation is to appropriate the full range of insights without the ideological baggage.

Chapter two of Greidanus's 1988 volume, *The Modern Preacher and the Ancient Text,* picks up the argument of Achtemeier and exposes some of the historicist presuppositions that fund historical-critical methodologies. These presuppositions, Greidanus shows, "assess the Bible from a standpoint, a worldview, grounded outside the Bible."[25] Since homiletics needs an

---

23. Achtemeier, *The Old Testament,* chs. 1-3. Again, in 1989, Achtemeier makes the same observation in *Preaching from the Old Testament,* see chs. 1-3. For other analyses of the gap between biblical studies and preaching see Paul Scott Wilson, "Biblical Studies and Preaching: A Growing Divide?" in *Preaching as a Theological Task: World, Gospel, Scripture. In Honor of David Buttrick,* ed. Thomas Long and Edward Farley (Louisville: Westminster John Knox, 1996); and Stephen Farris, "Limping Away with a Blessing: Biblical Studies and Preaching at the End of the Second Millennium," *Interpretation* 51, no. 4 (October 1997): 358-70.

24. Joseph Cardinal Ratzinger/Pope Benedict XVI, "Seven Theses on Christology and the Hermeneutic of Faith," *Letter and Spirit* 3 (2007): 207.

25. Greidanus, *Modern Preacher,* p. 35.

approach to Scripture marked by "a radical break" with these foundational assumptions, Greidanus proposes an alternative that is "shaped by the biblical worldview."[26] But a great deal of work remains to be done.

In the two decades since this important work was published, a good number of volumes on preaching the Old Testament have appeared. As Paul Scott Wilson helpfully reveals in *Preaching and Homiletical Theory,* these books apply a plethora of methods from biblical studies.[27] However, the work that Achtemeier called for, and Greidanus contributed to, has not been adequately developed. Homileticians continue to act with philosophical naiveté in the way in which they conceive of the relationship between homiletics and biblical studies.

The current volume goes a long way in mapping out the complex issues at play in biblical scholarship.[28] Bartholomew's chapter, "Philosophy and Old Testament Interpretation," for example, argues that "we need once and for all to reject the assumption that a neutral, autonomous reading of the Old Testament is possible or desirable."[29] An important corollary of this assertion and of the trinitarian hermeneutic outlined in his introductory chapter is that faith is indispensable to epistemology. The implications of this for biblical studies have not been sufficiently explored. Particularly helpful in this regard are commentaries that flag their presuppositions and do exegesis with a trinitarian hermeneutic, attending to the address of God. A great example of rigorous biblical studies in service to the church through commentary writing is Bartholomew's *Ecclesiastes* in the Baker Commentary on the Old Testament Wisdom and Psalms series. This volume is an excellent resource for the preaching of the Old Testament to appropriate more deeply a trinitarian hermeneutic.

Looking at the homiletical landscape today, one can identify various theoretical and methodological approaches to Scripture that, despite important differences, have enough in common to legitimatize identification as a singular constellation: conservative evangelical homiletics, new homiletics, postliberal homiletics, and (radically) postmodern homiletics. Broadly speaking, *conservative evangelical homiletics* typically approaches Scripture in terms of the historical-cultural gap between contemporary hearers and

---

26. Greidanus, *Modern Preacher,* p. 36.

27. Paul Scott Wilson, *Preaching and Homiletical Theory* (St. Louis: Chalice, 2004), chs. 2-3.

28. See also Craig Bartholomew et al., eds., *Renewing Biblical Interpretation,* SAHS 1 (Grand Rapids: Zondervan, 2000).

29. See Chapter 3 by Craig Bartholomew in the present volume.

the original recipients of the biblical texts; to overcome this gap, the preacher abstracts timeless truths from the text in order to apply these truths to the concrete situation of the contemporary congregation.[30] *New homiletics* approaches the Bible via the event of language as the universal key to being and understanding; the goal is evocation of a Word-event.[31] *Postliberal homiletics* understands the relationship of Scripture and reader narratively; in this approach the biblical story is carried forward into the contemporary world by incorporating the contemporary world into the world rendered by the biblical narrative.[32] Finally, *(radically) postmodern homiletics* erases all boundaries between Scripture and congregation; meaning is generated through participatory conversation.[33]

The differences between these four approaches to Scripture are deeper than a surface method. Such methodological pluralism is neither new nor

---

30. For example, Haddon Robinson, *Biblical Preaching: The Development and Delivery of Expository Messages,* 2nd ed. (Grand Rapids: Baker Academic, 2001), pp. 88-96; Bryan Chapell, *Christ-Centered Preaching: Redeeming the Expository Sermon* (Grand Rapids: Baker, 1994), pp. 40-44, 199-224; Greidanus, *The Modern Preacher,* pp. 131-40, 182-87, 224-27; Daniel Doriani, *Putting the Truth to Work: The Theory and Practice of Biblical Application* (Phillipsburg, NJ: Presbyterian & Reformed, 2001); John MacArthur, *Rediscovering Expository Preaching: Balancing the Science and Art of Biblical Exposition* (Dallas: Word, 1992), especially Part III: Processing and Principlizing the Biblical Text; Jay Edward Adams, *Truth Applied: Application in Preaching* (Stanley, NC: Timeless Texts, 1990).

31. For example, David Randolph, *The Renewal of Preaching: A New Homiletic Based on the New Hermeneutic* (Philadelphia: Fortress, 1969), p. 19; Fred Craddock, *As One without Authority: Revised with New Sermons* (St. Louis: Chalice, 2001), especially ch. 3; Fred Craddock, *Preaching* (Nashville: Abingdon, 1985), especially pp. 25-27, 85-86, 148-50, 194-209; Eugene Lowry, *The Homiletical Plot: The Sermon as Narrative Art Form* (Louisville: Westminster John Knox, 2001), especially pp. 74-79; Eugene Lowry, *Doing Time in the Pulpit: The Relationship between Narrative and Preaching* (Nashville: Abingdon, 1985), pp. 13, 23, 26, 32, 36, 82, 85.

32. For example, Charles Campbell, *Preaching Jesus: New Directions for Homiletics in Hans Frei's Postliberal Theology* (Grand Rapids: Eerdmans, 1997), pp. 250-57; Mark Ellingsen, *The Integrity of Biblical Narrative: Story in Theology and Proclamation* (Minneapolis: Fortress, 1990); Richard Eslinger, *Narrative and Imagination: Preaching Worlds That Shape Us* (Minneapolis: Fortress, 1995), especially ch. 1, "Our Home in the Narrative."

33. For example, John McClure, *Other-Wise Preaching: A Postmodern Ethic for Homiletics* (St. Louis: Chalice, 2001), pp. 13-26; Lucy Rose, *Sharing the Word: Preaching in the Roundtable Church* (Louisville: Westminster John Knox, 1997), pp. 98-113, 130-31; L. Bond, *Trouble with Jesus: Women, Christology, and Preaching* (St. Louis: Chalice, 1999); Christine Smith, *Preaching as Weeping, Confession, and Resistance: Radical Responses to Radical Evil* (Louisville: Westminster John Knox, 1992); Joseph Webb, *Preaching and the Challenge of Pluralism* (St. Louis: Chalice, 1998).

necessarily problematic for preaching. The various approaches to Scripture ultimately exhibit a deeper form of pluralism that is problematic. This type of pluralism operates at a subterranean level. It is rooted in issues not only of history (as Greidanus revealed), but also of language, epistemology, and textuality. Differences at this level are often irreconcilable. For example, John McClure's view of textuality, articulated in *Other-Wise Preaching,* is antipodal to Steven Mathewson's view expressed in *The Art of Preaching Old Testament Narrative.*[34] One cannot work with both views; they are mutually exclusive. To choose between the two is to choose a fundamental view of reality.

Language, epistemology, history, and textuality coalesce under the subject of thought that has been identified since the last half of the twentieth century as philosophical or contemporary hermeneutics.[35] Because this area of study addresses that which is foundational and formative for all theory construction, it is critical that Old Testament homileticians become proficient here.[36] In summary, until the methodologies of biblical studies utilized by homileticians and the homiletical theories of Scripture are consistent on a depth-philosophical level with a trinitarian hermeneutic, the much-needed reunion of preaching and Scripture will be hindered.

In his masterful work *The Desire of the Nations,* Oliver O'Donovan writes: "The passage from what God said to Abraham to what we are now to do about Iraq, is one which the intuition of faith may accomplish in a moment, and a preacher's exhortation in under twenty minutes. An intellectual account of it, however, can be the work of decades."[37] One is reminded of Sternberg's trenchant observation that biblical studies is "not a discipline by any stretch of the term but the intersection of the humanities par excel-

---

34. McClure, *Other-Wise Preaching,* pp. 13-26; Steven Mathewson, *The Art of Preaching Old Testament Narrative* (Grand Rapids: Baker Academic, 2002).

35. See Joel Weinsheimer, *Philosophical Hermeneutics and Literary Theory* (New Haven: Yale University Press, 1991), especially ch. 2; Jean Grondin, *Introduction to Philosophical Hermeneutics* (New Haven: Yale University Press, 1994); Josef Bleicher, *Contemporary Hermeneutics: Hermeneutics as Philosophy, Method, and Critique* (London: Routledge & Kegan Paul, 1980); Richard Palmer, *Hermeneutics: Interpretation Theory in Schleiermacher, Dilthey, Heidegger, and Gadamer* (Evanston: Northwestern University Press, 1969). For the specific issue of the bearing of a philosophy of language upon biblical studies, see Craig Bartholomew et al., eds., *After Pentecost: Language and Biblical Interpretation,* SAHS 2 (Grand Rapids: Zondervan, 2001).

36. See Aubrey Spears, *The Theological Hermeneutics of Homiletical Application and Ecclesiastes 7:23-29* (Eugene: Pickwick, forthcoming), for a depth analysis of these issues.

37. Oliver O'Donovan, *The Desire of the Nations: Rediscovering the Roots of Political Theology* (Cambridge: Cambridge University Press, 1999), p. ix.

lence." As a result, "the progress it so badly needs is conditional either on all-around expertise, not given to humans, or on a truly common pursuit of knowledge."[38] The sort of work Anthony Thiselton has done to explore the role of linguistics, philosophy, and theology of language in biblical studies has yet to be done with equivalent rigor in practical theology. Until such work is done, Richard Lischer's ironic comment will continue to be true: "It is as difficult to find ministers who are against biblical preaching as it is to find biblical preaching."[39]

Thesis 2: For the preaching of the Old Testament to fully appropriate the riches of a trinitarian hermeneutic that aims at hearing the voice of the living God, we must recover something like the four senses of Scripture in preaching.

For sixteen hundred years the church read the Old Testament and the New Testament as a single unified vision of Christ.[40] Henri de Lubac's magisterial survey of medieval exegesis demonstrates that such a profound union of the two Testaments could only be the result of "the all-powerful and unprecedented intervention of Him who is Himself at once the Alpha and Omega, the First and the Last. . . . Jesus Christ brings about the unity of Scripture, because he is the endpoint and fullness of Scripture. Everything in it is related to him. In the end he is its sole object. Consequently, he is, so to speak, its whole exegesis."[41] This understanding of the unity of the Old and New Testaments in Christ produced a unique hermeneutic — the fourfold reading of Scripture (also known as the *quadriga* or the four senses), which dominated Christian exegesis until the seventeenth century.

The four senses are the literal, allegorical, tropological, and anagogical. The trinitarian hermeneutic outlined in the current volume, combined with a robust biblical theology, enables one to explore the traditional four senses in a fresh way. The *literal* sense is the storyline of the Bible. The *allegorical* sense is the Christological meaning. The story of Scripture is fulfilled and fo-

---

38. Meir Sternberg, *The Poetics of Biblical Narrative: Ideological Literature and the Drama of Reading* (Bloomington: Indiana University Press, 1985), pp. 21-22.

39. Richard Lischer, *A Theology of Preaching: The Dynamics of the Gospel* (Eugene: Wipf & Stock, 2001), p. 57.

40. See especially in this volume Chapter 1 by Craig Bartholomew, Chapter 2 by Al Wolters on the history of Old Testament interpretation, and Chapter 6 by Mark Boda on biblical theology.

41. Henri de Lubac, *Medieval Exegesis: The Four Senses of Scripture,* vol. 1 (Grand Rapids: Eerdmans, 1998), pp. 236-37.

cused on Christ, who casts his light on the whole, and thus we see the New in the Old concealed and the Old in the New revealed. In addition, the allegorical sense is ecclesiological "because the church is the body of Christ, the community united to the incarnate Son."[42] The *tropological* sense is the morality and spirituality that flow from the passage rightly interpreted within the framework of the overarching story. Scripture instructs us how to live under Christ's reign. We live according to the story, in the in-between time, and we live in anticipation of the new heavens and the new earth. The *anagogical* sense, then, is the eschatological meaning; the ultimate destiny of the cosmos and of each person in this one true story of all things.[43]

Four characteristics of this approach are important to highlight. First, a trinitarian hermeneutic and biblical theology help us avoid the nature-grace dichotomy that is often in the background of the traditional approach to the four senses.[44] In this way, there is an organic unity throughout the senses. They intermingle with each other and cannot and should not be too strongly separated. The story that the Bible tells is not only the true story of the world; through it God also invites us to make this story our own. We do this through baptism by the Spirit into the body of Christ, and then we rightly read the story from this perspective of being in Christ.[45] The so-called spiritual senses, then, are actually implicit in the literal sense. Moreover, the so-called literal sense is actually spiritual because, as believers, we have already been persuaded by the Spirit that this is the true story of the whole world. The aim of the *quadriga*, therefore, is a rich take on the literal sense of Scripture. All the senses are "a single reality: the mystery of Christ lived at various levels."[46]

42. Peter Leithart, "The Quadriga or Something Like It: A Biblical and Pastoral Defense," in *Ancient Faith for the Church's Future*, ed. Mark Husbands and Jeffrey Greenman (Downers Grove: IVP Academic, 2008), p. 118.

43. Henri de Lubac, *Medieval Exegesis: The Four Senses of Scripture*, vol. 2 (Grand Rapids: Eerdmans, 2000), ch. 10.

44. For example, in Jean Leclercq's excellent book, *The Love of Learning and the Desire for God* (New York: Fordham University Press, 1982), a tension remains between scholastic and monastic interpretation; see especially pp. 3-4. However, configuring the four senses with a biblical theology and a trinitarian hermeneutic holds great resources for undermining this dichotomy.

45. For this way of reading the Bible see Bartholomew and Goheen, *The Drama of Scripture*; Wright, *The Mission of God*; Wright, *The New Testament and the People of God*. Also, see Joel Green's excellent commentary, *The Gospel of Luke*, NICNT (Grand Rapids: Eerdmans, 1997), as an outstanding example of interpreting the Bible in such a way.

46. Mariano Magrassi, *Praying the Bible: An Introduction to Lectio Divina* (Collegeville: Liturgical Press, 1998), p. 9.

Second, we see in this approach to Scripture the importance of a trinitarian soteriology: since Christians are in Christ, "scriptural interpretation participates in God's own teaching by participating in the teacher, Jesus Christ."[47]

Third, this reading of Scripture is a historical reading of Scripture because it organizes "all of revelation around a concrete center, which is fixed in time and space by the Cross of Jesus Christ."[48] The incarnation is a definitive moment in history.

Fourth, this way of reading Scripture is unique. As de Lubac argues, "nothing analogous can be found, even notionally, outside the Christian faith. What we have here is a theory that, even in its very form, owes everything to this Christian faith, and that, in its content, seeks to give it full expression."[49] The *quadriga* is not, as some have claimed, a borrowing from the Greeks. The New Testament "itself is the great exemplar of simultaneous literal and spiritual exegesis. Allegorical readings, for example, are plentiful in Paul's epistles and even identified as such in Galatians 4:24. In 1 Corinthians 5–11, Paul offers a tropological reading of the Old Testament. . . . The Apocalypse is, from end to end, an anagogical reading of salvation history."[50] Christ and the apostles, not Philo, are the fountainhead of interpretive theory picked up by the church fathers and passed down through the medieval ages.[51]

Why the demise of the traditional four senses? A full account of their loss is beyond the scope of this chapter. Suffice it to say that unrestrained allegorical readings in the patristic and the medieval periods, the onslaught of rationalism and its antisupernatural bias, the battle over interpretation between Catholics and Protestants, the Enlightenment prejudice against preju-

---

47. J. Todd Billings, *The Word of God for the People of God: An Entryway to the Theological Interpretation of Scripture* (Grand Rapids: Eerdmans, 2010), p. 159.

48. De Lubac, *Medieval Exegesis*, vol. 1, p. xi.

49. De Lubac, *Medieval Exegesis*, vol. 2, p. 225.

50. Scott Hahn, *Letter and Spirit: From Written Text to Living Word in the Liturgy* (New York: Doubleday Religion, 2005), p. 166.

51. For Jesus' spiritual reading of the Old Testament see Mary Healy, "The Hermeneutic of Jesus," unpublished paper. For a refutation of the common view that Origen learned more from Philo than from Paul with regard to spiritual interpretation see, among other places in his work, de Lubac, *Medieval Exegesis*, vol. 1, p. 148, and vol. 2, p. 4. For a brief discussion of the role of ontological issues (Who is God? How does he stand in relation to his creation? What is wrong and how must it be put right?) in the patristic interpretative approach to Scripture, see Gerald Bray, "The Church Fathers and Biblical Theology," in *Out of Egypt*, ed. Bartholomew et al.

dice, the scientistic turn to methodology, a nontranscendent understanding of history, and the rise of pragmatism together resulted in a loss of the "theological vision that provides the underpinning for the spiritual sense."[52] By the end of the eighteenth century, spiritual exegesis appeared to be a hopelessly outmoded, arbitrary, wildly subjective superimposition on the text by the interpreter.[53]

"Demise," however, is a misleading description. "Supposed demise" is more accurate.[54] J. Todd Billings has shown that, while Reformers like John Calvin did not organize their exegesis around the *quadriga*, they did rename the four senses and retain their content.[55] Today the four senses are present in the best of Christian homiletical practice. For example, Greidanus, Goldsworthy, Clowney, and Chapell have each drawn on a robust biblical theology in their advocacy of typology for theological interpretation in the service of preaching the Old Testament.[56] The use of the term "typology," in this case, over against the term "allegory," is intended to demarcate the former from the latter, which, in this case, is being identified as an unacceptable form of fanciful, nonliteral exegesis. However, as Peter Martens and others have demonstrated, this distinction is a modern one related to the overly historical concerns of modern biblical interpretation.[57] Of course, this does not mean that we should discard attempts to determine good allegorical inter-

52. F. Martin, "Spiritual Sense," in *Dictionary for Theological Interpretation of the Bible,* ed. Kevin Vanhoozer et al. (Grand Rapids: Baker Academic, 2005), p. 771.

53. Frances Young places the blame on modernist historicism. See her "Allegory and the Ethics of Reading," in *The Open Text: New Directions for Biblical Studies,* ed. Francis Watson (London: SCM, 1993); and Frances Young, "The 'Mind' of Scripture: Theological Readings of the Bible in the Fathers," *International Journal of Systematic Theology* 7, no. 2 (April 2005). See also Robert Louis Wilken, "Allegory and Interpretation of the Old Testament in the 21st Century," *Letter and Spirit* 1 (2005): 11-21; and Frei, *Eclipse of Biblical Narrative.*

54. Young makes the astonishing observation that historical-critical reading "may be regarded in some sense [as] allegorical in that it enabled the domestication of ancient texts to modern apologetic needs" ("Allegory and the Ethics of Reading," pp. 116-17).

55. Billings, *The Word of God,* p. 170.

56. Greidanus, *Modern Preacher;* Greidanus, *Preaching Christ from the Old Testament;* Greidanus, *Preaching Christ from Genesis;* Greidanus, *Preaching Christ from Ecclesiastes;* Goldsworthy, *Preaching the Whole Bible;* Clowney, *Preaching and Biblical Theology;* and Chapell, *Christ-Centered Preaching.*

57. See Peter Martens, "Origen the Allegorist and the Typology/Allegory Distinction" (paper presented at the Annual Conference of the Society for Biblical Literature, 2004), for a full bibliography of the development of this distinction and its critics. In Chapter 2 in the present volume on the history of Old Testament interpretation, Wolters affirms the modern distinction between allegory and typology.

pretations from bad ones. The point is that the current allegory/typology distinction hardly does justice to the complexity of successful nonliteral (narrowly conceived) exegesis and simultaneously prejudices us against a recovery of the full range of good allegorical interpretation that has existed for most of church history. Paul Scott Wilson's *God Sense* identifies various places in which one can find good allegory and the other spiritual senses, for that matter, in homiletics today.[58] Peter Leithart makes a similar point when stating: "No Christian preacher . . . will be content to recount the past. To the letter, therefore, we must add a spiritual sense. . . . As soon as we do . . . we have stepped, whether we know it or not, into the realm of the quadriga." In fact "all preaching that aims to cultivate faith, love and hope will end up working with something very like the quadriga."[59] The work of both Wilson and Leithart firmly establishes their point.

A full appropriation of the riches of a trinitarian hermeneutic that aims at hearing the voice of the living God must begin with a reevaluation of the whole notion of literal meaning. For example, in *The Authority of the Old Testament*, John Bright writes: "Let us say it clearly: The text has but one meaning, the meaning intended by its author; and there is but one method for discovering that meaning, the grammatical-historical method."[60] In *Preaching and Teaching from the Old Testament*, Walter Kaiser quotes and affirms Bright: "This is true, of course. It is the only way to rule out all subjective and personal readings of the text that are without authority or backing of the one who claimed to have received this word as a revelation from God."[61] Such a view is in line with a general drift of Old Testament hermeneutics since the Reformation in identifying the literal meaning with the grammatical-historical meaning. The problem here is twofold.

First, this view of the literal meaning is a reduction of what was meant by the literal sense throughout church history up to and including the Reformers.[62] Second, relegating the spiritual senses to "application" rather than understanding them as genuine meanings betrays important, though unacknowledged, theological presuppositions that militate against the renewal of Old Testament preaching. Mary Healy wisely asks a question of a related issue that focuses our attention on the theological shift involved in the reduction of meaning by Bright and Kaiser: "Does it sufficiently account for the

---

58. Wilson, *God Sense*, p. 86.
59. Leithart, "The Quadriga," p. 125.
60. John Bright, *The Authority of the Old Testament* (Nashville: Abingdon, 1971), p. 92.
61. Kaiser, *Preaching and Teaching*, pp. 2-3.
62. See, for example, Frei, *Eclipse of Biblical Narrative*.

relationship between the spiritual sense and the divine economy, the wise dispensation by which God ordered all history in stages toward its fulfill-ment in the mystery of Christ, which for the Fathers was the indispensable foundation of the spiritual sense?"[63] This is to say that the spiritual senses are inherent in Scripture "as part of the divine Author's intention: God puts them there."[64] They are "a deeper dimension of reality, one that . . . [is] con-tained within the historical event conveyed by Scripture."[65]

De-theologizing "meaning" so that it represents a narrow, objective grammatical-historical-literal sense of Scripture is theologically problem-atic. Are we willing to say that the literal meaning is what the text gives us (exegesis), while the Christological or ecclesiological or moral or eschatolog-ical sense is something we are reading into the text (eisegesis)? Are we will-ing to give the Christological or ecclesiological or moral or eschatological sense of Scripture a less authoritative role in the life of the church than the literal meaning of Scripture? Are we willing to surrender a transcendent un-derstanding of history and of the act of thinking itself? The modern reduc-tion of meaning has resulted in the loss of "a sense of the depth, the interior dimension, of history and the direction being given to it by God."[66]

While it is a mistake to misidentify the spiritual senses as application, it is also a mistake to confuse the spiritual senses with certain interpretive phe-nomena. For example, some homileticians have learned from contemporary hermeneutics that the impact of history shapes the interpreter no less than the text. As a result, there is a marked shift in homiletics to conceive of exe-gesis more in terms of an art than as a distinctly scientific method.[67] This has been a good and helpful corrective to the methodologically oriented ap-proaches that dominated homiletics throughout the nineteenth century and for most of the twentieth century. On the one hand, there is no completely objective standpoint that will guard the preacher as interpreter from subjec-tivity. On the other hand, despite this limitation, radical relativism is avoid-able. Philosophical hermeneutics helpfully opens our eyes to the nature of understanding a text, or anything for that matter, as the result of the en-counter between the interpreter and the object of interpretation. This philo-

63. Healy, "The Hermeneutic of Jesus."

64. Wilson, *God Sense*, p. 11.

65. Hans Boersma, *Nouvelle Théologie and Sacramental Ontology: A Return to Mystery* (Oxford: Oxford University Press, 2009), p. 151.

66. Martin, "Spiritual Sense," p. 771.

67. The excellent volume edited by Ellen Davis and Richard Hays, *The Art of Reading Scripture* (Grand Rapids: Eerdmans, 2003), is a good representation.

sophical insight, however, is fundamentally different from what the *quadriga* is getting at. Scripture's unique ontological relationship to Christ is what results in *its* pluriformity of meaning. The four senses are a function of "the prodigious newness of the Christian fact."[68]

A similar confusion has been highlighted by William Willimon in his description of a freshman seminar reading Augustine's *Confessions*. The students amaze their professor with how much they hear in the book, how much they see, as first-time readers, that Willimon has never seen. "This ancient book [speaks] . . . to them as vividly as Cicero's *Hortensius* spoke to Augustine when he was about their age."[69] Yet the phenomenon being described is more akin to George Steiner's description of the ability of a classic to speak when read well[70] than to the explosion of meaning that results from Christ. The spiritual sense of Scripture is not "an enterprise in literary artifice, but a matter of divine revelation."[71] The fourfold meaning is not a property of texts in general or classics in particular, but of history. Again, "the Spiritual sense does not refer to a literary relationship but an ontological relationship. It is founded on the unity of the two covenants within the divine economy of salvation. . . . Thus the spiritual sense is not an additional meaning retrospectively superimposed on the texts in the light of new events, but something that was *already hidden* in those things written about in the texts."[72]

Another inadequate treatment of the spiritual senses is exemplified in a growing group of pastors and homileticians who advocate various forms of "Christ-centered or gospel-centered" preaching.[73] Sidney Greidanus, previously mentioned, is the most prolific of this group. This "school" of preaching embodies an exciting recovery of theological interpretation in preaching that directly challenges grace-less moralistic and Christ-less interpretations of Scripture. However, as Jason Hood has pointed out, there is an inherent narrowness to this approach that focuses on Christocentric soteriology in

68. De Lubac, *Medieval Exegesis*, vol. 1, p. xix.

69. Willimon, *Conversations with Barth*, p. 33.

70. See George Steiner, *After Babel: Aspects of Language and Translation*, 3rd ed. (Oxford: Oxford University Press, 1998), p. 296; and George Steiner, *Real Presences* (Chicago: University of Chicago Press, 1989), p. 8.

71. Wilken, "Allegory and Old Testament Interpretation," p. 13.

72. Mary Healy, "Inspiration and Incarnation: The Christological Analogy and the Hermeneutics of Faith," *Letter and Spirit* 2 (2006): 34.

73. Representatives include Timothy Keller, Edmund Clowney, Bryan Chapell, Michael Scott Horton, R. Scott Clark, Graham Goldsworthy, and Sidney Greidanus.

such a way that sustained moral and doctrinal instruction in preaching is marginalized and even denigrated. In his sympathetic review of the Christ-centered "school" of preaching, Hood demonstrates that Scripture's own self-interpretation includes the modeling of moral and doctrinal interpretation of the Old Testament.[74]

Notice how the *quadriga* solves the problem Hood identifies in a way that honors the important insight of the Christ-centered "school" of preaching. De Lubac states the matter plainly: "Understood with its full force, it [the tropological sense] can . . . come only in third place."[75] The solution lies in the order of the spiritual senses. "Rectitude of faith is the precondition for purity of mind, and to the extent that this faith is not firm and solid, it would be vain to wish immediately to pass on to morality. 'For one is not made to come to faith by the virtues, but rather one is brought to pursue the virtues by means of faith.'"[76] As Leithart has argued, the rightly ordered four senses follow the New Testament order of redemption and sanctification.[77] De Lubac is again helpful: "one joins the soul with the . . . [S]pirit, so that from their union the 'good work' results."[78] Thus the *quadriga* has homiletical wisdom for those who would marginalize moral preaching. It also has wisdom for those who marginalize personal application in sermons.

Inasmuch as the Christ-centered "school" marginalizes moral preaching, the postliberal "school" marginalizes the individual. While helpfully naming and critiquing the tendency of much contemporary homiletics to be excessively individualistic, postliberal homiletics too often goes to the other extreme and becomes anti-individual. This is a result of casting a dichotomous either/or wedge between the homiletical options of individual application on the one hand and communal socialization on the other hand. The mistake is in polarizing community and individual.

The four senses of Scripture locate the church in the allegorical sense. "Scripture is about Christ, but the Christ of Scripture is not only himself but also his body. The Christ who is the subject matter of Scripture is the *totus*

74. Jason Hood, "Christ-Centered Interpretation Only? Moral Instruction from Scripture's Self-Interpretation as Caveat and Guide," *Scottish Bulletin of Evangelical Theology* 27, no. 1 (Spring 2009): 50-69.

75. De Lubac, *Medieval Exegesis*, vol. 2, p. 127.

76. De Lubac, *Medieval Exegesis*, vol. 2, p. 128. Citing Rabanus, *De Universo*, Bk. XIV, c. xxii (Migne, *Patrologia latina*, LXXVI, 1302 AB).

77. Leithart, "Quadriga," p. 118.

78. De Lubac, *Medieval Exegesis*, vol. 2, p. 128.

Christus."[79] The danger of individualism is avoided not by marginalizing the individual but by making the moral meaning pass through the allegorical meaning in both its Christological and ecclesiological senses. "Before I apply the text to myself, I apply it to Christ and the Church. That which took place in him and continues in his mystical Body needs only reverberate in me.... It is a christocentric and ecclesial spirituality, and yet it becomes deeply personal.... Christ, the Church, the individual: these are the steps through which the Word must pass."[80] In this vein Gregory the Great would often use the following transitional formula in his sermons: "What we have said of the Church in general, let us now see applied to each soul in particular."[81]

As we recover such a rich take on the literal meaning, earlier chapters in this volume identify important constraints. The story line of Scripture (see Mark Boda's chapter on biblical theology and Christopher Wright's chapter on mission and the Old Testament) and attention to philosophical paradigms (see Al Wolters's chapter on the history of Old Testament interpretation and Craig Bartholomew's chapter on philosophy and Old Testament interpretation) are especially crucial. In other words, I am not advocating that we copy the medieval or patristic approach exactly. No less an advocate than de Lubac has acknowledged as much:

> The use of these processes at times irritates or amuses us and at time ravishes us by the beauty of the symbolism it brings to light. From petty or tortuous subtlety to dazzling greatness, the whole range unfolds before our eyes. It is not necessary to speak too ill of the first of these two extremes, for it constitutes the inevitable price of the second. We sense, moreover, that any servile attempt at imitation could no longer have any virtue in an age that no longer participates in that "ancient aestheticism" in which Christian as well as pagan minds, all minds, bathed at that time.[82]

There is no question of becoming premodern, of retrieving the inexhaustible riches of premodern exegesis at the expense of the riches of modern critical study. We must receive the genuine progress achieved in the last three centuries as we explore more fully and deeply and boldly the riches of the

---

79. Peter Leithart, *Deep Exegesis: The Mystery of Reading Scripture* (Waco: Baylor University Press, 2009), p. 173.

80. Magrassi, *Praying the Bible*, p. 97.

81. Magrassi, *Praying the Bible*, p. 98.

82. Henri de Lubac, *History and Spirit: The Understanding of Scripture According to Origen* (San Francisco: Ignatius, 2007), p. 376.

fourfold reading of Scripture. In this direction lies a sensitivity to that "marvelous depth" of Scripture that inspired in Augustine a love mixed with dread. "O wondrous depth of your words, whose surface presents itself to us and pleases us like children, and yet what wondrous depth, my God, what wondrous depth! It makes one shudder to look into it — a shuddering of awe, but also a trembling of love!"[83]

Thesis 3: For the preaching of the Old Testament to fully appropriate the riches of a trinitarian hermeneutic that aims at hearing the voice of the living God, we must recover the role of prayer in the life of the preacher.[84]

As was discussed in the previous section, the essential livingness of Scripture is not a function of its literariness, but a unique ontological relationship. In breathing the Scriptures, God has made them alive (2 Tim. 3:16-17). But this breathing, this inspiration, is not limited to the origin of Scripture. Not only were the biblical authors inspired by the Spirit, but the Spirit continues to indwell Scripture. Inspiration "is an ongoing and ever-present influence at work within the Books themselves."[85] This is the traditional doctrine of Scriptural inspiration.

In the previous section of this chapter I pointed to the spiritual nature of all four senses. This points to an organic connection between inspiration and interpretation. As Jerome wrote of Galatians 5:19-21, Scripture must be read and interpreted "in the light of the same Spirit by whom it was written."[86] Reading the Bible is different from reading Dostoyevsky. While there is a sense in which one must approach Scripture as any other text, with the humility that is open to the other, the more important issue is that Scripture is not simply a text; it is God's book.[87] To properly read Scripture one must listen for God's address through his Spirit. Just as the human authors required the inspiration of the Holy Spirit to compose, so readers require the

---

83. Augustine, *Confessions*, 12.14, 17.

84. In reality, we must recover the role of prayer in the life of the preacher *and the congregation;* however, it is beyond the scope of this chapter to explore the relationship of the congregation's prayerful reading of Scripture to its reception of Scripture in the liturgy.

85. Magrassi, *Praying the Bible*, p. 27.

86. Jerome, *Commentaries on the Letter to the Galatians*, 5.19-21. Cited in Magrassi, *Praying the Bible*, p. 29.

87. See the eight volumes of the Scripture and Hermeneutics Seminar, especially Craig Bartholomew et al., *After Pentecost;* Craig Bartholomew et al., eds., *"Behind" the Text: History and Biblical Interpretation*, SAHS 4 (Grand Rapids: Zondervan, 2003); Craig Bartholomew et al., *Reading Luke: Interpretation, Reflection, Formation*, SAHS 6 (Grand Rapids: Zondervan, 2005); and Craig Bartholomew et al., eds., *Canon and Biblical Interpretation*.

inspiration of the Holy Spirit to understand. The heart of my third thesis for the renewal of Old Testament preaching in light of a trinitarian hermeneutic is that this principle must dictate the nature of our efforts to understand Scripture: faith has an epistemological edge.[88]

When a person reads Scripture and actually understands it, in the words of Origen, that person has received a "visit from Jesus."[89] This encounter

> does not consist in ideas, but it communicates the very reality of the One whose riches are unfathomable. . . . God does not appear as a distant third party with whom we could discourse or as the object of an impersonal contemplation; rather he presents himself to the soul in view of a dialogue of love. It presupposes ears cleaned of all the sounds of the world and sensitive to the steady sounds of the spirit that are the murmur of his call; unscaled eyes open to the delicate light of the signs by which he allows himself to be discerned.[90]

What an elegant description of the prayerful nature of interpreting Scripture! Unfortunately, as Craig Bartholomew and Robby Holt have noticed, this "relationship between prayer and biblical interpretation is neglected almost across the board. A perusal of books on biblical hermeneutics indicates that prayer is hardly ever listed."[91]

We have traveled so far from Origen's approach that Francis Martin can point out that reading the Bible in the light of Christ "has come to mean comparing texts in the light of a concept, rather than comparing realities mediated by the Holy Spirit through the texts, happening in the context of a faith experience of Jesus Christ."[92] On the rare occasion when prayer is ad-

---

88. Again, I am parting ways with the traditional Catholic approach over the nature-grace dichotomy. See the dialogue between Mark Noll and James Turner in which Turner argues that the Catholic position is that "[f]aith gives no *epistemological edge*," in their *The Future of Christian Learning: An Evangelical and Catholic Dialogue* (Grand Rapids: Brazos Press, 2008), p. 106. For an example of the way this debate plays out in the interpretation of Scripture see the exploration of the nature-grace relationship in the history of interpretation of Proverbs 31:10-31 in Al Wolters, *The Song of the Valiant Woman: Studies in the Interpretation of Proverbs 31:10-31* (Carlisle: Paternoster Press, 2001), pp. 15-29.

89. Origen, *Homilies on Isaiah*, hom. 6, 3. In *Die Griechischen Christlichen Schriftsteller der ersten drei Jahrhunderte. Origenes*, vol. 8, p. 274. Cited in de Lubac, *History and Spirit*, p. 382.

90. De Lubac, *History and Spirit*, pp. 382, 384.

91. Craig Bartholomew and Robby Holt, "Prayer in/and the Drama of Redemption in Luke: Prayer and Exegetical Performance," in *Reading Luke*, ed. Bartholomew et al., p. 351.

92. Martin, "Spiritual Sense," p. 771.

dressed in biblical studies or hermeneutics, it too often comes across as some kind of pious supplement to exegesis that adds nothing of substance to the interpreter's knowledge of Scripture.

For the preaching of the Old Testament to fully appropriate the riches of a trinitarian hermeneutic that aims at hearing the voice of the living God, we must recover the relationship of prayer and interpretation. There is an ancient tradition that holds great promise for such a recovery: *lectio divina.* Louis Bouyer helpfully describes this practice as "a personal reading of the Word of God during which we try to assimilate its substance; a reading in faith, in a spirit of prayer, believing in the real presence of God who speaks to us in the sacred text, while the [person reading Scripture] . . . strives to be present in a spirit of obedience and total surrender to the divine promises and demands."[93] Jean Leclerq provides a concise definition: "*lectio divina* is prayed reading."[94] The essence of this approach is found in both the Old Testament and the New Testament, and the church fathers frequently mention it, but the classic formulation of *lectio divina* was set down by Guigo the Second, prior of the Grande Chartreuse in the second half of the twelfth century.[95] He identifies four phases: *lectio, meditatio, oratio,* and *contemplatio.*

The starting point, *lectio,* is a slow, unhurried, disciplined, fully engaged reading of the Scripture in "an atmosphere of silence and inner calm."[96] Ambrose insisted that we "read . . . [the words] not in agitation, but in calm; not hurriedly, but slowly, a few at a time, pausing in attentive reflection."[97]

Meditatio is the slow and patient meditative entrance into the world of the passage. "The heart is the mouth in which the text is chewed . . . ruminated. We ponder each word in order to grasp its full meaning, imprint it on our memory and taste its sweetness, find joy and nourishment for our soul."[98] We move "from looking at the *words* of the text to entering the *world* of the text."[99] We begin to sense that Scripture is a living tissue, "a connected,

93. Louis Bouyer, *Parola, Chiesa e Sacramenti nel Protestantesimo e nel Cattolicesimo* (Brescia, 1962), p. 17. Cited in Magrassi, *Praying the Bible,* p. 18.

94. Jean Leclercq, *L'amour des lettres et le désir de Dieu: Initiation aux autueurs monastiques du moyen-âge* (Paris, 1957), p. 72. Cited in Magrassi, *Praying the Bible,* p. 18.

95. Guigo II, "The Ladder from Earth to Heaven," trans. Jeremy Holmes, *Letter and Spirit* 2 (2006): 175-88.

96. Magrassi, *Praying the Bible,* p. 63.

97. Cited in Magrassi, *Praying the Bible,* pp. 105-6.

98. Magrassi, *Praying the Bible,* p. 109.

99. Eugene Peterson, *Eat This Book: A Conversation in the Art of Spiritual Reading* (Grand Rapids: Eerdmans, 2005), p. 99.

coherent whole, not a collection of inspired bits and pieces."[100] The importance of biblical theology, with its attention to Scripture in its totality, is obvious. In time, "the Bible becomes second nature."[101] No longer tourists, we become inhabitants roaming freely within the world of the Bible as Jerome did: "He roamed through all the Scriptures with his thought and memory."[102]

Oratio is the soul leaving its reading to run to God in "meditative prayer" that "springs from the heart at the touch of the divine Word. . . . Having filled those words with all our thought, our love and our life, we repeat to God what he has said to us. The Word is not only the center of our listening; it is also the center of our response."[103]

Contemplatio, the summit of the whole process, is the "delicious fruit that ripens on the tree of Bible reading."[104] In the words of John of Fécamp, "the awestruck soul is rapt in contemplation; anxious, it is filled with wonder. Whereas before it spoke; now it is utterly speechless. Formerly enriched by its poverty, now it is impoverished by its riches. Amazingly, it becomes weak as it advances, but then in its weakness it advances further."[105] Here is the final stage of the journey that begins with reading and ends with astonishing intimacy with God.[106] *Lectio divina* requires an approach to the Bible "as the word of God actually addressed to the soul, rousing and creating the response in which the soul surrenders itself, as it recognizes the voice of the love who loved it first."[107]

Lectio divina is not a technique. The four phases are not methodical steps. It helps to think in terms of Eugene Peterson's description of one phase "calling forth another and then receding to give place to another, none in isolation from the others but thrown together in a kind of playful folk dance. . . . Each of the elements must be taken seriously; none of the elements may be eliminated; none of the elements can be practiced in isolation from the others. In the actual practice of *lectio divina* the four elements fuse,

---

100. Peterson, *Eat This Book,* p. 100.

101. Magrassi, *Praying the Bible,* p. 111.

102. Magrassi, *Praying the Bible,* p. 111.

103. Magrassi, *Praying the Bible,* p. 113.

104. Magrassi, *Praying the Bible,* p. 116.

105. John of Fécamp, *Confessio theologica,* in *Un maître de la vie spirituelle au XIe siècle: Jean de Fécamp,* ed. J. Bonnes and J. Leclercq (Paris, 1946), p. 182. Cited in Magrassi, *Praying the Bible,* p. 118.

106. Magrassi, *Praying the Bible,* pp. 118-19.

107. L. Bouyer, *The Spirit and Forms of Protestantism,* trans. A. Littledale (Princeton: Scepter Publishers, 2001), pp. 162-63.

interpenetrate."[108] Guigo himself provides a much-quoted metaphor that highlights the interpenetrating nature of each phase: "Reading places solid food in the mouth; meditation chews and breaks it; prayer extracts the flavor; contemplation is the very sweetness that gives joy and refreshes."[109]

Bouyer has reminded his Catholic brethren that the widespread Protestant practice of daily Bible reading leading on to private and personal prayer is closely akin to the ancient *lectio divina*. "What do they seek in this reading and in the prayer it inspires? We answer categorically: God speaking to the soul and acting in it."[110] However, speaking from experience, Protestants too often leave seminary having divorced this contemplative, prayerful, soul-nourishing Scripture reading from the disciplined and rigorous study of Scripture called exegesis.

In many seminaries the exegetical methods and the critical commentaries that are presented leave little or no room for prayer as a constitutive part of interpretation. Frequently one comes across suggestions such as David Dockery's: "The sermonic process begins with prayer. God's direction and enablement must be sought at each step."[111] In my homiletics course we began each class discussing the assigned reading from *Prayer*, by E. M. Bounds. But then, as in Dockery's essay, that was the end of prayer in the sense that there were no tools available for reuniting prayer and the exegetical method. As was mentioned earlier, biblical studies has given itself to methods structured by philosophical commitments antithetical to reading Scripture in order to attend to the address of God.

Hans Urs von Balthasar describes a similar scenario among Catholics:

> Some simply found food for their devotion in contemplating the gospel, without reference to their other studies. Others attempted, not always successfully, to make a synthesis between what it was their particular mission to proclaim and the traditional formulas of Scholasticism; or, if they could not assimilate these in their whole range . . . they selected particular stones from the building to use as the substructure for their own personal teaching.[112]

---

108. Peterson, *Eat This Book*, p. 91.

109. Guigo, "The Ladder from Earth to Heaven," p. 176.

110. Bouyer, *The Spirit and Forms of Protestantism*, p. 19.

111. David Dockery, "A Historical Model," in *Hermeneutics for Preaching: Approaches to Contemporary Interpretations of Scripture*, ed. Raymond Bailey (Nashville: Broadman, 1992), p. 39.

112. Hans Urs von Balthasar, *Explorations in Theology*, vol. 1: *The Word Made Flesh* (San Francisco: Ignatius, 1989), p. 189.

The problem becomes apparent when Balthasar compares this situation with the church fathers, who "found straightaway the appropriate dogmatic clothing for their very personal experience; everything became objective, and all the subjective conditions, experiences, fears, strivings, the 'shock' in a word, were made to serve a fuller understanding of the content of revelation, to orchestrate its great themes. Every form of spirituality, of mysticism was seen as serving a function in the Church."[113] We then see that recovering the traditional relationship between biblical studies and preaching, along with a recovery of a rich take on the literal sense, opens the door to recover the relationship between prayer and interpretation.

Marcellino D'Ambrosio describes one of de Lubac's most important insights when he writes, "Faith, not exegetical science, is the key to its [the spiritual sense's] discovery."[114] Balthasar's prescription for theology is right for us too: "Theology must always be conducted with rigorous precision. But it must also correspond at all points with its object, itself unique among objects of knowledge; and conform to its special content and method."[115]

De Lubac, wanting to surrender neither critical study nor the role of prayer in interpretation, insists that the two be properly related: biblical study, rightly conceived (in terms of the earlier section of this chapter), "prepares for it [*lectio divina*] and makes it more valuable because of the spiritual 'culture' it provides."[116] There is insight here. Magrassi makes the point: "Mystical contemplation is the end of a journey that begins with the sacred Book. It passes through the teaching of faith, leads to formation, creates moral attitudes modeled on the Word, and culminates in that 'sweetest experience of divine love, which with its ineffable sweetness unites us to the supreme God.' A true journey of reunion, it raises the human heart to the heart of God."[117] Notice the four senses: the *literal* is "a journey that begins with the sacred Book"; the *allegorical* "passes through the teaching of the faith, leads to formation"; the *tropological* "leads to formation, creates moral attitudes modeled on the Word"; and the *anagogical* culminates in that "sweetest experience of divine love." Here we have a fusion of the four senses and *lectio divina* in the study of Scripture. However, this should not be seen as a two-step process in which one begins with critical study and then moves

---

113. Balthasar, *Explorations in Theology*, p. 190.

114. Marcellino D'Ambrosio, "De Lubac's Hermeneutics of Tradition," *Letter and Spirit* 1 (2005): 152.

115. Balthasar, *Explorations in Theology*, p. 206.

116. Magrassi, *Praying the Bible*, p. 73.

117. Magrassi, *Praying the Bible*, p. 75.

on to spiritual insight. And yet there remains something of a dialectic between *lectio divina* and critical study, with both being able to correct the other.

The point at hand is that Scripture both instructs us and also is the means whereby we receive Christ and are remade into his image. Brian Daley argues that both Hilary of Poitiers and John Keble teach us that "the discovery of . . . holy things — which are Scripture's actual *content* and *meaning* — requires from the reader a process of purification and an attitude of reverence that are not simply the product of academic learning but belong to the life of worship and faith. The key to this attitude, for both authors, seems to lie in the sense that it is God who speaks through the biblical author and text and that our own engagement with the text is nothing less than a personal encounter with the Divine Mystery."[118] To adapt a phrase of Balthasar, *in so far as one is holy, one understands; in so far as one understands, one is holy.*[119] Such is the hermeneutical circle: the pure in heart see God, who are thereby purified in order to see God more clearly. The spiritual reading of Scripture is a spiritual discipline, a means for the transformation of the soul. A trinitarian hermeneutic, with its epistemological edge, paves the way for an integration of biblical study and *lectio divina* that will enable the preaching of the Old Testament to appropriate the riches of a trinitarian hermeneutic more fully.

Finally Arriving at the Beginning

The introduction to the second edition of Richard Lischer's homiletics reader contains an interesting modification of the first edition. In 1987 he wrote: "The church's reliance on and enjoyment of allegory appears to have disappeared for good."[120] In the 2002 edition Lischer writes: "Theological interpretation is once again displaying the riches of patristic exegesis, including allegory."[121] Another observation, unfortunately, remains the same despite the fifteen-year interregnum:

118. Brian Daley, "Is Patristic Exegesis Still Usable?" in *The Art of Reading Scripture,* ed. Davis and Hays, p. 80.

119. Balthasar, *Explorations in Theology,* p. 201.

120. Richard Lischer, *Theories of Preaching: Selected Readings in the Homiletical Tradition* (Durham: Labyrinth, 1987), p. 3.

121. Richard Lischer, *The Company of Preachers: Wisdom on Preaching from Augustine to the Present* (Grand Rapids: Eerdmans, 2002), p. xiv.

The person of the preacher . . . was of great importance to the medieval church but is now seldom discussed in homiletics. Most homiletical treatises from Augustine through the Middle Ages deal with the formation and holiness of the one appointed to preach. The same concerns are evident in seventeenth-, eighteenth-, and nineteenth-century classic texts, whether by Baxter, Herbert, Spener, or Schleiermacher. Despite the interest in spirituality in both the church and popular culture today, however, one does not discern a revival of the classical preoccupation with the holiness of the preacher.[122]

The preacher of Ecclesiastes concludes as follows: "The end of the matter; all has been heard. Fear God and keep his commandments, for this is the whole duty of man" (12:13). Developing the implications of a trinitarian hermeneutic brings us to the same point. In the words of de Lubac, "Understanding is not a matter of cleverness of mind, even a mind illumined by God, but of purity of heart, of uprightness."[123] Herein lies the direction we must go as we continue to recover from the eclipse of the Old Testament in the pulpit.

122. Lischer, *Company of Preachers*, p. xiv. Stephen Farris makes a similar comment: "The book for our time on the spirituality of the preacher is yet to be written." He goes on to suggest that such a book should include "a careful discipline of prayer and meditation." See Stephen Farris, *Preaching That Matters: The Bible and Our Lives* (Louisville: Westminster John Knox, 1998), p. 39.

123. De Lubac, *History and Spirit*, pp. 365-66.

Bibliography

Abbot, Abiel. "Traits of Resemblance in the People of the United States of America to Ancient Israel." In *The American Republic and Ancient Israel*, edited by J. Cellini. New York: Arno Press, 1977.

Achtemeier, Elizabeth. *The Old Testament and the Proclamation of the Gospel*. Philadelphia: Westminster, 1973.

———. *Preaching from the Old Testament*. Louisville: Westminster John Knox, 1989.

———. "The Canon as the Voice of the Living God." In *Reclaiming the Bible for the Church*, edited by Carl Braaten and Robert Jenson. Grand Rapids: Eerdmans, 1995.

Adam, A. K. M. *What Is Postmodern Biblical Criticism?* Minneapolis: Fortress, 1995.

Adams, Jay. *Truth Applied: Application in Preaching*. Stanley, NC: Timeless Texts, 1990.

Akenson, Donald Harman. *Surpassing Wonder: The Invention of the Bible and the Talmuds*. Chicago: University of Chicago Press, 2001.

Alexander, T. Desmond. *Abraham in the Negev: A Source-Critical Investigation of Genesis 20:1–22:19*. Carlisle: Paternoster, 1997.

———, and Brian S. Rosner, eds. *New Dictionary of Biblical Theology*. Downers Grove: IVP, 2000.

Alexander, William M. *Johann Georg Hamann: Philosophy and Faith*. The Hague: Martinus Nijhoff, 1966.

Alter, Robert. *The Art of Biblical Narrative*. New York: Basic Books, 1981.

———. *The Art of Biblical Poetry*. New York/Edinburgh: Basic Books/T&T Clark, 1985.

———. "Introduction to the Old Testament." In *The Literary Guide to the Bible*, edited by Robert Alter and Frank Kermode. Cambridge, MA: Harvard University Press, 1987.

———. *The World of Biblical Literature*. London: SPCK, 1992.

———. *Genesis: Translation and Commentary*. W. W. Norton, 1997.

———. *The David Story: A Translation with Commentary of 1 and 2 Samuel*. New York: Norton, 2000.

———. *The Book of Psalms: A Translation with Commentary.* New York: W. W. Norton, 2007.

———. *The Five Books of Moses: Translation and Commentary.* New York: W. W. Norton, 2008.

———. *The Wisdom Books: Job, Proverbs, and Ecclesiastes; A Translation with Commentary.* New York: Norton, 2010.

Amit, Yaira. *Reading Biblical Narratives: Literary Criticism and the Hebrew Bible.* Translated by Y. Lotan. Minneapolis: Fortress, 2001.

Anderson, Bernhard. *Understanding the Old Testament.* Englewood Cliffs: Prentice-Hall, 1986.

Anderson, Cheryl. *Ancient Laws and Contemporary Controversies: The Need for Inclusive Biblical Interpretation.* New York: Oxford University Press, 2009.

Aquinas, Thomas. *Summa Theologiae.* 3 vols. Turin: Marietti, 1962-63.

———. *Super Evangelium S. Ioannis Lectura.* Edited and translated by P. Raphaelis Cai. Casale Monferratto: Edizioni Piemme, 1972.

Athanasius. "Ad Serapion." In *Historical Tracts of S. Athanasius.* Translated by Miles Atkinson. Oxford: John Henry Parker, 1843.

Audet, J. P. "A Hebrew-Aramaic List of Books of the Old Testament in Greek Transcription." *Journal of Theological Studies* 1 (1950): 135-54.

Augustine, *Confessions.*

Augustine. *On Christian Teaching.*

Bäckersten, Olof. *Isaiah's Political Message: An Appraisal of His Alleged Social Critique.* FAT 2/29. Tübingen: Mohr Siebeck, 2008.

Bakan, David. *Disease, Pain and Sacrifice: Toward a Psychology of Suffering.* Chicago: University of Chicago Press, 1968.

Baker, David L. *Two Testaments, One Bible: A Study of the Theological Relationship between the Old and New Testaments.* Revised edition. Leicester: Apollos, 1991.

———. *Two Testaments, One Bible: The Theological Relationship between the Old and New Testaments.* 3rd edition. Downers Grove: IVP, 2010.

Balthasar, Hans Urs von. *Theologik II: Wahrheit Gottes.* Einsiedeln: Johannes Verlag, 1985.

———. *Theologik III: Der Geist der Wahrheit.* Einsiedeln: Johannes Verlag, 1987.

———. *Explorations in Theology, I: The Word Made Flesh.* San Francisco: Ignatius Press, 1989.

Bar-Efrat, Shimeon. *Narrative Art in the Bible.* Bible and Literature Series. Sheffield: Almond Press, 1989.

Barker, Paul A. *The Triumph of Grace in Deuteronomy: Faithless Israel, Faithful Yahweh in Deuteronomy.* Carlisle: Paternoster, 2004.

Barr, James. *The Semantics of Biblical Language.* Oxford: Oxford University Press, 1961.

———. *Biblical Words for Time.* Studies in Biblical Theology 33. London: SCM, 1962.

———. *Old and New in Interpretation: A Study of the Two Testaments.* London: SCM, 1962, 1966.

———. "Semantics and Biblical Theology: A Contribution to the Discussion." In *Congress Volume: Uppsala 1971,* edited by Henrik Samuel Nyberg. Leiden: Brill, 1972.

————. *Holy Scripture: Canon, Authority, Criticism.* Oxford: Oxford University Press, 1983.

————. *The Concept of Biblical Theology: An Old Testament Perspective.* Minneapolis: Fortress, 1999.

————. *History and Ideology in the Old Testament: Biblical Studies at the End of a Millennium.* Oxford: Oxford University Press, 2000.

Barram, Michael. *Mission and Moral Reflection in Paul.* Berlin: Peter Lang, 2005.

————. "The Bible, Mission, and Social Location: Toward a Missional Hermeneutic." *Interpretation* 61 (January 2007): 42-59.

Barth, Karl. "The Strange New World within the Bible." In *The Word of God and the Word of Man,* translated by Douglas Horton. London: Hodder and Stoughton, 1928.

————. *The Epistle to the Romans.* New York: Oxford University Press, 1968.

————. *Church Dogmatics.* 14 volumes. Edited by G. W. Bromiley and T. F. Torrance. Translated by G. W. Bromiley. London: T&T Clark, 2004.

Bartholomew, Craig G. "Review of Levenson, J. 1993. *The Hebrew Bible, the Old Testament and Historical Criticism.*" *Calvin Theological Journal* 30, no. 2 (1995): 525-30.

————. "*Three* Horizons: A Hermeneutics of the Cross/Hermeneutics from the Other End. An Evaluation of Anthony Thiselton's Hermeneutic Proposals." *European Journal of Theology* 5, no. 2 (1996): 121-35.

————. "Post/Late? Modernity as the Context for Christian Scholarship Today." *Themelios* 22, no. 2 (1997): 25-38.

————. *Reading Ecclesiastes: Old Testament Exegesis and Hermeneutical Theory.* Analecta Biblica 139. Rome: Pontificio Instituto Biblico, 1998.

————. "Introduction." In *Renewing Biblical Interpretation,* edited by Craig Bartholomew et al. SAHS 1. Grand Rapids: Zondervan, 2000.

————. "Uncharted Waters: Philosophy, Theology, and the Crisis in Biblical Interpretation." In *Renewing Biblical Interpretation,* edited by Craig Bartholomew et al. SAHS 1. Grand Rapids: Zondervan, 2000.

————. "Introduction." In *After Pentecost: Language and Biblical Interpretation,* edited by Craig Bartholomew et al. SAHS 2. Grand Rapids: Zondervan, 2001.

————. *Reading Proverbs with Integrity.* Grove Biblical Series B 22. Cambridge: Grove Books, 2001.

————. "Introduction." In *A Royal Priesthood? The Use of the Bible Ethically and Politically,* edited by Craig Bartholomew et al. SAHS 3. Grand Rapids: Zondervan, 2002.

————. "Introduction." In *"Behind" the Text: History and Biblical Interpretation,* edited by Craig Bartholomew et al. SAHS 4. Grand Rapids: Zondervan, 2003.

————. "Biblical Theology and Biblical Interpretation: Introduction." In *Out of Egypt: Biblical Theology and Biblical Interpretation,* edited by Craig Bartholomew et al. SAHS 5. Grand Rapids: Zondervan, 2004.

————. "In Front of the Text: The Quest of Hermeneutics." In *The Bible in Pastoral Practice: Readings in the Place and Function of Scripture in the Church,* edited by P. Ballard and S. R. Holmes. Grand Rapids: Eerdmans, 2005.

———. "Calvin, Barth, and Theological Interpretation." In *Calvin, Barth, and Reformed Theology,* edited by Neil B. MacDonald and Carl Trueman. Milton Keynes: Paternoster, 2008.

———. *Ecclesiastes.* Baker Commentary on the Old Testament Wisdom and Psalms. Grand Rapids: Baker Academic, 2009.

———. "The Tenth Commandment, René Girard, and the Good Neighbourhood of Proverbs." Forthcoming.

———. "The Theology of Ecclesiastes." In *Fresh Perspectives on Ecclesiastes,* edited by Mark Boda, Tremper Longman III, and Cristian Rata. Winona Lake, IN: Eisenbrauns, forthcoming.

———, and Michael W. Goheen. *The Drama of Scripture: Finding Our Place in the Biblical Story.* Grand Rapids: Baker Academic, 2004.

———, and Michael W. Goheen. "Story and Biblical Theology." In *Out of Egypt: Biblical Theology and Biblical Interpretation,* edited by Craig Bartholomew et al. SAHS 5. Grand Rapids: Zondervan, 2004.

———, and Robby Holt. "Prayer in/and the Drama of Redemption in Luke: Prayer and Exegetical Performance." In *Reading Luke: Interpretation, Reflection, Formation,* edited by Craig Bartholomew et al. SAHS 6. Grand Rapids: Zondervan, 2005.

———, and R. P. O'Dowd. *Old Testament Wisdom Literature: A Theological Introduction.* Downers Grove: IVP Academic, 2011.

Barton, John. *Oracles of God: Perceptions of Ancient Prophecy in Israel after the Exile.* New York: Oxford University Press, 1986.

———. *Isaiah 1–39.* OTG. Sheffield: Sheffield Academic Press, 1995.

———. *Holy Writings, Sacred Text: The Canon of Early Christianity.* Louisville: Westminster John Knox, 1997.

———. *Reading the Old Testament: Method in Biblical Study, New Edition.* London: Darton, Longman, and Todd, 2003.

———. *Understanding Old Testament Ethics: Approaches and Explanations.* Louisville: Westminster John Knox, 2003.

———. "The Imitation of God in the Old Testament." In *The God of Israel,* edited by R. P. Gordon. University of Cambridge Oriental Publications 64. Cambridge: Cambridge University Press, 2007.

———. *The Old Testament: Canon, Literature, and Theology.* Society for Old Testament Monograph Series. Aldershot: Ashgate, 2007.

———. *Oracles of God: Perceptions of Prophecy in Israel after the Exile.* New York: Oxford University Press, 2007.

Bass, Grace, and Lynda Anderson. *The Daniel's Fast Cookbook.* Brooklyn: A&B Publishers, 2008.

Bauckham, Richard. "Biblical Theology and the Problems of Monotheism." In *Out of Egypt: Biblical Theology and Biblical Interpretation,* edited by Craig Bartholomew et al. SAHS 5. Grand Rapids: Zondervan, 2004.

———. *Jesus and the God of Israel: God Crucified and Other Studies on the New Testament's Christology of Divine Identity.* Grand Rapids: Eerdmans, 2008.

Bavinck, Herman. *The Philosophy of Revelation: The Stone Lectures for 1908-1909, Princeton Theological Seminary.* New York: Longmans, Green, and Co., 1909.

———. *The Doctrine of God.* Translated by William Hendriksen. Edinburgh: Banner of Truth, 1978.

Beale, G. K., and D. A. Carson, eds. *Commentary on the New Testament Use of the Old Testament.* Grand Rapids: Baker Academic, 2007.

Beckwith, R. T. *The Old Testament Canon of the New Testament and Its Background in Early Judaism.* Grand Rapids: Eerdmans, 1985.

Beilby, James K., ed. *For Faith and Clarity: Philosophical Contributions to Christian Theology.* Grand Rapids: Baker Academic, 2006.

Beiser, Frederick C. *The Fate of Reason: German Philosophy from Kant to Fichte.* Cambridge, MA: Harvard University Press, 1987.

Bellis, Alice Ogden. *Helpmates, Harlots, and Heroes: Women's Stories in the Hebrew Bible.* 2nd ed. Louisville: Westminster John Knox, 2007.

Ben Zvi, Ehud. "Twelve Prophetic Books or 'The Twelve': A Few Preliminary Considerations." In *Forming Prophetic Literature: Essays on Isaiah and the Twelve in Honor of John D. W. Watts,* edited by James W. Watts and Paul R. House. JSOTSup 235. Sheffield: Sheffield Academic Press, 1996.

Bennett, Harold V. *Injustice Made Legal: Deuteronomic Law and the Plight of Widows, Strangers, and Orphans in Ancient Israel.* Grand Rapids: Eerdmans, 2002.

Berlin, Adele. *Poetics and Interpretation of Biblical Narrative.* Sheffield: Almond Press, 1983.

Berman, Joshua A. *Created Equal: How the Bible Broke with Ancient Political Thought.* Oxford: Oxford University Press, 2008.

Bienkowski, Piotr, et al., eds. *Writing and Ancient Near East Society: Papers in Honor of Alan R. Millard.* London: T&T Clark, 2005.

Billings, J. Todd. *The Word of God for the People of God: An Entryway to the Theological Interpretation of Scripture.* Grand Rapids: Eerdmans, 2010.

Bimson, J. *Redating the Exodus and Conquest.* JSOTSup 5. Sheffield: University of Sheffield Press, 1978.

Birch, B. C. *Let Justice Roll Down: The Old Testament, Ethics, and the Christian Life.* Louisville: Westminster John Knox, 1991.

———. "Divine Character and the Formation of Moral Community in the Book of Exodus." In *Bible in Ethics: The Second Sheffield Colloquium,* edited by J. W. Rogerson, M. Davies, and M. D. Carroll R. JSOTSup 207. Sheffield: Sheffield Academic Press, 1995.

Birch, B. C., and Larry L. Rasmussen. *Bible and Ethics in the Christian Life.* Minneapolis: Augsburg, 1989.

Bland, K. P. "The Rabbinic Method and Literary Criticism." In *Literary Interpretations of Biblical Narratives,* edited by K. R. R. Gros Louis, J. S. Ackerman, and T. S. Warshaw. The Bible in Literature Courses. Nashville: Abingdon, 1974.

Bleicher, Josef. *Contemporary Hermeneutics: Hermeneutics as Philosophy, Method, and Critique.* London: Routledge & Kegan Paul, 1980.

Blum, Erhard. *Die Komposition der Vätergeschichte.* WMANT 57. Neukirchen-Vluyn: Neukirchener Verlag, 1984.

Boda, Mark J. *Haggai/Zechariah.* NIVAC. Grand Rapids: Zondervan, 2004.

———. "Oil, Crowns and Thrones: Prophet, Priest and King in Zechariah 1:7–6:15." In *Perspectives on Hebrew Scriptures,* edited by Ehud ben Zvi. Piscataway, NJ: Gorgias Press, 2006.

———. *After God's Own Heart: The Gospel According to David.* Phillipsburg, NJ: Presbyterian and Reformed, 2007.

———. *A Severe Mercy: Sin and Its Remedy in the Old Testament.* Siphrut: Literature and Theology of the Hebrew Scriptures 1. Winona Lake, IN: Eisenbrauns, 2009.

———. "Legitimizing the Temple: The Chronicler's Temple Building Account." In *From the Foundations to the Crenellations: Essays on Temple Building in the Ancient Near East and Hebrew Bible,* edited by Mark J. Boda and Jamie R. Novotny. Alter Orient und Altes Testament 366. Münster: Ugarit-Verlag, 2010.

———. "Theological Commentary: A Review and Reflective Essay." *McMaster Journal of Theology and Ministry* 11 (2010): 139-50.

———. "Judges." In *Expositor's Bible Commentary,* volume 4, edited by David Garland and Tremper Longman III. Grand Rapids: Zondervan, forthcoming.

———. "Word and Spirit, Scribe and Prophet in Old Testament Hermeneutics." In *Spirit and Scripture: Examining a Pneumatic Hermeneutic,* edited by Kevin L. Spawn and Archie T. Wright. London: T&T Clark, 2012.

Boersma, Hans. *Nouvelle Théologie and Sacramental Ontology: A Return to Mystery.* Oxford: Oxford University Press, 2009.

Boff, Clodovis. "Epistemología y método en la teología de la liberación." In *Mysterium liberationis: Conceptos fundamentals de la teología de la liberación,* edited by I. Ellacuría and J. Sobrino. San Salvador: UCA, 1993.

Bond, L. Susan. *Trouble with Jesus: Women, Christology, and Preaching.* St. Louis: Chalice, 1999.

Bonhoeffer, Dietrich. *Ethics.* Translated by R. Krauss, C. C. West, and D. W. Stott. Dietrich Bonhoeffer Works 6. Minneapolis: Fortress, 2005.

Book of Common Worship. Louisville: Westminster John Knox, 1993.

Bos, Rein. *We Have Heard That God Is with You: Preaching the Old Testament.* Grand Rapids: Eerdmans, 2008.

Bouyer, Louis. *The Spirit and Forms of Protestantism.* Translated by A. V. Littledale. Princeton: Scepter Publishers, 2001.

Boyer, Paul. *When Time Shall Be No More: Prophecy Belief in Modern American Culture.* Cambridge, MA: Harvard University Press, 1992.

Brandt, Peter. *Endgestalten des Kanons: Das Arrangement der Schriften Israels in der jüdischen und christlichen Bibel.* Berlin: Philo, 2001.

Braudel, F. *On History.* Translated by S. Matthews. Chicago: University of Chicago Press, 1980.

Bray, Gerald. "The Church Fathers and Biblical Theology." In *Out of Egypt: Biblical Theology and Biblical Interpretation,* edited by Craig Bartholomew et al. SAHS 5. Grand Rapids: Zondervan, 2005.

Brett, Mark G. *Biblical Criticism in Crisis: The Impact of the Canonical Approach on Old Testament Studies.* Cambridge: Cambridge University Press, 1991.

―――. *Decolonizing God: The Bible in the Tides of Empire.* The Bible in the Modern World 16. Sheffield: Sheffield Phoenix, 2008.

Brettler, M. *The Creation of History in Ancient Israel.* London: Routledge, 1995.

Breytenbach, Cilliers. "The Minor Prophets in Mark's Gospel." In *The Minor Prophets in the New Testament,* edited by Maarten J. J. Menken and Steve Moyise. LNTS 377. London: T&T Clark, 2009.

Briggs, Richard S. *The Virtuous Reader: Old Testament Narrative and Interpretive Virtue.* Studies in Theological Interpretation. Grand Rapids: Baker Academic, 2010.

Bright, John. *The Authority of the Old Testament.* Nashville: Abingdon, 1971.

Brock, Brian. *Singing the Ethos of God: On the Place of Christian Ethics in Scripture.* Grand Rapids: Eerdmans, 2007.

Brown, W. P. *Character in Crisis: A Fresh Approach to the Wisdom Literature of the Old Testament.* Grand Rapids: Eerdmans, 1996.

―――. *Ethos of the Cosmos: The Generation of Moral Imagination in the Bible.* Grand Rapids: Eerdmans, 1999.

―――. *Seeing the Psalms: A Theology of Metaphor.* Louisville: Westminster John Knox, 2002.

―――, ed. *The Ten Commandments: The Reciprocity of Faithfulness.* Library of Theological Ethics. Louisville: Westminster John Knox, 2004.

Brownson, James V. *Speaking the Truth in Love: New Testament Resources for a Missional Hermeneutic.* Harrisburg: Trinity Press International, 1998.

Bruckner, James K. *Implied Law in the Abrahamic Narrative: A Literary and Theological Analysis.* JSOTSup 335. Sheffield: Sheffield Academic Press, 2001.

Brueggemann, Walter. *Theology of the Old Testament: Testimony, Dispute, Advocacy.* Minneapolis: Fortress, 1997.

―――. *An Introduction to the Old Testament: The Canon and Christian Imagination.* Louisville: Westminster John Knox, 2003.

Buckley, Michael. *At the Origins of Modern Atheism.* New Haven: Yale University Press, 1990.

Burgess, John P. *Why Scripture Matters: Reading the Bible in a Time of Church Conflict.* Louisville: Westminster John Knox, 1998.

Butterfield, H. *The Origins of History.* New York: Basic, 1981.

Buttrick, David. *Homiletic: Moves and Structures.* Philadelphia: Fortress, 1987.

Calvin, John. *Commentary on the Book of Psalms,* vol. 1. Edinburgh: Calvin Translation Society, 1845.

―――. *Institutes of the Christian Religion.* Translated by Henry Beveridge. Peabody, MA: Hendrickson, 2008.

Campbell, Charles. *Preaching Jesus: New Directions for Homiletics in Hans Frei's Postliberal Theology.* Grand Rapids: Eerdmans, 1997.

Caputo, John D. *Philosophy and Theology.* Horizons in Theology. Nashville: Abingdon, 2006.

Carr, D. M. *The Fractures of Genesis: Historical and Literary Approaches.* Louisville: Westminster John Knox, 2003.

———. *Writing on the Tablet of the Heart: Origins of Scripture and Literature.* New York: Oxford University Press, 2005.

Carroll R., M. Daniel. *Contexts for Amos: Prophetic Poetics in Latin American Perspective.* JSOTSup 132. Sheffield: Sheffield Academic Press, 1992.

———. "The Prophetic Text and the Literature of Dissent in Latin America: Amos, García Márquez, and Cabrera Infante Dismantle Militarism." *BibInt* 4, no. 1 (1996): 76-100.

———. "Blessing the Nations: Toward a Biblical Theology of Mission from Genesis." *BBR* 10, no. 1 (2000): 17-34.

———. "Liberation Theology: Latin America." In *The Oxford Illustrated History of the Bible,* edited by J. Rogerson. Oxford: Oxford University Press, 2001.

———. *Christians at the Border: Immigration, the Church, and the Bible.* Grand Rapids: Baker Academic, 2008.

———. "Imagining the Unthinkable: Exposing the Idolatry of National Security in Amos." *Ex Auditu* 24 (2008): 37-54.

———, and Jacqueline E. Lapsley, eds., *Character Ethics and the Old Testament.* Louisville: Westminster John Knox, 2007.

Carroll, Robert P. "Dismantling the Book of Jeremiah and Deconstructing the Prophet." In *"Wünschet Jerusalem Frieden": Collected Communications to the XIIth Congress of the International Organization for the Study of the Old Testament, Jerusalem 1986,* edited by Matthias Augustin and Klaus-Dietrich Schunck. BEATAJ 13. Frankfurt: Peter Lang, 1988.

Carson, D. A. *Exegetical Fallacies.* 2nd edition. Grand Rapids: Baker Books, 1996.

———. "Systematic Theology and Biblical Theology." In *New Dictionary of Biblical Theology,* edited by T. Desmond Alexander and Brian S. Rosner. Downers Grove: IVP, 2000.

Caven, William. *Christ's Teaching Concerning the Last Things and Other Papers.* Toronto: Westminster, 1908.

Chapell, Bryan. *Christ-Centered Preaching: Redeeming the Expository Sermon.* Grand Rapids: Baker, 1994.

Chapman, Stephen B. *The Law and the Prophets: A Study in Old Testament Canon Formation.* FAT 27. Tübingen: Mohr Siebeck, 2000.

———. "Reclaiming Inspiration for the Bible." In *Canon and Biblical Interpretation,* edited by Craig Bartholomew et al. SAHS 7. Grand Rapids: Zondervan, 2006.

Childs, Brevard S. *Biblical Theology in Crisis.* Philadelphia: Westminster, 1970.

———. *Exodus: A Commentary.* Philadelphia: Westminster, 1974.

———. "Reflections on the Modern Study of the Psalms." In *Magnalia Dei, the Mighty Acts of God: Essays in Memory of G. Ernest Wright,* edited by F. M. Cross, W. E. Lemke, and P. D. Miller Jr. Garden City: Doubleday, 1976.

———. "The Canonical Shape of the Prophetic Literature." *Int* 32 (1978): 46-55.

———. *Introduction to the Old Testament as Scripture.* Philadelphia: Fortress, 1979.

———. *Old Testament Theology in a Canonical Context.* Philadelphia: Fortress, 1985.

———. *Biblical Theology of the Old and New Testaments: Theological Reflection on the Christian Bible.* Minneapolis: Fortress Press, 1993.

———. "On Reclaiming the Bible for Christian Theology." In *Reclaiming the Bible for the Church,* edited by Carl E. Braaten and Robert W. Jenson. Grand Rapids: Eerdmans, 1995.

———. "Retrospective Reading of the Old Testament Prophets." *ZAW* 108, no. 3 (1996): 362-77.

———. "The Nature of the Christian Bible: One Book, Two Testaments." In *The Rule of Faith: Scripture, Creed, and Canon in a Critical Age,* edited by Ephraim Radner and George Sumner. Harrisburg: Morehouse, 1998.

———. *The Struggle to Understand Isaiah as Christian Scripture.* Grand Rapids: Eerdmans, 2004.

Clark, Gordon R. *The Word* Hesed *in the Hebrew Bible.* JSOTSup 157. Sheffield: JSOT, 1993.

Clark, Kelly J. *Return to Reason: A Critique of Enlightenment Evidentialism and Defense of Reason and Belief in God.* Grand Rapids: Eerdmans, 1990.

Clements, Ronald E. "Patterns in the Prophetic Canon." In *Canon and Authority: Essays in Old Testament Religion and Theology,* edited by George W. Coats and Burke O. Long. Philadelphia: Fortress, 1977.

Clines, David J. A. *The Theme of the Pentateuch.* JSOTSup 10. Sheffield: JSOT Press, 1978.

———. *Interested Parties: The Ideology of the Writers and Readers of the Hebrew Bible.* JSOTSup 205; Gender, Culture, Theory 1. Sheffield: Sheffield Academic Press, 1995.

———. "Methods in Old Testament Study." In *On the Way to the Postmodern: Old Testament Essays, 1967-1998,* vol. 1, edited by D. J. A. Clines. Sheffield: Sheffield Academic Press, 1998.

———. *Job 21–37.* WBC 18A. Nashville: Thomas Nelson, 2006.

———. *The Theme of the Pentateuch.* JSOTSup 10. Sheffield: Sheffield Academic Press, 2007.

Clive, J. *Not by Fact Alone: Essays on the Writing and Reading of History.* London: Collins Harvill, 1990.

Clouser, Roy A. *The Myth of Religious Neutrality: An Essay on the Hidden Role of Religious Belief in Theories.* Notre Dame: University of Notre Dame Press, 1991.

Clowney, Edmund P. *Preaching and Biblical Theology.* Grand Rapids: Eerdmans, 1961.

———. "Preaching Christ from All the Scriptures." In *The Preacher and Preaching,* edited by Samuel T. Logan. Phillipsburg, NJ: Presbyterian and Reformed, 1986.

Coccejus, Johannes. *Lexicon et Commentarius Sermonis Hebraici et Chaldaici Veteris Testamenti.* In *Opera Omnia Theologica, Exegetica, Didactica, Polemica, Philologica.* Amsterdam: P. & J. Blaeu, 1701-1706.

Coggins, Richard J. "Do We Still Need Deutero-Isaiah?" *JSOT* 81 (1998): 77-92.

Cohen, Raymond, and Raymond Westbrook, eds. *Isaiah's Vision of Peace in Biblical and Modern International Relations: Swords into Plowshares.* Culture and Religion in International Relations. New York: Palgrave Macmillan, 2008.

Collett, Donald C. "Prophetic Intentionality and the Book of the Twelve: A Study in the Hermeneutics of Prophecy." Ph.D. Diss., University of St. Andrews, 2007.

Collins, J. J. *The Bible after Babel: Historical Criticism in a Postmodern Age.* Grand Rapids: Eerdmans, 2005.

Collins, Terence. *The Mantle of Elijah: The Redaction Criticism of the Prophetical Books.* Biblical Seminar 20. Sheffield: Sheffield Academic Press, 1993.

Conrad, Edgar W. *Reading Isaiah.* OBT. Minneapolis: Fortress, 1991.

————. *Reading the Latter Prophets: Towards a New Canonical Criticism.* JSOTSup 376. London: T&T Clark, 2003.

Cornelius à Lapide. *Commentaria ad Sacram Scripturam. Editio Xysto Riario Sfortiae dicata.* 10 vols. Naples: Nagar, 1854-59.

Craddock, Fred. *Preaching.* Nashville: Abingdon, 1985.

————. *As One without Authority: Revised with New Sermons.* St. Louis: Chalice, 2001.

Creach, Jerome F. D. *Yahweh as Refuge and the Editing of the Hebrew Psalter.* JSOTSup 217. Sheffield: Sheffield Academic, 1996.

————. *The Destiny of the Righteous in the Psalms.* St. Louis: Chalice, 2008.

Crenshaw, James. *Education in Ancient Israel: Across the Deafening Silence.* New York: Doubleday, 1998.

————. "Qohelet's Understanding of Intellectual Inquiry." In *Qohelet in the Context of Wisdom,* edited by A. Schoors. Bibliotheca Ephemeridum Theologicarum Lovaniensium 136. Leuven: Leuven University Press, 1998.

Cross, F. M. "The Text Behind the Text of the Hebrew Bible." In *Understanding the Dead Sea Scrolls,* edited by H. Shanks. New York: Vintage, 1993.

Crossan, John Dominic. *The Birth of Christianity: Discovering What Happened in the Years after the Execution of Jesus.* San Francisco: HarperSanFrancisco, 1998.

Cuffey, Kenneth H. "Remnant, Redactor, and Biblical Theologian: A Comparative Study of Coherence in Micah and the Twelve." In *Reading and Hearing the Book of the Twelve,* edited by James D. Nogalski and Marvin A. Sweeney. SBLSymS 15. Atlanta: Society of Biblical Literature, 2000.

Cunningham, David S. *These Three Are One: the Practice of Trinitarian Theology.* Oxford: Blackwell, 1998.

Daley, Brian. "Is Patristic Exegesis Still Usable?" In *The Art of Reading Scripture,* edited by Ellen Davis and Richard Hays. Grand Rapids: Eerdmans, 2003.

Dalferth, Ingolf U. *Theology and Philosophy.* Eugene, OR: Wipf & Stock, 2001.

Dalley, Stephanie. *Myths from Mesopotamia: Creation, the Flood, Gilgamesh, and Others.* Oxford: Oxford University Press, 1989.

D'Ambrosio, Marcellino. "De Lubac's Hermeneutics of Tradition." *Letter and Spirit* 1 (2005): 147-57.

Daniélou, Jean. *Qu'est-ce que la typologie?* In *L'Ancien Testament et les chrétiens,* edited by P. Auvray et al. Paris: Éditions du Cerf, 1951.

————. "Judéo-Christianisme et Gnose." In *Aspects du Judéo-Christianisme. Colloque de Strasbourg, 23-25 avril, 1964.* Paris: Presses Universitiares de France, 1965.

Davies, Andrew. *Double Standards in Isaiah: Re-evaluating Prophetic Ethics and Divine Justice.* Biblical Interpretation Series 46. Leiden: Brill, 2000.

Davies, E. W. *Prophecy and Ethics: Isaiah and the Ethical Traditions of Israel*. Sheffield: JSOT Press, 1981.

———. "Walking in God's Ways: The Concept of *Imitatio Dei* in the Old Testament." In *In Search of True Wisdom: Essays in Old Testament Interpretation in Honor of Ronald E. Clements*, edited by E. Ball. JSOTSup 300. Sheffield: Sheffield Academic Press, 1999.

Davies, P. *In Search of Ancient Israel*. JSOTSup 148. Sheffield: Sheffield Academic Press, 1992.

———. *Whose Bible Is It Anyway?* JSOTSup 204. Sheffield: Sheffield Academic Press, 1995.

———. *Memories of Ancient Israel: An Introduction to Biblical History — Ancient and Modern*. Louisville: Westminster John Knox, 2008.

Davis, Ellen F. "Exploding the Limits: Form and Function in Psalm 22." *JSOT* 53 (1992): 93-105.

———. *Imagination Shaped: Old Testament Preaching in the Anglican Tradition*. Valley Forge: Trinity Press International, 1995.

———. "Job and Jacob: The Integrity of Faith." In *The Whirlwind: Essays on Job, Hermeneutics, and Theology in Memory of Jane Morse*, edited by S. L. Cooke, C. L. Patton, and J. W. Watts. JSOTSup 336. Sheffield: Sheffield Academic, 2001.

———. *Wondrous Depth: Preaching the Old Testament*. Louisville: Westminster John Knox, 2005.

———. "Demanding Deliverance." In *Preaching from Psalms, Oracles, and Parables*, edited by R. Alling and D. J. Schlafer. Harrisburg: Morehouse, 2006.

———. *Scripture, Culture, and Agriculture: An Agrarian Reading of the Bible*. Cambridge: Cambridge University Press, 2009.

———, and Richard Hays, eds. *The Art of Reading Scripture*. Grand Rapids: Eerdmans, 2003.

de Lubac, Henri. *Catholicism: Christ and the Common Destiny of Mankind*. San Francisco: Ignatius, 1947.

———. *Medieval Exegesis: The Four Senses of Scripture*. Vol. 1. Grand Rapids: Eerdmans, 1998.

———. *Medieval Exegesis: The Four Senses of Scripture*. Vol. 2. Grand Rapids: Eerdmans, 2000.

———. *Scripture in the Tradition*. New York: Crossroad, 2000.

———. *History and Spirit: The Understanding of Scripture According to Origen*. San Francisco: Ignatius, 2007.

Dempsey, Carol J. *Hope amid the Ruins: The Ethics of Israel's Prophets*. St. Louis: Chalice, 2000.

Dempster, Stephen G. "An Extraordinary Fact: Torah and Temple and the Contours of the Hebrew Canon." *Tyndale Bulletin* 48 (1997): 23-54, 191-218.

———. *Dominion and Dynasty: A Theology of the Hebrew Bible*. NSBT. Downers Grove: IVP, 2003.

———. "The Prophets, the Canon, and a Canonical Approach: No Empty Word." In

Canon and Biblical Interpretation, edited by Craig Bartholomew et al. SAHS 7. Grand Rapids: Zondervan, 2006.

———. "Adolf von Harnack." In *Encyclopedia of the Historical Jesus,* edited by Craig A. Evans. New York: Routledge, 2008.

———. "Canons on the Left and Canons on the Right: Finding a Resolution in the Canon Debate." *JETS* 52, no. 1 (2009): 47-77.

Dentan, R. C. "The Literary Affinities of Exodus xxxiv 6f." *VT* 13 (1963): 34-51.

de Wette, W. M. L. *Beitrage zur Einleitung in das Alte Testament.* 2 vols. Halle, 1806-1807.

Dillard, Raymond B. *2 Chronicles.* WBC 15. Waco: Word, 1987.

Dirksen, P. B., and Aad W. van der Kooij, eds. *Abraham Kuenen (1828-1891). His Major Contributions to the Study of the Old Testament.* Leiden: Brill, 1993.

Dockery, David S. "A Historical Model." In *Hermeneutics for Preaching: Approaches to Contemporary Interpretations of Scripture,* edited by Raymond Bailey. Nashville: Broadman, 1992.

———. "Typological Exegesis: Moving Beyond Abuse and Neglect." In *Reclaiming the Prophetic Mantle: Preaching the Old Testament Faithfully,* edited by George L. Klein. Nashville: Broadman, 1992.

Doriani, Daniel. *Putting the Truth to Work: The Theory and Practice of Biblical Application.* Phillipsburg, NJ: Presbyterian & Reformed, 2001.

Douglas, Mary. *Purity and Danger: An Analysis of Concepts of Pollution and Taboo.* London: Routledge, 1966.

———. *In the Wilderness: The Doctrine of Defilement in the Book of Numbers.* JSOTSup 159. Sheffield: Academic Press, 1993.

———. *Leviticus as Literature.* Oxford: Oxford University Press, 1999.

Downing, Barry H. *The Bible and Flying Saucers.* New York: Avon Books, 1968.

Duguid, Iain. "Messianic Themes in Zechariah 9–14." In *The Lord's Anointed: Interpretation of Old Testament Messianic Texts,* edited by P. E. Satterthwaite, R. S. Hess, and G. J. Wenham. Grand Rapids: Baker, 1995.

Duke, Paul. *Irony in the Fourth Gospel.* Louisville: John Knox, 1985.

Dumbrell, William J. *Covenant and Creation: A Theology of the Old Testament Covenants.* Nashville: Nelson, 1984.

———. *The Faith of Israel: A Theological Survey of the Old Testament.* 2nd ed. Grand Rapids: Baker Academic, 2002.

Dunn, James D. G. "The Problem of 'Biblical Theology.'" In *Out of Egypt: Biblical Theology and Biblical Interpretation,* edited by Craig Bartholomew et al. SAHS 5. Grand Rapids: Zondervan, 2004.

Eaton, J. H. *Kingship and the Psalms.* 2nd ed. The Biblical Seminar 3. Sheffield: JSOT, 1986.

Edinger, Edward F. *Ego and Archetype: Individuation and the Religious Formation of the Psyche.* Boston: Shambhala, 1992.

Ekblad, Bob. *Reading the Bible with the Damned.* Louisville: Westminster John Knox, 2007.

Elingsen, Mark. *The Integrity of Biblical Narrative: Story in Theology and Proclamation.* Minneapolis: Fortress, 1990.

Enns, Peter. *Inspiration and Incarnation: Evangelicals and the Problem of the Old Testament*. Grand Rapids: Baker Academic, 2005.

Eslinger, Richard. *Narrative and Imagination: Preaching Worlds That Shape Us*. Minneapolis: Fortress, 1995.

Evans, C. Stephen. *The Historical Christ and the Jesus of Faith: The Incarnational Narrative as History*. Oxford: Oxford University Press, 1996.

———. *Kierkegaard: An Introduction*. Cambridge: Cambridge University Press, 2009.

Farris, Stephen. "Limping Away with a Blessing: Biblical Studies and Preaching at the End of the Second Millennium." *Interpretation* 51, no. 4 (October 1997): 358-70.

———. *Preaching That Matters: The Bible and Our Lives*. Louisville: Westminster John Knox, 1998.

Fee, Gordon D. *God's Empowering Presence: The Holy Spirit in the Letters of Paul*. Peabody, MA: Hendrickson, 1994.

———, and Douglas Stuart. *How to Read the Bible for All Its Worth*. 3rd ed. Grand Rapids: Zondervan, 2003.

Finkelstein, Israel, and Neil A. Silberman. *The Bible Unearthed: Archaeology's New Vision of Ancient Israel and the Origin of the Sacred Texts*. New York: Free Press, 2001.

Firestone, Chris L., and Nathan Jacobs, *In Defense of Kant's Religion*. Bloomington: Indiana University Press, 2008.

Firestone, Chris L., and Stephen Palmquist, eds., *Kant and the New Philosophy of Religion*. Bloomington: Indiana University Press, 2006.

Fisch, Harold. "Ruth and the Structure of Covenant History." *VT* 32 (1982): 425-37.

Fishbane, Michael A. "Jeremiah IV 23-26 and Job III 3-13: A Recovered Use of the Creation Pattern." *VT* 21 (1971): 151-67.

———. *Biblical Interpretation in Ancient Israel*. Oxford: Clarendon, 1985.

Fowl, Stephen E. *Engaging Scripture: A Model for Theological Interpretation*. Challenges in Contemporary Theology. Malden, MA: Blackwell, 1998.

———. *Theological Interpretation of Scripture*. Cascade Companions. Eugene, OR: Cascade, 2009.

——— and L. Gregory Jones. *Reading in Communion: Scripture and Ethics in Christian Life*. Grand Rapids: Eerdmans, 1991.

Fox, Michael V. "Job 38 and God's Rhetoric." *Semeia* 19 (1981): 53-61.

France, R. T. *Jesus and the Old Testament: His Application of Old Testament Passages to Himself and His Mission*. Vancouver: Regent College Publishing, 1998.

Frankfort, Henri, John A. Wilson, Thorkild Jacobsen, and William A. Irwin. *The Intellectual Adventure of Ancient Man*. Chicago: University of Chicago Press, 1946.

Frei, Hans. *The Eclipse of Biblical Narrative: A Study in Eighteenth and Nineteenth Century Hermeneutics*. New Haven: Yale University Press, 1974.

Fretheim, Terence E. "Law in the Service of Life: A Dynamic Understanding of Law in Deuteronomy." In *A God So Near: Essays on Old Testament Theology in Honor of Patrick D. Miller,* edited by B. A. Strawn and N. R. Bowen. Winona Lake, IN: Eisenbrauns, 2003.

Freud, Sigmund. *The Interpretation of Dreams*. New York: Basic, 1955.

Friebel, Kelvin. "A Hermeneutical Paradigm for Interpreting Prophetic Sign-Actions." *Didaskalia* 12 (2001): 25-45.

George, Andrew. *The Epic of Gilgamesh: A New Translation.* New York: Barnes and Noble, 1999.

Gese, Hartmut. *Vom Sinai zum Zion: Alttestamentliche Beiträge zur biblischen Theologie.* Beiträge zur evangelischen Theologie 64. Munich: Chr. Kaiser, 1974.

Gibson, Arthur. *Text and Tablet: Near Eastern Archeology, the Old Testament and New Possibilities.* Aldershot: Ashgate, 2000.

Gibson, David. "The Answering Speech of Men: Karl Barth on Holy Scripture." Unpublished paper, 2010.

Gillingham, S. E. *The Poems and Psalms of the Hebrew Bible.* Oxford Bible Series. Oxford: Oxford University Press, 1994.

Girard, René. *Job: The Victim of His People.* Stanford: Stanford University Press, 1987.

———. *I See Satan Fall Like Lightning.* Translated by James G. Williams. Maryknoll: Orbis, 2001.

Gladson, Jerry A. *Retributive Paradoxes in Proverbs 10–29.* Ph.D. dissertation, Vanderbilt University, 1978.

Goldingay, John. *Theological Diversity and the Authority of the Old Testament.* Grand Rapids: Eerdmans, 1987.

———. *Models for Scripture.* Grand Rapids: Eerdmans, 1994.

———. *Models for Interpretation of Scripture.* Grand Rapids: Eerdmans, 1995.

———. *Old Testament Theology: Israel's Gospel.* Downers Grove: IVP, 2003.

———. *Old Testament Theology: Israel's Faith.* Downers Grove: IVP, 2006.

———. *Old Testament Theology: Israel's Life.* Downers Grove: IVP, 2009.

Goldsworthy, Graeme L. "'Thus Says the Lord': The Dogmatic Basis for Biblical Theology." In *God Who Is Rich in Mercy,* edited by Peter T. O'Brien and David Peterson. Homebush, Australia: Lancer, 1986.

———. *Preaching the Whole Bible as Christian Scripture.* Grand Rapids: Eerdmans, 2000.

———. "Relationship of Old Testament and New Testament." In *New Dictionary of Biblical Theology,* edited by T. Desmond Alexander and Brian S. Rosner. Downers Grove: IVP, 2000.

Goppelt, Leonhard. *Typos: The Typological Interpretation of the Old Testament in the New.* Translated by D. H. Madvig. Grand Rapids: Eerdmans, 1982.

Goshen-Gottstein, M. "'Sefer Hagu': The End of a Puzzle." *VT* 8 (1958): 286-88.

Gosling, F. A. "An Unresolved Problem of Old Testament Theology." *The Expository Times* 106 (1995): 234-37.

Gottwald, Norman K. "Theological Education as a Theory-Praxis Loop: Situating the Book of Joshua in a Cultural, Social Ethical, and Theological Matrix." In *Bible in Ethics: The Second Sheffield Colloquium,* edited by J. W. Rogerson, M. Davies, and M. D. Carroll R. JSOTSup 207. Sheffield: Sheffield Academic Press, 1995.

Gowan, Donald E. *Reclaiming the Old Testament for the Christian Pulpit.* Atlanta: John Knox, 1980.

Gray, Mark. *Rhetoric and Social Justice in Isaiah.* LHB/OTS 432. London: T&T Clark, 2006.

Green, Joel B. "The Challenge of Hearing the New Testament." In *Hearing the New Testament: Strategies for Interpretation,* edited by Joel B. Green. Grand Rapids: Eerdmans, 1995.

————. *The Gospel of Luke.* The New International Commentary on the New Testament. Grand Rapids: Eerdmans, 1997.

————. "Scripture and Theology: Uniting the Two So Long Divided." In *Between Two Horizons: Spanning New Testament Studies and Systematic Theology,* edited by Joel B. Green and Max Turner. Grand Rapids: Eerdmans, 2000.

————, and Max Turner, eds. *Between Two Horizons: Spanning New Testament Studies and Systematic Theology.* Grand Rapids: Eerdmans, 2000.

Greidanus, Sidney. *The Modern Preacher and the Ancient Text: Interpreting and Preaching Biblical Literature.* Grand Rapids: Eerdmans, 1988.

————. *Preaching Christ from the Old Testament: A Contemporary Hermeneutical Method.* Grand Rapids: Eerdmans, 1999.

————. *Preaching Christ from Genesis: Foundations for Expository Sermons.* Grand Rapids: Eerdmans, 2007.

————. *Preaching Christ from Ecclesiastes: Foundations for Expository Sermons.* Grand Rapids: Eerdmans, 2010.

Grenz, Stanley J. *Theology for the Community of God.* Grand Rapids: Eerdmans, 2000.

Grondin, Jean. *Introduction to Philosophical Hermeneutics.* New Haven: Yale University Press, 1994.

Grotius, Hugo. *Annotata ad Vetus Testamentum.* In *Opera omnia theologica in tres tomos divisa.* London: Pitt, 1679.

Guardini, Romano. *The World and the Person.* Chicago: Henry Regnery, 1965.

Guder, Darrell. "Biblical Formation and Discipleship." In *Treasure in Clay Jars: Patterns in Missional Faithfulness,* edited by Lois Barrett et al. Grand Rapids: Eerdmans, 2004.

Guigo II. "The Ladder from Earth to Heaven." Translated by Jeremy Holmes. *Letter and Spirit* 2 (2006): 175-88.

Guillaume, P. "A Reconsideration of Manuscripts Classified as Scrolls of the Twelve Minor Prophets (XII)." *Journal of Hebrew Scriptures* 7 (2007): 2-10.

Gunn, D. M. "New Directions in the Study of Biblical Hebrew Narrative." *JSOT* 39 (1987): 65-75.

————. "Narrative Criticism." In *To Each Its Own Meaning: An Introduction to Biblical Criticisms and Their Application,* edited by S. L. McKenzie and S. R. Haynes. Louisville: Westminster John Knox, 1999.

Gunneweg, A. H. J. *Understanding the Old Testament,* translated by J. Bowden. OTL. Philadelphia: Westminster, 1978.

Gurses, Derya. "The Hutchinsonian Defence of an Old Testament Trinitarian Christianity: The Controversy over Elahim, 1735-1773." *History of European Ideas* 29 (2003): 393-409.

Gutiérrez, Gustavo. *On Job: God-Talk and the Suffering of the Innocent.* Maryknoll: Orbis, 1987.

Hafemann, Scott. "Biblical Theology: Retrospect and Prospect." In *Biblical Theology: Retrospect and Prospect,* edited by Scott Hafemann. Downers Grove: IVP, 2002.

Hahn, Scott W. *Letter and Spirit: From Written Text to Living Word in the Liturgy.* New York: Doubleday, 2005.

———. "Worship in the Word: Toward a Liturgical Hermeneutic." *Letter and Spirit* 1 (2005): 101-36.

———. "Canon, Cult, and Covenant: The Promise of Liturgical Hermeneutics." In *Canon and Biblical Interpretation,* edited by Craig Bartholomew et al. SAHS 7. Grand Rapids: Zondervan, 2006.

Hall, Douglas John. *God and Human Suffering: An Exercise in the Theology of the Cross.* Minneapolis: Augsburg, 1986.

Halpern, Baruch. The *First Historians: The Hebrew Bible and History.* San Francisco: Harper and Row, 1988.

Ham, Clay Alan. "The Minor Prophets in Matthew's Gospel." In *The Minor Prophets in the New Testament,* edited by Maarten J. J. Menken and Steve Moyise. LNTS 377. London: T&T Clark, 2009.

Harnack, Adolf von. *Marcion: The Gospel of the Alien God.* Translated by J. H. Seeley and L. D. Bierma. Durham: Labyrinth Press, 1990.

Hasel, Gerhard F. *Old Testament Theology: Basic Issues in the Current Debate.* 4th ed. Grand Rapids: Eerdmans, 1991.

Hatton, P. T. H. *Contradiction in the Book of Proverbs: The Deep Waters of Council.* Society for Old Testament Study Series. Hampshire: Ashgate, 2008.

Hays, Richard B. *The Moral Vision of the New Testament: A Contemporary Introduction to New Testament Ethics.* San Francisco: HarperSanFrancisco, 1996.

———. "Can the Gospels Teach Us How to Read the Old Testament?" *Pro Ecclesia* 11 (2002): 402-18.

———. "Reading Scripture in the Light of the Resurrection." In *The Art of Reading Scripture,* edited by Ellen F. Davis and Richard B. Hays. Grand Rapids: Eerdmans, 2003.

Healy, Mary. "Inspiration and Incarnation: The Christological Analogy and the Hermeneutics of Faith." *Letter and Spirit* 2 (2006): 27-41.

———. "The Hermeneutic of Jesus," unpublished paper.

Hebbelthwaite, Brian. "Recent British Theology." In *One God in Trinity: An Analysis of the Primary Dogma of Christianity,* edited by P. Toon and J. D. Spiceland. London: Samuel Bagster, 1980.

Heim, K. M. *Like Grapes of Gold Set in Silver: An Interpretation of Proverbial Clusters in Proverbs 10:1–22:16.* BZAW 273. Berlin: de Gruyter, 2001.

Helmer, Christine. "Biblical Theology: Reality, Interpretation, and Interdisciplinarity." In *Biblical Interpretation: History, Context, and Reality,* edited by Christine Helmer and Taylor G. Petrey. Atlanta: Society of Biblical Literature, 2005.

———. "Introduction: Multivalence in Biblical Theology." In *The Multivalence of Bib-*

lical Texts and Theological Meanings, edited by Christine Helmer and Charlene T. Higbe. SBLSymS 37. Atlanta: Society of Biblical Literature, 2006.

Herder, J. G. *Vom Geist der ebräischen Poesie.* 2 vols. Leipzig: Barth, 1825.

————. "Spruch und Bild, insonderheit bei den Morgenländern." In *Werke,* vol. XV, 11. Munich: Hanser, 1953.

Hertzberg, Hans W. *Der Prediger.* Kommentar zum Alten Testament 17.4. Gütersloh: Mohn, 1963.

Heschel, Abraham J. *The Prophets: An Introduction.* 2 vols. New York: Harper & Row, 1962.

————. *The Prophets.* Perennial Classics Edition. San Francisco: HarperCollins, 2001.

Hess, Richard S., and David T. Tsumura, *I Studied Inscriptions from Before the Flood: Ancient Near Eastern, Literary, and Linguistic Approaches to Genesis 1–11.* Sources for Biblical and Theological Study 4. Winona Lake, IN: Eisenbrauns, 1994.

Hiebert, Theodore. *The Yahwist's Landscape: Nature and Religion in Early Israel.* Oxford: Oxford University Press, 1996.

Hildebrandt, Wilf. *An Old Testament Theology of the Spirit of God.* Peabody, MA: Hendrickson, 1995.

Hill, Andrew E. *Baker's Handbook of Bible Lists.* Grand Rapids: Baker, 1981.

Hinlicky, Paul R. *Paths Not Taken: Fates of Theology from Luther to Leibniz.* Grand Rapids: Eerdmans, 2009.

Hofius, Otfried. "Ist Jesus der Messias? Thesen." In *Der Messias,* edited by Ingo Baldermann et al. Jahrbuch für biblische Theologie 8. Neukirchen-Vluyn: Neukirchener, 1993.

Hood, Jason. "Christ-Centered Interpretation Only? Moral Instruction from Scripture's Self-Interpretation as Caveat and Guide." *Scottish Bulletin of Evangelical Theology* 27, no. 1 (Spring 2009): 50-69.

Horowitz, Elliott S. *Reckless Rites: Purim and the Legacy of Jewish Violence.* Jews, Christians, and Muslims from the Ancient to the Modern World. Princeton: Princeton University Press, 2006.

Horrell, David G., Cherryl Hunt, and Christopher Southgate. "Appeals to the Bible in Ecotheology and Environmental Ethics: A Typology of Hermeneutical Stances." *Studies in Christian Ethics* 21, no. 2 (2008): 219-38.

Hossfeld, Frank-Lothar, and Erich Zenger. *Psalms 2.* Hermeneia. Minneapolis: Fortress, 2005.

House, Paul R. *The Unity of the Twelve.* JSOTSup 77. Sheffield: Sheffield Academic Press, 1990.

————. "Endings as New Beginnings: Returning to the Lord, the Day of the Lord, and Renewal in the Book of the Twelve." In *Thematic Threads in the Book of the Twelve,* edited by Paul L. Redditt and Aaron Schart. BZAW 325. Berlin: Walter de Gruyter, 2003.

Houston, Walter J. "What Did the Prophets Think They Were Doing? Speech Acts and Prophetic Discourse in the Old Testament." *BibInt* 1 (1993): 167-88.

————. *Purity and Monotheism: Clean and Unclean Animals in Biblical Law.* JSOTSup 140. Sheffield: Sheffield Academic, 2003.

————. *Contending for Justice: Ideologies and Theologies of Justice in the Old Testament.* LHB/OTS 428. London: T&T Clark, 2006.

Howard, David M. "The Transfer of Power from Saul to David in 1 Sam 16:13-14." *JETS* 32, no. 4 (1989): 473-83.

Howard, Thomas A. *Religion and the Rise of Historicism: W. M. L. de Wette, Jacob Burckhardt, and the Theological Origins of Nineteenth-Century Historical Consciousness.* Cambridge: Cambridge University Press, 2000.

————, ed. *The Future of Christian Learning: An Evangelical and Catholic Dialogue — Mark A. Noll and James Turner.* Grand Rapids: Brazos, 2008.

Hugenberger, Gordon P. *Marriage as a Covenant: A Study of Biblical Law and Ethics Governing Marriage Developed from the Perspective of Malachi.* Leiden: Brill, 1994.

Humphreys, W. L. "Life-Style for Diaspora: A Study of the Tales of Esther and Daniel." *JBL* 92 (1973): 211-23.

Hunsberger, George. "Proposals for a Missional Hermeneutic: Mapping the Conversation." Paper presented at the annual meeting of AAR/SBL (2008). http://www.gocn.org/resources/articles/proposals-missional-hermeneutic-mapping-conversation.

Iggers, George G. "Historicism: The History and Meaning of the Term." *Journal of the History of Ideas* 56 (1995): 129-52.

Jackson, Robert H. "International Military Tribunal: Opening Address for the United States of America." *Department of State Bulletin* XIII, no. 335 (1945): 850-60.

Jacobson, Rolf A. "'The Faithfulness of the Lord Endures Forever': The Central Theological Witness of the Psalter." In *Soundings in the Theology of the Psalms: Perspectives and Methods in Contemporary Scholarship,* edited by Rolf A. Jacobson. Minneapolis: Fortress, 2011.

Jamieson, Robert, A. R. Fausset, and David Brown. *A Commentary, Critical, Experimental, and Practical, on the Old and New Testaments.* 6 vols. London: James Nisbet, 1864-1870.

Janzen, Waldemar. *Old Testament Ethics: A Paradigmatic Approach.* Louisville: Westminster John Knox, 1994.

Jeffrey, D. L. *People of the Book: Christian Identity and Literary Culture.* Grand Rapids: Eerdmans, 1996.

————, and C. Stephen Evans, eds. *The Bible and the University.* SAHS 8. Grand Rapids: Zondervan, 2007.

Jenkins, Philip. *The New Face of Christianity: Believing the Bible in the Global South.* Oxford: Oxford University Press, 2006.

Jepsen, A. "The Scientific Study of the Old Testament." In *Essays on the Old Testament,* edited by Claus Westermann, translated by J. Bright. Richmond: John Knox, 1971.

John of the Cross. *The Dark Night of the Soul.* London: Burns and Oates, 1976.

John Paul II. *Faith and Reason.* London: The Incorporated Catholic Truth Society, 1998.

Johnson, Luke Timothy. "So What's Catholic About It? The State of Catholic Biblical Scholarship." *Commonweal* 125 (1998): 12-16.

Jonas, Hans. *The Gnostic Religion: The Message of the Alien God and the Beginnings of Christianity.* Boston: Beacon, 1958.

Jónsson, Gunnlaugur A. *The Image of God: Genesis 1, 26-28 in a Century of Old Testament Research*. Stockholm: Almqvist & Wiksell International, 1988.

Jung, Carl G. *Mysterium Coniunctionis*. Collected Works, Vol. 14. Princeton: Princeton University Press, 1966-1979.

Justin Martyr. "The First Apology of Justin Martyr." In *The Ante-Nicene Fathers*, edited by Alexander Roberts and James Donaldson, 1:159-87. Grand Rapids: Eerdmans, 1973.

Kaiser, Walter C. *Toward Old Testament Ethics*. Grand Rapids: Zondervan, 1983.

———. *The Uses of the Old Testament in the New*. Chicago: Moody, 1985.

———. *Preaching and Teaching from the Old Testament*. Grand Rapids: Baker Academic, 2003.

Kant, Immanuel. *Religion within the Limits of Reason Alone*. Translated by Theodore Greene and Hoyt H. Hudson. New York: Harper & Brothers, 1960.

Katz, P. "The Old Testament Canon in Palestine." *ZNW* 47 (1956): 191-217.

Kearney, R. "Jacques Derrida." In *Dialogues with Contemporary Thinkers: The Phenomenological Heritage*, edited by R. Kearney. Manchester: Manchester UP, 1984.

———. *On Stories*. New York: Routledge, 2001.

Keck, Leander. "Will the Historical-Critical Method Survive?" In *Orientation by Disorientation: Studies in Literary Criticism and Biblical Literary Criticism, Presented in Honor of William A. Beardslee*, edited by R. A. Spencer. Pittsburgh: Pickwick, 1980.

Keown, Gerald L., Pamela J. Scalise, and Thomas G. Smothers. *Jeremiah 26–52*. WBC 27. Dallas: Word, 1995.

Kidd, Sue M. *When the Heart Waits: Spiritual Direction for Life's Sacred Questions*. San Francisco: Harper and Row, 1990.

Kitchen, K. A. *The Reliability of the Old Testament*. Grand Rapids: Eerdmans, 2003.

———. "Proverbs 2: Ancient Near Eastern Background." In *Dictionary of the Old Testament: Wisdom, Poetry, and Writings*, edited by Tremper Longman III and Peter Enns. Downers Grove: IVP Academic, 2008.

Kline, Meredith. "The Correlation of the Concepts of Canon and Covenant." In *New Perspectives on the Old Testament*, edited by J. Barton Payne. Waco: Word, 1970.

Knierim, Rolf P. *The Task of Old Testament Theology: Method and Cases*. Grand Rapids: Eerdmans, 1995.

Knight, W. S. M. *The Life and Works of Hugo Grotius*. London: Sweet & Maxwell, 1925.

Kofoed, Jens Bruun. *Text History: Historiography and the Study of the Biblical Text*. Winona Lake, IN: Eisenbrauns, 2005.

Kok, Johnson L. T. *The Sin of Moses and the Staff of God: A Narrative Approach*. Assen: Van Gorcum, 1997.

Koorevaar, Hendrik J. "Die Chronik als intendierter Abschluss des alttestamenlichen Kanons." *Jahrbuch für evangelikale Theologie* 11 (1997): 42-76.

Kraft, Robert. "Para-mania: Beside, Before, and Beyond Bible Studies." *JBL* 126 (2007): 3-27.

Kraus, Hans-Joachim. *Geschichte der historisch-kritischen Erforschung des Alten Testa-*

ments von der Reformation bis zur Gegenwart. Neukirchen: Verlag der Buchhand-lung des Erziehungsvereins Neukirchen Kreis Moers, 1956.

Kuenen, A. "Critical Method." *The Modern Review* 1 (1880): 461-88, 685-713.

Kugel, J. L. *The Idea of Biblical Poetry: Parallelism and Its History.* New Haven: Yale University Press, 1981.

Lane, William. *The Gospel According to Mark.* Grand Rapids: Eerdmans, 1974.

Lapsley, Jacqueline E. *Can These Bones Live? The Problem of the Moral Self in the Book of Ezekiel.* BZAW 301. Berlin: de Gruyter, 2000.

———. *Whispering the Word: Hearing Women's Stories in the Old Testament.* Louisville: Westminster John Knox, 2005.

Leclercq, Jean. *The Love of Learning and the Desire for God.* New York: Fordham University Press, 1982.

Lecureaux, Jason. "The Thematic Unity of the Book of the Twelve: The Call to Return and the Nature of the Minor Prophets." Ph.D. Diss., University of Gloucestershire, 2010.

Leithart, Peter J. *Deep Comedy: Trinity, Tragedy, and Hope in Western Literature.* Moscow, ID: Canon Press, 2006.

———. "The Quadriga or Something Like It: A Biblical and Pastoral Defense." In *Ancient Faith for the Church's Future,* edited by Mark Husbands and Jeffrey P. Greenman. Downers Grove: IVP Academic, 2008.

———. *Deep Exegesis: The Mystery of Reading Scripture.* Waco: Baylor University Press, 2009.

Lemche, Nils Peter. *The Old Testament between Theology and History.* Louisville: Westminster John Knox, 2008.

Lentricchia, Frank. *After the New Criticism.* London: Methuen, 1980.

Levenson, Jon D. *The Book of Job in Its Time and in the Twentieth Century.* Cambridge, MA: Harvard University Press, 1972.

———. *The Hebrew Bible, the Old Testament, and Historical Criticism.* Louisville: Westminster John Knox, 1993.

———. Review of C. A. Newsom, *The Book of Job: A Contest of Moral Imaginations. JR* 84 (2004): 271-72.

———. *Resurrection and the Restoration of Israel: The Ultimate Victory of the God of Life.* New Haven: Yale University Press, 2006.

Levy, Shimon. *The Bible as Theatre.* Brighton: Sussex Academic Press, 2000.

Lewis, J. P. "What Do We Mean by Jabneh?" *Journal of Bible and Religion* 32 (1964): 125-32.

Licht, Jacob. *Storytelling in the Bible.* Jerusalem: Magnes, 1978.

Liddell, Henry G., and Robert Scott. *Greek and English Lexicon.* Oxford: Clarendon Press, 1869.

Limburg, James. "Swords to Plowshares: Text and Contexts." In *Writing and Reading the Scroll of Isaiah: Studies of an Interpretive Tradition,* edited by Craig C. Broyles and Craig A. Evans. VTSup 70. Leiden: Brill, 1997.

Lincoln, Andrew. *Truth on Trial: The Lawsuit Motif in the Fourth Gospel.* Peabody, MA: Hendrickson, 2000.

Lindström, Fredrik. *Suffering and Sin: Interpretations of Illness in the Individual Complaint Psalms.* Coniectanea Biblica Old Testament Series 37. Stockholm: Almqvist & Wiksell International, 1994.

Lints, Richard. "Two Theologies or One? Warfield and Vos on the Nature of Theology." *WTJ* 54, no. 2 (1992): 235-53.

Lischer, Richard. *Theories of Preaching: Selected Readings in the Homiletical Tradition.* Durham: Labyrinth Press, 1987.

———. *A Theology of Preaching: The Dynamics of the Gospel.* Eugene, OR: Wipf & Stock, 2001.

———. *The Company of Preachers: Wisdom on Preaching, Augustine to the Present.* Grand Rapids: Eerdmans, 2002.

Liverani, M. *Israel's History and the History of Israel.* London: Equinox Publishing, 2005.

Lo, Alison. *Job 28 as Rhetoric: An Analysis of Job 28 in the Context of Job 22-31.* Leiden: Brill, 2003.

Lohfink, Norbert. *Qohelet: A Continental Commentary.* Translated by Sean E. McEvenue. Continental Commentaries. Minneapolis: Fortress, 2003.

Long, V. P. *The Reign and Rejection of King Saul: A Case for Literary and Theological Coherence.* SBLDS 118. Atlanta: Scholars Press, 1989.

———. *Art of Biblical History.* Foundations of Contemporary Interpretation 5. Grand Rapids: Zondervan, 1994.

———. "Reading the Old Testament as Literature." In *Interpreting the Old Testament: A Guide for Exegesis,* edited by C. C. Broyles. Grand Rapids: Baker Academic, 2001.

Longenecker, Richard. *Biblical Exegesis in the Apostolic Age.* Grand Rapids: Eerdmans, 1999.

Longman, Tremper, III. "Form Criticism, Recent Developments in Genre Theory, and the Evangelical." *Westminster Theological Journal* (1985): 46-67.

———. *Literary Approaches to Biblical Interpretation.* Foundations of Contemporary Interpretation 3. Grand Rapids: Zondervan, 1987.

———. *Ecclesiastes.* NICOT. Grand Rapids: Eerdmans, 1998.

———. *How to Read Exodus.* Downers Grove: IVP, 2009.

Lowry, Eugene. *Doing Time in the Pulpit: The Relationship between Narrative and Preaching.* Nashville: Abingdon, 1985.

———. *The Homiletical Plot: The Sermon as Narrative Art Form.* Expanded edition. Louisville: Westminster John Knox, 2001.

Lowth, R. *De sacra poesi Hebraeorum praelectiones academicae Oxonii habitae.* Oxford: Clarendon, 1753.

———. *Lectures on the Sacred Poetry of the Hebrews.* London: T. Tegg & Sons, 1835.

Lust, J. "Quotation Formulae and Canon in Qumran." In *Canonization and Decanonization,* edited by A. van der Kooij and K. van der Toorn. Studies in the History of Religions 82. Leiden: Brill, 1998.

Lutz, Christopher S. *Tradition in the Ethics of Alasdair MacIntyre: Relativism, Thomism, and Philosophy.* Lanham, MD: Lexington, 2004.

Lyons, Michael A. *From Law to Prophecy: Ezekiel's Use of the Holiness Code.* LHB/OTS 507. New York: T&T Clark, 2009.

Macdonald, Nathan. "Whose Monotheism? Which Rationality?" In *The Old Testament in Its World,* edited by R. P. Gordon and J. C. de Moor. Leiden: Brill 2005.

MacIntyre, Alasdair. *After Virtue: A Study in Moral Theory.* 2nd ed. Notre Dame: University of Notre Dame Press, 1984.

————. *Whose Justice? Which Rationality?* London: Duckworth, 1988.

Magrassi, Mariano. *Praying the Bible: An Introduction to Lectio Divina.* Collegeville: Liturgical Press, 1998.

Maier, Christl. *Jeremia als Lehrer der Tora: Soziale Gebote des Deuteronomiums in Fortschreibungen des Jeremiabuches.* Forschungen zur Religion und Literatur des Alten und Neuen Testaments 196. Göttingen: Vandenhoeck & Ruprecht, 2002.

Mandelbaum, Maurice. *History, Man, and Reason. A Study in Nineteenth-Century Thought.* Baltimore: Johns Hopkins Press, 1971.

Margolis, Max Leopold. *The Hebrew Scriptures in the Making.* Philadelphia: Jewish Publication Society of America, 1922.

Marlow, Hilary. *Biblical Prophets and Contemporary Environmental Ethics.* Oxford: Oxford University Press, 2009.

Marshall, Bruce D. *Trinity and Truth.* Cambridge: Cambridge University Press, 2000.

Martens, Elmer. "Reaching for a Biblical Theology of the Whole Bible." In *Reclaiming the Old Testament: Essays in Honor of Waldemar Janzen,* edited by Gordon Zerbe. Winnipeg: CMBC Publications, 2001.

————. "Old Testament Theology Since Walter Kaiser." *JETS* 50 (2007): 673-92.

Martens, Peter. "Origen the Allegorist and the Typology/Allegory Distinction." Paper presented at the annual meeting of the Society of Biblical Literature, 2004.

————. "Revisiting the Allegory/Typology Distinctions: The Case of Origen." *Journal of Early Christian Studies* 16 (2008): 283-317.

Martin, Francis. "Spiritual Sense." In *Dictionary for Theological Interpretation of the Bible,* edited by Kevin Vanhoozer et al. Grand Rapids: Baker Academic, 2005.

Mayhue, Richard, and Robert Thomas, ed. *Rediscovering Expository Preaching: Balancing the Science and Art of Biblical Exposition.* Dallas: Word, 1992.

Mays, James L. "Psalm 13." *Int* 34 (1980): 279-83.

————. "The Place of the Torah-Psalms in the Psalter." *JBL* 106 (1987): 3-12.

————. *Psalms.* Interpretation Bible Commentary. Louisville: John Knox, 1994.

————. *The Lord Reigns: A Theological Handbook to the Psalms.* Louisville: Westminster John Knox, 1994.

McCann Jr., J. Clinton. "The Psalms as Instruction." *Int* 46 (1992): 117-28.

————. *A Theological Introduction to the Book of Psalms: The Psalms as Torah.* Nashville: Abingdon, 1993.

————. "The Book of Psalms: Introduction, Commentary, and Reflections." In *The New Interpreter's Bible,* vol. 4. Nashville: Abingdon, 1996.

————. "Psalms, Book of." In *Dictionary for Theological Interpretation of the Bible,* edited by Kevin J. Vanhoozer et al. Grand Rapids: Baker Academic, 2005.

————. "The Shape of Book I of the Psalter and the Shape of Human Happiness." In *The Book of Psalms: Composition and Reception,* edited by Peter W. Flint and Patrick D. Miller. VTSup 99. Leiden: Brill, 2005.

———. "Toward a Non-Retaliatory Lifestyle: The Psalms, the Cross, and the Gospel." In *Character Ethics and the New Testament: Moral Dimensions of Scripture*, edited by Robert L. Brawley. Louisville: Westminster John Knox, 2007.

———. *Great Psalms of the Bible.* Louisville: Westminster John Knox, 2009.

———. "The Single Most Important Text in the Entire Bible: Toward a Theology of the Psalms." In *Soundings in the Theology of the Psalms: Perspectives and Methods in Contemporary Scholarship*, edited by Rolf A. Jacobson. Minneapolis: Fortress, 2011.

McClure, John. *Other-Wise Preaching: A Postmodern Ethic for Homiletics.* St. Louis: Chalice, 2001.

McConville, J. G. "Divine Speech and the Book of Jeremiah." In *The Trustworthiness of God: Perspectives on the Nature of Scripture*, edited by Paul Helm and Carl R. Trueman. Grand Rapids: Eerdmans, 2002.

———. *God and Earthly Power — An Old Testament Political Theology: Genesis-Kings.* LHB/OTS 454. London: T&T Clark, 2006.

———. "'How Can Jacob Stand? He Is So Small!' (Amos 7:2): The Prophetic Word and the Re-Imagining of Israel." In *Israel's Prophets and Israel's Past: Essays on the Relationship of Prophetic Texts and Israelite History in Honor of John H. Hayes*, edited by B. E. Kelle and M. B. Moore. LHB/OTS 446. New York: T&T Clark, 2006.

McDonald, L. M. *The Biblical Canon: Its Origin, Transmission, and Authority.* 3rd edition. Peabody, MA: Hendrickson Publishers, 2007.

McKane, William. *A Critical and Exegetical Commentary on Jeremiah.* Vol. 1. International Critical Commentary. Edinburgh: T&T Clark, 1986.

Mede, Joseph. *Dissertationum Ecclesiasticarum Triga: De Sanctitate Relativa, Veneratione Sacra, Sortitione & Alea, quibus accedunt Fragmenta Sacra.* London: Roycroft, 1653.

Mein, Andrew. *Ezekiel and the Ethics of Exile.* Oxford Theological Monographs. Oxford: Oxford University Press, 2001.

Menken, Maarten J. J. "The Minor Prophets in John's Gospel." In *The Minor Prophets in the New Testament*, edited by Maarten J. J. Menken and Steve Moyise. LNTS 377. London: T&T Clark, 2009.

———, and Steve Moyise, eds. *The Minor Prophets in the New Testament.* LNTS 377. London: T&T Clark, 2009.

Michalson, Gordon E. *Kant and the Problem of God.* Oxford: Blackwell, 1999.

Mieder, Wolfgang. *Proverbs Are Never Out of Season: Popular Wisdom in the Modern Age.* New York: Oxford University Press, 1993.

———, and Alan Dundes, eds. *The Wisdom of Many: Essays on the Proverb.* Madison: University of Wisconsin Press, 1994.

Milbank, John. *Theology and Social Theory. Beyond Secular Reason.* Oxford: Blackwell, 1990.

———. "Knowledge: The Theological Critique of Philosophy in Haman and Jacobi." In *Radical Orthodoxy*, edited by John Milbank, Catherine Pickstock, and Graham Ward. London: Routledge, 1999.

Miles, Jack. *Christ: A Crisis in the Life of God.* New York: Vintage, 2002.

Milgrom, Jacob. *Leviticus 1–16.* AB. New York: Doubleday, 1991.

Millard, A. R., J. K. Hoffmeier, and D. W. Baker, eds. *Faith, Tradition, and History.* Winona Lake, IN: Eisenbrauns, 1994.

Miller, J. M. "Israelite History." In *The Hebrew Bible and Its Modern Interpreters,* edited by D. A. Knight and G. M. Tucker. Philadelphia: Fortress, 1985.

―――, and J. H. Hayes. *A History of Ancient Israel and Judah.* Louisville: Westminster John Knox, 2006.

Miller, Patrick D. "The Theological Significance of Poetry." In *Israelite Religion and Biblical Theology: Collected Essays,* edited by P. D. Miller. JSOTSup 237. Sheffield: Sheffield Academic Press, 2000.

―――. "The Good Neighborhood: Identity and Community through the Commandments." In *Character and Scripture: Moral Formation, Community, and Biblical Interpretation,* edited by W. P. Brown. Grand Rapids: Eerdmans, 2002.

―――. "Theology from Below: The Theological Interpretation of Scripture." In *Reconsidering the Boundaries between Theological Disciplines/Zur Neubestimmung der Grenzen zwischen den theologischen Disziplinen,* edited by Michael Welker and Friedrich Schweitzer. Theology: Research and Science 8. Münster: Lit Verlag, 2005.

―――. *Theology Today: Reflections on the Bible and Contemporary Life.* Louisville: Westminster John Knox, 2006.

―――. *The Way of the Lord: Essays in Old Testament Theology.* Grand Rapids: Eerdmans, 2007.

Mills, Mary E. *Biblical Morality: Moral Perspectives in Old Testament Narratives.* Heythrop Series in Contemporary Philosophy, Religion and Theology. Aldershot: Ashgate, 2001.

Miranda, José Porfirio. *Marx and the Bible: A Critique of the Philosophy of Oppression.* Translated by J. Eagleson. Maryknoll: Orbis, 1974.

Moberly, R. W. L. *At the Mountain of God.* JSOTSup 22. Sheffield: JSOT Press, 1983.

―――. *The Old Testament of the Old Testament.* OBT. Minneapolis: Fortress, 1992.

―――. *The Bible, Theology, and Faith: A Study of Abraham and Jesus.* Cambridge Studies in Christian Doctrine. Cambridge: Cambridge University Press, 2000.

―――. *Prophecy and Discernment.* Cambridge Studies in Christian Doctrine. Cambridge: Cambridge University Press, 2006.

Möller, Karl. "Words of (In-)evitable Certitude? Reflections on the Interpretation of Prophetic Oracles of Judgement." In *After Pentecost: Language and Biblical Interpretation,* edited by Craig Bartholomew et al. SAHS 2. Grand Rapids: Zondervan, 2001.

―――. "The Nature and Genre of Biblical Theology." In *Out of Egypt: Biblical Theology and Biblical Interpretation,* edited by Craig Bartholomew et al. SAHS 5. Grand Rapids: Zondervan, 2004.

Montague, George T. *The Holy Spirit: Growth of a Biblical Tradition.* New York: Paulist, 1976.

Mosala, Itumeleng J. *Biblical Hermeneutics and Black Theology in South Africa.* Grand Rapids: Eerdmans, 1989.

Motyer, Steve. "Two Testaments, One Biblical Theology." In *Between Two Horizons:*

Spanning New Testament Studies and Systematic Theology, edited by Joel B. Green and Max Turner. Grand Rapids: Eerdmans, 2000.

Muilenburg, J. "Form Criticism and Beyond." *JBL* 88 (1969): 1-18.

Mulder, M. J., and Harry Sysling, eds. *Mikra: Text, Translation, Reading, and Interpretation of the Hebrew Bible in Ancient Judaism and Early Christianity.* Philadelphia: Fortress, 2005.

Müller, Mogens. *The First Bible of the Church: A Plea for the Septuagint.* Sheffield: Sheffield Academic Press, 1996.

Neill, Stephen, and N. T. Wright. *The Interpretation of the New Testament: 1861-1986.* Oxford: Oxford University Press, 1988.

Newbigin, Lesslie. *The Light Has Come: An Exposition of the Fourth Gospel.* Grand Rapids: Eerdmans, 1982.

———. *Foolishness to the Greeks.* London: SPCK, 1986.

———. *The Gospel in a Pluralist Society.* Grand Rapids: Eerdmans, 1989.

Newcome, William. *An Attempt Towards an Improved Version, A Metrical Arrangement; and an Explanation of the Twelve Minor Prophets.* Dublin: Marchbank, 1785.

Newsom, Carol A. "Job and Ecclesiastes." In *Old Testament Interpretation: Past, Present, and Future: Essays in Honor of Gene M. Tucker,* edited by J. L. Mays, D. L. Petersen, and K. H. Richards. Nashville: Abingdon, 1995.

Ngwa, Kenneth N. *The Hermeneutics of the "Happy" Ending in Job 42:7-17.* BZAW 354. Berlin: De Gruyter, 2005.

Nicholson, Ernest. *Interpreting the Old Testament: A Century of the Oriel Professorship.* Oxford: Clarendon, 1981.

———. *The Pentateuch in the Twentieth Century. The Legacy of Julius Wellhausen.* Oxford: Clarendon, 1998.

Niebuhr, H. Richard. *Christ and Culture.* New York: Harper Torchbooks, 1951.

Nihan, Christopher. "Saul among the Prophets (1 Sam 10:10-12 and 19:18-24): The Reworking of Saul's Figure in the Context of the Debate on 'Charismatic Prophecy' in the Persian Era." In *Saul in Story and Tradition,* edited by Carl S. Ehrlich and Marsha C. White. Forschungen zum Alten Testament 47. Tübingen: Mohr Siebeck, 2006.

Nogalski, James D. *Literary Precursors to the Book of the Twelve.* BZAW 217. Berlin: de Gruyter, 1993.

———. *Redactional Processes in the Book of the Twelve.* BZAW 218. Berlin: de Gruyter, 1993.

———. "Intertextuality and the Twelve." In *Forming Prophetic Literature: Essays on Isaiah and the Twelve in Honor of John D. W. Watts,* edited by James W. Watts and Paul R. House. JSOTSup 235. Sheffield: Sheffield Academic Press, 1996.

———. "Joel as 'Literary Anchor' for the Book of the Twelve." In *Reading and Hearing the Book of the Twelve,* edited by James D. Nogalski and Marvin A. Sweeney. SBLSymS 15. Atlanta: Society of Biblical Literature, 2000.

———. "The Day(s) of YHWH in the Book of the Twelve." In *Thematic Threads in the Book of the Twelve,* edited by Paul L. Redditt and Aaron Schart. BZAW 325. Berlin: de Gruyter, 2003.

Noll, Mark A. *The Civil War as a Theological Crisis.* Chapel Hill: University of North Carolina Press, 2006.

Nussbaum, Martha. *The Fragility of Goodness: Luck and Ethics in Greek Tragedy and Philosophy.* 2nd ed. Cambridge: Cambridge University Press, 2001.

O'Brien, Julia M. *Challenging Prophetic Metaphor: Theology and Ideology in the Prophets.* Louisville: Westminster John Knox, 2008.

Oden, Thomas C. *Requiem: A Lament in Three Movements.* Nashville: Abingdon, 1995.

—————, ed. The Ancient Christian Commentary on Scripture. 14 vols. Downers Grove: IVP, 2001-2009.

O'Donovan, Oliver. *Resurrection and Moral Order: An Outline for an Evangelical Ethics.* Grand Rapids: Eerdmans, 1994.

—————. *The Desire of the Nations: Rediscovering the Roots of Political Theology.* Cambridge: Cambridge University Press, 1996.

O'Flaherty, James C. *Johann Georg Hamann.* Boston: Twayne, 1979.

Ollenburger, Ben C., ed. *So Wide a Sea: Essays on Biblical and Systematic Theology.* Elkhart: Institute of Mennonite Studies, 1991.

Olson, Dennis T. *The Death of the Old and the Birth of the New: The Framework of the Book of Numbers and the Pentateuch.* Brown Judaic Studies 71. Chico: Scholars Press, 1985.

Otto, Eckart. *Theologische Ethik des Alten Testaments.* Theologische Wissenschaft 3/2. Stuttgart: W. Kohlhammer, 1994.

Palmer, Richard. *Hermeneutics: Interpretation Theory in Schleiermacher, Dilthey, Heidegger, and Gadamer.* Evanston: Northwestern University Press, 1969.

Pannenberg, Wolfhart. "Diskussionsbeitrag." *Evangelische Theologie* 44 (1984): 293-97.

Parry, Robin A. *Old Testament Story and Christian Ethics: The Rape of Dina as a Test Case.* Milton Keynes: Paternoster, 2004.

Pate, C. Marvin, and Calvin B. Haines Jr. *Doomsday Delusions: What's Wrong with Predictions about the End of the World.* Downers Grove: IVP, 1995.

Pelikan, Jaroslav. *Obedient Rebels.* New York: Harper and Row, 1964.

Pépin, Jean. *Mythe et allégorie. Les origines grecques et les contestations judéo-chétiennes.* Paris: Éditions Montaigne, 1958.

Perdue, Leo G. *Wisdom Literature: A Theological History.* Louisville: Westminster John Knox, 2007.

Perlitt, Lothar. *Vatke und Wellhausen.* BZAW 94. Berlin: Verlag Alfred Töpelman, 1965.

Perrin, Nicholas. "Dialogic Conceptions of Language and the Problem of Biblical Unity." In *Biblical Theology: Retrospect and Prospect,* edited by Scott Hafemann. Downers Grove: IVP, 2002.

Peters, James R. *The Logic of the Heart: Augustine, Pascal, and the Rationality of Faith.* Grand Rapids: Baker Academic, 2009.

Peterson, Eugene H. *Answering God: The Psalms as Tools for Prayer.* San Francisco: Harper and Row, 1989.

—————. *Eat This Book: A Conversation in the Art of Spiritual Reading.* Grand Rapids: Eerdmans, 2005.

Pixley, Jorge V. *On Exodus: A Liberation Perspective*. Translated by R. R. Barr. Maryknoll: Orbis, 1987.

Plaks, Andrew. "Afterword: Canonization in the Ancient World — The View from Farther East." In *Homer, the Bible, and Beyond: Literary and Religious Canons in the Ancient World*, edited by Margalit Finkelberg and Gedaliahu A. G. Stroumsa. Jerusalem Studies in Religion and Culture 2. Leiden: Brill, 2003.

Plantinga, Alvin. "Christian Philosophy at the End of the Twentieth Century." In *Christian Philosophy at the Close of the Twentieth Century*, edited by Sander Griffioen and B. M. Balk. Kampen: Kok, 1995.

———. "Two (or More) Kinds of Scripture Scholarship." *Modern Theology* 14, no. 2 (1998): 243-78.

———. *Warranted Christian Belief*. New York: Oxford University Press, 2000.

Pleins, J. David. *The Social Visions of the Hebrew Bible: A Theological Introduction*. Louisville: Westminster John Knox, 2001.

Popper, Karl R. "The Bucket and the Searchlight: Two Theories of Knowledge." In *Objective Knowledge: An Evolutionary Approach*. Oxford: Clarendon Press, 1972.

Provan, Iain W. *1 and 2 Kings*. NIBCOT. Peabody, MA: Hendrickson, 1995.

———. *1 and 2 Kings*. OTG. Sheffield: JSOT Press, 1997.

———. "On 'Seeing' the Trees While Missing the Forest: The Wisdom of Characters and Readers in 2 Samuel and 1 Kings." In *In Search of True Wisdom: Essays in Old Testament Interpretation in Honour of Ronald E. Clements*, edited by E. Ball. JSOTSup 300. Sheffield: Sheffield Academic Press, 2000.

———, V. P. Long, and Tremper Longman III. *A Biblical History of Israel*. Louisville: Westminster John Knox, 2003.

Quinn-Miscall, Peter D. *Reading Isaiah: Poetry and Vision*. Louisville: Westminster John Knox, 2001.

Rae, M. "Creation and Promise: Towards a Theology of History." In *"Behind" the Text: History and Biblical Interpretation*, edited by Craig Bartholomew et al. SAHS 4. Grand Rapids: Zondervan, 2003.

Ramsey, G. W. *The Quest for the Historical Israel*. London: SCM, 1984.

Randolph, David. *The Renewal of Preaching: A New Homiletic Based on the New Hermeneutic*. Philadelphia: Fortress, 1969.

Raphael, Rebecca. *Biblical Corpora: Representations of Disability in Hebrew Biblical Literature*. LHB/OTS 445. London: T&T Clark, 2008.

Ratheiser, Gershom M. H. *Mitzvoth Ethics and the Jewish Bible: The End of Old Testament Theology*. LHB/OTS 460. New York: T&T Clark, 2007.

Ratzinger, Joseph/Pope Benedict XVI. "Seven Theses on Christology and the Hermeneutic of Faith." *Letter and Spirit* 3 (2007): 189-209.

Redditt, Paul L. "The Production and Reading of the Book of the Twelve." In *Reading and Hearing the Book of the Twelve*, edited by James D. Nogalski and Marvin A. Sweeney. SBLSymS 15. Atlanta: Society of Biblical Literature, 2000.

———, and Aaron Schart, eds. *Thematic Threads in the Book of the Twelve*. BZAW 325. Berlin: de Gruyter, 2003.

Rendtorff, Rolf. *The Problem of the Process of Transmission in the Pentateuch.* Translated by J. J. Scullion. JSOTSup 89. Sheffield: JSOT Press, 1990.

————. "Alas for the Day! The 'Day of the Lord' in the Book of the Twelve." In *God in the Fray: A Tribute to Walter Brueggemann,* edited by Tod Linafelt and Timothy K. Beal. Minneapolis: Fortress, 1998.

————. *Leviticus 1,1-10, 20.* BKAT 3.1. Neukirchen: Neukirchener Verlag, 2004.

————. *The Canonical Hebrew Bible: A Theology of the Old Testament.* Translated by D. Orton. Tools for Biblical Study 7. Leiden: Deo, 2005.

Renz, Thomas. *The Rhetorical Function of the Book of Ezekiel.* VTSup 76. Leiden: Brill, 1999.

————. "Torah in the Minor Prophets." In *Reading the Law: Essays in Honor of Gordon J. Wenham,* edited by J. G. McConville and Karl Möller. LHB/OTS 461. London: T&T Clark, 2006.

Reventlow, H. G. *Problems of Biblical Theology in the Twentieth Century.* London: SCM, 1986.

Richter, Sandra L. "A Biblical Theology of Creation Care." *Asbury Journal* 62, no. 1 (2007): 67-76.

Ricoeur, Paul. *Philosophical Hermeneutics and Theological Hermeneutics: Ideology, Utopia, and Faith.* Center for Hermeneutical Studies in Hellenistic and Modern Culture 17. Berkeley: Graduate Theological Union and the University of California, 1976.

————. *Essays on Biblical Interpretation.* Edited by Lewis S. Mudge. Philadelphia: Fortress, 1980.

Ridderbos, Herman. *The Gospel of John: A Theological Commentary.* Translated by John Vriend. Grand Rapids: Eerdmans, 1997.

Roberts, Colin H., and T. C. Skeat. *The Birth of the Codex.* London: British Academy, 1987.

Roberts, J. J. M. "A Christian Perspective on Prophetic Prediction." In *The Bible and the Ancient Near East: Collected Essays,* edited by J. J. M. Roberts. Winona Lake, IN: Eisenbrauns, 2002.

Robinson, Haddon. *Biblical Preaching: The Development and Delivery of Expository Messages,* 2nd ed. Grand Rapids: Baker Academic, 2001.

Rodd, Cyril S. *Glimpses of a Strange Land: Studies in Old Testament Ethics.* OTS. London: T&T Clark, 2001.

Rogerson, John W. "Philosophy and the Rise of Biblical Criticism: England and Germany." In *England and Germany: Studies in Theological Diplomacy,* edited by Stephen W. Sykes. Studies in Intercultural History of Christianity 25. Frankfurt: Peter Lang, 1982.

————. *Old Testament Criticism in the Nineteenth Century: England and Germany.* Philadelphia: Fortress, 1984.

————. *W. M. L. de Wette, Founder of Modern Biblical Criticism: An Intellectual Biography.* JSOTSup 126. Sheffield: Sheffield Academic Press, 1992.

————. *The Bible and Criticism in Victorian Britain: Profiles of F. D. Maurice and William Robertson Smith.* JSOTSup 201. Sheffield: Sheffield Academic Press, 1995.

————. *Theory and Practice in Old Testament Ethics*. Edited by M. Daniel Carroll R. JSOTSup 405. London: T&T Clark, 2004.

————. *According to the Scriptures? The Challenge of Using the Bible in Social, Moral, and Political Questions*. Biblical Challenges in the Contemporary World. London: Equinox, 2007.

Rollins, Wayne G. "The Bible and Psychology: New Directions in Biblical Scholarship." In *Hearing Visions and Seeing Voices: Psychological Aspects of Biblical Concepts and Personalities*, edited by Gerrit Glas, M. H. Spero, P. J. Verhagen, and H. M. van Praag. Dordrecht: Springer, 2007.

Rose, Lucy. *Sharing the Word: Preaching in the Roundtable Church*. Louisville: Westminster John Knox, 1997.

Runia, David T. *Philo in Early Christian Literature: A Survey*. Minneapolis: Fortress, 1993.

Ryken, Leland. *Words of Delight: A Literary Introduction to the Bible*. Grand Rapids: Baker, 1992.

————. "The Bible as Literature: A Brief History." In *The Complete Literary Guide to the Bible*, edited by Leland Ryken and Tremper Longman III. Grand Rapids: Eerdmans, 1993.

Sailhamer, John. *An Introduction to Old Testament Theology: A Canonical Approach*. Grand Rapids: Zondervan, 1995.

Sandeen, Ernest R., ed. *The Bible and Social Reform*. The Bible in American Culture. Philadelphia: Fortress, 1982.

Sanders, James A. "Spinning the Bible." *Bible Review* 14 (1998): 23-29, 44-45.

Sandy, D. Brent. *Plowshares and Pruning Hooks: Rethinking the Language of Biblical Prophecy and Apocalyptic*. Downers Grove: IVP, 2002.

Sandys-Wunsch, John, and Laurence Eldredge. "J. P. Gabler and the Distinction between Biblical and Dogmatic Theology: Translation, Commentary, and Discussion of His Originality." *SJT* 33, no. 2 (1980): 133-58.

Sarna, Nahum J. *Exodus*. JPS Torah Commentary. Philadelphia: JPS, 1991.

Sawyer, J. F. A. *The Fifth Gospel: Isaiah in the History of Christianity*. Cambridge: Cambridge University Press, 1996.

Scalise, C. *From Scripture to Theology: A Canonical Journey into Hermeneutics*. Downers Grove: IVP, 1996.

Scharbert, J. "Formgeschichte und Exegese von Ex 34,6f und Seiner Parallelen." *Bib* 38 (1959): 130-50.

Schart, Aaron. *Die Entstehung des Zwölfprophetenbuchs: Neubearbeitungen von Amos im Rahmen schriftenübergreifender Redaktionsprozesse*. BZAW 260. Berlin: Walter de Gruyter, 1997.

————. "Reconstructing the Redaction History of the Twelve Prophets: Problems and Models." In *Reading and Hearing the Book of the Twelve*, edited by James D. Nogalski and Marvin A. Sweeney. SBLSymS 15. Atlanta: Society of Biblical Literature, 2000.

Schenke, L. *Das Markusevangelium*. Stuttgart: Kohlhammer, 2005.

Schifferdecker, Kathryn. *Out of the Whirlwind: Creation Theology in the Book of Job.* Harvard Theological Studies 61. Cambridge, MA: Harvard University Press, 2008.

Schiffman, Lawrence H. *The Halakhah at Qumran.* Leiden: Brill, 1975.

Schipper, Jeremy. *Disability Studies and the Hebrew Bible: Figuring Mephibosheth in the David Story.* LHB/OTS 441. London: T&T Clark, 2006.

Schniedewind, William M. *How the Bible Became a Book: The Textualization of Ancient Israel.* Cambridge: Cambridge University Press, 2005.

Schökel, L. A. *A Manual of Hebrew Poetics.* Subsidia Biblical 11. Rome: Pontifical Biblical Institute, 1988.

Scholder, Klaus. *The Birth of Modern Critical Theology: Origins and Problems of Biblical Criticism in the Seventeenth Century.* Philadelphia: Trinity Press International, 1990.

Schultz, Richard L. "The King in the Book of Isaiah." In *The Lord's Anointed: Interpretation of Old Testament Messianic Texts,* edited by P. E. Satterthwaite, R. S. Hess, and G. J. Wenham. Grand Rapids: Baker, 1995.

———. "The Ties That Bind: Intertextuality, the Identification of Verbal Parallels, and Reading Strategies in the Book of the Twelve." In *Thematic Threads in the Book of the Twelve,* edited by Paul L. Redditt and Aaron Schart. BZAW 325. Berlin: de Gruyter, 2003.

———. "How Many Isaiahs Were There and What Does It Matter? Prophetic Inspiration in Recent Evangelical Scholarship." In *Scripture in the Evangelical Tradition: Tradition, Authority, and Hermeneutics,* edited by Vince Bacote, Laura C. Miguelez, and Dennis L. Okholm. Downers Grove: IVP, 2004.

———. "Isaiah." In *Theological Interpretation of the Old Testament: A Book-by-Book Survey,* edited by Kevin J. Vanhoozer. Grand Rapids: Baker, 2007.

———. "Intertextuality, Canon, and 'Undecidability': Understanding Isaiah's 'New Heavens and New Earth' (Isa 65:17-25)." *BBR* 20 (2010): 19-38.

Schunck, Klaus-Dietrich. "Die Attribute des eschatologischen Messias: Struklinien in der Ausprägung des alttestamentlichen Messiasbildes." *TLZ* 111 (September 1986): 641-51.

Seitz, Christopher R., ed. *Reading and Preaching the Book of Isaiah.* Philadelphia: Fortress, 1988.

———. *Word without End: The Old Testament as Abiding Theological Witness.* Grand Rapids: Eerdmans, 1998.

———. "Christological Interpretation of Texts and Trinitarian Claims to Truth: An Engagement with Francis Watson's *Text and Truth.*" *SJT* 52, no. 2 (1999): 209-26.

———. *Figured Out: Typology and Providence in Christian Scripture.* Louisville: Westminster John Knox, 2001.

———. "What Lesson Will History Teach? The Book of the Twelve as History." In *"Behind" the Text: History and Biblical Interpretation,* edited by Craig Bartholomew et al. SAHS 4. Grand Rapids: Zondervan, 2003.

———. *Prophecy and Hermeneutics: Toward a New Introduction to the Prophets.* Studies in Theological Interpretation. Grand Rapids: Baker Academic, 2007.

———. *The Goodly Fellowship of the Prophets: The Achievement of Association in Canon Formation.* Grand Rapids: Baker Academic, 2009.

Sennett, James F., ed. *The Analytic Theist: An Alvin Plantinga Reader.* Grand Rapids: Eerdmans, 1998.

Seybold, Klaus. *Introducing the Psalms.* Translated by R. G. Dunphy. Edinburgh: T&T Clark, 1990.

Sharp, Carolyn. *Old Testament Prophets for Today.* Louisville: Westminster John Knox, 2009.

Shepherd, Michael B. "Compositional Analysis of the Twelve." *ZAW* 120 (2008): 184-93.

Sheppard, Gerald T. *Wisdom as a Hermeneutical Construct: A Study in the Sapientializing of the Old Testament.* BZAW 151. Berlin: de Gruyter, 1980.

———. "Canon." In *Encyclopedia of Religion,* Vol. 3, edited by Mircea, Eliade, pp. 62-69. New York: Macmillan, 1987.

Shiman, Lilian Lewis. *The Crusade against Drink in Victorian England.* London: Macmillan, 1998.

Sire, James. *Naming the Elephant: Worldview as a Concept.* Downers Grove: IVP, 2004.

Skehan, P. W., and A. A. di Lella. *The Wisdom of Ben Sira.* AB. New York: Doubleday, 1986.

Sloane, Andrew. *At Home in a Strange Land: Using the Old Testament in Christian Ethics.* Peabody, MA: Hendrickson, 2008.

Smalley, Beryl. *The Study of the Bible in the Middle Ages.* 3rd ed. Oxford: Blackwell, 1983.

Smith, Christine. *Preaching as Weeping, Confession, and Resistance: Radical Responses to Radical Evil.* Louisville: Westminster John Knox, 1992.

Soggin, J. A. *History of Israel: From the Beginning to the Bar Kochba Revolt, AD 135.* London: SCM, 1984.

Soulen, Richard N., and R. Kendall Soulen. *Handbook of Biblical Criticism.* 3rd ed. Louisville: Westminster John Knox, 2001.

Sparks, Kenton L. *God's Word in Human Words: An Evangelical Appropriation of Critical Biblical Scholarship.* Grand Rapids: Baker Academic, 2008.

Spears, Aubrey. *The Theological Hermeneutics of Homiletical Application and Ecclesiastes 7:23-29.* Eugene, OR: Pickwick Publications, forthcoming.

Spero, M. H. "The Hidden *Subject* of Job: Mirroring and the Anguish of Interminable Desire." In *Hearing Visions and Seeing Voices: Psychological Aspects of Biblical Concepts and Personalities,* edited by Gerrit Glas, M. H. Spero, P. J. Verhagen, and H. M. van Praag. Dordrecht: Springer, 2007.

Spinoza, Benedictus. *Tractatus theologico-politicus.* Translated by Samuel Shirley. Leiden: Brill, 1991.

Sprinkle, Joe M. *"The Book of the Covenant": A Literary Approach.* JSOTSup 174. Sheffield: Sheffield Academic Press, 1994.

———. *Biblical Law and Its Relevance: A Christian Understanding and Ethical Implications of the Mosaic Regulations.* Lanham, MD: University Press of America, 2006.

Spykman, Gordon J. *Reformational Theology: A New Paradigm for Doing Dogmatics.* Grand Rapids: Eerdmans, 1992.

Stassen, Glen H., and David P. Gushee. *Kingdom Ethics: Following Jesus in Contemporary Context.* Downers Grove: IVP, 2003.

Steiner, George. *The Death of Tragedy.* New York: Oxford University Press, 1961.

———. "The Good Books." *The New Yorker,* January 11, 1988, pp. 94-98.

———. *Real Presences.* Chicago: University of Chicago Press, 1989.

———. *After Babel: Aspects of Language and Translation.* Oxford: Oxford University Press, 1998.

Steinmann, Andrew. *The Oracles of God.* St. Louis: Concordia Academic Press, 1999.

Steins, Georg. *Die Chronik als kanonisches Abschlussphänomen. Studien zur Entstehung und Theologie von 1/2 Chronik.* Weinheim: Beltz Athenäum, 1995.

Sternberg, Meir. *The Poetics of Biblical Narrative: Ideological Literature and the Drama of Reading.* Indiana Studies in Biblical Literature. Bloomington: Indiana University Press, 1985.

Stiglmair, Arnold. "'. . . So spricht Jahwe . . .' — Prophetenwort als Wort Gottes." In *Die alttestamentliche Botschaft als Wegweisung: Festschrift für Heinze Reinelt,* edited by Josef Zmijewski. Stuttgart: Katholisches Bibelwerk, 1990.

Stockton, Ian. "Bonhoeffer's Wrestling with Jeremiah." *Modern Believing* 40 (1999): 50-58.

Stump, Eleonore. *Wandering in Darkness: Narrative and the Problem of Suffering.* Oxford: Clarendon Press, 2010.

Sugirtharajah, R. S. *The Bible and the Third World: Precolonial, Colonial, and Postcolonial Encounters.* Oxford: Clarendon, 2001.

Sundberg Jr., A. *The Old Testament of the Early Church.* Cambridge: Harvard University Press, 1964.

Swartley, Willard M. *Slavery, Sabbath, War, and Women: Case Issues in Biblical Interpretation.* Scottdale, PA: Herald, 1983.

———. *Homosexuality: Biblical Interpretation and Moral Discernment.* Scottdale, PA: Herald, 2003.

Sweeney, Marvin. *The Twelve Prophets.* Berit Olam. Collegeville: Liturgical Press, 2000.

———. *Faith and Intertextuality.* Tübingen: Mohr Siebeck, 2005.

Tappy, Ron E., and P. Kyle McCarter Jr., eds. *Literate Culture and Tenth-Century Canaan: The Tel Zayit Abecedary in Context.* Winona Lake, IN: Eisenbrauns, 2008.

Taylor, Charles. *Sources of the Self: The Making of the Modern Identity.* Cambridge, MA: Harvard University Press, 1989.

Thiselton, Anthony C. "Semantics and New Testament Interpretation." In *New Testament Interpretation: Essays on Principles and Methods,* edited by I. Howard Marshall. Carlisle: Paternoster, 1977.

———. *The Two Horizons: New Testament Hermeneutics and Philosophical Description.* Grand Rapids: Eerdmans, 1980.

———. *New Horizons in Hermeneutics.* Grand Rapids: Zondervan, 1992.

———. "New Testament Interpretation in Historical Perspective." In *Hearing the New Testament: Strategies for Interpretation,* edited by Joel B. Green. Grand Rapids: Eerdmans, 1995.

———. "Communicative Action and Promise in Interdisciplinary, Biblical, and Theological Hermeneutics." In *The Promise of Hermeneutics,* edited by Roger Lundin, Clarence Walhout, and Anthony C. Thiselton. Grand Rapids: Eerdmans, 1999.

Thompson, T. L. *The Historicity of the Patriarchal Narratives.* BZAW 133. Berlin: de Gruyter, 1974.

———. *The Mythic Past: Biblical Archaeology and the Myth of History.* New York: Basic Books, 1999.

Throntveit, Mark A. *Ezra-Nehemiah.* Interpretation Commentary Series. Louisville: John Knox, 1992.

Ticciati, Susannah. *Job and the Disruption of Identity: Reading Beyond Barth.* London: T&T Clark, 2005.

Toulmin, Stephen. *Cosmopolis. The Hidden Agenda of Modernity.* Chicago: University of Chicago Press, 1990.

Tov, Emanuel. *Textual Criticism of the Hebrew Bible.* Minneapolis: Augsburg Fortress, 2001.

Towns, Elmer E. *The Daniel Fast for Spiritual Breakthrough.* Ventura: Regal, 2010.

Trevaskis, Leigh M. *Holiness, Ethics and Ritual in Leviticus.* Hebrew Bible Monograph 29. Sheffield: Sheffield Phoenix, 2010.

Trible, Phyllis. *God and the Rhetoric of Sexuality.* OBT 2. Philadelphia: Fortress, 1978.

Troeltsch, E. "Über historische und dogmatische Methode in der Theologie." *Gesammelte Schriften.* Tübingen: Mohr, 1913.

———. "Historiography." In *Encyclopedia of Religion and Ethics,* vol. 6, edited by J. Hastings. New York: Scribner, 1914.

Tucker, Gene M. "Prophetic Superscriptions and the Growth of a Canon." In *Canon and Authority: Essays in Old Testament Religion and Theology,* edited by George W. Coats and Burke O. Long. Philadelphia: Fortress, 1977.

Tyndale, William. "The Obedience of a Christian Man." In *The Works of the English Reformers: William Tyndale and John Frith,* edited by Thomas Russell. London: Ebenezer Palmer, 1831.

Uhlig, Torsten. *The Theme of Hardening in the Book of Isaiah.* FAT 239. Tübingen: Mohr Siebeck, 2009.

Ulrich, Eugene. "The Notion and Definition of Canon." In *The Canon Debate,* edited by Lee M. McDonald and James A. Sanders. Peabody, MA: Hendrickson, 2002.

———. "Qumran and the Canon of the Old Testament." In *The Biblical Canons,* edited by J. M. Auwers and H. de Jonge. Leuven: Leuven University Press, 2003.

Van der Kooij, Arie. "The 'Critical Method' of Abraham Kuenen and the Methods of Old Testament Research Since 1891 up to 1991." In *Abraham Kuenen (1828-1891): His Major Contributions to the Study of the Old Testament,* edited by P. B. Dirksen and A. W. van der Kooij. Leiden: Brill, 1993.

van de Sandt, Huub. "The Minor Prophets in Luke-Acts," In *The Minor Prophets in the New Testament,* edited by Maarten J. J. Menken and Steve Moyise. LNTS 377. London: T&T Clark, 2009.

VanGemeren, Willem. *The Progress of Redemption: From Creation to the New Jerusalem.* Grand Rapids: Zondervan, 1988.

Van Harn, Roger E., and Strawn, Brent A., eds. *Psalms for Preaching and Worship: A Lectionary Commentary.* 3 vols. Grand Rapids: Eerdmans, 2009.

Vanhoozer, Kevin J. "Christ and Concept: Doing Theology and the 'Ministry' of Philosophy." In *Doing Theology in Today's World,* edited by John D. Woodbridge and Thomas E. McComiskey. Grand Rapids: Zondervan, 1991.

———. "The Spirit of Understanding: Special Revelation and General Hermeneutics." In *Disciplining Hermeneutics: Interpretation in Christian Perspective,* edited by Roger Lundin. Grand Rapids: Eerdmans, 1997.

———. *Is There a Meaning in This Text?* Grand Rapids: Zondervan, 1998.

———. "Exegesis and Hermeneutics." In *New Dictionary of Biblical Theology,* edited by T. Desmond Alexander and Brian S. Rosner. Downers Grove: IVP, 2000.

———. *The Drama of Scripture: A Canonical-Linguistic Approach to Christian Theology.* Louisville: Westminster John Knox, 2005.

———, ed. *Theological Interpretation of the Old Testament: A Book-by-Book Survey.* Grand Rapids: Baker Academic, 2008.

Vanier, Jean. *Drawn into the Mystery of Jesus through the Gospel of John.* Ottawa: Novalis, 2004.

van Itterzon, G. P. "Coccejus, Johannes." In *Christelijke Encyclopaedie,* edited by F. W. Grosheide and G. P. van Itterzon. Kampen: Kok, 1957.

Van Leeuwen, Raymond C. *Context and Meaning in Proverbs 25–27.* SBLDS 96. Atlanta: Scholars Press, 1988.

———. "Liminality and Worldview in Proverbs 1–9." *Semeia* 50 (1990): 111-44.

———. "Wealth and Poverty: System and Contradiction in Proverbs." *Hebrew Studies* 33 (1992): 25-36.

———. "Proverbs." In *A Complete Literary Guide to the Bible,* edited by Leland Ryken and Tremper Longman III. Grand Rapids: Zondervan, 1993.

———. "Scribal Wisdom and Theodicy in the Book of the Twelve." In *In Search of Wisdom: Essays in Memory of John G. Gammie,* edited by L. Perdue, B. B. Scott, and W. J. Wiseman. Louisville: Westminster John Knox Press, 1993.

———. "The Book of Proverbs." In *The New Interpreter's Bible,* vol. 5. Nashville: Abingdon, 1997.

———. "On Bible Translation and Hermeneutics." In *After Pentecost: Language and Biblical Interpretation,* edited by Craig Bartholomew et al. SAHS 2. Grand Rapids: Zondervan, 2001.

———. "Wisdom Literature." In *Dictionary for Theological Interpretation of the Bible,* edited by Kevin J. Vanhoozer et al. Grand Rapids: Baker Academic, 2005.

Van Seters, John. *Abraham in History and Tradition.* New Haven: Yale University Press, 1975.

van Wijk-Bos, Johanna W. H. *Making Wise the Simple: The Torah in Christian Faith and Practice.* Grand Rapids: Eerdmans, 2005.

———. *Interpreting the Prophetic Word.* Grand Rapids: Zondervan, 1996.

Venema, G. J. *Reading Scripture in the Old Testament: Deuteronomy 9–10, 31; 2 Kings 22–23; Jeremiah 36; Nehemiah 8.* Translated by Ch. E. Smit. Leiden: Brill, 2004.

Vitringa, Campegius. *Commentarius in librum prophetarum Jesajae*. Leeuwarden: Halma, 1714-1720.

von Rad, Gerhard. *Gesammelte Studien zum Alten Testament*. Theologische Bücherei: Neudrucke und Berichte aus dem 20. Jahrhundert 8. Munich: Chr. Kaiser, 1958.

———. *Deuteronomy: A Commentary*. London: SCM, 1966.

———. *The Problem of the Hexateuch and Other Essays*. London: Oliver & Boyd, 1966.

———. *Genesis: A Commentary*. Translated by John H. Marks. London: SCM, 1972.

———. *Wisdom in Israel*. Translated by J. D. Martin. Nashville: Abingdon, 1972.

———. *Old Testament Theology: The Theology of Israel's Historical Tradition*. Translated by D. M. G. Stalker. New York: Harper, 1985.

Walker-Jones, Arthur. *The Green Psalter: Resources for an Ecological Spirituality*. Minneapolis: Fortress, 2009.

Wall, Robert W. "Peter, 'Son' of Jonah: The Conversion of Cornelius in the Context of Canon." *Journal for the Study of the New Testament* 29 (1987): 79-90.

———. "Canonical Context and Canonical Conversations." In *Between Two Horizons: Spanning New Testament Studies and Systematic Theology*, edited by Joel B. Green and Max Turner. Grand Rapids: Eerdmans, 2000.

Waltke, Bruce K. *The Book of Proverbs*. 2 vols. NICOT. Grand Rapids: Eerdmans, 2004, 2005.

———, and Charles Yu. *An Old Testament Theology: A Canonical and Thematic Approach*. Grand Rapids: Zondervan, 2006.

Walton, John H. *The Lost World of Genesis One: Ancient Cosmology and the Origins Debate*. Downers Grove: IVP, 2009.

Watson, Francis. *Text, Church, and World: Biblical Interpretation in Theological Perspective*. Grand Rapids: Eerdmans, 1994.

———. *Text and Truth: Redefining Biblical Theology*. Grand Rapids: Eerdmans, 1997.

———. "The Old Testament as Scripture: A Response to Professor Seitz." *SJT* 52, no. 2 (1999): 227-32.

———. *Paul and the Hermeneutics of Faith*. London: T&T Clark, 2004.

Watson, W. G. E. *Classical Hebrew Poetry: A Guide to Its Techniques*. JSOTSup 26. Sheffield: JSOT, 1984.

Watts, Rikki E. *Isaiah's New Exodus and Mark*. Wissenschaftliche Untersuchungen zum Neuen Testament 2/88. Tübingen: Mohr Siebeck, 1997.

———. "'For I am not ashamed of the gospel': Romans 1:16-17 and Habakkuk 2:4." In *Romans and the People of God*, edited by Sven K. Soderlund and N. T. Wright. Grand Rapids: Eerdmans, 1999.

———. "Echoes from the Past: Israel's Ancient Traditions and the Destiny of the Nations in Isaiah 40–55." *JSOT* 28 (2004): 481-508.

———. "Emmanuel: Virgin Birth Proof Text or Programmatic Warning of Things to Come (Isa 7:14 in Matt 1:23)?" In *From Prophecy to Testament: The Function of the Old Testament in the New*, edited by Craig A. Evans. Peabody, MA: Hendrickson, 2004.

Webb, Joseph. *Preaching and the Challenge of Pluralism*. St. Louis: Chalice, 1998.

Webb, William J. *Slaves, Women, and Homosexuals: Exploring the Hermeneutics of Cultural Analysis.* Downers Grove: IVP, 2001.

Weinfeld, Moshe. *Deuteronomy 1–11.* AB. New York: Doubleday, 1991.

———. *Social Justice in Ancient Israel and in the Ancient Near East.* Minneapolis: Fortress, 1995.

Weinsheimer, Joel. *Philosophical Hermeneutics and Literary Theory.* New Haven: Yale University Press, 1991.

Weir, Jack. "Analogous Fulfillment." *Perspectives in Religious Studies* 9 (1982): 65-76.

Welch, John. *Spiritual Pilgrims: Carl Jung and Teresa of Avila.* New York: Paulist, 1982.

Welker, Michael, and Friedrich Schweitzer, eds. *Reconsidering the Boundaries between Theological Disciplines. Zur Neubestimmung der Grenzen zwischen den theologischen Disziplinen.* Theology: Research and Science 8. Münster: Lit Verlag, 2005.

Wellhausen, Julius. *Prolegomena to the History of Israel.* Translated by J. Sutherland Black and Allan Menzies. Edinburgh: Adam and Charles Black, 1885.

Wells, M. Jay. "Figural Representation and Canonical Unity." In *Biblical Theology: Retrospect and Prospect,* edited by Scott Hafemann. Downers Grove: IVP, 2002.

Wenham, G. J. *Genesis 1–15.* WBC 1. Waco: Word, 1987.

———. *Genesis 16–50.* WBC 2. Dallas: Word, 1994.

———. *Numbers.* OTG 5. Sheffield: Sheffield Academic, 1997.

———. "Pondering the Pentateuch: The Search for a New Paradigm." In *The Face of Old Testament Studies,* edited by David W. Baker and Bill T. Arnold. Grand Rapids: Baker, 1999.

———. *Story as Torah: Reading Old Testament Narrative Ethically.* Edinburgh: T&T Clark, 2000.

———. "Purity." In *The Biblical World II,* edited by John Barton. New York: Routledge, 2002.

———. "Toward a Canonical Reading of the Psalms." In *Canon and Biblical Interpretation,* edited by Craig Bartholomew et al. SAHS 7. Grand Rapids: Zondervan, 2006.

———. *Psalms as Torah: Reading Biblical Song Ethically.* Studies in Theological Interpretation. Grand Rapids: Baker Academic, 2012.

West, Gerald O. *The Academy of the Poor: Towards a Dialogical Reading of the Bible.* Interventions 2. Sheffield: Sheffield Academic Press, 1999.

Westbrook, Raymond. *Studies in Biblical and Cuneiform Law.* Cahiers de la Revue biblique 26. Paris: Gabalda, 1988.

———. *Property and the Family in Biblical Law.* JSOTSup 113. Sheffield: JSOT Press, 1991.

Westermann, Claus. *Genesis 1–11: A Commentary.* Translated by J. J. Scullion. Minneapolis: Augsburg, 1984.

Westphal, Merold. "Christian Philosophers and the Copernican Revolution." In *Christian Perspectives on Religious Knowledge,* edited by C. Stephen Evans and M. Westphal. Grand Rapids: Eerdmans, 1993.

Whiston, William. *An Essay Towards Restoring the True Text of the Old Testament and for Vindicating the Citations Made Thence in the New Testament.* London: Senex, 1722.

445

Whybray, R. Norman. *The Making of the Pentateuch: A Methodological Study.* JSOTSup 53. Sheffield: JSOT Press, 1987.

Wiles, Maurice. *The Making of Christian Doctrine: A Study in the Principles of Early Doctrinal Development.* Cambridge: Cambridge University Press, 1967.

Wilken, Robert Louis. *The Spirit of Early Christian Thought: Seeking the Face of God.* New Haven: Yale University Press, 2003.

———. "Allegory and Interpretation of the Old Testament in the Twenty-First Century." *Letter and Spirit* 1 (2005): 11-21.

Williams, Bernard. *Shame and Necessity.* Berkeley: University of California Press, 1993.

Williamson, H. G. M. "The Concept of Israel in Transition." In *The World of Ancient Israel,* edited by R. E. Clements. Cambridge: Cambridge University Press, 1989.

———. "In Search of the Pre-exilic Isaiah." In *In Search of Pre-Exilic Israel,* edited by John Day. JSOTSup 406. London: T&T Clark, 2004.

Willimon, William H. *Conversations with Barth on Preaching.* Nashville: Abingdon, 2006.

Wilson, Gerald H. *The Editing of the Hebrew Psalter.* SBLDS 76. Chico: Scholars, 1985.

———. "The Use of Royal Psalms at the 'Seams' of the Hebrew Psalter." *JSOT* 35 (1986): 85-94.

———. *Psalms,* vol 1. NIVAC. Grand Rapids: Zondervan, 2002.

Wilson, Paul Scott. "Biblical Studies and Preaching: A Growing Divide?" In *Preaching as a Theological Task: World, Gospel, Scripture. Essays in Honor of David Buttrick,* edited by Thomas Long and Edward Farley. Louisville: Westminster John Knox, 1996.

———. *God Sense: Reading the Bible for Preaching.* Nashville: Abingdon, 2001.

———. *Preaching and Homiletical Theory.* St. Louis: Chalice, 2004.

Witherington, Ben, III. *Jesus the Seer: The Progress of Prophecy.* Peabody, MA: Hendrickson, 1999.

Wolff, Hans Walter. "Schwerter zu Pflugscharen — Mißbrauch eines Prophetenwortes? Praktische Fragen und exegetische Klärungen zu Joël 4,9-12, Jes 2,2-5 und Mi 4,1-5." *Evangelische Theologie* 44 (1984): 280-92.

Wolters, Albert M. "The Centre and the Circumference." *Vanguard* (April 1980): 5-6.

———. *The Song of the Valiant Woman: Studies in the Interpretation of Proverbs 31:10-31.* Carlisle: Paternoster, 2001.

———. "Reading the Gospels Canonically: A Methodological Dialogue with Brevard Childs." In *Reading the Gospels Today,* edited by Stanley E. Porter. Grand Rapids: Eerdmans, 2004.

———. "The Text of the Old Testament." In *The Face of Old Testament Studies: A Survey of Contemporary Approaches,* edited by David W. Baker and Bill T. Arnold. Grand Rapids: Baker Academic, 2004.

Wolterstorff, Nicholas. *Reason within the Bounds of Religion.* Grand Rapids: Eerdmans, 1984.

———. *Divine Discourse: Philosophical Reflections on the Claim That God Speaks.* Cambridge: Cambridge University Press, 1995.

———. *Thomas Reid and the Story of Epistemology.* Cambridge: Cambridge University Press, 2001.

Wood, Allen W. "Rational Theology, Moral Faith, and Religion." In *The Cambridge Companion to Kant,* edited by Paul Guyer. Cambridge: Cambridge University Press, 1992.

———. *The Formation of Christian Understanding: Theological Hermeneutics.* Eugene, OR: Wipf & Stock, 2000.

Wood, Leon J. *The Holy Spirit in the Old Testament.* Grand Rapids: Zondervan, 1976.

Wright, Christopher J. H. *Living as the People of God: The Relevance of Old Testament Ethics.* Leicester: IVP, 1983.

———. *God's People in God's Land: Family, Land, and Property in the Old Testament.* Carlisle: Paternoster, 1990.

———. *Knowing Jesus through the Old Testament.* Downers Grove: IVP, 1995.

———. *Deuteronomy.* NIBCOT. Peabody, MA: Hendrickson, 1996.

———. *The Message of Ezekiel.* The Bible Speaks Today. Downers Grove: IVP, 2001.

———. "Mission as a Matrix for Hermeneutics and Biblical Theology." In *Out of Egypt: Biblical Theology and Biblical Interpretation,* edited by Craig Bartholomew et al. SAHS 5. Grand Rapids: Zondervan, 2004.

———. *Old Testament Ethics for the People of God.* Downers Grove: IVP, 2004.

———. *Knowing the Holy Spirit through the Old Testament.* Downers Grove: IVP, 2006.

———. *The Mission of God: Unlocking the Bible's Grand Narrative.* Downers Grove: IVP, 2006.

———. *Knowing God the Father Through the Old Testament.* Downers Grove: IVP, 2007.

———. *The Mission of God's People: A Biblical Theology of the Church's Mission,* edited by Jonathan Lunde. Biblical Theology for Life. Grand Rapids: Zondervan, 2010.

Wright, G. E. *God Who Acts.* SBT 1/8. London: SCM, 1952.

Wright, N. T. "How Can the Bible Be Authoritative?" *Vox Evangelica* 21 (1991): 7-32.

———. *The New Testament and the People of God.* Christian Origins and the Question of God 1. Minneapolis: Fortress, 1992.

———. *Jesus and the Victory of God: Christian Origins and the Question of God.* Minneapolis: Fortress, 1996.

Wright, T. R. *Theology and Literature.* Oxford: Blackwell, 1988.

Yancey, Philip. *The Bible Jesus Read.* Grand Rapids: Zondervan, 1999.

Yoder, John Howard. *The Politics of Jesus: Behold the Man! Our Victorious Lamb.* 2nd ed. Grand Rapids: Eerdmans, 1994.

Young, Frances M. "Allegory and the Ethics of Reading." In *The Open Text: New Directions for Biblical Studies,* edited by Francis Watson. London: SCM, 1993.

———. *Biblical Exegesis and the Formation of Christian Culture.* Peabody, MA: Hendrickson, 2002.

———. "The 'Mind' of Scripture: Theological Readings of the Bible in the Fathers." *International Journal of Systematic Theology* 7, no. 2 (April 2005): 126-41.

Younger, K. Lawson, Jr. *Ancient Conquest Accounts: A Study in Ancient Near Eastern and Biblical History Writing.* JSOTSup 98. Sheffield: JSOT Press, 1990.

Zaharopoulos, Dimitri Z. *Theodore of Mopsuestia on the Bible: A Study of His Old Testament Exegesis.* Mahwah, NJ: Paulist Press, 1989.

Zaman, Luc. *The Bible and Canon: A Modern Historical Inquiry.* Studia Semitica Neerlandica 50. Leiden: Brill, 2008.

Zenger, Erich. *A God of Vengeance? Understanding the Psalms of Enmity.* Translated by Linda Maloney. Louisville: Westminster John Knox, 1995.

———. *Das Erste Testament. Die jüdische Bibel und die Christen.* Düsseldorf: Patmos, 1998.

Zimmerli, Walther. "Zur Struktur der alttestamentlichen Weisheit." *ZAW* 51 (1933): 177-204.

———. "Place and Limit of Wisdom in the Framework of the Old Testament Theology." *SJT* 17 (1964): 146-58.

———. "Prophetic Proclamation and Reinterpretation." In *Tradition and Theology in the Old Testament,* edited by Douglas A. Knight. Philadelphia: Fortress, 1977.

Zimmerman, Frank. *The Inner World of Qohelet.* New York: Ktav, 1973.

Zimmermann, Jens. *Recovering Theological Hermeneutics: An Incarnational-Trinitarian Theory of Interpretation.* Grand Rapids: Baker, 2004.

Index of Authors

Index of Subjects

Alexandrian school, 27-28
Allegory, 24-25, 27-28, 33, 38, 140-41, 393-94, 396-97, 400, 408
Animals, 238-39
Anthropology, 57, 253
Antiochene school, 27-28
Application, 398
Apocrypha, 34
Archaeology, 100-101, 104-5
Author, focus on, 73
Authority of the Old Testament, 206-10
Authorship, 99
Autonomy, 61

Bible, 161; as any other book, 71; as unlike any other book, 71
Biblical criticism, 45-46, 52-54, 356
Biblical theology, 9, 122-53, 236, 341, 372, 386-87, 393-94; and systematic theology, 125
Blessed, 296-98
Blessing, 354; and curses, 251-52; of the nations, 270
Book of the Twelve, 356-79

Canon, 9, 26, 154-78, 183, 219, 268, 324, 383; canonical approach, 43, 154-55, 351, 359; canonical context, 348; canonical criticism, 233-34, 338; canonical form, 217-19, 279; canonical hermeneutic, 56; canonical shaping, 279, 345; canonical trajectories, 222-24; final form, 218, 338
Centrist histories, 109-11
Character-consequence structure, 307
Characters: and characterization, 81-83; three types of in Hebrew narrative, 81-82
Christian community, 211-13
Christian ministry, 42
Christocentric, 3-4, 41
Christological, 38
Christotelic, 144-46
Chronicles, book of, 173, 259-61
Comedy, 319
Communion, 16-17
Community, 182, 186, 334
Conservative Evangelical homiletics, 390
Continuity, 149-50
Correlation, 6
Covenant, 39, 183
Creation, 15, 63, 146-47, 183, 202, 270, 354, 356, 364, 372; ancient Near Eastern accounts of, 235-37; new creation,

Index of Scripture References